A Quest for Glory

Robert J. Schneller, Jr.

QUORUM PARS FUI.

A Quest *for* *Glory*

A Biography of
Rear Admiral John A. Dahlgren

NAVAL INSTITUTE PRESS   *Annapolis, Maryland*

Library of Congress Cataloging-in-Publication Data
Schneller, Robert John, 1957–
    A quest for glory : a biography of Rear Admiral John A. Dahlgren /
Robert John Schneller, Jr.
        p.   cm.
    Includes bibliographical references (p.   ) and index.
    ISBN 1-55750-762-7 (alk. paper)
    1. Dahlgren, John Adolphus Bernard, 1809–1870. 2. Admirals—
United States—Biography.   3. United States. Navy—Biography.
4. Charleston (S.C.)—History—Siege, 1863. I. Title.
E467.1.D13S36   1995
359'.0092—dc20   95-20085

Printed in the United States of America on acid-free paper ∞
03 02 01 00 99 98 97 96   9 8 7 6 5 4 3 2

For Zach and Noah

Contents

Illustrations

Preface

In 1864 Rear Admiral John A. Dahlgren watched the opportunity he had always dreamed of slip through his fingers. His command, the South Atlantic Blockading Squadron, was the Union navy's most powerful fleet, and it was poised to strike at Charleston, birthplace of the rebellion. Victory would fulfill his lifelong ambition for glory. Although Dahlgren already enjoyed an unprecedented reputation, it had not brought him the power he wanted. He was chief of the Bureau of Ordnance, guns that bore his name armed almost every ship in the Union navy, and naval officers recognized him as the foremost ordnance expert in America, if not the world; yet his superiors had still meddled in the development of American naval armament, which he regarded as his exclusive bailiwick. Assistant Secretary of the Navy Gustavus V. Fox's insistence that he design a 15-inch cannon for the *Passaic*-class monitors had been the last straw. With help from his friend Abraham Lincoln, Dahlgren had abandoned ordnance work to pursue glory at Charleston. But command of the South Atlantic Blockading Squadron was not turning out as he had hoped. In his view, too many obstacles stood in the way: uncooperative superiors, a scheming partner in command, the strongest defenses of any Confederate port. As a result, the campaign had degenerated into a stalemate. Nevertheless, Dahlgren clung quixotically to the hope of leading his ironclad fleet in a heroic charge into Charleston harbor, whether he won a great victory or died in the attempt.

To win glory and power, to be renowned throughout posterity—such ambition drove Dahlgren to excel. And excel he did. He went down in history as a maker of the American naval tradition, as one of the five great Union admirals of the American Civil War, and, most significantly, as the father of American naval ordnance.[1] His name is synonymous with naval armament during the Civil War era, and he is an immortal figure in the pantheon of American naval heroes.

Unlike those whose fame stemmed from heroic feats in battle, Dahlgren made his mark in technical work. He invented a heavy naval smoothbore cannon derived from scientific research in ballistics and metallurgy, and manufactured and tested under the most comprehensive system of quality control seen in the United States Navy to that time. Because its predecessors had been copies of European designs, the "bottle-shaped" Dahlgren gun was the first truly American naval cannon, and it enjoyed a sparkling and well-deserved reputation as the world's most powerful and reliable piece of naval ordnance. Dahlgren's guns were the standard weapon on board Union naval vessels during the Civil War, and they armed the *Monitor,* the *Virginia,* and the *Kearsarge,* the ship that sank the greatest American commerce raider of all time, the CSS *Alabama.* His were the last smoothbores the navy ever adopted.

Dahlgren was an innovator and entrepreneur who pioneered a new style of research and development in the navy. In the process of developing the Dahlgren gun, he created the first organization in American naval history designed to improve a naval weapon systematically, thereby contributing the idea of institutionalized innovation to the American naval tradition.

During the Civil War he commanded successively the Washington Navy Yard, the Bureau of Ordnance, and the South Atlantic Blockading Squadron. In the last he had the dubious distinction of presiding over the navy's greatest disappointment during the war, the failure to capture Charleston.

Dahlgren was nothing if not controversial. Personal rivalries plagued his career. He took offense at the slightest insult. Twice he nearly resorted to dueling to defend his honor. Those who criticized his work he scorned as "old fogies." Abraham Lincoln so enjoyed his company that he became a regular fixture at the Washington Navy Yard, the site of Dahlgren's ordnance work, and made Dahlgren his principal adviser on naval matters. But Lincoln's favor made him unpopular among fellow naval officers such as Du

Pont and Farragut. Quincy A. Gillmore, the commanding general of Union army forces at Charleston who ordered the ill-fated July 1863 attack on Fort Wagner, conducted a secret campaign to blame Dahlgren for the Union's failure to capture the city. Gillmore denounced Dahlgren to the press behind his back while lying about it to his face.

Poignancy and tragedy filled Dahlgren's family life. He lost his first wife in the midst of a professional crisis that threatened to ruin his ordnance career. He nearly suffered a nervous breakdown while commanding the fleet at Charleston when his son Ulric, a colonel of Union cavalry, was killed during a famous and ill-fated raid to free Federal prisoners of war from Richmond's Libby Prison. Although Dahlgren loved his other children, they disappointed him in the end. For example, his daughter fell in love with the son of his archrival Thomas J. Rodman, the renowned United States Army ordnance innovator.

Dahlgren was a great man whose greatness was eclipsed, in part, by his own actions. Sadly, he saw his fame and reputation decline toward the end of his life. Nevertheless, his ambition for glory and his skill in political manipulation proved decisive not only to the ultimate existence of his gun but also to his legacy.

There has been no good biography of Dahlgren. The basis of much of the secondary literature on him is the *Memoir of John A. Dahlgren*, published in 1882 by his wife Madeleine Vinton Dahlgren. The *Memoir* contains large, often revealing chunks of Dahlgren's personal papers, but its value is limited by the fact that Madeleine sought to portray her husband in the best possible light. The only recent full-length biography is C. Stewart Peterson's *Admiral John A. Dahlgren: Father of U.S. Naval Ordnance*, published in 1945. It is essentially a condensed version of Madeleine Dahlgren's book. Biographical sketches appear in sources like the *Dictionary of American Biography* and the *National Cyclopaedia of American Biography*. The best sketches are those by Joel T. Headley and David K. Allison in, respectively, *Farragut and Our Naval Commanders* and *Captains of the Old Steam Navy: Makers of the American Naval Tradition*. Most other secondary works that discuss Dahlgren do so from a limited perspective—for example, considering only his role in the lives of his contemporaries or in the history of ordnance.[2]

Given the vast quantity of source material available, it is amazing that Dahlgren remains only superficially known. His papers are preserved in repositories across the United States. The most important collections are those in the Library of Congress and in the George Arents Research Library at Syracuse University. The Library of Congress has some ten thousand items, ranging from unpublished reports to calculations written on scraps of paper. This collection contains many important documents that are not filed in chronological order. Researchers who do not sift through every scrap will inevitably miss key items. (That is why my citations from this collection are longer than the others.) Syracuse University's George Arents Research Library has most of Dahlgren's often devastatingly candid diary. Other repositories have the remaining extant portions of the diary, which spans Dahlgren's entire naval career. Needless to say, it is a gold mine. The National Archives has a wealth of materials pertaining to the Dahlgren guns in Record Group 74, the navy Bureau of Ordnance records. *The Official Records of the Union and Confederate Navies in the War of the Rebellion* documents Dahlgren's command of the South Atlantic Blockading Squadron during the Civil War. Dahlgren himself wrote several books, the most important of which is *Shells and Shell Guns*. That such a wealth of data has survived stems in part from the fact that Dahlgren valued his papers highly and took great pains to preserve them. And recently unearthed Dahlgren family papers, which have been locked in a safe-deposit box for the last fifty years, shed new light on aspects of his life.

Many people helped me with this book. Bill Still suggested the Dahlgren gun as the topic for my masters thesis at East Carolina University. Bill not only nurtured my study of Dahlgren through its infancy but also convinced me that I could become a historian. Alex Roland patiently plowed through several iterations of the present work, which began as my doctoral dissertation at Duke University. Alex's candid and detailed analyses of these and other writings have made me a better historian.

I thank Bill Dudley, I. B. Holley, Jr., and Sey Mauskopf for their comments on my dissertation. Bob Browning, Chuck Haberlein, Mike Palmer, Clark Reynolds, Spencer Tucker, and Gary Weir have my gratitude for casting a critical eye on an entire draft of this work. I thank Dean Allard, Jeff Barlow, Bob Cressman, Frank Duncan, Kevin Foster, Bob Gordon, Bert Hall, Mark Hayes, Glenn Helm, Jean Hort, Wendi Karppi, Ed Marolda, Tonya Montgomery, John Rumm, Rick Russell, Bill Thiesen, Curtis Utz, Steve Wise, Mark Wertheimer, and Peter Wood for variously providing sources and insights, reading and commenting on writings related to this book, or suffering through frequent monologues on the subject. These folks helped make the book better than it otherwise would have been. Responsibility for any errors or flaws, however, remains with me.

Numerous archivists and librarians at the American Swedish Historical Museum, Georgetown University Library, Hagley Museum and Library, Historical Society of Pennsylvania, Library of Congress, National Archives, Naval Academy Museum, Naval Historical Center, New-York Historical Society, New York Public Library, Nimitz Library, and Syracuse University Library went above and beyond the call of duty in providing assistance when I visited their institutions. Their professionalism and enthusiasm made researching this book a pleasure. The staffs at the other manuscript repositories mentioned in the bibliography have my thanks as well. I would like to express my gratitude to Julie Anne Young Johnson for sharing her family papers with me, to Charlie Peery for providing the portrait of Madeleine Dahlgren, and to Rod Lee and Kate Mason for drawing the maps of the South Atlantic coast.

I am grateful to the Naval Historical Center and to the American Society of Arms Collectors for providing grants that funded portions of the research for this book. I thank my agent, Fritz Heinzen, for finding a publisher, and the crew at the Naval Institute Press for getting this book into print.

I am deeply indebted to my mother, Joanne Green, and most of all to my wife, Rebecca. Without their love, support, and understanding, this book would never have come to be.

1

THE YOUTH

1

The Quest Begins
1809–1826

The Dahlgrens were not your average Swedes. While most preindustrial folks farmed, the Dahlgrens earned their living as civil servants. Wealth, close ties to the Swedish monarchy, and higher education in the sciences figured prominently in the family history.[1]

John Dahlgren's grandfather, Johan Adolf Dahlgren, was born in 1744 in Norrköping, a town southwest of Stockholm near the Baltic coast. After receiving a basic education from private tutors, Johan became a protégé of the naturalist Linnaeus and studied chemistry and pharmacy with the Swedish admiralty chemist in Stockholm. In 1764 he enrolled as a student at the University of Uppsala, the preeminent Swedish university. Eleven years later he graduated with a degree in medicine, which Linnaeus signed. Dr. Dahlgren was an active and energetic man who wrote many highly regarded professional works. In 1789 he became chief physician of the province of Finland, then part of the Swedish empire. He earned the respect of rulers and the love of common people as a highly skilled practitioner of medicine. He died in 1797.[2]

His son, Bernhard Ullrik Dahlgren, charted a different course in life. Born on 12 May 1784, Bernhard grew into a broad-shouldered man standing 6 feet 4^1/$_2$ inches tall. He too received an education at Uppsala, but he enjoyed

3

adventure and travel as much as studying and frequently trekked to the mountains. Rather than serve the monarchy as had his father, Bernhard Dahlgren rebelled against it. In 1804, authorities caught him handing out pamphlets that advocated republican principles.[3]

Distributing such literature in a monarchy was tantamount to treason. Republican ideas ran counter to the king's ends, not to mention his very existence. The crown confiscated Bernhard Dahlgren's property and forced him to flee. In the winter of 1806–7, after many months of traveling, he arrived in Philadelphia. He immediately applied for naturalization papers and soon became a U.S. citizen.[4]

In his adopted country, Bernhard Dahlgren met and fell in love with Martha Rowan. Her family had emigrated from Ireland among Pennsylvania's earliest settlers. Her father, James Rowan, had served in the Revolutionary War as a supply officer and fought at the battles of Germantown and Princeton. He used a good deal of his own money to finance his unit, but the government never repaid him. Like Bernhard Dahlgren, James Rowan had made sacrifices for his republican principles. The details of the courtship between Bernhard Dahlgren and Martha Rowan have been lost. They married on 19 November 1808.[5]

Bernhard earned a living as a merchant and involved himself in numerous enterprises. He engaged in the slave trade, joined a banking company, and speculated in real estate. When the Pennsylvania government decided to move the state capital from Philadelphia to Harrisburg, he signed a petition for permission to build a bridge across the Susquehanna River, in anticipation of increased traffic. The big Swede understood capitalism as well as republican principles.[6]

Bernhard Dahlgren was a solid, upstanding citizen whose motto was "Candor and Fidelity." He joined the party of Thomas Jefferson, became a respected officer in Philadelphia's Masonic institutions, and took an interest in the theater. People from all walks of life called on him to decide their disputes so as to avoid formal litigation. His friends thought him a "man of strong mind," "highly respectable," "a man of high character," and "unquestionably one of our most respectable and worthy citizens."[7]

Physically and financially, the Dahlgren family lived on the fringe of Philadelphia's socioeconomic elite. Jacksonian America was very much a class society. There existed in almost every city a socioeconomic aristocracy, and Philadelphia's was the most exclusive. Bernhard Dahlgren had business dealings and social connections with the Cadwalader family, who along with the Biddles, Mifflins, Whartons, Willings, Wistars, and others made up the highest stratum of Philadelphia society. A Wharton, a Willing, and a Wistar numbered among John Dahlgren's boyhood friends. More than half of the city's leading families lived on a few blocks of Walnut, Mulberry, and Chestnut Streets. The Dahlgrens lived on the corner of Front and Walnut, not far away. The elite enjoyed theater, Italian opera, soirées, and musical evenings. Bernhard shared their interest in the theater. The overwhelming majority of wealthy Americans were descended from families who combined affluence with high social status. Although Bernhard's family remained in Sweden, the Dahlgren family traditions of education, wealth, and social status certainly gave him more in common with the upper stratum of society than with any other.[8]

The eldest of Bernhard and Martha's five children, John Adolphus Bernard, was born on 13 November 1809. Family lore had it that just before John was born his nurse dreamed that Martha gave birth to a boy with six toes on each foot. According to the nurse's superstition, this meant that John "would live to be a great man." John's brother Charles Gustavus was born in 1810. As a man Charles lived in Natchez, Mississippi, and sided with the Confederacy during the Civil War. Another boy, Washington, born in 1817, died a year later. Martha Matilda, whom the family nicknamed Patty, was born in 1818. She lived in Philadelphia and Washington and married Matthew P. Read in the fall of 1867. She idolized John, and the two remained close throughout his life. William Theodore, born in 1820, was the black sheep of the family. After Bernhard's death William drew heavily upon his mother and her estate until 1842, when John forced him to sell his interest in the estate. This so upset William that he vowed never to be known as Dahlgren again. He changed his name to De Rohan, the name of his mother's Irish ancestors. He went abroad and served as a soldier of fortune in the Turkish, Argentine, British, and Chilean navies. Although anxious to fight for the Union in the Civil War, he decided not to, because he feared being assigned to John's command. Following the war he served with Garibaldi in the wars of Italian unification. He became an admiral in the Italian navy and spent all of his large fortune on warships, for which the Italian government never reimbursed him. William returned to America and died a poor man.[9]

John Dahlgren spent the bulk of his boyhood, he later recalled, as "a hard student under his father's eye." Bernhard Dahlgren valued education highly and spared no pains or expense to educate his children. He sent John to a school called Rand's Writing Academy and to a Quaker school on Fourth Street near Chestnut, where the boy studied Spanish, Latin, and mathematics. Philadelphia Quakers, who had been instrumental in founding the city's American Philosophical Society, encouraged education in science because they believed it would improve the physical condition of people's lives. Bernhard chose this school because it fit nicely into the Dahlgren family tradition of scientific education. The Quaker teachers surely gave the boy a dose of moral philosophy as well. Bernhard sometimes sat in on John's classes, taking a seat near the schoolmaster. One can imagine him casting a critical eye on the teacher as well as on his son, who must have endured ribbing from the other boys because of his father's presence. Bernhard tutored the boy at home as well. John later remembered that "Latin and Mathematics were got by hard study." As an eleven-year-old he read histories of Greece and Rome, variously praising or criticizing the morality of the ancient heroes, and took first prize in a Latin competition for a translation of Virgil. He studied trigonometry, algebra, navigation, surveying, and geography. One of his mathematics notebooks has survived. It is meticulously neat and carefully rendered. It contains definitions, rules, axioms, postulates, and problems in geometry and algebra. It has none of the doodles or scribblings of a schoolboy's notebook. Instead, fancy letters printed in different styles spell out captions and headings, most of which are underlined with a flourish. There are no mistakes, strike-throughs, or erasures. John must have copied it from a rough draft. The notebook was painstakingly fashioned by a hardworking boy who took himself quite seriously. His teachers praised his character, conduct, disposition and achievements.[10]

One application for mathematics that John learned early was accounting. Entries in a journal he kept when he was fourteen focused on money. John purchased a flying squirrel for 12.5 cents. The squirrel seemed feeble, so the next day he sold it for the same price and purchased a heartier one for 18.5 cents. He kept the new pet in a box in his brother's room, but the animal gnawed through the twine lattice he had fashioned as a window covering. John estimated that a stronger box would cost $4. "At my time of life," he lamented, "money was scarce being not quite $2 in ready money." He sold the squirrel to a friend for 25 cents. The fourteen-year-old Dahlgren kept his money in three separate "funds": one for general expenses that he called the "contingent" fund, one for purchasing the plays of his favorite comedian, and one for buying other playbooks at auction. He listed the amount in each fund, noting that his mother owed him $1.25 and would pay him 12.5 cents every Saturday until the debt was retired. Dahlgren no doubt used part of the "contingent fund" to buy the squirrel. This preoccupation with money would be a lifelong trait.[11]

John Dahlgren recalled childhood as his "happy days." In later years he wistfully remembered himself as a "little white-haired urchin with a world no greater than State House Square and some half-dozen squares near it, a happy child, only envious of the possession of a pair of little white bantams in his grandmother's yard." He recalled fondly how his grandmother regaled him with stories from her past.[12]

Yet Dahlgren was not altogether pleased with his upbringing. While most Americans came from rural backgrounds, Dahlgren grew up in the city. Cities were the centers of American commerce, industry, finance, politics, wealth, art, and learning, and they typically housed the state's most influential people. But they also embodied danger, violence, corruption, dirt, disease, filth, and crime. Densely populated, smelly, poorly cleaned and drained, their streets covered with horse manure, cities were not attractive places. Dahlgren revealed his true feelings about growing up as a "hard student" in the city through his ideas about raising his own children. The countryside, he noted, was a far better place for a child. Diet, exercise, and "country air" were of paramount importance. Education, if begun too early, could rob a child of his or her health. A child should avoid "every task imposed by mental labor until the chest, stomach & frame are full & well developed. Study is the greatest consumer of physical capability and if begun too soon, prostrates the system forever." Dahlgren suffered from periodic illness throughout his life and no doubt blamed it on his upbringing.[13]

John Dahlgren's childhood ended abruptly with the sudden death of his father. Heart disease ran in the family, but the cause of Bernhard Dahlgren's death remains uncertain. What is certain is that he died on 19 July 1824, before John turned fifteen. Bernhard had been a generous man, generous to a fault. He had given so much to charity that his death left his wife and four children in financial straits. John Vaughan, an influential family friend, put it thus: "Had [Bernhard] lived a few years longer[, he] would have left his family in excellent circumstances had his talents and industry continued to yield what he was in the receipt of at the time he died. As it is the children must as early as possible free themselves from dependence on the Mother."[14]

Thrust unexpectedly into the world of work, John Dahlgren set out to fulfill his boyhood dream: to join the United States Navy. "That my thoughts should have been turned seaward," he reflected later in life, "may be readily accounted for by several early associations which…had taken deep root in my young fancy." He had grown up within sight of Philadelphia's wharves at a time when commerce boomed and tall ships were commonplace. On holiday visits to the Philadelphia Navy Yard, the frigate *Raritan* and the giant ship of the line *Pennsylvania* deeply impressed him. Many of his schoolmates had chosen a maritime career. In 1820 his father had taken him and his brother Charles on a trip to Brandywine, Delaware, to discuss business matters with Victor Marie du Pont. While there, Samuel Francis Du Pont,[15] then sixteen years old, returned home from his first cruise with the navy, resplendent in his midshipman's uniform. As Charles later recalled, Du Pont's "uniform was so attractive to the eyes of the little boy [John] of less than 11 years of age that, as he told me long years after, it gave him his first idea of the Navy." Finally, as John Dahlgren later recalled, James Fenimore Cooper's "beautiful sea-tale" *The Pilot* "captivated" his imagination.[16]

The Pilot is the most interesting and important of Dahlgren's childhood associations, for it reveals much about his dream. *The Pilot,* Cooper's fourth novel, introduced the sea story as a distinct genre in literature. It was the first full-length novel in which the ocean was the principal setting and in which seamen were the main characters. Cooper asserted that its purpose was to rescue naval figures from obscurity. With considerable artistic license *The Pilot* recounts the exploits of John Paul Jones, although it never mentions him by name. It also extols American democracy and virtues and glorifies naval life by portraying seamen as stalwart American heroes. It was the first of Cooper's novels in which he tried to foster an American maritime nationalism and argue that America's manifest destiny lay upon the ocean. Young Dahlgren may not have grasped Cooper's thesis, but the virtuous pilot who calmly led his ship through danger may well have reminded him of the heroes of ancient Greece and Rome.[17]

The popular American perception of victory in the War of 1812 must have been another great source of inspiration. As one literary magazine put it in 1813, "the glorious achievements of our navy" had "kindled a new and holy spirit of nationality, and enabled the humblest citizen among us boldly to say to the world that he too has a country." These "brilliant deeds of heroism" were set down in writing to "make the remembrance of the old become the cause of future victories." The War of 1812 was a fertile source of popular songs, such as those that narrated Oliver Hazard Perry's victory on Lake Erie or the *Constitution*'s victory in her epic duel with the *Guerriere.*[18]

The American naval tradition of the Jacksonian era rested upon the daring exploits of heroic individuals rather than on an institution that had built and defended an empire, such as the Royal Navy. James Biddle, Stephen Decatur, Jesse D. Elliot, Thomas Macdonough, and Charles Morris rose rapidly to the highest naval rank because the navy and the nation identified them as heroes. Decatur, Elliot, and Macdonough had been commanding officers in spectacular naval victories; Biddle and Morris had been first lieutenants in such victories. The navy viewed promotion based on heroic deeds—acts of conspicuous bravery or those that promoted the national interest—as the consummate form of recognition for merit.[19] Writers emphasized America's naval successes and ignored its failures, and the nation worshipped a pantheon of naval heroes. So deep is their imprint on the American consciousness that many of their names—Decatur, Perry, Macdonough, Bainbridge—remain familiar today.

A quest for glory had motivated many of the naval heroes of the 1812 generation. Thomas Macdonough and Stephen Decatur passionately sought military glory. Edward Preble lusted for fame. David Porter's thirst for glory so impaired his reasoning that in one battle he deliberately engaged a superior force, at the cost of 60 percent of his people. "How were these officers to gain glory?" asked Herman Melville in a sea novel of a type different from Cooper's: "How but by a distinguished slaughtering of their fellow men." Most popular literature, however, portrayed the American naval officer as a virtuous hero of strong moral fiber who defeats the villainous foe in a single-ship duel. It was a neo-chivalrous image rooted in Homer's *Iliad*.[20]

To seek immortal fame through war was a respectable ambition in the eighteenth and nineteenth centuries. Since the time of Homer, glory achieved in battle had allowed the warrior to live beyond death. The heritage of fame in Western society sprang from classical ideals of public service, civic virtue, and national glory. In the eighteenth century, preoccupation with personal immortality expressed itself in the desire to fix one's name and image for posterity. Since the eighteenth century, fame has been connected more with achievement and social mobility than with inherited position. Nineteenth-century America emphasized social mobility and the self-made man. Desire for glory embodied desire both for transcendence and for social mobility. In the United States a man could achieve glory entirely through his own efforts. Glory won in battle enabled a man to rise above his status at birth and assured social survival and immortal fame.[21]

John Dahlgren sought a berth in the United States Navy in order to win glory and achieve immortal fame. The "recognition he most ardently desired," recalled Madeleine Dahlgren, his second wife, was "the recognition of posterity."[22] A naval career offered him a chance to recoup or perhaps transcend the status and security he had lost when his father died. Bernhard Dahlgren had sacrificed not only social status in Sweden in the name of republicanism but also the money he had earned in America for the sake of charity. In America admission to the social aristocracy often depended on the amount of one's fortune.[23] In Philadelphia the Dahlgrens lived on the fringe of the socioeconomic aristocracy rather than on the inside because Bernhard had given away the admission ticket. Perhaps subconsciously John Dahlgren realized that he could regain lost status for the family name through heroic naval service to the American state. Fame and glory won as a naval hero would allow him to rise above the vulgar necessity of wealth. In short, John Dahlgren embarked on a quest for glory in order to transcend his social status and to make his mark in history.

But his immediate reason for joining the navy was the practical necessity of earning a living. Virtually the only route to a commission in the nineteenth-century navy was through service as a midshipman; few if any enlisted men rose from the ranks. Obtaining a midshipman's warrant was the first step. This was a matter of politics. The navy possessed virtually no standards for selecting midshipmen. Appointments were the prerogative of the secretary of the navy and the president. The political needs of the administration in power were the primary consideration. The government paid little attention to the navy's actual requirements, and there were no specified ratios for officer grades.[24]

Dahlgren applied for a midshipman's warrant in the winter of 1824–25. His teachers and his father's friends—including John Vaughan, D. H. Willing, and other prominent Philadelphians—sent glowing recommendations to the secretary of the navy on his behalf. The letters noted Dahlgren's achievements in Latin and mathematics and praised his "almost unequalled personal merit," his "uncommon intellectual dispositions," and his "chastened morals, disciplined understanding, and cultivated mind." Moreover, forty-seven members of Pennsylvania's General Assembly signed a petition in support of the application. It was an impressive mustering of influence.[25]

The navy turned him down. "It is not probable that the wishes of Mr. Dahlgren can be gratified very soon," explained the secretary of the navy. "The number in the service already from Philadelphia, with other causes, will, I fear, prevent it for some time."[26]

Disappointed but not crushed, Dahlgren signed on board the merchant brig *Mary Beckett* in hopes that experience at sea would improve his chances the next time. On 28 March 1825 he registered as a seaman. The certificate of registration describes him as fifteen years old, 5 feet 6 ½ inches tall, with light hair and complexion, blue eyes, and a scar on his forehead between the eyebrows. The *Mary Beckett* set sail for Trinidad de Cuba two days later and arrived there after a three-week passage.[27]

Dahlgren had recently begun to record his thoughts and experiences in a diary, a habit he would keep up for the rest of his life. He had much to say about his first trip away from home. Although Trinidad de Cuba and the surrounding area looked beautiful from afar, everything was filthy up close. The fort guarding the harbor was "wretched"; a company of militia could storm it in "five minutes." Corrupt customs officials pocketed part of the import duty paid on each barrel of beef, pork, and flour. Spanish men suffered from "cowardice," and the women from "want of modesty" because they smoked cigars. The few available books in the town were exorbitantly priced, "and both the Books & news-paper are so confined in their ideas and bigoted in their opinions on Politics and Religion &c. that they soon disgust the reader." On 23 May the *Mary Beckett* departed from Cuba. Six days out she was struck by a severe gale, lost her sails, and drifted to the west coast of Florida. Dahlgren reached Philadelphia on 18 June 1825.[28]

He spent the next several months reading and working as a secretary for the pastor of the Old Swedes' Church. He launched a second campaign to become a midshipman that fall. It resembled the first in that he gathered recommendations from influential family friends. But this time influential Philadelphians visited the secretary of the navy in person to recommend the boy.[29]

Dahlgren's determination, persistence, hard work, and connections paid off. On 1 February 1826 Secretary of the Navy Samuel L. Southard appointed him a midshipman in the United States Navy.[30]

2

The Reefer, the Sailing Navy, and the Steam Navy
1826–May 1834

The word *generation* commonly refers to a chronological frame of reference, but it can also denote groups of contemporaries who share common experiences. Alexis de Toqueville observed in democracies that "each generation is a new people." Arthur M. Schlesinger perceived a generational impulse when he described the history of American politics as a series of alternating shifts between liberal and conservative periods, occurring roughly every seventeen years.[1]

The common experience of officers who joined the navy in the seventeen years following 1798, the year the Navy Department was created, was war: the Quasi War with France, the Barbary Wars, and the War of 1812, which ended in 1815. The next major war, the war with Mexico, occurred thirty-one years later. Different experiences shaped the outlook of the officers who joined the navy after the War of 1812: dissatisfaction with the service, introduction of new technology, and reform in organization. If war defined the pre-1815 generation, frustration and change defined Dahlgren's generation after 1815. However, the two generations were socialized into the navy in the same way: on board sailing men-of-war.

An apprenticeship as a midshipman was the first step toward a commission as an officer in the United States Navy. Historian Christopher McKee has painted a composite portrait of the typical midshipman of the pre-1815 navy. The odds ran about one in three that the father was dead when the son decided to seek a midshipman's warrant. The decline in family income resulting from the father's death shaped that decision. While alive, the father had been either a federal officeholder or a businessman. Although the midshipman usually inherited a modest sum of money if any at all, his parents had given him a strong formal education, including Latin or Greek. His literary and mathematical training prepared him for the task of continuing self-education that the navy would impose. He went to sea in a merchantman before sailing on a naval vessel. And he received his warrant with the help of political connections.

The training, education, and socialization program for young officers of the pre-1815 navy sought to instill in them obedience, attentiveness, activity, industriousness, zeal, ambition, practical and theoretical knowledge of ships and the sea, and gentlemanly behavior—defined as ethical conduct; internalized discipline; avoidance of indulgence or self-destructive excess; courteous and harmonious relationships with peers; manners; the habit of associating with or emulating one's social equals (or even better, those of superior social status); and proper conduct in regard to social inferiors (that is, the maintaining of social distance). The officers of the pre-1815 navy viewed enlisted men as socially inferior and their behavior as childlike or adolescent.[2]

Historian Peter Karsten's composite portrait of the typical naval officer of the period 1845–1925 resembles McKee's pre-1815 officer in many ways. The later officer came from the upper echelon of the American social order. His well-to-do Anglo-Saxon parents enjoyed a significant measure of political influence. He was politically, socially, and professionally conservative. He saw man as a Hobbesian savage and believed that the races were all slightly different species, with Anglo-Americans being the best. He saw himself as a man of virtue battling vice.[3]

Soon after receiving notification of his appointment, the midshipman went to sea on board a naval vessel. The first six months were probationary. If the midshipman performed adequately, he received his midshipman's warrant, back-dated to the time of the original appointment, and the rank "acting midshipman." After a second cruise, the acting midshipman was eligible to take an examination for promotion to the rank of "passed midshipman." The would-be officer served in this nebulous grade until a commissioned berth opened up, a wait that could last six or seven years.[4]

Midshipmen, who were nicknamed reefers, learned their trade in the hard school of experience. Naval tradition dictated that the only place to educate an officer was on the deck of a sailing ship. There was no better school for practical seamanship, the main subject. It was not the only subject. On the starboard side of the gun deck, forward of the captain's cabin, the ship's "professor," usually the chaplain, hung canvas to partition off a classroom in which he taught writing, navigation, French, and mathematics. "It was only in cases of fortunate accident," says one historian of the salty schoolmasters, "that [the professors] knew anything about a subject before they were called to teach it." Apart from seamanship, naval education was not often taken seriously. The quality varied with the schoolmaster's knowledge and the captain's attitude.[5]

Midshipmen were quasi officers. They ranged in age from the early teens to the early thirties; most were about sixteen. All hands addressed them as Mister. Their duties included standing watch, assisting at gun drill, inspecting clothes and hammocks, supervising deck-cleaning details, and climbing aloft in all weather to shout orders from the yards to the top men. Their chief duty was to carry messages.[6]

On board frigates, as many as twenty reefers lived in the steerage, a place fraught with noise, rowdiness, hilarity, pranks, hazing, bullying, and fighting. A new midshipman coming below after a night watch on deck might find a pig trussed up in his hammock, or when he climbed into his bed he might discover that the clews had been arranged to slip and tumble him to the floor. Simply put, reefers were still boys.[7]

These boys did not enjoy the best of reputations. They were the most active participants in duels, and as a group they were one of the most troublesome and turbulent elements in the navy. Enlisted men despised them for their immaturity, lack of knowledge, and inexperience as leaders. Some indulged in petty tyranny and displayed a callous disregard for the feelings and comfort of the enlisted men. A marine private on board one ship was repelled by the right of young midshipmen "to command, to insult, to strike in the face men old enough to be their grandfathers." Many reefers were the wilder and less dutiful sons of prominent politicians, who packed them off to sea to keep them out of trouble until discipline and maturity curbed their spirit. Those such as Dahlgren who made fine junior officers partially offset the poor reputation that the bad apples gave to the group as a whole.[8]

Midshipmen learned their trade on board active-duty vessels. The primary peacetime mission of the United States Navy during the nineteenth century was the protection of American commerce. This meant that the navy fought pirates, suppressed smuggling, performed limited diplomatic duties, and showed the flag to powers that might otherwise discriminate against it. The navy did this by scattering its two to three dozen warships around the globe on distant stations. To each station the navy sent a squadron that consisted of a frigate and several sloops or schooners. Seldom did a squadron operate as a unit. Normally each ship went its own way so that the flag was shown in as many ports as possible. The distant-station squadrons gave moral and physical support to American shipping and commercial interests abroad and provided valuable nautical and geographical experience for officers and men.[9]

On 12 April 1826 Secretary of the Navy Southard ordered Dahlgren to report to Captain James Barron in Norfolk for duty on board the *Macedonian,* bound for the Brazil station. The *Macedonian* was a thirty-eight-gun frigate, built in Britain in 1810 and captured by the forty-four-gun frigate *United States,* Commodore Stephen Decatur, on 25 October 1812. Following the War of 1812 she fought against the Barbary pirates and patrolled in the Mediterranean, off the Atlantic coast of the United States, and off the Pacific coast of South America. The cruise on the Brazil station would be her last. She departed from Norfolk on 11 June 1826.[10]

The *Macedonian*'s final voyage had all of the color and romance of nineteenth-century life at sea. During her cruise up and down the east coast of South America and visits to the various ports of call, her crew witnessed a battle between Brazilian and Argentine vessels, boarded slave ships, sighted whales, weathered storms, and chased a buccaneer. In his diary Dahlgren wrote dispassionately about floggings, grog, and duels. He later recalled pride in wearing his "much prized" insignia and joy at being "in daily proximity" to heroes of the War of 1812. The *Macedonian* "had been one of the finest frigates in the British Navy, and by the valor of Decatur…graced our list." The squadron commodore was a "stern disciplinarian," and "the very atmosphere of the ship was that of 1812 with all its historic association." Dahlgren's new life was a colorful one.[11]

Everyday life at sea had its own color. Drinking water, for example, was usually green. Stored in wooden casks, the water rapidly became home to all sorts of living slime. Ben Sands, a contemporary of Dahlgren who rose to the rank of rear admiral, recalled that "we strained [the water] through our teeth"; it smelled like "sulphuretted hydrogen." Bread, beef, pork, dried vegetables, and cheese served as the principal items of seafaring diet until just before the Civil War. The beef, which many sailors called salt junk, was prepared ashore, cut into 10-pound slabs, salted heavily to preserve it, and stowed in white-oak casks. It was so hard that sailors could use it for scrimshaw work, carving it into little boxes and picture frames. The bread, known as ship's biscuit or hardtack, was baked ashore and stowed on board in a quantity to last the entire cruise. Each hard-crusted loaf weighed a pound. Hardtack served as home for weevils, which could be laboriously picked out or unceremoniously eaten. Sailors often raced the weevils, picking their favorites and placing their bets. Sands recalled "the hard tack being rather animated, the 'salt junk' a little rusty, the salt pork a wee bit rancid, and the butter tasting of the oak of the keg." But "even the pork, if not too rancid, was delicious to a hungry reefer when covering a good cake of hard tack and topped by a coat of red pepper!" As quasi officers, the midshipmen ate better than enlisted men. They were able to purchase livestock for their mess, as well as garlic, onions, and peppers to add spice to their diet.[12]

In his diary Dahlgren took little note of everyday life at sea, but he revealed himself through remarks about matters of social class, naval custom, and rank. On 29 July 1826 the *Macedonian* crossed the equator on her voyage southward. This was an eagerly anticipated event because it brought a welcome break from routine: the tradition of "initiating" men who were crossing the equator for the first time. The initiation ceremony included mock pagan rituals, speeches, processions, and a play in which crewmen performed the roles of King Neptune and his court. The highlight of the ceremony came when all the officers and men who had not crossed the line before were ducked in a pool of equatorial water, "lathered" with tar brushes, and "shaved" with iron-hoop "razors." Although sprains and broken bones sometimes resulted, the line-crossing ceremony remained a popular shipboard diversion throughout the navy's history. But Commodore Biddle, commander of the Brazil Squadron, forbade the crew of the *Macedonian* to stage the ritual. Dahlgren agreed with this point of view, considering such rituals "subversive of true discipline." The navy was an authoritarian organization. Principles of discipline and domination were central to it. Some officers considered diversions such as the line-crossing ceremony important for morale. Others viewed enlisted men with contempt and considered them to belong to the lowest class of humanity; officers like these believed that the men could be controlled only by the threat of punishment, and they ran their ships with an iron hand. Dahlgren's view of the line-crossing ceremony marks him with the latter stripe and suggests that he viewed enlisted men as inferiors.[13]

Indeed, young Dahlgren considered himself a member of the upper class. On 13 October 1826, American merchants living in the Bahia province of Brazil gave a ball for Commodore Biddle and his officers. Dahlgren was impressed by the sum the merchants had spent on the affair, but not by the merchants themselves. Dahlgren said this about the affair:

> The manner in which we were treated, was highly displeasing and satisfied us that riches, alone, never will constitute the gentleman: these men, obscure, and of low standing, in the U. States, like many others left it, as unknown and low adventurers, thro' the most wonderful good fortune, had amassed considerable wealth…their never having mixed with genteel society in their own country, will however be sufficient excuse, for their ignorance of the common rules of politeness.[14]

Dahlgren also expressed contempt for those who he thought wielded unmerited influence. The *Macedonian* entered the harbor of Rio de Janeiro on 7 November. A court-martial that Dahlgren attended there led him to reflect on the nature of political influence. He was incensed that boys who "scarcely [had] a grammatical knowledge of their own language" were given midshipman's warrants. "Never should the defence of our Country," he fumed, "be entrusted to any but those, who are really worthy of that honor: Influence, however predominates." Furthermore, Dahlgren was upset by the fact that some of his unworthy peers were already receiving pay, while meritorious lads like himself had to wait until the end of the probationary period. Dahlgren had amassed a fair amount of influence to secure his own appointment as midshipman, but he believed that he truly deserved it.[15]

Dahlgren objected to the United States Navy's system of rank as well. The highest rank was captain. Squadron commanders, given the honorary title of commodore, were formally listed as "post captains." The American government considered this the equivalent of a European admiral, but the Europeans did not see it that way. According to international maritime etiquette, an admiral was entitled to a fifteen-gun salute, whereas a post captain rated only nine guns. Dahlgren was dismayed when a French admiral returned Commodore Biddle's salute with fewer guns. "This ranks among the chief disadvantages of our present Naval System," he complained. "They will not make Admirals until fatal Experience has convinced them of their Error."[16]

Dahlgren was a serious lad, but he liked to have fun as much as any teenaged reefer. On 24 May 1827 the master's mates and midshipmen of the

British ship *Warspite* paid a visit to their counterparts on the *Macedonian*, then anchored in the harbor at Rio. The Americans provided "Punch, Wine, & grog," as Dahlgren noted in his diary, and the British "staid til Sundown and did honor to our cheer in such a manner that another half hour would have made them feel rather funny. By the time we parted we were as friendly as if our acquaintance had existed for years." Several days later the *Warspite* reefers paid another visit to the *Macedonian*. A drinking contest between the American and British lads ensued. Dahlgren noted that "the drunken Englishmen beat us out & out—for to crown the glory of the day, One of them b— himself."[17]

Dahlgren spent his free time calling on ladies ashore and writing letters to his mother and influential friends. On one occasion he secured permission to take one of the *Macedonian*'s boats and four men for a three-day sail around Rio's harbor. The trip inspired Dahlgren to wax poetic about the quality of the light as "the rays of the setting sun gleaming on the water…appeared to be a sheet of liquid fire from the orb of the bright luminary."[18]

Life at sea also had its dark side. The two-year cruise came to an end, and on 29 August 1828 the *Macedonian* departed Rio for home. Smallpox had broken out among the crew. Within a few days forty-five men were reported on the sick list. Dahlgren remarked upon their "offensive" and "hardly endurable" odor. He contracted a mild case of smallpox himself. Men who died were buried at sea. To Dahlgren's horror, "the splash of water was but the signal for myriads of sharks to rush to the spot for all that was left of poor humanity." Even the *Macedonian* herself was ill. She had become structurally decrepit, hogging excessively.[19] "The weakness of the ship," noted Dahlgren, "was such as to render every exertion necessary to ensure her safety at sea." The ordeal ended on 31 October 1828, when the *Macedonian* dropped anchor at Hampton Roads.[20]

The next day Dahlgren was granted a leave of absence. He returned to Philadelphia and rented a garret in a boardinghouse on Seventh Street, where his mother now lived. On 1 December 1828 he received his long-awaited midshipman's warrant. He spent the time ashore visiting old friends and working hard. He desired a copy of the expensive book *Riddle's Navigation* but could not afford to buy one. He borrowed one instead, took it to his unheated garret, and copied it by hand during the cold Philadelphia winter. Like a character in a Russian novel, he wrapped himself up in an overcoat and wrote until his fingers became too cold to go on. By the spring he had copied everything he wanted. Eager to return to active duty, he applied for sea service.[21]

On 5 June 1829 Dahlgren received orders to report to Commodore Chauncey in New York City for duty on board the *Ontario,* bound for the Mediterranean, the navy's most important distant station. The Mediterranean Squadron had been established early in the nineteenth century as a reminder to Barbary corsairs that depredations to the Stars and Stripes would not be tolerated, but this mission faded with the passing years. The primary mission of the Mediterranean Squadron was now to show the flag in various ports in order to remind Europeans that the United States had a potentially dangerous fleet. Dahlgren later recalled the Mediterranean as being the best school for an officer because it provided experience in handling ships close to shore, in entering and leaving crowded harbors, and in dealing with the French and English navies.[22]

Dahlgren arrived in New York shortly after receiving his orders. The sixteen-gun sloop *Ontario,* built in 1813, had seen service in the War of 1812 and had sailed in the Mediterranean, Pacific, and Caribbean. Dahlgren described her as "a light o' keel, rakish rover of a craft." The *Ontario* set sail for Gibraltar on 22 August 1829, a clear and pleasant day.[23]

The *Ontario* visited Gibraltar, Algiers, Port Mahon, Tunis, Majorca, Minorca, Barcelona, Marseilles, Livorno, and Smyrna. She encountered merchant and naval vessels from Britain, France, Austria, Holland, Sweden, and Spain. She carried dispatches and diplomats on her rounds. On one occasion she accidently backed into a British packet. On another, a round she fired to salute an Austrian commodore accidently passed through the rigging of a Dutch brig, damaged the spars of a French brig, and struck the side of an Austrian merchantman. Dahlgren had charge of a deck, occasionally worked the ship, and did lieutenant's duty.[24]

The Mediterranean rewarded him with rich experience. On his first visit to Algiers he donned his cocked hat and sword and went ashore. Eyes peered at him through holes in the walls as he picked his way through the narrow streets, guided by a native, on his way to visit the American consul general. The consul took him on a tour of the city. Dahlgren saw ferocious lions in the dey's menagerie, noting that they were "very little like the poor sheepish lions and tigers palmed off on us at home." He gave money and tobacco to French sailors who had been shipwrecked and subsequently imprisoned by the dey. In Port Mahon he sampled date-and-fish soup and monkey-and-woodcock soup, both of which proved a welcome change from salt junk and

USS *Ontario* (Naval Historical Center)

hardtack. He marveled at the international flavor of the port, and at the beggars who flocked around naval officers. Tailors, shoemakers, launderers, and food vendors also flocked around the officers. Dahlgren thought the Mahonese a "neat, tidy, painstaking people."[25]

Another bout with illness tainted Dahlgren's Mediterranean experience. Chest pain had been plaguing him for several months, and he began to spit blood. The *Ontario*'s surgeon declared him unfit for active duty. On 8 September 1831 the captain transferred him to the *Constellation,* which was due to sail for home. The sources do not name his ailment.[26]

The illness was not the only thing threatening his life. Back in the fall of 1829 Dahlgren, then on board the *Ontario,* had had a misunderstanding with a midshipman from the *Constellation* named Henry Walker. Walker had challenged him to a duel, but the *Constellation* had sailed before they could resolve the matter. Soon after Dahlgren stepped on board the *Constellation* in September 1831, Walker reissued the challenge. Dahlgren's new messmates took a keen interest in the affair. One of them, a reefer named J. P. Parker, sided with him. In the process of defending him, Parker managed to insult yet another party, and a challenge for a second duel was issued. The whole affair ended peacefully when the various parties untangled the web and discovered that no one's honor had been slighted after all.[27]

Honor was all-important to the nineteenth-century naval officer. It guided him in delicate affairs like paying debts and dealing with insults. It told him how to behave. Its ingredients included physical courage, a balance of obligation and reward, gentlemanly conduct, personal fealty to the commander, a sense of brotherhood, and the pursuit of glory. Honor placed the individual above the group. Dueling was the ritualistic expression of honor, the code of gentlemen. Moreover, on shipboard, the crowded decks, endless days upon the sea, bad food, and slimy water tended to blow trivial matters like Dahlgren's misunderstanding with Walker out of proportion.[28]

Shortly after the misunderstanding was sorted out, the *Constellation* set sail for home, arriving in Norfolk on 12 November 1831. Dahlgren was given a three-month leave of absence. He decided to spend it at the Norfolk Naval School preparing for the examination for promotion to the rank of passed midshipman. First held in 1819, this exam was an early step toward establishing professional standards in the officer corps. It covered seamanship, gunnery, navigation, and higher mathematics. To pass meant that a midshipman was qualified for the rank of lieutenant. Schools to prepare reefers for the exam were set up at the Washington, Boston, New York, and Norfolk

Navy Yards. Ben Sands, recalling his own experience at the Norfolk Naval School in 1833, noted that although the reefers took their studies seriously, they rounded out their education with "fun and mischief," grand balls, and falling in love with Norfolk's young women.[29]

Even the rowdiest reefers buckled down as exam time drew near. Ben Sands described the tension as "worse than going into battle." The orally administered exam was a "trying ordeal." Each candidate appeared alone before the board for a grilling on the various subjects. Immediately afterward the board notified him whether he had passed. Sands quipped that his classmates either congratulated or consoled him with a mint julep.[30]

Dahlgren prepared with characteristic resolve. The notes he left behind contain specific questions: "How do you get on a Bowsprit cap at sea?" "A shoal is discovered close a-head, it is doubtful whether there be room to back or veer; what do?" Dahlgren highlighted questions that certain members of the examining board were known to ask. He wrote detailed answers to each one.[31]

Dahlgren passed the exam in April 1832, placing ninth among the thirty-one midshipmen who took it. His classmate Raphael Semmes, who would become the notorious commander of the Confederate raider *Alabama,* placed first. Dahlgren firmly believed that his own seven-year apprenticeship had qualified him for some sort of command, and he fully expected to get one. When he did not, he complained privately, took the next several months off, and returned to Philadelphia.[32]

In January 1833 Dahlgren applied for active duty in his home town. The navy assigned him to the receiving ship *Sea Gull* at the Philadelphia Navy Yard the following April. It was easy duty. In his relatively ample spare time Dahlgren studied law, making detailed notes on Blackstone and other luminaries in the field. The study of law, at least according to lawyers, was an upper-class thing to do. Blackstone held that knowledge of the law is the proper accomplishment of every gentleman, and an almost essential part of a polite education.[33]

But Dahlgren was unhappy in his new assignment. The *Sea Gull's* commanding officer, a Lieutenant Charles Guantt, ordered Dahlgren and the two other officers to remain on board every night, forbidding them to rotate ashore. Moreover, Guantt discharged one of their mess servants. Dahlgren and the others addressed a letter to Guantt's commanding officer, Captain James Barron, Dahlgren's commanding officer on the *Macedonian,* asking him to reinstate the servant and to allow two of them to go home each night.

In support of the latter request, they cited a naval regulation. In the navy, reporting one's superior for misconduct was insubordination. It was also a maxim never to disagree with one's superior. Respect for authority was considered essential to the military way of doing things. Predictably, Barron addressed a harsh reprimand to the three for writing the letter. Barron said that it jeopardized their careers, and that Dahlgren and his mates "must either be extremely deficient in their knowledge of discipline, or entertain very little respect for the Laws of their Country, or the dignity of the Station of a Commander." Needless to say, he did not grant their requests. The incident is significant because it was the first time Dahlgren went over a superior's head to try to get what he wanted. It would not be the last.[34]

In June 1833 illness forced Dahlgren to take an unwelcome leave of absence, which he spent in Philadelphia. The nature of this ailment is also unknown, but by early the next year his health had improved enough for him to return to active duty. On 10 February 1834 the secretary of the navy assigned him to the United States Coast Survey. The head of the survey would order him to report for duty when a place became available.[35]

Annoyed by the wait and by the fact that he had not yet received a command afloat, Dahlgren began to think critically about his occupation. He took out his frustration by publishing a series of anonymous essays, addressed to the chairman of the Senate Naval Affairs Committee and signed only "Blue Jacket," in the Philadelphia *National Gazette*. In the essays Dahlgren attacked a new code of regulations that had been devised by a group of senior officers. The regulations based promotions on seniority, empowered senior officers to promote juniors to fill vacancies in the ranks, and permitted seniors to revoke such promotions as they pleased. Dahlgren condemned this as "aggrandizement of a few at the expense of the subordinate grades." He decried another regulation that forbade officers to express their opinions, even in private correspondence. Predicting that the new regulations would foster an evil abuse of power, he demanded reform. Dahlgren's identity as "Blue Jacket" was never discovered. Although the articles did not lead to any changes, Dahlgren had risked his career in an attempt to redress grievances.[36]

Dahlgren pondered the navy's shortcomings as he awaited orders to join the coast survey. The rate by which officers advanced in grade had become notoriously slow since the War of 1812. "From Captain to midshipman," he wrote, "the cry is promotion." He applauded the rumored plan of Andrew Jackson to institute a retirement program for senior officers, thus enabling juniors to advance: "While former administrations have been content that the Navy should drag on its wearied march groaning under the tyranny and arbitrary ideas and exploded notions of a few old Captains, Jackson at once calls into action the fire and originality of the younger officers, which had so long been rebuked by the timid, time worn policy of old men." Dahlgren had begun to despise the heroes he had once worshipped.[37]

If the promotion system was not changed, Dahlgren reasoned, officers who remained in a junior rank for a long time should receive higher pay. "What might be considered a fair compensation for a young man just entering life," he wrote, "would be entirely inadequate to meet the increasing demands upon one who is burdened with the maintenance of a family." He blamed the pay situation on the secretary of the navy, the height of whose ambition was, as he put it, "to save a copper." The navy needed "a statesman and a philosopher" at the helm, not a "clerk of estimates."[38]

The promotion rate was a major difference between Dahlgren's generation and the generation that had fought the War of 1812. The pre-1815 navy offered marvelous opportunities for advancement. It was a young organization, almost continuously involved in or on the brink of warfare. Viewing the pre-1815 navy as a whole, the median age of an officer upon promotion to lieutenant was twenty-two; the median age was twenty-nine upon promotion to the next grade, master commandant, and thirty-two upon promotion to captain, the highest grade.[39]

But in the post-1815 navy the rate of promotion to higher grades slowed to a glacial pace. Honor obliged the naval officer to do his duty to the best of his ability, and in return he expected promotion; rank was the most important thing to him. But there was no system of retirement. Young officers had to rely on death to provide vacancies in the top ranks, and the navy was simply too small to provide a berth for every reefer. Matthew Fontaine Maury, a contemporary of Dahlgren, estimated that a midshipman appointed in 1839 could expect to reach the rank of lieutenant by 1870. Many officers remained in the rank of lieutenant for ten years or longer. Common gossip had it that such lieutenants developed a list to starboard from carrying the one epaulette on the right shoulder. Advancement to captain, which provided the other epaulette, was the only way to restore them to an even keel. Matthew Calbraith Perry, another contemporary, described the promotion system as one of "death-like stagnation." Perry blamed this on the lack of a rank above captain. Fear of establishing a naval aristocracy, democratic resentment of the title admiral, and the tendency of every politician with militia connections to call himself a general kept Congress from authorizing higher ranks.[40]

For most of the first half of the nineteenth century, the generation of officers that had fought in the War of 1812 dominated the navy. These officers were intense individualists, jealous of their own rights, quick to resent an affront, prone to suspect malice or envy in others, and sensitive to the least criticism. Pathologically preoccupied with personal honor, they proved incapable of sacrificing private considerations for the good of the service. Feuds, cliques, squabbling, and tension tore the ranks apart. Some commanders lacked concern for the letter of the law in naval regulations except where it concerned their own prerogatives. Senior officers showed contempt for new ideas. Junior officers complained about the tyranny of superiors. The aura of hero worship that surrounded the old veterans protected them from the charges of their subordinates. Senior officers were virtually immune from serious punishment. Given this gloomy atmosphere, it is not surprising that many junior officers resigned their commissions in despair and chose other occupations. But among those who remained in the navy were young men dedicated to improving both the service and their own future.[41]

Naval reform after 1815 stemmed from a nationwide impulse toward reform. The spirit of reform swept America in the 1830s and 1840s as never before. American minds pondered numerous schemes for moral and social reform. All across the nation there sprang up religious cults and utopias; efforts to reform education, prisons, and the care of the poor, the blind, and the insane; and crusades for temperance, peace, women's rights, and the abolition of slavery. Reformers in this period often repudiated "old fogies" and their values.[42]

The national reform wave manifested itself in the armed services in what historian Samuel P. Huntington calls the American Military Enlightenment. The fifteen years from the end of Andrew Jackson's first administration to the beginning of the Mexican War saw an outpouring of military thought and writing. Military societies sprang up, military journals emerged for brief but active lives, military officers published significant and original books, and the idea of a military profession was expounded and defended. Military and naval reformers advocated such issues as technological change, the creation of professional standards, a regularized system of promotion by merit, and professional education.[43]

Matthew Fontaine Maury was known for his efforts to reform naval administration. Robert Stockton, Matthew C. Perry, and Franklin Buchanan led a devoted band of officers in the belief that steam propulsion and shell guns were fast making sailing navies obsolete. Perry, who also dedicated himself to the education of his fellow officers, founded the Naval Lyceum in the New York Navy Yard and published the *Naval Magazine.* Samuel Francis Du Pont and Alexander S. Mackenzie fostered efforts to curb the dictatorial powers of their seniors and retire the obviously unfit. Each issue was identified with the individual officers who promoted it.[44]

Naval reformers shared similar views on three basic issues: administrative reform, naval education, and technological change, particularly the introduction of steam propulsion into warships. The impetus for almost every innovation came from civilian officials and junior officers, with senior officers lining up in opposition.[45]

The first major naval innovation of the American Military Enlightenment was the introduction of steam propulsion into warships. Fits and false starts marked the early history of the steam navy. Experiments with steam propulsion began during the War of 1812, when the government built a steam-driven war vessel generally described as a "steam battery," known both as the *Fulton I* and the *Demologos.* She was the first steam-driven warship ever constructed for any navy. Laid up after the War of 1812, she was destroyed by an accidental explosion in 1829. The Navy Act of 1816 authorized three more steam batteries, but the Board of Navy Commissioners, the administrative triumvirate of senior officers at the top of the naval hierarchy, had not seen fit to build them. The pre-1815 generation, led by the commissioners, tended to resist steam power. They detested the very thought of a navy dominated by cumbersome steam vessels that did not demand a high level of seamanship and created endless noise and dirt. They enjoyed the support of politicians such as Secretary of the Navy James K. Paulding and President Martin Van Buren, who was quoted as saying that "this country [requires] no navy at all, much less a steam navy."

Congress, however, was apprehensive about the increasing use of steam power in the French and British navies and authorized the construction of steam warships. A vessel named the *Fulton II,* launched in 1837, marked the real beginning of the steam navy of the United States. In March 1839 Congress authorized three additional steam warships. Matthew C. Perry, a pioneer in steam navigation, was largely responsible for the success of the first two of these vessels, the paddle-steamers *Mississippi* and *Missouri,* completed in 1842. A war scare with England over the Maine–New Brunswick boundary, the energetic leadership of Abel P. Upshur, who became secretary of the navy in October 1841, and Stockton's efforts led to the construction of the first screw-propelled naval warship, the *Princeton*. As the steam movement gathered momentum, Congress authorized four more war steamers in March 1847.[46]

Advocacy of steam propulsion was the one thing that virtually all the officers who joined the navy after 1815 had in common. For this reason Dahlgren and his peers may be referred to as the "steam generation," to distinguish them from the generation of officers who joined the navy before 1815.

Dahlgren expressed his generation's view of steam propulsion in a pamphlet published in 1838. The pamphlet conjured up images of an America driven by an impulse toward change, before which "the red man and the forest have receded like the mist of the morning before the rising sun." Rich and growing cities took their place in a vast and mighty America. A similar change was inevitable upon the sea. Soon, "snug reefs and leeway will be things of another time, and in their stead, we tighten the screw, oil the machinery, and poke the fire. Among the mighty agents of this change none can compare with steam." Dahlgren was fully aware that steam power was as yet in its infancy. Years would pass before its full potential could be realized. Nevertheless, "the haughty three-decker…is doomed, after all, like the steel-clad knight, or the mammoth, to be but the wonder and the riddle of another age."[47]

The introduction of steam power into the fleet exposed serious flaws in naval administration and brought about the second major naval innovation of the American Military Enlightenment: the creation of the bureau system. The Board of Navy Commissioners, established in 1815 to assist the secretary of the navy on matters relating to the building, arming, equipping, and employing of ships of war, had long outlived its usefulness, but Congress had ignored suggestions for changes. The trenchant pen of Matthew Fontaine Maury supplied the impetus for change. In articles published in the *Southern Literary Messenger* between 1838 and 1841, Maury expressed the discontent of the steam generation and subjected the whole naval organization to brilliant and merciless criticism. The articles played an important part in the reorganization that followed. Secretary Upshur believed that the commissioners were indecisive, deliberate, and unresponsive to new ideas. He instituted a plan for reform that divided the duties of the commissioners among several separate bureaus. They were charged with the responsibilities indicated by their names: Navy Yards and Docks; Ordnance and Hydrography; Construction, Equipment, and Repairs; Medicine and Surgery; and Provisions and Clothing. On 31 August 1842 Congress passed a bill that implemented this change. The heads of the bureaus were appointed by the president with approval of the Senate, but it was the secretary of the navy who determined their duties and to whom they were responsible. No term for their chiefdom was specified. No attempt was made to form the bureaus into a board; the secretary was the only unifying force. Upshur left the Navy Department in 1843 to become secretary of state. For the next ten years the administration of the navy fell to a series of short-term secretaries, with the result that naval reform was sporadic. As was the case with other naval reforms, administrative changes resulted largely from individual efforts.[48]

The third major naval innovation of the American Military Enlightenment was Secretary of the Navy George Bancroft's single-handed initiative in founding the United States Naval Academy in 1845. Senior officers tended to believe that "you could no more educate sailors in a shore college than you could teach ducks to swim in a garret." But within five months of assuming office, Bancroft started the academy without benefit of congressional authorization. He obtained the obsolete Fort Severn in Annapolis, Maryland, from the War Department as the site for the new school. He appointed a council of officers, including Perry, to discuss the curriculum. By legitimate exercise of the secretary's authority, Bancroft ordered in professors of mathematics from various warships and transferred midshipmen from ships and naval schools to Annapolis. Thus, the Naval Academy as well came into being through the initiative of a determined individual.[49]

In the sailing navy the traditional path to the top of the profession lay in service afloat, particularly in a fighting berth. The lack of traditional opportunities in the steam navy led officers to choose nontraditional career paths. Steam-generation officers promoted reform in naval technology, administration, and education in part because the rapid promotion rate available to the pre-1815 generation proved unavailable to them. They sought to legitimize their service by elevating nontraditional career paths to the status of service afloat. In this way distinguished service in science, technology, reform, education, and diplomacy joined heroic performance in battle in the American naval tradition. However, it was not until well into the twentieth century that officers who made contributions in these new fields achieved the same status as those who distinguished themselves in combat.

3

The Young Officer
May 1834–1846

In May 1834 the disgruntled Dahlgren finally received orders to join the United States Coast Survey. Ferdinand Rudolf Hassler, superintendent of the survey, was a towering figure in the history of American science. His signal contribution was the highly accurate instrumentation he designed for surveying. Not only did Hassler teach Dahlgren much of the science that the naval officer later adapted to ordnance work, but he also became a father figure to the young man.[1]

Hassler was born in the German part of Switzerland on 7 October 1770. His biographer considered him "a man of high intellectual qualities, almost a genius, a man of unlimited enthusiasm and devotion to his science, as honest and upright a man as God ever made, a proud spirit, independent, fretting under restraint, a true son of William Tell." Hassler studied mathematics and the science of geodesy at the Political Institute of Bern, known later as the University of Bern. In 1791 he began working for his mathematics professor on a survey of the Bern canton. When French soldiers interrupted the project, Hassler emigrated to America. In 1805 he arrived in Philadelphia, where he befriended members of the American Philosophical Society, including John Vaughan, the same man who had helped Dahlgren get into the navy. Through his connections with the American Philosophical Society, Hassler became head of the coast survey.

Because of the lack of suitable instruments in America, Hassler traveled to London, then home to the world's greatest manufacturers of precision instruments. He ordered theodolites, chronometers, and telescopes and helped design and build them. He spent four years in Europe and disbursed $5,000 more than the $50,000 Congress had appropriated for the purpose. He began the survey in the spring of 1816 and the next year had a specially designed carriage built to transport the precious and delicate instruments.

Although Hassler wanted to make a contribution to geodesy on par with European science, members of Congress wanted charts and things for saving mariners' lives and increasing merchants' profits. Politicians grumbled about Hassler's expenditures of time and money, and in 1818 Congress passed an act providing that only army or navy officers could be employed on the survey. Hassler was out of a job because Congress was used to the quick but less accurate results obtained with chains and compasses.

The struggle between Hassler's vision of science and the government's demand for results shaped the subsequent history of the coast survey. Between 1818 and 1832 the survey alternated between stagnation and false starts under a series of army and navy officers. Congress, meanwhile, had gained a clearer understanding of the need to support practical scientific endeavors such as surveying and exploration, endeavors that were in tune with the main task of the American people during this period: the conquest of a continent. In 1832 Hassler was asked to return as head of the coast survey. He agreed on the condition that the work be done in order to make a contribution to science. Congress acceded on the condition that he employ army and navy officers as assistants.[2]

Hassler devoted a great deal of time and effort to training his assistants. He kept officers on the survey long enough for them to acquire a fine scientific education, fine even by European standards, because only in this way would they be useful to him. He gave his charges a firm grounding in mathematics and physics, provided textbooks, and gave them on-the-job training in the use of delicate instruments and the application of mathematics to geodesy. He often worked until two or three in the morning, checking calculations made by his assistants to ensure that no mistakes slipped through. He maintained good personal relations with the officers assigned to him and established a fine esprit de corps. Service on the coast survey became popular in the navy. Ben Sands, John Rodgers, and David D. Porter numbered among Hassler's better-known students. Service under Hassler was as close as the navy came to providing graduate education in science.[3]

The Swiss geodesist was always on the lookout for suitable officers. Dahlgren had expressed an interest in pursuing some occupation connected with science. John Vaughan, a friend to both, recommended Dahlgren to Hassler, who in turn pulled the strings necessary to have the passed midshipman attached to the survey.[4]

On 15 May 1834 Hassler ordered Dahlgren to report to James Ferguson in Greenwich, Connecticut. Ferguson, engaged in the secondary triangulation of Connecticut, worked his crew seven days a week. Dahlgren was so busy on his first days of survey duty that he rarely found time to write in his diary. When he did write, he noted how little free time he had.[5]

The survey was a pleasant assignment. In warm months officers enjoyed duty on schooners and camping adventures on shore near triangulation points. Surveyors ate meals of fresh fish and fowl and in the evenings sang songs around campfires. Dahlgren delighted in visiting historic sites connected with the Revolutionary War. Hassler slept with his instruments in their specially designed carriage and criticized his subordinates' penmanship while checking the accuracy of their calculations. Ben Sands remembered Hassler as genial, accessible, and appreciative of a good joke.[6]

Dahlgren spent three years on the survey. In summers he did fieldwork, making triangulations by day and astronomical observations by night. He spent many an evening plotting points and making calculations by candlelight. In winters he calculated triangles and mapped geographic projections. He worked as a crew member on triangulation parties in Connecticut, New York, New Jersey, and Maine, and he was chief of a plane-table crew on Long Island. He learned both practical and pure science and gained an appreciation for fine instruments.[7]

Dahlgren and Hassler soon developed a close personal friendship. In April 1835 Hassler ordered Dahlgren to Washington to assist in making calculations. By the following fall the precise geodesist had begun to entrust this young officer with work he lacked the time to do himself. By the end of the year he had begun to confide in Dahlgren about family matters and the politics of running the survey. The two had much in common: European heritage, an affinity for math and science, and a penchant for overwork. Hassler's emphasis on education and high standing in the scientific community must have reminded Dahlgren of his own father.[8]

Nevertheless, in his second year Dahlgren found cause for discontent. Hassler used a system of quasi ranks to determine the duties of his people, but the navy determined the pay and rank of naval officers assigned to the survey. Dahlgren performed the duties of a second assistant, a coast survey grade usually occupied by naval officers of higher rank than passed midshipman. Dahlgren wanted equal pay for equal work. In August 1835 he embarked on a campaign for either a raise in pay or a promotion, or both. With Hassler's assistance he brought his case before the secretary of the navy. Hassler wrote a letter stating that Dahlgren deserved a promotion because he did the same work as naval officers of a higher grade. The secretary of the navy denied the promotion on the grounds that Dahlgren had not lately been to sea and therefore did not rate a promotion. He denied Dahlgren higher pay because naval law did not permit officers to receive more pay than they rated. He pointed out that duty on the coast survey was voluntary. If Dahlgren did not like his situation, he was free to seek another. Dahlgren drafted a reply in which he quoted naval law, argued that equal work merited equal pay whether on shipboard or on land, and virtually demanded at least a temporary promotion, but he did not send the letter. The *Sea Gull* experience had taught him the perils of such action. But he did not give up.[9]

Dahlgren renewed his campaign for higher pay in the spring of 1836. He now commanded a plane-table crew, the only naval officer ever to do so. It was a tribute to the excellence of his work. But as a passed midshipman, he received little more than half the pay of his civilian counterparts. He persuaded Hassler to ask the secretary of the navy to redress the inequity. The secretary agreed that the situation was unjust but argued that it would be equally unfair for officers on the survey to receive higher pay than officers of equal rank on other duty. He again denied the request. Dahlgren concluded that the whole system of naval rank needed to be reformed. "Merit alone," he grumbled, "unaided by influence or the chances of War, seldom goes beyond a Lieutenancy."[10]

The secretary of the navy gave Dahlgren a chance to obtain his promotion "legitimately," by service afloat. In September 1836 he offered Dahlgren duty as sailing master on a ship assigned to a squadron about to embark on a scientific exploring expedition. Dahlgren declined for reasons of decorum. Lieutenant Charles Wilkes was slated to lead the expedition. Such a command was usually reserved for higher-ranking officers. Moreover, an officer senior to Wilkes was to be placed under Wilkes's command. Such arrangements violated Dahlgren's sense of military propriety. Instead of accepting the assignment, he argued that service on the coast survey should count as sea duty for the sake of promotion and pay. The secretary still refused to promote him.[11]

Dahlgren still did not give up, and Hassler fully supported him. The coast survey had been attached to the Navy Department since 1834. The geodesist had objected to military control and had protested vehemently. In 1836 President Andrew Jackson placed the survey under the Treasury Department. That September, Hassler asked Secretary of the Treasury Levi Woodbury to raise Dahlgren's pay from $750 to $3,000 per year. The following spring Woodbury and Hassler took Dahlgren's case to the president. The geodesist argued that while most naval officers lived on board naval vessels, Dahlgren's duties kept him on land, where he incurred greater living expenses. Therefore, he should receive a corresponding increase in pay. The president agreed and made it so. As of March 1837, duty on the coast survey counted as service at sea for purposes of pay and promotion. Dahlgren received both the raise and the higher rank.[12]

Lieutenant Dahlgren had learned a great deal on the coast survey, not only about science but also about politics. Initiative, persistence, and influence proved the key lessons. Dahlgren took the initiative in righting what he perceived as a wrong, used Hassler's influence to get himself heard, and persisted despite opposition from the secretary of the navy. Most important, he overcame opposition by appealing to a higher authority. Merit did much better when coupled with influence.

Ill health nearly erased his gains. Following the promotion, Dahlgren received sailing orders. But the years of hard, close work at the plane table by day and the drawing table by night had taken their toll on his eyesight, threatening him with blindness. Instead of sailing on board a ship, Dahlgren spent the summer of 1837 at the naval hospital in Philadelphia. Although cared for by one of the best oculists in the United States, his vision failed to improve.[13]

In September, Dahlgren asked Hassler for a leave of absence to go to Paris for treatment under a world-famous oculist. He reasoned that because he had incurred the injury in the line of duty, he should receive full pay while on leave. Hassler agreed. To justify Dahlgren's pay, Hassler prepared a list of survey-related errands for him to run in Paris. Hassler forwarded the request to the secretary of the treasury in late September. Woodbury discussed Dahlgren's case with the president. They decided to grant the request, provided the absence did not extend beyond the following spring.[14]

Dahlgren left for Europe in November 1837. He remembered to take letters of introduction to American ambassadors but forgot Hassler's list of errands. In Paris the work of Henri Joseph Paixhans, a French ordnance expert, captivated Dahlgren's imagination. The French navy was in the process of adopting a type of cannon that Paixhans had invented for firing explosive shells. Despite his vision problems, Dahlgren studied Paixhans so thoroughly that he was able to publish a ninety-two-page translation of the Frenchman's work after returning to America. So much for resting his eyes. He entitled the work *An Account of the Experiments Made in the French Navy for the Trial of Bomb Cannon* and distributed it to American naval officers at his own expense. The pamphlet was well received and earned Dahlgren a reputation as an ordnance expert.[15]

Dahlgren returned to Washington on 19 May 1838. Shortly thereafter he paid Hassler a visit. The geodesist thought that Dahlgren had come back too soon, for his eyes had improved little. Dahlgren planned to resign from the survey and relinquish the pay he had received while abroad because he had failed to run the errands he was supposed to. More concerned about his friend's vision, Hassler told him not to worry about the errands. He persuaded Dahlgren to stay on the survey and to keep the money. Several days later, Dahlgren visited the secretary of the navy. At first the secretary thought that Dahlgren was reporting for duty. Dahlgren explained that he was making a formal courtesy call; his eyes had not improved enough for him to go on active duty. The secretary gave him a three-month leave of absence and put him on half pay.[16]

Dahlgren's visit to the secretary nearly cost him his career. Hassler had warned him to keep quiet about the errands. The geodesist smelled trouble, because the errands had been the justification for the pay Dahlgren had received in Europe. But the fact that he had not run them had surfaced in Dahlgren's unfortunate visit to secretary of the navy. The secretary in turn relayed the news to his counterpart in the treasury. The treasury secretary examined the facts. Dahlgren had not run the errands in Paris. He was as yet unable to work because of his eyes. The term of his leave with full pay, according to the original agreement, should have expired the previous spring. The secretary decided to remove him from the coast survey.[17]

A navy surgeon examined Dahlgren's eyes and diagnosed his affliction as "amaurosis," the partial loss of sight arising from disease of the optic nerve. The surgeon pronounced him unfit for duty and advised him to take a long rest in the country. Secretary of the Navy James K. Paulding suggested that Dahlgren take a furlough until he recovered. An officer on furlough received half pay. Dahlgren objected strenuously to this suggestion in letters to the secretary. "Will the Department permit me to inquire if this be the course

Early portrait of Dahlgren (Syracuse University Library)

usually adopted," he wrote, "in case of disability incurred by an officer in the line of his duty." He argued that furloughs were for officers who at their own discretion wanted to retire from duty temporarily. Half pay would not meet his needs. If the department forced him to take a furlough, he would apply for active duty, even though the surgeon estimated that he would not be ready for another eight to twelve months. Dahlgren had been willing to relinquish the errand pay, but a furlough was a different matter altogether. He felt entitled to full pay during recovery because he had sustained the injury in the line of duty. He was incensed at being treated this way after making such a sacrifice.[18]

He wrote about the predicament to his congressman, who in turn referred the matter to the committee on invalid pensions. Dahlgren told a senator that the navy was unfairly pressuring him into the furlough. The senator in turn told the president that Dahlgren had been given two alternatives: sea duty, which meant that he would probably lose his sight altogether, or a furlough on half pay. Secretary of the Navy Paulding caught wind of this latter move. He obtained a copy of the senator's letter to the president and sent it to Dahlgren, asking if he had "authorized" it. Dahlgren replied that he had simply mentioned his problem to the senator "in the course of such conversation as might naturally arise among friends." Paulding seethed with anger at Dahlgren's audacity. "Perhaps the best in your case," Hassler advised the young officer, "might be to let boiling substances cool down."[19]

But the gamble paid off. Although not on active duty, Dahlgren received full pay for the duration of his recovery, a period lasting several years. Instead of a furlough, he was given a leave of absence, renewable every three months provided a certificate from a navy surgeon pronounced him unfit for duty. Once again he had overcome resistance by appealing to higher authorities.[20]

Dahlgren purchased an 86.5-acre farm near Hartsville in Bucks County, Pennsylvania, where he lived while his eyes got better. On 8 January 1839 he married his sweetheart of the past seven years, Mary Clement Bunker. "Your change of the single state into the more sociable one," Hassler wrote him, "is in my opinion proper & I hope good. You have my best wishes for it." Dahlgren had first seen Mary while living in Philadelphia after the midshipman exam. She was then a dark-haired girl of fifteen. He remembered her as "much amused with a school companion and coyly avoiding the observation which she could not fail to attract." Since then Mary had grown into a young woman whom Patty Dahlgren described as "beautiful in person...lovely in disposition and noble in character." In 1833 John Dahlgren penned a poem about her:

Methought within the deep dark dye
    And sparkling glances of that eye
Reason and feeling shone supreme
    Yielding their deepest, brightest beam
But yet I saw that beauty's spill
    Upon that form so truly fill
None could superior seem
    Kind mercy, there too, lent her say
Effulgent as the orb of day
    Reflected from in the mirror'd stream

Later in life he wrote of Mary, "She was one who, to every charm of rare beauty and a lovely presence, added the attractive graces of refined social life, and a Christian piety that never failed to win the admiration of her friends and the affectionate attachment of her family." When duty called Dahlgren away, Mary expressed great sorrow at their parting and sorely missed him during his absence. The Dahlgrens truly loved each other.[21]

From a social as well as a professional standpoint, John Dahlgren had chosen well. Mary's father, Nathan Bunker, was an influential Philadelphia merchant. Because members of families belonging to the socioeconomic elite of the Jacksonian Northeast tended to marry within their own class, social acceptability as well as love graced John and Mary's marriage. Naval officers assumed that a cultivated gentlewoman naturally would improve the moral fiber of her mate. Moreover, such a wife was desirable because family influence, power, and connections were good for the status and social position of the officer and benefited the navy at large.[22]

The new husband approached life on the farm with characteristic vigor. He raised chickens, clover, wheat, oats, and timothy. He had horses, cattle, and an apple orchard. He and Mary employed a man, two women, and a girl to help with the chores. He repaired fences and chopped firewood. He treated a cut on the leg of his horse "Monkey" by washing it out with Irish whiskey and molasses, then applying a paste of water and shaved Castile soap. He kept detailed records of the weather, his finances, and activities on the farm. He and Mary also made babies. Their first three children, Charles Bunker, Elisabeth, and Ulric, were born on the farm, respectively, in 1839, 1840, and 1842. Dahlgren would remember these days as the happiest of his life.[23]

He returned to active duty in May 1842. His eyesight had improved somewhat, but not fully. He commuted to Philadelphia, where again he served on board a receiving ship. He sold the farm a year later and moved his family to Wilmington, Delaware. On 29 August 1843 he requested duty as flag lieutenant of the *Cumberland,* bound from Boston as flagship of the Mediterranean Squadron. The navy granted his request.[24]

On 26 September, Dahlgren departed for Boston. The *Cumberland,* a fifty-gun frigate, had been launched the year before. This would be her maiden voyage. She is known to history as a victim of the Confederate iron-clad *Virginia.* Dahlgren wrote Mary about his first impressions of the new assignment. Everything seemed familiar to him as he walked about the *Cumberland.* It was as though nothing had happened since his last cruise. His messmates were "all agreeable clever men." The other officers, evidently familiar with his translation of Paixhans, thought that he should be assigned to the ship's shell guns.[25]

During the day Dahlgren and other officers supervised raw recruits, experienced seamen, and navy yard workmen in fitting out and provisioning the *Cumberland* for sea. Night life included the teas, dinners, and receptions common to a navy town. Dahlgren was particularly impressed by his host at one such occasion. The Ticknors, a wealthy Boston publishing family, invited Dahlgren and two other officers to dinner. Dahlgren was struck by their magnificent home. "The beauty, taste and costliness of every thing around," he wrote Mary, "could only be equalled by the perfect breeding of the company we met." At the table, the wine, food, and conversation delighted him. After dinner the company retired to the library, which contained thirteen thousand books. Coffee was served, and there was entertainment at the piano. Dahlgren was thoroughly at ease among people like the Ticknors.[26]

On 20 November 1843 the *Cumberland* sailed for the Mediterranean. Dahlgren bid an emotional good-bye to his beloved wife. "Farewell darling, farewell," he wrote her. "I cannot desire that time should fly as I used to do, when younger—for now go with it health and strength—and we draw nearer to the grave—the moments we wish to fly, may at the dread hour be a boon prayed for, that no earthly power may grant. But oh! may they go happily with all that I love."[27]

At sea Dahlgren turned his attention to duty. A lieutenant had greater

USS *Cumberland* (United States Naval Institute)

responsibilities than a midshipman. Lieutenants served as watch and division officers. As a watch officer, Dahlgren took duty in rotation on the quarterdeck as the officer of the deck, in nominal charge of the ship. As a division officer, he had charge of men and equipment. He was responsible for the cleanliness of the decks and gear in his division. He inspected his men, drilled them at the guns, and trained them in small arms. His duties included service on courts of enquiry and courts-martial.[28]

Dahlgren's division included the *Cumberland*'s four shell guns. The state of naval gunnery at that time shocked him. The range tables that the navy used were disgracefully inaccurate, most commanders shamefully neglected gun drill, and ships wasted hundreds of rounds on salutes while target practice took place only once in six months. He determined to improve the situation, drilling and exhorting his division to be the *Cumberland*'s best. He thought that the standard navy lock was too complicated, so he designed a simpler one. He noticed that during practice in still weather, as smoke enveloped the gun deck after each discharge, the men did not properly elevate their pieces for the next round because the smoke obscured their vision. He solved the problem by devising a new way to sight guns. All of this enhanced Dahlgren's reputation as an ordnance expert.[29]

Joseph Smith, circa 1863 (United States Naval Institute)

Meanwhile, his old friend Hassler had died. Mid-November 1843 found the geodesist still at work in the field. The weather had turned, but Hassler was not ready to end the field season, despite the cold and snow. While he was en route to a new location one day, a severe hailstorm struck. The wind blew the canvas off the precious instruments. Hassler tried to cover them with his body but fell down and struck his chest on a rock. He lay in the cold and rain for several hours until the storm passed. The exposure brought on an illness that forced him to return to Philadelphia. Despite his misery, he insisted on doing paperwork. His condition worsened, but he refused to rest, working until he was too weak to continue. He died on the day the *Cumberland* had set sail for the Mediterranean. Dahlgren wrote Mary that he was "much distressed" by the death of his "poor old friend," whom he considered a "son of genius." He reflected with pleasure upon the many hours they had spent together.[30]

Dahlgren made an important new friend on board the *Cumberland.* Commodore Joseph Smith was commander of the Mediterranean Squadron. The two had met when Dahlgren first arrived in Boston. Shortly after the *Cumberland* departed for the Mediterranean, illness confined Smith to his bed. Dahlgren spent an hour or two each morning chatting with him while he recovered. The lieutenant and the commodore often dined together. Dahlgren accompanied Smith on most official visits to diplomats at the various ports of call. It is important to remember that Dahlgren had asked specifically for duty on board the flagship of the Mediterranean Squadron, still the most prestigious squadron in the fleet. He undoubtedly pursued a friendship with Smith at least in part because of the political benefits he could reap. Dahlgren would in fact profit from their friendship.[31]

Dahlgren met another important officer on board the *Cumberland:* Lieutenant Andrew Hull Foote. In fact, by the end of the cruise Foote had become his best friend. "Foot is a warm friend to me," he wrote Mary, "and never suffers any chance to pass of manifesting his feelings. His high standing as an officer & a man make this very valuable to me."[32]

Foote was an ardent social reformer. He developed an interest in the seaman's cause after being called to religion during a cruise in 1827. He became a member of the American Seaman's Friend Society, an organization dedicated to the improvement of sailors' lives ashore. Just before the *Cumberland* had departed from Boston, several crewmen had broken into her store of whiskey, gotten drunk, and assaulted an officer. For this they had been heavily flogged. It seemed ridiculous to Foote that the navy encouraged alcoholism with its "grog tub" while on the other hand it punished those who broke the rules to slake their addiction. He determined to act.[33]

Encouraged by Commodore Smith, Foote formed a temperance society among his fellow officers. He showed them pictures of human stomachs ruined by alcohol. He preached about the evils of drink in religious services he held on Sundays. The temperance movement spread to the crew. By the end of the first year of the voyage, all of the sailors had agreed to accept cash in lieu of their grog ration. The *Cumberland* had become the first temperance ship in the United States Navy.[34]

The movement to abolish grog stemmed from the national temperance crusade and the larger reform wave that swept across the United States in the 1830s and 1840s. Many naval officers and officials strongly opposed

Andrew Hull Foote, circa 1862 (United States Naval Institute)

abolishing grog. They feared that it would lead to illicit indulgence in alcohol, violations of discipline, and increased difficulties in recruiting. Supporters of naval temperance argued that it would improve sailors' lives, health, discipline, and efficiency. Moreover, some linked alcohol with flogging, a punishment that reformers viewed as repugnant and inhumane. Most floggings occurred because of drunkenness. Eliminate grog, they reasoned, and there would be no flogging. Naval temperance was one of the most sensitive and controversial issues of the day.[35]

Dahlgren fully supported the temperance crusade on board the *Cumber-*

land. Foote gave Dahlgren much of the credit for its success. At various dinners given by Captain Breese, the *Cumberland*'s commanding officer, Dahlgren drank wine sparingly or not at all to set an example for his fellow officers. He supported Foote despite the hostility that greeted their crusade. During a visit to Port Mahon the crew of the USS *Columbia* challenged the *Cumberland*'s crew to a boat race. During the race, crews of two onlooking American vessels rooted against the *Cumberland*'s boat because of her crew's temperance pledge. The *Cumberland*'s boat won the 2.5-mile race by 150 yards. Dahlgren observed:

> It is mournful to contemplate how the effort to better the condition of seamen by making them sober, has excited a deep seated hostility of officers & men in other ships. But when they attempted to prove that a crew necessarily deteriorated for want of grog & failed in every essential of seamanship, the result proved a mistake.… [The] Cumberland has always taken the lead & there is a very wholesome determination among the crew to keep it.

Foote claimed that during the second year of the cruise the sober sailors did superior duty in sailing the *Cumberland,* keeping her clean, and exercising her guns, and the ship gained a reputation for excellent discipline.[36]

Dahlgren's support of naval temperance stemmed as much from class consciousness as from genuine concern for the welfare of the enlisted men, whom many officers viewed as members of the lowest class of society. "The application of moral discipline," he wrote Mary, "seems to be of great aid in sustaining order." Enlisted men were easier to control and discipline if sober.[37]

Similarly, discipline and class consciousness informed Dahlgren's position on shipboard theater for enlisted men. Because officers made few efforts to sponsor activities to boost morale, the men themselves occasionally provided their own diversions, usually in the form of amateur theatricals. With the approval of their commanding officer, the crew put on skits, plays, songs, and other amusements. Many officers disapproved of such events because they often lampooned the officers or even the lordly commodore, either subtly or mercilessly. The resulting hilarity completely overwhelmed the normal spirit of iron discipline, if only for a few hours.[38]

Dahlgren opposed such events. In January 1845, encouraged by the second lieutenant, the *Cumberland*'s sober sailors started a theatrical association in the navy yard of Port Mahon, where the ship lay at anchor. Some of her officers supported it, but not Dahlgren, who wrote Mary:

> My belief is, that any association in a military body is likely to mar discipline—therefore I object to them: it matters little whether the object be good or bad. The law is sufficient to ensure order, religion, & morality…and if the officers show a good example and do their duty in enforcing the law, obedience, sobriety and attendance at the customary religious service must follow. If the men lack amusement it is their fault—for they have liberty to their content & a liberal allowance of money—far beyond the practice of other ships. When they want sport, they can play ball or have other manly exercises ashore.[39]

Dahlgren wrote Mary regularly during the cruise. His letters provide insights into his character and personality. He was, for example, a hopeless romantic. His nickname for Mary was Polly. Sentimental passages like this one abound:

> Three months have elapsed since I left you, and they have weighed on me like years. All my pleasure has been centered in one, and now that I am exiled from this, how indifferent does all else seem to me…. Yesterday was Christmas!—how my heart swells as I write the word that conveys so much—Does it not tell me of our fireside, of our country home—of my own Mary, the light of my heart, the love of my early days, the blessing of a later time, and of our children. What matter if the snow whitened the landscape and the seal of stern winter was on all around—Within all was peace and comfort and love—Now see the contrast to this happy picture. Far away on a distant shore the weary pilgrim, yearns toward those he has left behind him—his soul is sad to think how long it must be ere he can rejoin those dearest to him.[40]

Dahlgren was not always so melancholy but was quite capable of enjoying himself, as shown in this passage about a wedding reception for a fellow officer:

> If uniform could make the affair brilliant there was surely a sufficiency…. You certainly would not have recognized the rustic of Hartsville tricked out in a flashy uniform and going the "light fantastic" with Spanish

doññas. I thought however you would be pleased, remembering that you never relished my turn for a simple life & plain dress. Though I believe that these would exert a happier influence on the destinies of our children both here and hereafter.[41]

Dahlgren loved his children dearly and had firm opinions on how they should be raised. He intended for Mary to read parts of his letters aloud to the children: "Kiss all the babies for Papa and bid them be good and do as Mama tells them—I have no separate remembrance for either, they are all alike—Charley is Papa's boy—Sissy is the one little duck—Ully is bandy and Mister 4—has a black noddle—Good and sufficient reasons I am sure why Papa should be very fond of them." Dahlgren missed playing with his children, carrying them piggyback up and down the stairs. He wanted them to grow up in the country, far from the wickedness of city life. Country life would free their minds "to receive instruction & example from the source designed by Providence." He did not want his children confined in school before proper diet, exercise, and fresh air had built strong constitutions. Such remarks indicted his own boyhood in the city.[42]

Dahlgren never saw his fourth child, who was born and died while he was at sea. The loss saddened him deeply. He grieved hour after hour, alone in his stateroom, shedding bitter tears. He wrote Mary, "My child—my child—what have I done that you should be taken from me thus—Have not afflictions sufficient been heaped on me already but that death must strike down one of my little flock—and make desolate a stricken heart—Spare them, oh spare them, they are the treasure of a lone & sorrowful soul—In mercy let me be called first."[43]

Although Dahlgren reserved his deepest emotions for his family, the Mediterranean inspired him as well. "As usual with the Mahomitan cities on the Mediterranean," a visit to Tripoli prompted him to write, "the people are but slaves and the slaves of savages too—mere brutes who hold power but to wring the hard earned [illegible] from the starving people." Dahlgren found the appearance of the French soldiers and sailors whom he encountered in the Mediterranean "so inferior to the stout athletic proportions and soldierly bearing of the English Austrian & German troops" that he was surprised "that with such *personal* [*sic*] Napoleon planted the Eagles of Empire on the capital cities of Spain, Germany, Austria, and Prussia, and swept away opposing armies as if they had been chaff." Dahlgren openly admired the British. He remarked of Malta, "The streets are regular and well arranged, the houses handsome & well built of the white soft stone peculiar to the island and the shops filled with every commodity, purchaseable at low rates. Order and no small degree of activity prevail, and on the whole the English have given to it the wholesome condition, which they rarely fail to impress where they have the power." Such racist characterizations anticipated the social-Darwinian defense of imperialism that emerged later in the century.[44]

Visits to places connected with the history of the United States Navy inspired Dahlgren's most patriotic musings. At Tripoli he wrote:

> Here it was that the young Republic made its first effort against the pirates of the Mediterranean. And nobly was the honor of the flag sustained by the infant Navy—for four years were measures prosecuted against the Pacha. His fort was closely blockaded—his gun boats repulsed & destroyed—his town battered by the ships and his very power threatened until he was glad to treat on the terms proposed. It was here that the Philadelphia frigate had the misfortune by grounding to fall into the enemy's hands—but that could cause little regret which occasioned one of the most brilliant & daring feats ever performed. Anchored under the very batteries of the Dey, crowded by his troops, the ship was carried sword in hand by Decatur & his retreat lighted by the blaze of the trophy he could not remove.

Dissatisfaction with the realities of service in the United States Navy had not dimmed his zest for the heroic feats of its past.[45]

Dahlgren nearly got involved in another duel during this cruise. On the occasion of his promotion, an officer of the *Cumberland* gave a supper for his fellows. As Dahlgren wrote Mary, it "had the appearance of a general affair." But Dahlgren did not receive an invitation, an affront that "wore the aspect of intentional uncivility." He confronted the perpetrator of this indignity and expressed his sense of injury, fully expecting "a mortal quarrel." But instead the officer "made such explanation" that Dahlgren "could harbor no farther thought of the matter." "I know you would not have me tamely to submit to an insult, wherever I might be compelled to appeal for redress," he wrote Mary. "What indeed can be so degraded as a man without courage, unless it be a woman without virtue."[46]

A crisis with Mexico brought the cruise to an end. In October 1845, in anticipation of war, the *Cumberland* set sail for home, closing the chronicle of Dahlgren's Mediterranean adventure.[47] He returned to his family in

Wilmington on 12 November. He found Mary and the children seated at the dinner table. He hardly recognized the children, they had grown so. Mary looked beautiful to him. The couple lost no time becoming reacquainted. Almost nine months to the day after he returned from sea, their fifth child, a son, was born.[48]

Dahlgren awaited orders in Wilmington until 6 January 1847, when he received instructions to report to Washington for duty in the Bureau of Ordnance and Hydrography. His friend Commodore Smith, who had been impressed by his ordnance expertise on the *Cumberland,* had arranged this assignment, marking the beginning of the longest single phase of his career, and the one in which he would produce his signal achievements.[49]

Dahlgren's experiences as a young officer would shape his ordnance career. He reveled in the historic ambience of the *Macedonian,* and on the *Cumberland* he wrote stirringly of the burning of the *Philadelphia.* In between he had learned about the naval realities of slow promotion and dominance by senior officers. But it was not a contradiction that he remarked disparagingly on the "time worn policy of old men" while still admiring their heroism. It was not the heroes themselves that Dahlgren loved; it was their reputation.

The quest for glory drove him to seek recognition for his accomplishments: a midshipman's warrant for excelling in his boyhood studies; a command for completing his naval apprenticeship and passing his midshipman's examination; pay and rank commensurate with his duties on the coast survey. His need for power and recognition, in turn, drove him to effect reform. The "Blue Jacket" articles decried the power of senior officers at the expense of junior officers. On the coast survey, Dahlgren fought for what he viewed as the just rewards for service rendered: promotion and higher pay.

Dahlgren used connections to get what he wanted. He mustered an impressive array of important people to support his application to join the navy. He used his friendship with the influential John Vaughan to obtain the assignment to the coast survey. He relied upon Hassler's support in the fight for promotion to lieutenant. Although he rankled at undeserving chaps who used influence, he used it himself because he truly believed that he deserved what he sought.

Dahlgren followed a pattern in getting what he wanted. He defined the problem, then tried to solve it by working within the immediate authority structure. If this approach failed, he worked even harder and used any influence he could muster above the immediate authority structure. Persistence, hard work, and influential connections proved the keys to his success. He did not get into the navy on the first try. He sublimated his ambition in hard work, mustered the influence of his supporters, and tried again. In his fight for the right to go on leave with full pay after returning from Paris, he did not get what he wanted from the secretary of the navy, so he went over the secretary's head, through a senator, to the president. Going over opponents' heads to higher authorities became Dahlgren's signature tactic. He had learned an important element of the art of politics.

Dahlgren, himself a determined individual, used the same sort of methods to effect reform as his steam-generation fellows. Like Maury, he expressed his discontent with the navy publicly, in newspapers. (Incidentally, Dahlgren's use of this device predated Maury's.) Like Perry and Stockton, Dahlgren benefited from the support of higher authorities for his efforts. His publication of *Bomb Cannon,* invention of a lock, and development of a new way to aim cannon began to earn him a reputation as an ordnance expert in the same manner that Perry's work in education and Stockton's development of steam propulsion gave them reputations as experts in their fields.

But Dahlgren swam in the current of reform largely in order to benefit his own reputation. This was perfectly consistent in a naval culture in which individual deeds became institutional tradition and in which honor, the concept governing officers' behavior, placed the individual above the group. Although he published views on steam power and shell guns because he believed that these developments would enhance the power of the fleet, his greatest efforts so far had been undertaken on his own behalf, and he placed his own needs first. The "Blue Jacket" articles expressed his frustration with the slow rate of promotion in the officer corps. He took on the secretary of the navy in various efforts to obtain promotions and pay increases to advance his own career. He applied hard-learned lessons in the art of politics to the pursuit of personal ends. His brand of reform aimed less at benefiting the navy than at improving his own position and reputation.

Dahlgren's ambition, his education in science and mathematics, his upbringing in the sailing navy amid the traditions of 1812, his ordnance expertise, and his mastery of politics would bring him glory during his assignment to the Bureau of Ordnance and Hydrography, but not to his satisfaction.

2

THE INNOVATOR

4

American Naval Ordnance before 1850

For Dahlgren, ordnance was the foundation of naval affairs. In the process of developing his guns, the first American naval cannon not based on European designs, he articulated an unusually comprehensive conception of naval ordnance, embracing the role of the navy in national policy, naval strategy and tactics, and doctrine. His interests extended into virtually every aspect of making and using naval cannon. He did research on ballistics, metallurgy, and the destructive capabilities of cannon. As an advocate of steam propulsion, he devised doctrine for what he considered the optimum balance of steam, sail, and ordnance in naval vessels. He designed guns, oversaw their manufacture, and trained men to use them. He worked at improving all kinds of ordnance equipment, including locks, sights, carriages, gun barrels, and even the rope used for breeching tackle.

Dahlgren worked in the context of what has been called the "nineteenth-century naval revolution," which historians describe in terms of six technological developments: steam propulsion, shell guns, rifled guns, iron hulls, screw propellers, and armor plate.[1] This revolution occurred within the context of a longstanding naval tradition. "Shell guns, steam engines, and the screw propeller," notes one historian, "were all introduced into a sailing battlefleet dominated by the material, the men and the philosophy of the sailing navy."[2] To understand Dahlgren's role in these developments, it is necessary to examine the state of naval warfare on the eve of the Civil War.

THE STATUS QUO IN NAVAL WARFARE

The fundamental units of naval power in the early nineteenth century were ships of the line—which Dahlgren and his contemporaries called "liners"—and those "below." Liners usually carried seventy-four or more guns on two or more gun decks. Below them were thirty- to forty-gun frigates, used for cruiser duties. Ships of the line were so named because they formed the line of battle.[3]

Warship technology alternated between periods of stagnation and innovation between the seventeenth and mid-nineteenth centuries, the heyday of the ship of the line. Beginning in the eighteenth century, French naval architects received training in mathematics and theory, resulting in some advantages for French liners and frigates. British shipbuilders still learned their trade in the workshops, but Royal Navy officers were never universally convinced that French ships were superior. Although the shape of the bow and stern, the method of construction, the form of the underwater lines, the arrangement of the decks, and the size of ships of the line changed significantly between 1810 and 1840, the size and strength of ships remained limited by the size of trees and the strength of wood. The upshot was that early-nineteenth-century ships of the line "were almost completely unchanged in principle," as historian Brian Lavery puts it, "and there was little aboard them that…even Drake would not have recognized and understood." In essence, liners were still floating wind-powered wooden gun platforms designed to carry as many cannon as possible.[4]

A ship's striking power depended on the projectile weight of its broadside and the distance the guns could hurl the metal. In the early nineteenth century the principal naval weapon was the cast-iron smoothbore cannon, which fired round shot. Projectile weight was limited by the size of naval cannon, which in turn was limited by the knowledge and techniques of the craftsmen who manufactured them, by the weight-bearing capacity of the wooden ships that carried them, and by the strength of the men who served them. Until the late 1830s the heaviest shot a standard shipboard gun could fire weighed 48 pounds, while the largest common projectiles weighed 30 to 36 pounds. The effective range of such ordnance was 300 to 600 yards.[5]

Naval battle rested upon a tradition of close, brutal engagement. From the late seventeenth century until the last quarter of the eighteenth century, warships usually fought in line-ahead formation. After 1782, British naval commanders sought to break the enemy line, a tactic that often resulted in a melee. In most cases, whatever the formation, ships usually fought within the 300- to 600-yard effective range of their cannon. The notion of the ship-killing gun was a myth. The range and striking power of shipboard guns changed but little between the seventeenth and early nineteenth centuries, and the 2-foot-thick oak sides of big ships remained almost impervious to round shot. Holes below the waterline in wooden ships were partially self-sealing. The result was that smoothbore cannon did not sink ships; they turned them into floating charnel houses. Battles degenerated into butchery. Lord Nelson won Trafalgar by slaughtering French and Spanish sailors, not by sinking their ships. There, as in other sea fights during the age of sail, opposing ships slugged it out "yard-arm to yard-arm." Solid shot smashed into wooden walls, showering sailors with deadly jagged wooden splinters. The outcome usually hinged upon the rate of fire of a ship's cannon, which in turn depended upon the training, discipline, and quality of the crew.[6]

On the eve of the nineteenth-century naval revolution, Great Britain possessed more ships of the line than any other nation. Britain's policy of naval supremacy was the status quo. Because Britain was an insular maritime power, economically dependent on overseas trade, this policy arose from necessity. The Royal Navy had ruled the waves since the late seventeenth century because Britain outbuilt its opponents, because of the excellence of the British sailor, and because the fleet could innovate technologically and tactically, when necessary.

THE AMERICAN NAVAL DOCTRINE OF QUALITATIVE SUPERIORITY

American naval policy stemmed from demands different from those that shaped the Royal Navy's doctrine of naval supremacy. In the colonial era, because of frequent warfare with neighboring French and Spanish settlements, the temptation of smuggling, and the constant menace of piracy, American shipbuilders emphasized speed under sail and ordnance power. Ships were designed to outrun what they could not outgun, or to outgun what they could not outrun.[7]

Independence in 1783 meant that American politicians had to ask themselves fundamental questions about naval power. They could no longer rely upon the Royal Navy to protect their trade. The central naval policy issue before the War of 1812 was not whether to build a navy, but how to use one. At stake was not only the navy's force structure but also America's role in world affairs.

"Antinavalists" opposed building a powerful peacetime fleet to use as a political instrument, whether to deter war or influence the policy of other nations. They believed that a big navy would not only be expensive but might also lead to unwanted involvement in European affairs, or even to war. Thomas Jefferson best articulated this view. His desire for a fleet of small gunboats, instead of a fleet of liners, stemmed from a national defense policy based on local militias and a determination to challenge Europe on the seas.

"Navalists," on the other hand, wanted to build a strong blue-water fleet not simply to deter aggression but to gain for the infant nation the honor, prestige, and diplomatic clout they thought naval power would bring. In their view, a navy should not merely defend the coast and chase pirates but should also show the flag in foreign ports and protect American economic interests abroad. When navalists asked for a fleet of twelve liners in 1798, they asked in effect that the United States begin to participate in the international balance of power.

International and domestic politics shaped the debate, but in the end the antinavalists won a majority in Congress. Until the last quarter of the nineteenth century, American naval policy stemmed from the militia concept. A few vessels patrolled far-flung stations while citizens at home remained confident that if an overt threat should develop, citizen sailors would volunteer in droves to serve on board makeshift warships or to work coastal artillery.[8]

The American navy now had to devise a doctrine to fit this policy. Doctrine guides the procurement, design, and development of weapons and the conduct of war. It guides the structure of forces and their employment in battle. It embodies assumptions about potential threats and the nature of the strategic environment in which forces will operate in war.[9]

American naval doctrine stemmed from an unbroken string of successes. At least that was how those who formulated doctrine saw it.

The Revolutionary War implanted into the American naval mind the idea of the lone big, fast, heavily gunned frigate. Continental frigates were faster and more heavily gunned than comparable types in other navies, and when they could get to sea, they proved effective commerce raiders. Their success began a trend in naval construction that made the United States, as historian Howard I. Chapelle puts it, a "frigate nation." The emphasis upon superior ships intended to operate alone, rather than upon a well-integrated fleet or squadron, dominated naval shipbuilding in the United States for the rest of the age of sail. Because of this emphasis, the United States developed some of the largest and finest frigates the world had seen.[10]

The doctrine formulated for the first ships of the United States Navy stemmed from this preference for big, fast, heavily gunned frigates. While navalists and antinavalists debated about what type of navy the United States should have, the dey of Algiers plundered American merchant shipping in the Mediterranean. The debate shifted to whether large frigates would be more economical than negotiation in stopping the piracy. On 27 March 1794 Congress passed an act authorizing the construction of six frigates, three of which were to carry forty-four guns. This act founded the United States Navy. It was not a manifestation of the views of either side in the debate but an expedient to deal with the pirates. Shipbuilder Joshua Humphreys was appointed to design the three forty-four-gun vessels. He discussed them in a letter to Robert Morris:

> As our navy must be for a considerable time inferior in the number of its vessels to [those of Europe], we are to consider what size ships will be most formidable, and be an overmatch for those of an enemy. Such frigates as in blowing weather would be an overmatch for doubledecked ships, or in light winds may evade coming to action by outsailing them. Ships built on these principles will render those of an enemy in a degree useless, or will require them to have a superiority in number before they attack our ships.... If we build our ships of the same size as the Europeans, they having so great a number of them, we shall always be behind them. I would build them of a larger size than theirs, and take the lead of them, which is the only safe method of commencing a navy.

Humphreys intended to build them with scantlings as thick as those of seventy-four-gun liners. The forty-four-gun frigates *United States, Constitution,* and *President* were built in accord with the American tradition of qualitative superiority, which Humphreys now established as doctrine.[11]

This doctrine applied to ordnance as well as ship size. The forty-four-gun frigates carried not only more guns than their European counterparts but also heavier guns. Their main armament consisted of 24-pounders, while 18-pounders constituted the main armament of British frigates.

During the War of 1812 the young United States Navy shocked the Royal Navy by winning a series of brilliant single-ship actions against British frigates. For many Americans these duels confirmed the wisdom of the doctrine of qualitative superiority. Success was attributed to heavier guns, heavier scantlings, and better crews. Charles B. Boynton, a naval historian writing in the mid-nineteenth century, declared that American superiority in weight of broadside from the big frigates, more than two-thirds that of British liners, "was decisive, and the results gave an *éclat* and character to the American navy which it has never lost. It was the first triumph of American sagacity on the ocean, and it has shaped since their whole naval policy." Such histories reflected many Americans' belief that their navy won the War of 1812. This perception confirmed the doctrine that American ships should carry the heaviest possible guns. Frederick P. Stanton, chairman of the House Committee on Naval Affairs (1849–53), put it best: "The war of 1812 established a new era in the navies of all the States of Christendom. So far as naval architecture and armaments were concerned, that war left the United States far in advance of the times. We introduced larger ships and heavier metal, demonstrated by sea-fights the superiority of both, and thus rendered the whole navy of England almost entirely *effete*."[12]

However, Americans did not ignore the fact that by the war's end, the Royal Navy had blockaded their coast and bottled up the big frigates in their harbors. In the words of British historian Andrew Lambert, the United States saw her trade "destroyed, her coastal cities and capital assaulted and her coast defence flotilla shown up as an ideologically motivated fraud."[13] In response, in legislation passed in 1813 and 1816, Congress authorized construction of a total of fourteen ships of the line and eighteen forty-four-gun frigates. This was no play for naval supremacy, for in June 1812 the Royal Navy possessed some 120 liners and 116 frigates. Nevertheless, seven of the American liners were completed by 1828 and saw regular service on distant stations.[14] In keeping with the doctrine of qualitative superiority, they were big, well-armed ships. The *Ohio*, for example, by British standards of measurement, was larger and more heavily gunned than a first-rate liner like HMS *Caledonia*. The doctrine of qualitative superiority, resting on a foundation of perceived success, would also provide a framework for responding to future threats.[15]

THE SHELL GUN

Unlike the Americans, the French harbored no perception of victory in their recent war with the British. In fact, the Royal Navy had bested the French navy for more than a century. Following Napoleon's hundred days in 1815, the French renewed the search for a way to defeat the British fleet. One of Napoleon's artillery officers, Henri Joseph Paixhans, believed he had found the answer. Born in Metz in 1783, Paixhans passed through the École polytechnique and during the Napoleonic Wars rose to the rank of chef de battalion. In about 1820 he proposed "to use guns which shall drive the heaviest bombs [shells] horizontally, like a cannon shot, and with equal force and accuracy. The explosion of the bomb would make a large breach in the hull of the ship, if it take place there, or cause great mischief within." In short, he proposed to arm French vessels with shells and shell guns.[16]

Shell guns and cannon both fired projectiles on a relatively flat trajectory. What distinguished a shell gun from a cannon was the projectile fired. Cannon fired solid shot. Shell guns fired shells: hollow projectiles filled with gunpowder and fuzed to explode on target. Being hollow, shells were lighter than solid shot of the same diameter. For a given projectile weight, shells had a larger diameter. Thus, the bore diameter of a shell gun was often larger than that of a cannon. Shells were fired with smaller charges than solid shot for two reasons. First, the shell itself, being hollow, could not bear the shock of firing as well as solid shot. Second, because shells weighed less, a smaller charge of powder could still achieve an adequate muzzle velocity. Solid shot were not generally fired from shell guns. A shot of a diameter large enough to fit into a shell gun would have weighed substantially more than a shell. To fire such a shot, a larger charge would have been called for. Gun-founders did not know how to produce cast-iron guns strong enough to bear the added strain.

The idea of firing explosive projectiles horizontally from shipboard guns did not originate with Paixhans. Like the introduction of steam propulsion into the United States Navy, the early history of shells and shell guns was one of fits and false starts. Before the nineteenth century the use of shells was sporadic, widely scattered, and short-lived. In various times and places, shells appeared, achieved noteworthy successes, and promptly disappeared. It is said that the Chinese had used shells as early as the twelfth century. Edward Gibbon described the use of shells at the siege of St. Boniface in

Corsica in 1421. Voltaire stated that the French first used shells at sea during the bombardment of Algiers in 1681. Eight years later, English naval shellfire disabled a French vessel at the battle of Bantry Bay. In 1788, Russian naval shellfire devastated a superior force of Turkish vessels at the mouth of the Liman River in the Sea of Azov. None of these sporadic appearances of shells and shell guns spawned an intentional, systematic, evolutionary, or long-lasting line of development.[17]

During the French Revolution and Napoleonic Wars, Frenchmen gave serious consideration to the possibilities of shellfire. The chief stumbling blocks were the dangers inherent in carrying explosive projectiles on board wooden ships and in firing shells. Shells on board French vessels frequently exploded accidentally. Some four or five liners, six frigates, and several smaller vessels either burned, blew up, or were so terribly damaged by their own explosive ordnance that they were incapable of further action. To fire a shell, French gunners lit the fuze, stuffed the shell down the barrel, and touched off the gun, all the while praying that the shell would not explode before flying well away from the ship. British and American gunners relied on the flames from the gunpowder to ignite the fuze when they fired the gun, and tried to delay the explosion of the shell by loading it with the fuze pointed toward the muzzle. The development of better fuzes after 1815 reduced the risk of both carrying and firing shells and paved the way for the widespread adoption of shell guns.[18]

In 1821 and 1824 Paixhans tested shells and shell guns of his own design for a French naval commission. His *canon-obusier* weighed nearly 8,000 pounds, about as much as a French 36-pounder, but threw a shell as large as an 80-pounder solid shot. Paixhans fired it at the hulks of old liners. The gun achieved good range and accuracy, and the shells wrought havoc on the targets. One shell blasted a 12-foot-square hole in the side of one of the hulks. Although the tests were demonstrations rather than scientific experiments, they provided convincing evidence of the destructive capabilities of the shell gun. The naval commission was impressed and recommended placing a few shell guns on a few French liners.[19]

Paixhans published his ideas in *Nouvelle force maritime et artillerie* (1822) and *Expériences faites sur une armé nouvelle* (1825). These works put forth two main principles: standardization of caliber (bore diameter), and shellfire. Paixhans proposed that the French adopt one caliber of gun in several different sizes (weights of gun) instead of the several calibers then used on French ships. This system would offer the same flexibility as several different calibers yet would simplify procurement and supply.[20]

Paixhans was less interested in the guns themselves than in what France could do with them. Shell guns, he argued, would revolutionize naval warfare. An explosive shell would inflict far more damage on a ship, round for round, than solid shot. No tar-impregnated wooden warship could long withstand the explosive and incendiary effects of shellfire, even at 1,300 yards, a far greater distance than the 300-yard effective range of solid shot. Thus, he concluded, shells and shell guns would spell the doom of wooden ships of the line.[21]

In 1837 the French navy established the 80-pounder shell gun as a part of every ship's battery. It adopted the 36-pounder cannon, in different sizes, as the standard caliber of shipboard ordnance. But the French did not go as far as Paixhans advocated. Shells did not supplant solid shot. Two calibers appeared on French ships, not one. Cannon remained the main armament; the French considered shell guns as auxiliaries.[22]

The Royal Navy followed suit. In 1839 it adopted an 8-inch shell gun as an auxiliary shipboard weapon and six different weight classes of 32-pounder cannon as the main weapons. By this time Denmark, Holland, Russia, and Sweden had also adopted shell guns.[23]

The United States Navy followed Europe's lead. In 1838 a squadron of French frigates forced the formidable castle of San Juan de Ulúa at Vera Cruz, Mexico, to surrender. This feat of arms caused a sensation. The duke of Wellington remarked that it was the only example known to him of a strong fort falling to sea power alone. The instrument of French success was Paixhans's shell guns. Commander David G. Farragut witnessed the event from the USS *Erie* and later reported it to the Navy Department. That same year a twenty-six-gun French vessel armed entirely with shell guns visited several American ports, exciting great interest in naval circles. These events led Secretary of the Navy James K. Paulding to wonder whether America had dropped behind Europe in naval developments.[24]

In 1839 and 1840 Paulding ordered Matthew C. Perry to conduct gunnery experiments on a proving ground at Sandy Hook, New Jersey. Perry built targets, firing platforms, and storage sheds. He set up targets on shore at distances of between 800 and 1,200 yards from the firing platforms. He also mounted guns on board the steamer *Fulton II*. He fired both shot and shells at the targets and carefully recorded the results. Shells proved both safe and effective. Perry concluded that the navy ought to adopt shell guns but emphasized that most American naval officers knew little about shells.

Paulding agreed. The secretary subsequently attached as many officers to the *Fulton II* as possible to train them in the use of shells and shell guns.[25]

In 1841 the Navy Department let contracts for 8-inch shell guns. The new guns appeared on board American frigates and liners, usually four per deck. Like the Europeans, the Americans adopted shell guns as auxiliaries, keeping solid-shot guns as the main armament.[26]

AMERICAN GUN-FOUNDING

Starting with the authorization of the first frigates in 1794, the United States Navy contracted with private firms for its ordnance. By midcentury four firms were producing most of the navy's heavy cannon: Tredegar Ironworks in Richmond, the Fort Pitt Foundry in Pittsburgh, Cyrus Alger and Company in Boston, and the West Point Foundry in Cold Spring, New York. These firms numbered among the largest industrial enterprises in America. In 1850 the West Point Foundry employed four hundred men who worked by the discipline of the clock rather than by the rhythms of nature. It included iron and brass foundries, a pattern shop, a smith's shop featuring a 7-ton triphammer, a machine shop housing twenty-eight turning lathes and three planing machines, and a boiler shop. The West Point Foundry produced steam engines as well as cannon for the army and navy.[27]

Gun-founding was a complicated process. Naval smoothbores were cast solid, then bored out. The iron was extracted from its ore by smelting in blast furnaces fueled by charcoal. The molten metal was channeled into a number of small molds, where it cooled. This was called pig iron. Meanwhile, the founder made a mold from a full-scale model of the gun, then placed the mold upright in a pit, breech side down. To cast a gun, the founder remelted the pig iron in a blast furnace. When a sufficient quantity of molten metal had collected, the founder tapped the furnace, and the mold filled from the bottom up. After the casting had cooled in the pit, it was extracted from the mold, then the chamber was bored.[28]

Before the navy paid for the gun, it had to pass "proof." First, an assistant inspector of ordnance, a naval officer, examined the gun inside and out for defects and to ensure that it had the proper dimensions. Then he fired the gun, usually three times, with increasing charges of gunpowder. The final charge weighed the same as the projectile and was substantially higher than would be used in combat. If a gun survived, it was thought safe enough to accept for service.[29]

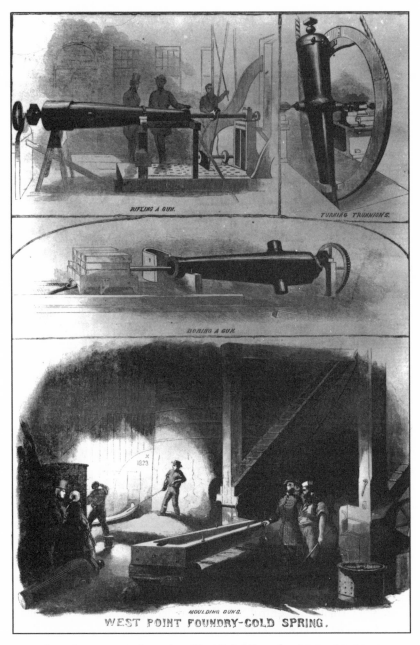

Steps in gun manufacturing, West Point Foundry (National Archives)

Although advances in science were beginning to affect the foundryman's craft in the mid-nineteenth century, metallurgy largely remained a mystery. Foundrymen had no explanations for such elementary operations as the reduction of ores to metal, the formation of alloys, or the conversion of cast iron into wrought iron or steel. Many knew what would make good castings, but not why. No one could explain why one iron was better than another. Founders guessed at the quality of a metal from its appearance. Most problems in iron casting arose from ignorance about what happened chemically, not thermally or mechanically.[30]

The entire process of gun-founding relied upon the knowledge of the foreman of the foundry. Ironmasters behaved like craftsmen, jealously guarding their art and skill, keeping certain knowledge in their heads, not on paper, and passing secrets and tricks of the trade by word of mouth from father to son, from master to apprentice. They also acted like modern engineers, solving practical problems and producing books filled with solid technical information and current best practice. The mid-nineteenth-century foundry foreman was a metallurgist, patternmaker, chemist—indeed, everything. With raw materials, a little equipment, common sense, and most of all experience, he blended his own special mixture of iron ores that he "knew" would yield a strong product, tapped the furnace to pour the casting at the "right" moment, and extracted the casting from the mold when he "figured" it had cooled enough.[31]

Myriad problems arose with guns produced this way. The quality of pig iron varied widely. Different furnaces produced iron with different properties, some more brittle than others, some more malleable. For each kind of casting the founder memorized certain proportions of pigs from different foundries. With no theory relating the chemical composition of pig iron to the structure into which it solidified, founders had no idea before trying it whether a new kind of iron or technique would produce good cannon. Certain furnaces and combinations of ore, fuel, and flux happened to produce iron with the proper proportions of alloying elements that resulted in good cannon. When an ironmaster chanced upon a suitable product, he was loath to tinker with the materials or technique that produced it. The navy exercised virtually no control over the founders' methods. The particulars varied from one ironmaster to the next, and as a result, quality varied widely in guns produced in different foundries, and even in guns produced in the same foundry. Proof often failed to expose bad guns. On numerous occasions guns made with poor-quality metal survived proof and were issued to the fleet. Thus, the navy played ordnance roulette. Most guns withstood hundreds of firings, but occasionally a cannon exploded after only a few.[32]

SCIENCE AND GUNNERY

In the sixteenth century, scientists and mathematicians began experimenting with cannon to learn more about natural phenomena and to improve gunnery. Nicolo Tartaglia, known as "the father of ballistics," published a treatise on the subject in Venice in 1537. Ballistics, the science of projectile motion, has two aspects: interior ballistics, concerned with the combustion of the gunpowder and the motion of the projectile inside the gun, and exterior ballistics, which considers the projectile in flight. Tartaglia argued that "to shoot by rule and not haphazardly," the gunner should be able to calculate the range to the target and should know the range of his piece at various elevations. Toward these ends Tartaglia described and probably first devised the method using a form of gunner's quadrant.

During the seventeenth century the publication of several textbooks written by practical gunners, scientists, and mathematicians reflected an increasingly scientific approach to the problems of artillerymen. In the first half of the eighteenth century the French and the British conducted numerous experiments with guns, gunpowder, and projectiles. They learned that heavier projectiles had greater range than lighter ones, and that increasing the weight of the gunpowder charge did not consistently produce a proportional increase in range for a given weight of projectile. A trend toward larger calibers reflected these findings.[33]

An English mathematician, Benjamin Robins, pushed the envelope farther. Robins, born in 1707, was said to have mastered Archimedes, Huyghens, and Newton as a child. As an adult he taught mathematics and built bridges, mills, and harbors. He soon developed an interest in ballistics and studied the available books on the subject. He discovered that although English authors carped at Tartaglia's belief that air resistance affected the flight of projectiles, none had examined the idea by experiment.

Robins decided to do just that. He invented a ballistic pendulum to measure the velocity of a projectile as it exited the barrel. This allowed him to ascertain the effect of such variable factors as the charge, windage (the clearance between the projectile and the gun barrel wall), and gun length. Then, following the projectile in flight, he observed that air resistance, contrary to accepted dogma, was a highly significant factor in trajectory. His work attracted the attention of Lord Anson, head of the Admiralty, who enabled him to experiment with all sorts of British naval guns.

The results led Robins to propose sweeping changes in the Royal Navy's ordnance. In 1747 he published a pamphlet entitled *A Proposal for Increasing the Strength of the British Navy, by Changing All Guns from 18-Pounders downwards into Others of Equal Weight but of Greater Bore.* The pamphlet argued for dispensing with all superfluous metal not contributing to the strength of guns. A cannon could thus be made with a larger bore for the same weight of metal. Such a cannon would fire a heavier projectile. For safety's sake, a smaller charge would be used. But owing to the heavier weight of the larger projectile, there would be no corresponding loss in momentum. A heavier shot traveling at the same velocity as a lighter shot inflicted greater damage to the side of a ship. In short, by redistributing the metal in a gun, a greater caliber could be attained for a given weight with no loss in safety. However, Robins's proposals did not lead to any immediate changes in Royal Navy ordnance.[34]

Principles of internal ballistics learned in the latter half of the eighteenth century supported Robins's arguments for redesigning naval ordnance. Previously the size, shape, and ornamentation of guns had varied with the taste of the founder. Ironmasters made cannon with double or triple reinforces of metal, so that the exterior surface was stepped longitudinally from breech to muzzle. Recent experiments, however, indicated that gunpowder acted uniformly, not in steps. Ordnance experts reasoned that a gun should have a cylindrical bore with its outer contour shaped in a slightly concave curve, corresponding presumably to the curve of powder pressure. Experts realized that determining the curve exactly would be difficult, so they recommended a sloping straight line from breech to muzzle as sufficient.[35]

In the nineteenth century, European scientists and ordnance experts accelerated the trend of using science to improve ordnance. In France, for example, Guillaume Piobert, educated at the École d'application de l'artillerie et du génie, did research in internal ballistics to correct what he diagnosed as dangerously excessive pressures in French cannon as well as experimentation with gunpowder. In Britain Sir Howard Douglas studied both the theory of ballistics and the practical problems of gunnery at sea. His famous *Treatise on Naval Gunnery,* in which he published his findings, became the standard British text on the subject for the remaining years of the wooden navy. The Royal Navy adopted many of his recommendations for improving gunnery at sea, including a training program for officers and men conducted on board a ship reserved exclusively for the purpose.[36]

SCIENCE AND THE UNITED STATES ARMY ORDNANCE DEPARTMENT

In the United States the army took the lead in using science to improve ordnance. The army's Ordnance Department, a staff bureau created in 1812, procured, tested, stored, maintained, and distributed weapons, ammunition, and related equipment. It also recruited and trained ordnance specialists for attachment to units in the field or in garrison. It controlled two armories, fifteen arsenals, and four depots. The most important arsenals were located in Washington, Pittsburgh, and Watervliet, New York, where carriages were built and ammunition manufactured. The barrels were cast at private foundries and mounted at these arsenals.[37]

In 1832 the army established an ordnance board to develop a standard American system of artillery. Before then, United States Army ordnance stemmed from British and French designs. Creating a new system entailed not only determining uniform types, calibers, dimensions, weights, and materials of field, siege, and coastal artillery, but also doing the same for carriages, limbers, caissons, ammunition chests, and all of the other necessary equipment. Most important, the job entailed designing, testing, and evaluating this equipment. Army ordnance experts worked on the new system throughout the 1830s.

One such expert, Alfred Mordecai, was typical of what historian Stanley Falk calls "soldier-technologists." Mordecai and his army colleagues led the way for technical military research and the practical application of science to the military arts in the United States. At age fifteen Mordecai enrolled in the Military Academy, where he studied physics, chemistry, drawing, engineering, and the arts of war. After graduation he served in the Army Corps of Engineers until 1832, when he was appointed a captain in the Ordnance Department. As an ordnance officer, Mordecai tested gunpowder and small arms, experimented in ballistics, worked on the army's system of artillery, and served on the ordnance board. He would become an important figure in Dahlgren's life during the latter's early years at the Bureau of Ordnance and Hydrography.

Toward the end of the 1830s a disagreement arose between Secretary of War Joel R. Poinsett and the members of the ordnance board about whether cast iron should replace bronze in field artillery. Bronze had been the material of choice because of its relative strength, but iron was cheaper. In April 1840 Poinsett dispatched Mordecai, Major Rufus L. Baker, Captain Benjamin Huger, and William Wade to Europe "to obtain such practical knowledge of the treatment of iron, that the Ordnance Department may dictate rules to the founders so as to ensure the selection of good metal, and the fabrication of good guns." Baker and Huger were army officers serving with Mordecai on the ordnance board. William Wade, a former army ordnance officer and part owner of the Fort Pitt Foundry, was interested in finding a way to make stronger iron castings. The researchers visited arsenals, foundries, mines, powder mills, and other installations in Britain, Norway, Sweden, Germany, Russia, Belgium, and France. The Swedes permitted them to make a thorough study of gun-founding methods in their country. Because of its rich iron mines and excellent foundries, Sweden numbered among the few European states capable of manufacturing and using cast-iron field artillery. The researchers took careful notes on every phase of production, from the initial mining and preparation of the ore through the smelting, molding, casting, and boring processes.

As a result of these observations, in 1842 the Ordnance Department stationed a representative at every private iron foundry that made guns for the army. This "attending agent" monitored ordnance production to ensure that the foundries produced high-quality guns. The Ordnance Department issued a detailed set of instructions for the attending agent as well as a comprehensive set of specifications for the founders. The attending agent oversaw the selection of metals as well as the production process itself and was empowered to reject any gun he deemed unfit for service. For the first time in the history of American artillery production, the Ordnance Department prescribed and enforced specific rules for selecting and preparing metals and for manufacturing artillery. These quality-control measures materially improved army artillery. Incidentally, the army decided to retain bronze in its field artillery but continued to use cast iron in its heavy seacoast artillery.

Wade applied what he had learned in Europe to develop a standard procedure for testing iron to determine whether it was strong enough to be used in cannon. The procedure consisted of casting a 9-pounder trial gun of the metal in question and firing it until it failed. The procedure included making detailed records, including the location of the mines, the amount of iron melted to pour the gun, the melting time, the fusion time, and the cooling time.[38]

The army Ordnance Department also did research in internal ballistics. Chief of Ordnance Lieutenant Colonel George Bomford designed an experiment to determine the pressures inside the barrel of a gun during firing. Bomford drilled a series of holes along the length of a cannon barrel, secured a pistol barrel in each hole, and place a bullet in each barrel. When he fired the cannon, the force of the exploding gunpowder shot the bullets at ballistic pendulums, thereby registering the force of the explosion at each point. From these findings he plotted a curve representing the variation in pressure as the projectile moved down the barrel.

Bomford used this curve to design coastal artillery for the army's new system. He proportioned the thickness of metal along the barrel so as to correspond to the relative internal pressure at each point. In 1844 the army introduced into service two such weapons, the 8- and 10-inch "columbiads" (the generic name for heavy coast-defense cannon). These weapons retained the moldings, longitudinal steps, and other traditional earmarks of ordnance design but conformed more closely to the curve of internal pressure than any previous weapon. The model 1844 columbiad was the first American cannon based on the results of research in internal ballistics.[39]

By early 1847 the ordnance board had completed most of the details of the artillery system. The board assigned Mordecai the job of preparing its work for publication. By this time Mordecai had added to his ordnance résumé service as an assistant attending agent and work with William Wade in strength-of-metals testing. He had become one of the premier ordnance officers in the United States, if not the world. In 1849 his final report on the new artillery system was published as a full-length book entitled *Artillery for the United States Land Service, as Devised and Arranged by the Ordnance Board.* That year the secretary of war officially adopted the new system of artillery.[40]

THE *PRINCETON* CATASTROPHE

The United States Navy followed the army's lead in using science to improve ordnance. In 1841 the House Committee on Naval Affairs reported that the Navy Department "should be clothed with power to test the value of such improvements as have been, or may hereafter be, made in naval ordnance and construction." But it was the forward-thinking Abel P. Upshur who best articulated the impulse toward science. In his 1842 report to Congress he demanded that "*the very best guns which can be made,* and none others, should ever be used." He believed that only "by the union of science with practical skill" could the quality of ordnance be improved:

> The application of scientific principles in the mechanical arts is now universal. The mere artisan, whose skill is derived only from practice, is far behind the times. Science is now lending her aid to the arts, in all their departments—expanding their powers, multiplying their uses, and perfecting their works.... The knowledge which we obtain from *experience* is always slow, always costly, and *not* always sure; that which we obtain from *experiment,* particularly in physical science, rarely deceives, and seldom fails richly to repay us.[41]

The *Princeton* catastrophe accelerated the use of science to improve American ordnance. In 1841 Captain Robert F. Stockton, a man of tremendous political influence, persuaded Congress and the Navy Department to build the USS *Princeton,* the navy's first screw-propelled steamer. Two 12-inch wrought-iron cannon were the centerpieces of her armament. Both the screw propeller and the 12-inchers had been designed by the Swedish inventor John Ericsson, but Stockton took all the credit.[42]

Stockton made extraordinary claims for this vessel: The innovations she embodied were the greatest since the invention of gunpowder. The 12-inch guns, named the Peacemaker and the Oregon, were perfect. They were so accurate that they would reduce the art of gunnery to a mathematical certainty. They had greater endurance and destructive power than any gun in service. Thus, the *Princeton* could do battle with any vessel afloat, no matter how large. Stockton intended to modernize the navy by building several vessels like the *Princeton,* all based on the doctrine of qualitative superiority.

On 28 February 1844 Stockton staged a gala event to show off the *Princeton* and her guns. Over five hundred people including President John Tyler, cabinet members, foreign ministers, congressmen, senators, army and navy officers, and their wives thronged on board the *Princeton* for a dinner party and a demonstration of the ship. Stockton fired the Peacemaker twice to show off its power. Someone asked him to fire the gun again. He did. Without warning the Peacemaker exploded, killing, among others, the secretary of the navy, the chief of the Bureau of Construction, Equipment, and Repairs, and Upshur, who was then secretary of state. It is hard to imagine a worse blow to Stockton's prospects. The next day the House Naval Affairs Committee crushed Stockton's proposal to build more ships like the *Princeton*. No more guns like the Peacemaker were made. The explosion of the Peacemaker was a disaster unparalleled in the history of American naval ordnance.

As a result of the *Princeton* tragedy, the U.S. government sponsored extensive experiments by ordnance experts and gun-founders on metals and ways to strengthen guns. The army, which did not want to experience its own ordnance disaster, also launched a program to test the strength and durability of guns already in service. Army and civilian ordnance experts often worked together, using equipment such as transverse breaking machines[43] to determine tensile strength, and methods such as the application of hydrostatic pressure and failure testing to determine durability. They concluded that the properties of iron varied with the casting method. Moreover, they found a correlation between the density and tensile strength of the metal and the durability of the gun. Metal with a higher density and tenacity seemed to result in a more durable gun. The purpose of these experiments, like Wade's experiments, was to enable the founder to select metal of known strength and durability for cannon.[44]

THE 1845 NAVAL ORDNANCE BOARD

Inspired by the army's example and horrified by the *Princeton* tragedy, the navy stepped up its own efforts to use science to improve ordnance. In June 1844 Secretary of the Navy John Y. Mason sent two naval officers abroad to study the standardization of ordnance and the adoption of shell guns in the French and British navies, a move reminiscent of the army's mission to Europe four years earlier. In March 1845 the secretary appointed a board of officers to examine European ordnance innovations, to evaluate the navy's proof procedures, and to study the ballistics of naval ordnance. The board included William M. Crane, chief of the Bureau of Ordnance and Hydrography; Captain Lewis Warrington, chief of the Bureau of Yards and Docks; Captain Charles Morris, chief of the Bureau of Construction, Equipment, and Repair; Captain William B. Shubrick, chief of the Bureau of Provisions and Clothing; and Captain Alexander S. Wadsworth.[45]

The fact that the navy appointed this board raises a number of important points. There was no career path in ordnance. Until the institution of the bureau system in 1842, the navy had no permanent ordnance organization such as the army's Ordnance Department. Ordnance duty fell to officers who were interested in it, but there were no minimum requirements in education or experience. Thus, the people who decided the fate of ordnance proposals were not always qualified to do so. The Board of Navy Commissioners had handled routine ordnance matters such as supplying ships with ammunition. The secretary of the navy appointed individuals or temporary, ad hoc boards to study nonroutine problems when they arose. For example, in 1837 the secretary had appointed a board to determine whether 24-pounder cannon made in 1826 were still safe enough for shipboard use. As noted above, Matthew Perry was assigned to study shell guns. This way of doing things enabled individuals to take the initiative in suggesting innovation, such as Robert Stockton in the case of the Peacemaker, but it also meant that innovation depended on the initiative, influence, and abilities of those individuals. In the absence of the dynamic leadership of men such as Abel Upshur or the initiative of highly motivated officers such as Perry, American naval ordnance remained stagnant.

Because of this ad hoc way of doing things, there was no consistency in naval ordnance. Before 1815 the navy had procured its cannon from a variety of sources, including the United States Army, Great Britain, France, private manufacturers, and even smugglers. Naval guns made in America since the War of 1812 followed French or British designs.[46]

There were two reasons why the navy appointed a board to study ordnance in 1845 instead of relying on the Bureau of Ordnance and Hydrography. Crane, the ordnance bureau chief, blamed himself for the *Princeton* disaster. Although the decision to build the *Princeton* and her deadly guns had been made before his office had even been created, he was chief of the bureau charged with all matters relating to ordnance, and he considered himself ultimately responsible for the disaster. In March 1846 he resigned his position, locked himself in his office, and slashed his own throat.[47] The second reason stemmed from the fact that all of the first bureau chiefs had joined the navy before 1815, and many had been navy commissioners. Although the naval organization had a new form, its leaders preferred doing things the old way.

The board submitted its first report on 29 May. It recommended that the navy designate a frigate as a gunnery ship in order to establish a uniform system of drill, to determine a standard means of arraying and stowing ammunition, to train gunners, and to determine the ranges and penetration of the different types of American naval guns. It also recommended establishing a practice battery ashore for ranging guns. In its second report, which came out in June, the board issued regulations that tightened quality control in the production of the new guns. The regulations specified not only tests to ensure that the iron used in cannon was sound, but also the proof that guns had to pass before the navy would accept them.[48]

With the approval of the secretary of the navy, the 1845 board adopted a new system of shipboard ordnance. Like the Royal Navy, it adopted the 32-pounder as the basic gun, in six different sizes. It also adopted a second, lighter pattern of 8-inch shell gun to supplement the one that entered service in 1841. Captain Wadsworth designed the new guns on the British model. New regulations doubled the number of shell guns to be mounted on all classes of warships. For the next several years a substantial number of the new guns entered the fleet. One of the most interesting aspects of the 1845 armament was that the United States Navy accepted qualitative equality with the Europeans in naval ordnance, in contrast to its prior doctrine of qualitative superiority.[49]

Navy and army ordnance experts worked together in a spirit of warmth and cooperation in the wake of the *Princeton* tragedy. Naval officers attended army-sponsored ordnance experiments, army officers attended navy experiments, and both services worked closely with private gun-founders. In fact, both services employed the same foundries to manufacture their heavy ordnance. The services freely shared testing equipment, reports on experiments, and ideas. The navy was the junior partner in the use of science to improve ordnance. For example, the navy based its quality-control regulations on the army's European-influenced rules for selecting, preparing, and testing metals and manufacturing artillery.[50]

Three naval ordnance officers captured this community spirit in a letter to the chief of the naval ordnance bureau written in 1849:

> Let us not omit to render justice to the genius of Bomford, who…has in so many…ways improved our ordnance; nor to say that to Wadsworth we owe the present excellent modification of Bomford[']s and other constructions, which are seen in the New Navy Guns. The first is beyond the reach of our humble tribute to his worth, but to the last, it may be gratifying to know that his labors have been appreciated, and will be known to future generations.

They also paid tribute to William Wade and to Cyrus Alger, owner of the Boston foundry. Moreover, the naval officers recommended the adoption of a device Mordecai had designed for testing gunpowder.[51]

By establishing contacts with European ordnance experts and gun-founders on their missions to Europe, army and navy ordnance officers also participated in an international ordnance community. European and American ordnance experts had similar backgrounds in training and experience, shared ideas, and relied on record keeping, mathematics, and systematic experiment to advance gunnery and gunmaking. The nineteenth-century naval revolution depended not only on things such as shell guns but also on ideas for using them, organizations to develop them, and science to improve them. This was the scene when Dahlgren appeared on the stage.

5

Inventing the Dahlgren Gun
1847–1850

During his first five years at the Washington Navy Yard, Dahlgren conceived of what he considered his most important contributions: the heavy Dahlgren shell gun, the Dahlgren boat gun, and the "Ordnance Establishment," the organization he created to test, improve, and manufacture naval ordnance. But had someone told him in January 1847 that he would accomplish all of this, he would not have believed it. When he received his assignment to the Washington Navy Yard, he had no idea that he would become an innovator.

Like most naval officers, Dahlgren would have preferred a command afloat. A reputation for heroism was made afloat, not ashore. For example, Percival Drayton, who would become a famous monitor skipper in the Civil War, looked upon shore duty as "a disgusting business altogether" and considered it "a pity that any gentleman should be obliged to dirty his fingers with it." Service ashore came roughly once in every three tours of duty. Although Dahlgren had not served a lengthy tour ashore since the coast survey, he felt due for service afloat. Even though he had obtained the assignment to ordnance through the influence of his friend Joseph Smith, he applied for service in the Gulf of Mexico in command of a "shell vessel." The request was denied. Dahlgren resigned himself to another tour ashore, per-haps comforted by the maxim that a cruise in Washington was worth two around Cape Horn. "My main purpose in seeking ordn. duty," he later recalled, "was to fit myself more fully for sea service."[1]

On 12 January 1847 Dahlgren reported for duty to Commodore Lewis Warrington, chief of the Bureau of Ordnance and Hydrography. Warrington gave him a cold reception. Usually a bureau chief approved the people assigned to him, but Warrington had not been consulted about Dahlgren. He told Dahlgren that he would send for him when he wanted him. It was an inauspicious start for the father of American naval ordnance.[2]

THE ORDNANCE ESTABLISHMENT

Initial Duties and the Founding of the Ordnance Establishment

Ordnance and Hydrography was the bureau charged with all matters relat-ing to ordnance, but Dahlgren worked at the Washington Navy Yard, an installation controlled by the Bureau of Yards and Docks. After the War of 1812 the Washington Navy Yard became the navy's principal industrial cen-ter. Anchors, tackle blocks, ammunition, small arms, chain cables, and gun carriages were manufactured there. By 1846 it had also become the navy's foremost metalworking center. The yard housed a rolling mill, a tilt ham-mer, and a foundry as well as blacksmith, plumber, anchor-maker, rigger, and painter shops. Although the chief of Ordnance and Hydrography was not in charge of the yard, he officially sponsored all of the ordnance work done there. The commandant of the navy yard, a subordinate of the chief of Yards and Docks, was responsible for any activity that took place within his command. Though Dahlgren answered to two commanding officers, his pri-mary responsibility was to Warrington.[3]

Lewis Warrington was a hero of the 1812 generation. He entered the navy as a midshipman in 1800 and developed his sea legs in the Mediterranean under Commodore Edward Preble. The beginning of the War of 1812 found him a first lieutenant on board the thirty-eight-gun *Congress,* one of Humphreys's superfrigates. At the suggestion of Stephen Decatur, Warrington was given command of the new twenty-gun sloop *Peacock.* On a dark night in March 1814 the *Peacock* slipped past the British blockaders off New York for a cruise in the West Indies. On 28 April she encountered

Washington Navy Yard, circa 1850 (Naval Historical Center)

the British eighteen-gun brig-sloop *Épervier* off Cape Canaveral. The *Peacock* won the ensuing battle, making Warrington's reputation. After returning to New York in October to fit out for another cruise, Warrington led his ship into the East Indies, where he captured four prizes. When he returned to New York in November 1815, he found that he had been promoted to captain. During the next few decades he commanded the *Macedonian* on a cruise in the Mediterranean, helped rid the West Indies of pirates as commander of the sloop *John Adams,* served as a navy commissioner, and headed the Bureau of Yards and Docks. When he took command of the Bureau of Ordnance and Hydrography in 1846, he was a senior officer of great stature. The sober, able, and energetic Warrington had a knack for avoiding controversy, but this did not prevent him from advocating steam propulsion; he understood the traditions of the sailing navy as well as the need for progress. Such understanding was an important trait for a man in charge of an organization in which innovation depended on the initiative, influence, and abilities of individuals.[4]

Warrington knew that Secretary of the Navy John Young Mason had a particular fondness for war rockets invented by the Englishman William Hale. In the fall of 1846 Joshua Burrows Hyde, a Connecticut-born engineer who had met Hale in London, offered to sell Hale's rockets to the U.S. government on the Englishman's behalf. The army's Ordnance Department

Lewis Warrington, circa 1848 (Naval Historical Center)

asked General Winfield Scott what he thought of the idea. Scott remembered the British war rockets fired against his forces at the battles of Chippewa and Lundy's Lane during the War of 1812 and approved. Adoption was contingent upon the results of tests with the rockets conducted by a joint army-navy board that November. Although the results impressed the army officers, including none other than Alfred Mordecai, Warrington, who was one of the naval officers on the board, voiced "strong objections" to the rockets because of "the danger of accidental ignition,…the inconvenience of transport, and the difficulty of giving them a right direction when a vessel is in motion." But the majority of the board disagreed with Warrington, and Mason ordered him to begin manufacturing rockets for the navy. Warrington resented the Hale rocket project because it had been foisted upon him over his objections. On 27 January 1847 he summoned Dahlgren to his office and assigned him the task.[5]

The next day Alfred Mordecai accompanied Dahlgren to look at the ordnance facilities at the Washington Navy Yard. Dahlgren could hardly have had a more experienced ordnance officer to show him the ropes. The ordnance facilities at the navy yard included a press for loading propellant into rockets housed in the end of a timber shed, a space in the plumber's shop for making and fitting fuze stocks, locks, and shells, and a laboratory directed by a civilian, Benjamin Coston. These were meager facilities by army standards.[6]

Fortunately, Dahlgren benefited from Mordecai's vast experience during his early days at the yard. The two officers were "on the best of terms," according to Foote. For Dahlgren it was the beginning of a long and profitable relationship. With Mordecai's help he began test-firing rockets in mid-February.[7]

While Dahlgren developed the rockets, the question of who had control of the ordnance lab became a matter of contention. Although Dahlgren considered Coston "a very clever person," he preferred to direct projects himself. When Coston refused to obey an order, Dahlgren appealed directly to Warrington to clarify their respective spheres of authority. Warrington, who had begun to respect the lieutenant for his knowledge, determination, and progress with the rockets, declared that the prerogative of command at the yard should rest with naval officers. From now on Coston was to consider himself subordinate to Dahlgren.[8]

With his authority clarified, Dahlgren set about improving the facilities at the yard. In April he received permission to build an ordnance workshop. He installed a press, boring machine, ball cutter and finisher, cap cutter, lathes, musket pendulum, and other machines. He later added a planing machine, a drill press, and a machine for making cones and nipples. The workshop was the first step in transforming the Washington Navy Yard into a first-rate ordnance establishment.[9]

Dahlgren's duties began to expand. In addition to developing the rockets, Warrington assigned him the responsibility of inspecting and preparing ordnance equipment for the Home Squadron, engaged in blockading Mexico's Gulf coast ports. In July, Matthew Perry, commander of the squadron, sent Warrington a letter praising the equipment he had received. Warrington was immensely pleased. Within a month he had placed Dahlgren in charge of all ordnance work at the yard, including the new machinery, the development of war rockets, and the inspection and preparation of primers, percussion caps, and shells.[10]

Dahlgren's new position empowered him to tinker with ordnance and machines. He read up on gunpowder and found a way to improve fuzes. He noticed the tendency of shells to rust and solved the problem by instituting a new procedure for handling them. He worked out a way to apply steam power to a hydrostatic press, enabling one man to operate it instead of five.[11]

Dahlgren's work attracted the attention of Secretary Mason. In October 1847 Mason offered to make him head of the gunnery department at the newly founded Naval Academy in nearby Annapolis, Maryland. Foote wanted his friend to accept the offer and "teach the youngsters how to shoot." He thought that Dahlgren's "literary—scientific—& moral" attainments would be a fine example for "young men just at the turning point of character." But Dahlgren did not want the job. The ordnance assignment was far more interesting than he had anticipated, and he did not want other duties to intrude. Nevertheless, the secretary prevailed upon him to teach classes at the academy twice a week.[12]

Although Dahlgren did not welcome the added burden, he was prepared for it. As "Professor of Gunnery," he revealed an extensive knowledge of ordnance hardware and a familiarity with the important literature in the field. He lectured the midshipmen on guns, projectiles, charges, and carriages and on how to equip, handle, and maintain a ship's battery. In lectures he cited the work of such luminaries as Paixhans, Ben Robins, Count Rumford (the inventor of a ballistic pendulum), British ordnance expert T. F. Simmons, and Mordecai. Dahlgren also set up a battery to teach practical gunnery. The midshipmen, as Foote put it, formed "golden opinions" of their gunnery professor.[13]

Development of a Precise and Systematic Testing Framework

Dahlgren received yet another assignment that fall. The 1845 ordnance board had recommended a program for improving the accuracy of naval gunnery. The program involved preparing and distributing range tables and adopting tangent sights for the new guns. A tangent sight, mounted on the breech of a gun, featured a graduated scale of ranges. It improved aim by enabling the gunner to elevate his piece according to the estimated distance to the target. It allowed a commander to set all of a ship's guns for a given range regardless of how they were mounted. To mount a tangent sight properly, one would have to know the ranges of the gun at various elevations. The navy, however, did not have this information. Warrington assigned Dahlgren the task of finding the range of each class of new gun in order to construct the range tables and mount the tangent sights.[14]

Dahlgren studied methods that others had used to find ranges. He read

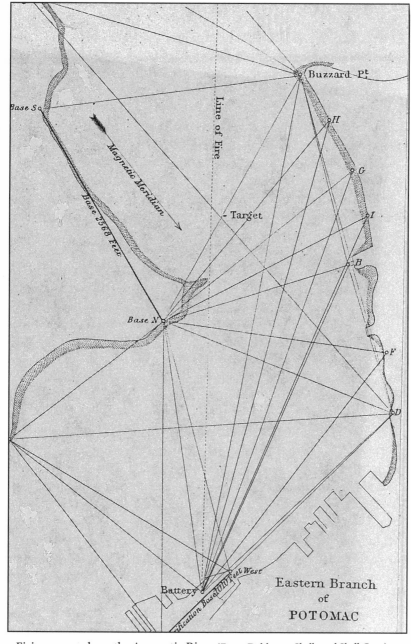

Firing range along the Anacostia River (From Dahlgren, *Shells and Shell Guns*)

works by Sir Howard Douglas, who had constructed range tables for the Royal Navy. He examined works of other French and British ordnance experts. The English tables omitted the height of sight and elevation of the bore. The French tables did not list individual shots, only the mean of many shots. "Therefore there is no internal evidence of the accuracy obtained," concluded Dahlgren, and "consequently no certainty as to the dependence to be given."[15]

Therefore, he devised his own technique, applying what he had learned on the coast survey as head of a triangulation party and as a student of Hassler's dedication to pure science. He proposed a two-part program. First, to find the ranges, he would fire the guns and systematically record the results. For each round he would log the height of the sight, the height of the gun above the water, the elevation of the barrel, the time and distance to the first and last grazes, the total number of grazes, and the recoil of the gun, and include detailed information about the particular piece used. He intended to fire the cannon over water and use two plane tables, one placed on either side of the line of fire, to find the distance from the gun to the grazes. He surveyed the test area to locate exactly the position of the firing platform. With the data from the two plane tables, each a check on the other, he could calculate the ranges by triangulation. Second, he would determine the effects of different projectiles by firing them at targets built to resemble the side of a ship. He would measure the lateral and vertical deviation of the projectile from the line of sight, the penetration of the projectile, and the effect of shells.[16]

Dahlgren tested the feasibility of the method in November. He borrowed two plane tables from the Naval Observatory and modified them for his own purposes. He placed two guns on a wharf and fired 101 rounds over the course of eight days. Each plane-table operator tracked the projectiles with an alidade, marking paper laid on the plane table for the jet of water produced by each graze. Dahlgren concluded that the method worked simply, quickly, and accurately. Historian Edward W. Constant has noted that testing is a key element in applying scientific methods to technology, and that the construction of testing apparatus in itself is worthy of note. The plane-table method was Dahlgren's first direct application of scientific methods to American naval ordnance.[17]

During the next several years Dahlgren used the plane-table method to range each class of 1845 ordnance. He did not range guns on windy days. The method worked better in calm weather because the jets made when the projectiles struck the water were easier to see. He added refinements as he went along, such as using muslin screens measuring 20 feet wide by 10 feet high with vertical lines painted down the center to measure accuracy. The firing range was established over the Anacostia River, the eastern branch of the Potomac. The guns were mounted on a firing platform resembling the deck of a ship and were fired by a navy gun crew, led by an officer. Civilian "Ord. Mechanics" from the shop worked the plane tables. To fire, the crew maneuvered the gun to a mark on the deck, checked the line of sight, inserted a gunner's quadrant to obtain the elevation, signaled the plane-table operators to stand ready, and pulled the lock lanyard. The men stood about the gun during firing as though on board ship. Dahlgren designed special instruments for the job, including gunner's quadrants, a micrometer for measuring distances, and an alidade with a spring-loaded punch for marking the grazes.[18]

Dahlgren and his plane-table method so pleased Warrington that he decided to show them off to the makers of naval policy. In October 1848 the bureau chief invited President James K. Polk down to what had come to be known as the "experimental battery" for a demonstration. Dahlgren fired six rounds at a wooden target for Polk, the secretaries of the navy and the treasury, the commandant of the Washington Navy Yard, and Warrington.[19]

On 1 November, in a beautifully crafted report, Dahlgren communicated the results of his work with the 32-pounder of 32 cwt. The report was thorough, succinct, easily understood, and well conceived. It included hand-drawn color pictures of guns, projectiles, and some of the testing equipment employed as well as a map of the firing range. Dahlgren put the purpose and results of the experiments up front, then explained the testing method in detail. He added a few observations on similar French and English experiments and included raw measurements in tabular form. The bulk of the report expounded the virtues of the plane-table method, which provided a precise and systematic framework for observing the performances of the various guns and projectiles Dahlgren tested.[20]

The Ordnance Establishment Grows

When the weather did not permit ranging, Dahlgren performed myriad other duties. He inspected ordnance materials produced by private firms, tested ordnance inventions, and proposed changes in the way ordnance materials were handled. As the ranging progressed, he went on board ships to affix tangent sights to the guns.[21]

Dahlgren took good care of his subordinates at the yard. He was in charge of the mechanics and foremen who worked in the ordnance shops and the secretary and clerk who worked in the office. These people were civilians. He was also in charge of the sailors who served the guns at the experimental battery. Dahlgren praised individuals in reports to Warrington. He asked the commandant of the yard to increase the civilian workers' pay. On one occasion he asked his chief for a 50-cent per diem allowance for the shop mechanics who worked the plane tables: "It seems to have been of no consequence to them, that the service is not in the line of their usual work, they go to it cheerfully—notwithstanding that the exposure to heat, cold, and dampness along the low shores of the stream has more than once occasioned sickness among them." Dahlgren created new positions for some of the more specialized work, established minimum standards and job descriptions for his people, and made sure that they received adequate training. He wrote Warrington:

> Two good seamen are much wanted for the usual labor in the Gunner's gang strapping shells, inspecting shot & shells & many other items— These could be drafted from Norfolk—and should be young intelligent men who have served one *entire* cruise as Capts of Fore-top—which would be the best certificate of their sailor-ship—they should be able to read and write—and above all be habitually sober. The pay here of an ordinary laborer which is $1.00 would be ample no doubt when compared with any ships rate—one year here would make capable Quarter Gunners of them & their places could be supplied by other seamen.

By attending to the needs of his men, Dahlgren produced a cadre of loyal ordnance specialists.[22]

Trained personnel proved a central element in what Dahlgren was creating. His "Ordnance Establishment" was becoming an organization analogous to the army's Ordnance Department. No comparable organization had existed in the navy before. Dahlgren created it without a master plan, devising and institutionalizing its components to meet demands as they arose. The work of the organization fell into three broad categories: manufacturing ammunition and equipment, inspecting ordnance received from foundries, and testing ordnance and inventions. Dahlgren instituted the machine shop for manufacturing and the experimental battery for testing during his first two years at the Washington Navy Yard. His work ethic, expertise, scientific training under Hassler, and ability to write attractive reports, as well as the appeal of the method he devised to range guns, had pleased Warrington and attracted the attention and recognition of policy-makers. This attention and recognition gave Dahlgren the bureaucratic pull he needed to create the Ordnance Establishment.

The Development of the Boat Gun

Dahlgren's Ordnance Establishment soon demonstrated the capability to develop new weapons. A demand for a light boat howitzer had arisen during the Mexican War, when carronades and army howitzers had proven inade-quate for boat operations in shallow waters. Characteristically, Dahlgren took the initiative. In September 1847 he proposed to Warrington that the navy develop a light bronze gun for boat operations in support of landings or of forces on shore. It was to be used "almost entirely against uncovered masses of men," firing shells and shrapnel. He cited a French precedent: a single French boat gun had stopped a Mexican cavalry charge at the battle of Vera Cruz and had deprived Santa Anna of a leg in the process.[23]

Dahlgren completed a design for a boat gun in February 1848 but did not receive Warrington's permission to make one until the following September. He attributed the delay to "fogies" who for various reasons had objected to the boat gun. One "fogy," Lieutenant A. B. Fairfax, a naval officer who had worked with ordnance, argued that it was too light to endure the rigors of service, and that shells carried in boats would inevitably get wet. To answer these charges, Dahlgren cited French and English sources on the practica-bility of similar pieces in their navies. He drummed up support from friends and exhibited the boat gun in public demonstrations. On one occasion he put on a show for the secretary of the navy, the secretary of war, Warrington, two other bureau chiefs, and the commandant of the yard. A boat gun mounted on a field carriage was fired six times in fifty-five seconds. Afterward Dahlgren conducted the dignitaries on a tour of the ordnance workshops and lab. He won authorization to develop his system of boat guns.[24]

Dahlgren intended to produce the boat guns at the Washington Navy Yard rather than contract with private firms. Warrington's support enabled him to implement this ambitious and unprecedented proposal. He intended to create an establishment similar to army arsenals, putting himself in charge. He concentrated all the machines and equipment necessary to make ammunition for the boat guns in one building. He also built a furnace to cast the guns. There was already adequate machinery at the yard to bore and finish them. The Ordnance Establishment now included a gun factory, with Dahlgren its manager.[25]

Dahlgren developed not only hardware and a plant but also doctrine. He devised drills to simulate amphibious landings, firing the boat gun at targets ashore as the boat approached. Upon beaching, the boat crew switched the gun from its boat carriage to a field carriage and moved inland. Dahlgren was far more concerned with how the gun handled and its rate of fire than with accuracy or range.[26]

The navy formally adopted Dahlgren's system of boat guns on 17 December 1850. By general order of the secretary of the navy, several classes of boat guns were approved for liners down to sloops. Dahlgren had overcome resistance to the guns by persistence, hard work, influence, and the merit of the weapons themselves. This was becoming a characteristic style of his undertakings.[27]

THE INVENTION OF THE DAHLGREN GUN

The capability of Dahlgren's Ordnance Establishment to develop new weapons led not only to the boat gun but also to the Dahlgren gun, which was a heavy cast-iron muzzleloading smoothbore shell gun. Although the U.S. and European navies already had guns of this description in service, several conceptual and structural components distinguished the Dahlgren gun from other types of ordnance: Dahlgren's hypothesis of round-projectile ballistics, the exterior shape, the casting method, and the quality-control procedures used in the manufacturing process. The first component Dahlgren conceived of was the hypothesis of round-projectile ballistics. The idea occurred to him as he was ranging the 1845 ordnance.

The Hypothesis of Round-Projectile Ballistics

While banging away with the 32-pounder of 57-cwt., Dahlgren perceived a flaw in the conception of the 1845 ordnance. He had been ranging the 57 cwt. class intermittently since January 1849. The following October he noted that "the circumstances under which this practice was executed could not have been more favorable, and yet the inaccuracy is surprising when compared with that of the 32 of 32 cwt." Dahlgren measured the relative accuracy of the guns by firing them from a constant range at targets measuring 40 feet wide by 20 feet high. The greater the proportion of hits per round

Dahlgren boat gun. *Top,* boat carriage; *bottom,* field carriage (not to scale). (From U.S. Navy Department, Bureau of Ordnance, *Ordnance Instructions for the United States Navy*)

fired, he reasoned, the more accurate the gun. When equal proportions were obtained, he measured how close each hit came to the vertical line painted down the center of the target. He reasoned that the closer the average hit was to the line, the more accurate the gun. He found that the heavier 32-pounders were less accurate than the lighter ones. On 15 October 1849 he reported to Warrington that the range of the 32-pounder of 57 cwt. increased with the powder charge, but beyond a certain weight of charge its accuracy was inferior to that of lighter 32-pounders. What Dahlgren had observed was that above a certain muzzle velocity (heavier charges produced greater muzzle velocities), the accuracy of a round projectile decreased dramatically. "The limit referred to," he wrote, "approaches the velocity which is generally supposed to produce a vacuum behind a moving body."[28]

This became the basis of Dahlgren's hypothesis of round-projectile ballistics. Here is how he reasoned it out: The accuracy and range of a projectile depend to a large degree on its momentum, a product of its mass and velocity. Above a certain velocity, air resistance to a round projectile increases dramatically, causing it to wobble from its intended trajectory. Thus, the optimum velocity for a round projectile is less than the maximum velocity attainable. Given the existence of an optimum velocity, lower than that attained by the heavier 32-pounders, the proper way to increase the momentum and therefore the range of a round projectile is to increase its weight. To increase momentum by increasing only the velocity reduces the accuracy when the optimum velocity is exceeded. Dahlgren considered this, as he noted in his diary, "an important discovery."[29]

In the 15 October report on the 32-pounder of 57 cwt., he proposed casting a 9-inch shell gun to test this hypothesis. The 9-incher would fire a heavier projectile than the 32-pounders or 8-inchers of the 1845 system. Dahlgren must have reasoned that if his hypothesis of round-projectile ballistics was correct, the 9-incher would be more accurate and have greater range than the 1845 guns. Moreover, the 9-inch shell would be more destructive than the 8-inch shell because of its greater weight.[30]

Dahlgren believed that his hypothesis of round-projectile momentum would change the face of the United States Navy. He wrote Warrington:

> I am aware that the principle now evolved if established would lead to an entire reorganization of the ordnance and to great changes in the arrangements of ships which are to receive new metal: But neither of these considerations ought to be of weight in view of the advantages attributable

to superior efficiency—Especially if it not be overlooked that, with the exception of a single frigate, we have not a model of a Liner or Frigate less antique than the third of a Century.

In the course of perfecting the 1845 system of ordnance, Dahlgren believed, he had discredited it. He was suggesting that the United States Navy adopt heavier ordnance. And as the 1845 system was based on the European model, the new ordnance would be heavier than that carried on French and British vessels. With these pen stokes, Dahlgren called for a return to qualitative superiority in American ordnance.[31]

The Bottle Shape

The lieutenant also arrived at the shape of his gun in the context of testing the 1845 ordnance, but by a different path.

Dahlgren spent his fortieth birthday, 13 November 1849, as he usually spent a windless day, at the guns. Between 9:30 and 10:00 A.M. he fired seven rounds from a 32-pounder of 57 cwt. At ten a group of army ordnance experts arrived for a tour of the Ordnance Establishment. Dahlgren fired an 8-inch shell gun and a boat howitzer for the party, then took them on a tour of the lab. At 2:30 P.M. he returned to the 32-pounder. Three rounds were fired. A fourth was loaded and the gun pointed as usual. Dahlgren turned to the gunner and asked if he was ready. "Ready Sir," the gunner replied. They were his last words. Dahlgren recorded what happened next:

> I said "Fire"—An unusual explosion took place instantly, the Battery was filled with smoke, and a great crash of timber was heard—Behind me I heard the ground ploughed up and of the things that fell, something grazed my heels, which afterwards proved to be part of the Breeching. Much stunned by the noise & the confusion, my attention was first attracted by the cries of a lad; but seeing that he would not be much hurt, I turned to the Battery—amid the smoke, yet lifting slowly, the first object [I saw] was the body of the unfortunate Gunner stretched on the deck & quite dead.

Dahlgren had narrowly escaped death himself. He immediately reported the tragedy to Warrington, requested a court of inquiry to discover the cause of the explosion, and discontinued the ranging program until the results were in.[32]

Warrington ordered three officers to conduct the investigation forthwith. He was certain that Dahlgren was blameless. The gun had burst on the 116th round. The chase—that part of the barrel between the trunnions and muzzle—had broken off intact and simply fell to the ground. The breech had broken into two large pieces, one of which weighed 2,000 pounds and flew 81 feet. The investigating officers postulated that the accident had resulted from bad metal in the gun. They warned that the consequences of a similar explosion on shipboard could be catastrophic. Moreover, as the defective 32-pounder had passed proof, the incident cast a shadow of doubt on the safety of every gun in service.[33]

Dahlgren launched a retrospective-testing program to forestall another such explosion. He cut small samples of metal from the muzzle faces of selected guns in service as well as samples from every one of his boat guns. He tested the density and tensile strength of the samples, checking for indications of bad metal. Army ordnance experts had used a similar program to test their own guns following the Peacemaker explosion. They had found that the method was reliable. Dahlgren also subjected a few of the older navy guns to extreme proof to determine if age, density, or tensile strength of metal affected the durability of a gun.[34]

Warrington also ordered Dahlgren to conduct his own investigation of the explosion. The lieutenant submitted his conclusions in a report dated 4 March 1850. In short order he blamed the accident on the quality of the metal, then spent the bulk of the report proposing stricter standards of proof. He cited three instances during the Barbary wars and the War of 1812 in which guns had exploded on shipboard, killing crewmen. "The ill effects of such a catastrophe on the minds of a ship's crew," he wrote, "may easily be imagined." He proposed that in the future the quality of iron should be judged by its density, tensile strength, color, and character of fracture when a sample was put in the transverse breaking machine. He recommended setting minimum standards for each criterion as well as a more extensive program for testing the guns already in service.[35]

These proposals, like the retrospective-testing program, were based on army experiments conducted in the wake of the Peacemaker tragedy to determine the strength of metals. Dahlgren studied the reports on the army experiments extensively. His program for testing the strength of metals as well as his proposals for proof standards stemmed directly from the conclusions of the army reports.[36]

Dahlgren used the explosion of the 32-pounder as an opportunity to push through his proposal to build the experimental 9-inch gun. On 9 January 1850 he submitted to Warrington a drawing of the 9-incher. The gun depicted had a peculiar shape. Concave lines swept down from an exaggerated breech along a slim chase. The gun looked like a soda-water bottle.[37]

Dahlgren believed that although the exterior shape of a gun had no effect on the accuracy, force, or range of the projectile, it determined the safety of the gun. Experience had shown that the navy's proof methods did not always expose a gun made with weak metal. When such a gun failed, as in the case of the 32-pounder, the chase usually dropped off intact while the breech flew to pieces. If a Dahlgren gun made with weak metal failed, the slim chase was supposed to rupture instead of the thick breech. On a ship, a gun was run out so that most of its chase was outboard when firing. The characteristic exaggerated breech and slim chase of Dahlgren's bottle-shaped design were intended to reduce the danger to the crew. Dahlgren told Warrington that by redistributing the metal, he could "exercise a *greater* amount of *ordnance power with a given weight of metal,* and with more safety to those who manage the gun, than any other piece then known of *like weight.*"[38]

There is controversy over exactly how Dahlgren arrived at this peculiar shape. One historian claims that he carried out an experiment in which he drilled a series of holes along the length of a cannon barrel and installed pressure gauges in each one. When the gun was fired, the gauges showed the varying levels of pressure on the barrel. Dahlgren allegedly graphed the readings, basing his design on the resultant curve. Another historian asserts that he drilled holes along the barrel of an 8-incher, plugged all but one, and placed a bullet in the open hole. When the cannon was fired, the force of the exploding powder shot the bullet at a ballistic pendulum, thereby registering the force of the explosion at that particular hole. By repeating the experiment at each hole, Dahlgren supposedly generated the signature curve.[39]

Remember that George Bomford had conducted experiments with bullets fired from pistol barrels secured in holes drilled in a gun barrel to show the variations in internal pressure. Major Thomas J. Rodman, who became Dahlgren's archrival, later confirmed Bomford's findings with a similar experiment.[40]

Dahlgren himself emphatically denied conducting experiments to determine the curve for the design of his gun. In a memorandum dated 20 December 1865 he wrote that "the models which I proposed" were "deduced—*not from experiment* as has been supposed—but from such principles as I believed were correct. I drew and completed the models without assistance from anyone." When asked what specific thought led him to invent his cannon, he said, "I observed a law of nature, and making a mathematical application of it, made a gun which was an invention, and in no wise a result of experiment." In a letter written to an English ordnance expert and dated 28 December 1859, Dahlgren noted that "the pistol-barrel experiment does not belong to me, and so far from developing such models as mine, it would…father that of the Columbiad."[41]

Nevertheless, it is generally accepted that Dahlgren designed his gun to correspond to variations in internal pressure produced by the expanding gases from the exploding gunpowder as they drove the projectile down the barrel. But where did he get the idea? Dahlgren's papers do not contain the definitive answer. Charles Cowley, who served on Dahlgren's staff during his command of the South Atlantic Blockading Squadron during the Civil War, said that Dahlgren had told him he had "obtained the idea of the formation of his unrivalled gun from observing the formation of the soda-water bottle." In truth, Dahlgren might have borrowed the curve of pressure from army experiments, just as he had borrowed information on strength-of-metals and proof testing. Dahlgren knew Mordecai well, had cited his and other army works in his Naval Academy ordnance lectures, and was familiar with Wade's strength-of-metals testing. It is likely that he was also aware of Bomford's experiments on internal ballistics. Dahlgren claimed that the design of his gun was original with him, but he did not claim credit for originating the idea of shaping the exterior of a gun to correspond to fluctuations in internal pressure. It would appear that he applied the results of the army experiments to the design of his gun. The design was original, but the idea behind it stemmed from army research.[42]

The First 9-Incher

Dahlgren described how he arrived at a caliber of 9 inches:

> The calibre of IX" was the result of deductions from the single datum 1st *That a broadside gun should be as heavy as could be conveniently worked at sea* and about 9000 lbs was assumed in round numbers as a suitable weight for first trial. Computing the weight of projectile which could be thrown from a gun of this weight with proper velocity of proj. and convenient recoil of gun there resulted 72 lbs and a charge of 10 lb of powder—from this weight of projectile resulted the IX" shell which when loaded weighed 72 lbs.[43]

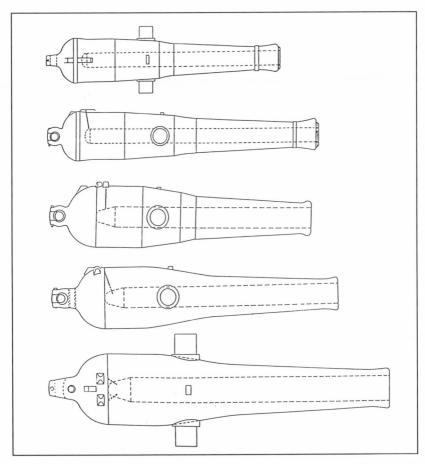

Top to bottom: 32-pounder of 42 cwt., 32-pounder of 57 cwt., the first 9-inch Dahlgren gun, 9-inch Dahlgren gun, 11-inch Dahlgren gun (approximately to scale). (From Canfield, *Civil War Naval Ordnance*)

Critics resisted the unusual gun, which seemed a radical departure from traditional design. The sources do not name the critics. Presumably they were officers interested in ordnance. Although the recent trend had been to thicken the breech and reduce the chase metal, critics did not believe that Dahlgren's chase would survive the strain of firing.[44]

At this time, however, Dahlgren was more interested in testing his hypothesis of round-projectile ballistics than in demonstrating the safety of a slim chase. He wanted to determine the accuracy, range, and destructive power of a gun with a 9-inch bore. If it proved superior in these respects to the 1845 guns, it would verify his hypothesis. The safety of a slim chase, a separate question, would have to be answered with subsequent models. To overcome the critics' resistance to the 9-incher, he compromised on the design of the exterior, shortening and thickening the chase. The West Point Foundry cast it without further ado.[45]

Although the casting of the first 9-incher marked the translation of the Dahlgren gun from an idea into a piece of hardware, the Dahlgren gun of Civil War fame had not yet emerged. Dahlgren would devise the casting method and quality-control procedures, the other unique structural and conceptual components of his gun, later.[46]

The Dahlgren Gun as a "Scientific Invention"

Three months before Dahlgren submitted the design of the 9-incher to Warrington, Lieutenant Henry A. Wise, who would later play an important role in Dahlgren's life, remarked to Foote that he considered Dahlgren "the most scientific officer in the Navy." Captain H. H. Cocke, commander of the sloop *St. Louis,* disapproved of Dahlgren's innovations in ammunition but hesitated to express his dissatisfaction to Warrington because "it might be thought that I possess no *science,* and am a quarter of a century behind the age of *improvements.*" Dahlgren was well on the way to earning a reputation as a "scientific inventor."[47]

What did this mean?[48] An "invention" is a thing, usually a new combination of familiar elements. "Invention" is also the process of inventing; it is primarily a mental process. One philosopher observed that "invention causes things to come into existence from ideas."[49] The process of invention translates ideas into objects or practices.

Dahlgren's method of invention embodied elements of science, engineering, and craft. Artisans converted ideas into objects with their hands, their tools, and the materials available to them. The emphasis on manual skill made their methods more artistic than mechanical, more individualistic than organized. Craftsmen learned by doing, not from books.

Artisans and engineers were both creative workmen whose stock in trade consisted of ideas and techniques. Engineers converted ideas first into drawings, then into objects. Engineering knowledge included knowledge based on experimental evidence and on empirical observations of materials and systems. As engineering emerged as a profession based on formal education and written knowledge, craft secrets came to be embedded in patents.

Science in mid-nineteenth-century America remained closely associated with craft traditions and was not yet established as a profession, but it differed from the crafts in several respects. Science depended heavily on formal education and its own literature for the transmission of knowledge. A scientist was more of a social being than an individualistic craftsman. Scientists organized themselves into international communities of practitioners and freely exchanged ideas.

Science was a process, the goal of which was understanding. Scientists developed theories about nature. They observed phenomena within the ordered framework of a paradigm, formulated hypotheses to explain these phenomena, and devised tests to validate their hypotheses. Some of the hallmarks of science were the quest for pure knowledge, participation in a community of practitioners with access to that knowledge, and testing and measuring apparatus.

The scientific inventor's skill, like that of the engineer, was both intellectual and manual. He learned his occupation both by doing and from books. For the oral traditions passed from master to apprentice the scientific inventor substituted education, a community of practitioners, and a technical literature patterned on those of science. The application of mathematics, systematic record keeping, a subscription to theory, and an experimental approach were the main functional differences between craftsmen on the one hand and engineers and scientific inventors on the other. Craftsmen's empirical knowledge and use of testing enabled them to learn *that* something worked better than something else, but not *why.* They were rarely able to venture outside the realm of experience. Theories and experiments designed to test those theories helped scientific inventors discover the *why.* Scientific methods and knowledge enabled the new breed of inventors to draw, calculate, and design things outside the range of prior experience and allowed them to explore possibilities beyond the point where craft intuition could offer guidance. With its ethic of openness and free access to ever-increasing quantities of knowledge, science also enabled innovators to invent and improve things much faster than craftsmen who kept to themselves.

The institutional context in which Dahlgren worked also shaped his role as a scientific inventor. Like Thomas Edison's Menlo Park laboratory, Dahlgren's Ordnance Establishment featured talented and trained individuals, machine tools, library resources, and scientific instruments. It was a context that fostered invention. Dahlgren created this organization virtually from scratch, modeling it after the army's Ordnance Department. Thanks to Dahlgren, the navy now had an organization capable of manufacturing, developing, and testing weapons.

Although Dahlgren created the Ordnance Establishment to facilitate work on the 1845 ordnance, the systematic framework he devised to test that ordnance exposed flaws in its conception. Dahlgren's interest in understanding what happened when he fired 32-pounders was a scientific interest in external ballistics. To observe this phenomenon systematically, he drew upon his coast survey experience and the community of ordnance practitioners to develop the plane-table method and its associated instruments. This method enabled him to observe that heavier 32-pounders were less accurate than lighter ones. To explain this phenomenon, he formulated a hypothesis about round-projectile ballistics. He designed the 9-inch gun in part to serve as an instrument to test this hypothesis.

The 9-inch gun was a new combination of familiar elements. "The limits of any design are culture bound," notes historian Eugene Ferguson. "All successful designs rest solidly on specific precedents."[50] The peculiar shape of the Dahlgren gun stemmed from recent army research in internal ballistics, and it had been a trend since the eighteenth century to design guns with thinner chases and thicker breeches. Another trend since the eighteenth century had been the use of increasingly heavy projectiles. In the mid-eighteenth century Benjamin Robins had published the idea of designing guns with larger bore diameters for a given weight of gunmetal. And although shells had been around for centuries, Paixhans had sparked the worldwide adoption of shell guns. Dahlgren combined all of these familiar yet disparate elements into the new invention known as the Dahlgren gun. But as Ferguson puts it, "The inevitability of the old in the new is no check to originality.... The possible combinations of known elements exceed comprehension, and the combination of elements is subject to endless variation."[51] The Dahlgren gun was Dahlgren's invention, and Dahlgren's alone.

Dahlgren was fortunate to have Warrington as a patron. Although he was a member of the pre-1815 generation, Warrington appreciated the importance of innovation to the navy. Without Warrington's approval Dahlgren would not have been able to procure an experimental 9-incher. Had Dahlgren never overcome the bad start with his chief, the Dahlgren gun might never have been more than an idea floating around inside Dahlgren's head.

6

Early Development
1850–1851

Invention is often conceived as the first step in the process by which things come to be. When, exactly, did Dahlgren invent the Dahlgren gun? Was it on 15 October 1849, when he proposed to fabricate a 9-inch gun to test his hypothesis of round-projectile momentum? Was it on 9 January 1850, when he submitted the first design of a bottle-shaped gun to Warrington? Or was it several years later, when he devised the casting method and quality-control procedures that distinguished his gun from other types of ordnance? As this exercise shows, it is difficult to date precisely the invention of the Dahlgren gun. It is also futile, for the gun's structural and conceptual components did not appear wholly conceived in Dahlgren's mind with a flash of insight and a shout of "Eureka!" Ideas for a new gun began to occur to him in the late 1840s, but Dahlgren guns were not mounted on board U.S. naval vessels until 1855.

What happened during the interim? Historians often conceive of technological change in terms of invention, development, and innovation. One model of technological change characterizes invention, development, and innovation as chronological phases that simply follow one another. It defines *invention* as the idea upon which the inventor takes out a patent; *development* as the phase culminating in a workable, full-scale device; and *innovation* as the introduction of the device into commercial markets. In applying these definitions to the case of naval ordnance, *innovation* can be conceived as the introduction of a new weapon into a ship engaged in normal operations. Although the period between invention and innovation is commonly identified as development, it is better to think of invention and development as processes or activities rather than chronological phases.[1] Development entails converting an invention into a usable piece of hardware. During the process of development, hardware is designed, built, and tested, and part or all of it is repeatedly reinvented, retested, and rebuilt until it is capable of functioning in the environment for which it was intended.

Development in the case of the Dahlgren gun also had a political aspect. Before the gun could be mounted on a ship—indeed, even before it could be developed—Dahlgren had to convince the makers of naval policy that it was worth developing and mounting. In other words, he had to sell his gun to the navy, and the navy had to buy or adopt it. To paraphrase historian Donald MacKenzie, Dahlgren had to engineer not only a cannon but also bureaucrats and politicians. He had to overcome their doubts and persuade them to provide the resources necessary to develop the gun.[2] Dahlgren had to be not only a scientific inventor but also a bureaucratic entrepreneur.

Dahlgren's 15 October 1849 proposal to procure an experimental 9-incher to test his round-projectile-ballistics hypothesis marked the beginning of his efforts to sell a new gun to the navy. "I am aware that the principle now evolved if established," he wrote, "would lead to an entire reorganization of the ordnance."[3] He must have figured it would be a tough sell. He believed that in the course of developing the 1845 system of ordnance, he had discredited it. For the next several years he would argue that the navy should retire the 1845 ordnance and adopt his own in its place.

NAVAL POLICYMAKERS

To sell the gun, Dahlgren would have to create a constituency for it among key makers of naval policy. The Constitution divided policymaking between the executive and legislative branches of government. The executive branch conceived and executed naval policy; the legislative branch controlled the purse. Decisions on procurement fell under the domain of internal policy. Internal policy decided what the navy should be: how big the fleet should be and what types of ships and guns it should have or develop. A proposal for a new ship or gun could come from almost anywhere: the secretary of the navy, congressional committee members, bureau chiefs, or junior officers. The proposal was followed by political interplay among the rest of the policymakers, and its fate depended on the persistence of the sponsor and the degree of sympathy, apathy, or hostility it encountered along the way.[4]

The hierarchy of policymakers in the Navy Department ran downward from the president of the United States, the secretary of the navy, the chiefs of the naval bureaus, and the officers assigned to those bureaus. The president as commander in chief of the armed forces usually delegated supreme control of naval affairs to the secretary of the navy, a hand-picked cabinet member. The secretary was responsible for the administration of the Navy Department and for all of its activities. He directed the maintenance of the fleet, superintended its operations, and dealt with Congress. Maintenance was divided among the five bureaus under the supervision of naval officers responsible to the secretary.[5]

Congressional authority stemmed from control of the budget. Congress entrusted its decisions on the navy to the Naval Affairs Committee in each house. Virtually every bill on a distinctly naval topic came before these committees. The fate of the bills depended upon the ability of their sponsors to sell them to Congress.[6]

The principal agent of liaison between the navy and Congress was the secretary of the navy. Congress funded the navy through appropriations based on estimates submitted by the secretary. Toward the end of each year the secretary presented the estimates in a report that reviewed the accomplishments of the Navy Department for that year. Each bureau chief wrote up the section on his own bureau for the report. Their recommendations served as a natural basis for legislation.[7]

NATIONAL IMPULSES

To create a constituency for his gun among makers of naval policy, Dahlgren would have to link it to their interests. Three national impulses of the 1840s and 1850s shaped the argument Dahlgren used to sell his gun: the memory of the War of 1812, an admiration for science, and a movement for naval expansion.

As has been seen, the national memory of the War of 1812 focused on the brilliant American victories in one-on-one duels with British vessels, such as the *Constitution*'s victory over the *Guerriere.* Histories such as Charles B. Boynton's *The Navies of England, France, America, and Russia* reflected the perception that the United States had won the war in part by means of such victories.[8] These victories in turn were attributed to American qualitative superiority in ships and guns.

Mid-nineteenth-century Americans applauded the use of science to advance "the practical arts" and equated science with progress. Along with the builders of steamships, factories, and railroads, the investigators of boiler explosions, and Americans who exhibited gadgets and machinery at London's Crystal Palace, Dahlgren rode the wave on which "scientific inventors" began to replace artisans and craftsmen. This atmosphere heightened the interest that the makers of naval policy took in the lieutenant, whose work and reputation as a scientific officer were already known to the bureau chiefs, secretaries of the navy, and presidents who had come down to the Washington Navy Yard for demonstrations of his ranging method.[9]

Historian Samuel Eliot Morison has noted that America experienced a national euphoria during the 1840s and early 1850s. The tough war with Mexico had been brilliantly won, Texas secured, California and New Mexico annexed, and a lion's share of the Oregon country wrested from Britain. The California gold rush created an upsurge in the economy. Dreams of Pacific Empire began to unfold. Pacific islands, and perhaps all of the Far East, seemed ripe for being brought under the aegis of Western civilization. Territorial acquisitions added hundreds of miles to the American coast and raised the problem of defending two widely separated seaboards fronting on two oceans. This in turn stimulated demands for a trans-isthmian canal and a larger navy to defend it all. The canal agitation and a southern impulse to expand in the Caribbean made that sea a focus of American interests and international rivalry. American activities there produced fresh collisions with the vested interests and entrenched power of the British Empire. These activities and collisions together with a rapid growth of overseas commerce led to the movement for naval expansion.[10]

Naval expansionism manifested itself in Congress in demands for new war steamers. In 1846, congressional navalists began securing and publishing reports from the Navy Department that painted an alarming portrait of the state of the country's defenses upon the sea. The reports contained detailed statistical summaries of the world's navies, lists of the United States Navy's deficiencies, and possible strategies for a war with Great Britain. They pointed out that Britain had 141 war steamers (built or building) mounting a total of 698 guns and that France had 68 steamers with 430 guns. The United States, on the other hand, had only seven steamers mounting a total of thirty-nine guns. The reports led to the authorization of four new war steamers in 1847. For many navalists, however, it was not enough.[11]

Justifying the Dahlgren Gun

In February 1850 David L. Yulee, chairman of the Senate Naval Affairs Committee, wrote Dahlgren a letter asking what type of war steamers the navy should have and how such vessels should be used. Yulee, who must have heard of the lieutenant's work at the yard and might even have attended a demonstration of the ranging method, sought information to bolster the navalist argument in a congressional debate about whether to build more war steamers.

The next month Dahlgren replied with a paper that addressed five major topics.[12] The first was what type of ships the navy should have. The lieutenant described three different classes of steam warships: first-class vessels, which maximized steam power at the expense of the battery to achieve the greatest speed, such as the USS *Powhatan,* a paddle-wheeler authorized in 1847, and HMS *Terrible;* second-class vessels, which carried an auxiliary steam engine, a full rig for sailing, and the heaviest possible battery, such as the British frigates *Termagant* and *Arrogant;* and small, fast, third-class steamers, which carried a few of the longest-range guns. In each class the battery, engine, and sailing rig competed for the ship's carrying capacity and space. Dahlgren believed that motive power should be subordinate to ordnance power, which he considered the most important aspect of a naval vessel. He said that new second-class steamers should have screw propellers instead of paddle wheels, which interfered with placement of ordnance. He considered the second-class vessel, which anticipated the *Merrimack* class of steam frigates in its crucial respects, as the ideal ship for the United States Navy.

Dahlgren's second topic involved doctrine. Second-class warships would operate alone, or in tandem with a third-class vessel. If alone, a second-class warship would be able to hold faster enemy vessels at bay, assuming it carried superior ordnance. If in tandem, the third-class vessel would harass and cripple an enemy ship with its long-range guns, then the second-class vessel would move in for the kill. This doctrine rested on the assumption that American warships would meet enemy vessels in situations analogous to the single-ship encounters of the War of 1812. Dahlgren did not explain how a string of single-ship victories would produce victory in war, nor did he speculate on what would happen if single American warships met an enemy squadron or fleet.

Dahlgren did not think exclusively in terms of lone ships in those days, however. In a paper written less than two years later he set forth an idea about how the navy could use a fleet of two hundred steamers against Britain: "It would no longer be an object to defend our own ports, but to capture and destroy the enemy's ships in distant seas, while protecting his colonies and trade—to intercept his commerce everywhere—to dispute the command of the high seas with his mightiest fleets, and blockade every naval station of his island empire."[13] These words foreshadowed those written by American naval prophet Alfred Thayer Mahan nearly forty years later, but Dahlgren did not pursue the ideas they embodied, because he knew that Congress would not buy such a large fleet in the early 1850s.

The third topic in Dahlgren's paper for Yulee was naval strategy and policy. In war, second-class vessels would defend the larger northern harbors. Third-class steamers would be stationed in southern coastal waters where they "would readily command the narrow passage between Cuba and Florida, through which so valuable a portion of the Southern and Western produce passes to market." Their object would be to prevent enemy warships from attacking American merchant shipping. This strategy recognized the importance of the Caribbean to American maritime commerce, and the importance of maritime commerce to the American economy. Dahlgren emphasized the necessity of defending the coast, protecting commerce, and keeping open sea lines of communication.

Fourth, Dahlgren addressed naval-industrial relations. He asserted that building engines of 800 to 1,000 horsepower for first-class steamers required the investment of more capital than most American industrial firms had at their disposal. Therefore, only a few of the largest firms could offer bids for such engines. But the construction of smaller steam engines for second- and third-class warships "would bring into the field a large share of the mechanical industry and skill of the whole country, and as a consequence bring the cost and quality of work and time of execution to the true standard. Besides the indirect benefit resulting from the development of resources on which reliance might be placed at any time." The construction of second- and third-class warships, Dahlgren reasoned, would best utilize the existing civilian industrial base, and at the same time develop its potential for the future.

Finally, Dahlgren discussed ordnance. Armed according to the regulations of 1845, the *Congress* carried 203,000 pounds of 32-pounders on her gun deck and 105,000 pounds of 32-pounders and 8-inch shell guns on her spar deck. Dahlgren proposed replacing this battery with 202,000 pounds of 9-inchers on the gun deck and 94,000 pounds of 11-inch guns on the spar deck. The new battery would consist of twenty-eight guns instead of fifty and would weigh 5.5 tons less, but it would be more powerful because the 9- and 11-inchers would be qualitatively superior to the 32-pounders and 8-inchers.

This last argument rested on a foundation of sheer speculation. The guns Dahlgren recommended did not yet exist. The experimental 9-incher had not yet been cast. The 11-inch gun appeared out of the blue. It was the first time Dahlgren had ever mentioned such a caliber. Why he mentioned it is unclear.

Nevertheless, the paper fit new technology—steam power and ordnance—into the traditional American conception of naval power. The argument about second-class vessels reflected the American naval tradition of qualitative superiority. The argument about doctrine envisioned future naval combat in terms of the single-ship duel, a means of combat that the United States Navy had used to such good effect in the late eighteenth and early nineteenth centuries. The argument about strategy mirrored the long-standing policy that the navy should be used for defense. Dahlgren had written a prescription to win a midcentury version of the War of 1812. He had provided congressional navalists with a vision of what new war steamers should be and how they should be used. And he had justified his own ordnance. By integrating it into a traditional framework, he made it appear less radical. By identifying it with currents of naval expansion in Congress, he made it appealing to those with the power of the purse.

His conception of the ideal warship differed from the traditional American superfrigate in one crucial respect. Although the superfrigate was faster than European frigates, Dahlgren did not expect his ideal ship to outrun enemy vessels. He sacrificed superior speed to gain a decisive superiority in ordnance. "*Speed*," he later wrote, "is an essential requisite for a...ship of war, *but essential only to go into action, not out of it!*"[14] His entire system of ship design, propulsion, and doctrine sought to maximize the potential of the gun—his gun. His ideal ship could outgun anything afloat.

The paper was a milestone. It marked the first appearance in print of the idea that Dahlgren guns should supplant the 1845 ordnance. Dahlgren originally conceived the 9-inch gun as an instrument to test his hypothesis of projectile ballistics, but it was now becoming more than that. He began to see the 9-incher not only as a means to experiment in external ballistics but also as a way to enhance his own reputation. The development and adoption of the 9-incher would become an end in itself, not a means to an end. Similarly, the Ordnance Establishment, which Dahlgren originally instituted as a means to expedite his assignments, would also become a way to persuade the navy to adopt the Dahlgren gun. The lieutenant began to equate his own future and reputation with that of his gun. This paper was the opening move in a protracted struggle.

Selling the Gun

Dahlgren's argument was based on reason, not facts. Testing would provide the hard evidence necessary to convince policymakers that the navy should have his gun. When the 9-incher arrived at the Washington Navy Yard that May, he set it up at the experimental battery. During the summer he fired 120 rounds from the gun at various elevations and with different charges, using the plane-table method to document the results. At the same time, he continued to range the 1845 ordnance.[15]

Soon after firing the first few rounds from his gun, Dahlgren began expounding its virtues to naval officers and policymakers. He figured that the best way to ensure its adoption was to link it to proposals for naval construction and expansion. The gun stood a better chance if it could sail through Congress on the deck of a ship. On 31 July he wrote to Commodore Charles W. Skinner, chief of the Bureau of Construction, Equipment, and Repair. Skinner was considering a plan to "razee" the sailing ship of the line *Franklin*—to convert her into a heavy frigate by removing her upper deck and guns. The *Franklin* was also slated to receive a steam engine for auxiliary power. The modifications would transform the old liner into a second-class warship of the type Dahlgren envisioned as ideal for the navy. He sent Skinner a sketch of the 9-incher, claiming that it was more powerful than either 32-pounders or 8-inchers and proposing to arm the *Franklin* with his own guns. Skinner was impressed and incorporated Dahlgren's ideas into his section of the secretary of the navy's report for 1850.[16]

Dahlgren's sales campaign soon spilled over into an effort to get a raise. That fall the secretary of war granted Mordecai an increase in pay to $4,000 per year because of his "literary & scientific" work. Dahlgren, who had been using the army's Ordnance Department and arsenals as models for the navy's Ordnance Establishment, believed that he too deserved a raise, and with Warrington's help he persuaded the secretary of the navy to put the matter before Congress. In his report to Congress for 1850 the secretary recommended raising Dahlgren's pay to the equivalent of commander at sea, a jump from $1,500 to $3,500 per year. The report now included a ship, a gun, and a raise connected to Dahlgren's name. His campaign for his gun had also become one of self-promotion.[17]

Dahlgren sought to ensure that Congress would approve the secretary's recommendations. In January 1851 he fired off a barrage of letters to congressmen, arguing that he deserved equal pay for equal work. The United States Army had arsenals, a "scientific corps," and a trained "ordnance corps," and it breveted officers for ordnance work. Dahlgren implied that he, as a scientific naval officer and creator of the naval Ordnance Establishment, deserved the same sort of recognition. Moreover, he argued, in Europe "money is poured out like water, and fleets of Steamers dot every shore with black clouds of smoke, while new and heavy ordnance are produced and the invention of their officers [is] taxed to bring forth any improvement in Ordnance equipment—who are amply rewarded for success in any one detail." Again, Dahlgren implied that he merited the same sort of recognition. Congress would decide the issue of his pay in March 1851, when it voted on the appropriations bill for the next fiscal year.[18]

Meanwhile, Dahlgren prepared a report on the experiments with the 9-inch shell gun and submitted it to Warrington on 30 January. He argued that the experiments with the 9-incher had verified his hypothesis of round-projectile ballistics: "The results have been highly satisfactory, and I think will fully confirm the idea presented to the Bureau in Sept. [*sic*] 1849. Namely:— That in projecting shot there is a velocity which cannot be exceeded without injuriously affecting the accuracy, so far as the purposes of Sea Ordnance are concerned." The most effective ordnance, he suggested, would be the heaviest manageable guns that fired the heaviest manageable shells with charges low enough so as not to exceed the optimum velocity.[19]

He again argued that the ideal ship would be a second-class frigate equipped with a full rig for sailing, an auxiliary steam engine driving a screw, and a battery of his own design. Such a vessel would be economical on long cruises in distant seas and would have maximum defensive power. The battery he proposed for this vessel was similar to the one he had proposed for the *Congress*. The gun deck should have twenty-eight 9-inchers mounted on broadside carriages, fourteen per side. The spar deck (the upper deck) should have long-range guns mounted on pivot carriages so that they could be trained on either side. Dahlgren proposed developing an 11-inch shell gun for the pivot carriages and mounting seven of them on the spar deck. He compared such a vessel with a typical American eighty-four-gun liner armed according to the regulations of 1845. Dahlgren's frigate fired 500 pounds more metal in a broadside.[20]

Congressman Frederick P. Stanton liked Dahlgren's frigate. Stanton was a Democrat and an advocate of naval expansion, steam propulsion, and science. He entered the House in 1845 as a representative from Memphis, Tennessee. Assigned to the Committee on Naval Affairs, he became its chairman in December 1849. Dahlgren, as a scientific officer and a proponent of steam, had a double-barreled appeal for the congressman. It seems that the two met during a test of the 9-inch gun. The lieutenant allowed Stanton and Congressman Hugh White to aim three of the rounds fired that day. It was a brilliant ploy. Stanton became one of Dahlgren's most ardent supporters.[21]

In February and March 1851, during the debates on the appropriations bill, Stanton put Dahlgren's views before the House. "Take shells of eleven inches in diameter, which will inevitably be used hereafter in naval battles," he said, "and plant one of them in the side of a ship, and she is gone inevitably." He proposed to amend the bill to include an appropriation for a war steamer of the kind Dahlgren had described in the report on the 9-incher. The ship would, of course, mount Dahlgren guns.[22]

The pending bill included the secretary's recommendation to raise Dahlgren's pay. In the House, opponents of the raise argued that Dahlgren's duties were not arduous and that his pay of $1,500 per year was sufficient. Dahlgren's advocates pointed out that both the secretary of the navy and the secretary of war had recommended the raise. Thomas Bayly, one of the congressmen Dahlgren had written to in January, said that he was "a very meritorious officer" who could have patented his improvements but had chosen not to. Stanton said that Dahlgren deserved the raise because his ordnance work had revolutionized the navy. Robert Toombs, another congressman Dahlgren had written to in January, said that he deserved the raise because his work demanded "high scientific acquirements." The House voted to give him the raise. Debate in the Senate ran along similar lines. John P. Hale, who would become chairman of the Senate Naval Affairs Committee in 1861, argued that such an extravagant raise would be favoritism. David Yulee, to whom Dahlgren had sent his paper on ships, doctrine, strategy and policy, naval-industrial relations, and ordnance, noted that the lieutenant deserved a raise because he lived in Washington at his own expense. When the issue came to a vote, Dahlgren got the raise. The proposal for the steamer, however, was defeated.[23]

The First 11-Incher

A few days later, Dahlgren submitted to Warrington a design for an 11-inch shell gun. He had arrived at this caliber by assuming arbitrarily that the heaviest loaded shell that could be handled at sea would weigh about 135 pounds. He calculated that the diameter of a 135-pound projectile would be 11 inches. Using a one-tenth scale model, he calculated that an 11-inch shell gun would weigh roughly 16,000 pounds. He designed the 11-incher with a slim chase, much like the original design of the 9-incher, so that if the gun failed because of bad metal, the chase would give way instead of the breech, minimizing the danger to the gun crew. Warrington agreed to have the gun cast.[24]

Cyrus Alger of Boston, with whom Warrington contracted for the 11-incher, asserted that its chase was too slender and thought it unwise to cast the gun. Alger, the proprietor of one of the principal foundries that produced guns for the navy, was known for casting techniques that produced iron of exceptional strength, and his opinion carried great weight. He expressed his doubts to Warrington, who in turn told Dahlgren.[25]

But this time Dahlgren refused to compromise his design. Warrington backed him fully. The lieutenant devised an alternative way to demonstrate the safety of a slim chase. He had an 8-incher turned on a lathe so that its dimensions were proportional to those of the 11-incher. He fired the modified 8-incher 220 times, sometimes with two projectiles per round. The gun showed no signs of failing. Dahlgren reasoned that if an 8-incher with a slim chase could survive, so could an 11-incher. The demonstration convinced Alger, who cast the 11-incher in July.[26]

Adoption Seems Imminent

As 1851 drew to a close, Dahlgren was receiving the recognition he so desperately craved. Fellow steam-generation officers applauded his work on boat guns, heavy ordnance, and tangent sights. On 17 September 1851

President Millard Fillmore visited Boston to see a parade in which industrialists showed off their latest products. Included in the procession was Dahlgren's recently finished 11-inch shell gun, mounted on a carriage drawn by three huge horses. The secretary of the navy's report to Congress for 1851 said, "Improvements and discoveries in ordnance and gunnery have been introduced, by means of which, in the opinion of well informed officers, a ship of inferior rating, say of thirty-two guns, may be so built and rigged, and armed, as to prove more than a match for the stoutest line-of-battle ship of the old construction and armament." Dahlgren must have rejoiced. The navy seemed on the verge of adopting his guns and ideas.[27]

Warrington's death on 12 October 1851 cast a pall on this optimism. Dahlgren remembered calling on him about a month before he died:

> He never looked in better health—his vigorous and massive frame seemed untouched by age,—the keen searching glance still undimmed,—and the thick dark hair, somewhat frosted by advancing years, alone marked the inroad of time. I was never to see him again.... The Commodore was one of those sea-warriors who so gallantly upheld the credit of our flag in 1812—and no less in after years by a long course of honorable and devoted service—he was a man in the fullest sense of the word, honest, sincere to all,—faithful to his friends and fearless in the discharge of duty.[28]

7

Overcoming Entrenched Resistance
1851–1853

Charles Morris, Warrington's successor as chief of the Bureau of Ordnance and Hydrography, was a bona fide naval hero. He had become a midshipman in 1799 and had served in the Quasi War with France and in the Mediterranean against the Barbary pirates. Stephen Decatur selected him to take part in the daring run into Tripoli harbor to burn the frigate *Philadelphia*, which had fallen into enemy hands. On the night of 15 February 1804 Morris leapt onto the deck of the *Philadelphia*, the first of Decatur's party to board her. Decatur followed but did not realize that he had been preceded. Thinking that Morris was a pirate, Decatur raised his cutlass to strike him down. Morris stayed Decatur's hand and whispered the password "Philadelphia." The two then turned to face the enemy. In the War of 1812 Morris engineered the famous escape of the becalmed frigate *Constitution* from a British naval squadron, and he directed the *Constitution*'s gunfire in her victorious duel with the *Guerriere*. He was severely wounded in the battle. Later in the war he captured ten prizes while commanding the sloop *John Adams*.[1]

Following the War of 1812 Morris rose to the top of the naval establishment. He successively commanded the Mediterranean, Gulf, and Brazil Squadrons, thereby earning the honorary title "commodore" for life. As commander of the sloop *Brandywine,* he returned the marquis de Lafayette to France. He served more than a dozen years as a dominant member of the Board of Navy Commissioners. He headed the Bureau of Construction, Equipment, and Repair from 1844 until Warrington's death, when he took charge of the ordnance bureau. Morris was considered the most capable officer in the navy, its intellectual leader, and the most scientifically minded of its senior officers. During a long career near the top of the naval hierarchy, Morris devised and executed much of the naval policy of the day. Both as a fighter and an administrator, he embodied the traditions of the sailing navy.[2]

Dahlgren had met him during the *Cumberland* cruise, when Morris turned over command of the Mediterranean Squadron to Joseph Smith in January 1844. Ben Sands, who had served under Morris in the Mediterranean, recalled that the commodore "did not earn the good will of the squadron he commanded, conceiving himself to be the great reformer and retrencher." But Dahlgren noted of him, "In deportment it would be difficult to conceive of a better model for an officer of rank—dignified without haughtiness—affable and easy without familiarity—intelligent without affectation—he bears well the honors of his present position as well as of his earlier days." Morris was one of the naval heroes Dahlgren had worshipped as a boy. Soon the hero would become an implacable foe.[3]

Morris had a love-hate relationship with Dahlgren's work. As a scientifically minded officer, the commodore appreciated the high standards the lieutenant brought to his duties. But Morris had been a key figure on the board that had instituted the 1845 ordnance system, and he had a vested interest in the very guns Dahlgren intended to eliminate.

In January 1852 Morris ordered Dahlgren not to allow other work to interfere with the completion of the range tables for the 1845 guns, and to submit an interim report on his progress. These were reasonable orders. The tables took a long time to finish because Dahlgren ranged the guns only on calm days. But the orders robbed him of much of the time that Warrington had given him to work on his own guns. Morris also arranged for Dahlgren to be retained indefinitely at the Washington Navy Yard to superintend the manufacture of boat guns, to prepare ordnance equipment, and to range the 1845 ordnance. Dahlgren's assignment was now a virtually permanent post.[4]

Morris not only robbed Dahlgren of time to develop his gun but also tried to entrench the 1845 ordnance in the navy by applying Dahlgren's idea of upgunning a vessel without increasing the overall battery weight. In June he

Charles Morris, circa 1851 (Naval Historical Center)

issued orders to replace two of the *Independence*'s heavy 32-pounders with two 8-inch shell guns. The new armament achieved greater destructive power per pound of gun than the old but remained within the 1845 ordnance system. Morris subsequently upgunned other vessels in a similar fashion.[5]

Despite Morris's resistance, Dahlgren did not lose hope of getting his gun adopted by linking it to proposals for naval construction. Stanton intended to include funds for a new vessel in the current appropriations bill. In August he asked Dahlgren to reiterate his views on the "most modern and improved model for ships." Stanton wanted not only to pass legislation for new construction but also to test "what is believed to be the most powerful and efficient armament." It was virtually the same proposal that had been defeated the previous year.[6]

Dahlgren replied with his lengthiest unpublished piece of writing to date, a forty-nine-page paper entitled "Reorganization of the U.S. Naval Ordnance." Although Stanton was primarily interested in ships, Dahlgren emphasized guns, stressing that experimental evidence proved the 9-incher to be more accurate and powerful than the 1845 guns. The 32-pounder of 57 cwt., which had too high a muzzle velocity, was, according to Dahlgren's hypothesis of round-projectile ballistics, "constructed in entire violation of the law which controls the accuracy of military projectiles."

Dahlgren reiterated the position that the ideal ship for the navy would be about 240 feet long and not less than 2,000 tons burden; it would carry "an armament of the greatest power," have "a sailing speed equal to the highest yet attained," and carry auxiliary steam power capable of moving the vessel at 10 knots. Protocol dictated that the paper pass through the hands of the commodore and the secretary of the navy on its way to Stanton.

Morris, who rightly regarded the paper as a threat to the 1845 ordnance, forwarded it to Stanton along with a critique. He agreed that the navy needed fast new sailing ships equipped with auxiliary steam engines and pointed out that the ordnance board of 1845 had recommended such vessels. He noted that while the efficiency of the 9-incher had been "sufficiently established," its endurance had not yet been tested. The 11-incher had not yet been tested at all, except for proof. "The extensive use of very large guns in our ships," he concluded, "cannot be recommended before their strength and endurance has been more thoroughly tested." This sounded reasonable, but Morris gave Dahlgren less time to test his guns than Warrington had. Nevertheless, Stanton now had two opposing points of view to consider.[7]

On 17 August, in a speech to Congress, Stanton proposed building new war steamers and arming them with Dahlgren guns:

> I think I can say with entire truth that the practicability of using these guns at sea, and their immense superiority over the armaments now in use, may be considered settled questions—settled by experiment, as well as sustained by theory.... It would be a great oversight not to apply the new and fertile principles evolved by the genius of a young American officer, to the defense of our country.... I believe it will present to the world a ship which will have the effect not only of remodeling the whole of our own navy, but which will render necessary the alteration or rebuilding of every other Navy which expects to occupy a respectable position upon the ocean, and to cope with the enginery supplied to ships of war by modern science.

Stanton quoted extensively from Dahlgren's paper and completely ignored Morris's critique. The speech married Dahlgren's guns to the very idea of any new construction.[8]

But the proposal did not pass. Dahlgren later recalled that "the opposition…was too strong—and one of our oldest officers boasted to me of the influence he had used to defeat the measure." It is likely that the officer was Morris.[9]

Regardless of whether Morris used connections in Congress to defeat the proposal, the commodore certainly took other steps to undermine the Dahlgren gun and entrench the 1845 ordnance. Several days after the vote, Morris ordered his friend Commander David G. Farragut to conduct experiments at Old Point Comfort near Fort Monroe. Then an assistant inspector of ordnance, Farragut had worked with Dahlgren's boat guns and had also helped prepare an ordnance manual. The commodore ordered him to test each class of gun in service, including the only 9-inch Dahlgren gun then in existence. The stated purpose was to test the endurance of the various classes. Farragut was to fire round after round from each gun until it failed. With the only extant 9-incher thus doomed, Dahlgren could not continue his own experiments with it. Farragut would spend nearly a year conducting these tests. Morris emphasized Farragut's experiments in the ordnance bureau section of the secretary of the navy's report to Congress for 1852 but barely mentioned Dahlgren's work.[10]

Dahlgren recaptured official attention in the spring of 1853 with the publication of *Naval Percussion Locks and Primers, Particularly Those of the United States*. The book had been in preparation for more than a year. Commodore Smith had read the manuscript and thought it "perfect." Morris also read it and thought it publishable. The secretary of the navy ordered five hundred copies for the navy.[11]

Dahlgren's 125-page *Locks and Primers* described the evolution of the percussion lock, the different types of locks in service in the American, British, and French navies, and how they all worked. Dahlgren preferred to mount locks on cannon by means of lock lugs cast onto the barrel, as in his own ordnance, rather than by attaching a complicated and expensive lock piece. The Hidden lock, which had a hollow hammerhead to allow the gases escaping from the vent to pass through, was his favorite. The book was a thorough and competent piece of writing.[12]

Locks and Primers was not Dahlgren's first published book. That distinction fell to *The System of Boat Armament in the United States Navy*, first published in 1852. This 217-page book (1856 revised edition), divided into thirteen topical chapters, described Dahlgren's boat guns and gave instructions for their use. Dahlgren included the story of how the boat guns came to be, a brief description of the Ordnance Establishment, and a historical sketch of light artillery dating back to the seventeenth century. It was a very informative work that went through several editions.[13]

Dahlgren made sure that people noticed his books. He gave copies to the Library of Congress and to naval officers. The books were well received. One officer, thanking Dahlgren for a copy of *Locks and Primers*, wrote, "Your professional friends have much reason to rejoice in the progress you are making, & causing the whole service to make, in that important branch of our business." Distribution of books was a brilliant tactic in Dahlgren's campaign of self-promotion.[14]

Stanton's ongoing campaign in Congress for war steamers also kept Dahlgren in the official eye. On 23 February 1853 Stanton introduced a bill in the House to build three screw frigates and three sloops, arguing that the United States should keep abreast of the latest developments. The United States must not only be prepared for war with a European power, he argued, but also be wary of war among European powers. He reminded Congress of the events of 1800–1812, when the Europeans had trampled upon American commerce. The recent acquisitions of Texas, California, and Oregon would increase American commerce, both between coasts and in the Pacific. The navy should be expanded so that it would be strong enough to command the Gulf of Mexico and the Caribbean Sea. No resolution was reached on the bill at that time. Secretary of the Navy John P. Kennedy, a lame-duck Whig, had not developed sufficient clout in Congress during his short tenure in office to push the proposal through. For the time being, Dahlgren's plan to bring the gun into the navy on the deck of a new ship was thwarted.[15]

He pressed on nevertheless. In May he submitted to Morris plans for a 9-incher to replace the one sent to Farragut. The second 9-incher had a longer and slimmer chase. Dahlgren reasoned that the performances of the 11-incher and modified 8-incher had demonstrated the safety of a slim chase, enabling him to draw the second 9-incher as he had originally drawn the first. He included a nine-page paper arguing that he be allowed to expand the testing of his own ordnance. He asked the commodore to order two 9-inchers for shipboard tests in addition to the one for the experimental battery. He also asked him to include twenty 9-inchers and six 11-inchers in the estimates for the upcoming year. He asserted that Morris's recent change in shipboard armament "can only be regarded as a more judicious arrangement of existing forces, and by no means remedies the inherent inferiority of our present batteries; because that inferiority arises from a defect in principle."[16]

The commodore agreed to procure one 9-incher, contracting with the West Point Foundry for it. Robert P. Parrott, the superintendent, thought that the gun would be difficult to cast because of its peculiar shape. Parrott had attended the United States Military Academy and had served as an ordnance officer in the army. He had resigned his commission in 1836 to become superintendent of the foundry and was now a renowned ordnance expert. Dahlgren persuaded him to proceed with the gun as designed, and it was cast that summer.[17]

Dahlgren followed up the nine-page paper with an even longer work entitled "Reorganization of the U.S. Naval Ordnance No. 2."[18] The thrust of "Reorganization 2," which incorporated the results of recent experiments with the 11-incher, was that 11-inchers should replace 32-pounders and 8-inchers on the spar decks of frigates. Dahlgren argued that a battery of six 11-inchers mounted on pivot carriages would weigh 11,000 pounds less than the battery of twenty broadside-mounted 32-pounders and 8-inchers specified by the regulations of 1845, yet would fire 160 pounds more metal in a broadside. He claimed that the 11-inch battery would be more accurate and would attain a comparable rate of fire. Moreover, an 11-inch projectile had greater powers of penetration and explosion than 32-pound shot and 8-inch shells, and would drive more splinters from the side of a ship into the interior. He based these claims on theoretical calculations as well as on data obtained in experiments. To illustrate his point, he used the familiar image of a ship armed his way winning a duel with a ship armed the old way.

Part of Dahlgren's argument rested on the assumption that ships would engage each other at greater distances in the future than they had in the past. Early in the nineteenth century, ships fought within the 300- to 600-yard effective range of their guns. Dahlgren cited the battle of Vera Cruz in 1838 as a precedent for longer ranges. A French fleet had engaged a Mexican fort at a distance of 1,300 yards. At that range the lighter Mexican shot had little effect on the French vessels, whose heavier shells overcame the fort. A heavier projectile, Dahlgren explained, has greater range than a lighter one because its greater weight enables it to overcome air resistance better and therefore maintain more of its velocity over a longer distance. Thus, "with heavy shells it is not necessary to close in order to act with power." Dahlgren was trying to reshape the parameters of doctrine to fit the new guns.

Morris forwarded "Reorganization 2" to the secretary of the navy along with a detailed criticism raising objections to mounting spar-deck guns on pivot carriages instead of on traditional broadside carriages. He reasoned that pivot carriages would deprive a ship of space to store large boats, interfere with the hatches that provided access to the lower decks, and get in the way of crewmen trying to work the sails. Moreover, he felt that a 16,000-pound 11-inch gun was too heavy for shipboard use.[19]

Morris preferred a battery mounting a larger number of lighter guns. He reasoned that the more guns, the better the chance of hitting the target. He argued, "The advantages which have been sometimes claimed for heavier and for lighter calibres by their respective advocates, in consequence of the different effect produced in actions between ships, seem to have been more properly due to the skill and accuracy with which they were used than to their relative calibres and weights." The victories of American 24-pounder frigates over British 18-pounder frigates during the War of 1812 were attributable to superior gunnery, not superior guns. Morris pointed out that possession of heavier guns had not enabled the French to defeat the Royal Navy between 1793 and 1815.

Morris also questioned the assumption about the range at which future battles would take place. He pointed out that Dahlgren had conducted his experiments on dry land. A rolling ship was a far less stable gun platform and therefore would have to engage targets at shorter ranges than Dahlgren had envisioned. At close range, two 32-pounder shot could inflict greater damage than one 9-inch shell because they could disable two enemy gun crews instead of just one. The commodore asserted that the French admiral had chosen a range of 1,300 yards at Vera Cruz because shoals prevented him from moving closer. He concluded, "Enough may have been advanced, and supported by experiments on shore and by inferences from them, to justify experiments on a moderate scale, in sea going vessels, as the only proper tests of practical purposes; but there is not yet sufficient evidence presented to justify any extensive and still less any general change, in the character of the armaments of our ships of war."

Meanwhile, Farragut was finishing the endurance experiments at Old Point Comfort and submitted a report to Morris in August. If the commodore had hoped that Farragut would turn up conclusive evidence to discredit the Dahlgren gun, he was disappointed. The 9-incher withstood nearly a thousand rounds, a remarkable performance in a day when naval cannon were not expected to last much beyond five hundred. This outstanding performance represented a victory for Dahlgren's adoption campaign.[20]

The next victory proved decisive. With the inauguration of Franklin Pierce had come a new secretary of the navy, James C. Dobbin. Shortly after

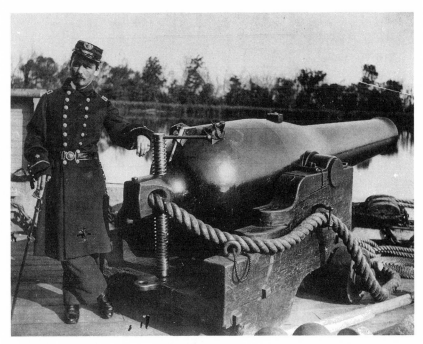

Nine-inch Dahlgren gun on Marsilly carriage. Note the gun sight, elevating screw, and percussion lock and lanyard on the right lock lug. After January 1856, Dahlgren guns were cast with two lock lugs for two vents. Only one vent was open at a time. After five hundred firings the original vent was sealed with zinc and the second vent bored. Before firing, the gunner inserted a percussion primer into the vent. To fire, he pulled the lanyard, causing the hammer to strike the percussion primer, which in turn ignited the charge. The photo was taken on the gunboat *Hunchback* on the James River, circa 1864. The identity of the person is unknown. (National Archives)

taking office, Dobbin had appointed Morris, Joseph Smith, naval constructor John Lenthall, and two other naval officers to confer "upon the character proper for a vessel, and for her armament, which would be desirable as a substitute for the U.S. Ship 'Franklin.'" The real function of this board, known as the *Franklin* board, was to begin designing the war steamers Congress had been debating since 1850.[21]

The Navy Department now considered some sort of new construction as imminent. The election of 1852 had put a Democrat in the White House and increased the Democratic majorities in both houses of Congress. Pierce was determined to restore internal unity by a prudently aggressive assertion of American claims and interests abroad. Naval expansion dovetailed nicely with this program.[22]

The *Franklin* board decided that the "substitute" should be a sailing frigate with an auxiliary steam engine driving a screw propeller. It was Dahlgren's ideal ship, the type suggested by the ordnance board in 1845 and the type under consideration in Congress since 1850. The board chose twenty-eight 9-inch Dahlgren guns for her gun deck, and for her spar deck, twenty 8-inchers mounted on broadside carriages, with one pivot gun aft and one or two pivot guns forward, the caliber as yet undetermined. In essence the navy had adopted the 9-inch gun for new vessels. Morris did not attempt to block this decision, because he could not deny the superiority of the 9-incher.[23]

The secretary of the navy's report for 1853 capped the victory. Although Morris failed to mention Dahlgren in the ordnance section, Secretary Dobbin praised him: "The indefatigable efforts of Lieutenant Dahlgren to give accuracy and greater effectiveness to gunnery, and to improve the ordnance of the navy, have succeeded well, and none can doubt the advantage the service will experience therefrom." More important, Dobbin recommended that Congress authorize six new war steamers. If Congress did so, the 9-incher and its inventor would receive a great deal of exposure.[24]

8

Arming the Fleet
1853–1854

Dahlgren might have rejoiced over the decision to adopt the 9-incher, but he did not. In fact, he was so upset that the navy had not adopted his plan for pivoting 11-inchers on spar decks that a friend felt the need to console him.[1] Dahlgren was selling not only a gun but also a plan for arming the fleet with his 9- and 11-inch cannon. Getting a new gun on ships was one thing, but persuading the navy to arm the fleet exclusively with new guns was another thing entirely. In the ordnance bailiwick, Dahlgren's political connections and growing reputation as the nation's leading naval ordnance expert carried a great deal of weight. But in the realm of the fleet, the question of how to arm ships also involved the shipbuilders, who had their own political connections, vested interests, claims to expertise, and traditions.

The *Franklin* board's decision meant that the navy had only adopted Dahlgren's gun-deck armament; the jury was still out on the spar deck, particularly the 11-inch gun. In struggling for the adoption of his armament plan, Dahlgren would test the limits of bureaucratic entrepreneurship.

Unsatisfied with only a partial victory, Dahlgren wrote a third paper on rearming ships. Unimaginatively entitled "Reorganization of the U.S. Naval Ordnance No. 3," it aimed at convincing Secretary of the Navy Dobbin that the *Franklin* board had erred grievously in adopting 8-inch carriage guns instead of 11-inch pivot guns for the spar decks of new ships.[2] Dahlgren was determined that the navy should adopt his ship armament plan in its entirety: 9-inchers on the gun deck and 11-inchers pivoted on the spar deck. He strenuously objected to the fact that Morris had "summarily dispose[d]" of the 11-incher "without trial."

The paper was based on an experiment comparing the accuracies of a 32-pounder of 57 cwt., an 8-incher of 63 cwt., a 64-pounder, a 9-incher, and an 11-incher at a range of 1,300 yards. Dahlgren fired ten rounds from each gun at muslin screens measuring 40 feet wide by 20 feet high. Although he would have preferred to have fired more rounds, he believed that the results were reliable. He concluded that the 9- and 11-inchers and the 64-pounder were more accurate at 1,300 yards than the 8-incher and 32-pounder. However, the power of the 64-pounder was "very disproportionate to the weight." The 32-pounder, he asserted, "should be entirely dispensed with."

Dahlgren noted that the power of French and British batteries depended on the number rather than on the caliber of guns. He used the familiar hypothetical single-ship duel to argue that on a U.S. ship rearmed as he envisioned, the reverse would be true: the power of a battery would depend on caliber rather than number. He envisioned a battle between the new British 101-gun screw steamer *Saint Jean d'Acre* and the refurbished *Franklin,* assuming their speeds under steam to be equal. If the *Franklin* kept out of range of the *Acre*'s shorter-range gun-deck battery, victory would depend on the accuracy of the *Franklin*'s long-range guns. Again, Dahlgren was trying to reshape accepted doctrine to fit the new gun. His argument foreshadowed the one used to sell the all-big-gun dreadnought of a later generation. Dahlgren asserted that the U.S. ship could win with 11-inchers on her spar deck, but she would lose if armed as specified by the *Franklin* board, because American 8-inchers were inferior in range to the heaviest British guns.[3]

Morris forwarded a copy of "Reorganization 3" to Secretary Dobbin and sent him a critique of it several days later. The commodore argued that the number of guns in a ship's battery was more important than their caliber because naval combat would necessarily occur at closer distances than Dahlgren had envisioned. Morris was arguing within the parameters of accepted doctrine. He noted that comparative accuracy tests conducted ashore did not reflect the reality of combat at sea, where the margin for error was much greater. "The chances of hitting an enemy," he reasoned, "will be

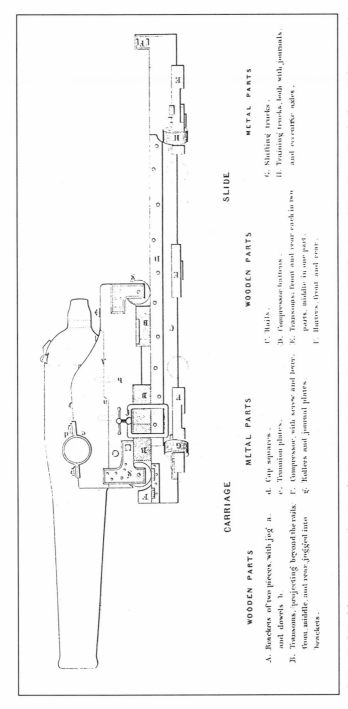

Eleven-inch Dahlgren gun on pivot carriage. (From U.S. Navy Department, Bureau of Ordnance, *Ordnance Instructions for the United States Navy*)

more in proportion to the number of projectiles fired from the different guns than his battery practice shews." Morris doubted that the United States could build a fleet "in which each and every vessel should have equal speed with the best of all other nations." Therefore, an American commander might not have the luxury of choosing the range at which combat would occur. An enemy of superior speed would close with the American ship in order to bring his entire battery within effective range. Morris admitted that an 11-inch shell was more powerful than an 8-inch shell, but because a spar-deck battery of 8-inch guns contained a greater number of pieces than a battery of 11-inchers, the 8-inch battery would throw more shells and hit the target more often in a given period of time. "This absolute power united to greater number of hits," he argued, "may be fairly urged as an advantage for the armament proposed by the [*Franklin*] board."[4]

Dahlgren responded to Morris's critique of "Reorganization 3" with "Reorganization of U.S. Naval Armament No. 4," an impassioned plea for the 11-incher arguing that accuracy of gunfire was more important than volume. Dahlgren asserted that the careful training of gun crews would enable them to fire accurately at longer ranges. He believed that accurate fire from the spar-deck battery he was proposing would offset the advantage of the more rapid fire of an enemy battery that mounted a larger number of lighter guns. He argued that the regulations of 1845 placed the spar-deck guns in broadside mounts, where the gunports prevented them from being elevated to achieve maximum range.[5]

"Reorganization 4" revealed the extent of Dahlgren's frustration with Morris's resistance to the 11-incher. He asserted that the system of armament adopted in 1845 was underpowered and that it underutilized shells. He suggested arming a ship his way and comparing its performance against an old hulk with that of a ship armed with 1845 ordnance. This was tantamount to challenging the old system to a duel. If the navy insisted on a broadside spar-deck battery in new ships, 9-inchers should be used instead of 8-inchers. Not only would this be a more powerful battery; it would also be logistically simpler, for the ship would carry one caliber instead of two.

As before, Morris sent a critique of the paper to the secretary. The commodore was willing to consider mounting 9-inchers in place of 8-inchers on the spar deck, but he adhered to the position that a battery mounting a larger number of lighter guns was better than one mounting fewer, heavier guns. He believed that volume of fire was more important than accuracy. The wily commodore then raised the specter of the Peacemaker:

The superior accuracy of very large and heavy projectiles, beyond certain distances, is also well established. This and its power was particularly shown by the shore practice in 1842, with the wrought iron 12 inch gun proposed by Capt. Stockton. It induced that officer to state officially, "I have now the most perfect and formidable gun ever made, and it is ready for proof;" and shortly after to express the "opinion that there ought to be but one calibre in the Navy; and two kinds of gun, the heavy gun and the Carronade, all of 12 inches and made of wrought iron."

But neither these shore experiments nor those of Lt. Dahlgren can be safely admitted as conclusive for general sea service, without some confirmation by experience founded on the results of varied practice at sea.[6]

On 6 April 1854 Congress authorized the six war steamers that Secretary Dobbin had recommended the previous December. The bill embodying the proposal had passed the Senate without debate but had provoked a spirited discussion in the House. Its chief sponsor, Thomas S. Bocock, who had replaced Stanton as chairman of the House Naval Affairs Committee, argued that naval expansion was necessary to keep pace with recent American territorial and commercial expansion. Moreover, American ships were rapidly becoming obsolete. Pointing to the Crimean War, Bocock said that the United States needed a stronger, more modern navy to forestall aggression by belligerents against neutral American commerce. Furthermore, an impressive display of power would facilitate further expansion of American commercial interests in the Far East and acquisition of the island of Cuba. House Democrats voted three to one in favor of the bill; House Whigs voted two to one in its favor. The *Merrimack* class was born. Five of the new vessels would be steam frigates; the sixth, the *Niagara*, would be built as a sloop.[7]

On the day the Senate passed the bill, Dahlgren went to Dobbin's office to ask permission to arm one of the ships his way. He subsequently raised the issue throughout the spring and early summer whenever he chanced upon the secretary outside his office. He even went to Dobbin's house one evening to stump for his armament plan. By early July, construction of the five frigates had begun. The lieutenant called on the secretary once more to ask for one of the ships. Dobbin told him to arrange a meeting with John Lenthall, chief of the Bureau of Construction, Equipment, and Repair, to discuss the matter.[8]

Lenthall was a distinguished naval architect. Born in 1807, he learned the trade of ship carpenter at the Washington Navy Yard and around 1827 became an assistant and draftsman at the Philadelphia Navy Yard for Samuel Humphreys, Joshua Humphreys's son. Lenthall rose to the position of assistant naval constructor in the Philadelphia Navy Yard in 1838, chief naval constructor there in 1849, and chief of the Bureau of Construction, Equipment, and Repair in 1853. Although Lenthall fully embraced the American naval tradition of big, fast-sailing ships, he did more than perhaps any other American shipbuilder of his generation to introduce steam into the United States Navy. He was in charge of designing and building the five new frigates.[9]

Dahlgren met him on 8 July. They discussed both the *Franklin* board's plan of armament and Dahlgren's. Lenthall, visibly uncomfortable in the presence of the intense lieutenant, was not about to mount six 11-inch pivot guns on one of his spar decks. He preferred the traditional broadside arrangement for the spar-deck guns. He also raised objections to Morris's plan of mounting a pivot gun on the after end of the spar deck, because it would interfere with a mechanism that hoisted the propeller to facilitate sailing. This astonished Dahlgren, who wondered how the stern would be defended.[10]

Three days later, Dahlgren and Lenthall met with Dobbin in the secretary's office and spent an hour discussing pivot guns. Dobbin remained undecided about what caliber of pivot gun to mount on Lenthall's ships, as well as whether to allow Dahlgren to arm one his way.[11]

Commodore Morris, who objected to the 11-incher as a pivot gun because of its great weight, ordered Dahlgren to design a 10-incher as a substitute. Dahlgren rankled at having to compromise. The 10-incher would weigh roughly 12,000 pounds, the same as the navy's 64-pounder pivot gun (a solid-shot-firing weapon with an 8-inch bore) and nearly 2 tons less than the 11-incher. The 10-inch shell weighed only about 100 pounds, a big difference from the 135-pound 11-inch shell, the size Dahlgren had chosen specifically to test his ideas on heavy ordnance.[12]

Nevertheless, clinging tenaciously to his desire to develop an 11-inch pivot gun for shipboard use, Dahlgren tried again to persuade Dobbin to arm the *Niagara,* which George Steers was to build, with 11-inchers. Steers built fast ships. He had designed the famous racing yacht *America* and the ships of the Collins Line, the favorite of transatlantic travelers, and had kept up with the latest developments in steam propulsion.[13]

On 29 July, Dobbin summoned Dahlgren to his office to meet Steers. Dobbin introduced the ordnance expert to the shipbuilder, then the three bent over Steers's plan for the *Niagara.* Dahlgren, who expected to see another frigate, was surprised to see a sloop. The *Niagara* had no gun-deck battery; only the spar deck would have cannon. Steers was far more interested in speed than in armament and had eliminated the gun-deck battery to save weight. After studying the plans, Dahlgren took Steers to the yard to show him guns. Steers listened to Dahlgren's pitch and agreed that the *Niagara* should be armed with 11-inch shell guns pivoted on her spar deck.

Although Steers had agreed to the 11-incher, Dahlgren was disappointed that none of the new ships would be armed according to his plan. "So after all that is the result," he lamented in his diary. "The Bureau takes my plan for the Gun deck—and Steers takes the spar deck.... The Sec. is evidently reluctant to interfere with the Bureaus [Lenthall and Morris], and so saddles me on Steers—whose ship *can* only take one half of my plan."[14]

Nevertheless, Dahlgren did not give up. He dogged Dobbin and Lenthall, trying to persuade them to arm one of the frigates his way. He even tried to persuade Dobbin to direct Steers to mount a gun-deck battery of 9-inchers on the *Niagara.*[15]

In mid-September, Dobbin made the final decision on the armament of the new vessels. Each frigate would receive 9-inchers on its gun deck and broadside 8-inchers and two 10-inch pivot guns on its spar deck. Dobbin had sided with the older bureau chiefs rather than with the younger lieutenant after all. Dahlgren lamented that Lenthall and Morris "had borne him down by their own narrow views." The only consolation was that Dobbin had decided to arm the *Niagara* with 11-inch guns on an experimental basis. Thus, Dahlgren's guns were adopted, but not his armament plan.[16]

Dahlgren's success in selling his guns to the navy demonstrated the power of his bureaucratic entrepreneurship.

Dahlgren owed a great debt to Warrington. This old commodore had given the young lieutenant the leeway to innovate, helped him create the Ordnance Establishment, supported his effort for a raise, backed his requests for the experimental 9- and 11-inchers, and, most important, arranged for politicians, bureaucrats, and officers to meet him and observe him at work.

In effect, Warrington had introduced the seller to the buyers. When the makers of naval policy found that Dahlgren's background in science and his views on naval expansion and qualitative superiority paralleled their own interests, they lent him their support for his gun. Dahlgren thus established a constituency for his gun among naval policymakers, a constituency from above. With Warrington's support, Dahlgren's proposals gathered a good deal of institutional momentum.

Morris would have crushed Dahlgren's ship rearmament proposals if he could have. The commodore disliked them for several reasons. He had been a key figure in developing the 1845 ordnance, the very guns Dahlgren meant to replace. Dahlgren's insistence that the 1845 ordnance was unsound must have been unsettling. Furthermore, the commodore genuinely believed that the 11-incher was too unwieldy for shipboard use, and that a battery of a larger number of lighter guns was superior to a battery of fewer, heavier guns.

Morris had the best interests of the navy in mind; he was not merely a jealous old man. It is unlikely that he considered Dahlgren a threat to his position, for he was virtually an institution himself. In fact, he supported Dahlgren in many ways. For example, he permitted publication of Dahlgren's *Locks and Primers* and helped institute the Ordnance Establishment and experimental battery by extending Dahlgren's tour at the Washington Navy Yard indefinitely. He came to accept the 9-inch gun.

Morris objected mainly to the 11-inch gun and employed numerous means to block its development. He forced Dahlgren to focus on the range tables for the old ordnance at the expense of the time and resources needed to develop the 11-incher. In the ordnance section of the secretary of the navy's annual reports, he downplayed or ignored Dahlgren's work. He raised the specter of the Peacemaker in a move calculated to raise doubts about Dahlgren's big gun. He sent official criticism of Dahlgren's "Reorganization" papers to the secretary of the navy and to congressmen.

Dahlgren employed his own tactics to overcome Morris's resistance. He packaged his ideas in attractive documents. He circulated his publications to fellow officers and made them available to civilian policymakers by donating copies to libraries. He maintained contacts with key congressmen. He took his proposals right over the commodore's head to congressmen and cabinet officials. He inundated them with an endless stream of reports based on his experiments. He couched his proposal in terms that reflected the impulses of the day. Ships armed with his guns always won the 1812-style duels he envisioned on paper. He mustered support by reconciling political power and ordnance principle.

Dahlgren spent years patiently chipping away at Morris's resistance. He succeeded in getting his ordnance adopted by the familiar pattern of dogged persistence, back-breaking work, the masterful use of influence, and the sheer merit of the guns themselves. Dahlgren's salesmanship was just as important as the quality of the gun, if not more so, in the face of Morris's strong, conservative resistance. Despite the demonstrated merits of his guns,

Dahlgren's sales campaign probably would have failed if he had been less of an entrepreneur.

His failure to sell the armament plan to the navy revealed the limits of the power of bureaucratic entrepreneurship. His struggle to develop the 9- and 11-inch guns occurred inside the ordnance bailiwick. It boiled down to a struggle between Morris and Dahlgren. Dahlgren was able to muster enough political power to win. In the realm of the fleet, however, Dahlgren met resistance on two fronts. The best he could do was to effect a compromise. The struggle to arm the *Merrimack* class involved the Bureau of Construction, Equipment, and Repair as well as the Bureau of Ordnance and Hydrography. Despite the secretary of the navy's enthusiasm for Dahlgren's work, Lenthall and Morris, as Dahlgren had lamented, "had borne him down by their own narrow views." Dahlgren simply lacked the clout with Dobbin to overcome the resistance of two bureau chiefs.

9

The Crises of 1855
October 1854–October 1855

Eighteen fifty-five was a tough year for Dahlgren. "Job with all his amiability," he remarked, "would have lost character in 1855." At first Dahlgren focused attention on the production of his guns, which began in February. But what he would remember most about 1855 were the crises that devastated his life and threatened his career.[1]

PRODUCTION BEGINS

Dahlgren's Ideas about Metallurgy

While Dahlgren had been fighting for the adoption of his ordnance, he had also been studying metallurgy. Warrington had collected the army's reports on the strength-of-metals experiments conducted in the wake of the Peacemaker tragedy. Dahlgren had studied them all, notably those prepared by army ordnance officers George Bomford and Thomas J. Rodman.[2]

Dahlgren had also acquired one of William Wade's transverse breaking machines for the Ordnance Establishment. He and physicist Joseph Henry, who had become head of the new Smithsonian Institution in 1846, had used it to conduct their own experiments on the strength of metal. The results led Henry to conjecture that "the form of the material ought to have some effect upon its tenacity."[3]

After reflecting on the army experiments as well as his work with Henry, Dahlgren concluded that the strength of a gun depended on how it was cast, particularly on the shape of the casting. This conclusion led him to devise a casting method that he believed would produce stronger guns. Rather than casting guns in the traditional manner, in their finished form, he intended to have them cast with excess metal on the chase, then to have them turned on a lathe to their bottle shape. The unfinished casting would be a right cone, almost a cylinder, with straight lines running from the thickest part of the breech to the thinnest part of the muzzle rather than concave curves. The addition of metal at the chase, he reasoned, would make the shape of the casting more uniform and would promote a more regular solidification of the metal.[4]

He was right. It is now known that the physical properties of iron in a casting depend in part on the rate at which the metal cools. In a casting that varies in thickness, such as that of a 32-pounder, both the cooling rate and the properties of the metal vary with the thickness. This is section effect. The thicker parts have a different density and tensile strength from the thinner parts, for example. On the other hand, a uniformly shaped casting cools more evenly, resulting in greater consistency in the properties of the metal throughout the casting. Cylinder casting apparently reduced section effect.[5]

Production Monitoring

On 30 October 1854 Morris called a meeting in Washington to discuss the possibility of using the cylinder-casting method to manufacture the new guns. The meeting was attended by Commodore Charles Skinner, former chief of the naval construction bureau; Colonel Craig, chief of the army ordnance bureau; William Wade and Charles Knap, owners of the Fort Pitt Foundry; Joseph R. Anderson, owner of the Tredegar Iron Works; Cyrus Alger; Robert Parrott; Morris; and Dahlgren. Morris expressed approval of cylinder casting and asked for the others' opinions. Everyone concurred.[6]

Commodore Morris issued contracts for the new guns early in December. Dahlgren helped prepare the final copies. The contracts specified a minimum amount of excess metal to be cast on the chase of a gun. Each founder could, at his own discretion, add more than the minimum to the chase.

Dahlgren recommended making them as cylindrical as possible. Morris ordered fifty 9-inchers each from Tredegar and Fort Pitt, and twenty-eight 9-inchers, seven 10-inchers, and seven 11-inchers each from Alger and Parrott. The founders were to deliver all of the guns to the navy on or before 15 October 1855.[7]

Production was to be regulated by the contract between the founders and the navy and by the navy ordnance manual issued in 1852. The regulations dealt with inspection of the iron before the guns were cast and inspection and proof of the guns themselves. The founder was to collect enough cold-blast pig iron to make all of the guns contracted for. The Bureau of Ordnance and Hydrography would send an assistant inspector of ordnance to examine the metal and report to the chief, who would decide whether or not to approve it.

After the guns were cast, the assistant inspector would supervise extraction of samples of metal from the castings, examine the guns, and supervise proof. The founders usually submitted guns for inspection and proof in lots of ten. The samples taken from the castings were to be sent to the bureau and tested for density, tensile strength, and hardness. The contracts for the Dahlgren guns specified a minimum density and tensile strength of 7.22 pounds per cubic inch and 30,000 pounds per square inch, respectively. The assistant inspector would then examine each gun individually. Each gun had to conform to the dimensions specified in the drafts supplied by the bureau. The ordnance manual listed tolerances for variation in the dimensions. The chief of ordnance would determine the method of "powder proof" later; the contract did not specify a method. Powder proof was a standard test of newly completed cannon to determine their fitness for service by firing them several times. The founder would provide the proving ground, and the navy would bear the cost of proof. The assistant inspector was to supervise proof and recommend whether or not to accept each gun. The final decision rested with the chief.

The production regulations dealt with what happened before and after the casting process, not with the casting process itself. It was up to the founder to decide what metal to use and in what proportion, provided it had passed inspection; what fuel to use in the furnace; how long to keep the metal in fusion; how much excess metal to cast on the chase; whether to heat the cooling pit or not; and how long to cool the casting. As has been seen, in the past this kind of discretion had resulted in considerable variation in the quality of naval guns.[8]

Percival Drayton, circa 1863 (Naval Historical Center)

The inspector from the nearest navy yard was to monitor production at each foundry. The bureau assigned an assistant inspector to a navy yard for a three-year tour of duty. The regulations required him to attend the foundry only for specific tasks: inspection of the pig iron, extraction of samples from the casting, and supervision of proof; they did not require him to observe the actual production process. He would spend the bulk of his time at the navy yard performing other duties.[9]

One officer nicknamed the assistant inspectors of the mid-1850s "smart young fellers." It was an apt choice of words. These "smart young fellers" were generally reform-minded steam-generation officers who objected to the glacial rate of promotion in the navy, to the seemingly unlimited power of the senior officers, and to senior officers' resistance to new developments in

Henry Augustus Wise, circa 1864 (Naval Historical Center)

steam power, ordnance, naval education, and naval administration. Most of the "fellers" were Dahlgren's friends. Among them were Lieutenant George Sinclair in Norfolk, Lieutenant Henry Augustus Wise in Boston, and particularly Lieutenant Percival Drayton in New York, whom Dahlgren later referred to as his "well-tried and old comrade." Their views, expressed in letters to Dahlgren, reflected the friction between the pre-1815 and steam generations. Drayton remarked that senior naval officers were "tyrants" who were "all dreaming of the past instead of looking to the present or future." "There is at present such an amount of uneasiness restlessness and desperate disgust in the Navy," he believed, "that I really think like the French in '89 a spark is only necessary to blow the whole concern sky high." Sinclair remarked that "we will never be freed of old fogyism, except through the grave. Railroad collisions & retiring boards seem alike inadequate to the task."[10]

Dahlgren believed that the inspectors should oversee the entire production process, and he sent Morris a memo to that effect. He had borrowed this idea, as he had borrowed so many for his gun and for the Ordnance Establishment, from the army's Ordnance Department. In 1842 the army had instituted a post called "attending agent," whose function was to monitor army ordnance production at private foundries to ensure that high-quality guns were produced. The ordnance board drew up a detailed set of instructions for the attending agent as well as a detailed set of specifications for the founders. The attending agent oversaw the selection of metals as well as the production process itself and was empowered to reject any gun he deemed unfit for service. These quality-control measures, which the army had itself borrowed from European practice, materially improved the quality of army artillery.[11]

In February 1855, shortly after the founders began producing the Dahlgren guns, Morris asked the navy yard commanders to send assistant inspectors to nearby foundries to "witness and carefully note...every thing which may be considered of interest in connection with the varieties of metal used, its origin and mode of treatment—appearances of fracture—embracing color size &c &c of crystals—proportions of the kind used in the gun metal and mode of treatment and any further points likely to be interesting."[12] Wise did not fully understand these instructions and wrote to Dahlgren for clarification. He quipped that the workers at Alger's foundry found Dahlgren's "pot bellied monsters" to lack aesthetic appeal.[13]

The colorful Wise soon became a central figure in Dahlgren's life. He had become a midshipman in 1834, worked at the Depot of Charts, and served several tours on the coast survey. In his spare time he wrote popular adventure stories. He described himself as a "young man with a good character" who "can turn his hand or legs at anything" and who has "no objections to travel and takes beer with his vittals."[14]

Dahlgren replied promptly to Wise's query. He was glad that Wise was enthusiastic about his "awfully dry" assignment and instructed him to record "the *exact* history of the process used in making" each piece, "from the smelting to the final solidification." He wanted a sort of biography of each gun. Such data would prove useful in evaluating various types of iron and foundry techniques. To the gibe about the aesthetics of his guns he replied, "The guns are as you say not sightly; they do not conform to our conventional notions in such things. But if the workmen who find them ugly had had one of the prettiest flying about their ears, and killing somebody close by, as befel me, it is probable that they would find the beauty of such things to lie in their fitness."[15]

Wise sent informal progress reports to Dahlgren in addition to the formal reports he sent to Morris. In a mid-March report he told Dahlgren that he lacked knowledge of how Alger had smelted his iron. He knew that the iron came from the Greenwood mines near West Point, New York, and included information about Alger's casting method.[16]

Dahlgren wanted more details. Wise did some research, made a few inquiries, compiled a more thorough report on the goings-on at Alger's foundry, and sent it to Dahlgren on 4 April. Alger used excess metal from previous castings for the new guns. The metal remained in fusion for three and a half hours. Alger used less excess metal on the chase than Dahlgren would have preferred.[17]

Morris's unclear instructions and Dahlgren's need for specific information reflected the naval tradition of ad hoc arrangements for monitoring the production of guns. Ordnance contracts had been let intermittently since the founding of the navy, and it seemed that a new set of regulations had appeared with each contract. Dahlgren noted that the navy had no organization comparable to the army's ordnance corps. He believed that the amount of time officers served as assistant inspectors was not long enough for them to learn all they needed to know. At the end of an assistant inspector's tour, when he was just beginning to perform his duties adequately, he was shipped off to another post. Dahlgren thought that the navy suffered under such procedures, which he attributed to overly strict adherence to routine. In a letter to Drayton he referred to routine as the "devil," and he lamented that "general reform is never accomplished except gradually and in detail."[18]

In a report to Morris in May, Dahlgren recommended changes in the arrangements for monitoring production. He asked that no personnel substitutions be made at this time, despite the fact that some of the officers were due for rotation. He argued that the quality of production monitoring would drop while new people were being trained. He wanted to attain the highest possible level of quality control for his guns.[19]

In June, four months after the first gun had been poured, Morris implemented Dahlgren's suggestions and tightened up the organizational arrangements for production monitoring. To each foundry he assigned an assistant inspector whose exclusive duty was to monitor production. He ordered the inspectors to keep a detailed record for each gun and specified exactly what information to include. This clarified the duties and responsibilities of the inspectors, whose reports would provide a uniform database on the guns.[20]

Dahlgren's memo to Morris not only improved production monitoring but also planted the seeds of a social constituency for his gun from below. In effect, the assistant inspectors of ordnance would invest a portion of their careers in producing the new Dahlgren gun. The inspectors thus equated the success of the gun with their own success in this tour of duty.

Production moved at a heady pace. Parrott's casting pits averaged five Dahlgren guns a week. Alger's produced five every fortnight, but that shop was also making columbiads for the army. To speed things along, Alger had hissing-hot guns removed from the molds to free the pits for the next casting. Alger's machine shop worked eighteen-hour days.[21]

DAHLGREN'S PERSONAL CRISIS

Dahlgren's family life suffered during his stint at the Washington Navy Yard. Ranging 32-pounders, inspecting ordnance, building a factory, developing new guns, fighting for their adoption, studying metallurgy, and gearing up for production absorbed most of his attention. During 1847 he returned home to Wilmington only four times. His sixth child, Eva, born on 19 March 1848, had been conceived during one of these visits. The family moved to a little house on 4½ Street in Washington near the navy yard the following May. Dahlgren delighted in his children during his rare appearances at home. He loved to watch them sledding at Christmas, kept an account of each new tooth, and saw that they received a proper education. During the summer of 1849 his vision, which had troubled him since the coast survey, suddenly improved, enabling him to dispense with his glasses for the first time in ten years. He attributed it to "homoeopathy." On 12 November 1850 his seventh child, Lawrence, was born. Tragically, Lawrence died seven months later. In the summer of 1853 Dahlgren sent Mary and the children to the country to escape the city heat. He did not see his family at all that summer. On Christmas Day, 1854, Dahlgren worked at the yard from 7:30 A.M. to 4:00 P.M. signing bills, checking the dimensions of the plans for the screw elevator, writing a few pages of a "Reorganization" paper, and meeting with private inventors. He returned home "wearied in soul & body," as he put it, to spend what was left of Christmas with his family.[22]

Mary Dahlgren's health had been declining steadily during these years. In the fall of 1854 she suffered the first in a series of attacks from a disease that her husband described as "stricture of the bowels." On 27 March 1855 what would be the last of these attacks began.[23]

Her condition seesawed over the next two months. Doctors, friends, and family members visited her often. Sometimes she was nervous and impatient and preferred to be alone; at other times she was almost herself. She occasionally spoke of plans for the future. But on 21 May she realized for the first time that she was going to die. The doctors concurred. She suffered little, but her interest in food and in her surroundings declined steadily.[24]

Dahlgren described her last day, Wednesday, 6 June 1855:

About 3ºᶜ before daylight she asked to have me called to help turn her in bed. She had a restless spell, complained of oppression in breathing:—raised her in a sitting position & fanned her. In half an hour she was easy; laid her down—she then insisted on my going back to bed—I slept in the next room, the large folding doors open, so as to make one room. About 5¹/₂ she had me called again to turn her—after which I dressed as usual walking about both rooms—Dear Mary lay with her eyes closed mostly the nurse easing her position at times—appeared to have no severe pain. After dressing I sat down by the bed side giving such little attendance as she needed, and occasionally making a remark, which she would notice or speak of, but did not seem disposed to talk. About 7 breakfast was ready and I went down, without any apprehension—Returning she was uneasy, and talked more but rather incoherently which I attributed to the exhaustion of the opiate.... I sent round to Dr. May (Dr. Hall being sick) asking that he would please come in soon after breakfast. He did so about 9—thought the opiate not wanted, and dear Mary said she did not feel any need of it—I had to rouse her a little when the Dr. came in, & being asked if she knew him, she said oh yes. Her remarks were now by no means coherent and the muscles of the face did not seem entirely at command. The Dr. said to me aside on going out that she would not last long.... She lay still, and I sat down by her side, smoothing her hair.... Spoke to her at intervals—"Mary do you know me?"—She would open her eyes and say "my darling"—The children had now gathered about the bed of their dear mother—The mind when her notice was aroused was clear as to persons, but the idea of things seemed confused. Presently I called the youngest & said—"Mary who is this?"—She turned her head on the pillow to the child with the sweetest smile and her lips out, which Eva kissed—saying "little E"—and looking at her asked "what ruffle have you on".... Eva laughed & said it was only her apron—The dear sufferer closed her eyes, soon after clasped her hands across her bosom and slipt out of life so quietly that I could not say when the breathing ceased.

Dahlgren stayed by Mary's side until nightfall.[25]

The next day he and his son Ully sat with her body until it was time to go to the funeral parlor. At 5:00 P.M. family and friends gathered there to hear a service read by an Episcopal minister.[26]

On Friday, Dahlgren, three of his children, his sister, and several other family members and friends accompanied the coffin on the train to Philadelphia. The funeral was held that afternoon at Laurel Hill Cemetery. Dahlgren spent the weekend in Philadelphia, taking his sons Charley and Ully on a tour of family landmarks. He showed the boys the house where his mother had lived in 1832, the place where he was born, and the neighborhoods of his youth. After the tour Dahlgren paused to reflect on Mary's beauty, her joys and sorrows, their various homes together, and her "many virtues." Her death pained him deeply.[27]

Dahlgren loved Mary and grieved for her, but her death did not incapacitate him. He dealt with his grief in typical Dahlgren fashion, confronting it head-on. He allowed himself to feel the pain; he did not try to hide from it or deny it. He acknowledged his feelings, worked through them, and was soon ready to go on with his life. He wrote about how he felt and helped his children through their own grief. The little time Dahlgren spent with his family was spent well.

DAHLGREN'S PROFESSIONAL CRISIS

While Dahlgren weathered his personal crisis, a professional crisis loomed on the horizon. In March 1855 the lieutenant received reports that columbiads cast for the army at the Cold Spring foundry had failed powder proof. Parrott blamed the failures on bad metal and resolved to recast twenty. He realized that this would delay the production of Dahlgren's guns, but he took great pride in his work and did not wish to saddle the army with unsafe cannon.[28] Dahlgren neither minded the delay nor worried about the failures. He figured that some sort of accident was to blame.[29]

At the end of June, Dahlgren received word of more problems. Several other Cold Spring columbiads had failed powder proof. Parrott now faced the loss of forty guns instead of twenty. On the twenty-eighth, Wise reported that two of the columbiads cast in Boston had failed in spectacular explosions, "some of the pieces flying off laterally, and one large fragment some distance to the rear over the heads of the bystanders." Wise noted that these guns "were made under precisely the same treatment, proportions [of metal] and phases as those for the Navy.... The Lord only knows what devil has been at work in the mines or furnaces."[30]

Dahlgren now perceived that a crisis was at hand. Guns made with bad metal might pass proof, then the navy would have to pay for them. Worse, the navy might unwittingly issue bad guns to the fleet. Images of the *Princeton* must have haunted his thoughts.

On 30 June, Dahlgren wrote to Morris expressing fear that whatever had caused the failure of the columbiads at Boston and Cold Spring stood a good chance of vitiating his own guns. Moreover, he claimed that the founders had adhered to neither his design nor his casting method. The guns were being made with a central vent, not a side vent as he had intended, and the founders were not casting as much excess metal on the chase as he had envisioned. He wanted the founders, not himself, to receive the blame in the event of failure.

To detect unsound metal in the guns, Dahlgren suggested implementing a special course of "extreme proof" at both foundries. Extreme proof was a test of endurance in which a gun was fired repeatedly until it failed, or until a predetermined number of rounds had been reached. Dahlgren wanted to fire at least one gun from each foundry a thousand times with service charges, a procedure Wade had recommended. Theoretically the performance of each test piece would indicate what endurance the navy could expect from the other guns made of the same metal.[31]

But instead of taking steps to avert a crisis, Morris disputed Dahlgren's contentions. He argued that Dahlgren had specified the central vent and had agreed to allow the founders to determine the amount of excess metal to cast onto the chase. Morris neither acknowledged the existence of a crisis nor responded to Dahlgren's pleas for additional tests. Weeks would pass before he would make a decision on special extreme proof.[32]

Drayton consoled Dahlgren about the delay:

> I sincerely sympathise with you in your many troubles, which I can see no end to however, so long as we persist in permitting the men [of] past times and prejudices to shape our present. it is a piece of stupidity which there is only one way to account for.... [From] the time of Galileo, I am sorry to say, that stupidity with power, has proved itself too much for genius without it, and that with so many examples of the ill effects of such a state of things, we can of all people persist in referring to worn out systems, for our government, is only another instance of how slowly the world progresses.[33]

Meanwhile, Dahlgren tried to convince Morris that the crisis was real and that steps must be taken to avert catastrophe. He wrote the commodore a letter asserting that the columbiads had failed because they had been made with bad metal. He pointed out that the founders were using the same metal in his own guns. It would be unwise to issue these guns to the fleet without more rigorous testing.[34]

Dahlgren also tried to persuade the commodore to cease proving guns with excessive charges and to adopt "service charges" for both powder and extreme proof. The service charge was the amount of gunpowder the cannon would normally fire, both in peace and in war. Morris had established the powder proof for 9-, 10-, and 11-inch Dahlgren guns the previous May. Each piece was to be fired twice, the first round with an excessive charge, the second with the service charge. The commodore left it to the inspector to decide whether to fire a third round with the service charge. Morris objected to proof by service charges because it cost more, took longer, and used up more gunpowder and shells. Dahlgren considered proof by excessive charges to be "a sheer waste of the gun." He believed that this practice weakened a cannon and reduced its life, yet another idea he had derived from army ordnance research. Furthermore, he felt that his gun was simply not designed to handle a larger charge. He feared that bad guns might withstand Morris's two or three rounds, then the navy would have to accept them under the terms of the contract, and they would have been weakened by excessive proof charges to boot. Dahlgren wanted to change powder proof to ten rounds with service charges. He believed that although it would be more expensive than Morris's two to three rounds, it would provide a better indication of quality.[35]

Dahlgren hoped that the unusual longevity of the original 11-inch gun would convince Morris that excessive charges reduced the service life of guns and that proving should instead be done with service charges. With Morris's permission Dahlgren had initiated extreme proof of the gun in October 1854. Dahlgren's method for endurance testing differed from the one Farragut had used at Old Point Comfort. Dahlgren built a similar testing battery, complete with a bunker to shelter the three- to four-man crew during firing. But unlike Farragut, Dahlgren never fired the 11-incher with excessive charges, and he fired only one projectile at a time. The gun endured 1,958 rounds, 655 with solid shot, a truly remarkable performance. On the next round, fired on 18 July 1855, the 11-incher split into three pieces. The chase broke off intact and dropped straight down, the left side of the breech flipped over with the carriage, and the right side flew 90 feet. The breech had failed, not the chase, contrary to Dahlgren's intention, but the gun had endured magnificently.[36]

Nevertheless, the commodore refused to use service charges in proof. On 26 July 1855 Dahlgren went to Richmond to observe the regular proof of several 9-inch guns recently finished there. They were all fired with excessive charges in accordance with Morris's orders, and they all passed.[37]

In late August, Morris decided to implement a course of extreme proof for 9-inch guns at each foundry. At Richmond he allowed Dahlgren not only to use service charges but also to try a new method. The test piece would be suspended from a frame, like a pendulum, and fired into an earth-filled butt. More shells could be salvaged and reused this way. As usual, Dahlgren had gotten the idea from the army. But at Boston, Pittsburgh, and Cold Spring, Morris insisted on excessive charges. At each of the northern foundries, one 9-incher was to be fired 160 times with service charges and 350 times with greater-than-service charges. The commodore remained undecided about extreme proof for 11-inchers and gave no ground on powder proof for any caliber.[38]

By the end of the summer each of the foundries had completed the 9-inch Dahlgren guns and submitted them for inspection. Powder proof commenced in September. The Richmond guns fared best in both regular and extreme proof. One 9-incher made there endured 1,681 rounds without failing. The navy rejected only three guns produced in Richmond under the first contract. Extreme proof at the other foundries went badly. One of the Pittsburgh 9-inchers failed on the 206th firing, another on the 120th. A Cold Spring 9-incher exploded on the 244th round. In Boston a 9-incher exploded on the very first pull of the lanyard. Powder proof of the first lots did not go well either. In Boston several 9-inchers survived, but the firing scarred the metal in the bore. Morris rejected all forty-three guns submitted for powder proof in Pittsburgh because of defective trunnions. Compared with the remarkable endurance of the original 11-inch gun, these performances were abysmal.[39]

In response to the failures, the Bureau of Ordnance and Hydrography instituted Dahlgren's regular and extreme proof methods for the remaining guns, but the orders did not come from Morris's pen. The commodore had evidently been taken ill and was away from his post when the orders went into effect. Dahlgren's old friend Joseph Smith, who had assumed temporary command of the bureau, issued them in Morris's absence.[40]

It did not help. The guns still performed miserably. A Pittsburgh gun broke apart on the 122d firing. All of the Boston guns were "indented like the devil," as Wise put it, and two showed signs of splitting open at the vents.[41]

The one bright moment during these dark days came on 14 September, when Dahlgren rose to the rank of commander. Wise quipped that the promotion increased his "prospects of commanding a dam ole cockroach gun brig on the coast of Africa."[42]

But Dahlgren was in no mood to celebrate. The crisis he feared had materialized. He must have worried that critics would point to the failures as evidence that his soda-water-bottle design was indeed unsound. Such a charge could nip his ship armament program in the bud. At worst it could wreck his reputation, not to mention his career.

10

Development during Production
October 1855–August 1856

Why the guns failed was a vexing question. Wise wrote Dahlgren that "the iron is beyond doubt extremely darn bad, though no one here has as yet found out how or why it is so." The founders at Boston, Pittsburgh, and Cold Spring had recently been making most of their guns with iron from the Greenwood mines near West Point, New York. Wade, Parrott, and Alger suspected that the Greenwood iron might be the cause of the failures, and they stopped using it in cannon. What puzzled everyone was that Greenwood met if not exceeded the standards for density and tensile strength spelled out in the contracts. Neither Wade nor Parrott thought that density alone was a reliable indicator of strength, but Wade believed that moderate density and high tenacity indicated sound metal.[1]

Parrott reasoned out two explanations for the failures. Like Dahlgren, he suspected that the use of excessive proof charges had fatally weakened the guns. He also suggested that the guns had been proven too soon after being cast. He believed that the longer a gun rested before being fired, the better its endurance. He reasoned that time enabled the structure of the iron to recover from the strain of cooling, during which the outer layers of metal compressed the inner layers. The Dahlgren guns, he figured, had not rested sufficiently. The strain of firing added to the unreleased tension of compression during cooling and had contributed to the failure. Wade agreed with both explanations. Dahlgren had no opinion on the effect of time on the strength of metal but deemed the question worthy of experiment.[2]

The founders at Pittsburgh blamed the failures on Dahlgren's bottle-shaped design. Drayton quipped that this was "about as reasonable as the people of Tuscany attributing the grape disease to Railroads, or war to the appearance of a comet."[3] Dahlgren did not take the explanation from Pittsburgh so lightly. "It hardly seems handsome in our friends at Pittsburgh," he wrote Drayton, "to arraign the model of the IX" when the quality of the iron is notoriously unfit." He was certain that the failures did not stem from faulty design.[4]

THE SOLUTION: PRODUCTION AND PROOF SPECIFICATIONS

On 31 October, Dahlgren wrote Morris, formally expressing his views on why the Boston, Pittsburgh, and Cold Spring 9-inchers had failed.[5] He attributed the failures to three causes. First, he blamed the warm-blast technique used to smelt the Greenwood iron. In warm blasting, air was heated as it was pumped into the furnace. Dahlgren reasoned that the higher the temperature of the blast, the greater the tendency of the metal to contract upon cooling. Greater contraction meant greater strain, thus weakening the metal. Dahlgren noted that each of his own guns as well as the army cannon that had failed had been made with varying proportions of Greenwood iron. He knew that in the past, iron produced by a cold or unheated blast of air had made good gunmetal, and he reminded Morris that this was why the regulations specified the exclusive use of "'Cold Blast' charcoal pig iron" in naval cannon.

Second, he blamed the "position of the vent." He noted that despite his objections, the failed guns had been made with central vents, located in what he called the "plane of projection," perpendicular to the axis of the bore. He argued that a central vent was subject to greater strain and damage during firing than the side vent he had recommended, which entered the chamber diagonally. He believed that a central vent reduced the life of a gun by one-third.[6]

Third, he blamed the form of the casting. The contracts had allowed each founder to decide for himself how much excess metal to cast about the chase. Knap and Wade had cast only 3 extra inches in diameter onto the chases of the 9-inchers. Although this added over 1,200 pounds of metal that had to be lathed off, it was less than the minimum amount specified by the red lines on the plans supplied to each foundry. Parrott had cast more than the minimum amount of metal onto the muzzles but had sought to alter the form of casting in other respects. Thus, the shapes of the castings varied from one foundry to the next—exactly the situation Dahlgren had sought to redress. He asked Morris to order the founders to cast the guns strictly according to the red lines on the drawings, to ensure both the uniformity of properties throughout each gun and the uniformity of guns from one foundry to the next. He pointed out that Parrott planned to use the cylinder-casting method not only for subsequent navy guns but for army guns as well. By this time Dahlgren considered the cylinder-casting method to be as integral to the definition of a Dahlgren gun as the soda-water-bottle shape.[7]

In short, Dahlgren blamed the founders for the failures. "As for the present results with the IX^{in} guns," he wrote Lieutenant John S. Missroon, an assistant inspector stationed in Boston, "I am in no-wise responsible."[8]

Dahlgren was confident that guns of cold-blast pig iron, cast with the exact amount of excess metal on the chase specified by the red lines on the drawings and made with side vents, would have a service life of a thousand rounds. He asked Morris to refuse any gun that did not meet these specifications. Parrott and Alger were finishing up the 11-inchers and getting ready to submit them for inspection. Dahlgren worried that these guns had not been made as the contracts had specified, and that Morris would reject them before submitting them to powder proof.[9]

Morris replied the next day. Ignoring Dahlgren's explanation, he simply ordered him to go to Boston and inspect any 11-inch gun Alger submitted, whether or not it had been made according to Dahlgren's specifications. However, he permitted Dahlgren to use his own method of proof.[10]

Then for some unknown reason the commodore changed his mind about proof. On 10 November he ordered Dahlgren to select the weakest 11-incher in Boston and prove it with one excessive charge and one service charge. Later he ordered that all 10- and 11-inchers should be proven with one excessive and one service charge. Despite well-informed opinion that excessive charges weakened a gun, the commodore could not bring himself to break with tradition.[11]

Meanwhile, evidence mounted in favor of Dahlgren's ideas. Parrott had sealed the central vent of a 9-incher undergoing extreme proof at Cold Spring and drilled a side vent instead. As of 9 November the piece had withstood 1,402 rounds. The new vent "wears both inside & outside *very much less* than the old one," Parrott wrote Dahlgren. "The difference is so remarkable that its importance must lead to the adoption of the side vent." Drayton, who was supervising the proof of this piece, wrote Dahlgren:

> How in the face of all this which is known they can stick to the old fashion, can only be explained by the very old fogies, and then not comprehensibly to any one but themselves. Some of these days, your gun vent and all, will be stolen by some travelling artillerist, and coming back to us from Europe will be received by the ancients with delight, but having no confidence in their own judgement, they dont like to acknowledge any on this side of the Atlantic.

By 13 November the gun had reached 1,602 rounds. Drayton, disappointed by a recent order from Morris to stop the firing, felt that the gun would have endured two thousand rounds.[12]

The weight of evidence finally forced Morris to relent. Dahlgren sent him a report on the results of the Boston 11-incher that he had ordered proven with an excessive charge. The gun had failed on the first round. On 22 November the commodore ordered Dahlgren to draw up specifications to "secure the fabrication of [11-inch] guns of greater strength and endurance than if made according to the provisions of [the present] contracts." He also ordered Dahlgren to specify proof. New contracts embodying these specifications and proof procedures would be drawn up and issued to the founders.[13]

Dahlgren had won a significant victory. The crisis caused by inferior metal had forced Morris to institute changes in production and proof. This victory hardened Dahlgren's resolve to see his plans through. "If I am to be accountable for the XI^{in} guns," he wrote Drayton, "rely upon it, I will not stop half way."[14]

Dahlgren forwarded the specifications on 24 November. They included the following: The founder should collect a sufficient quantity of metal to cast twenty cannon. It should be charcoal-smelted cold-blast pig iron; no scraps, turnings, or remelted cannon were allowed in the mix. The cylinder-casting method should be used; the shape of the chase was to be a right cone of specified dimensions, the superfluous metal to be turned off after cooling. The castings should be cooled as slowly and regularly as possible, remaining in the cooling pit at least ten days. A single 11-incher was to be cast in this way and subjected to a proof of ten service rounds. If it passed, the navy would pay for it and subject it to a total of one thousand rounds with service charges. If it endured, the founder could then produce the rest of the guns in the contract. Each was to be made in the same way and from the same iron as the first gun and had to meet the same standards of density and tensile strength. Subsequent guns that did not meet these standards would be rejected. Regular proof would be ten service rounds. Any rejected guns would be broken up. The contractor was not allowed to use Dahlgren's design or casting method for other purposes.[15]

These specifications embodied Dahlgren's ideas about metallurgy, derived from army strength-of-metals studies. The central idea was that the properties of iron in a gun depended upon the casting method. Dahlgren concluded that the cylinder-casting method, which entailed the shape of the casting, the smelting process, and the mode of solidification, was the best way to obtain strong guns.

On 27 November, Morris wrote to Alger and Parrott, rejecting the 11-inchers already made and offering them the opportunity to make new 11-inchers to Dahlgren's specifications, which he forwarded with the letters.[16]

Alger objected to the specifications and tried to persuade Morris to drop some of them. He argued that the metal could not be treated in exactly the same manner for each gun. The amount of time necessary for metallization (separation of impurities in the iron by heating in the furnace) varied with the weather conditions and was a decision best left to the founder. Alger also wanted to use remelted castings and scraps in new guns if made of the same metal in the same way. He objected to the amount of time specified for a gun to remain in the cooling pit, arguing that the crystalline structure of metal does not change after cooling to red-hot. Again, he reasoned that the founder knew best when to remove a casting from the pit. Alger did not mention that leaving it there for ten days would slow production, but the thought must have crossed his mind. Parrott raised similar objections.[17]

The founders rankled at the degree of control over the production of cannon that the specifications promised to usurp from them. Alger and Parrott had learned their trade at the mouth of a furnace. Dahlgren, on the other hand, had learned about iron founding by reading in his office. As an outsider to the ironmaster's craft, he was more willing than the insiders to change the way of doing things.

Morris forwarded the gun-founders' objections to Dahlgren. The lieutenant defended every point under dispute, yielding no ground. The commodore ordered him to compromise with Alger and Parrott. Dahlgren visited Boston and Cold Spring in January 1856. Upon finding the seventy-six-year-old Alger too ill to do business, he conferred with younger executives. A week later he traveled by train and by sleigh across the frozen Hudson to visit Parrott. Dahlgren persuaded the founders to cast his guns exactly as he had specified. His victory was complete.[18]

When included in subsequent contracts, Dahlgren's specifications bound gun-founders to a standard prescription in making Dahlgren guns. The specifications focused on the casting method, which formerly had been chosen by the founders—the master craftsmen of the iron industry. In effect, they transferred much of the control over the production process from the subjective knowledge and experience of the craftsmen to provisions spelled out in the government contract. They brought greater uniformity and more rigorous quality control to naval ordnance than had ever been attained before. Dahlgren's imposition of standardized procedures on the gun-founders represented the impingement of both science upon craft and government upon industry.

Ironically, ironmasters and ordnance experts soon learned that coke-smelted hot-blast iron actually produced stronger cannon than charcoal-smelted cold-blast iron.[19] But because his guns proved so reliable, Dahlgren never tested his ideas about smelting fuel and blast temperature.

MORRIS DIES

When Dahlgren returned from the foundries, Morris was dead. Dahlgren had called on the commodore the day before he left Washington. He recounted the meeting in his diary: "Com. Morris was sitting at his table with hat & overcoat on—a stout wrapper about the neck to the ears and moccasins. He did not look well...he had taken a cold and felt it all over him:—I remarked that he ought not to have left home and had better return and be cared for.... *It was to be the last time I ever should see him alive.*" Morris had died on 27 January 1856 of pneumonia combined with pleurisy and acute bronchitis. Dahlgren was convinced that stress arising from the ordnance crisis had killed him. "The trouble and anxiety arising from the difficulties with the Founders had preyed on him," Dahlgren wrote in his diary, "and in my opinion made the system unable to resist the disease—which may be well conceived at 72."[20]

Obituaries remarked upon Morris's impeccable character and brilliant career. The president, the secretary of the navy, Dahlgren, and other highly placed politicians and distinguished citizens attended his funeral on 29 January, which was held, according to the commodore's wishes, without military pageantry.[21]

The next day the secretary of the navy summoned Dahlgren to his office. Dobbin said that he would like to make him chief of the Bureau of Ordnance and Hydrography. Dahlgren, however, did not want the position. A bureau chief dealt more with administrative details than with the kind of work he had come to love.[22] He was far more interested in perfecting and institutionalizing his gun as head of the Ordnance Establishment he had created. "My main purpose in seeking ordnance duty," he wrote a friend, "was to fit myself more fully for sea service. In so doing I have become more interested in the pursuit than intended at the outset, and identified with innovation which however viewed by others, seemed to me essential."[23]

Dahlgren had joined the navy to win glory but had been denied command of a ship, the traditional means to that end. This had frustrated him immensely. But now ordnance work promised to fulfill his ambition for fame and recognition. Dahlgren wanted to achieve immortality through the success of his invention. His own reputation had become synonymous with that of his gun.

Dahlgren Exploits Morris's Death

Dahlgren moved quickly in the wake of the commodore's death to implement measures that the old man had resisted. As he later recalled, the fact that his friend Joseph Smith was temporarily appointed bureau chief gave him "control of the whole business." Smith, who had taken over a few days before Morris died, began to institute Dahlgren's measures almost immediately. On 25 January he ordered the founders to adhere strictly to Dahlgren's specifications in the manufacture of 11-inch guns. On 6 February, Dahlgren asked him to extend the specifications to the 9- and 10-inch guns as well. Smith complied. All subsequent Dahlgren guns had side vents and were cast with a specific amount of excess metal on the chase. Thus, the navy fully implemented Dahlgren's quality-control program.[24]

Dahlgren also used the opportunity created by Morris's death to fulfill a longstanding desire to improve gunnery procedures in the fleet. Drayton had summarized the problem in a letter to Dahlgren in June 1850:

Gunnery may be considered an occasional divisional exercise, where the guns are run in and out with the least possible trouble to officers and men. Target firing is a tradition, and shells a mystery which it is supposed will be explained some of these days. In the mean time poor Jack looks upon them with a mixture of fear and awe, and a Lieut. not very long ago, asked me privately, what composition was inside to cause the explosion, not seeming to dream, that so simple an agent as gunpowder could be used.

There was no standard gunnery drill in the navy. It varied from ship to ship and often from division to division within a ship. Dahlgren sought to change the situation by developing a program to train officers as ordnance specialists, one of whom would be assigned to each ship in the fleet. He believed that regular practice and standard drill would vastly improve shipboard gunnery.[25]

Dahlgren launched the program late in January 1856. Specially trained ordnance officers were assigned to each of the new war steamers. These officers had served a tour of duty as assistant inspectors of ordnance as part of their training. From now on, shipboard gunnery would be under the charge of a specialist in ordnance.[26]

Dahlgren had a vested interest in assigning such specialists to the new ships. Each specialist was a "smart young feller" and thus thoroughly familiar with the Dahlgren guns. It was important to Dahlgren that his own men "fit the new guns," as he put it, because "no small responsibility...attaches to the innovation, and I naturally feel solicitous to come out square." He realized that his reputation was riding on the success of his ordnance. He sought not only to improve gunnery but also to ensure that any problems with the new guns could be kept within the family, so to speak. Because the assistant inspectors had spent a significant portion of their careers working on Dahlgren guns, they too had a vested interest in their success.[27]

"I am glad to hear that you have arranged for an ordn officer in the steamers," Drayton wrote Dahlgren; "without such a person I am satisfied that they will come back with a report that the guns wont work, which being examined into will prove that no one ever gave themselves any trouble about the matter." Drayton recommended assigning the job to

the youngest Lieuts from the School [the Naval Academy], who having nothing to unlearn and bringing habits of study would pick up more with you in three months, than their older Brethren in that number of years.... I am convinced...from observation that if you want your ideas and those of the modern school fully carried out you must take up younger men [because] the others have too much to unlearn. it is I think very important to get the proper kind of people.[28]

The first shipboard ordnance specialist was an assistant inspector named Catesby Jones, who was assigned to the *Merrimack* at Dahlgren's request. Lieutenant Jones had been appointed midshipman in 1836 and had served on board several vessels and at the Depot of Charts and Instruments. Since 1853 he had served under Dahlgren at the experimental battery.[29]

Dahlgren's shrewd choice soon paid dividends. The *Merrimack* was commissioned in Boston on 20 February 1856. She then cruised to Norfolk, where her fitting out was completed. Jones had test-fired her 9-inchers en route. It was the first time Dahlgren guns had ever been fired at sea. The carriage for mounting the 9-inchers was a copy of the French Marsilly carriage, which had only two trucks (wheels) instead of four. In place of rear wheels, the Marsilly carriage featured wooden skids to reduce recoil and facilitate reloading. The carriage was moved about with traditional breeching tackle and a new device called a roller handspike, a sort

USS *Merrimack,* circa 1856 (Naval Historical Center)

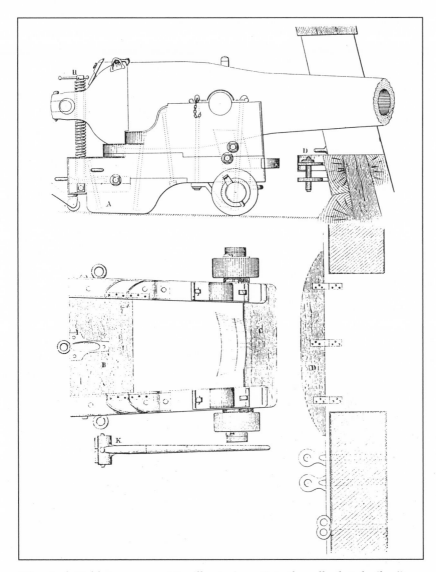

Nine-inch Dahlgren gun on Marsilly carriage. Note the roller handspike (item *K* in the drawing). (From U.S. Navy Department, Bureau of Ordnance, *Ordnance Instructions for the United States Navy*)

of wheeled lever. Jones reported that the roller handspike was difficult to use and scarred the decks. He wrote Dahlgren that he was "not at all sure the IX inch would not have been reported against equipped as they were if there had not been someone on board who understood their management and was interested in their success." Jones, of course, submitted a positive report on the 9-inchers.[30]

Finally, Dahlgren tried to use his newfound power to arm the spar decks of the *Merrimack* class his own way. The fact that the navy had not adopted his shipboard armament plan in its entirety still rankled. As he put it to one of the assistant inspectors:

> I have dislodged the 32 Pdrs. and only a few of the old 8 in guns find place in the new ships—their batteries being chiefly composed of my IX in and X in shell guns. Still the presence of these 8 in is a blemish and a weakness.... Whether I may not be finally worn out and used up by this continued and unnecessary struggle remains to be seen. But it must and will come right in the end.[31]

On 9 April, Dobbin ordered Dahlgren to Norfolk to run another test of the *Merrimack*'s battery. The *Merrimack* weighed anchor on 14 April and steamed about off Norfolk. Dahlgren had the guns fired at a fixed target from various ranges while the ship was both under steam and standing still. Five days later the *Merrimack* picked up the president, the secretary of the navy, and their entourage in Annapolis. Dahlgren had his guns fired for the visitors. Unlike the infamous demonstration of the Peacemaker, though, the Dahlgren guns fired blanks.[32]

On 25 April, Dahlgren sent Dobbin a report on the test. In the first three pages he concluded that the test had been a success. He spent the next five pages arguing that two 11-inchers and ten 9-inchers would be a more powerful, efficient, and economical battery for the spar decks of the *Merrimack*-class frigates than the fourteen 8-inchers and two 10-inchers they now carried. No immediate changes to the *Merrimack* class resulted from this effort, but Dahlgren did succeed in rearming the older sidewheeler *Powhatan* with his guns.[33]

All in all, Dahlgren had made significant progress while Smith was in charge of ordnance. He initiated the program of assigning specially trained ordnance officers to naval vessels, and he gained complete control over the design of his guns and the methods used to produce and test them.

THE FIRST ORDNANCE CRISIS ENDS

At the end of March 1856 Captain Duncan Nathaniel Ingraham took command of the Bureau of Ordnance and Hydrography. Ingraham had fought in both the War of 1812 and the Mexican War. Unlike Morris, Ingraham had little experience with ordnance. Dahlgren had never seen him before but had heard pleasant things about him.[34]

The ordnance crisis ended anticlimactically. In the spring of 1856 the West Point Foundry began producing 11-inchers to the new specifications. By 21 July one of the new 11-inchers put to extreme proof had endured one thousand service rounds without injury. That month Ingraham nullified the navy's contract with the Fort Pitt Foundry. After rejecting forty-three of the fifty guns originally contracted for, the bureau had offered Knap and Wade another contract. When it became clear that they would be unable to deliver the guns on time, Ingraham offered the contract to other foundries. Production resumed in Boston late in September 1856. The delay had been caused by difficulties in collecting metal. By the year's end the foundries had delivered all of the Dahlgren guns ordered in the first contracts.[35]

These and subsequent Dahlgren guns were manufactured and tested under the most rigorous and comprehensive program of quality control seen in the United States Navy to that time. The program embodied the latest developments in the science of metallurgy and included detailed specifications for the production of cannon, personnel to monitor the production process, and a rigorous system of proof testing.

Dahlgren had derived his quality-control program from army research as well as from the experiments he and Joseph Henry had conducted. The institution of these specifications was the final milestone in the development of 9-, 10-, and 11-inch Dahlgren guns. Like cylinder casting, quality control had become integral to the definition of the Dahlgren gun.

Morris resisted Dahlgren's program not only because he disliked change but also because he was cautious. The commodore fought Dahlgren's program almost to the bitter end because it cost more than the old way, because he identified with the 1845 ordnance that Dahlgren meant to supplant, and because he simply could not bring himself to break with tradition until overwhelming evidence in favor of the new way compelled him to do so. "Routine is the death of any institution," Dahlgren observed, "but it is not the peculiar attribute of age—you will find young-fogies as well as old fogies; and more of them—some men's ideas never grow old, those of others are never young."[36] There were no faceless bureaucrats in charge of the Bureau of Ordnance and Hydrography. The pace and direction of change depended not only on the drive of the led but also on the vision of the leaders.

Because Morris questioned and resisted Dahlgren's ideas, Dahlgren considered him an old fogy. Dahlgren was critical of anyone who disagreed with him; it was one of the defining traits of his character. On the other hand, Dahlgren got along well with people like Warrington who supported his ideas.

While the constituency from above facilitated the gun's adoption, the constituency from below facilitated its perfection. As a social constituency whose career success depended on the gun's success, the assistant inspectors strove to attain the highest standards both as production monitors and as shipboard ordnance officers. As Catesby Jones had implied, men without a stake in the Dahlgren gun might not have striven so hard to ensure its success.

And there would have been no Dahlgren gun had Dahlgren not worked so hard to overcome the various organizational and technical hurdles he encountered. Dahlgren had done so because he had come to equate the success of his gun with his own reputation. This was why he had stumped so hard for his ship armament plan. It was why he had taken offense when workmen in Boston made fun of the gun's shape. It was why he had objected so strenuously when founders attempted to tamper with his design or specifications. It was why he had spent so much time away from his beloved wife and children. Dahlgren had come to perceive the gun as his ticket to glory.

11

Dahlgren's Star Rising
1856–1859

In the years following the ordnance crisis, Dahlgren rose from relative obscurity in the Bureau of Ordnance and Hydrography to international renown as a scientific ordnance expert. Leo Braudy has pointed out that it is not only accomplishment that accords renown but also public recognition of that accomplishment. Publicity for a deed is as important as the deed itself.[1]

Before the navy had chosen his guns for the *Merrimack*-class frigates, Dahlgren had publicized his deeds in order to sell his gun. He continued to seek publicity for three reasons. First, the navy had adopted his 9- and 10-inch guns, but not the 11-incher. The 11-inch gun was still "experimental." Second, although the navy's leaders and several assistant inspectors of ordnance were acquainted with his ordnance, the rest of the navy remained unfamiliar with it. Most sailors and officers had not yet laid eyes upon a bottle-shaped gun; 9- and 10-inchers were just beginning to trickle into the fleet. The Dahlgren gun had been adopted but not institutionalized.

And then, of course, there was glory. Dahlgren had come to equate renown as an innovator with glory won in combat. He wanted the navy to celebrate his accomplishments and endow him with the honor he so desperately desired. But the navy still looked askance at officers like him who specialized in "sideline" fields; sea duty remained paramount. As Andrew Foote put it, the ranking of service afloat above all other kinds was an "old fogy idea" in need of revision.[2] Dahlgren shared this belief. He lamented to a friend:

> It is probable that the common opinion attaches more value to my ser-vices as a Sea officer than as an ordnance officer, though my own opin-ion is that the latter duty is very much underrated, not in my own proper case, but generally, and I doubt whether in future any officer will incur the risk of being ostracized, in order to cultivate the knowledge which nine years of steady labor convinces me is not sufficient to master the Art.[3]

Dahlgren was blazing the trail for a new breed of "specialist" officers whose importance to the navy stemmed from their expertise in a particular field, not from heroic feats of combat. He was fighting to institutionalize not only his guns but also the idea of the specialist officer. In the process, he would institutionalize his own name.

Dahlgren truly felt that he deserved such recognition. He boasted in a memorandum that the 9-incher had achieved "*a greater amount of Ordnance power with a given weight of metal,* and with more safety to those who man-aged the gun, than any other piece then known of *like weight.*"[4] To Stephen Mallory, chairman of the Senate Naval Affairs Committee from 1855 to 1860 and future Confederate secretary of the navy, he said that his guns would remain the best "until some entire Revolution supersedes them, which will not be soon."[5] On the anniversary of his arrival at the Washington Navy Yard, he wrote in his diary, "This day Ten Years [ago], I began my career in the ord-nance—all alone, and unassisted then and for some time—There was not the first vestige of the present establishment, except the Laboratory.... The Mechanical Dept—the Foundry, the new Armam. of Ships and of Boats are my work exclusively."[6] In another diary entry he referred to the building where he worked during his early days at the yard as the "cradle of the ord-nance." This comment suggests that he harbored paternal feelings about his work. His title "father of naval ordnance" may well have originated with him.[7]

Many naval officials and officers already recognized Dahlgren's contri-bution. Mallory told Congress that "under [Dahlgren's] zealous and scien-tific researches and attention our naval ordnance at this time is unsurpassed by any in the world."[8] Secretary Dobbin heaped praise upon him in his 1856 report to Congress:

The experimental establishment at the Washington Navy Yard, has been for many years an admirable adjunct to the Bureau. Having at its head an officer of high order of intellect and indefatigable energy, aided by a small corps of assistants, the Department has found it a shield of protection against the novelties of visionary inventors. No innovation has been recommended until subjected to the severest tests; yet progress, and an eagerness to be in the foreground of improvement, have been manifest. The recent adoption on the new frigates of the 9, 10, and 11-inch shell guns to the exclusion of shot, was by no means inconsiderately or hastily made.... The six new frigates presented at once the question of supplying them with the guns after the usual old model or in accordance with the suggestions of our able ordnance officer, tested by years of much consideration. After investigation, I unhesitatingly sustained the recommendation to fit out the new frigates with their present formidable battery. It is true the guns are very heavy, but experience and practice, and the aid of labor saving inventions daily made, will render them as manageable as 32-pounders were twenty years ago.[9]

Commander Thomas Turner, an assistant inspector of ordnance assigned to the Philadelphia Navy Yard, told Foote:

It is time that our best officers should know Dahlgren's merits and acknowledge them. I would, for my part, like to see him, this minute, Chief of Bureau, and to have all Navy Officers kicked out of the service, who, are opposed to his advancement.... [The] Navy will be ruined if old fogies try to keep such men as Dahlgren from standing just where their weight of character ought to place them.[10]

Dahlgren did what he could to spread such views throughout the fleet. He sent a copy of a "Reorganization" paper to Samuel F. Du Pont, who was regarded as one of the navy's best officers. He had his initials stamped onto the instruments the assistant inspectors used to examine shells. He asked his friends Catesby Jones, Joseph Smith, and Matthew F. Maury, the renowned scientist of hydrography, to take charge of his papers in the event of his death and use them to publicize his work. When important people praised him in writing, whether in letters, newspapers, or official reports, he excerpted the complimentary passages and filed them away for future self-publicity campaigns.[11]

Dahlgren found ships to be excellent vehicles for publicity. Ships on distant-station duty put in at ports around the world and received hundreds of visitors, particularly American and foreign naval officers. Innovations invariably attracted a great deal of attention. Following a shakedown cruise in the West Indies, the *Merrimack* departed for Europe in the fall of 1856, visiting Lisbon, Southampton, Brest, Toulon, and other ports. It was the first time Dahlgren guns were carried on a vessel engaged in normal operations. The guns excited comment from American and European naval officers alike. One American captain, whose ship was armed with 1845 ordnance, said that 32-pounders were better than the Dahlgren guns, which he considered "shams, not properly proved." His opinion was the exception. Catesby Jones, the ordnance officer on board the *Merrimack,* noted that "the IX in grow in favour, most [American officers] think all of our broadside should be IX in and that we should have more of them." An article in the British *United Service Journal* said that the *Merrimack*'s guns had three times the broadside power of the British frigate *Shannon* of circa 1812 and threw 214 pounds more metal in a broadside than an eighty-gun British liner like the *Majestic.* The *Merrimack*'s designation as a frigate reminded the author of the Americans' "smart practice" in the War of 1812, for he considered her "equal to a line-of-battle ship in everything but name." Jones observed that British naval officers admired Dahlgren's guns and believed them "constructed upon proper principles." The British repeatedly asked for their dimensions.[12]

Trying to obtain the dimensions of the Dahlgren gun had become something of a tradition among the British. In the spring of 1855 a Captain Cox of the Royal Artillery paid several visits to Alger's foundry. Visiting foreign establishments was a common practice in the international ordnance community. As the navy's representative in Boston, Henry Wise briefed Cox on Dahlgren's guns. The Englishman was quite impressed by the "Iron Leviathans," as Wise put it. Dahlgren had instructed Wise to keep Cox and other European visitors in the dark about the dimensions of the guns. "Some day the guns will speak for themselves," he boasted. On a visit to the foundry that June, Cox asked to see plans of the guns. Wise politely refused but was called away to the machine shop, leaving Cox alone in the office. Wise returned to find him busily measuring plans of the 11-incher. At the end of the day Wise took the Englishman out for a drink. At the tavern he noticed notches on Cox's swagger stick, which he assumed were measurements taken from the plan. "In the beguilement of Mint Juleps," as he put it in a letter to Dahlgren, Wise pared off the notches with a penknife and cut others in their place. He thought it was "the cutest thing" he had ever done. Such was the state of military intelligence in 1855.[13]

Cox proved to be the vanguard of an army of European ordnance experts who descended upon the United States in 1856. That year "scientific" officers from Britain, France, Russia, Sweden, and other countries visited Dahlgren at the Washington Navy Yard, eager to learn more about his work. The fact that European experts were seeking out an American naval officer certainly enhanced Dahlgren's prestige.[14]

Dahlgren's writings also enhanced his stature and proved to be another excellent medium for publicity. A London bookseller noted that his report on the 32-pounder of 32 cwt., which had since been published, had sold well in Britain, France, Prussia, and Russia. The bookseller thought that Dahlgren's *Boat Armament* would do as well.[15]

Shells and Shell Guns, Dahlgren's magnum opus, crowned his reputation. Dahlgren had financed the book with his own money and had finished a draft by August 1856. Dobbin read it and ordered three hundred copies. The book, which Dahlgren dedicated to his best friend Foote, appeared in print in March 1857.[16]

Dahlgren opened the book with a brief history of the use of shells at sea, citing Paixhans as the inventor of horizontal shellfire as then practiced. He then launched into a technical and theoretical discussion of ordnance, reiterating most of the arguments he had been putting forth since 1847. His implicit thesis was that his guns were based on infallible principles. He ended the book with a review of the Crimean War.[17]

Shells and Shell Guns received worldwide critical acclaim. A British naval officer regarded it as "the best work on ordnance that ever has been written."[18] A writer for the London *Morning Post* gave a typical review:

> To no one—not even to Paixhans himself, it may be—is the naval shell system more indebted than to the author whose able and interesting work now lies before us. Paixhans, indeed, had the intelligence to perceive the application of shells fired from long guns, and employed in naval warfare, but Dahlgren was the first to carry it out as an exclusive system of naval armament.... This great revolution of naval armament is chiefly attributable to the authority of Commander Dahlgren.[19]

Dahlgren must have glowed when he read this. His reputation had risen above that of Paixhans, whose work had been a seminal influence on his own career and had changed the shape of the world's navies. Dahlgren had achieved international recognition as a leading authority on naval ordnance.

THE FIRST *PLYMOUTH* CRUISE

Basking in the glow of his newfound fame, Dahlgren looked forward to a long-awaited cruise, which, if successful, would accelerate the institutionalization of his gun and name. Back in February 1856 Secretary Dobbin had placed the sloop *Plymouth* at his disposal as a "Gunnery-Practice-Ship." The stated purpose was twofold. First, Dahlgren would train officers and men in gunnery. As noted before, there was no standard gunnery drill in the navy. Ship captains selected leaders for the gun crews on the basis of interest or experience in the job. There was no standard set of qualifications. Drill occurred at the whim of the captain. Many U.S. ships would have been woefully unprepared in the event of war. In contrast, sailors in the Royal Navy drilled as thoroughly and regularly in gunnery as British soldiers drilled in musketry. Dahlgren intended to raise the standard of American gunnery to a similar level. Every year the gunnery ship would turn out a new class of specially trained officers and sailors, who in turn would spread their knowledge throughout the fleet. The second stated purpose of the *Plymouth* was to help Dahlgren determine whether the 11-incher was suitable for shipboard use. Morris had never given him an opportunity to test the 11-incher at sea. Dobbin allowed Dahlgren to mount one 11-incher, four 9-inchers, and three boat guns on the *Plymouth*.[20]

From Dahlgren's perspective, the *Plymouth* had two additional purposes. First, using his ordnance to train new classes of officers and seamen in gunnery each year would not only increase the navy's familiarity with his gun but also broaden the gun's social constituency. Second, successful results with the 11-incher would remove its "experimental" status, making it a standard shipboard weapon.

On 22 June 1857 Dahlgren received sailing orders from Isaac Toucey, who had become secretary of the navy when President James Buchanan took office. Toucey ordered him to cruise for six months and to visit the Azores, Lisbon, France, the Netherlands, Britain, and Bermuda. He gave Dahlgren leeway to experiment with the guns, to call at other ports, and to visit "the most important Arsenals of the different countries." The *Plymouth* set sail a few days later.[21]

Eleven-inch Dahlgren gun. This is the after pivot gun on board the USS *Kearsarge*, with Acting Master Eben M. Stoddard (left) and Chief Engineer William H. Cushman. (Naval Historical Center)

Dahlgren conducted gunnery practice during the cruise with three goals in mind: (1) to prove that the 11-incher was manageable at sea, (2) to refine the 11-incher's pivot carriage and associated hardware, and (3) to develop drill procedures for the 9- and 11-inchers. The crew fired at floating targets several hours a day during July and August. Dahlgren turned the practice into a competition, awarding prizes to the three individuals most skilled at handling the guns and for the three best shots.[22]

He also gathered intelligence on European ordnance and installations during the cruise. In Britain he visited the arsenal at Woolwich, the Royal Small Arms Factory at Enfield, the Royal Gunpowder Factory at Waltham Abbey, and the dockyards at Woolwich, Chatham, and Portsmouth. In Belgium he visited the cannon foundry and small-arms plant at Liège. The *Plymouth* returned home in early November.[23]

Dahlgren declared the cruise a complete success. The crew had fired 121 shells from the 11-incher and 230 shells from the 9-inchers during gunnery exercises. He concluded that the 11-incher was as manageable a pivot gun as the 64-pounders carried on U.S. steamers. His report to Secretary Toucey argued that "there should be no objection to restoring that part of my plan or armament which assigned a tier of eleven-inch guns to the spar decks of the screw frigates.... Certainly the present spar deck batteries of the Merrimac class are altogether unworthy of being placed there." He also used the report to tout gun-crew training and steam power, and to relate what he had seen of European ordnance.[24]

Naval officials agreed with Dahlgren's assessment of the *Plymouth* cruise. In his first report to Congress Toucey stated, "The result of the operations of the Plymouth seems to dispel all remaining doubt whether the heavy cannon which she carried would be manageable, and not only to justify the previous adoption of such ordnance in the steam frigates recently built, but also to render it expedient to extend this plan of armament."[25] Mallory said of Dahlgren in a letter to Wise, "I really do not know any living man who has done so much to make our naval ships formidable, nor one who more decidedly merits his country's approbation & reward."[26]

The *Plymouth* cruise had indeed accelerated the institutionalization of the Dahlgren gun. Toucey had not only lifted the experimental status from the 11-incher but also approved a measure that broadened the social constituency for the new ordnance. In December 1857 Dahlgren established a three-year training program for gun-crew captains on board the gunnery practice ship. It was, in effect, a program to create more "smart young fellers."[27]

Dahlgren reflected in his diary, "Most of the objections to the heavy guns were as flimsy as cobwebs.... Thus have I begun at the beginning & from the germ carried out the entire plan—ending with triumphant proof on the high seas."[28]

THE SECOND *PLYMOUTH* CRUISE

On 28 May, Toucey ordered Dahlgren to take the *Plymouth* on a second cruise. This time the mission was more typical of the operations the navy conducted during the nineteenth century. The Royal Navy had been boarding and searching American merchantmen in the Caribbean suspected of engaging in the slave trade. Dahlgren's mission was to patrol in the vicinity of Cuba to prevent further depredations to the American flag.[29]

The *Plymouth* set sail on 3 June. Upon visiting the Cuban port of Sagua, Dahlgren learned that the British cruiser *Styx* had boarded several American merchantmen anchored there. He patrolled off Cuba for six weeks, tracking the movements of the *Styx* but never sighting her. He received no further reports of British boardings during that time. By mid-July the tension between Britain and the United States over the boardings had abated.[30]

On 22 July, Dahlgren received orders to proceed to Navassa, a tiny Caribbean island about 45 miles from Santo Domingo and 70 miles from Jamaica. An American merchant named E. K. Cooper had applied to the Navy Department for protection when two Haitian warships stopped his guano-extracting operation on the island. Cooper claimed that because no nation owned the island, he had a right under American law to extract the guano. Commodore McIntosh, commander of the Home Squadron, Dahlgren's superior on this cruise, ordered the *Saratoga* and *Plymouth* to Navassa to protect the American's interest there. They arrived on 7 August, assessed the situation, and then set sail for Port-au-Prince to warn the Haitian government not to interfere with Cooper. The show of force worked; Cooper resumed operations unmolested. The secretary of the navy then ordered the *Plymouth* to Vera Cruz.[31]

Dahlgren sailed for a Mexico racked by civil war. From 1858 to 1861 the War of the Reform ripped Mexico apart. The Anticlerical liberals under Benito Juarez had managed to pass an act stripping the Catholic church of much of its land and power, and in 1857 they put forth a liberal constitution. These moves were anathema to the conservative Clericals, who included the large landowners and most of the armed forces. They struck under the leadership of General Miguel Miramón. The Juaristas fought back. By the spring of 1858 Tampico had come under the control of General Juan José de la Garza and his Anticlerical troops.[32]

The *Plymouth* arrived at Vera Cruz on 19 September. Dahlgren's original mission was to return the American consul posted there to the United States. On 1 October he received word from Franklin Chase, the American consul at Tampico, that the Anticlericals had seized $200,000 worth of American merchandise and were demanding repayment of duties that had already been paid to the Clericals. Chase noted that a "respectable" American citizen had recently been incarcerated in a "loathsome prison" for refusing to pay a "forced loan." He asked Dahlgren for help.[33]

The *Plymouth* anchored off Tampico on 3 October. Chase and Dahlgren paid a visit to General Garza. Dahlgren protested the Anticlerical outrages to American citizens. No doubt his study of law on board the *Sea Gull* proved useful in these negotiations. Garza agreed to take the matter up with his superiors.[34]

Several days later, Dahlgren returned to Vera Cruz. On his own initiative he decided to speak directly to President Juarez about the situation at Tampico. On 14 October, Dahlgren and several American diplomatic officials met with Juarez in his office. Dahlgren reiterated his protest. Juarez concurred and ordered Garza to redress the grievances. Garza did so.[35]

Dahlgren had proven to be an able negotiator. "You have done more for the commerce of this place than all the ships or Squadrons belonging to the U. States have done since I have had charge of this Consulate," Chase wrote to him. "I have made honorable mention of your name to Mr. Cass [the secretary of state], and I am determined to make your efficient and valuable services known in other parts of the U. States."[36] Dahlgren could do no wrong.

The *Plymouth* set sail for home on 29 October. Dahlgren arrived in Washington in early December, after a brief stop in Mobile Bay. On the eighth, Toucey ordered him to resume his ordnance duties in Washington.[37]

THE INSTITUTIONALIZATION OF DAHLGREN'S GUNS

Dahlgren returned to find the institutionalization of his gun an accomplished fact. The self-publicity campaign, the constituency from below, and the sheer excellence of the guns themselves had won them acceptance throughout the fleet.

While Dahlgren had been cruising in the Caribbean, a Boston-made 9-incher had turned in an amazing performance in extreme proof, enduring 1,531 rounds. The assistant inspector fired the first 1,509 rounds with ordinary service charges, thereafter increasing the amounts of powder and numbers of shot. The round that finally split open the barrel consisted of 20 pounds of powder and ten 90-pound shot, nearly filling the gun to the muzzle. *Scientific American* reported that this "formidable engine of war" had consumed a total of 15,400 pounds of gunpowder during the proof. Morris must have rolled over in his grave at the expense. Nevertheless, Dahlgren's production specifications and quality-control procedures had paid off. His guns were earning notoriety as not only the world's most powerful naval cannon but also the world's strongest.[38]

This reputation led the navy to arm its newest ships with the new guns. In June 1858, shortly after Dahlgren had sailed for Cuba, southern senators and representatives, some of whom were agitating openly for war with Britain because of the depredations to American merchantmen, drove a bill through Congress authorizing seven shallow-draft steamers. The Navy Department equipped them with 9- and 11-inch Dahlgren guns. Subsequent vessels authorized before the Civil War were also armed with 9-, 10-, and 11-inchers. Ships now served not only as vehicles for success but also measures of success. The Dahlgren gun had become standard shipboard ordnance.[39]

The Russians paid an offhand tribute to the new guns. Shortly after returning from the second *Plymouth* cruise, Dahlgren heard a rumor that Alger and Company had manufactured guns of his design for the Russian frigate *General Admiral,* an allegation the company promptly denied. The Navy Department ordered an investigation. A group of American naval officers visited the Russian vessel and measured her two pivot guns. The external dimensions of the guns matched those of the 11-incher, but they had $10^3/_4$-inch bore diameters. Alger and Company admitted producing the guns but claimed that they were not Dahlgren guns, because of their caliber.[40]

This was not an isolated incident. Alger had sold the pasha of Egypt two 9-inch guns that the United States Navy had rejected as unfit for service. Two of Dahlgren's guns were also seen at Woolwich.[41]

Dahlgren was outraged that his guns had been sold to foreigners. The contracts for 11-inchers stipulated that any guns the navy rejected were to be broken up. The idea was to prevent foreign powers from obtaining the U.S. design. Dahlgren believed that this provision extended in principle to all calibers.[42]

Determined never to allow such a thing to happen again, he took out a patent the next day. He had not done so before because he thought that gunfounders were bound, by both honor and the law, not to sell rejected guns to foreigners. He also thought it dishonorable to profit from serving his country. He took out a patent now because "the breach of faith thus committed is an encroachment on the right of property to my grievous detriment," as he explained to Toucey, "for after the service of a life in my profession, this alone constitutes the entire dependence of my children if accident should deprive them of my assistance."[43]

He defined his invention with a list of ten specific points. The first four dealt with the internal and external design of the gun. The fifth dealt with the side vent. The sixth through eighth covered the cylinder-casting method. The last two points mentioned lock lugs and the screw elevator. He claimed as original inventions everything but the design of the chamber, the heated cooling pit, and a provision for not removing the crust of the casting on the breech.[44]

He then sought to punish Alger and Company for its transgression. He informed Secretary Toucey that a provision in the contract had specified that the dimensions of his guns were to be kept secret from "strangers." He claimed that the 10³/₄-inch guns, despite their unusual caliber, were indeed Dahlgren guns because of their shape. He asked "that the Department...not permit this Firm to manufacture any more cannon of my model, under future contracts." Toucey seemed to agree.[45]

The affair more or less ended with Dahlgren's official protest. The navy made no other contracts with Alger and Company before the Civil War, but not necessarily because of Dahlgren's wishes. There were only three contracts for Dahlgren guns let in 1859 and 1860, two to the West Point Foundry and one to the Tredegar Iron Works. Alger and Company was a major producer of Dahlgren guns during the war. As for the guns Alger had sold to the Russians, Dahlgren need not have worried that they might be copied. When the *General Admiral* returned home, one of the guns was mounted on shore for a demonstration. After a few rounds had been fired, the gun exploded, knocking the legs off the Grand Duke's horse. Apparently Alger and Company had not adhered to Dahlgren's specifications in manufacturing guns for the Russian navy.[46]

But gun-founders did adhere to Dahlgren's specifications when producing guns for the United States Navy, and by the eve of the Civil War the Dahlgren gun was no longer a mystery to most American naval officers and officials. Some remained unconvinced that Dahlgren's guns were better than the 32-pounders and 8-inchers they were meant to replace. Farragut, for one, still preferred a battery that incorporated more of the lighter cannon, and he said so in a report to Dahlgren's boss, Duncan Ingraham. Characteristically, Dahlgren sent Ingraham a twelve-page rebuttal of the report and told Drayton that Farragut "got the cart before the horse." Nevertheless, for the rest of his life Farragut held on to his conviction that gunnery depended as much on the "eye and practice of the Gunner" as on the gun itself.[47]

But the prevailing winds blew in Dahlgren's favor. "The Dahlgren gun," wrote the superintendent of Alger and Company, without intending the irony, "is so good a thing that all attempts to localize it, we fear, will prove unavailing, and his name & fame will go along with it to other countries."[48] Captain Samuel F. Du Pont, commander of the *Minnesota* (*Merrimack* class), noted that the new weapon "defied criticism."[49] Secretary Toucey said in his report for 1858, "We have aimed to select and adopt the arm which combines the greatest strength, range, accuracy, and power. In the Dahlgren gun we have found what we want, and it is believed there is no gun in any service that surpasses it in these qualities."[50] In 1859 a board of naval officers appointed to examine naval installations reported that thanks to Dahlgren, American naval ordnance was "equal, if not superior, to [that of] any navy afloat."[51] As usual, Dahlgren copied the complimentary passages of many of these documents on separate pieces of paper and filed them away for future use.[52]

By the end of 1859 Dahlgren had become a regular guest at state dinners, rubbing elbows with foreign ministers, diplomats, cabinet members, and the president of the United States.[53] Joseph Smith wrote him, "You stand on a high pinnacle & you are always cautious to prevent virtigo from upsetting you; whether you have arrived at the apex or have still a loftier eminence to mount is to be seen. Your career is onward, the record will come sooner or later, therefore keep your weather eye open."[54]

By the eve of the Civil War, Dahlgren's star had reached its zenith. Both his ordnance and his name had become American naval institutions. "Seldom have the technical knowledge and innovative mind of a naval officer been so universally recognized in his own time," observes historian Albert Christman. "[His] name and 'ordnance' were synonymous."[55] The Dahlgren gun, an American original, enjoyed a reputation as the world's most powerful and reliable naval cannon. Many Europeans held Dahlgren to be more significant than Henri Joseph Paixhans. Although his self-publicity campaign assured him a place in naval history, his renown rested on a solid foundation: the demonstrated power and reliability of his ordnance. He had invented heavy cannon, boat guns, an ordnance establishment, experimental methods, and quality-control procedures. His masterpiece, *Shells and Shell Guns,* had won worldwide acclaim. He had achieved an unprecedented level of international renown as an American scientific ordnance inventor. It would not be enough in the end.

12

The Rifle Question
1859–1860

The Dahlgren gun was the last smoothbore cannon the United States Navy adopted as standard shipboard ordnance. While Dahlgren was stumping to institutionalize his gun, Europeans were striving to perfect rifled cannon. Rifled cannon were one of the principal technological catalysts of the nineteenth-century naval revolution, fueling a race between ordnance and armor that lasted well into the twentieth century. The development of naval rifled cannon culminated in a 150-ton 18.1-inch rifle, nine of which the Japanese mounted on their superbattleship *Yamato*.[1] These guns dwarfed Dahlgren's 8-ton 11-inch smoothbore in all respects. Wrought-iron rifles first appeared on ships in the 1850s, while Dahlgren was grappling with Morris and the gun-founders over production and proof specifications, but they did not reach full maturity until 1880, when, as historian Marshall J. Bastable puts it, "steel replaced wrought iron in the making of armaments and set off another wave of technological innovations in military and naval weapons."[2]

Although his smoothbore was the foundation of his reputation, Dahlgren did not ignore rifled ordnance. In fact, he tried to begin developing a rifled gun of his own for the United States Navy even before the smoothbore was fully institutionalized. He failed to do so because he was fettered by organizational restraints. Despite his stature as an internationally renowned ord-

166

nance expert, he did not wield sufficient bureaucratic power to tackle new projects as he saw fit. Although he would develop rifled cannon in the end, he was disquieted by the fact that he had been restrained at all. Stature without power seemed to him a dubious achievement.

Like the introduction of steam propulsion into the United States Navy and the development of shells and shell guns, the history of rifled ordnance was one of fits and false starts. Rifling is said to have been invented by Gaspard Zoller of Vienna in about 1500, but the technology necessary to produce cheap and reliable rifled artillery simply did not exist until the nineteenth century.[3]

It was the shell gun that precipitated the development of rifled naval ordnance. The Crimean War (1853–56) proved two things: the existence of shell guns necessitated armor to protect warships, and the existence of armor necessitated a more powerful cannon to sink warships.

During the siege of Sebastopol (1854–55) Russian soldiers armed with rifled muskets were able to pick off French artillerists without fear of return fire because their weapons outranged the French smoothbore cannon. This prompted Napoleon III to order experiments with rifled artillery. After rifled bronze pieces proved effective in colonial skirmishes in Africa and Indochina, Napoleon III ordered all French smoothbore bronze field pieces to be rifled on a plan devised by Colonel Treuille de Beaulieu, a pioneer in rifling. The French extended this plan to naval armament and by 1860 had converted their 30- and 50-pounder naval smoothbores into rifles.[4]

The British committed themselves to an entirely new kind of ordnance. In 1854 William Armstrong, a prominent English industrialist, began development of a wrought-iron breechloading rifled cannon constructed by the famous "built-up" method whereby wrought-iron hoops of various diameters were shrunk onto a core. Armstrong did not invent any of these features, but he combined them into one type of cannon, which was subsequently named for him. Joseph Whitworth and Captain Alexander T. Blakely also developed rifled ordnance, also named after them, for the Royal Navy in the latter 1850s. Armstrong and Whitworth became great competitors.[5]

Dahlgren kept abreast of these developments as an active member of the international community of ordnance practitioners. He habitually read European journals, gathered reports of American naval officers abroad, and corresponded with European ordnance experts, particularly the Belgian Colonel Charles

Guillaume Bormann, inventor of the Bormann fuze and author of a book on the use of the shrapnel shell in the Crimean War. Occasionally foreign gunmakers offered to sell him their products. In March 1856, for example, a representative of the Prussian firm Krupp inquired whether the navy was interested in a demonstration of one of his company's new cast-steel cannon.[6]

From these sources Dahlgren collected information about guns, shells, fuzes, and other ordnance equipment. He knew, for example, that French 30-pounder rifles far outranged comparable smoothbores but could only endure 350 to 680 rounds. He also compiled data on individual foreign ships, including tonnage, number and type of guns, and speeds under sail and steam. This information enabled him to assess accurately the capabilities of America's potential adversaries. He realized that Britain and France were, as he put it, "engaged in unprecedented efforts to improve their ordnance, particularly by introducing Rifled Cannon."[7]

He concluded that the United States Navy should develop its own rifled ordnance. On 16 August 1856 he submitted a design for a rifled gun to Captain Duncan Nathaniel Ingraham, the new chief of the Bureau of Ordnance and Hydrography. The gun would weigh approximately 16,000 pounds, have a 9-inch bore, and fire a 100-pound projectile. Ingraham ignored it. He did not even answer Dahlgren's letter. Dahlgren resubmitted the request in June 1857, but Ingraham ignored it again.[8]

By any stretch of the imagination, the new chief was no ordnance expert. Ingraham had become a midshipman in 1812 at the age of nine. The highlight of his otherwise undistinguished career came in 1853, when, in command of the sloop *St. Louis,* he freed a man named Martin Koszta from an Austrian ship. Koszta, a Hungarian rebel, had come to New York in 1851 and declared his intent to become a U.S. citizen. After two years' residence, he had gone to Turkey on allegedly private business and was seized by Austrian hirelings and imprisoned on board the brig *Hussar* in the harbor of Smyrna. Although facing a superior force, Ingraham cleared the *St. Louis* for action and demanded that Koszta be set free. A fight appeared inevitable, but at the last minute the Austrians turned Koszta over to the French consul general pending diplomatic settlement, resulting ultimately in his release. Ingraham's deed popped right out of the mold of traditional American naval heroism. The U.S. government wholeheartedly approved his action; New Yorkers turned out in droves to welcome him home in 1854; Congress gave him a gold medal; and the navy made him chief of the Bureau of Ordnance and Hydrography, a position for which he had no qualifications whatever.[9]

Duncan Nathaniel Ingraham, circa 1856 (United States Naval Institute)

Dahlgren was outraged at his superior's behavior. Ingraham not only ignored his rifle proposal but also interfered with Dahlgren's ship armament plans by allowing older naval vessels to retain their model 1845 guns. "A more miserable & stupid administration of affairs can hardly be imagined," Dahlgren blustered in his diary.[10] Catesby Jones noted that Ingraham followed "the beaten track; not changing or originating anything."[11] Dahlgren later wrote of his new boss:

> It would be difficult to find a man more unfit for a duty which he desired to perform fully & honestly—All progress was impossible.... Upon the most imperfect grounds he quickly came to a resolution, and was then most inflexible in adhering to it—His fear of expenditure was a real disease—such another in his time can hardly exist.... It will be difficult however to repair his blunders in Rifled Cannon.[12]

Dahlgren was perturbed that the navy would permit a relic of the pre-1815 generation with no expertise to interfere with his ordnance work.

Experimental battery, Washington Navy Yard. Note the breechloader on the left. The gun on the right is probably a Dahlgren 11-incher. (United States Naval Institute)

Despite his dismay, Dahlgren did not fight for rifles as he had fought for his smoothbores. Mary's death and the years of struggling for smoothbores had worn him down. He had spent the better part of 1857 and 1858 at sea on the *Plymouth*, working on his smoothbores and chasing British vessels. While ashore, he devoted his energies to running the Ordnance Establishment and resolving the affair with Alger and the Russians. He simply did not have the time to devote to rifles.

He finally secured permission to develop rifled cannon in the spring of 1859. He did so in typical Dahlgren fashion by appealing directly to Secretary Toucey, right over Ingraham's head. Ingraham did not resist this time, because, as Dahlgren put it, "the surprising results of Armstrong were astonishing the public mind." Armstrong had recently demonstrated several calibers of breechloading rifles that appeared to be superior in range, accuracy, and power of penetration to smoothbores of the same calibers. By 4

April, Dahlgren had completed the designs for three different calibers of rifles and had patented a design for an elongated projectile for rifled ordnance. He began experimenting with rifles shortly thereafter.[13]

Dahlgren used the same basic framework in testing rifles as he had in testing smoothbores, but the tests themselves were an empirical search for data. He had based the design, production specifications, and quality-control procedures for his smoothbores upon prior research, often approaching problems in ballistics and metallurgy armed with hypotheses. He relied more on original research in developing rifles but generally tackled problems without first constructing hypotheses. Throughout 1859 he tested guns of the same caliber but with different pitches (number of turns in the spiral of rifling per unit length of barrel) to see which worked best. By the end of the year he had obtained greater range than Armstrong had reported and equal penetration, but only half the accuracy.[14]

Dahlgren's rifles had a familiar appearance. They featured the same soda-water-bottle shape as his smoothbores but were cast without trunnions. Dahlgren believed that corners or angles in the surface of cast iron made it more liable to break. The trunnions were secured to the barrel by means of a breech strap.[15]

Dahlgren made his rifles of familiar materials. He regarded the strength of metal as the "principal difficulty" in developing rifled ordnance. "The real bar to progress lies in strain on gun," he noted; "they burst." He knew that Europeans were using steel, wrought iron, and other materials for rifles because cast-iron barrels could not safely bear the extra pressure of gases behind the tighter-fitting projectiles when the rifle was fired. The greater windage (difference between projectile and bore diameters) of smoothbores allowed a larger proportion of these gases to escape. The solution seemed to lie in finding a metal strong enough to bear the added strain, but Dahlgren was unwilling to experiment with wrought iron, steel, or other materials. "In view of the very superior character of our own cast iron," he wrote Franklin Buchanan, commandant of the Washington Navy Yard, "I am unable to concede its inability to furnish what may be required." His success in making cast iron work in heavy smoothbores convinced him that he could also make it work in rifles.[16]

Meanwhile, Armstrong was developing a better solution. He attained greater strength by using several layers of wrought iron. First he forged wrought-iron bars into a tube. Next he fabricated a second tube whose inner diameter was smaller than the outer diameter of the first. Then he heated the second tube until its inner diameter had expanded enough to slide over the first cold tube. As the outer tube cooled, it shrank tightly onto the inner tube, thereby compressing it. By the same procedure Armstrong "built up" the gun with one or more additional layers, with larger calibers having more layers. He used thicker tubes near the breech, where the internal pressure from the explosion of the charge was greatest. The inward pressure of the tubes was directed against the forces exerted on the barrel when the gun was fired. Built-up breechloading rifled cannon soon became the primary armament of British battleships.[17]

Dahlgren rightly believed that rifled cannon would be the ordnance of the future. The day of the 9-inch gun "is likely to be a short one," he wrote Du Pont in August 1859, "and before long Rifled Cannon may replace them." But "there is much to be done yet," he wrote Drayton, "before Rifled Cannon can be established beyond doubt."[18]

Dahlgren found Ingraham's conservatism, inflexibility, and incompetence to be the greatest obstacle he himself faced in developing rifled ordnance. "The Rifle Cannon progress," he wrote Drayton, "but I see no sign of the Chief's intent to try them in service; in fact he does [not] believe in Rifle Cannon of any kind, thinking that their shortcomings more than balance the advantages—the entire unreliability of their ricochet, for instance."[19]

Dahlgren had little confidence in Secretary of the Navy Toucey's ability to rectify the situation. He complained in his diary that Toucey was "always favorable, but is finally overruled in action; therefore a cipher."[20] Historian Robert G. Albion considers Toucey one of the worst secretaries in American naval history.[21] In an organization in which progress depended on the competence of those at the helm, a secretary such as Toucey plus a bureau chief such as Ingraham was a formula for stagnation. But it was Ingraham whom Dahlgren would blame for the navy's lack of reliable rifled ordnance at the beginning of the Civil War.[22]

With his progress in rifle development stalled, the winter of 1859–60 was a winter of discontent for Dahlgren. He rankled at Ingraham's interference, for he regarded naval ordnance as his exclusive bailiwick. To his friend David D. Porter, who would win fame in the Civil War, he complained that paperwork and red tape were keeping him from his experiments. To his friend Drayton he complained that he was working hard but "doing nothing— time, labor used up on mere gimcracks of fancied Inventors, while really important matters are passed by." To Toucey he complained that Lieutenant

Simpson's book on ordnance for the Naval Academy did not properly acknowledge his own works. In various notes he complained that Congress demanded too much of the navy and provided too little in the way of funding, and that the navy was run badly at top levels. He was dissatisfied with the entire naval organization.[23]

As a solution, in December and January he sent Toucey proposals for reorganizing the Ordnance Establishment at the Washington Navy Yard. He argued that the "Ordnance Department," as he now called the experimental battery, the gun factory, and everything else under his charge, should be removed from the jurisdiction of the commandant of the yard. This would promote efficiency by cutting down on useless paperwork, which had been an unfortunate feature of his life since Morris had taken command of the ordnance bureau back in 1851. The yard's current commandant, Captain Franklin Buchanan, whom Dahlgren considered a martinet, adhered strictly to form in administrative matters. "The [Ordnance] Department as now constituted does not answer the best ends of its creation," he wrote a friend; "it is helpless & crippled." He contended that increases in the amount of work and the number of personnel at the yard rendered it "absolutely necessary" to simplify the administration. Toucey ignored the proposal.[24]

Dahlgren channeled his ire elsewhere. Also discontented with his pay, he sought another raise. In February and March he sent letters to senators and congressmen to drum up support in his own inimitable fashion. It was the first time since 1851 that he had sought a raise. Now, he argued, as head of a branch within a bureau he was entitled to the same pay as his friend Matthew F. Maury, the head of the Naval Observatory. He also argued for the raise on the basis of his accomplishments. His ordnance was a "radical change," as he put it, and "more powerful than any carried elsewhere." In June, Congress raised his pay to $4,200 per year. It was a spring thaw to warm his heart after the winter of discontent.[25]

That fall another event warmed Dahlgren's heart. Ingraham left the ordnance bureau in September to take command of the *Richmond*, one of the *Hartford*-class screw sloops armed with Dahlgren smoothbores authorized in 1857. Dahlgren had higher hopes for Captain Magruder, Ingraham's successor, who seemed more amenable to rifled ordnance. As he put it to Drayton, "We have a better prospect of doing something than for some time past."[26]

That assessment proved correct. By the end of 1860 Dahlgren had completed ballistics tests on three calibers of rifles: a 15-pounder, a 50-pounder,

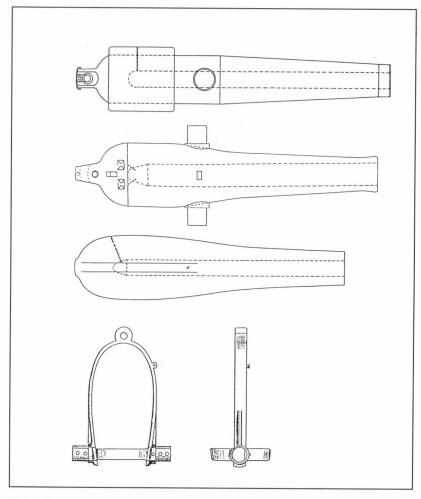

Top to bottom: 150-pounder (8-inch) Parrott rifle, 11-inch Dahlgren smooth-bore, 150-pounder (7.5-inch) Dahlgren rifle, breech strap for Dahlgren rifle (approximately to scale). The *x* in the drawing of the Dahlgren rifle indicates the position of the trunnion. The 150-pounder (7.5-inch) Dahlgren rifle was never used in service. (From Canfield, *Civil War Naval Ordnance,* and Holley, *Treatise on Ordnance and Armor*)

and an 80-pounder (designated by weight of shot). He believed that the 50- and 80-pounders were ready for introduction into the fleet for long-range work as supplements to his smoothbores. He intended to mount four 80-pounders per gun deck and two per spar deck on sloops and frigates. The 50-pounders were for smaller vessels.[27]

Dahlgren not only made progress with his own work but also encountered a unique opportunity to check up on the competition. On 14 September 1860 a Mr. Joseph Allen approached him with a complete set of plans of the Armstrong gun that he had obtained by bribing a draftsman. "I told him frankly that I was opposed to this mode of obtaining information," wrote Dahlgren in his diary, "and never would use it." He suggested that Allen take the matter to his superior, who in turn sent him to the secretary of the navy. Toucey did not know how to handle this situation, so the matter dropped. Such was the state of industrial espionage in 1860.[28]

In December, Dahlgren submitted a report to Congress arguing for the adoption of rifled ordnance on board U.S. naval vessels. He pointed out that Britain and France were spending enormous amounts on the development of rifled cannon. Moreover, the effects of heavy shells "may be nullified, more or less, by the use of iron ribs or plates." The French had already launched an ironclad, the *Gloire*. Although the ship was "far from perfect," she represented the future of naval power. Dahlgren believed that rifled ordnance would make iron armor "less effectual." He declared that "rifled cannon are now about to share a place with the smooth bores, if they do not replace them entirely." Dahlgren rifles were subsequently introduced into the fleet on a limited basis.[29]

One might expect Dahlgren to have rejoiced over the navy's adoption of his rifles, but there is no evidence that he did. Despite his international reputation as an ordnance expert, he had experienced great difficulty overcoming Ingraham's resistance. During his winter of discontent he realized that his renown was not accompanied by the power to institute organizational change. Because he lacked sufficient clout, his effort to develop rifled ordnance had faltered and his effort to reorganize the Ordnance Establishment failed. His raise offered small consolation. Despite his unprecedented reputation and record of success, the navy had proven reluctant to follow the course he wanted set for ordnance. It frustrated him immensely. To paraphrase Joseph Smith, he would keep a weather eye open for a loftier eminence to mount.

13

Dahlgren and Lincoln
1860–1861

The fact that power did not accompany renown rankled Dahlgren. While men such as Ingraham won accolades for a shining performance in a single moment, frustration still dogged Dahlgren despite years of hard work and self-sacrifice. Nevertheless, Dahlgren continued his quest for glory within his own bailiwick. Success, he came to believe, would require a reorganization of the Bureau of Ordnance and Hydrography. The friendship he developed with Abraham Lincoln early in the Civil War promised to aid him in his quest.

The Civil War is the central event in American history. No event has received more historical attention. Despite enormous literature on the topic, however, historians have been unable to agree upon why the Civil War happened in the first place. Some argue that it resulted from fundamental differences in American society, differences that were irreconcilable by any other means. Many see slavery as the root cause but disagree about the precise role it played. Others view the war as the result of a fundamental conflict between an industrial North and an agrarian South for control of the Union. The fact is that during the 1850s, events and issues such as the abolition of slavery, the emergence of the Republican party, "bleeding Kansas," the Sumner-Brooks incident, the financial panic of 1857, the Dred Scott case, and John Brown's raid on Harpers Ferry drove wedges of separation between the North and South. At the meeting of the Republican state convention at Springfield, Illinois, on 16 June 1858, Abraham Lincoln, whose own star was rising, struck a note that vibrated through the coming years: "'A house divided against itself cannot stand.' I believe this government cannot endure, permanently half *slave* and half *free*." Lincoln was no Garrisonian abolitionist, but he believed that slavery was an "unqualified evil to the negro, to the white man, to the soil, and to the State." Southerners, pointing to Lincoln's statements as evidence that the Republican party intended to make war upon slavery, asserted that Republican success in the election of 1860 would lead to secession. Northerners came to believe the abolitionist charge that the insatiable "slavocracy" would not be satisfied until slavery had been made legal in every state.[1]

From Dahlgren's perspective, storm clouds began to appear on the horizon near the end of 1859. A few days before Christmas he wrote Drayton:

> The mere *form* of Union may not disappear at this time, but it is certain that the good feeling which is in reality *the* Union has been sadly shocked, and the idea of separation more strongly impressed on the Southern mind than ever. It has always been my earnest wish never to live so long as to witness such an event, but to me Northern man as I am, there seems more danger of civil strife by keeping together than by [severing] the ties at once—: it is painful to entertain such a sentiment—But madness rules the hour and fanaticism stalks unrebuked in the North—hand in hand with blasphemy—God help them![2]

Dahlgren later expressed his views on slavery in a letter to Foote:

> As a system I find [slavery] permitted through the whole of the two dispensations [Testaments], and I cannot believe it would have escaped our Saviour's denunciation if a tithe were true that is *now* urged against it— It is also to be considered that this was the Slavery of white men, whereas with us it is the Slavery of an inferior race, developing resources of rich soils, which white men cannot work—The abuses of a system are no argument against the system itself—Uniforms cover cowards, Canonicals, hypocrisy and the highest places, shelter corruption and infamy—But you would not for that abolish these professions & institutions.... It is of no

use now to enquire who is to blame for the present troubles—But to endeavor to allay them in such a manner as to preserve the rights of all sections, under the Constitution. In so doing it is not to be forgotten that the North can yield more than the South, because the latter are exposed to a perilous liability in case their Negroes become excited.

Dahlgren had confidence that Abraham Lincoln, the lawyer from Springfield and Republican candidate for president in the upcoming election, could resolve the question of slavery peacefully. If not, Dahlgren believed, there would be war.[3]

On 6 November 1860 Lincoln was elected the sixteenth president of the United States. Dahlgren was enchanted by his "rail-splitter" image, so firmly established during the campaign. Born in a log cabin and raised on a farm, Lincoln never tried to disguise the country flavor of his manners and speech. In his accent, homespun turn of phrase, and way with people, he was the quintessential westerner, careless of ceremony and endowed with a charming sense of humor. His lanky frame, spindly legs, weather-beaten face, unruly hair, and firm but cautious stride suggested the American pioneer.[4]

Lincoln had received only a sprinkling of popular votes in the South. On 20 December, South Carolina seceded from the Union. This event troubled Dahlgren deeply. He wrote his son Ulric, "It may do for old fogies to argue the abstract right of secession but practical men will deal with facts, and when the danger is imminent must see how it is to be avoided peaceably. No American with the feelings of a man can fail to regard the present crisis with the deepest solicitude." On Christmas Eve, 1860, he wrote Ulric:

> I have a good opportunity of noting the current of feeling as well as of events. Most of the prominent men I know intimately. One evening I pass with a Northern Senator and hear the Republican view—no trepidation—no misgiving, but he & his friends behold the coming tempest with firm hearts. Some[times] I spend the evening with a Southern extremist;—Tombs [Robert Toombs] and Jeff Davis &c are there—as I am perhaps the only outsider [to whom] they speak freely—the question in all its bearing is treated without the least temper or disrespect to the other side. But so decidedly that all hope seems to vanish.[5]

During January and February 1861, Mississippi, Florida, Alabama, Georgia, Louisiana, and Texas joined South Carolina in secession. On 4 February a convention of the seven states met in Montgomery, Alabama.

Abraham Lincoln, circa 1862 (Library of Congress)

Three days later they adopted a provisional constitution for the Confederate States of America.

As the stars dropped from the constitutional firmament, to paraphrase his expression for secession, Dahlgren resolved to do whatever his country asked of him. On 9 January he wrote a friend that Washington was "likely to be the scene of a row.... A number of ugly-looking customers are to be seen about the streets. No one knows whence they came or on what errand, but like stormy petrels they are generally seen in advance of trouble." Nine days later he wrote Drayton:

> It is to be hoped that Providence will not punish the madness of the hour by allowing madness to desolate their prosperous & happy land with fire & sword—But difficult as a peaceable solution seems, I do not despair of it. For myself I think & care little[, for I have reached] the great purposes of [my] life…, and I am almost indifferent to its termination.

Dahlgren was a Northern man and a Union man who intended to do his duty, even if it meant glorious death.[6]

In January rumors ran rampant that the Confederates would try to seize the capital. Officials made plans for defense, but without coordinating their ideas, actions, or resources. On the eighth, Buchanan told Dahlgren of a rumor that a mob might try to seize the arms stored at the Washington Navy Yard to prevent Lincoln's inauguration. He ordered Dahlgren to prepare defenses in secret. The yard was not to be surrendered without orders from the secretary of the navy. In the event of an attack, it was to be defended "to the last extremity." If the defenses seemed about to be overwhelmed, the magazine and armory should be blown up. Dahlgren placed eight howitzers, eight hundred small arms, and the yard's ammunition supply in the attic of the main building, turning it into a fortress.[7]

While awaiting the rumored attack, Dahlgren tried to railroad several measures through Congress. On 11 February he appealed directly to Freeman H. Morse, chairman of the House Naval Affairs Committee, and James W. Grimes, chairman of the Senate Naval Affairs Committee, to authorize trials of ordnance against armor. He also recommended construction of an armored warship. In the same letters he proposed drastic changes in the organization of the navy, changes that reached far beyond simply reorganizing the Bureau of Ordnance and Hydrography. He called for the abolition of the bureau system, "which has failed utterly," and recommended replacing it with a board of admiralty consisting of at least five captains or commanders, no doubt with a view toward occupying one of the berths himself. Congress, obviously preoccupied with the crisis of the Union, took no action on any of these proposals at that time, deepening Dahlgren's frustration.[8]

The crisis, meanwhile, kept worsening. Dahlgren noted without comment that the "Cotton States" had "confederated" and had elected Jefferson Davis as their president. A friend, depressed about the state of the country, shot himself with a pistol Dahlgren had lent him. On 4 March, Dahlgren attended Lincoln's inauguration, which went off without the rumored attack.[9]

The next month Dahlgren met the new president. On 3 April he attended the wedding of Franklin Buchanan's daughter. Lincoln was there too. Dahlgren was introduced to him. The president took Dahlgren's hand in both of his. They conversed for half an hour. Dahlgren noted in his diary that the wedding was "a very brilliant party." Brilliant, perhaps, like the last rays of light on a beautiful summer day. But the sun was about to set on an era. It was to be a bloody sunset.[10]

Within days the long-approaching conflict engulfed the United States. Quiet had rested on the banks of the Potomac for a month following Lincoln's inauguration. Tension rose in early April when it became apparent that the Lincoln administration had decided to resupply Forts Pickens and Sumter. Gideon Welles, Lincoln's secretary of the navy, instructed all officers in the Navy Department and at the navy yards in Washington and Norfolk to prepare for the possible secession of Virginia. Welles suspected that some of the senior naval officers, including Maury, Magruder, and Buchanan, planned to resign their commissions if Virginia seceded.[11]

Events moved quickly. On the evening of 13 April, Washington learned via the telegraph that Fort Sumter had surrendered. The next day Dahlgren noted "great excitement" in the city, with "people almost stunned by the news." On the fifteenth, Lincoln called upon the loyal states to supply seventy-five thousand militiamen to subdue what he now considered a rebellion. Four days later he proclaimed a blockade of the Southern ports. Dahlgren noted, "It has now leaked out that Virginia seceded…secretly, in order to grab the public property that is within her borders.… Every one believes too that a body of men are on the way to take Washington, and the alarm is intense." Rebel flags appeared over Alexandria; rumors spread of Confederate scouts on the bridge approaches to the district; and tales were told of mobs coming from Richmond, Baltimore, and even Harpers Ferry to sack the capital.[12]

DAHLGREN TAKES COMMAND OF THE WASHINGTON NAVY YARD

On 22 April, Dahlgren found himself in command of the Washington Navy Yard. At about ten that morning Welles's son came to his office with a note from the secretary. Dahlgren was ordered to "assume temporary command" and to "discharge all suspected persons upon satisfactory evidence of their disloyalty to the Government, and place the yard in the best possible state of defense." Soon afterward Buchanan sent for Dahlgren to show him his resignation. Dahlgren spent the day arming and fitting out the Potomac River steamers *Baltimore*, *Mount Vernon*, and *Philadelphia* and shoring up the land defenses. The next day Buchanan assembled the men and formally turned command over to Dahlgren.[13]

Dahlgren was the most senior officer assigned to the yard who did not "go South." As he later put it in a book about his son Ulric:

For quickly, upon the secession of the border States [Virginia, Arkansas, Tennessee, and North Carolina], the officers of the Washington Navy Yard, who happened to belong to them, abandoned their duty, to join the standards of what they considered their paramount allegiance; and the command of the most important position thereby devolved upon Captain Dahlgren, who alone remained faithful to his trust.

Command fell to him because he was in the right place at the right time.[14]

Dahlgren shone in the new job. As a military position, Washington had no natural strength; it was vulnerable from every side. Lincoln's call for volunteers on 15 April had fanned the flames of secession in Maryland. For a time the capital stood isolated from the North, with Confederate territory threatening to encircle the city. Rebels severed telegraph lines and burned railroad bridges north of Baltimore. Business in the district came to a virtual standstill. Dahlgren at first had only about 150 men at his command. Tension eased on 25 April with the arrival of the Seventh New York Regiment. The next morning the Eighth Massachusetts and portions of the First Rhode Island arrived. The Seventy-first New York marched into the Washington Navy Yard on 27 April, and within a few days four other units took up positions in the city. Dahlgren remained calm and worked hard, eat-

Union troops drilling at the Washington Navy Yard (Naval Historical Center)

ing and sleeping in a room across the hall from his office. His kindness and courtesy impressed the men of the Seventy-first. He fed and quartered the troops and commanded ships in ferrying soldiers, accompanying transports, and patrolling the Potomac. He also received important visitors, including Welles, Secretary of War Simon Cameron, and President Lincoln.[15]

Dahlgren worked furiously as commander of the Washington Navy Yard and Ordnance Establishment. Until 1863 the defense of the Potomac rested largely on the ships under his command. The small, unsung Potomac Flotilla kept the river open by removing mines, patrolling, and neutralizing Confederate shore batteries in Virginia. Dahlgren drove the ordnance department 'round the clock, lighting the shops with gas lights at night. The department turned out two hundred shells, twenty-five thousand percussion caps, and thirty-five thousand Minié and musket balls every day, besides casting, rifling, finishing, and mounting boat guns. Dahlgren also drilled men, improved the defenses of the yard, filled ordnance requisitions for naval vessels, tested gadgets made by private inventors, and monitored the production of heavy ordnance. He worked seven days a week.[16]

Newspaper reporters visited the yard during these hectic days. N. P. Willis, a reporter from the *Home Journal*, published a piece about Dahlgren, who, he noted, was "acknowledged throughout Europe to be the great master of the projectile science." Willis wrote:

> The great inventor is too famous a person to escape the usual penalty of pre-eminence, and he will forgive me, therefore, if I tell the public what it wishes to know of his *personnel*. He is a light complexioned man of perhaps forty years of age [he was fifty-one], slight and of medium height, pale and delicate-featured. His countenance is exceedingly thoughtful and modest, and expresses complete unconsciousness of being observed; while his eye is inevitably keen and his thin nostrils expand as he talks with a look of great enthusiasm. A practiced physiognomist would at once pick him out for a man of distinguished abilities, though his destructive branch of science would hardly be guessed under a demeanor so quiet and amiable.[17]

DAHLGREN AND LINCOLN

Dahlgren knew that he was rendering invaluable service as commander of the Washington Navy Yard and the Ordnance Establishment, and he brashly

Dahlgren as commandant of the Washington Navy Yard, circa 1862 (Naval Historical Center)

demanded a reward from the president. On 28 April he went to the White House and pointed out to Lincoln that Buchanan had deserted his post and had thrown down his commission as captain. He declared that in doing Buchanan's duty, he had earned the right to his commission. Lincoln seemed amenable to the demand but remarked that he must not go "across lots." The president was beginning to like this brash, efficient naval officer.[18]

Lincoln's lanky figure soon became a familiar sight at the Washington Navy Yard. The president came down to the yard on 9 May for a concert given by the Seventy-first to celebrate the easing of tension inside the capital. A thirty-four-gun salute heralded Lincoln's arrival. His carriage rolled up to the concert hall, a big storeroom decorated with banners. A crowd of over two hundred, including cabinet officials and top army and navy officers, listened to a musical program of marches and sentimental ballads.

There was much applause. After the concert Lincoln asked to see an 11-inch Dahlgren gun fired. Dahlgren took the president and his party on board the *Pensacola* to watch. The river sparkled in the sunlight of a springtime afternoon, and the water rippled gently under a fresh breeze from the northwest. The 11-incher, mounted ashore, was fired at a wooden target in the river. John Hay, one of Lincoln's private secretaries, described the occasion in his diary: "The splendid course of the 11-inch shell flying through 1300 yards of air, the lighting, the quick rebound, & flight through the target with wild skips, throwing up a 30 ft. column of spray at every jump, the decreasing leaps and steady roll into the waves were scenes as novel and pleasant to me as to all the rest of the party. The Prest. was delighted." Dahlgren too had noticed Lincoln's delight in the 11-incher and subsequently had a miniature Dahlgren gun made for the president's sons. The pleasant afternoon ended with the firing of a salute, then the presidential carriage rolled out through the Navy Yard gate to the tune of "Hail to the Chief," played by the Marine Band.[19]

Three days later the president dropped by the yard unexpectedly. There was no formal occasion this time; he simply wanted to visit. Dahlgren took him for a pleasant jaunt down the Potomac. On 18 May the president dropped by for another unannounced visit, this time ostensibly about ordnance business. In truth, Lincoln simply liked gadgets, weapons, and munitions, and these things abounded at the Washington Navy Yard. As he stepped out of Dahlgren's office, men were test-firing breechloading carbines nearby. The president walked over, picked up one of the pieces, and fired a shot. He found visiting the yard to be a relaxing diversion from the war.[20]

The somber circumstances of the president's next visit, however, reflected the stark reality of war. Early on the morning of 24 May, Major General Charles W. Sanford of the New York militia mounted a three-pronged Federal assault on the Virginia shore to secure Washington's defenses. Dahlgren commanded the ships that transported and supported the troops. Most of the Confederate defenders had evacuated, except for a small group that was soon captured. The only casualty was Lincoln's close friend, Colonel Elmer Ephraim Ellsworth of the New York Fire Zouaves. Ellsworth had tried to remove a secessionist banner from an Alexandria hotel. This action offended the proprietor of the establishment, who killed Ellsworth with a shotgun. An enlisted man promptly bayonetted the proprietor. Dahlgren, who had accompanied Ellsworth across the Potomac to Virginia, accompanied his body back to the capital on the same ship. He had Ellsworth laid out in a building at the yard. Lincoln came down and asked Dahlgren to accompany him to see the body. The death of a close friend saddened the president.[21]

But Lincoln had found a new friend in Dahlgren. "The President often comes to see the Yard," Dahlgren noted in his diary on 9 June, "and treats me without reserve." Percival Drayton noted that "the Navy Yard here seems a favourite lounging place of Old Abe and his wife, who are here almost every day." Sometimes Lincoln drove down to watch a new invention being tested, but more often he came just for coffee, cigars, and a chat with his favorite naval officer. He visited the yard almost every week during the first two years of the war and usually brought along cabinet members and other top officials. Dahlgren entertained them with food, drink, and shipboard jaunts down the Potomac. He was spending so much time with the president and his cabinet that Welles began to consider him a courtier. Lincoln relished Dahlgren's company and invited him to the White House often. For his part, Dahlgren genuinely enjoyed the company of the president. Their friendship soon became so close that it was nothing for the officer to drop in at the White House without an appointment. Lincoln grew closer to Dahlgren than to any other officer in the navy.

Dahlgren and the president had reached their positions along very different paths. Lincoln learned reading, writing, and arithmetic by firelight in a log cabin on the frontier. His father wanted him to be a farmer. Dahlgren learned Latin and mathematics at the better schools in a major city. His father wanted him to choose a field in the sciences. Lincoln held numerous jobs on his way to the White House: day laborer, flatboatman, clerk, lawyer, postmaster, politician. Dahlgren was first and foremost a naval officer, but one whose duties kept him ashore.

Their personalities differed as well. The president was quick with a joke and always ready to poke fun at himself. Dahlgren, quick to take offense at the slightest insult to his reputation, was as serious as Lincoln was jocular. He cared deeply about family and friends but was not someone to slap on the back and joke around with much.

But Dahlgren and Lincoln also had much in common. Both were born in 1809. Both read voraciously in their youth. The teetotaling Lincoln might have heard of Dahlgren's temperance cruise on the *Cumberland*. Like Dahlgren, Lincoln had worked as a surveyor. And both delighted in machinery. Lincoln loved machines, not simply as a rail splitter might love a circular saw but also as a mathematician loves a neat solution to an equation. During the 1850s, steam engines pounded and gas lights hissed in

Springfield. Ready-made clothes piled up on its counters while reapers clattered on the surrounding farms. Fascinated by these machines, Lincoln talked with inventors and read about inventions in the *Annual of Scientific Discovery*. His greatest success as a lawyer had come from his work with railroads, which brought him a greater understanding of the impact of technology on human life. During the course of his friendship with Dahlgren, which would span his presidency, he would learn about the technology of taking life.

Despite his growing perception of Dahlgren as a courtier, Secretary of the Navy Gideon Welles encouraged the friendship. Unofficially, Dahlgren served as the president's naval aide. Lincoln often sought his opinion on the latest military or naval development, not only in matters of hardware but also concerning operations. "I must see Dahl," the president was known to remark when considering naval operations. Lincoln also freely discussed plans and operations of the War Department with Dahlgren, who in turn passed the information along to Welles, who rarely received such information through official channels or from his colleagues in the cabinet.[22]

This friendship paid dividends at once. Toward the end of July 1861 several navy captains sought command of the Washington Navy Yard. They argued that Dahlgren was not legally entitled to the post because it was a captain's billet, and he was only a commander. The president would not hear of it. "The Yard shall not be taken from [Dahlgren]," said Lincoln; "he held it when no one else would, and now he shall keep it as long as he pleases." On 2 August, Congress amended the law so that Dahlgren could hold the post as a commander. Dahlgren called the vote "the best compliment I ever received."[23]

Dahlgren's "compliment" rankled other naval officers. "I had to serve twenty-two years at sea before I could get a navy yard," Du Pont wrote his wife; "now a commander who [has] not yet commanded a sloop of war is eligible." Du Pont disdained such "special legislation for individuals at the expense [of] all military propriety and justice." Dahlgren's peers were beginning to resent his relationship with Lincoln.[24]

On 5 August, Welles summoned Dahlgren to his office and offered him command of the Bureau of Ordnance and Hydrography. George Magruder had gone to Canada after a period of agonized indecision over his own allegiance, leaving the bureau temporarily headless. Dahlgren declined Welles's offer on the spot. The job entailed too much administration, he explained; he preferred experimental work. At Dahlgren's recommendation, Welles gave the chief post to Dahlgren's friend Andrew A. Harwood, who took care of the administrative side of the house and deferred to Dahlgren in technical matters.

What Dahlgren really wanted was what every naval officer wanted most: a promotion. After the chat with Welles he dropped by the State Department to raise the subject with Secretary of State William Seward. Seward spoke to Lincoln about it and later that afternoon told Dahlgren that he would be given the next available vacancy. "I will make a Captain of Dahlgren," Lincoln said to Welles on 15 November, "as soon as you say there is a place." The president expressed the desire to promote Dahlgren on other occasions, but Welles consistently opposed it. The secretary did not want the shadow of favoritism to darken his department. Nevertheless, Dahlgren had gained a powerful ally in the president.[25]

Meanwhile, Dahlgren arranged his personal life to allow full concentration on his duties. Since Mary's death in 1855 he had lived in the house on 4½ Street with his sister Patty, who helped him raise his children. His sons Charles and Ulric spent a lot of time at the Washington Navy Yard, studying quietly in their father's office and swimming and rowing in the Anacostia River with "ordnance seamen." When the Civil War broke out, Dahlgren sent his sister and daughter to Wilmington, Delaware, so that he "might have mind and body free to do my own duty fully and free from all personal considerations." But Patty preferred Washington and soon returned to the house on 4½ Street. Accordingly, Dahlgren took up residence in the commandant's house at the yard. He moved back to 4½ Street in the summer of 1862.[26]

By night, Dahlgren lived the life of a Washington insider. He moved easily in the highest circles. He spent many evenings at formal state dinners or informal gatherings of top government officials and foreign dignitaries. A typical entry from his diary, dated Thursday, 26 September 1861, reads:

> The fast day proclaimed by the President,—the first day in which there has been a suspension of labor in this Yard since I took the command.
>
> The Prince de Joinville is here with other French Princes;—so there are some dinners &c. On Monday a party at Lisboa's the Brazilian Minister,—Tuesday, dinner at Secr. of State's, where we had besides de Joinville, the Count of Paris heir to the French throne and the Duke de Chartres his brother. Gen. McClellan was present: the party at Lisboa's was an exhibition of the melancholy wreck of our social circle,—only half a dozen ladies could be mustered.

Yesterday I dined at the President's with some of his friends,—the only notability there was Mr. Holt, late Secretary of War to Buchanan.... Hannah (Mrs Paul) is here with me for a few days. In the evening, I took her to the Sec. of State's,—we talked with the ladies, and were soon joined by the French Princes and Mr. Seward: then came in the President and we had a very chatty evening.[27]

Dahlgren was no stranger to cabinet officials, senators, and congressmen. He lived his life in daily contact with America's political power elite. He knew the trend-setters of his day. He himself was one of them. And he had forged the ultimate political tool: a friendship with President Lincoln. Although he had not deliberately sought Lincoln's friendship to further his quest for glory, he would not hesitate to use it for that purpose as their friendship grew.

In January 1862 Lincoln asked Dahlgren's opinion about the organization of the ordnance bureau. Dahlgren replied that the chief should have an assistant to handle the administrative end so that he could focus his attention on research and development. Lincoln tacitly understood these as being Dahlgren's conditions for accepting the post as chief with Henry Wise as his assistant. He forwarded Dahlgren's recommendations to Senator John Hale, the chairman of the Senate Naval Affairs Committee. Hale included them in a bill to reorganize the Navy Department into eight bureaus, which he introduced into Congress on 24 January.[28]

Dahlgren must have been ecstatic. It seemed that the Bureau of Ordnance and Hydrography would be reorganized according to his wishes after all. Being the chief yet remaining free to do R&D would be a fitting reward for his hard work and self-sacrifice as an innovator.

But power to shape the future of American naval ordnance would elude him. While Congress was debating the proposed reorganization of the Navy Department, the Confederates were converting the *Merrimack* into an ironclad warship. In the process they were transforming the showplace for Dahlgren's ordnance into its nemesis.

14

Monitor versus *Virginia*
February 1861–March 1862

"Every American schoolboy knows the story of the historic battle between the *Merrimac* and the *Monitor*," wrote historian Bernard Brodie in his classic *Sea Power in the Machine Age*.[1] It was the first battle between armored warships in history. For Dahlgren, the event had disquieting import. The famous duel between the *Monitor* and *Virginia* on 9 March 1862 proved his gun inadequate against armored ships.

THE UNION NAVY

The slugfest at Hampton Roads occurred against the backdrop of the blockade of the Confederacy. Establishing and maintaining the blockade was the Union navy's primary task during the Civil War. Since the Confederate coast extended some 3,400 miles from the Chesapeake Bay to the Mexican border, the Union needed a large fleet. On 4 March 1861 the navy had only thirty old sailing vessels and twelve relatively new steam warships in commission, with several more building. By the end of the Civil War the fleet had ballooned in size to 670 vessels, ranging from East River ferryboats to ironclads. Between 1861 and 1865 the number of officers rose from 1,300 to

Gideon Welles (Naval Historical Center)

6,700, the number of men increased from 7,500 to 51,500, and annual expenditures skyrocketed from $12 million to $123 million.[2]

Secretary of the Navy Gideon Welles presided over this greatly expanded fleet. A politician with no naval experience save for a brief stint as chief of the Bureau of Provisions and Clothing (1846–49), Welles was an excellent administrator. He seemed modest and unassuming, but he vigorously asserted the navy's policies inside Lincoln's cabinet, and within the Navy Department he took a businesslike approach to administration. He was an unusually good judge of character and generally chose well in filling naval command billets. Never brilliant, he was always competent, faithful, and honest.[3]

Assistant Secretary Gustavus Vasa Fox was an equally important figure in the Navy Department during the Civil War. Fox served in the navy and merchant marine for eighteen years before resigning in 1856 to accept a position as a business agent. In May 1861 he rejoined the department when Welles appointed him chief clerk. Fox became the navy's first assistant secretary in

Gustavus Vasa Fox (Naval Historical Center)

July, and not long afterward he took over direction of naval operations. He was often genial, but he could also be autocratic, ruthless, and vindictive. Naval officers liked him because he could communicate with them in navy parlance, and most of them had known him for years. The Lincolns also liked Fox. Welles encouraged Fox's close relations with the president for the same reason he encouraged Dahlgren's friendship with Lincoln, for Fox told Welles what he learned from the president about the goings-on in the War Department. Fox was a man of action, but he shied away from the study, planning, and follow-through that operations required. Instead he preferred plans that seemed to offer easy solutions. After the successes at New Orleans and Port Royal, he became so sure of himself that he would neither take advice nor brook resistance. He was wont to rewrite orders from Welles to bureau chiefs and sign his own name to them.[4] Welles ascribed this behavior to Fox's need to be a man "of authority."[5] Fox shunned interservice cooperation even when sound strategy demanded it, because he believed that the navy never received due credit in joint operations. "I feel my duty is two fold," he wrote to one naval officer, "first to beat our Southern friends; second to beat the Army."[6] Fox made as many enemies as friends. He also made many grievous errors.

Abraham Lincoln pretty much allowed Welles and Fox to run their own show. As a matter of course the secretary and assistant secretary consulted the president when undertaking major operations, but Lincoln rarely intervened in naval affairs, in sharp contrast to how he handled the War Department. Welles and Fox remained at the helm for the duration of the Civil War.[7]

The *Virginia*

The Confederacy had no navy at all at the outset of the war and had to improvise one from scratch. On 20 February 1861 the Confederate congress established the Confederate States Navy. The next day Jefferson Davis appointed Stephen R. Mallory, former Senate Naval Affairs Committee chairman, as the Confederacy's secretary of the navy. Although Mallory intended to purchase cruisers abroad and use them against Northern commerce, he viewed harbor and river defense as the Confederate navy's primary mission.[8]

The early capture of the Gosport Navy Yard in Norfolk, the country's biggest, proved a great windfall to the Confederacy. The Norfolk yard had deepwater wharves, large dry docks, and an industrial plant. It held some three hundred cannon, fifty of which were 9-inch Dahlgren guns. On 20 April 1861, Union forces partially destroyed the yard's facilities to prevent them from falling into Confederate hands. They burned five ships to their waterlines; four of these, including the *Merrimack,* sank. The Confederates distributed captured guns to ships and forts throughout the South.[9]

In the time-honored American tradition, the Confederate navy attempted to compensate for numerical inferiority with qualitative superiority. On 30 May 1861 the Confederates raised the *Merrimack* and began converting her into the ironclad ram *Virginia.* Her upper works had burned, but her lower hull and machinery remained in fairly serviceable condition. Shipwrights rebuilt her charred hull up to the level of the berth deck and added a massive 4-foot-long cast-iron ram to the bow. They built a casemate of 20-inch pine, sheathed with 4 inches of oak planking and armored with 4 inches of iron, atop her deck. The casemate sloped at an angle of 36 degrees, to cause enemy shots to ricochet. The *Virginia* carried six 9-inch Dahlgren guns and four Brooke rifles, converted from 32-pounders. Her engines had been condemned by the prewar navy and slated for replacement; their saltwater soaking had not helped. The *Virginia's* 22-foot draft prevented her from operating in shallow water, while her unseaworthiness prevented her from standing out to the open sea. Nevertheless, the *Virginia* inspired hope in the South and caused consternation in the North. The Confederate navy commissioned the *Virginia* on 17 February 1862. Captain Franklin Buchanan, Dahlgren's old boss, took command of her. Mallory ordered Buchanan to take the *Virginia* past Old Point and ascend the Potomac to Washington to strike fear into the "public mind."[10]

THE UNION IRONCLAD PROGRAM

The Union initially launched its own ironclad program in response to developments in Europe. On 26 June 1861 Dahlgren reported to Welles that Britain was building nine ironclads. France had the *Gloire* and was building thirteen other ironclads. In July, Welles informed Congress of Dahlgren's report. Early in August, Congress appropriated $1.5 million for the "construction or completion of iron or steelclad steamers or steam batteries." Welles published an advertisement for contractors to submit plans and appointed Commodore Joseph Smith, Commodore Hiram Paulding, and

Commander Charles H. Davis to the "ironclad board" study them. On 16 September, after examining numerous proposals submitted by private contractors, the board recommended construction of the *Monitor, Galena,* and *New Ironsides.* The board's report indicated that these vessels would be used for coast defense, river service, and passing fortifications. The *Galena* and *New Ironsides* carried guns in traditional broadside mounts.[11]

The *Monitor,* designed by John Ericsson, was a radical ship. Instead of a standard ship's hull, the *Monitor* had a 172-foot-long overhanging armored raft supported by a lower section measuring 122 feet in length. The entire hull was made of iron and floated with less than 2 feet of freeboard. The ship featured numerous innovations, including forced-draft ventilation and a protected anchor. But the most important innovation was a revolving centerline turret, 20 feet in diameter, 9 feet high, encased in 8 inches of armor, and housing two 11-inch Dahlgren guns. The *Monitor*'s turret, 11-foot draft, and 7-knot speed gave her maneuverability and versatility. Nevertheless, many naval officers condemned her as a "cheesebox on a raft" and "Ericsson's folly." Early in March 1862 the navy dispatched the *Monitor,* the first Union ironclad completed, to Hampton Roads.[12]

THE BATTLE OF HAMPTON ROADS

Meanwhile, rumors circulated in Washington that the Confederates had finished converting the *Merrimack* into an ironclad warship. On Saturday, 8 March 1862, Fox and Henry Wise went to Old Point to see whether there was any truth to these rumors. At eleven that morning, to the cheers of crowds gathered on nearby wharves, the *Virginia* cast off and steamed down the Elizabeth River toward Hampton Roads.[13]

Five Union ships mounting a total of 219 guns guarded the mouth of the James River at Hampton Roads: the *Minnesota, Roanoke, St. Lawrence, Congress,* and *Cumberland.* The last three were sailing ships. The first two were *Merrimack*-class steam frigates, at that time the navy's most powerful class of oceangoing ships. The blockaders swung gently at their anchors, unaware of the *Virginia*'s approach. A storm had just passed, and the weather was clear and bright. Washed clothes hung on the lines.

At one o'clock the *Virginia* emerged from the mouth of the Elizabeth River. An officer on board the *Congress* spotted her through his spyglass. "That *Thing* is coming down!" he shouted. The Confederate ironclad stood

CSS *Virginia* sinks USS *Cumberland,* Hampton Roads, 8 March 1862 (Beverley Robinson Collection, United States Naval Academy Museum)

first for the *Cumberland,* firing several shells into her side before ramming her and sending her to the bottom. Meanwhile, the *Congress* and *Cumberland* fired broadside after broadside, which "struck and glanced off" the *Virginia,* in the words of a Northern observer, "having no more effect than peas from a pop-gun."[14] Then the *Virginia* went after the *Congress.* The commanding officer of the doomed Union ship was Joseph B. Smith, Commodore Joseph Smith's son. The *Virginia* raked her with broadsides and set her afire. The *Congress* struck. When Commodore Smith heard of the surrender, he said, "Then Joe is dead." He was right; young Joseph was killed before the *Congress* surrendered. But the Confederates never took possession of her. The fires eventually reached the powder magazine and blew up the *Congress.* The *Minnesota* ran aground, preventing the deep-draft Confederate craft from closing. The *Virginia* threw a few shells into the *Minnesota* and drew off as night fell. Not until the Japanese attack on Pearl Harbor, seventy-nine years later, would the United States Navy endure losses of such magnitude in a single day.[15]

An officer on board the *Congress* described the effects of the Confederate ironclad's gunfire:

One of her shells dismounted an eight-inch gun and either killed or wounded every one of the gun's crew, while the slaughter at the other guns was fearful. There were comparatively few wounded, the fragments of the huge shells she threw killing outright as a general thing. Our clean and handsome gun deck was in an instant changed into a slaughter-pen, with lopped off legs and arms and bleeding, blackened bodies scattered about by the shells.... One poor fellow had his chest transfixed by a splinter of oak as thick as the wrist, but the shell wounds were even worse.

The *Virginia*'s shell guns were brutally effective against the wooden ships. About 241 of the 810 officers and men on board the *Congress* and *Cumberland* died. Return fire had little effect on the *Virginia*. An observer on shore noted that projectiles fired by the *Congress* "rattled on the armored *Merrimack* without the least injury." The pilot of the *Cumberland* noted that the shells fired by his own ship bounced off the *Virginia*'s armored casemate "like India-rubber balls." The Confederate ironclad suffered only two killed.[16]

Word of the *Virginia*'s debut reached Washington early the next morning. Dahlgren sat in his office at the Washington Navy Yard, regretting that he had not gone to church. When Lincoln arrived at 10:30, Dahlgren went outside to greet him. "Frightful news," said the president, then told Dahlgren about the catastrophe at Hampton Roads. Lincoln worried that the *Virginia* might ascend the Potomac to bombard the capital. Dahlgren said that the river must be blocked if the *Virginia* attempted to ascend to Washington.

The president then drove Dahlgren to the White House in his carriage. Upon arriving, they entered Lincoln's private room. Welles, Seward, Secretary of War Edwin M. Stanton, Lincoln's private secretary John G. Nicolay, Quartermaster General Montgomery C. Meigs, Major General George McClellan, and the assistant secretary of war were already there. Dahlgren noted that "there was a hasty and very promiscuous emission of opinion from every one without much regard to rank." Meigs remained despondent and silent. McClellan expressed concern about the troops at Newport News. Seward seemed perfectly composed. Stanton paced back and forth, his eyes glued to Welles. The secretary of war feared that the *Virginia* would destroy every Union vessel and every city on the coast, then steam to Washington, disperse Congress, and destroy the capitol and other public buildings. Welles told him that the *Monitor* had just arrived at Hampton

Roads and expressed confidence in her ability to resist and perhaps even overcome the *Virginia*. Stanton derived no comfort from the fact that the *Monitor* carried only two guns. He and Lincoln went repeatedly to the window to see if the *Virginia* was steaming up the river. Dahlgren doubted that the *Virginia* could come that far, her 22-foot draft being too deep for her to cross Kettle Bottom Shoals. He suggested dispatching the *Wabash* to Hampton Roads, posting a steamer at the mouth of the Potomac to send word if the *Virginia* appeared, and making preparations to block the river. Lincoln directed Dahlgren, McClellan, and Meigs to do the last.[17]

Dahlgren left the White House at about two and returned to the yard. He spent the rest of the afternoon piecing together what had happened at the Roads from five military telegrams and a full account written by a newspaper reporter.

Just as he finished eating dinner, Seward and Stanton arrived. Dahlgren took them down the river in a steamer to see where the *Virginia* might appear. Stanton gave Dahlgren full authority to command army soldiers and cannon to defend the river and ordered him to obstruct the channel with sixty canal boats laden with stone. They returned to the yard. At nine Dahlgren telegraphed both Lincoln and Welles that he had begun to place obstructions as ordered and had established batteries at narrow points along the river.[18]

An hour later, Dahlgren learned that the *Monitor* had fought the *Virginia* to a standstill. Fox had wired the message over the recently completed telegraph line from Fort Monroe to Washington. The *Monitor* had arrived at Hampton Roads on the night of 8 March, her way lighted by the burning *Congress*. When the Confederate ironclad appeared the next morning to finish off the wooden blockaders, the *Monitor* engaged her. For two hours the two ironclads hammered away at each other, hull to hull, fighting at such close range that five times the two ships collided, as the men inside, half-blinded by smoke, loaded and fired, loaded and fired. Neither ship inflicted serious damage on the other. The *Virginia* retired at noon.[19]

At two the next morning Welles wired Dahlgren to stop placing obstructions in the river. Eight hours later, Dahlgren, Welles, Stanton, and other cabinet members and Wise, who had just arrived from Hampton Roads, met with Lincoln. Wise gave a spirited account of the two-day battle. It did not alleviate Stanton's fears. Affecting calm but in a voice trembling with emotion, Stanton asked Welles if he had countermanded the order to obstruct the Potomac. Welles said yes, arguing that it was important to keep com-

Monitor versus *Virginia,* Hampton Roads, 9 March 1862 (Beverley Robinson Collection, United States Naval Academy Museum)

munications open. Stanton blustered, but the president accepted Welles's judgment. Dahlgren then asked Welles to place him in command of the *Monitor,* since her skipper, Captain John L. Worden, had been wounded during the duel. Welles refused, telling him that he would be of more use in Washington.[20]

THE SECOND ORDNANCE CRISIS

Stanton's panic and fear were symptomatic of the flood of emotions unleashed by the *Virginia*'s appearance. William H. Parker, who had commanded the Confederate gunboat *Beaufort* during the battle of Hampton Roads, recalled:

Upon our return to Norfolk, which was on Sunday, March 9th, the whole city was alive with joy and excitement. Nothing was talked of but the *Merrimac* and what she had accomplished. As to what she could do in the future, no limit was set to her powers. The papers indulged in the wildest speculations, and everybody went mad, as usual. At the North the same fever prevailed. No battle that was ever fought caused as great a sensation throughout the civilized world. The moral effect at the North was most marvelous; and even now I can scarcely realize it. The people of New York and Washington were in hourly expectation of the *Merrimac's* appearance off those cities, and I suppose were ready to yield at the first summons. At the South it was expected that she would take Fortress Monroe when she again went out.[21]

Dahlgren perceived Hampton Roads as a watershed. "The *defence* has been gradually making slow way against ordnance," he noted. "But the events of this day will definitively shape the future in such matters.... Now comes the reign of iron—and cased ships are to take the place of wooden ships."[22]

The battle of Hampton Roads heralded a revolution in naval architecture that eventually spelled the doom of wooden fleets. It also represented a victory of armor over the gun. During the duel between the ironclads the concussion of projectiles striking the *Virginia's* sides causing bleeding from the crew's noses and ears. Three men inside the turret of the *Monitor* who were leaning against the wall were stunned when a Confederate projectile struck the outside, but no one in the turret was seriously injured. Another of the *Virginia's* shells exploded directly outside the *Monitor's* pilothouse, partially raising its heavy iron cover and driving powder fragments into Worden's eyes as he peered through the narrow vision slit. A gunner in the *Virginia,* when asked why he had momentarily ceased firing, replied that he could do as much damage to the *Monitor* by snapping his fingers every three minutes. No one on board either ironclad died during the slugfest, in stark contrast to the carnage on the *Congress* and *Cumberland* the previous day. The battle of the ironclads seemed to demonstrate that the 9-inch Dahlgren guns on the *Virginia* and the 11-inch Dahlgren guns on the *Monitor,* the Union navy's most powerful cannon, were virtually useless against armor. Dahlgren's second ordnance crisis had arrived.[23]

15

The Last Straw
March–July 1862

The battle of Hampton Roads revealed a need for further innovation in naval weaponry. Despite Dahlgren's unparalleled international reputation, Gustavus V. Fox, a man without ordnance expertise of any kind, took it upon himself to initiate development of cannon he deemed capable of destroying Confederate ironclads. For Dahlgren, Fox's interference in his bailiwick was the last straw. He finally realized that the navy would never empower him to determine the future shape of naval ordnance unfettered. Sea service remained the true path to glory and power; being an internationally acclaimed ordnance expert was simply no substitute for old-fashioned heroic feats of combat. Therefore, Dahlgren sought a new berth where he could win glory.

FOX AND THE SOLUTION TO CONFEDERATE IRONCLADS

Fox and Henry Wise spent the morning of 9 March 1862 in a tugboat at Hampton Roads, with ringside seats for the historic encounter between the *Monitor* and *Virginia*. When the battle ended, they boarded the *Monitor* to congratulate Captain John Worden, who lay bleeding on a couch in his cabin.

201

Fifteen-inch Rodman gun at Battery Rodgers, Alexandria, Virginia (National Archives)

"Have I beat her off?" asked Worden. "Jack! You have saved your country," replied Wise. Fox shared Wise's enthusiasm. Fox thought that the ironclad duel was the greatest naval battle on record. He considered the *Monitor* a "gem." In his passion over what he perceived as a clear-cut victory for the Union contestant, he became a devoted Ericsson disciple. But Fox realized that the *Virginia* had not been materially damaged. "Our present calibres," he noted, "are entirely inadequate to destroy such vessels." Stepping ashore at Fort Monroe, he saw a 15-inch gun that had been designed by army ordnance expert Thomas J. Rodman. Right then and there, Fox decided that it was the answer for combating armored warships. "We must have more of these Boats [monitors]," he wired Dahlgren two days later, "with fifteen inch guns."[1]

Fox's ardor for monitors reflected popular opinion in the North. After his first trip ashore following the duel, Frederick Keeler, the *Monitor*'s paymaster, wrote, "You cannot conceive of the feeling[;]...the *Monitor* is on every one's tongue & the expressions of gratitude & joy embarrassed us they are so numerous.... It was told from one to another as I passed along—'he's an officer from the *Monitor*'—& they looked at me as if I was some strange being." The *Monitor* drew crowds of visitors when she arrived in Washington for repairs. Ericsson became immensely popular both in the North and in his native Sweden. Journalists promoted the *Monitor* as an unsurpassed new weapon. Poets, government authorities, soldiers, sailors, and the civilian public began to consider the ironclad as a tool for achieving victory. Fox was convinced that the *Monitor* was a superweapon.[2]

The *Monitor* craze inspired the Union navy to build a fleet of turreted ironclads. On 25 March, Welles asked Congress to increase the appropriation for ironclads from $12 million to $30 million. Ericsson was in such high favor that he and his associates obtained contracts for six of the ten previously planned *Passaic*-class ironclads, which were larger, improved versions of the original *Monitor*.[3] Welles had little trouble selling monitors to Congress, for they were cheap, novel, and perceived as successful. The *Passaic* was commissioned on 25 November 1862. Most of the ships in her class had been launched by the spring of 1863.[4]

DAHLGREN AND THE 15-INCH GUN

Characteristically, Fox had decided on impulse to arm the *Passaic* class with 15-inch guns. In a letter to Ericsson he wrote that Dahlgren secured the trunnions to his guns by means of straps, and that the trunnions could therefore be shifted to any position. He apparently did not know that Dahlgren used trunnion straps only on rifles. He obviously had no idea of the importance of trunnion location to the preponderance of a gun.[5] In fact, he had little understanding of ordnance at all.[6]

On 17 March 1862 Dahlgren received orders to design 15- and 20-inch guns for the new monitors. The next day Fox, Secretary of State Seward, Secretary of War Stanton, and Dahlgren took a cruise to Alexandria to visit General McClellan, who was preparing the Army of the Potomac for a march on Richmond from a landing point on the peninsula between the York and James Rivers. The men chatted about ordnance over a bottle of champagne. "15^{in} were nothing," Dahlgren sarcastically noted of the conversation, "20 at least & He of War suggested a 30^{in}[.] Go it—The National Team has run off—& stand clear."[7]

Dahlgren opposed Fox's hasty decision to produce a 15-incher. Although Dahlgren had never tested ordnance against armor, Fox conceived the gun for use against armored vessels. "A subject so important cannot be perfected with out much reflection and extensive experiment," Dahlgren wrote Harwood on 19 March. "But we lack almost the preliminary information

USS *Passaic* (Naval Historical Center)

indispensable to commence with. We do not know what size and kind of projectiles are needed to pierce, dislocate or dislodge iron plates of different thicknesses placed perpendicularly or obliquely to the blow."[8]

Fox had chosen the 15-inch gun without considering doctrine for ordnance against armor. During the Civil War two opposing schools of thought arose as to the best means of destroying armored warships. The "racking" school held that projectiles should smash against the ship, distributing the force of the blow along the whole side and dislocating the armor. Once the armor had been shaken off, the vessel would be vulnerable to shellfire. The "punching" school held that the projectile should penetrate the armor, showering the ship's interior with deadly splinters in the process. Once inside, it would bounce around, wreaking general havoc. The debate raged around questions of rifled and smooth bores, heavy and light projectiles, high and low muzzle velocities, and the strain on the gun produced by various projectile weights and powder charges. Neither American nor European ordnance experts resolved these questions during the war. In contrast, Dahlgren had fully worked out the doctrine for the 9- and 11-inch guns before the navy adopted them.[9]

Fox had also chosen the 15-incher without reference to metallurgical or ballistic principles. Dahlgren lacked data on the endurance and safety of so large a caliber. He did not know whether a cast-iron cannon could be made strong enough to endure the strain of repeatedly firing 15-inch projectiles.

Furthermore, Dahlgren entertained doubts about the method used to cast the 15-incher that Fox had seen at Fort Monroe.[10] The method had been devised by the United States Army's premier ordnance expert, Thomas J. Rodman. His method involved casting guns on a hollow core through which water circulated, cooling the interior as rapidly as possible. The idea of hollow casting was not new, but the water-cooling idea and the rationale behind the method were. Hollow casting was to Rodman guns what cylinder casting was to Dahlgren guns: a successful attempt to increase the endurance and safety of cannon by increasing their internal uniformity.

Rodman had graduated from the Military Academy in 1841 and was commissioned in the ordnance corps. He had developed his method in the wake of the Peacemaker disaster. In 1847 he worked out a business agreement with Charles Knap of the Fort Pitt Foundry, trading his patent on hollow casting for the resources needed to perfect the method. During the 1850s Rodman ran a series of experiments in which he cast guns from the same metal in pairs, one by his method and the other solid. He then compared the endurances of the pairs in extreme proof. During these experiments he found that the model 1844 columbiads were structurally weak, a finding reinforced by their poor performance in proof in 1855. Rodman consequently developed model 1858 and model 1861 columbiads. All were coastal artillery pieces; the model 1861 appeared in 8-, 10-, 13-, 15-, and 20-inch calibers. They were all commonly known as Rodman guns.

In 1859 Secretary of War John B. Floyd ordered that all army guns be cast by Rodman's method. The order included a provision that the army ordnance bureau pay Knap, the holder of the patent, a 20 percent royalty on all guns cast by Rodman's technique. Tredegar's ironmaster refused to adopt the Rodman method. The founders at the West Point Foundry, Alger and Company, and the Bellona Foundry resisted hollow casting at first but later admitted that it was an improved technique.[11]

Dahlgren had learned of Rodman's work in 1851, when Warrington sent an assistant inspector to Pittsburgh to observe and report on Rodman's experiments. Dahlgren had read these reports during his study of metallurgy prior to the crisis of 1855. In the spring of 1856 he had two boat howitzers cast hollow, then tested their strength. He concluded that Rodman's casting technique was inferior to his own.[12]

Despite his objections, Dahlgren followed orders and began designing a 15-inch gun. But he made it clear to Harwood, the ordnance chief, that he regarded the 15-incher as an interim weapon for use against armored vessels. He recommended experimenting with armor and ordnance to determine the best type of projectile "to pierce injure or destroy plates of the thickness in use or likely to be used," and to base the ultimate caliber of the anti-armor gun on the projectile that performed the best. He did not foresee the coming race between armor and ordnance.[13]

Harwood, eager to follow Dahlgren's advice, wrote Dahlgren that he would "listen with the deference due to your experience to every suggestion you may make." Dahlgren thereupon recommended that he order the 15-inch guns from the Fort Pitt Foundry, where Rodman's 15-incher had been produced. Harwood complied, ordering fifty of them on 20 March. Although Dahlgren finally answered to a bureau chief who recognized his expertise, it was vexing to him that Fox was not so pliable.[14]

THE DAHLGREN-RODMAN DISPUTE

Dahlgren had another personal reason for resisting a 15-inch navy gun. The only 15-incher then in existence was an army weapon, a columbiad, a Rodman gun. The proud and vain Dahlgren did not wish to appear to be following in anyone's footsteps, particularly Rodman's, for there was bad blood between the two.

Their dispute was rooted in the ordnance crisis of 1855. In July of that year, during the period between the failures of the recently cast model 1844 columbiads and his own 9-inchers, Dahlgren drew up a proposition for replacing the model 1844 columbiads with his 11-inch guns. He showed Jefferson Davis, then secretary of war, drawings of the 11-incher and a 10-inch columbiad. He argued that the 11-incher was superior to the columbiad because it fired a heavier shell and because its breech was stronger, safer, and more reliable. Davis summoned Colonel Craig, the army chief of ordnance, to his office to hear Dahlgren's argument. For reasons that were not made clear, Craig rejected the idea. Dahlgren never officially filed his written proposal.[15]

In March 1858 Dahlgren used a report on tests of his own guns as a platform from which to launch another attack on the model 1844 columbiads. "The...*shape* of the Army gun, both in its finished and unfinished state," he argued, "is unfavorable to its endurance." He believed that the "disadvantageous" design of the army guns increased "contractile strains" on them. He argued that "accidental causes" such as unusually good iron accounted for the occasional good performance of a columbiad.[16]

In November 1859 Dahlgren dropped by the army ordnance office for information about shells and chanced upon Rodman and William Wade of the Fort Pitt Foundry studying the drawing of a model 1858 columbiad. Dahlgren noticed the plan's "familiar shape," as he put it. "This is something of a cross," said Rodman, meaning that it resembled Dahlgren's design. "It is the thing itself," said Dahlgren. The two argued. Rodman pointed out differences between the columbiad and the Dahlgren gun; Dahlgren pointed out similarities.[17]

On 13 October 1860 Dahlgren wrote to the secretary of war, formally charging Rodman with plagiarism. He included a photograph of the 15-inch Rodman gun, then undergoing tests near Fort Monroe, and an outline of an 11-inch Dahlgren gun drawn on tracing paper. He noted that "by placing the latter on the photograph" one could see that "the similarity of model is so close as to make the external form practically identical."[18]

Rodman denied the charge. In a letter to the chief of ordnance written in September 1861, he pointed out that the photo of the 15-incher that Dahlgren had used had distorted the true lines of the gun, as photos often do. The fact that the photo of the 15-incher and the drawing of the 11-incher were not to scale, he argued, had also misled Dahlgren. Rodman enclosed full-scale drawings of his 15-incher, an 11-inch Dahlgren gun, and a 10-inch model 1858 columbiad, along with tables of dimensions. He asserted that his 15-inch gun had more in common with the model 1858 columbiad than with Dahlgren's 11-incher.[19]

Rodman then charged Dahlgren with plagiarism, noting that Dahlgren had designed his gun "to so distribute the metal that all parts of the gun should be equally strained at each discharge." He pointed out that this principle was not original with Dahlgren, but with Major Wade and Colonel Bomford, who had used it to design columbiads in the 1840s. He asserted that his own design was in fact superior to Dahlgren's. He recommended casting two guns of equal caliber from the same metal, one by his design and casting method and the other by Dahlgren's, and comparing their endurance in extreme proof.[20]

On 31 March 1862, in the midst of designing his own 15-inch gun, Dahlgren responded to Rodman's assertions in an eighteen-page letter to the secretary of war. He repeated his original charge of plagiarism, illustrating his argument with the data Rodman had supplied in the letter of September 1861. He did not respond to any of Rodman's other charges or remarks.[21]

Rodman's charge of plagiarism ran closer to the truth than Dahlgren's. Dahlgren had borrowed from army research the idea of shaping a gun according to the progression of internal pressure resulting from the discharge of a projectile. Although Rodman's guns bore a strong resemblance to Dahlgren's, they differed in both caliber and proportion. In truth, it appears that Dahlgren and Rodman both derived their designs from the work of George Bomford.

Even disregarding the allegations of plagiarism, the controversy bore no good for either the army or the navy. Before Dahlgren's name became synonymous with naval ordnance, army and navy ordnance experts had worked together in a spirit of warmth and cooperation, exemplified by the three navy assistant inspectors of ordnance who paid tribute to Bomford in 1849, and by Dahlgren's relationship with Mordecai in the late 1840s and early 1850s. But as Dahlgren and Rodman grew more powerful in their respective services, the army-navy ordnance relationship degenerated into bitter interpersonal and interservice rivalry. Although the services faced similar problems in developing rifled cannon and heavy ordnance during the war, this rivalry prevented them from pooling their resources and working together toward solutions. Neither ordnance prima donna wanted to appear as the follower; both wanted to be hailed as leaders.

The Dahlgren 15-Inch Gun

Dahlgren completed plans for the navy 15-inch gun in early April. On 4 April he sent a copy of the plans to Ericsson to ensure that the 15-incher would fit inside the monitor turrets. Three days later, Dahlgren sent copies to Harwood, who forwarded one to the founders. Harwood specified that the founders use the same type of iron and the same casting method— Rodman's—that were used to produce the army 15-inch gun. Dahlgren went along with Rodman's method to "adhere as closely as possible to the method practiced in manufacturing the only 15-inch gun yet made."[22]

On 7 April Dahlgren sent Harwood another memorandum reiterating his objections to the 15-inch gun. He added a warning that the consequences of a 15-inch gun exploding inside a monitor turret would be "disasterous [*sic*] and conclusive." He raised the question as to whether a 12-, 13-, or 14-inch

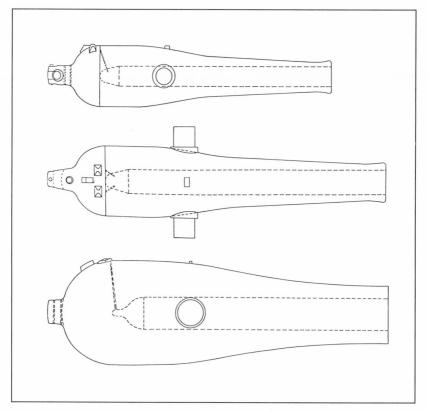

Top to bottom: 9-, 11-, and 15-inch Dahlgren guns (approximately to scale) (From Canfield, *Civil War Naval Ordnance*)

gun might be sufficient to deal with the thicknesses of armor then appearing on warships; even the 11-incher might prove sufficient. He recounted how the 170-pound shot fired from the *Monitor*'s 11-inch guns had put the *Virginia* out of action for three weeks. He wondered whether a larger number of 11-inch shot might have disabled the *Virginia* entirely. Dahlgren wrote this memorandum not only to reiterate his apprehension over the 15-inch gun but also to protect his reputation. It amounted to a disclaimer, absolving him of responsibility for the gun if it failed.[23] Incidentally, during the battle of Mobile Bay on 5 August 1864, the Union ironclad *Chicasaw* nearly stove in the aft end of the CSS *Tennessee*'s casemate with 11-inch fire, using heavier powder charges than the *Monitor* had fired.

THE CRISIS PASSES

As events unfolded following the battle of Hampton Roads, Dahlgren grew increasingly disgusted with the 15-inch gun, with Fox's interference in his bailiwick, and with the whole ordnance crisis. "The people have gone mad on ordnance, here and in England," he noted in a personal memorandum entitled "Ordnance Panic":

> The action of M. and M [*Monitor* and *Merrimack*/*Virginia*] first drove Fox head long to 15"...guns—So the contracts have actually been made for these monstrosities—But the work is hardly begun when comes news from England that Armstrong has shivered to pieces at a shot the hitherto invulnerable iron target.... *So away we go again*—And Fox now shifts his ground from the 15", because he fears its Velocity is insufficient[.]
>
> It is melancholy to witness this vacillation and uncertainty among the high authorities & the experts—All arising from the lack of due experiment.... [Meanwhile] the public panic is increased by every blatant ass.[24]

In the weeks following the *Virginia*'s debut, Dahlgren showed no sign of panic. Instead of working furiously to develop the 15-inch gun or some other counter to armored vessels, he spent much of his time on board ships, taking trips down the Potomac with the president. He certainly did not allow the crisis to affect his lifestyle as a Washington insider. He spent most evenings with Lincoln and cabinet members discussing the war. During this period he devoted far more space in his diary to the position of Union armies, boat rides, and chats with top officials than to ordnance and ironclads.[25]

Panic and fear abated in the North with the *Virginia*'s destruction. On 10 May, Union forces captured Norfolk and reoccupied the navy yard there. As the *Virginia* drew too much water to retire up the James River, the ranking Confederate officer reluctantly ordered her blown up.

Welles celebrated her demise by taking a small party on a six-day cruise. With Dahlgren in command, Welles, Seward, Attorney General Edward Bates, and members of their families left the Washington Navy Yard on Tuesday, 13 May, on the steamer *Baltimore*. The next morning they ascended the Pamunkey River, a branch of the York, past mile-long strings of anchored transports, to McClellan's command post. The general, accompanied by French observers dressed as aides, provided mounts for the men and ambulances for the women for a tour of his camp. He also put on a parade. The party returned to the ship that evening.

On Thursday, in the rain, the *Baltimore* steamed around to Norfolk, a town of empty streets and shuttered windows. The next day they surveyed the ruined ships and burned buildings of the Gosport Navy Yard. Dahlgren took note of some "badly cast" Confederate-made rifled cannon. On the trip back to Fort Monroe they sailed past the wreck of the *Virginia*. Only one large timber of the once dreaded warship was visible. On Saturday they chugged up the James River, past the wrecks of the *Congress* and *Cumberland,* and witnessed the occupation of an abandoned Confederate battery by a unit of marines.

In buoyant spirits they pressed upriver until they encountered two Union vessels bearing news that the *Monitor* and *Galena,* which had gone up the James to bombard Richmond, had stopped 8 miles short of the city and had been badly battered at Drewry's Bluff. Dahlgren thought it "curious" that everyone's spirits were "quelled" by this "little reverse." He noted that Seward "began to remember reasons for returning." Dahlgren persuaded the party to venture onward. After grounding once or twice, the *Baltimore* arrived at Jamestown and anchored. At four o'clock Sunday morning, Dahlgren was awakened from a sound sleep by urgent banging on his door. It was Seward, in his gown, demanding to be taken to Washington immediately for "state reasons." Dahlgren had hoped to continue upriver to have a look at the *Monitor* and *Galena,* but Seward insisted.

Dahlgren upped anchor and headed for Washington, stopping briefly at Newport News and Fort Monroe. When the *Baltimore* arrived back at the yard on Sunday, Seward admitted that he had been afraid of being captured. This amused Welles, who had also been amusing himself by teasing Bates incessantly about a rat that had made off with his cravat. The cruise was a fitting end to the panic and tension caused by the *Virginia.*[26]

DAHLGREN REDIRECTS HIS QUEST

But the cruise did nothing to ameliorate Dahlgren's opinion of Fox. As he later noted of the assistant secretary:

> [Fox exercises] an insufferable tyranny over the Navy—and has entirely deranged it in fastening his notions upon everything—Retiring officers,

and assigning duty without regard to anything but his own will—absorbing every function of the Depart—filling the Bureaus with his own creatures, and spending money in every fancy that entered his pate.... Nothing could exceed the insolent tyranny of Fox.[27]

In spite of his disgust with the assistant secretary, the 15-incher, and the ordnance panic, Dahlgren pressed forward with his effort to reorganize the ordnance bureau. On 24 March 1862 he wrote to Senator John Hale, chairman of the Senate Naval Affairs Committee. The bill to reorganize the Navy Department, which Hale had introduced into Congress on 24 January, was still under consideration, and Dahlgren wanted to ensure that the senator understood his plan for the ordnance organization. He proposed replacing the Bureau of Ordnance and Hydrography with an organization he called the "Directorship of Ordnance." This proposal would alter the ordnance hierarchy so that experimental work would take precedence over management. A "Director of Experiments," a post Dahlgren intended for himself, would replace the bureau chief, traditionally an administrative post, as the ranking officer. He also wanted to free the Washington Navy Yard from the Bureau of Yards and Docks.[28]

On 29 May, Hale wrote Dahlgren asking if the Union Navy had a sufficient supply of heavy ordnance and how the government could help meet the current demand. In his letter of reply Dahlgren said that the supply of guns was insufficient, forcing him to arm ships with obsolete 32-pounders and 8-inch shell guns. He noted that it had always been difficult to provide the navy with guns and blamed the difficulty on the organization of the ordnance department. "That now existing," he wrote, "would neutralize the abilities of the most skillful Ordnance expert in this or any other Country. It is evident that there is no royal road to the art of making proper cannon." He suggested a three-part remedy: extending the government plant to meet one-quarter of the current demand, stockpiling a large supply of iron for heavy ordnance, and reorganizing the navy's ordnance department.[29]

Dahlgren accelerated his quest. He sought not only to reorganize the Bureau of Ordnance but also to get himself promoted to the highest rank. A bill had arisen in Congress the past February to promote nine commanders and captains who had distinguished themselves in battle to the rank of flag officer. This designation, created in 1857 by Congress, had simply replaced the seemingly less grandiose title of commodore. Dahlgren had written to Charles B. Sedgwick, chairman of the House Naval Affairs

Committee, arguing that the promotion list should not be limited to combat veterans. He reasoned that he too should be considered because of his ordnance work and service in defense of the Washington Navy Yard. The onset of the *Virginia* crisis had temporarily diverted him from his campaign for a promotion. With the *Virginia* sunk, Dahlgren renewed the effort in earnest.[30]

He wrote letters to congressmen in May and June 1862, arguing a case based on his command of the Washington Navy Yard early in the war. It had been the closest he had come to battle. Here is part of his letter to Congressman William D. Kelley:

> The peculiar hardship of the case is that I supposed I had rendered as important service to the US. as I could render, by the faithful & successful maintainance [*sic*] of my duties at this Yard, when it was abandoned by its Commandant and officers, at the most critical period of the Rebellion.
>
> Doubt and disloyalty were all around—the public buildings were provisioned and garrisoned. The President was guarded in his own residence. Baltimore had severed our communications,—the City was held by a mere handful of men and its fate depended more on the firm bearing of leaders than on any actual power at their command.
>
> The Navy Department, through the President has official[ly] stated to the present Congress that my "services are as valuable to the country and entitled to as high regard as those of the most successful Flag Officer who commands a Squadron."[31]

Here is part of his letter to Congressman J. M. Phelps:

> Upon me had been devolved one of the most important tracts that could be held by any Naval Officer, when the continuance of this Union seemed to tremble in the Balance.... The Navy Yard was the key of the whole position on the left[;]...it contained stores of Artillery & Ammunition, that of themselves might have decided the fate of the city. Had Washington then been lost, the very Union might have been despaired of.[32]

These letters mark a turning point in Dahlgren's quest. He was arguing for promotion not on the basis of ordnance work but on the basis of what amounted to an operational command. He had come to the realization that the navy would never, at least during his lifetime, accord ordnance work status equal to that of a winning combat record.

Dahlgren was not alone in this realization. Harwood complained to him in a letter of 19 March, "The most experienced [ordnance] Inspectors in the service are applying for an opportunity of signalizing themselves afloat, and are entirely distracted from the consideration of duties which making no show yield no adequate recompense."[33] They were right. Percival Drayton, for example, is remembered not for his years of service as an assistant inspector of ordnance in New York, but for his shining moment during the battle of Mobile Bay, when Admiral David G. Farragut allegedly shouted, "Damn the torpedoes! Full speed ahead Drayton!"[34] This failure to recognize, acknowledge, and reward technological work remained a flaw in the American military establishment as a whole until well into the next century. It was only toward the end of World War II that the military began to appreciate the importance of managers and technologists as well as heroic leaders.[35] Until then the establishment consistently obstructed the paths of innovators who sought to develop new weapons, such as breechloading muskets, machine guns, and submarines.

For Dahlgren, Fox's interference was the last straw. Dahlgren now knew that the navy would not give him full authority over ordnance development, despite his unparalleled reputation as an expert. Renown without such power seemed to him a dubious achievement. A reputation made in a bureau simply did not measure up to glory won at sea. Dahlgren began to divorce himself from ordnance and to seek a berth where he could win traditional glory.

But he was between the horns of a dilemma. He sought not only glory but also promotion. Although nothing was more gratifying to an officer than rank, Gideon Welles was a firm believer in basing promotion exclusively on combat service.[36] Thus, Dahlgren had a dual motivation for seeking a fighting command. His problem was that Welles wanted to keep him in ordnance. The secretary's wishes, however, did not keep him from trying. After all, he was known for circumventing superiors.

During lunch on 25 May, Dahlgren received an urgent telegram to dispatch cannon from the Washington Navy Yard to Harpers Ferry. He went over to the Navy Department to find out what was going on and learned that Confederate troops under Major General Thomas J. "Stonewall" Jackson were threatening the town. It was part of Jackson's famous Shenandoah Valley Campaign, aimed at preventing Major General Irvin McDowell's corps from linking up with McClellan's army on the peninsula. Dahlgren ran into Secretary of War Stanton and immediately volunteered for duty at Harpers Ferry. Stanton offered to make him chief of artillery, if the Navy Department would agree. Not surprisingly, Welles objected. Dahlgren then asked Lincoln, who at first assented to the request, but when Fox added his objection, the matter was dropped.[37]

The president sought to mitigate his friend's disappointment. On 6 June he wrote Stanton, "I need not tell you how much I would like to oblige Capt. [*sic*] Dahlgren. I now learn, not from him, that he would be gratified for his son Ulric Dahlgren, to be appointed a lieutenant in the Army. Please find a place for him."[38] Stanton made Ulric Dahlgren, who had just turned twenty, a captain in the army.[39]

On 5 July, Congress passed the bill reorganizing the Navy Department. The Bureau of Ordnance and Hydrography was split into the Bureau of Navigation and the Bureau of Ordnance. That morning Dahlgren was summoned to the War Department, where he met with Lincoln, Welles, and Fox. Confederate forces had deflected McClellan's peninsular thrust toward Richmond. In seven days of fighting, which had begun on 25 June, the Confederates had suffered more than twenty thousand casualties to the Union's sixteen thousand. Although the Army of the Potomac was neither destroyed nor seriously crippled, General McClellan determined that he had been defeated and decided to withdraw. The president, anxious about the fate of the Army of the Potomac, asked Dahlgren if communications along the James River could be kept open. Dahlgren said that he would guarantee it if the president would place him in command there and provide sufficient forces. Lincoln must have been surprised, for according to their understanding of the previous January, Dahlgren was slated to head the new Bureau of Ordnance. Dahlgren repeated his proposal to Welles. The secretary objected at once, arguing that Dahlgren could not be spared from ordnance work. Dahlgren, worried that the James River command might be his last opportunity to earn a promotion to flag rank, said he was willing to give up both the yard and the Ordnance Establishment for the opportunity to fight. Welles flatly refused. Dahlgren turned to the president. Lincoln thought hard about the matter but decided to go along with Welles. Dahlgren was to remain in ordnance. Welles nominated him head of the Bureau of Ordnance. In separate meetings Fox told Dahlgren that the position entailed the administrative work he loathed, not the developmental work he loved. Dahlgren thereupon asked Welles that his name be withdrawn. The secretary told him to ignore Fox; he would be allowed to retain control of weapons development if he accepted the position. Dahlgren took a few days to consider the offer.[40]

As consolation, Lincoln tried to get his friend promoted. The designation of flag officer in the promotion bill had recently been changed to rear admiral because the prewar rank system had proven inadequate. Ranking army officers tended to interfere with naval officers during joint operations. A clause in the pending promotion bill made a congressional vote of thanks a prerequisite for promotion to rear admiral. On 12 July, Lincoln recommended Dahlgren for a vote of thanks. Four days later the House voted him one. But in the Senate, James W. Grimes, a member of the Naval Affairs Committee, managed to get the vote postponed until the next session.[41]

Grimes, who later proved a generous and effective friend to the navy, postponed the vote for perhaps two reasons. Hale's leadership of the Naval Affairs Committee was so poor that several senators sought to resign from it. It seems that Grimes got the vote postponed in the course of a murky political game with Hale.[42] Grimes might also have wished to prevent Dahlgren's promotion. He considered Dahlgren a courtier who had attained his position on the strength of his social skills in soirées. Dahlgren considered Grimes a "mean rascal" for postponing the vote. In any case, Grimes's action prevented him from becoming a rear admiral at that time.[43]

Reluctantly, Dahlgren decided to accept command of the Bureau of Ordnance. He became chief on 21 July. As he had wished, the Ordnance Establishment was separated from the jurisdiction of the Washington Navy Yard, and he was allowed to retain control over the experimental work. Harwood, the former ordnance chief, became commandant of the yard. On 5 August, Dahlgren was promoted to captain. Welles had won, for now.[44]

16

The Bureau of Ordnance
July 1862–June 1863

Ultimately, the chief of the Bureau of Ordnance was responsible for everything having to do with naval armament. Since Dahlgren's arrival in Washington in 1847, the chiefs had done the administrative work and allowed Dahlgren to preside over research and development. Although Charles Morris and Duncan Ingraham had interfered in the development of Dahlgren's heavy smoothbore and rifled ordnance, they had given him leeway to run most other aspects of the Ordnance Establishment his way, including determining ranges of cannon, testing inventions and gunpowder, and fitting ordnance to ships. As chief of the bureau during the Civil War, however, Dahlgren broke with tradition and assumed a dual role, presiding over both administration and innovation.

Dahlgren maintained a fairly routine daily schedule as chief of ordnance. He left home at eight for his office at the Navy Department, where he spent the morning doing the administrative work he loathed. At 12:30 he left the department, stopped by his house for lunch, then went on to the yard, where he spent the afternoon doing the experimental work he loved. He returned home at five, read the mail, and ate dinner. He usually spent the evening with politicians and diplomats.[1]

THE DEVELOPMENT OF THE 15-INCH GUN

Although Dahlgren was now chief of ordnance, Fox's order to develop a 15-inch gun remained in force. The assistant secretary wanted a cannon capable of destroying any ship that could cross the ocean. In 1862 the threat of European intervention on the Confederate side seemed as real to many Union officials as the threat posed by enemy ironclads.[2]

In the spring of 1862, when not cruising the Potomac with Lincoln, Dahlgren spent much of his time reluctantly developing the 15-incher. He remained doubtful of the capability of cast-iron guns to endure the strain of firing 15-inch projectiles. Nevertheless, the Navy Department wanted him to rush 15-inch guns to production so that they would be available to arm the new monitors when they came off the ways. Welles and Fox were anxious to send the ironclads to Charleston, South Carolina, as soon as possible.[3]

It had become apparent early in the Civil War that places such as Charleston could not be blockaded continuously if the ships had to return north for fuel and supplies. Blockaders often spent nearly as much time cruising back and forth to bases as they did on station. Welles had appointed a board of naval officers, headed by Captain Samuel F. Du Pont, to study the problem. The board recommended establishing two blockading squadrons in the Atlantic and capturing bases for them on the Southern coast. Du Pont became commander of the South Atlantic Blockading Squadron, whose area of responsibility stretched from the North Carolina–South Carolina border to the southern tip of Florida. Port Royal, South Carolina, was captured by a joint army-navy expedition in November 1861, with Du Pont commanding the naval forces. Port Royal became the base for the blockade of Charleston.[4]

But a mere blockade did not satisfy everybody. Northern editors shouted "on to Charleston," scorning the city as a "hot-bed of secession" and a "viper's nest and breeding place of rebellion." Welles wrote that "there is no place that the American people would so delight to see captured as Charleston." Fox likened the fall of the city to "the fall of Satan's kingdom." Fox linked the Charleston mania to the monitor craze. Ten days after the battle of Hampton Roads, he told a congressional committee that the navy "would have no hesitation in taking the *Monitor* right into Charleston." He fixated on the idea that the city should fall to a naval force alone. Jealousy pervaded his reasoning, for he believed that the army had received a disproportionate share of the credit for capturing Forts Hatteras and Donelson

Fifteen-inch Dahlgren gun at the experimental battery, Washington Navy Yard
(Library of Congress)

earlier in the war. Charleston under the guns of technologically advanced
Federal warships would be an unparalleled propaganda coup for the navy.
In the fall of 1862 the Navy Department began planning an attack on
Charleston. Success would depend largely on the new ironclads and their
new cannon.[5]

Production of 15-inch Dahlgren guns began in June 1862. It soon became
apparent that there would not be a sufficient number ready in time. By the
end of August, two new *Passaic*-class monitors were ready to receive their
ordnance. Each was slated for two 15-inch guns, but a total of only three were
on hand. Ericsson found army 15-inchers to be unsuitable for the turrets
because they were too big. Dahlgren suggested using 11-inchers until more
15-inchers were finished. Ericsson preferred mounting one 11-incher and
one 15-incher in each turret. "With only one of the large guns in each vessel,"
he said, "we shall be able to destroy all rebel craft, inspire a whol[e]some
dread in rebeldom and prove to foreign powers that we can punish any intentional meddling." Dahlgren acquiesced.[6]

The rush to production and the Navy Department's mania to take Charleston prevented Dahlgren from testing 15-inchers as thoroughly as he had tested his other calibers before they entered service. Time constraints forced him to establish regular proof for 15-inchers before determining their endurance as a class. Charles Knap, the owner of the Fort Pitt Foundry, had invested $30,000 in the first 15-incher. He did not want the proof to be so severe that it would threaten his investment. He assumed that regular proof for navy 15-inchers would be the same as for army 15-inchers: three rounds of 50 pounds of powder and a 315-pound shell. When Dahlgren hinted at a more rigorous proof, Knap threatened to stop production of 15-inchers until a firm agreement was concluded. Dahlgren was more concerned with the safety of navy gun crews than with Knap's money, but he agreed to the army proof in order not to delay production. If a 15-incher survived the three rounds, the navy would be obliged to pay for it. Before issuing 15-inchers to ships, however, Dahlgren had each one proven with twenty-five additional rounds of 30 pounds of powder and a 330-pound shell.[7]

A private firm thus forced the navy to accept inferior standards of quality control. But given the uncertainty as to whether the 15-inch gun would succeed as a class, the navy could not reasonably expect a private firm to assume the financial risk. Several private firms had refused the navy's offer to produce the big guns, probably for this very reason.[8]

Time constraints also prevented Dahlgren from determining the ballistic characteristics and endurance of 15-inch guns before individual pieces were issued to the fleet. In contrast, his 9- and 11-inch guns had been thoroughly proven and tested, with several pieces going over a thousand rounds, before any had been mounted on board ships. The first navy 15-incher produced was slated for testing and arrived at the Washington Navy Yard early in October. Dahlgren began firing the gun on the twelfth. *Passaic*-class vessels received 15-inch guns that same month. By 26 October the 15-incher at the experimental battery had been fired 250 times.[9]

Civilian policymakers marveled at the big new gun. The 15-incher was larger than anything in the United States Navy's ordnance inventory. The 11-inch gun—formerly the navy's largest cannon—weighed about 16,000 pounds and fired a 136-pound shell with 15 pounds of gunpowder. But the 11-incher paled in comparison with the 15-incher, which weighed nearly 42,000 pounds and fired a 350-pound shell with 35 pounds of powder.[10] That fall Lincoln and Welles frequented the Washington Navy Yard to see the new cannon test-fired.[11] Even Du Pont seemed impressed. He wrote his wife,

"The gun makes the effect upon you, in size, to all other guns you have seen, great as some of these are, that the elephant in a menagerie does, in comparison with the small quadrupeds around it."[12]

Despite its impressiveness, the 15-incher suffered numerous teething troubles. Experiments at the Washington Navy Yard revealed that the big gun's best rate of fire was only one-third that of the 11-incher.[13] Furthermore, numerous difficulties arose in melding 15-inch guns and *Passaic*-class ships into effective fighting units. Ericsson had originally designed the gunports of the *Passaic*-class turrets for smaller weapons, and although he had received plans of the 15-incher in April, he never redesigned the gunports to accommodate the larger piece. As a result, the muzzle of the 15-inch gun was too large to fit through the gunports of the *Passaic* and her sister ships. In late October, Welles sent Dahlgren to New York, where the *Passaic* was building, to have her gunports cut to the proper size. Ericsson protested that enlarging the gunports would weaken the turret wall, so he improvised what he called a "smoke box," which was a closetlike structure bolted inside the turret to isolate the muzzle so that the gun could be fired inside the turret. A muzzle ring connected the gun to the turret side, to direct to the outside of the ship the smoke and concussion that resulted from firing.[14]

Percival Drayton, now the *Passaic*'s commanding officer, hated the smoke box. The first few times he fired her 15-incher, the blast from the muzzle blew the thing apart. Drayton half joked to a friend that the gun might soon blow the turret open. Dahlgren attended one of these tests. He found that the turret crew could not stand the gun's noise, smoke, and concussion. He told Ericsson that the smoke box was a failure. Ericsson's solution was a stronger smoke box. Drayton admitted that it was an improvement, but he would have preferred the larger gunport. Both Fox and Welles, however, hailed the strengthened smoke box as a success.[15]

Dahlgren, however, moved to distance himself from the 15-inch gun. He had no wish to stake his reputation on a weapon that Fox had ordered him to design against his better judgment, that was proving troublesome to develop, and whose endurance was problematic. Ericsson recalled that Dahlgren repeatedly claimed that he had "nothing to do with the project" and that he had "simply carried out instructions" in designing the big guns. By 5 January 1863 he had fired only 260 rounds from the 15-incher at the experimental battery. Although the piece showed no signs of weakness, Dahlgren thought it prudent to issue a circular letter of caution about 15-inch guns. The circular said that they were the largest cannon ever used on

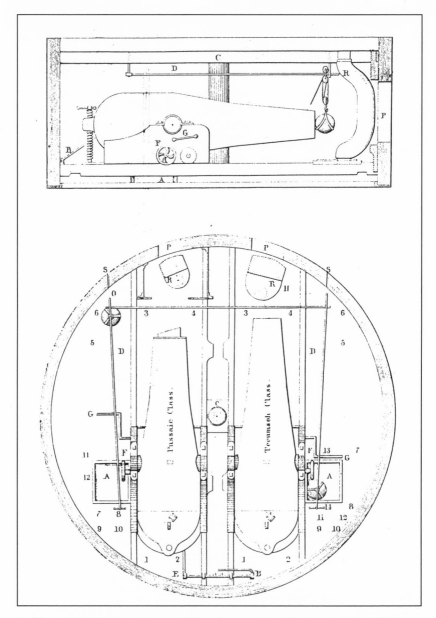

Inside a monitor turret. *Bottom:* Note the muzzle collar (wedge-shaped structure on muzzle of gun labeled "Passaic Class") and smoke-box structures (lines around structure *R* forward of *Passaic*-class gun). (From U.S. Navy Department, Bureau of Ordnance, *Ordnance Instructions for the United States Navy*)

shipboard, and that their endurance was unknown. It warned that if one exploded inside a monitor turret, it might sink the ship. The circular included special instructions to minimize the danger. As Welles later noted, Dahlgren was a prudent, cautious man, careful to avoid danger, and careful to provide the means of escaping from it. The circular was a second disclaimer, absolving Dahlgren of responsibility for the gun if it failed.[16]

WARTIME PRODUCTION

Developing the 15-inch gun was but one of many things Dahlgren did as chief of the Bureau of Ordnance during the Civil War. His responsibilities fell into three broad categories: developing weapons, testing weapons and inventions, and supplying the fleet with ordnance and related materials.

American naval ordnance was produced on a far greater scale during the Civil War than at any previous time in American history. By the end of 1862, ordnance appropriations had skyrocketed to twenty times the prewar level. Seven firms now manufactured cannon for the navy: Knap and Rudd in Pittsburgh; Alger and Company in Boston; Hinckley, Williams, and Company, also in Boston; R. P. Parrott in Cold Spring, New York; the Portland Company of Portland, Maine; Builders' Iron Foundry in Providence, Rhode Island; and the Scott Foundry in Reading, Pennsylvania.[17]

Expanding production to meet the unprecedented increase in demand for ordnance and supplies proved to be a difficult administrative task. Shortly after taking command of the bureau, Dahlgren realized that the supply of nitre—also called potassium nitrate or saltpeter, the basic ingredient of gunpowder—was critically short. The navy's prewar supply had come from the British, who in 1862 appeared sympathetic to the South. After Captain Charles Wilkes had precipitated a diplomatic crisis by forcibly removing Confederate commissioners James Mason and John Slidell from the British ship *Trent,* Her Majesty's government detained a large shipment of nitre bound for the Union, threatening the entire Northern war effort. Without nitre there could be no gunpowder.[18]

Dahlgren also faced a shortage of cannon. Before the war the Navy Department usually issued contracts for new cannon only when building or refitting ships. Once the ships received their metal, few new guns remained to be stockpiled. As a result, the wartime surge in demand for cannon forced

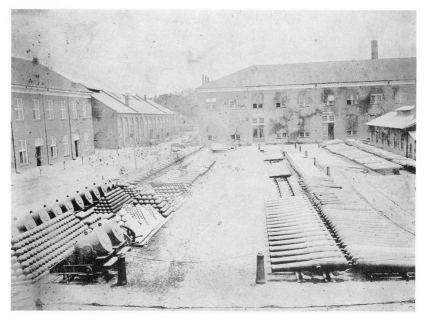

Various ordnance in the Washington Navy Yard (Naval Historical Center)

Dahlgren to arm many ships, particularly those engaged in operations along the Mississippi, with old 32-pounders and 8-inch shell guns.

The Bureau of Ordnance suffered not only materiel shortages but also personnel shortages. With more firms producing naval cannon, more assistant inspectors of ordnance were needed to monitor production. The exodus of the most experienced inspectors to fighting berths exacerbated the problem. If Dahlgren's program of quality control was to be maintained during the war, new inspectors would have to be recruited, trained, and persuaded to stay on the job. There was also a shortage of clerical help in the offices at the Washington Navy Yard.[19]

Dahlgren took measures to solve these problems. He worked in conjunction with Henry du Pont and the New Haven Chemical company to develop domestic sources of nitre. By the summer of 1863 the navy's supply of nitre was assured. Dahlgren quintupled the clerical staff at the Washington Navy Yard, increased their pay, and established quarters for officers there. He ran the shops at the Washington Navy Yard day and night to produce boat guns, fuzes, carriages, and other ordnance and equipment. He oversaw a tremendous increase in production of heavy cannon. In March 1861 the navy possessed 305 9-inchers and 32 11-inchers. By 1 November 1863, Union foundries had turned out 503 new 9-inchers and 291 new 11-inchers, an increase of 165 percent in the number of 9-inchers and 909 percent in the number of 11-inchers. Union foundries had also turned out 200 mortars, 36 15-inch guns, and 691 new Parrott rifled cannon for the navy, all produced under the eyes of new assistant inspectors of ordnance.[20]

RESEARCH AND DEVELOPMENT

Of all the facets of ordnance work, Dahlgren loved R&D best—provided he was doing work of his own choosing. Besides the 15-incher, another onus imposed on him from above was the testing of weapons and gadgets invented by private individuals. He examined over sixty such inventions during one eight-month period in 1862.[21]

Lincoln and his entourage attended many of these tests, often held on Sunday afternoons and followed by brunch. Although Lincoln was serious about finding and developing new weapons to help the Union win the war, one disaffected officer who viewed the tests as means to impress the president dubbed them "champagne experiments." On one such occasion Lincoln, Seward, and Treasury Secretary Chase attended a demonstration of a Hyde war rocket. The eminent onlookers stood only a few steps away while the fuze was lit. But instead of shooting up over the water, the rocket blew up where it stood. Dahlgren must have been horrified. But when the smoke cleared, he saw that the president and the two cabinet members were unhurt. Despite several such accidents over the years, Dahlgren had failed to institute adequate safety precautions.[22]

Although he rankled at testing others' inventions as a distraction from his own work, Dahlgren prided himself on giving each one a fair shake. Inventors, however, often blamed him if their inventions proved failures. In fact, an unknown person approached one of the clerks at the yard for information that would damage Dahlgren's career. The individual told the clerk that because Dahlgren had opposed certain inventions, an organization of disgruntled inventors was raising funds to mount a campaign in Congress to have him removed from the bureau. The clerk promptly told his boss. "This," Dahlgren ranted, "is a sample of the unscrupulous scoundrels that infest the Gov. whose sole aim is to rob the U.S." Scarcely a month after becoming ord-

nance chief, he asked Welles to give someone else the "onerous" duty of testing these inventions, but nothing came of the request.[23]

Dahlgren's primary interest as chief of the Bureau of Ordnance remained
experimenting with cannon. When not annoyed by superiors and private
inventors, he focused R&D efforts on two areas: testing ordnance against
armor and the rifle question. He had begun testing ordnance against armor
in May 1862. At first he worked exclusively with an 11-inch gun, for he was
bent on proving the caliber effective against armor in order to vindicate its
reputation. For example, because the *Monitor*'s 11-inchers had failed to
destroy the *Virginia,* the First Lord of the British Admiralty had declared the
guns "idle against armor plate." Dahlgren sought evidence to rebut such rep-
utation-damaging criticism. He also sought evidence to bolster his argument
against developing the 15-incher. If the 11-inch gun proved adequate
against armor plate, the larger cannon would seem unnecessary. He fired
the 11-incher from a range of 80 to 90 feet at various wooden targets covered with iron plates. He also fired the gun with larger charges than it was
designed for. He found that it could safely bear 30 pounds of gunpowder,
twice the service charge. In the Bureau of Ordnance section of Welles's 1862
report to Congress, Dahlgren stated that the 11-incher was sufficient for racking purposes. He implied that if the *Monitor*'s 11-inchers had been fired with
30-pound charges, they would have destroyed the *Virginia* on 9 March.[24]

Dahlgren subsequently used armored targets to test as many different
types and calibers of guns as he could get his hands on, including the 15-
incher, various British cannon, and rifled ordnance. He also tried new cannon of his own, designed specifically for use against armored warships,
including a 13-incher, an 11-incher with a straight muzzle, and a 16,000-
pound 10-inch gun designed to fire solid shot. All were bottle-shaped
smoothbores; only the 11-incher eventually saw active duty. By the end of
1862 Dahlgren concluded that racking was more effective against armored
vessels than punching. Racking favored his low-velocity smoothbores over
high-velocity rifled cannon.[25]

The rifle question had hung over the Union Navy at the beginning of the
Civil War. At first the question focused on the superior range of rifles over
smoothbores. Many captains of rifle-less sailing warships were terrified by
the prospect of encountering enemy vessels possessing rifled ordnance, creating a minor ordnance panic at the onset of hostilities. "Without a rifle can-

Armor test pieces, Washington Navy Yard (Naval Historical Center)

non," wrote the *Portsmouth*'s captain, "the ship, in a calm, would be at the mercy of any rebel steamer armed with one rifle cannon of long range."[26] In a letter marked "private" the *Constellation*'s captain virtually begged for rifles for his ship:

> Two or three days since I reported for the Command of the Constellation at this Yard [Portsmouth Navy Yard], and very much regretted to learn that she was not to be allowed a rifled gun upon her spar deck in place of one of her former pivot smooth bores. Please tell me if it is not possible to allow her at least one 18 or 24 pound rifle, or if not possible to do this, can you not give me two rifled howitzers, indeed anything to give me a fair chance against an enemy Steamer, which would of course choose a position to windward, at such a distance as to render my 8 in broadside guns entirely unavailable and indeed place me at her mercy, and without the power of reaching her, I beg of you my dear sir to comply with my request if in your power, so that I may have an opportunity of rendering some small service during the cruise which I am about to undertake.[27]

Although most captains did not sound so desperate, a blizzard of similar letters had blanketed the ordnance bureau.

Dahlgren had been pressing forward with the development of his own rifled ordnance since the beginning of the Civil War. By the end of 1862 he had completed designs for four rifled guns: a 4.4-inch 30-pounder, a 5.1-inch 50-pounder, a 6-inch 80-pounder, and a 7.5-inch 150-pounder. The ordnance foundry at the Washington Navy Yard produced a number of 30-, 50-, and 80-pounders, while other Dahlgren rifles were cast at private foundries and rifled at the yard. A few 150-pounders were produced, but none saw service. On 7 February 1862 an 80-pounder on board the *Hetzel* exploded during the assault on Roanoke Island, resulting in the withdrawal from service of fourteen 80-pounders and twelve 30-pounders. According to Dahlgren, the Fort Pitt Foundry had used inferior metal in these guns. Production of Dahlgren rifles ceased in early 1864. The Dahlgren rifle was a failure.[28]

During the Civil War the navy also procured rifled ordnance designed by Robert P. Parrott. The Parrott rifle was a muzzleloader whose distinctive feature was a wrought-iron reinforcing band that wrapped around the breech of the cast-iron barrel. Parrott produced his first rifle in 1860; the navy adopted several classes of his rifles in the spring of 1861. By January 1864 the navy had in service some 650 Parrott rifles of various sizes, including a 4.4-inch 30-pounder, a 5.3-inch 60-pounder, a 6.4-inch 100-pounder, and an 8-inch 150-pounder. A year later, one-fifth of the guns in service were Parrott rifles. The lighter calibers were cast solid and bored out; the heavier calibers were produced by the Rodman method. Instead of contracting for a specific number of guns, the navy had agreed to buy rifled cannon from Parrott as fast as he could manufacture them. During the war Parrott's Cold Spring Foundry produced his rifles exclusively.[29]

In Europe research and development of rifled cannon focused on the question of combating armored vessels. By 1862 William Armstrong had risen to preeminence in the field of naval rifled ordnance. The Royal Navy had adopted six different classes of his rifles, ranging from 6- to 110-pounders. While Americans were fighting the Civil War, Armstrong and his competitors continued testing larger and larger rifled cannon against thicker and thicker iron plates. The race between ordnance and armor was on.

Although Dahlgren had been enthusiastic about rifled ordnance before the Civil War, as chief of ordnance he began to sing a different tune. In the Bureau of Ordnance section of Welles's 1862 report to Congress, he noted that despite numerous tests, the British had "arrived at no final decision" in regard to the effectiveness of rifled ordnance against armored warships. After examining data from tests of the latest Armstrong rifles against armor with data from his own experiments, he concluded that his 11-inch gun "bears comparison with the best forged British guns of the latest design."[30]

In short, Dahlgren had determined his 11-incher to be adequate against armor and equal to the Armstrong rifle.

Dahlgren's effectiveness as chief of the Bureau of Ordnance during the Civil War depended upon his performance in each of his two leading roles: administrator and innovator. With Dahlgren at the helm, the Bureau of Ordnance successfully met the increased demand for ordnance during the Civil War. During his tenure as bureau chief, no ship or squadron was delayed in its movements by the lack of ordnance or ordnance supplies.[31] His greatest contribution to Civil War naval ordnance was in the guns and quality-control procedures he had introduced before the war.

Dahlgren once told a fellow officer that "a state of war was a most unfavorable period for experiments."[32] The demands of administering production left him with relatively little time for innovation. Much of his research effort was aimed at raising doubts about Fox's 15-incher and polishing the reputation of his own 11-inch gun, which had become tarnished in the wake of the *Monitor*'s failure to disable the *Virginia* and British progress in developing rifled ordnance. His own heavy rifle was a failure, the first real failure of his ordnance career. Other than the modified 11-incher, his effort to develop alternative weapons for monitors was halfhearted. As an innovator, Dahlgren did not turn in a shining performance during the Civil War.

Contemporaries thought even less of his performance as an administrator. John S. Missroon, an assistant inspector of ordnance at Boston, commented in a letter to Wise on Dahlgren's "unfitness" to head a bureau. Percival Drayton believed that Dahlgren lacked "the administrative talent" to head the bureau. Charles B. Sedgwick, chairman of the House Naval Affairs Committee during the first two years of the Civil War and someone who considered himself Dahlgren's friend, thought that Dahlgren was "not *up* to [the] business details & affairs" of managing the bureau.[33]

How can one account for the discrepancy between Dahlgren's success in meeting the wartime demand for ordnance on the one hand and his peers' disparagement of his management talents on the other? In taking charge of both administration and innovation, Dahlgren had spread himself too thin.

Before the Civil War each was a full-time job; management was the bureau chief's responsibility, and research and development was Dahlgren's. Despite the Civil War's extra demands, however, Dahlgren tried to do both jobs by working half a day on each. His subordinates must have had to work extra hard to pick up the slack. Dahlgren solved the nitre and ordnance shortages because they were the most crucial problems facing the Union. Everything else, particularly innovation, suffered.

Instead of personally presiding over development of the 15-incher, hosting the champagne experiments, overcoming the nitre shortage, increasing production to meet demand, and researching the rifle and armor questions, he might have delegated one or more of these tasks to subordinates, increasing their prestige by increasing their responsibility while lightening the load on himself. In the navy, however, the chief was ultimately responsible for everything that happened inside his bureau. Thus, with his reputation more or less on the line for each facet of ordnance work, Dahlgren was loath to delegate responsibility, for it would have meant staking his reputation on someone else's work. Nor did he want to share with anyone else the credit for success. So he tried to do it all himself.

17

Dahlgren's Star Ascendant
October 1862–June 1863

One other fact has to be considered in assessing Dahlgren's effectiveness as chief of the Bureau of Ordnance. He did not really want the job. He was simply biding his time, waiting for an opportunity to get a command afloat and a chance at real glory. He set his sights on command of the South Atlantic Blockading Squadron, potentially the most prestigious berth in the fleet.

ON TO CHARLESTON

If the cradle of the rebellion fell to a naval attack, the commander of the South Atlantic Blockading Squadron would become the most famous naval officer in the Union. Despite the problems besetting the Bureau of Ordnance, Dahlgren could not resist this opportunity. At the moment when his country needed him most for his unique expertise, he stood ready to forsake ordnance work. There was simply no glory in it. On 1 October 1862 he applied formally to Welles "for command of the forces that are to attack Sumter & the other Charleston forts." The secretary, however, had already chosen Rear Admiral Samuel Francis Du Pont to lead the attack.[1]

Dahlgren was not deterred. Characteristically, he went right over Welles's head and appealed directly to his friend the president for the command. "As Admiral Dupont has reaped so many laurels," he told Lincoln, "I am sure he would not object."[2]

Dahlgren also appealed, indirectly, to Du Pont. Probably at Dahlgren's request, Andrew Foote and Henry Wise approached Du Pont and asked him to give his command to Dahlgren. Du Pont was astounded and enraged. He wrote Fox:

> Simply observing that Dahlgren is a diseased man on the subject of prefer-ment and position—As I told Foote he chose one line in the walk of his profession, while F. [Foote] & I chose another; he was licking cream while we were eating dirt & living on the *pay* of our rank. Now he wants all the honors belonging to the other but without having encountered its jolt-ings—it is a disease and nothing else.

Du Pont flatly refused to hand the South Atlantic Blockading Squadron over to Dahlgren.[3]

Fox thought that Dahlgren deserved a crack at the enemy, but Welles did not want him to give up ordnance work. On 8 October the secretary sum-moned Dahlgren to his office and officially denied his request to lead the attack on Charleston, stating that he could not deprive Du Pont of the honor. He offered Dahlgren two alternatives: command of a single ironclad, or the position of ordnance officer in the attacking fleet. In either case Dahlgren would have to remain chief of the Bureau of Ordnance. Welles assured him that his presence at the capture of Charleston as fleet ordnance officer would accord him honor second only to Du Pont's. But Dahlgren was insulted, believing both alternatives beneath an officer of his stature. He hinted that he might resign from the bureau and accept command of an ironclad. The secretary said that he would not permit his resignation. After Dahlgren left the office, Welles wrote in his diary:

> Dahlgren is grieved with my action in his case. He desires, beyond almost any one, the high honors of his profession, and has his appetite stimulated by the partiality of the President, who does not hesitate to say to him and to me, that he will give him the highest grade if I will send him a letter to that effect, or a letter of appointment. Title irregularly obtained cannot add to Dahlgren's reputation, yet he cannot be reasoned with…. He is not conscious of it, but he had Dahlgren more than the service in view.

Welles thought that Dahlgren was seeking a command afloat only to make himself eligible for promotion to rear admiral.[4]

DAHLGREN'S PROMOTION TO REAR ADMIRAL

Dahlgren, however, wanted it all: a fighting berth as well as advancement to the highest rank. In January 1863 he renewed his campaign for promotion to rear admiral by sending a remarkable letter to Senators David Wilmot and E. Cowan. His old friends Foote and Joseph Smith hand-delivered it for him.[5] The letter began innocuously enough. Dahlgren noted that the president had recommended him for a vote of thanks and that the resolution had passed the House without a dissenting vote. As the resolution now stood before the Senate, he asked Wilmot and Cowan "to urge its favorable consideration."

Dahlgren then recited the litany of his accomplishments. Guns bearing his name had "been borne by the national vessels over every sea, sustaining our flag and the great interests it represents." They had provided the means for the "brilliant successes" at Hatteras, Port Royal, and New Orleans. "I should certainly have preferred to appear before you with claims for service rendered in Battle," he explained, "but it is not the province of an officer of the Navy to dictate to the Department how he shall be employed." He quoted at length from the collection of testimonials and praises he had amassed over the years, for he had kept clippings of virtually every positive comment made about him. He also recounted his role in the defense of the capital in 1861. "No public officer," he declared, "held a more responsible charge than confided to me." If the capital had fallen, "no subsequent naval victories would have retrieved the loss." He then came to the point, arguing that he should not be denied a deserved promotion just because he had not rendered service afloat during the war.

Dahlgren got a little help from his friend. Lincoln had often promised to promote him as soon as a spot became available. "Well, Mr. Welles," the president had more than once remarked to the secretary, "I am ready to sign Dahlgren's commission whenever you send it in."[6] Lincoln joined Dahlgren in urging the Senate to pass the vote of thanks. The Senate did so early in February, and the president signed the bill on the seventh. Dahlgren's way to the rank of rear admiral was clear; all he needed now was to be nominated and then confirmed by the Senate. On 17 February the president summoned him to the White House to examine inventions. Dahlgren reminded Lincoln of his promise to promote him. The president seemed "willing enough," as Dahlgren noted in his diary. Shortly thereafter Lincoln nominated Dahlgren for rear admiral and recommended that the Senate confirm the appointment.[7]

The Senate did so at 10 P.M. on 27 February. Dahlgren dropped by the White House the next day "to present the new admiral & shake hands." He noted in the diary, "So I am at last an Admiral of the Republic. There are five above me, Farragut[,] Goldsborough, Du Pont, Foote and Davis." Dahlgren received his commission on 11 March. "This jump," he noted, "raised me over half the Captains, and all the Commodores."[8]

Dahlgren's promotion precipitated a storm of indignation. In making him a rear admiral the president had circumvented not only Welles's policy of advancing only those who had distinguished themselves in battle but also the naval tradition of basing promotion on sea service and seniority. Lincoln had essentially rewarded him for his ordnance work. While Dahlgren certainly deserved such an accolade, the navy was not yet ready to make admirals of nonfighters. Friends like Foote, of course, wholeheartedly supported Dahlgren's advancement. But it did not sit well with many officers, who began to refer to Dahlgren as "Mr. Lincoln's admiral." Fox strongly opposed it and had told Dahlgren so in plain language. Charles Knap, who felt threatened by Dahlgren's efforts to establish a national foundry, deplored his "constant readiness to wait upon and devote himself to whomsoever may be in power." Du Pont wrote his wife that "Dahlgren is a man of great merit, but ought never to have been made an admiral." Du Pont adhered firmly to the doctrine that promotion should be based on seniority and service afloat. Farragut shared this belief. He wrote Du Pont, "How must those poor fellows feel who have had Dahlgren put over their heads.... It is, in my opinion, a great perversion of the law, but he must be a great man to be able to make Congress make the law to suit his case and give him the rank of admiral over the heads of men who have been fighting for their country ever since the commencement of the war." When Dahlgren stopped by Welles's office to thank him for the promotion, the secretary "told him to thank the President, who had made it a specialty;...I did not advise it."[9]

DU PONT'S ATTACK ON CHARLESTON

Meanwhile, the navy was preparing to attack Charleston, the most heavily fortified port in the Confederacy. British officers who visited the place reported that its defenses were stronger than those of Sevastopol during the Crimean War. The city itself lay at the extremity of a peninsula formed by the Ashley and Cooper Rivers. Numerous narrow but deep rivers and creeks divided the surrounding terrain into a patchwork of islands, which the Confederates fortified to defend the city against a land attack. In command was General Pierre Gustave Toutant Beauregard, one of the Confederacy's finest military engineers. Beauregard believed in unity of command and to a significant degree exercised operational control of Confederate naval forces in South Carolina and Georgia, his area of responsibility. Charleston harbor itself resembled a cul-de-sac. Beauregard's engineers ringed its perimeter with fortifications and batteries, the most prominent being Fort Wagner on Morris Island at the southern end of the entrance to the harbor, and Fort Moultrie on Sullivan's Island at the northern end. Fort Sumter, standing almost midway between James and Sullivan's Islands, covered the surrounding batteries. In turn, the island batteries could produce a great "wall of fire" to cover Sumter. Beauregard had buoys placed in the harbor so that his gunners would know the exact range to attacking enemy ships.[10]

A small naval flotilla complemented the fortifications. In addition to a few small wooden gunboats, Charleston's fleet eventually included four ironclads, but they were all slow, difficult to handle, mechanically unreliable, and unseaworthy. These examples of Confederate high technology posed a relatively limited threat to attacking enemy ironclads.[11]

Confederate low technology, in the form of underwater defenses, posed a much greater threat. The Confederate government actively funded underwater warfare and established a "torpedo station" in Charleston. That city's underwater defenses consisted of mines (called torpedoes in those days), heavily constructed rope and log booms stretched across the channel to prevent ships from passing and to entangle their propellers, and pilings arranged to keep attacking ships in the main channel under the guns of the shore batteries. Shortages of materials and strong winds and tides made these obstructions difficult to maintain, but they were cheap and effective.[12] As historian Rowena Reed has put it, "The harbor's organic defensive system was the strongest in North America."[13] Du Pont described Charleston harbor as a "porcupine hide with quills turned outside in and sewed up at one end."[14]

In September 1862 Welles summoned Du Pont to Washington to discuss the attack. The secretary believed that a fleet of monitors could run past Beauregard's ring of forts and, once inside the harbor, compel the city to surrender by threat of bombardment. Du Pont disagreed. His fleet had out-

Samuel Francis Du Pont, 1863 (Naval Historical Center)

gunned the enemy at Port Royal, but the monitors would be outgunned at Charleston. Sailors of his day operated by the rule of thumb that to silence shore batteries, an attacking fleet required a fifteen-to-one superiority in numbers of guns. Each of the new *Passaic*-class monitors had only two guns; Fort Sumter and the batteries on Morris and Sullivan's Islands alone mounted over seventy cannon. Du Pont thought that the ironclads would be unable to take the city unless the forts fell first. The monitors could not reduce the forts by themselves, he reasoned, because they lacked sufficient firepower. He viewed the repulse of the *Monitor* and *Galena* at Drewry's Bluff in May 1862, which had so unnerved Seward during the cruise with Dahlgren following the *Virginia*'s demise, as proof that ironclads alone could not overcome well-sited fortifications. He felt that the attack should be made by a joint force including twenty-five thousand troops to capture the forts.[15]

Du Pont's trepidations fell on deaf ears. The winter of 1862–63 was the darkest period for the Union in the war. Major General Ambrose E. Burnside's Fredericksburg campaign had recently been added to the list of Union disasters, no progress had been made on the inland waters since the capture of Memphis the previous summer, and the initial operations at Vicksburg had failed. For political reasons the Union needed a victory now. Besides, both Welles and Fox were convinced that the monitors were invulnerable.[16] As Rear Admiral Stephen B. Luce, founder of the Naval War College, put it, "The Monitor and Merrimac fight had given an exaggerated idea of the military value of [the *Monitor*] class of vessels."[17] On 6 January 1863 Welles ordered an attack on Charleston without delay.

Unfortunately, the prognosis for a naval attack on Charleston was not good. Drayton and the other skippers of the new monitors had problems not only with their guns but also with their ships. Soon after taking command of the *Passaic,* Drayton wrote a friend that the vessel seemed "carelessly and cheaply" built. He told another friend that as fast as the crew could fix one breakdown, another would appear. Worse, living conditions on these craft were wretched. A hot sun beating down on the iron deck turned a monitor into a veritable oven. Temperatures in the engine room reached as high as 130 degrees Fahrenheit. The air in the living quarters was an almost unbreathable thick fog. Everything was wet, both from condensation and from innumerable leaks. Worst of all, monitors were practically unseaworthy. En route to South Carolina the *Passaic* nearly foundered. The original *Monitor* foundered on 31 December 1862.[18]

None of this augured well for the attack on Charleston. Drayton expressed reservations about the attack to Dahlgren. Ericsson believed that monitors were the wrong kind of ships for such an operation and doubted that they would succeed. Although he was perfectly confident of their ability to destroy enemy vessels, he shared Du Pont's view of their limitations against forts. In a letter to Fox, Ericsson said that if the assault did succeed, it would not be "a mechanical consequence of your 'marvellous' vessels, but because you are marvellously fortunate." Dahlgren shared these views. The proper way to take Charleston, he believed, was with fifty thousand troops.[19]

Du Pont thought it prudent to test the mettle of the ironclads before attacking Charleston. On 27 January 1863 he sent the *Montauk* up the Ogeechee River, just south of the Georgia line, to attack Fort McAllister, a modest nine-gun sand fort serving as part of Savannah's defenses. The *Montauk* bombarded the fort for four hours but failed to silence its guns.

Other attacks by the *Montauk* on 1 February and by the *Passaic, Nahant,* and *Patapsco* on 3 March yielded similar results. Du Pont concluded that the monitors' big guns were ineffective against forts. Their low rate of fire, coupled with the fact that each monitor carried only two guns, meant that the ironclad fleet simply could not produce the volume of gunfire necessary to destroy an enemy fort in a single attack. He reported this view to Welles and reiterated his conviction that troops would be necessary to take Charleston. Moreover, Du Pont found that 15-inch guns could not fight for more than a day without needing repairs. The big cannon were particularly hard on their smoke boxes and carriages, both of which still had plenty of bugs in them.[20]

Du Pont was particularly upset by a decree Dahlgren issued establishing the service life of 15-inch guns at only three hundred rounds. A far cry from the thousand-round service life of 9- and 11-inchers, the three-hundred-round limit reflected Dahlgren's uncertainty about the endurance of the big guns and his concern for the lives of the gun crews as well as for his own reputation. Apprehensive monitor skippers believed that they would certainly fire more than three hundred rounds from their 15-inchers at Charleston.[21]

Nevertheless, Lincoln wanted the monitor fleet to do *something.* He had relieved Major General George B. McClellan the previous November for not taking offensive action with the Army of the Potomac, and he was beginning to wonder if Du Pont was a naval McClellan. Furthermore, the navy had built the monitor fleet at tremendous cost, and Lincoln wanted to show the public that it was worth the investment. But most important, Northern editors were beginning to call on the government to sue for peace. Du Pont's misgivings about the attack would prove meaningless if the Union war effort collapsed before he even made the attempt. On 29 March, a bright and windy Sunday, Dahlgren found the president in the chief clerk's office at the Navy Department. Lincoln complained that Du Pont was asking for ironclads as fast as they could be built yet had made no progress at Charleston. Dahlgren tried to console his friend. Lincoln brooded that public support for the war was dwindling. He tried making a couple of jokes, but his mood did not lighten.[22]

Lincoln and his cabinet pressured Du Pont into action despite the latter's apprehension. The government had dispatched troops to participate in the assault, but the army commanders could not agree on a plan of attack. Their wrangling left the navy to attack the city by itself. Du Pont devised a plan for a reconnaissance in force. He would steam into the harbor with the ironclads in line ahead, reducing the fortifications in turn, with Sumter as the

Du Pont's attack on Charleston, 7 April 1863. Note the USS *Keokuk,* which resembles a double-turreted vessel, and the broadside ironclad USS *New Ironsides,* on the left side of the picture. (Naval Historical Center)

initial target. If the enemy proved to be too strong, he would withdraw. If not, he would press the attack. Convinced that the monitors were invulnerable, Fox actually tried to persuade Du Pont not to fire on the forts at all, but to steam defiantly and silently to the city's wharves to demand surrender. Du Pont listened to this idea with restrained amusement until he realized that the assistant secretary was deadly serious and that the government considered this plan practicable. Although Du Pont believed that Fox's plan would certainly fail and that not even his own plan would force the city to surrender, he determined to try, fearing that the department would transfer the ironclads to the North Atlantic Blockading Squadron for an attack on Wilmington, North Carolina.[23]

Du Pont attacked on 7 April 1863. Nine ironclads steamed toward Fort Sumter in line ahead, with the monitor *Weehawken* in the lead. Affixed to her bow was a 50-foot-long raft designed by John Ericsson to clear mines and obstructions. Union commanders hoped that Ericsson's "torpedo rake" would enable the *Weehawken* to sweep a lane into the harbor for the rest of the column. The contraption succeeded in detonating a mine, damaging the ship, but it made the already unwieldy monitor almost impossible to steer, and the *Weehawken*'s skipper had to cast it loose.[24]

The ironclads bombarded Fort Sumter for some two hours. Every Confederate gun in range hammered the attackers. Ninety shot and shell perforated the lightly armored *Keokuk,* which later sank. Five monitors suffered extensive damage. The *Weehawken* fired twenty-six rounds and received fifty-three hits. In spots her side armor was fragmented and the wood exposed. Thirty-six of the cast-iron bolts that held her turret armor together snapped off. The *Passaic* fired thirteen shells and received thirty-five hits. A shot landing at the base of her turret jammed together the rails of a gun carriage, putting half of her two-gun battery out of action. Broken boltheads flew like bullets inside the *Nahant*'s pilothouse, one of them fatally wounding the helmsman. And so on down the line. The disparity of fire was tremendous. The Confederates fired more than twenty-two hundred shots. The entire ironclad squadron managed only 154 rounds because shot striking the monitors' turret bases and port stoppers put their guns out of action. Sumter was damaged but far from destroyed. Du Pont withdrew. The monitors proved difficult to maneuver, and their complicated machinery proved vulnerable to concentrated gunfire. As Du Pont had warned, their striking power was inadequate for strictly naval operations against forts.[25]

The first reports from Charleston blamed the failure on the hardware. Drayton wrote a friend that had the monitors remained under fire for an hour longer than they did, the fleet would have suffered a disaster. He told Dahlgren that to renew the attack would be "madness," a view shared by all of the other ironclad skippers. Commander Daniel Ammen, skipper of the monitor *Patapsco,* concluded that the short range of the 15-incher made it impossible for monitors to operate against forts without sustaining serious damage from return fire.[26]

Du Pont was furious. He had not expected a victory and had launched the attack only because he had been ordered to. "A silly faith in monitors," he wrote a friend, "and a more absurd *want* of faith in the insuperable nature of obstructions in such a harbor, have led to a great blunder—the greatest, I think, of the war." Du Pont reasoned that renewing the attack without the cooperation of a land force to occupy the forts could conceivably cost half of the monitors. The Confederates might subsequently repair them and turn them against the blockaders. To attack again, he told his wife, would be "sheer folly." He decided against a second effort. "The monitor people will be my worst enemies," he rightly predicted.[27]

USS *Patapsco*. Note damage to armor from Confederate projectiles, the smoke box for the 15-inch gun (left), and the rifling visible in the muzzle of the 150-pounder (8-inch) Parrott rifle (right). (National Archives)

Welles, who had staked his reputation on the monitor-building program, not to mention the reputation of the Navy Department and the Lincoln administration, did not buy Du Pont's explanation. After all the great preparations and expense, the secretary was distressed that Du Pont apparently intended to abandon the attack after a two-hour fight and the loss of only one man. Welles had been confident of Du Pont's ability but was now disappointed in him. He was also disappointed in himself for believing that Du Pont would press the attack.[28] Lincoln too was disappointed in Du Pont, whose dispatches and movements reminded him of McClellan.[29]

Both Welles and Fox believed that ironclads were the key to victory and remained blind to their shortcomings. Welles had been fully prepared to sacrifice a few monitors to take Charleston. He ordered Chief Engineer Alban Stimers to inspect the damaged vessels. Stimers concluded that Du Pont and the skippers were to blame for the failure, not the ironclads. An examining board under Rear Admiral F. H. Gregory reached the same conclusion. The newspapers caught wind of these investigations and venomously denounced

Du Pont. The newspaper attack prompted a joint letter to Welles from the monitor skippers denying the published assertions. Du Pont, bristling at the newspapers' accusations of incompetence and cowardice, forwarded the skippers' letter with one of his own. Welles criticized Du Pont for worrying too much about the press when he should have been attacking. Du Pont demanded permission to publish his own account of what had happened. Welles refused. He could not afford the political backlash from assertions that the monitors were flawed. Furthermore, publishing the truth about the ironclads would undermine their psychological value. The secretary wanted Du Pont to take the blame for the failure.[30]

Meanwhile, Du Pont railed about Dahlgren's 15-incher and fretted about the prospect of losing his command. "Dahlgren made an admiral," he lamented to a friend, "in part for a gun which is a greater failure than the monitor which carries it—[Dahlgren] never stood behind one in action—while I presume I shall be damaged for having at the risk of honor and life found it worthless."[31]

In May, Welles began to consider replacing Du Pont. The secretary knew that Du Pont had strong ties in Congress, and he had been warned that Du Pont was a "shrewd intriguer." But Welles was shrewder. He knew that firing Du Pont would be tantamount to blaming him for the failure of the attack. Du Pont would defend himself by blaming the monitors. It all boiled down to a showdown between Du Pont, his command abilities, and his friends in Congress on the one hand and Welles, the monitors, Navy Department policy, and the Lincoln administration on the other. The secretary decided to accept the risk. Because Du Pont refused to be a willing scapegoat, and because he refused to renew the attack, Welles relieved him on 3 June.[32]

Dahlgren defended Du Pont. The two had been friends. At least, Du Pont had written nice things about Dahlgren. Perhaps Dahlgren felt he owed Du Pont a favor. He reminded Welles that Du Pont "was a judicious & brave officer and that the Capts. of the Iron Clads who were chosen officers concurred with D."[33] At the same time, Dahlgren went after Du Pont's former command.

DAHLGREN GETS A COMMAND AFLOAT

Meanwhile, Welles was wrestling with the problem of finding a successor to Du Pont. Rear Admiral David G. Farragut was his first choice, but Farragut was already commanding the Gulf Blockading Squadron. Rear

Admiral David Dixon Porter and Foote were possible candidates. Foote was not only Dahlgren's friend but also a longtime friend of Welles. And, of course, Welles knew that Dahlgren ardently desired the post. He thought Dahlgren deserved a chance to prove himself in combat but believed that giving him command of the South Atlantic Blockading Squadron would outrage his fellow officers.[34]

Welles decided to replace Du Pont with Foote. The secretary summoned Foote to his office and offered him the job. Foote accepted eagerly. Welles said that it would be good for the nation and the fleet if Dahlgren went along as second-in-command. Foote agreed but doubted that Dahlgren would consent. Welles sent Fox over to the Bureau of Ordnance to offer Dahlgren the job. Fox asked Dahlgren if he would volunteer to go to Charleston as second to Foote. Dahlgren said that he would obey an order to that effect but would not volunteer because he believed that having two admirals in one command would create disputes. He told Fox that he had his "own opinions as to the mode of conducting the business, and would not yield them to any one."[35]

Fox recounted the conversation to Welles. The secretary was disappointed. He doubted that Dahlgren would ever get a better opportunity to prove himself in a fighting command. Foote offered to try to persuade Dahlgren to go. Welles doubted that he could.[36]

On 2 June, Welles, Fox, and Dahlgren were working in the department. Welles brought up Charleston. Dahlgren proposed making the attack on the city a separate command from the blockade. He said that he would go if Welles would let him lead the attack. Fox responded enthusiastically, suggesting that Dahlgren immediately go to New York to see if Foote would agree.[37]

Dahlgren did so and the next day met Foote at the home of publisher David Van Nostrand. Foote complained of a terrible headache. Dahlgren laid out his proposal for dividing the command. Foote agreed that Dahlgren should command the ironclads. And so it was decided that Foote would succeed Du Pont in command of the South Atlantic Blockading Squadron, and Dahlgren would lead the ironclads in the next attack on Charleston. Dahlgren's lifelong dream of a fighting command afloat had come true.[38]

Foote never made it to Charleston. The headache he had complained of at Van Nostrand's was a symptom of something far worse. While on business in New York on 19 June, Dahlgren read in the morning paper that his old friend was dangerously ill. He went to the Astor House, the luxurious hotel where Foote was staying, and learned that his friend was dying from a wound he had received during the attack on Fort Donelson the previous

February. Dahlgren entered Foote's room. Foote was glad to see him but began to have difficulty breathing. Dahlgren left. Foote was as pleasant as ever when Dahlgren visited that afternoon. Dahlgren came back the following day, but Foote had lost consciousness. Saddened, Dahlgren returned to Washington in the evening.[39]

The next day was Sunday, 21 June. Dahlgren went to church. A messenger appeared in the middle of the service to summon him to Welles's home. When Dahlgren arrived, the secretary told him that he would be in sole command of the South Atlantic Blockading Squadron, adding that he seemed "destined" for the post. Welles said that he would have to pick a new staff because some of the officers who had seen more duty at sea would resent serving under him. The secretary made it clear that he was giving Dahlgren this command because Lincoln had pressured him into it. He added that Dahlgren would retain command of the Bureau of Ordnance, with Wise acting as chief. Dahlgren urged him to appoint a new chief. The secretary refused, because Dahlgren was so well qualified for the post. He wanted Dahlgren to remain chief of ordnance indefinitely. He gave Dahlgren full authority to conduct operations, but no specific instructions.[40]

The secretary and the admiral met twice on 23 June to discuss the latter's new command. Afterward Welles expressed his opinion of Dahlgren in a long diary entry:

> My intercourse and relations with Dahlgren have been individually satisfactory. The partiality of the President has sometimes embarrassed me and given D. promotion and prominence which may prove a misfortune in the end. It has gained him no friends in the profession, for the officers feel and know he has attained naval honors without naval claims or experience. He has intelligence and ability without question; his nautical qualities are disputed; his skill, capacity, courage, daring, sagacity, and comprehensiveness in a high command are to be tested. He is intensely ambitious, and, I fear, too selfish. He has the heroism which proceeds from pride and would lead him to danger and to death, but whether he has the innate, unselfish courage of the genuine sailor and soldier remains to be seen. I think him exact and a good disciplinarian, and the President regards him with special favor. In periods of trying difficulties here, from the beginning of the Rebellion, he has never failed me. He would, I know, gallantly sustain his chief anywhere and make a good second in command, such as I wished to make him when I proposed that he should be associated with Foote. As a

bureau officer he is capable and intelligent, but he shuns and evades responsibility. This may be his infirmity in his new position.[41]

Senator Grimes reached a similar conclusion. He wrote Du Pont:

I see it is stated that Dahlgren is to be the man [to replace you]. I hope not. I have no affection for the man and not much respect. He is a courtier; he is doubtless brave; but he is, in my conviction, the most conceited man in the Navy. He was made an admiral professedly for improvements in ordnance, but really for his attention to ladies in Washington.[42]

On 24 June, Dahlgren left for New York, where he would catch a steamer to Port Royal. Foote's illness meant that he would be heading south at least a month earlier than he had anticipated. The next day he went to see his old friend. Foote was delirious. He said, "Who will fight for Dahlgren?" then lapsed into unconsciousness. Foote had been unable to recognize anyone else. Dahlgren returned for a brief visit on the twenty-sixth. Foote was "very low," as Dahlgren put it in his diary. Foote died at ten that evening. "The grave never closed on a better man," noted Dahlgren. "Bosom friends we had been for 20 years and one week since when our last conversation took place he expressed his high opinion of me, and added 'I would not say this *now* unless I believed it.'"[43]

Dahlgren spent the next few days with his daughter Eva, who was now fifteen and living with her aunt Patty, Dahlgren's sister. He thought of such moments as "bright spots in life." On 30 June, the day he departed for the South, he reflected on his children: "Take leave of my little daughter—Shall we meet again and how? or where! A scattered family truly—Charley at Vicksburgh[,] Ully in the Army, Paully at sea and Eva at Newport. I too on the move—so that Patty alone occupies what was once home, bright and happy with hope and vocal with the voices of little children. Alas!"[44]

Dahlgren's nostalgia did not dampen his enthusiasm for his new command, however. Percival Drayton, en route to a new post as fleet captain of the West Gulf Blockading Squadron under Farragut, saw Dahlgren in New York that morning. Having commanded the *Passaic* during Du Pont's attack on Charleston, Drayton proceeded to fill Dahlgren in on some of the difficulties he was about to face. Dahlgren simply gave him an "incredulous" smile. "I only hope that you will prove us all to have been wanting," Drayton told him.[45]

Incidentally, on the eve of his departure for the South, Dahlgren changed his mind about the 15-inch gun. On 17 June the *Atlanta*, a Confederate iron-clad resembling the *Virginia*, sortied from her base in Savannah on a mission to attack the blockading fleet. Du Pont had stationed two *Passaic*-class monitors, the *Weehawken* and the *Nahant*, each armed with one 11- and one 15-inch gun, in Wassau Sound, southeast of Savannah, to await the *Atlanta*'s appearance. At 4:19 that morning, Union observers spotted the *Atlanta* steaming down the Wilmington River. The two monitors steamed upstream to meet her. Unfortunately for the rebels, the *Atlanta* ran aground. She managed to fire six rounds at the approaching monitors, but they all missed. The *Weehawken* opened fire at 300 yards. Two rounds from her 15-incher forced the *Atlanta* to surrender before the *Nahant* even opened fire. Newspapers, which had once condemned the 15-inch gun, now heaped praise upon it. The Navy Department published a letter of appreciation to the *Weehawken*'s commander. The letter cited Rodman as the inventor of the gun. Although Dahlgren had divorced himself from the gun, he now sought reconciliation and immediately sent the Department a letter of his own. "I beg leave to state that the 15-inch gun carried by the Weehawken in her late contest with the Atlanta," he wrote, "was designed by my direction under my own eye." He could not bear to miss an opportunity to bask in the limelight.[46]

The United States Navy's culture and traditions infused its officers with the idea that to seek glory was the noblest quest. Dahlgren had defined glory in terms of international reputation as an ordnance expert, power to direct the development of ordnance, and promotion to high rank. His quest had driven him to overcome the entrenched resistance of hidebound superiors in order to innovate in naval ordnance. As a result, the United States Navy had gained its first research and development establishment, a crop of ordnance specialists, and, for a shining moment, the world's most powerful and reliable naval cannon.

Unfortunately for both Dahlgren and the navy, tradition dictated that the quarterdeck of a fighting ship at sea, not a bureau in Washington, was the place to find glory. Dahlgren achieved international recognition as an ordnance expert, but he gained neither the power to shape the development of ordnance nor what he perceived to be an adequate reward for his service. As a result, the navy began to lose the lead in ordnance it had gained over the Europeans, lagging behind in solving the rifle and armor questions, and causing Dahlgren to redefine his quest for glory in traditional terms. The effort he expended in seeking command of the South Atlantic Blockading Squadron surely detracted from his performance at the Bureau of Ordnance.

Gideon Welles recognized the value of Dahlgren's work to the navy, but because Dahlgren had not won a great victory, and because Welles believed that the interests of the fleet would be served best if Dahlgren remained chief of ordnance, the secretary resisted both his promotion to rear admiral and his bid for a fighting command. Welles failed on both counts because of Dahlgren's luck, his skill as a bureaucratic entrepreneur, and his friendship with Abraham Lincoln.

The result was that Dahlgren set sail for Charleston under enormous pressure. The press and the public demanded retribution against the cradle of the rebellion. The political means by which Dahlgren had won promotion and assignment to the South Atlantic Blockading Squadron made him enormously unpopular among certain politicians, many brother officers, and key superiors. Only success would vindicate him in their eyes. Dahlgren had staked his reputation on achieving a great victory.

3

THE ADMIRAL

18

Morris Island and Fort Sumter

July–December 1863

The South Atlantic Blockading Squadron was a large-scale command. Geographically, its area of responsibility extended from the North Carolina–South Carolina border down some 300 miles of coastline to the southern tip of Florida. There were twenty-three principal ports, inlets, sounds, and rivers capable of supporting commerce along this coastline, including Charleston and the base at Port Royal. Under Dahlgren the squadron ranged in size from seventy to ninety-six vessels.[1]

Dahlgren's mission was threefold: capturing Charleston, blockading the South Atlantic coast, and defending the fleet and base at Port Royal. To accomplish this mission he would have to conduct four distinct types of operations: supporting ground troops, naval attack on land fortifications, blockading, and underwater warfare.[2]

Dahlgren would draw on past experience to devise and execute operations in order to carry out his mission. Although he never received formal instruction in tactics, he was not ignorant of the subject. His translation of Paixhans, the ordnance lectures at the Naval Academy, and the wealth of material he produced in the 1850s to support the development of the Dahlgren gun emphasized tactical doctrine. Unfortunately, these works focused on duels between wooden ships on the open sea; they had little to

251

do with the littoral operations he would conduct at Charleston. And as with most of his peers, there was nothing in his experience to prepare him for blockading or underwater warfare.

But Dahlgren's background did include some knowledge of joint operations and attacking land fortifications. He had developed ways to support ground troops while working on the boat guns. His 1851 paper on coast defense included a study of fortifications. In *Shells and Shell Guns* he had discussed actions of allied fleets against Russian shore batteries during the Crimean War. Especially applicable was his study of the French use of armored floating batteries against Russian forts at Kinburn. He had also taken a keen interest in the effect of heavy shells on masonry during the November 1856 bombardment of the Barrier Forts in Canton, China, by U.S. vessels.[3] Most of this was theoretical knowledge, however. Dahlgren had been assigned one of the navy's largest commands, but he had no combat experience at all.

MORRIS ISLAND AND FORT SUMTER

By June 1863 Welles had come to accept Du Pont's contention that Charleston would not fall to a naval force alone; it would have to be a joint navy-army operation. Although he would have preferred sending the ironclads to Farragut for an attack on Mobile, Alabama, he conceded that Charleston remained important from a political standpoint. To capture the city would not only redeem the navy's honor in the wake of Du Pont's failure but also boost Union morale, which was sagging under the weight of financial difficulties, the draft, and the disaster at Chancellorsville, Robert E. Lee's greatest victory. Furthermore, the monitors, on which the Navy Department had spent enormous sums of money, proved to be useless for operations on the open sea. Barely able to remain afloat outside protected coastal waters, they could neither pursue enemy commerce raiders nor escort valuable cargo vessels such as those carrying California gold. Only by taking the remaining Confederate seaports, or at least by occupying their harbors, could more seaworthy blockaders be released for such duties. Since Charleston and Wilmington tied up the most ships, Welles accorded their capture the highest priority.[4]

Dahlgren's counterpart in the Union army would be Quincy A. Gillmore. Gillmore had graduated first in his class at West Point in 1849, built seacoast

Quincy Adams Gillmore (National Archives)

fortifications, and in 1856 received the coveted job of heading the army engineer office responsible for the defenses of New York City. During the Civil War he served as chief engineer of the Port Royal expedition during the winter of 1861–62, reduced Fort Pulaski at the mouth of the Savannah River in April 1862, and won a victory at Somerset, Kentucky, the next month. At Fort Pulaski, Gillmore proved the ability of rifled ordnance to destroy masonry fortifications and thereby established a reputation as the Union army's foremost artillery and engineering officer. Twice breveted for gallantry and meritorious services, he rose to the rank of brigadier general of volunteers.[5]

Gillmore's ego was matched only by his vanity. He posed for photographs with his hand inside his coat, à la Napoleon, as did many other officers of his day. Upon being promoted to major general in the summer of 1863, he had a military band follow him around for a day or so, playing loudly all the while, as if he believed his movements should be set to music.[6] His concern for his reputation outmatched even Dahlgren's, and as time would tell, he would stoop to almost anything to protect it.

In May 1863 Gillmore learned that his superiors in Washington were considering him for operations against Charleston. He wrote a letter asking for the job to his friend Brigadier General George W. Cullum, who was serving as chief of staff to Major General Henry W. Halleck, general in chief, United States Army. Halleck thereupon summoned Gillmore to Washington.[7]

Later that month, in a series of conferences with Fox, Secretary of War Stanton, and Halleck, Gillmore proposed a general four-step plan for joint operations against Charleston. The army would (1) make an amphibious landing on Morris Island, (2) capture Fort Wagner, and (3) knock Fort Sumter to pieces. The navy would then (4) remove the harbor obstructions, enter the channel, steam up to the wharves past the remaining enemy batteries, and demand the surrender of the city. Welles, Fox, and Stanton applauded the plan. Even Halleck, who generally disapproved of joint operations, seemed to like it. On 12 June 1863 Gillmore took command of the Department of the South, the army counterpart to the South Atlantic Blockading Squadron.[8]

Dahlgren arrived at Port Royal at 7:30 on the morning of 4 July. Two and a half hours later, he climbed on board the *Wabash*, Du Pont's flagship. Du Pont received him with the proper fanfare and treated him cordially. Two days later, Du Pont formally turned over command of the South Atlantic Blockading Squadron. He then boarded the steamer *Augusta* and headed north, never to command at sea again.[9]

Dahlgren had received but one specific instruction from Welles: "Please afford [Gillmore] all the aid and assistance in your power in conducting his operations."[10] Other than that, he "was to consider himself clothed with full powers" in planning and executing his own operations.[11]

The success of the campaign would depend on Dahlgren's and Gillmore's ability to cooperate and to solve problems themselves. There was no overall Union joint commander at Charleston. Dahlgren had command of the naval forces and Gillmore the army forces. Neither had authority over the other. The navy chain of command ran upward from Dahlgren to Fox to Welles to Lincoln. Similarly, the army chain ran up from Gillmore to Halleck to Stanton to Lincoln. Like Dahlgren and Gillmore, Welles and Halleck had different ideas about the campaign. Welles had begun to entertain doubts

Rear Admiral John A. Dahlgren and his monitors (United States Naval Institute)

that an attack on Charleston would succeed but had failed to convey his misgivings to anyone else. Halleck remained confident that the city could be taken yet seemed ready to withdraw the army forces there and dispatch them to Vicksburg. There were other problems. Fox's distaste for joint operations stemmed largely from Halleck's claiming exclusive army credit for the victories at Forts Henry and Donelson.[12] Furthermore, no written plans for a joint attack on Charleston existed when Gillmore and Dahlgren assumed their respective commands.[13]

Dahlgren and Gillmore met on 4 and 5 July to discuss operations. The general wanted to attack Morris Island as soon as possible. A month earlier the admiral had considered a purely naval attack against Charleston, but he thought one feasible only if the Navy Department gave him six or seven more monitors in addition to the seven already under his command. Since Welles had told him that no new monitors would be ready before October, Dahlgren considered his primary role to be support of army operations ashore. In none of these initial meetings between the two commanders did Gillmore mention his grand four-phase plan. "Morris Island…alone,"

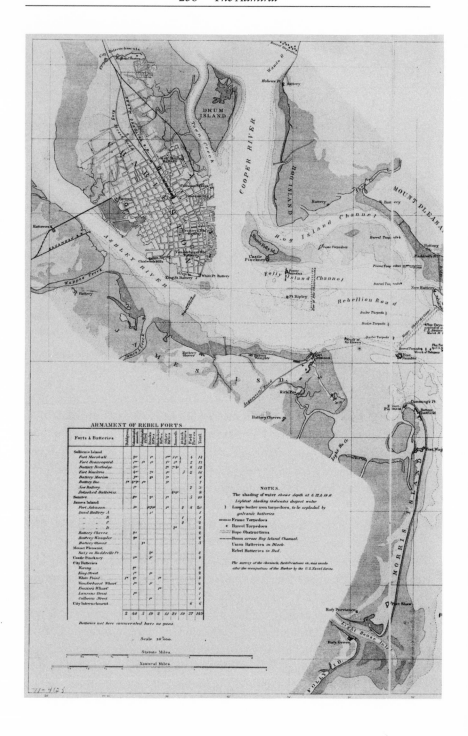

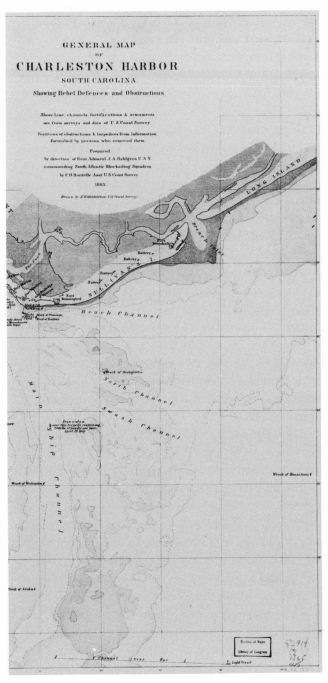

Charleston's fortifications and underwater defenses. "Prepared by Direction of Rear Admiral J. A. Dahlgren, U.S.N. commanding South Atlantic Blockading Squadron...1865." (Library of Congress)

Dahlgren later recalled, "was the subject of arrangement." Although Dahlgren clearly understood that a naval assault into the harbor was in the offing, he believed it would come later rather than sooner. Gillmore, however, viewed the upcoming Morris Island operations strictly within the framework of his larger plan. Thus, the two commanders miscommunicated from the start.[14]

Four days after Dahlgren assumed command of the South Atlantic Blockading Squadron, Federal forces attacked. At five o'clock on the morning of 10 July, twenty-five hundred Union troops landed on the southern end of Morris Island and began moving north. The monitors *Nahant, Montauk, Weehawken,* and *Catskill,* in which Dahlgren wore his flag, opened fire at 6:15 to cover the advance. Small craft armed with Dahlgren boat guns provided close-in support. Well-aimed gunfire from the vessels drove the Confederates from their positions. Shell and canister inflicted heavy casualties on the defenders as they retreated toward Fort Wagner. By nine o'clock the Federals occupied three-fourths of the island, with skirmishers in range of Wagner. The troops, exhausted by the heat and by four hours of combat, went no further. The monitors moved up to bombard Wagner, maintaining a steady fire until six that evening. Confederate gunners in Wagner and Fort Sumter concentrated their return fire on Dahlgren's flagship, scoring sixty hits. Dahlgren rode in the *Catskill*'s pilothouse, located on top of the turret, the most exposed part of the ship. A flying bolthead driven off by a Confederate hit barely missed him.[15]

At dawn the next day Gillmore's troops assaulted Fort Wagner. The Confederates beat them back, inflicting 339 casualties. The attack failed because the Union forces were outnumbered. Dahlgren first learned of the attack at six. Three hours later, Gillmore asked him for gunfire support. The admiral sent four monitors, but by then it was too late. Nevertheless, in an after-action report to Welles, Dahlgren praised both the monitors and Gillmore's effort. Welles thought that Gillmore had attacked prematurely and with insufficient forces.[16]

Dahlgren and Gillmore decided to soften up Fort Wagner with a heavy bombardment before launching another attack. For a week Dahlgren's ironclads kept up a steady fire on the fort while Federal troops constructed batteries on Morris Island. Dahlgren kept in constant communication with the army commanders and eagerly concentrated twenty-one warships for the upcoming assault. By 17 July Gillmore's engineers had established forty guns on the island in four batteries.[17]

The next day Federal naval and land forces bombarded Fort Wagner for eleven hours. Confederate commanders estimated that the Federal forces fired nine thousand shells at the rate of about fourteen per minute. Dahlgren wore his flag in the *Montauk,* which, along with four other monitors and the *New Ironsides,* closed to within 300 yards of Wagner. "Such a cracking of shells and thunder of cannon and flying of sand and earth into the air," the admiral noted in his diary. The bombardment seemed to be tearing Wagner to shreds, but in reality the fort's sand walls absorbed most of the punishment and protected those inside. Late in the afternoon Gillmore signaled that he intended to storm the fort at sunset, when the dim light would make it difficult for Confederate gunners on the islands across the harbor to see their targets. The Federal cannonade ceased as the sun set, and six thousand attacking troops moved forward in a dense column. Dahlgren watched darkness envelop the mass of men. The thirteen hundred defenders in Fort Wagner and nearby Confederate batteries poured a withering fire into the attackers. At the climax of the battle, a few soldiers of the Fifty-fourth Massachusetts, the most famous black regiment of the Civil War, made it to the top of the parapet. There most of them fell. Dahlgren saw flashes of light and heard the sharp rattle of musketry and cannon but did not allow the fleet to fire on the fort because he could not distinguish friend from foe. The attackers retreated after a fierce fight, leaving behind fifteen hundred casualties. The Confederates lost 188 men. The next day a truce was declared so that both sides could bury their dead and tend their wounded. In his after-action report to Welles, Dahlgren attributed the failure to "a manifest lack of force."[18]

Gillmore settled down to siege operations. His engineers constructed a series of zigzag trenches approaching Fort Wagner while his gunners bombarded the fort day and night. Nearly every morning the fleet would close in and pound it all day with its own heavy ordnance, stopping only for lunch. The navy gunners became expert with their fire, placing shells almost anywhere they wanted. The gunners even devised a way to reach the center of the fort by ricocheting shells off the water. No doubt having the United States Navy's principal ordnance expert as their commanding officer had something to do with their performance.[19]

Nevertheless, doubts began to arise among Union leaders about whether the siege would go on. Gillmore kept asking Halleck for more troops, but the general in chief had no wish to send them. In dispatches to Welles, Dahlgren expressed concern that the campaign might end if no additional troops

Fort Sumter, April 1861 (United States Naval Academy Museum)

arrived. Halleck refused even to discuss the matter with Fox, so Welles raised the issue with Lincoln. The president agreed that reinforcements were necessary and ordered Halleck to send ten thousand men to the Department of the South. As one of Gillmore's subordinates put it, "Charleston is too important to be lost when so nearly won." Halleck, miffed about Lincoln's interference, upbraided Gillmore for requesting additional men. "Had it been supposed that you would require more troops," Halleck wrote Gillmore, "the operations would not have been attempted with my consent."[20]

By 8 August the Federals had opened a parallel 500 yards from Wagner. This brought the sappers within range of Fort Sumter's barbette guns, whose projectiles arced over Wagner and fell almost vertically into the Union trenches. Federal progress stopped cold. Unless Sumter's barbette batteries were silenced, Wagner might hold out until sickness and attrition compelled a Federal withdrawal from Morris Island.[21]

On 17 August, Dahlgren's ironclads and Gillmore's guns on Morris Island, the war's largest concentration of heavy ordnance, opened up a week-long bombardment of Fort Sumter. The cannonade pounded Sumter's brick walls into rubble and silenced its guns, allowing Union sappers to press closer to Wagner.[22] The general requested support from the ironclads almost daily. Dahlgren cooperated fully[23] but warned Gillmore that the monitors' cannon were wearing out. The general agreed that the guns should not be used up against Wagner and Sumter but should be "kept for the interior defenses of Charleston."[24]

The bombardment of Sumter climaxed on 23 August. At about three that morning the monitors *Weehawken, Montauk, Nahant, Passaic,* and *Patapsco* took up a position approximately 800 yards from the fort and opened fire. Confederate batteries in Fort Moultrie fired back, scoring several hits. The monitors had fired a total of seventy-one rounds before day broke and fog obscured the view on both sides. "Finding Sumter pretty well used up," Dahlgren noted, "I concluded to haul off, for the men had been at work two days and two nights and were exhausted."[25]

Later that day Gillmore wrote Dahlgren, "I consider the offensive power of Sumter entirely destroyed from to-day's firing. I do not believe they can serve a single gun."[26] The general later recalled that Sumter was "reduced to the condition of a mere infantry outpost, alike incapable of annoying our approaches to Fort Wagner, or of inflicting injury upon the iron-clads." He believed that Dahlgren was free to launch an attack into the harbor and fully expected him to do so. As he saw it, the army had eliminated the threat to the fleet; it was now up to the navy to deliver the city.[27]

Joint bombardment of Fort Sumter, August 1863 (Beverley Robinson Collection, United States Naval Academy Museum)

Fort Sumter, November 1863 (United States Naval Academy Museum)

But the general had overlooked three important developments. First, the condition of the fleet had deteriorated. On 23 August, Dahlgren could muster only five of the seven monitors under his command and the broadside ironclad *New Ironsides* for an attack against Charleston. One of the two unavailable monitors was on station in Wassau Sound, keeping her eye on a Confederate ram building in Savannah; the other was having her pilot-house repaired at Port Royal. All had been in service for six to seven months and were the worse for wear. In the actions off Morris Island the monitors had fired approximately eight thousand rounds and received 882 hits. Their 15-inch guns were fast approaching the upper limit of their three-hundred-round service life, and only a few 11-inchers were available as replacements. Enemy shot had bent many armor plates, loosened turret packing, and sheared off dozens of nuts and bolts. Lying close inshore during often foul weather had strained their hulls, causing some to leak badly. Their bottoms had become fouled with barnacles and grass, reducing their speed to between 3 and 3½ knots. Dahlgren eventually had to shuttle the monitors, two at a time, to the navy's repair facilities at Port Royal.[28]

The second development was that during the two weeks following 23 August, the Confederates systematically removed all of Fort Sumter's serviceable heavy cannon and distributed them among the James Island batteries, Fort Moultrie, and the city of Charleston. This made the inner defenses more formidable than the outer "wall of fire" that had wrought such havoc on the ironclads during Du Pont's attack.[29]

Finally, and most important, while Union cannon were pounding Fort Sumter to rubble, the Confederates had been strengthening their underwater defenses. To gather intelligence on the enemy's underwater defenses, Dahlgren used active measures such as sending vessels to reconnoiter the harbor and passive measures such as interrogating deserters and examining obstructions washed down by heavy weather. He learned that the enemy's underwater defenses included various kinds of mines, nets, rafts, and booms—even booms made of railroad iron. The mines could be detonated electrically from shore or by contact with ships, and they ranged in size from metal cylinders filled with about 40 pounds of gunpowder to steam boilers filled with 1,000 to 2,000 pounds of powder. Dahlgren concluded that these obstructions would have to be removed before his ships could pass into the harbor without undue risk. In sum, the defenses of Charleston had grown stronger and the ironclads weaker since Du Pont's attack of 7 April.[30]

Nevertheless, Dahlgren intended to launch a naval attack into the harbor. Early in the evening of 26 August, he assembled the skippers of the ironclads to explain his plan. "Smart seamen" working from small boats and a steam tug would use "tackles, straps, fish hooks, saws, augurs, chisels, hammers, and anything else deemed necessary" to clear a lane through the obstructions between Forts Wagner and Sumter, then the monitors were to pass the forts and attack into the harbor. If Fort Moultrie or any other Confederate fort opened fire while the tug and boat crews were at work, the monitors were to move up to shield them with their turrets.

Captain Stephen Clegg Rowan, skipper of the *New Ironsides,* vehemently denounced the plan. Dahlgren noted in his diary that Rowan was "a great drawback, full of objections,…and is ready to cavil at anything." None of the other ironclad skippers dissented.

After the meeting, Dahlgren hoisted his flag in the *Weehawken.* The ironclads got going at nine that night but had difficulty making headway against the strong flood tide. After about two hours the weather took a turn for the worse. Strong winds buffeted the boats and the tug while torrents of rain soaked their crews. The *Weehawken*'s pilot declared that a southeaster was coming. Dahlgren called off the attack.[31]

He intended to try again on 29 August but canceled the operation because of reports of Confederate gunfire from Fort Sumter. The success of a naval attack, he reasoned, depended upon absolute silence from the fort. Even musket fire from Sumter would hinder efforts to clear the obstructions, and he considered it impossible to enter the harbor while they remained in place.

Thus, Dahlgren still regarded Sumter as a viable threat. From the Confederate viewpoint the underwater defenses, covered by fortifications on shore and in the harbor, were keeping Union warships out.[32] Dahlgren and Gillmore never did figure out a way for their men to remove the harbor obstructions under fire. "Lack of attention to this single detail," according to historian Rowena Reed, "rendered all the rest of their preparations worthless."[33]

Dahlgren finally attacked on 1 September. His purpose, however, was not to enter the harbor but to knock out Sumter. At about ten that night Dahlgren hoisted his flag in the *Weehawken* and led the ironclads up the channel. A couple of hours of slow steaming brought the ships to a position 500 yards from Sumter. They opened fire on the fort, which replied with only two rounds. Fort Moultrie, however, "blazed away in full style," as Dahlgren put it in his diary. In five hours of action the ironclads fired a total of 245 shells, receiving 71 hits in return. One Confederate shot hit the base of the *Weehawken*'s turret and drove off an iron splinter that broke the leg of Dahlgren's fleet captain, Captain Oscar C. Badger. The vessels withdrew at daylight when the flood tide came in. Instead of resuming operations "with a view of forcing a passage," Dahlgren wrote in his after-action report to Welles, "General Gillmore is now ready for another movement and I propose to assist him first."[34]

Gillmore's sappers had pushed their siege lines to within 150 yards of Fort Wagner. The general decided that the time had come to complete the seizure of Morris Island. Unable to understand why Dahlgren would not attack into the harbor, Gillmore intended to mount batteries on Cummings Point to provide covering fire for the ironclads and, he hoped, to prod the navy into action. Dahlgren offered him naval support for the final assault on Fort Wagner. Gillmore accepted.[35]

At dawn on 5 September the general's artillery and the admiral's ships opened up a forty-two-hour bombardment of Wagner. The Union forces used calcium lights to illuminate the fort at night. As the shells began to fall, the Confederates on Morris Island numbered nine hundred to the Union's eleven thousand. The bombardment cut the defenders down to four hundred effectives. Gillmore had scheduled the final assault for the morning of 7 September, but the Confederates had evacuated Morris Island the night before.[36] At about 5:10 on the morning of the seventh, Gillmore signaled Dahlgren, "The whole island is ours, but the enemy have escaped us."[37]

In an attempt to exploit any ensuing confusion or loss of morale in the Confederate ranks, Dahlgren demanded the immediate surrender of Fort

Sumter. "Come and take it" was the reply.[38] Dahlgren intended to do exactly that. He ordered Commander T. H. Stevens to lead an amphibious assault on the fort. Stevens said that he knew nothing about amphibious operations. "There is nothing but a corporal guard at the fort," Dahlgren replied, "and all we have to do is go in and take possession." The admiral spent most of 8 September preparing for the assault, set for that night. He signaled Gillmore of his intention. The general sent word that he was planning the same thing and suggested that Dahlgren place his force under army command to coordinate the effort and prevent mistakes. Dahlgren turned down the suggestion flat. He did not want to share the glory with Gillmore.[39]

Dahlgren did not know that his plan was doomed. On 4 September the Confederates had replaced the artillerymen in Fort Sumter with infantry, who fashioned a strong fortification out of the rubble in almost no time at all. Worse, in April the Confederates had recovered a code book from the wreck of the *Keokuk,* enabling them to read the signals exchanged between Dahlgren's flagship and Gillmore's headquarters. They intercepted the admiral's signal on the afternoon of the eighth and prepared a hot reception.[40]

In the wee hours of the ninth, small boats containing Dahlgren's force of five hundred sailors and marines rowed toward Fort Sumter, completely unaware that Confederate eyes watched their every move. When the boats had drawn to within a few yards of the fort, the Confederates fired a withering blast. Union sailors who struggled ashore met a deluge of hand grenades and musket fire. Then the Confederate ironclad *Chicora* opened up on them, as did the artillery across the harbor. Unable to scale the walls, the Union forces sheltered in the recesses, realizing that they had fallen into a trap. Those who could, surrendered. The rest withdrew, leaving behind 127 sailors and marines. The Confederates lost nobody. Gillmore's assault never got started. His men had gathered at a rendezvous point in a creek west of Morris Island, but when the general realized that the sailors had failed, he canceled the operation.[41]

Dahlgren had intended to observe the attack in person, but it went off while he was still a quarter of a mile away. Nevertheless, he was close enough to realize that it had failed. He must have been shocked, for he had felt almost certain of success. He spent the rest of the night in a small boat, ready to render any aid he could. He sent an after-action report to Welles on 11 September. The secretary considered the attack "a hasty and not very thoroughly matured movement." Du Pont, who heard of the attack a few days later, thought it "the silliest and worse-managed affair" he had ever heard of.

He suspected that Dahlgren's wretched health may have contributed to the failure.[42]

Du Pont may have been right. Gastritis had stricken Dahlgren about two months after his arrival in the South. The following excerpts from his diary chronicle his condition:

12 August Feel badly—Stomach does not act—hot weather—weakens me very much—Must hold out.

15 August Nothing but the will has kept me up—my head swam and I could hardly walk five minutes

26 August One of these debilitating days such as I have seen no where else; I was so feeble that I could hardly rise from the chair and walk across the room.

28 August ... the debility increases so that to-day it is an exertion to sit in a chair—I feel like lying down—My head is light—I do not see well— How strange—no pain, but so feeble that it seems like gliding away to— death—How easy it seems—Why not, to one whose race is run—?

2 September Got up at 2—just able to dress and sit in chair life seemed to be passing away without pain

19 September I have been much prostrated, and not a doctor to say why.[43]

Rumors circulated in Gillmore's command that Dahlgren was too sick to do his duty. "Some lying asses of sojers," Henry Wise wrote Dahlgren, "have been writing letters in the papers, saying you had been ill abed for 10 days." Dahlgren admitted to Wise that he indeed had been ill but wrote, "I am getting very much better and will be all right in a few days—never took the steel out of me. During the night of Sumter I was up throughout. Went up to the scene of action & was in a five oared boat from midnight to daylight the day before I was hardly able to cross the cabin."[44]

The physical and mental stress of command probably caused Dahlgren's illness. He had to contend not only with the strain of almost constant operations but also with his unpopularity among his fellow officers and their belief that he was no fighter. The illness, which his habit of hard work probably exacerbated, might have clouded his judgment, not only about the boat attack but also about all the operations he had conducted since the beginning of August.

As he recovered he began to despair about the state of affairs at Charleston. On a bright, beautiful Sunday near the end of September he paused to reflect on his life. He daydreamed fondly of his childhood in Philadelphia, his early days in the navy, and his time with Mary and the children. He wrote in his diary:

> How happily those years rolled away—a little overcast now & then, but still as bright as blaze of noon day—That home!—it was a home—and the little toddlers!—they are grown now.... Then passed away the dream—and I was alone miserable—have never been otherwise since—trouble has never ceased to be my companion—together with name and high rank—And now I look perhaps at the end, tho I am in the vigor of life—But it is in truth only the lees of life—there is nothing to give one a moment's real pleasure, such as I used to know.

Dahlgren realized that the tests of war were more severe than he had anticipated. The war was far less glamorous at the front than it had seemed in Washington. Command of the South Atlantic Blockading Squadron was not yielding the glory he so ardently desired.[45]

THE *DAVID*

The Confederates added to Dahlgren's woes with a new twist in their practice of underwater warfare. On the night of 5 October they made their first attack on a Union warship with a torpedo ram. The Confederate craft, appropriately named the *David,* went after the largest enemy vessel in sight, the 3,486-ton *New Ironsides.* The *David* plunged her torpedo against the Union ship's starboard quarter. The explosion shook the *Ironsides* and threw up an immense column of water, which put out the fire in the *David*'s boiler. The *David*'s captain and one of her crew, believing that their vessel was doomed, jumped overboard. They were subsequently picked up by the blockaders. The *David*'s engineer, however, managed to relight the boiler, and the ram made it back to Charleston.[46]

The next day Dahlgren interrogated the captured Confederate crewman. The prisoner described the *David* as a cigar-shaped vessel, 50 feet in length and about 6 feet in diameter, with an engine capable of driving her at 8 to 10 knots and a crew of four. A 10-foot-long spar affixed to her bow mounted

CSS *David,* aground in Charleston harbor, 1863 (Naval Historical Center)

a percussion torpedo that held 60 pounds of powder. No one in the Union fleet at that time knew what had become of the *David.* The *New Ironsides* suffered damage but remained on station until May 1864, when she headed north for repairs.[47]

In response to this new menace, Dahlgren ordered outriggers affixed to the monitors at night. He suggested to Welles that the Union employ vessels similar to the *David* to attack the Confederate ironclads in Charleston harbor. "Nothing could have been more successful as a first effort," he wrote in his diary. "The secrecy, rapidity of movement, control of direction and precise explosion," he wrote Fox, "indicate I think the introduction of the Torpedo element as a means of certain warfare—It can be ignored no longer." He asked Fox for "a quantity of these torpedoes" to turn against the enemy, pointing out that "we can make them faster than they can."[48]

Confederate torpedoes did not dampen Dahlgren's zeal for renewing the attack on Charleston. He was less worried about fixed torpedoes than about those mounted on vessels like the *David.* "They may exist or they may not, may act or not when resorted to, and may be anywhere," he wrote Welles, but they "will not prevent a suitable force from entering and penetrating to Charleston." He considered the worst threat to an attack to be the obstructions covered by gunfire from Forts Moultrie and Johnson. At this point in the channel the forts were out of range of the monitors' guns, but the monitors were vulnerable to plunging fire from the forts. Dahlgren could not guarantee the success of an attack with the seven monitors available to him. But if five more monitors were added to his fleet, he told Welles, "there would be every reason to look for success." He suggested the following mode of attack: "To enter the harbor directly with the ironclads, passing Moultrie, Johnson, and the obstructions, defeating or driving back the three [Confederate] ironclads, knocking down Ripley, silencing Pinckney, and taking position off Charleston."[49]

Welles replied on 9 October, praising Dahlgren's command ability, judgment, and bravery and promising to send four new monitors as soon as they were completed. He noted that because of construction delays, however, it would take another two months. He did not think that attacking before then was a good idea, because he did not want to risk losing the nation's only ironclad fleet while the possibility of other operations along the Southern coast or the possibility of a foreign war existed. He admonished Dahlgren not to allow public impatience to force him into a hasty and premature attack.[50]

DAHLGREN AND GILLMORE

With operations against Charleston thus delayed, rumors about bad blood between Gillmore and Dahlgren began circulating. Welles heard that Gillmore had requested to be relieved of his command because of a dis-

USS *New Ironsides,* circa 1863 (Naval Historical Center)

agreement with Dahlgren. That rumor soon appeared in the newspapers along with another that the two commanders did not get along. Gillmore assured Dahlgren that the rumors were false. In a letter to Dahlgren published in the newspapers, the general attributed the rumors to "some scribbling sensationalist." Not everyone believed him. Du Pont, for one, firmly believed that Gillmore had indeed threatened resignation and had even "declaimed against Dahlgren" to top officials.[51]

Dahlgren believed Gillmore. "Our own papers have caught the infection and lie too," Dahlgren wrote his son Ulric. "They talk of a difficulty between the Gen. and myself—not a word of truth in it—we are as we have been on the most cordial terms. The Gen. came on board to see me the day before yesterday and said how this world is given to lying!"[52]

Gillmore, however, was not at all pleased with Dahlgren. He had fully expected the admiral to enter Charleston harbor and attack the city after 23 August, the date he considered the offensive power of Sumter destroyed. Between that date and Wagner's fall, the general reasoned, Forts Wagner and Sumter posed no threat to the ironclads because they no longer mounted heavy cannon.[53] The cynical words of one infantry officer reflected the general's mood: "One story is that the Rebs have a couple of men with revolvers (Colts Navy). One on Fort Sumter and the other on Fort Moultrie and that the Monitors are afraid to go up least their fire should sink them!"[54] Gillmore was so frustrated by 27 September that he offered to remove the obstructions in the harbor himself. Dahlgren declined the offer because he viewed the task as "my proper work."[55] Nevertheless, the longer Dahlgren delayed the final attack, the more Gillmore's ire grew.

Gillmore pressed him to renew the offensive. On 15 October the general proposed a joint operation against the interior defenses of the harbor. Dahlgren put the matter before Welles. Because of Gillmore's insistence and the public demand for action stirred up by the press, the secretary reconsidered the option of attacking before the new monitors arrived. He ordered Dahlgren to poll the opinion of his officers. Dahlgren held a council of war on the 22 October to discuss the risks and possible benefits of attacking with the seven available monitors. Present were the monitor skippers, the skipper of the *Ironsides,* and two staff officers. After a six-hour discussion Dahlgren put the question to a vote. The four junior officers voted for an attack; the six senior officers voted against one. Dahlgren shared the majority view that the attack should be postponed until the new monitors arrived. He forwarded the minutes of the meeting to Welles.[56]

The secretary replied on 2 November. He agreed that Dahlgren should avoid undue risks. "Although delay is annoying," he wrote, "a failure would be more so. Success is the great and paramount consideration, and the Department will acquiesce in any reasonable delay to insure it." Welles left the final decision up to Dahlgren.[57]

Dahlgren decided to follow the predominant naval view and postpone the attack until the new monitors arrived. He told all of this to Gillmore on 11 November as the two walked the beach at Morris Island. The general said that he supported the decision.[58]

The press, meanwhile, perceiving that the monitors had suffered little damage in the operations off Charleston, had criticized the navy for not attacking. The admiral could not admit the truth about the damage the monitors had sustained without politically damaging the Navy Department and the Lincoln administration. Such information might also prove useful to the enemy. It was the same sort of dilemma Du Pont had faced. Dahlgren's reputation suffered.[59]

Because many of the newspaper accounts seemed to originate from Gillmore's headquarters, Dahlgren began to suspect that the general was behind them. He confronted Gillmore. The general denied any role in it, attributing the bad press to sensational journalism and disgruntled officers. His easy manner allayed Dahlgren's suspicions. How could someone he got along with so well in person be condemning him behind his back?[60]

But Gillmore was doing exactly that. Two of the general's subordinates had gone to Welles's office on 24 October. The secretary was certain that Gillmore had sent them. The officers denounced Dahlgren as "incompetent, imbecile, and insane," declared that he was totally unfit for his command, and hinted that he should be relieved. They submitted some of the correspondence between Gillmore and Dahlgren as evidence of the admiral's inability. Welles disagreed with their assessment, writing in his diary, "[Dahlgren's] cold, selfish, and ambitious nature has been wounded, but he is neither a fool nor insane as those military gentlemen represent and believe. Both Dahlgren and Gillmore are out of place; they are both intelligent, but they can better acquit themselves as ordnance officers than in active command."[61] By definition, an honorable officer should not have lied as Gillmore had done. Dahlgren had given him the benefit of the doubt and would continue to take him at his word until incontrovertible evidence exposed him as a liar.

It did not take long. On 14 December an article in the *New York Tribune* attributed the delay in the naval attack on Charleston to "instructions from

Washington," a reference to Welles's letters of 9 October and 2 November advising Dahlgren to postpone the naval attack until the new monitors arrived. The only people who had seen those documents were Dahlgren, the ironclad skippers, and Gillmore. The article cited the general's headquarters as its source. Dahlgren, however, still refused to believe that Gillmore was responsible. "It is another evidence of the unscrupulous propensity with which some writers are oppressed to make news," he wrote Welles, "if they can not collect it." He would not realize the truth until the following spring.[62]

Welles knew it all along. The visit from Gillmore's officers convinced him that the general was behind Dahlgren's bad press. He told the president what was going on. Upon hearing the suggestion that Dahlgren be relieved, the president exclaimed that he "would be damned if he would do anything to discredit or disgrace John A. Dahlgren."[63] Lincoln, Welles, and even Fox believed that the admiral had done all that could be done with the forces available to him. Four days before Christmas the president censured Gillmore for his behind-the-scenes denunciation of Dahlgren.[64] Gillmore had maintained a mask of cordiality in Dahlgren's presence but secretly had done all he thought he could get away with to undermine him. The egotistical general did not wish to be blamed for the lack of progress at Charleston and had sought to make Dahlgren the scapegoat.

Indeed, Quincy Gillmore bears a good deal of the responsibility for the Union's failure to take Charleston in 1863. Numerous shortcomings offset his successful siege of Fort Wagner and his reduction of Fort Sumter. He failed to explain his four-phase plan in full to Dahlgren. He failed to concentrate his forces for the first two assaults on Fort Wagner. He failed to request naval gunfire support for the 11 July assault on Wagner, probably because he felt confident of success and did not wish to share the glory with the navy.

Worse, Gillmore understood neither the limitations nor the capabilities of the monitors. Until Dahlgren pointed it out to him, he seemed oblivious to the fact that his constant requests for naval gunfire support were wearing the monitors out. He also failed to realize that the monitors' two-gun batteries and low rate of fire limited their effectiveness against fortifications. Historian Herbert W. Wilson believed, rightly, that expecting Dahlgren to take Charleston with ironclads alone was expecting the impossible. Captain Stephen B. Luce, who commanded the monitor *Nantucket* under Dahlgren in 1864, considered this task "hopeless."[65]

Worst of all was Gillmore's ego, manifested in his effort to make Dahlgren the scapegoat for the failure to take Charleston. It eventually poisoned the waters between them, ruining any future chance of cooperation—the essential ingredient of success in joint operations, during the Civil War or at any other time in military history.

Dahlgren, on the other hand, had done reasonably well. He had proven an excellent team player. It is true that his unwillingness to share with the army the glory of capturing Fort Sumter helped to botch the boat attack, but he answered Gillmore's every call for naval gunfire support, despite being ill much of the time. His principal shortcoming was his failure to devise a way for his men to clear the harbor obstructions while under Confederate fire.

Officials in Washington were reasonably pleased with Dahlgren's performance. Wise wrote him, "Fox says, you have done 'nobly' and even should nothing else be effected, the mere fact that you have closed the Port of Charleston is of immense importance and value to the cause.... Everybody from the President down backs you up here; and the Navy Department are doing all possible for your fleet." Wise assured him he would "make a name to last forever in Naval fame."[66] Gideon Welles doubted whether even Farragut, whom Lincoln regarded as the navy's best officer, could have done better at Charleston.[67]

As 1863 drew to a close, Dahlgren paused to reflect on its events. Charleston remained in Confederate hands. The press had accused him of inaction. He could not reply without revealing vital information, so he had to suffer the blow to his reputation in silence. It was a trying experience. Wise tried to console him, assuring him that everyone in Washington believed that he had done all that could be done with the forces available to him.[68]

But Dahlgren was inconsolable. "I am much wearier with the delay of the new Monitors," he wrote, "and sometimes almost despair—It would be easier to fight a dozen battles than stand their postponements."[69] On New Year's Eve he lamented in his diary, "Thus endeth the old year—1863—one that has witnessed my highest advancement—but not my happiness—for I have been loaded with responsibilities that no one could hope to lead to a favorable issue—the best possible of which would ruin the reputation of any man—and now what is there to look forward to."[70]

19

Stalemate
January–November 1864

To paraphrase historian Leo Braudy, in the face of a situation beyond one's control, the only alternatives seem to be withdrawal, resignation, or a glorious death that forever frames one in a heroic posture.[1]

The dawn of 1864 found Dahlgren at such an impasse. On 11 January, Welles reminded him that he had the authority to conduct operations as he saw fit. Five days later, Gillmore told him that the War Department had refused the request for reinforcements and had no intention of doing anything else at Charleston. Therefore, the army could not mount offensive operations against the remaining Confederate forts, even if the ironclads entered the harbor. In light of their experience, the two commanders agreed that the forts would not fall to naval action alone.[2]

Nevertheless, Dahlgren intended to enter the harbor to shell the forts and perhaps engage the enemy ironclads once the new monitors arrived.[3] He so relished the prospect of winning glory in a naval attack that he could not bring himself to abandon the idea. He might even have harbored a fantasy of dying in a blaze of glory, as implied in this letter to Henry Wise: "When we go in you may be sure there will be some severe hammering. My own life I do not set at a pin's fee,—I have had all from it that's worth having,—but I want to do that piece of work in the best manner if I never do another.…

Won't it be magnificent when we go in—there will be some firing then, Wise."[4]

But the new monitors would never arrive in Charleston. By the end of 1863 the War Department had abandoned the idea of capturing the city.[5] In 1864 Welles also abandoned the idea of capturing Charleston and sent the ironclads elsewhere. Stephen B. Luce put it this way: "The government's policy was to keep only just enough troops in and about that district to occupy the attention of the Confederate authorities and prevent them from sending the troops for the defense of Charleston, to re-enforce the army under Lee."[6] Instead of launching a glorious naval attack on the cradle of the rebellion, Dahlgren spent the year mired in the routine of blockade, coping with Confederate mines and submersibles, defending his reputation, refighting old battles, and mourning the death of his son.

THE *HUNLEY*

Confederate torpedo craft proved a constant annoyance to the Union blockaders. In the wake of the *David*'s attack on the *New Ironsides,* Dahlgren implemented effective countermeasures to defend his ironclads against future torpedo attacks. Every night the monitors steamed to a position in shallow water in the outer harbor and dropped anchor. Sailors hung heavy nets from their fenders while boats towed log booms around them. Less valuable craft shielded the monitors by anchoring alongside. Dahlgren increased the numbers of lookouts standing watch and boats patrolling nearby. Calcium searchlights swept the surrounding waters. For the remainder of the war, Union sailors off Charleston stood to their guns by night and slept by day.[7]

Early in January, deserters from the city told Dahlgren that the *David* and a second vessel of its class were ready for action. They said that nine other "Davids," which had become a generic name for such craft, were in various stages of construction. They had also seen a second kind of torpedo boat, which they called the *Diver*. Unlike the Davids, it operated completely underwater. They said that the *Diver* had passed successfully under surface vessels on three separate occasions. But in other trials, three crews had drowned. Dahlgren immediately warned the ironclad skippers. Night after night they nervously awaited an attack.[8]

The Confederates struck on the night of 17 February. At about 8:45 the officer of the deck on board the USS *Housatonic* spotted what appeared to be a plank closing on his ship from 100 yards off the starboard side. He sounded the alarm. All hands came to quarters, the chain was slipped, and the engine backed. Three minutes later an explosion ripped through the ship. The *Housatonic* settled into the water stern-first, heeling to port as she sank. The ship went down in less than five minutes. Most of the crew saved themselves by scrambling into the rigging. Five men died. Despite Dahlgren's warning, the attack took the Union squadron by surprise. The *Housatonic* was a wooden screw-steamer, not an ironclad. The Confederates had targeted her because the monitors were so well protected.[9]

Dahlgren dispatched an official report to Welles two days later, mistakenly identifying the attacker as a David. It was actually the *Hunley*, the vessel the deserters had referred to as the *Diver*. Dahlgren feared that "the whole line of blockade will be infested with these cheap, convenient, and formidable defenses." He suggested that the Department offer a prize of $20,000 to $30,000 for each David captured or destroyed.[10]

Dahlgren believed that the loss of the *Housatonic* would force Union authorities to take underwater warfare seriously. "Torpedoes have been laughed at," he wrote in his diary, "but this disaster ends that." He also thought that the Confederates had wasted a golden opportunity. "You have heard by this time of the disaster to the Housatonic," he wrote his son Ulric. "I have cried Wolf, wolf!—until tired—and no one but a few seem[ed] to regard the danger as real—*Now*, it has come and a heavy blow it is,—Yet if the Rebs. had been wiser they might have made it almost irremediable by striking at several vessels, and those of more value—Everyone will be wide awake now and they will not get another chance very soon again."[11]

Dahlgren took additional countermeasures against torpedo attacks, ordering all ships either skirted with booms and nets or kept constantly under way each night. Dahlgren told Welles that torpedoes constituted "the most formidable of the difficulties in the way to Charleston."[12]

The *Hunley*'s success granted the Confederates a significant measure of control in their defense of Charleston. Dahlgren's countermeasures prevented further torpedo-boat attacks from succeeding but ceded control of Charleston harbor to the Confederates at night, enabling them to beef up their fortifications and underwater defenses in the inner harbor. Dahlgren entertained various proposals for mine- and obstruction-clearing contraptions from private inventors, but apparently none of them worked out. He never tried to interfere with the Confederates' efforts to strengthen their underwater defenses, and he mounted operations to remove the obstruc-

CSS *Hunley* (Naval Historical Center)

tions only when launching an attack. On one such occasion the monitor *Patapsco*, sent to cover small craft engaged in clearing obstructions and rigged with a variation of Ericsson's torpedo rake, struck a mine and went down with sixty-two officers and men. Dahlgren never did find an effective counter to Confederate underwater defenses.[13]

The Confederate successes in underwater warfare demoralized Dahlgren's officers. Four days after the *Hunley*'s attack, Dahlgren noted in his diary, "It is evident that I am very indifferently supported—no zeal—just a look out for bread & butter—the officers are against the War."[14]

Washington Interlude

Despite his officers' lack of enthusiasm, or perhaps because of it, the loss of the *Housatonic* increased Dahlgren's eagerness to launch a Union attack. "I am very weary of delay more so than the nincoms. who cry out, apathy!" he wrote Ulric. "We have a Wolf by the ears, and we cannot let him alone,— if we do not attack, they will,—when they are ready." But the admiral found himself in an ambiguous position. He had been given the authority to conduct operations at his own discretion and believed that the Navy Department wanted him to go on the offensive, but he construed Welles's communication of 2 November 1863 as an admonition not to attack unless success was guaranteed. "It rarely happens that a Commander can promise even to himself an absolute certainty of success," he wrote Welles, "unless his advantage of numbers or position are decided." Still expecting reinforcements, Dahlgren wanted to launch the attack with at least ten monitors. If Welles would not dispatch reinforcements, Dahlgren figured that he would need at least six monitors to maintain the blockade.[15]

Dahlgren decided to go to the Navy Department to discuss these options with Welles in person. The secretary agreed that it was a good idea. Dahlgren boarded his flagship, the *Harvest Moon,* and departed for Washington after midnight on 27 February.[16]

The trip exhilarated him. On 2 March a hard, cold, northwest wind blew while the ship entered the Potomac. "I feel a different man," Dahlgren wrote in his diary. "There is vitality in a Northern atmosphere." As no pilot could be found for the ascent of the river, the admiral decided to guide the ship himself. Snow streaked the banks of the Potomac as the *Harvest Moon* steamed upstream. Pleased with himself, Dahlgren noted that the ship touched bottom only once because a buoy was out of place. He arrived at the Washington Navy Yard at five that evening, ate dinner, and afterward paid a visit to Welles's home. The secretary and his family gave him a warm welcome. He then visited Fox, who also seemed glad to see him.[17]

The next day Dahlgren's skin tingled in the politically charged atmosphere of the capital as he headed for the Navy Department. The city was "alive with crowds," he noted, "making money on the War." Another chat with the assistant secretary soon dampened his mood. Fox opposed an attack on Charleston unless the admiral was certain of success. He said a defeat would hurt the government, the Navy Department, and Dahlgren's reputation. He suggested that Dahlgren hand the monitors over to Farragut for the upcoming attack on Mobile. After Mobile fell, Dahlgren could have the monitors and anything else needed to attack Charleston.

Dahlgren visited Lincoln that evening. They talked about Charleston. Although Dahlgren was upset by Fox's revelation about the change in plans for the new monitors, he did not burden his friend with it. Nevertheless, the admiral could not resist grumbling about what the newspapers were saying about his conduct of the campaign. The president smoothed Dahlgren's ruffled feathers. "Well, you never heard me complain," said Lincoln. "No, I never did," said Dahlgren. The two friends had a pleasant chat that lasted almost until midnight.[18]

Dahlgren fretted over Fox's suggestion for the next day and a half. He concluded that the attack on Charleston would be postponed indefinitely. He decided that there was no glory in presiding over a stalemate. On 5 March he called on Welles to resign his command of the South Atlantic Blockading Squadron.[19]

The secretary was utterly astonished. Dahlgren had pulled a lot of strings for this command. Although Welles had opposed giving it to Dahlgren, he doubted whether even Farragut could have done better at Charleston. Furthermore, the secretary no longer regarded capturing the city as essential. Strategically, the blockade was sufficient, although capturing the cradle of rebellion would certainly boost Northern morale. Welles told Dahlgren that he was perfectly satisfied with the job he had done and flatly refused to relieve him.[20]

Dahlgren thereupon argued that he should receive the new monitors instead of Farragut. The ironclads stood a better chance of success against any objective if concentrated into one fleet. Because it was necessary to keep at least a few monitors at Charleston to prevent the Confederate ironclads there from making a sortie against the wooden blockaders, all of the new monitors should be sent to him, along with fifteen thousand to twenty thousand more ground troops. If such a force was assembled and put into action immediately, the campaign would be over by June, freeing an ironclad fleet and an army for use elsewhere. Welles agreed to consider the proposal.[21]

Three days later, the second anniversary of the *Virginia*'s debut at Hampton Roads, Lincoln summoned Dahlgren to the White House. Dahlgren arrived promptly. The president said that he had just received a telegram: Ulric Dahlgren had been killed.[22]

"Like father, like son," goes the old saying. Life had impelled Ulric Dahlgren to embark on his own quest for glory. The Civil War gave him what he sought, but it cost him everything.

As a boy "little Ully" studied Latin, mathematics, and surveying, but he reserved his passion for horses and became a skilled and graceful rider. When his mother died, Ulric sat with his father during his all-night vigil in her room. Afterward Ulric spent many a day at the Washington Navy Yard and often accompanied his father on cruises down the Potomac, including the *Merrimack*'s happier version of the *Princeton* cruise. At age seventeen Ulric wanted to try his own way in the world as a surveyor, but he succumbed to his father's wishes that he study for the bar at an uncle's law firm in Philadelphia.

Ulric Dahlgren, circa 1862 (National Archives)

Like his father, Ulric Dahlgren saw the Civil War as an opportunity to fulfill a dream of glory. After Lincoln got him appointed captain in the army, Ulric served as an aide to Brigadier General Franz Sigel and saw service in the Shenandoah Valley, on the Rappahannock, at Second Bull Run, and along the defenses of Washington. Ulric was a good soldier, compiled a spotless military record, and earned a reputation as an honorable man. In November 1862 he attacked Fredericksburg at the head of Sigel's bodyguard of fifty-seven men, held the town for three hours, and returned with prisoners. Ulric later served with Major General Joseph Hooker at Chancellorsville and Major General George Meade at Gettysburg. On 2 July 1863, during the battle of Gettysburg, Ulric captured a Confederate courier with a dispatch from Jefferson Davis to Robert E. Lee. The dispatch said that it would be impossible for the Confederates to gather another army at Culpepper, Virginia, to threaten Washington and thereby draw off part of the Union army facing Lee. Ulric made a fast 30-mile ride over the mountains and delivered this message to Meade, who supposedly used the intelligence in his decision to fight it out where he was. On 6 July, Ulric was leading a cavalry charge in pursuit of retreating Confederates near Hagerstown, Maryland, when a Confederate musket ball struck his right foot. Too proud to allow a mere foot wound to unsaddle him, Ulric ignored it until the loss of blood forced him down. Three days later he was carried to his father's home in Washington on a litter. By the end of July the doctors had found it necessary to amputate his right leg below the knee.[23]

John Dahlgren tried to comfort his son. "There is nothing good that could happen to me," he wrote Ulric, "which by any possibility could compensate for a serious evil to any of my children." Indeed, the admiral feared for his son's life. "I am…distressed beyond measure by Ully's misfortune," he wrote Wise; "it weighs on me incessantly—to myself it would have been nothing—for my career is nearly run—But he is so young."[24]

Many prominent soldiers and officials visited Ulric while he lay abed, including General Hooker and Secretary of War Stanton. The latter came to tell Ulric that he had been promoted to the rank of colonel for his gallantry. Ulric had skipped the grade of major to become the youngest colonel in the Union army. Lincoln visited Ulric too, to offer "kindly words of heart-felt sympathy." The president had grown fond of his friend's son and felt sorry for both of them.[25]

To Dahlgren's relief, Ulric's condition improved in August. The youth sent his worried father an optimistic note. Dahlgren replied, "I have had nothing so welcome as your letter,—It is not so much what we have in this world as the use we put our means to—You can do a great deal more, minus a foot than most young men who have two—It is no small matter to have fought your way to a colonelcy at 21, and that must lead to more."[26]

By mid-October, Ulric was able to move about on crutches. In November he traveled to Charleston to visit his father. The admiral was delighted to see him but grieved for him. Dahlgren later recalled how he felt upon seeing his son for the first time after the amputation:

I knew of all his suffering—knew that my bright brave boy, had been shorn of his fair proportions,—and yet when he stood at his full manly height before me, I felt that I had not realized *my* loss,—felt yet as one seldom feels in a whole life—it seemed as if a dagger were in my heart,—and I could scarcely refrain from uttering a cry—but I did—he smiled could I dare let him know what I felt! How should any father feel? I had looked on the graceful figure of that gallant son for more than 20 years—graceful & active and manly now alas!—maimed & crippled—My son, my son, how I longed to fall on your neck and weep my welcome.[27]

Ulric made the rounds of command with his father, learning all about the admiral's predicament. He also met Gillmore. War had taken its toll on the general. Gillmore smoked incessantly and complained of difficulty sleeping. Ulric disliked his "foxy" appearance.[28] Perhaps because they shared blood, Ully shared his father's view of the military situation. He wrote Henry Wise:

Father is a little impatient to go in.... It is rather hard...to have all the abuse which has been heaped upon him without a word in reply.... Our attack here must be perfectly successful—we cannot afford to lose or be checked in the smallest way. The power of the Iron Clads must not be shown at a disadvantage—Suppose we should fail—Foreign nations would see our weak points & take advantage of them as quickly as we do. But let more Iron Clads be sent here & Father is confident of perfect success.[29]

Ully left Charleston in January 1864. It was the last time the admiral would see his son alive.

On 1 March 1864 Colonel Ulric Dahlgren set out for Richmond, leading a force of Union cavalry. The operation was the brainchild of twenty-eight-year-old Hugh Judson Kilpatrick, who had risen to the rank of brigadier general just three years after graduating from West Point in 1861. Nicknamed "Kilcavalry," Kilpatrick had a reputation for being aggressive to the point of carelessness. He dreamed of emerging from the war a hero and, ultimately, becoming president of the United States. Toward these ends he devised a two-pronged raid on Richmond to free the thousands of Union soldiers held prisoner on Belle Isle and in Libby Prison. When Ulric Dahlgren caught wind of the raid, he could not resist the temptation to join in, despite the loss of a leg. Kilpatrick's plan sounded foolproof. He would strike from the north, Ulric Dahlgren from the west.[30] Just before the start of the ride, Ulric told his men, "If there is any man here who is not willing to sacrifice his life in such a great and glorious undertaking, let him step out, and he may go home to the arms of his sweetheart and read of the brave who swept through the city of Richmond." To his father he wrote, "If we do not return, there is no better place to give up the ghost."[31] Kilpatrick's plan failed utterly, and Confederate home guardsmen shot Ulric Dahlgren in the back.

"A more gallant and brave-hearted fellow was not to be found in the service," Gideon Welles wrote in his diary. "His death will be a terrible blow to his father, who doted on him and not without reason."[32]

Upon hearing the awful news from the president, Dahlgren asked permission to go to Fort Monroe for confirmation. "Go," said Lincoln. "I authorize it. Ask no one. I will stand by you."[33] Lincoln grieved for Dahlgren's loss. He knew what it was like to lose a son. Two years earlier, death had taken his boy Willie. Dahlgren left Washington that afternoon, hoping that there had been a mistake, praying that his son was still alive.

There was no mistake. Dahlgren arrived at Fort Monroe the next night. Newspapers from Richmond carried accounts of Ulric's death. Dahlgren learned that someone had stripped the body and cut off a finger to get the gold ring that Ulric had worn in remembrance of his sister Lizzie. The Richmond press denounced Ully because of documents allegedly found on the body, purported to be orders to his men calling for the destruction of Richmond, the assassination of Jefferson Davis, the slaughter of livestock, and the like. "Henceforth the name of Dahlgren is linked with eternal infamy," said the *Richmond Examiner,* "and in the years to come defenseless women and innocent children will peruse, with a sense of shrinking horror, the story of Richmond's rescue from the midnight sack and ravage led by Dahlgren."[34]

"May an avenging God pursue them," John Dahlgren wrote of the Richmond press in his diary. He wondered whether there was any truth in the newspaper accounts about the documents. Kilpatrick told him that they were genuine, except for the part about killing Jefferson Davis and burning Richmond. The Northern press claimed that this section was a forgery, designed to inflame Southern hatred of the enemy and to secure foreign aid.[35]

Dahlgren later concluded that the papers were a "shameless imposture." Upon examining a photograph of the documents, he noticed that the signature read "U. Dalhgren." Not only was the last name misspelled, but Ulric had always written out his first name when signing things. This was sufficient evidence for the admiral. "I always told him," he wrote his sister Patty, "that I gave him no middle name in order that he should write his name in full."[36]

Dahlgren remained at Fort Monroe until 15 March, desperately hoping to recover his son's body, but each day brought only frustration and despair. Dahlgren had lost children before: the son he never saw, his son Lawrence, and his daughter Lizzie. He had grieved for them, and for Mary as well, but none of those deaths had upset him as much as Ulric's death did now. The Confederates were assailing not only his son but also the honor, reputation, and very name of Dahlgren. In a letter to Patty the admiral condemned Confederate leaders for condoning the treatment of Ulric's body. The leaders were worse than the "ignorant and unfeeling brute" who cut off the finger, because they at least claimed to be high-minded, honorable gentlemen, while the thief knew no better:

> My son fell like a true man in the lead of his men,—no one in advance of him,—having risked all in an attempt to rescue his fellow soldiers from a horrible captivity—But neither this, nor the evidence of having been maimed in previous battle, nor his humanity at Fredericksburg could create a kind or generous sentiment in the hearts of these terrified cowards who had been too much exasperated by their fears to forgive—
>
> The bravest might be proud of his young, brief, blazing career—And so am I—Would that I had a dozen such to stand up before the world and do battle for a good cause, as he has done—
>
> He has given limb and now life for his country.

Dahlgren vowed to recover his son's body, no matter how long it took; to erect a statue in honor of him, even if no one else helped pay for it; and to write a biography of him, in order to resurrect Ulric's honor and reputation.[37]

Dahlgren returned to Washington on 17 March and spent the next few days in his house on 4^1/$_2$ Street gathering every scrap he could find about his son for the book. A few close friends stopped by to offer their condolences. Articles praising Ulric came out in the Northern papers almost daily. Ulric's friends sent reminiscences and even poetry about the youth. Henry Wise had Ulric's amputated leg sealed inside the cornerstone of a gun foundry being built at the Washington Navy Yard to honor the only portion of the youth's remains that the Confederates had not defiled.[38]

On 25 March Dahlgren thought that he had better go to the Navy

Department and attend to business. He saw Fox first. He reminded the assistant secretary that the Department had been promising him the new monitors for the past six months. Fox said that ironclads had to remain available should Major General Ulysses S. Grant need them to operate in the James River in support of his upcoming campaign in Virginia. Fox doubted that an attack on Charleston would succeed in any case. "A trial should be made," said Dahlgren. Fox replied that Washington had abandoned the idea of capturing Charleston. Dahlgren then saw Welles, who agreed that at least a few of the new ironclads should be reserved to support Grant.[39]

Meanwhile, rumors were running rampant in Washington that Dahlgren was planning to resume his position as chief of the Bureau of Ordnance. Dahlgren had retained nominal charge of the bureau as a condition for getting the South Atlantic Blockading Squadron. Henry Wise, whom Welles considered only a temporary replacement, had done the lion's share of the work while Dahlgren was in South Carolina. No doubt Dahlgren's month-long stay in the capital fueled the rumors of his return to the bureau. There might also have been talk of his request to be relieved of command of the squadron.

The weight of opinion fell decidedly against his returning to the bureau. Charles B. Sedgwick, who had been chairman of the House Naval Affairs Committee in 1861 and 1862 and who considered himself Dahlgren's friend, wanted Wise to be chief. Wise's friend Robert Townsend agreed. "You are just the man for the place," he wrote Wise. Townsend considered Dahlgren more suited to "the development of the theory, and improvement of the materiel and the practice of Gunnery" than to managing the bureau. John S. Missroon, who had been an assistant inspector of ordnance at Boston, wrote Wise that he was "pained to learn that the Dept may possibly deem it necessary to re-place Dahlgren at the head of the Bu: & to put you in some other position—there can be no doubt of his unfitness for a Bu: & that he is far inferior to yourself as a head of that Dept." Another of Wise's friends, R. A. Watkinson, expressed a similar view:

I see the Admiral still keeps himself in the papers as *rumored* to be about to take charge of the Bureau again, as though the ordnance of the country was suspended on the end of his tail. For my part I think it a humiliating position for the Navy Department that the old fogy gentleman that wears that white wig [Welles] is so afraid of offending a few of the Washington City officers.[40]

As usual, the bewigged Welles knew what was really going on. He wrote in his diary that Wise was "almost insane for the appointment of Chief, and, like too many, supposes the way to promotion is by denouncing those who stand in his way, or whom he supposes stand in his way. Mr. Everett writes to old Mr. Blair against Dahlgren. Admiral Stringham and Worden called on me yesterday in behalf of Wise and both opposed D. They were sent by Wise." Wise, who had supported his friend when things went awry at Charleston, had turned against him.[41]

Dahlgren remained unaware of Wise's actions. He was too preoccupied by Ulric's death to notice. In fact, Ully had become an obsession. Dahlgren considered him a "heroic patriot" who had died on a holy mission of sublime purpose. "A purer life, a nobler breast has not been laid on the Altar of the great cause," he wrote, "since it was proclaimed throughout the land." During the first two weeks of April he focused nearly all of his attention on Ulric. His diary entry of 5 April characterizes the period:

> Occupied in collecting every item about dear Ully—old letters &c every day some extracts sent me showing how deeply the brave fellow had taken hold of the feelings everywhere—
>
> Letter from Capt Mitchell 2[d] NY Cavalry, who was in his command and saw much of him—took his meals with him and assisted him off & on his horse writes in glowing terms of the noble boy so brave under fire,—so enduring of hardship—and his presence so influential with the men—Dear Ully you have fought your last battle—Rest my son in peace.[42]

People began to worry about Dahlgren's sanity. Welles visited him on the evening of 8 April. Dahlgren was inconsolable. The secretary advised him "to get abroad and mingle in the world, and not yield to a blow that was irremediable." Secretary of War Stanton ran into Dahlgren on the street ten days later. All the admiral could talk about was Ulric's remains. Stanton thought Dahlgren "had better be quiet for a while."[43]

By mid-April, Welles had decided that the time had come for Dahlgren to return south. Dahlgren met with Welles and Fox several times between the eighteenth and the twenty-third to discuss the Bureau of Ordnance and operations against Charleston. Dahlgren told Welles that he wanted to sever his connection with the bureau, and that Wise wanted to be chief. The admiral said that he would like to "retain the modelling fabrication &c," but would not serve under Wise, whom he outranked. Welles assented and made

Wise chief. Dahlgren remained unaware of his friend's plot. Fox said that Grant definitely wanted naval aid in the James; therefore, a full-scale attack on Charleston was out of the question. On 23 April, Welles ordered Dahlgren to sail for Port Royal.[44]

As Dahlgren wound up his affairs in the capital, a man named Robert Orrock paid him a visit. Orrock said that a Union sympathizer named Lohman had removed Ulric's body from its original grave and had reburied it on his farm. Dahlgren would recover Ulric's remains from Lohman's farm after the war.[45]

Dahlgren Returns South

Just before leaving Washington, Dahlgren stopped in at the Navy Department and the White House to say good-bye. He was unhappy about his prospects. He told Welles not to expect any real progress unless he received the monitors he had been promised. He told Lincoln that all he could do with the forces at his disposal was to hold on. He then went down to the Washington Navy Yard and boarded the *Harvest Moon*. The flagship left the wharf and headed downstream. Dahlgren felt none of the exhilaration he had experienced while steaming up the river two months earlier. "My beloved Ully will never hear from me again," he wrote in his diary. "How little did I dream on entering these waters that I was to suffer this deep sorrow—God help me." The *Harvest Moon* reached Port Royal at noon on 2 May.[46]

The next day Brigadier Generals George H. Gordon and John P. Hatch called on Dahlgren. Gillmore, along with the army's Tenth Corps, had been transferred to the Army of the James. Gillmore had requested the transfer because he did not think Dahlgren intended to attack; Hatch now commanded the Department of the South. The admiral noted that the generals "seemed inclined to pitch in to Gillmore." Dahlgren returned their visit on 4 May. Gordon denounced Gillmore as "untruthfull, selfish and insane for notoriety." He told Dahlgren that Gillmore had encouraged the press campaign against him and had been trying to set him up as a scapegoat for the failure to capture Charleston. "Here is patriotism for you," Dahlgren wrote in his diary, "and honor & honesty!"[47]

But the revelation did not really surprise him. He had begun to suspect as early as January that Gillmore had condoned the newspaper attacks on him, and he had expressed this suspicion to Welles in March. But until now no one had spoken about it as a matter of fact. Dahlgren realized that Gillmore had been lying to him all along. Gillmore would remain an enemy for the rest of his life.[48]

There was also trouble in Dahlgren's own camp. On 6 May his chief of staff, Lieutenant Commander J. M. Bradford, told the admiral a disconcerting tale about his fleet captain, Captain Stephen Clegg Rowan, who had commanded the South Atlantic Blockading Squadron during Dahlgren's Washington interlude. According to Dr. Duvall (the surgeon of the *New Ironsides*), Captain Rowan and his executive officer, Lieutenant George E. Belknap, "had been speaking illy" of the admiral in his absence. This was insubordination.

Dahlgren returned to Charleston two days later but did not confront his flag officer immediately. Rowan stepped on board the flagship and greeted Dahlgren with a smile and a warm handshake. The two conversed freely and spent what Dahlgren considered "a most cordial evening." After Rowan left, the admiral wrote in his diary that he doubted that Rowan had said or done anything against him, "for to act the friend to my face & stab me behind was not possible." How quickly Dahlgren had forgotten that Gillmore had done just that!

The next day Rowan sent Dahlgren a package of letters from Duvall to the Navy Department that accused Rowan, Belknap, and other officers of openly criticizing Dahlgren and demoralizing the entire squadron. Rowan denied the charge and accused Duvall of lying. Dahlgren ordered a court of inquiry on board the *New Ironsides*. The court found that no one had spoken disrespectfully of Dahlgren after all. Duvall was later court-martialed, but Welles and Fox saved him from dismissal. In retrospect Dahlgren can be criticized for his offhand handling of the matter, but officers often grumbled among themselves about their superiors during the Civil War. The morale issue, however, was a serious one, as Dahlgren would soon learn.[49]

After dealing with Duvall's charges, Dahlgren assessed the naval situation. He had seven monitors in good condition. The *New Ironsides* was due for repairs. No new ironclads would be arriving anytime soon. From deserters he learned that the Confederates were maintaining a garrison of 150 men at Fort Sumter and were building bombproofs and mounting guns on the channel faces. He concluded that the fort should be attacked to disrupt the work.[50]

Dahlgren held two counsels of war with Bradford and the skippers of the eight ironclads to discuss the idea. Stephen B. Luce, skipper of the *Nantucket*, recalled of the conferences:

Steven Clegg Rowan, circa 1864 (National Archives)

While operations of some sort seemed advisable, the object to be gained by attacking Sumter was not quite clear. To me, individually we were groping in the dark; and the other members of the council impressed me as being pretty much in the same state of mental obscurity. There was no one present who seemed to understand the problem to be solved and able to state it in precise terms.[51]

At the end of the second meeting, Dahlgren put the matter to a vote. Seven of the nine officers opposed attacking Sumter.[52]

The officers' attitudes were no more surprising to Dahlgren than learning the truth about Gillmore had been. He had frequently complained in his diary that they were despondent and lacked enthusiasm. He had gone to Washington at a time when morale among his officers was particularly low. It had not improved during his absence.[53]

Dahlgren reassessed the situation. His officers did not support even a limited attack against Charleston's defenses. There were only 14,500 troops left in the army command, a force he considered insufficient for offensive operations. He had come to believe that when the monitors reserved for the James River finished operations there, they would be sent to Mobile instead of to him. All of this left him "with nothing to do," as he put it in his diary. The Charleston campaign had become more deeply mired in stalemate. The press was accusing him of inaction, a charge that some might construe as one of cowardice. Enthusiasm for the campaign had waned in Washington. Therefore, on 14 May he again asked Welles to relieve him of command. The secretary would not reply to this request for two months.[54]

THE ROUTINE OF BLOCKADE

Dahlgren kept busy in the interim. As the prospect of launching a naval attack faded, blockading became his first priority. During the first two years of the Civil War, Charleston had served as the home port for the majority of the Confederacy's blockade-running companies. Sleek blockade runners congested the harbor, and the tons of war materials and luxury goods they delivered lay in heaps on the docks. The city so dominated blockade running that Thomas Dudley, the U.S. consul in Liverpool, claimed that its capture would be regarded as the deathblow to the rebellion. In fact, the fall of Morris Island and the reduction of Fort Sumter ended Charleston's reign as the Confederacy's premier blockade-running port. Dahlgren posted picket boats, tugs, and monitors just outside the obstructions, leaving open only a small area close to shore. From batteries established on Cummings Point, Union artillerists could blanket the harbor with gunfire whenever they saw a signal light flashing on Sullivan's Island. From September 1863 to March 1864 there was no blockade-running activity in the city. Although blockade runners were entering and leaving the city as late as February 1865, many of them failed in the attempt.[55]

Dahlgren found blockading to be "dull work." He lacked sufficient vessels to cover each location along the coast all of the time. Ships ran out of supplies, engines broke down, bottoms became fouled, and storms blew blockaders off station. Dahlgren therefore had to juggle his ships among the various locations and Port Royal, where they received supplies and maintenance. Each time a vessel moved, her skipper informed Dahlgren about the movement in writing. The admiral required his officers to acknowledge receipt of all printed orders in writing. He sent weekly reports to Welles and issued circulars, announcements, and the results of courts-martial to each of his ship captains. All of this produced a mound of paperwork, an amount comparable to that generated by a naval bureau.[56]

Dahlgren hated the paperwork and frequently complained about it in his diary, but he knew that it was important. "I am so taxed with incessant labor that to write even a note is an effort," he wrote his sister Patty. "There is no rest and the worst of it is that all one does is so important to somebody that the utmost care is needed to avoid raising the devil—Talk of power,—I would not be a ruler for the fee simple of a whole country."[57]

The admiral maintained a grueling work schedule to keep up. "He must have...a steel plated, iron constitution," noted Joshua D. Warren, skipper of the *Harvest Moon* during most of 1864, "for he [is] the last man to *sleep,* and the first to *awake....* [He] takes more hours of labor, and less hours for rest, than any man in his fleet." Warren later recalled that Dahlgren spent most of his nights dictating orders for the fleet to several clerks seated around him.[58]

Dahlgren delegated as much administrative work as he could to his staff, which by the war's end included a fleet captain, a fleet surgeon, a fleet engineer, a fleet pilot, a paymaster, and numerous clerks, secretaries, and aides. He placed a high value on these people and rewarded them with promotions and pay increases.[59]

The admiral valued his enlisted men as well. Roughly 80 percent of his enlisted people were greenhorns who had to be trained on the job. When recruits' terms of enlistment expired, vessels remained undermanned until replacements arrived. In the fall of 1863 Dahlgren enforced an act of Congress that allowed commanders to retain seamen beyond their term of enlistment. At best, such seamen grumbled. At worst, they refused to obey orders. Some were insubordinate. On one occasion a group of seamen on board the *New Ironsides* hanged an effigy of Dahlgren from the rigging. None of these problems, however, should be viewed as an indictment of his leadership. Sailors always complain. Dahlgren was hanged in effigy for

Dahlgren and his staff, 21 April 1865. *Left to right:* unknown, Lieutenant Commander Oscar C. Badger (fleet ordnance officer), Paymaster J. O. Bradford, Lieutenant Commander J. M. Bradford (fleet captain), Dahlgren, Ensign LaRue P. Adams (staff signal officer), Fleet Surgeon William Johnson, Chief Engineer Robert Dabney (fleet engineer), unknown. (United States Naval Institute)

enforcing a congressional law in wartime. Personnel problems are a universal feature of military organizations.[60]

On the whole, Dahlgren did well by his enlisted men. He tried his best to keep up their morale. He frequently visited sailors and marines who had shore duty. He assigned a chaplain the task of corresponding with navy people held prisoner in Charleston. He rewarded conspicuous acts of bravery with on-the-spot promotions and issued circulars recounting the deeds. The circulars mentioned the men by name and were read aloud on board every ship in the squadron. Dahlgren also issued circulars announcing Union military and naval victories in other theaters.[61]

Dahlgren took pains to look after his people's health. Illness not only reduced the number of men available for service but also lowered morale. Dahlgren ordered the commanders and paymasters of his ships to pay special attention to diet and encouraged them to submit requisitions for food without delay. He took pains to procure vegetables in order to prevent scurvy. He tried to prevent the spread of other diseases as well. Upon entering Port Royal, each vessel received a visit from a medical officer. If the officer found evidence of disease, the vessel was quarantined. Dahlgren ordered each medical officer to inspect the sanitary condition of his ship daily. He recommended frequent use of "disinfectants" such as "chloride of lime" and "nitrate of lead." He warned ship commanders and medical officers that they would be punished if their vessels did not meet his standards of cleanliness.[62]

Dahlgren particularly worried about the crews of his ironclads. Monitors were damp, smelly, dirty, cramped, dark, and poorly ventilated. A monitor's deck was awash while under way in anything but a flat calm, forcing the crew to remain below with hatches battened down. The only place where the men could find relief was atop the turret, but only when out of range of Confederate weapons. Because of these conditions, monitor crews suffered excessively from illness. In the summer of 1863, for example, an average of 20 percent of the *Nahant*'s crew were hospitalized at any one time. Many of the men lapsed into despondency.[63]

Dahlgren tried to ease their burdens. His fleet surgeon suggested that the men in the turrets be given whiskey to compensate for "the extraordinary draft on their strength." Dahlgren agreed and ordered six barrels of whiskey, but since grog had been outlawed, William Whelen, the navy's chief of the Bureau of Medicine and Surgery, overturned the order. Other measures went through, however. Dahlgren saw to it that monitor crewmen received a 25 percent pay increase, special ice rations, and extra allowances for clothing, which was quickly ruined on board their vessels. Dahlgren periodically rotated monitor crewmen to a hulk for rest.[64]

Despite his myriad duties and responsibilities, Dahlgren found some time to enjoy life's simpler pleasures. Each day around sunset he went ashore for a walk on the beach. He supplemented the bland navy diet of bread, meat, and potatoes with catsup, herring, tea, canned asparagus, and macaroni. He tried to avoid working on Sunday whenever possible, but duty usually kept him busy seven days a week.[65]

REFIGHTING OLD BATTLES

Dahlgren found relief from the routine of blockade in answering congressional queries. The Joint Committee on the Conduct of the War, created in December 1861 by the radical faction of the Republican party in Congress,

USS *Passaic* in South Carolina waters (United States Naval Institute)

was one of the most controversial and feared bodies ever to operate in Washington. Formed amid the outrage in the wake of the Union defeats at the battles of Bull Run and Ball's Bluff, the committee was empowered to inquire into any aspect of the war. It devoted most of its attention to the army but undertook several investigations of the Navy Department and a few naval campaigns. The committee tended to conduct its investigations of the navy with a hostile spirit, aiming to discredit Gideon Welles. The radicals disliked and distrusted Welles because he was a Democrat and because he opposed the radical aim of speedy emancipation.[66]

During the summer and fall of 1863 Welles and Du Pont had exchanged barbed letters over the secretary's refusal to publish Du Pont's reports, which blamed the monitors for the failure of his April 1863 attack on Charleston. Du Pont's friend Henry Winter Davis, the acknowledged leader of the opposition to Lincoln in Congress, saw this as an opportunity to attack the administration. Hoping to discredit Welles and the Lincoln administration, Davis—together with Senator Benjamin F. Wade, chairman of the Joint Committee on the Conduct of the War—secured a joint resolution calling for a congressional investigation into Du Pont's attack and the Navy Department's ironclad policy.[67]

Welles devised a plan to turn the tables on Du Pont and Davis. He decided to provide the committee not only with Du Pont's reports but also with massive documentation defending the monitors. He intended to shift the focus from the Navy Department to Du Pont, characterize Du Pont as incompetent, and crush him with the weight of evidence. For the plan to work, Welles had to secure favorable reports from officers who had experience with ironclads. Dahlgren was the most experienced.[68]

On 12 January 1864 the secretary wrote Dahlgren a remarkable letter. He said that a plan was afoot "in certain quarters" to "give a false impression" of the ironclads "and of the officers and others connected with them." But since taking command of the South Atlantic Blockading Squadron, Dahlgren had "vindicated their reputation." Dahlgren had made "what was but an imperfect blockade an efficient and thorough one." The press had deluded the public into believing that "the seat of rebeldom would be overwhelmed at once." But Dahlgren was "working out a name in connection with the iron-clads" that would "amply compensate" him "for the wicked attacks and misrepresentations that have been made." The world was watching Dahlgren with great interest, more for the novelty of the ironclads than for the mere capture of Charleston: "The character of that portion of your fleet which is before Charleston gives a marked character to your acts and will cause your labors to stand out prominent in history. Success will insure more than ordinary fame. Your reputation is identified with the Monitors, and the assaults that have been made included both yourself and that class of vessels." Congress had issued "a very broad call for facts and information" in regard to the monitors. Welles intended to make "full replies." He ordered Dahlgren to prepare a report on the ironclads for the congressional committee.[69]

Welles could not have written a more persuasive letter. It appealed directly to Dahlgren's vanity, ambition, and desire to go down in history as a hero. In representing the attacks on the monitors as attacks on the admiral's reputation, Welles struck at his most sensitive nerve. If Dahlgren bought the argument, he would certainly praise the ironclads in his report.

Dahlgren found Welles's letter to be "prodigiously flattering," as he noted in his diary, "and asking for good character to the monitors." Dahlgren saw the congressional inquiry as a golden opportunity to defend himself against the onslaught of Gillmore and the press. He finished the report within a week. The first part recounted his operations against Charleston during 1863. Support of army operations, he said, was his primary mission during the first two months. He argued that had the army used more troops in either of its frontal assaults on Fort Wagner in July, the fort probably would have fallen, followed by Fort Sumter. The ironclads would not have been beaten up supporting the siege operations and would have met only light opposition in a subsequent move into the harbor. But the assaults had failed, and the two months of the siege had allowed the defenders to beef up the interior defenses considerably, building new fortifications and placing formidable obstructions in the main ship channel. In short, Charleston might have fallen in 1863 if the army had not bungled the frontal assaults on Fort Wagner.[70]

The second part of the report dealt with the monitors. Dahlgren addressed five specific points about their performance, then assessed their overall value. First, endurance. In the Morris Island operations nine iron-clads had fired a total of 8,000 projectiles and had received 882 hits. "The battering received was without precedent," he argued. "It is not surprising that they should need considerable repair after sustaining such severe pounding for so long a time, but only that they could be restored at all to a serviceable condition." Second, ordnance. Dahlgren criticized the 15-inch gun for its low rate of fire, arguing that two 11-inchers would better arm a monitor than one 11- and one 15-incher. Third, he said that the 11 1/2-foot draft of the *Passaic*-class monitors enabled them to operate in most channels. Fourth, he said that monitors had "respectable" speed, that their steerage was "not difficult of control," and that they were able to "pivot with celerity and in less space than almost any other class of vessel." Fifth, he remarked that the eighty-man crew of a monitor was "very moderate." He admitted that the monitors had their defects but asserted that those could be fixed easily. He concluded that monitors were the best possible type of vessel for shallow-water operations.[71]

Dahlgren's paper became part of a monumental report on all armored ships. Welles declared that monitors were experimental vessels and admitted their faults but argued that their proven strengths far outweighed their weaknesses. Carefully selected documents from Dahlgren and many other officers supported these contentions, defended the Navy Department's policies, and cast Du Pont in the worst possible light. The massive report, reprinted under the title *Armored Vessels* and issued by the thousands, stopped Du Pont and Davis in their tracks. It sacrificed Du Pont's reputation for the sake of public confidence in the government's prosecution of the war.[72]

Their shot having bounced off the ironclads, the radicals took aim at a new target. In May the Committee on the Conduct of the War addressed a letter to Welles asking why the navy had failed to capture Charleston. The secretary forwarded the communication to Dahlgren.[73] This time Welles did not have to flatter him to get a favorable response. Dahlgren wrote a friend:

I never was more glad in my life to have a chance of being heard fairly—the hard part being—that my own afflictions first occupied my time,—and now the public business gives me not a moment of leisure—the papers look at me daily, untouched Now what shall a man do? the people cry out *In to Charleston!* Well if I could get there and do that work, I would be willing that it should serve as my monument—But the tools to do it are not in my hands yet—When you see my paper I think you will be satisfied—No man can be more anxious than myself to put such a mark on that accursed nest of treason, as will serve throughout time.[74]

On 20 June, Dahlgren sent the committee a paper of sixty-one handwritten pages, highlighting the navy's accomplishments and repeating his argument that Gillmore was to blame for the Union's failure to take Charleston in 1863.[75]

Both of Dahlgren's reports to the Committee on the Conduct of the War pleased Welles. Dahlgren had not only supplied evidence to use against Du Pont and Davis but also shifted away from the navy the blame for the failure to take Charleston. However, the admiral had done so at the price of escalating the feud between himself and Gillmore. The political cost to Welles, on the other hand, was nil. Although Dahlgren was a master of the politics of innovation, Welles was his master in the politics of government. The feud with Gillmore would last for the rest of Dahlgren's life and would shape his attitude toward ordnance after the war.

Charleston, July–November 1864

In July, Welles replied to Dahlgren's request to be relieved of command. The secretary attributed the two-month delay to "embarrassments to the Department in relation to the several commands." He noted that some reshuffling of commands would soon take place. The letter ended with an ambiguous sentence: "Your application to be detached relieves the Department of any difficulty that might have intervened in your case, and will be borne in mind in any new arrangement that may be ordered." Dahlgren inferred that Welles had already chosen a successor.[76]

Welles permitted Dahlgren neither to lead a major attack nor to resign. The secretary considered Dahlgren a prudent, courageous, intelligent, and cautious man who was careful to avoid danger, who evaded responsibility, and whose vanity and ambition made him difficult to reason with. Although he believed that Dahlgren lacked the innate fighting qualities of Rear Admirals David G. Farragut and David D. Porter, he defended Dahlgren when others criticized him and was satisfied with the job he was doing. Although he had originally opposed giving Dahlgren command of the South Atlantic Blockading Squadron, he would not now let him give it up.[77]

The secretary targeted Wilmington, North Carolina, located near the mouth of the Cape Fear River, for the next major naval attack. With Charleston closely blockaded, Wilmington was the last logistically useful Confederate port that blockade runners still stood a reasonable chance of making. Goods run through the blockade there reached Lee's army via the excellent rail connections between Wilmington and Richmond and other points inland. The dual approaches to the mouth of the Cape Fear River, the notoriously dangerous Frying Pan Shoals off Smith's Island, and the comparative remoteness from Union bases made the maintenance of a close blockade there especially difficult. To close Wilmington, Welles proposed a joint attack on Fort Fisher, the city's principal fortification.[78]

Welles wanted Farragut to lead the attack on Fort Fisher. On 9 September the secretary wrote Dahlgren that Farragut would arrive at Port Royal by the end of the month with a force slated to attack Wilmington. He ordered Dahlgren to place himself under Farragut's command, turn four monitors over to Farragut, and create the impression that Charleston was the target. By the time Dahlgren received the communication on 21 October, Farragut had declined command of the Fort Fisher expedition because of failing health and near exhaustion, and Porter was appointed in his place.[79]

These plans should have convinced Dahlgren that Welles did not intend to launch a major attack against Charleston, but the admiral clung desperately to the hope of mounting one. In a letter to Henry Wise written in September he spoke of a climactic battle for the city in which he would triumph or die. On 10 November he sent Welles a proposal for an attack requiring fifty thousand troops. This was so out of line with the department's obvious intentions as to suggest that the admiral was losing touch with reality. Dahlgren had not gone over the edge, however. After all he had been through, he simply could not bear the thought of abandoning his chance at glory.[80]

Eighteen sixty-four dealt Dahlgren one final blow. In mid-November he learned that his old friend Henry Wise had proposed casting his 9- and 11-inch guns by Rodman's hollow-casting method. Dahlgren was stunned. He believed that Wise owed his position to him. This outrageous proposition struck at the very basis of his fame and reputation as an ordnance expert. On 20 November he sent Welles a twenty-two-page letter objecting to what he called the "Rodmanizing" of his guns. He argued that the 9- and 11-inchers were so good that no change in the casting method was necessary, that hollow casting was not a superior method, and that Rodman had plagiarized his design. Dahlgren felt that Wise, the original "smart young feller," had betrayed him.[81]

Eighteen sixty-four was turning out even worse than 1863. Instead of a triumphant ride into Charleston or a glorious death during the attack, fate had dealt Dahlgren a stalemate, consigning him to the tedium of blockade duty. There was no glory in not attacking, so Dahlgren twice tried to resign.

But Welles would not allow it. Dahlgren had become useful to him at Charleston. Not only was he doing an adequate job maintaining the blockade and defending his fleet against Confederate submarines, but he also served as a useful pawn in the game against the radicals in Congress. And as the year drew to a close, Dahlgren assumed additional utility in distracting Confederate attention from the upcoming attack on Fort Fisher.

For Dahlgren, nothing—not the failure to take Charleston, not the blows to his reputation, not Wise's betrayal—was worse than Ulric's death. In the privacy of his cabin in the flagship he lamented:

> Full & bitter tears do I shed for my dead boy,—and very often—my own lonely bedroom is my only refuge then,—just as I used to weep for his dead sister dear Lizzie,—in the solitude of my cabin in the Plymouth,— how often Lord will thou afflict me and sear my broken heart—Dear son is not every part of this vessel alive with your memory—? how little you thought when sitting with me, that in a brief space we should part forever—We waived hands—and never met again,—my beloved boy![82]

20

The Fall of Charleston and the End of the War
November 1864–July 1865

Despite the suffering he had endured in 1864, Dahlgren had good reason to celebrate Thanksgiving. On 22 November he received word that Major General William T. Sherman and fifty thousand troops had left Atlanta and were marching on Savannah. Welles ordered him to render any assistance he could. Dahlgren sent vessels up rivers and estuaries to reconnoiter Confederate positions and to watch for Sherman's arrival.[1] The approaching juggernaut promised to break the deadlock. On 25 November Dahlgren wrote in his diary:

> Last night I ordered illumination for the Public thanksgiving,—but really that the People were firm to their right, and Sherman coming like a thunderbolt and retribution seemed nigh,—it was a fitting remembrance for my son[.] So the vessels gleamed in light—and the Naval buildings and Rockets shot into the air—and the signal lights shewed their bright colors.[2]

THE FALL OF CHARLESTON

Sherman made contact with the South Atlantic Blockading Squadron on 12 December, when a steamer picked up one of his officers carrying a dispatch announcing the army's arrival in the vicinity of Savannah. Dahlgren immediately informed Welles and Lincoln that Sherman had almost reached the sea.[3] The admiral steamed to Wassau Sound in the *Harvest Moon* in case the Confederate ironclads based in Savannah tried to make a run for it now that a Union army threatened from behind.

Two days later, as Dahlgren paced the deck of his flagship, an approaching steamer signaled that Sherman was on board. The *Harvest Moon* dropped anchor. The steamer drew alongside. Dahlgren jumped on board and walked into the cabin. Sherman greeted him cordially and later remembered him as "a most agreeable gentleman." "I was not personally acquainted with [Dahlgren] at the time," the general recalled, "but he was so extremely kind and courteous that I was at once attracted to him. There was nothing in his power, he said, which he would not do to assist us, to make our campaign absolutely successful."[4] Dahlgren wrote of the event, "The Cabin being filled with officers [Sherman, Major General John G. Foster, now in command of the Department of the South, and Dahlgren]…[we] were the centre & all listened to what was said among us. It would be impossible to repeat even the substance of what passed and yet every word was of profound interest."[5] Sherman's arrival revived Dahlgren's spirit, renewed his sense of purpose, and resurrected his ego.

Sherman spent the rest of the day with Dahlgren, who took him on a tour of Wassau Sound. Hundreds of sailors, perched in the yards of their ships, cheered as the general passed by. After breakfast the next morning, Dahlgren

Making contact with Sherman's army (Naval Historical Center)

William Tecumseh Sherman (Naval Historical Center)

and Sherman inspected Fort McAllister, which had fallen to a Federal assault on 12 December. "Our soldiers looked worn and dirty," Dahlgren noted of Sherman's troops; "they never seem to notice the presence of their officers,—even Sh. passed with no more than a stare." Dahlgren then took Sherman to a point upriver, where he rode off to rejoin his troops.[6]

Sherman regarded the fall of Savannah as inevitable now that Fort McAllister had been taken. While he invested Savannah on the land side, the navy maintained a presence on the rivers, creeks, and sounds. During the night of 20–21 December, Confederate forces evacuated Savannah. Sherman was on board the *Harvest Moon* with Dahlgren at the time, returning from a conference with Foster on Hilton Head. Strong winds blew the steamer onto a mud bank. Sherman continued the voyage in the admiral's barge. At about three o'clock on the afternoon of the twenty-first, a tug steamed up with a telegram announcing that Savannah had been taken.[7] Sherman sent Lincoln a famous letter the next day: "I beg to present you as a Christmas-gift the city

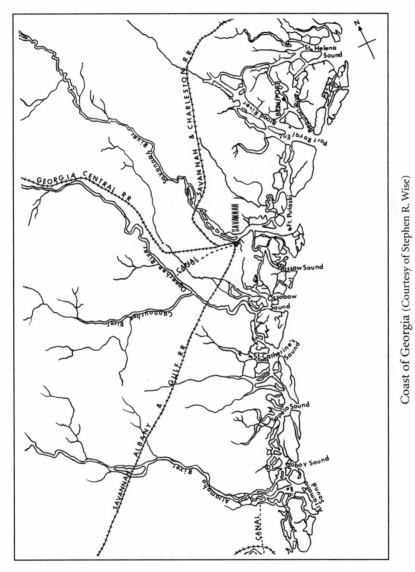

Coast of Georgia (Courtesy of Stephen R. Wise)

Coast of Georgia and northern Florida (Courtesy of Stephen R. Wise)

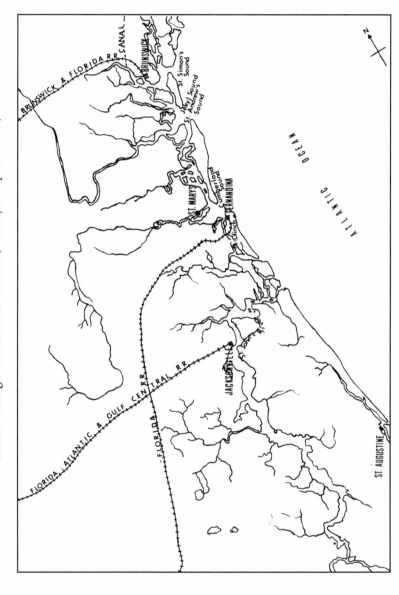

of Savannah, with one hundred and fifty heavy guns and plenty of ammunition, also about twenty-five thousand bales of cotton."[8]

Dahlgren spent the next few weeks examining Savannah's defenses and discussing operations with Sherman. From Savannah the general intended to march inland to Columbia, South Carolina, then up into North Carolina, eventually linking up with General Grant's army. He did not intend to turn toward Charleston, for he believed that the city itself had little military value. "Charleston is now a mere desolated wreck," he wrote Grant, "and is hardly worth the time it would take to starve it out."[9] Besides, Sherman saw no need for an attack on the city. As he put it to Stephen B. Luce, "You navy fellows have been hammering away at Charleston for the past three years. But just wait till I get into South Carolina; I will cut her communications and Charleston will fall into your hands like a ripe pear."[10] Sherman asked Dahlgren to make demonstrations up the Edisto and Stono Rivers, hoping to pin down Charleston's defenders and divert Confederate attention from his march. He suggested not sending the ironclads into Charleston harbor because of its strong defenses.[11]

Dahlgren left Savannah on the night of 12 January and arrived in Charleston two days later. After breakfast on the fifteenth he summoned the ironclad skippers for a council of war and told them that Sherman wanted the squadron to make a diversionary move against Charleston. He proposed three alternatives: attacking Sullivan's Island, attacking Fort Johnson, or attacking the city itself. The latter two proposals were essentially frontal attacks on strong enemy positions and stood quite out of line with Sherman's suggestion. In either case the fleet would have to run the gauntlet of Confederate fire from the forts lining the inner harbor. Dahlgren still sought glory in a naval attack. His officers, however, were diffident. "Not a fire eater among them," he lamented in his diary. They decided that the best alternative was to attack Sullivan's Island.[12]

Dahlgren received a letter from Sherman three days later. The general disapproved of attacking Sullivan's Island. He preferred the navy to make a feint at Bull's Bay, roughly 22 miles up the coast from Charleston. He advised the admiral not to expose his vessels to Confederate gunfire or torpedoes. The idea was to convince the Rebels that the army was heading toward Charleston instead of Columbia, but to do so without risking the fleet in a frontal assault. Dahlgren acceded. Sherman marched out of Savannah on 24 January. Dahlgren's ships operated in the rivers nearby, covering the army and compelling the Confederates to spread out their forces.[13]

Coast of South Carolina (Courtesy of Stephen R. Wise)

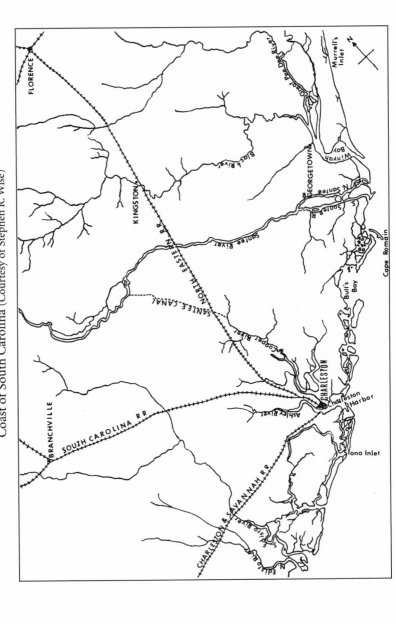

On 6 February a steamer brought an unexpected passenger to Charleston. It was Quincy A. Gillmore, who had returned to command the Department of the South. He was replacing Foster, who was going north to get treatment for an old wound. Dahlgren wondered how he could be expected to cooperate with a man who had "harbor[ed] scribblers to lampoon me," as he noted in his diary, "and den[ied] their assertions to my face."[14]

The next day one of Dahlgren's officers brought him a copy of Gillmore's recently published book, *Engineer and Artillery Operations against the Defences of Charleston Harbor in 1863; Comprising the Descent upon Morris Island, the Demolition of Fort Sumter, the Reduction of Forts Wagner and Gregg*.[15] The admiral paged through it, reading here and there, and quickly became outraged. He noted in his diary:

> [Gillmore's book appears] to be a vindication of himself, from something, at my expense.… Is it not a heart-burning shame that a man who is educated, with high rank, and intrusted with grave responsibilities, should be incapable of pursuing the plain, straight path to duty, without permitting baser motives to mingle in his thoughts, and swerve head and hand from the true course? Gillmore was a Captain of Engineers with the rank of Volunteer Brigadier-General, an ephemeral, fleeting thing. Of course he would like to be a Major-General, and this demanded some brilliant performance. This he thought he could not achieve without having the entire credit. The Navy must not be allowed any share, and the howl that Charleston was not taken came like a shock. Did he fear that he would fail to be a Major-General, and find it necessary to place the failure upon me? He took Morris Island (by his own account); I did not even help. Now I must take Charleston![16]

Dahlgren concluded that he could not work with Gillmore. For the sake of harmony between the services, he wrote to Welles, asking for the third time to be relieved of command.[17]

On 11 February, Gillmore boarded a boat bound for Dahlgren's flagship to greet the admiral officially. When the gig drew alongside the flagship, Gillmore climbed the gangway and came over the side. He doffed his hat. Dahlgren raised his own hat. The general stepped forward, offering his hand. Dahlgren bowed. "Please walk into my cabin," he said, turning to show the way. No one else seemed to notice that he had refused to shake the general's hand. Gillmore left after a brief discussion of the operation at Bull's Bay.[18]

Joint operations at Bull's Bay, February 1865 (Naval Historical Center)

Over the next several days the squadron supported diversionary operations against Secessionville, James Island, and Bull's Bay. Dahlgren had perfected this kind of joint operation over the previous year. In February 1864, near Jacksonville, Florida, he had supported army operations along the St. John's River. In the vicinity of Charleston he had supported attacks up the Stono River in July; up the Ashepoo and South Edisto Rivers in May; and up the Broad River in November and December. Most of these operations followed a general pattern: the army landed, the Confederates repulsed its attack, then the navy covered its retreat. These defeats disgusted Dahlgren, but his naval gunfire support enabled the troops to make clean getaways. The Bull's Bay operation broke the mold, however; the landing force drove the Confederates from their positions and pushed inland. Meanwhile, ships of the South Atlantic Blockading Squadron also covered the army at various river and stream crossings.[19]

Dahlgren received a communication from Sherman on 13 February. Rain had so muddied the roads that the general thought he might have to turn toward Charleston after all. Dahlgren immediately withdrew his request to be relieved of command. The chance for the glory of finally taking Charleston outweighed the indignity of working with Gillmore. "Now I must…fight it out with the Rebs. in front and Gillmore in the rear," he noted in his diary.[20] In the end, Sherman marched inland, bypassing Charleston as planned.

The Confederate high command believed that losing Charleston's garrison would be worse than losing the city itself. Rebel forces abandoned the city on the night of 17–18 February, leaving new flags flying over Fort Sumter, Fort Moultrie, and Castle Pinckney. As the last Confederate pickets left the city on the morning of the eighteenth, the magazine at Battery Bee on Sullivan's Island exploded with a deafening roar. Dahlgren's ironclads gingerly approached the entrance of the harbor. The monitor *Canocious* steamed opposite Moultrie and fired two rounds into the fort. There was no reply. The *Canocious*'s crew had just fired the last shots of the 587-day siege of Charleston. A detachment from the Twenty-first United States Colored Troops raised the Union flag over Fort Sumter.[21]

The morning of 18 February found Dahlgren on board his flagship, engaged in directing operations on the Stono River. At 10:45 he received word that the Confederates had evacuated Sullivan's Island. He immediately made for Charleston. On the way he learned that the Confederates had also abandoned James Island. The *Harvest Moon* reached Fort Moultrie at two. Monitors crowded around the entrance to the harbor. A boat brought news that Union troops had entered the city. Dahlgren decided to enter the harbor, despite the torpedoes. The flagship steamed past the once deadly Rebel batteries, up the Cooper River, and anchored near a wharf. The admiral and members of his staff stepped ashore and walked to the Arsenal, then turned down King Street. The city was closed up tight. Fires, set by retreating Rebels, raged in every building containing cotton. Dahlgren returned to the *Harvest Moon* in order to dispatch a report to Welles and to write in his diary:

> The "City by the Sea" that the proud chivalry swore they would burn before we should enter—we should walk on its ashes, and they were going to die &c &c—the braggarts would not fire one shot for, nor lose a life— All the better.... [It] was the hot bed of the Rebellion and for half a century has striven by word & deed to produce Rebellion—the whirlwind came,—Blood & treasure flowed as if they were water—for four years our efforts were jeered at & taunted—at last comes fate—And the wretched lying, boasting crew sneak away from their dear City and will not risk its bricks nor their own hides—Go in ignominy & disgrace.

He then wrote Patty:

> The Rebel flags of two Forts lie on the carpet near my feet as I write—The game is played out—The leaders may struggle on so long as there are fools

to follow, but their last die is cast and the end is on them—It would have been a great satisfaction to me to have entered this harbor amid the smoke of battle—but this was not to be and I must ever bear the disappointment as I can.[22]

DAHLGREN THE COMMANDER

Dahlgren might also have reflected on his performance as commander of the South Atlantic Blockading Squadron. Despite his frustration at Charleston's falling without a glorious naval attack, he had much to be proud of.

Personality

Leadership is in part a function of personality. In his study of great commanders of the Royal Navy, historian John Horsfield points out that leadership is a social activity. A commander's ability to get along with his peers and subordinates makes or breaks him. Offensive instinct and the ability to recognize and exploit opportunities are also essential. In his brilliant study of Civil War combat, Gerald Linderman argues that in Dahlgren's time, courage was considered a man's most important attribute.[23]

How did Dahlgren measure up? His courage came under particularly close scrutiny because of Lincoln's role in his rise to the rank of rear admiral and command of the South Atlantic Blockading Squadron, and because of his relative lack of sea experience. Dahlgren certainly was offensive-minded; he kept proposing attacks on Charleston even after Welles had made it clear that attacking was not on the agenda. He was a firm believer in leading from the front. Time and again he led attacks on Confederate forts from a monitor's pilothouse, the most exposed part of the ship. Doubts about his courage soon receded. On the other hand, his vision never extended beyond a frontal assault on the defenses at Charleston.

Like many of his contemporaries, Dahlgren was motivated by the chance to win glory. He twice requested permission to resign when it became clear that offensive operations would be postponed. He withdrew his third request when Sherman's army resurrected the promise of glory. He did not want the command unless it would benefit his reputation.

Dahlgren got on well with some officers. He and Sherman developed a lasting friendship. Upon taking leave of the Department of the South, Brigadier General Alexander Schimmelfennig expressed high esteem for Dahlgren,

Portrait of Dahlgren, circa 1865 (Naval Historical Center)

thanked him for "the uniform courtesy and invaluable coöperation" the admiral had shown him, and remarked on the "good feeling and true comradeship" that existed between army and navy officers at Charleston. One navy officer noted that Dahlgren's subordinates spoke of him in the "warmest terms." Charles Cowley, who served on Dahlgren's staff from May 1864 to the summer of 1865, "respected and honored" Dahlgren "as a son would a father." "To me his presence was like a morning star," noted Joshua D. Warren, skipper of the *Harvest Moon*, "the forerunner of a bright and cheery day. I loved him like a brother. He had a frame of iron and a Daniel Webster brain." Warren worked closely with the admiral for most of 1864 and "never [received] an unpleasant remark or dissatisfied look from him."[24]

Dahlgren did not get on so well with other officers. His problems with Gillmore never ended. He frequently complained in his diary that his iron-clad skippers were despondent and lacked enthusiasm. Some of the officers, in turn, had a low opinion of Dahlgren. According to Samuel Preston, a member of Dahlgren's staff, his poor treatment of the chief of staff, Lieutenant Commander Bradford, hindered his command and strained his relationships with other officers. One officer told Dahlgren that he "was not supported by the Capts. of vessels." Dahlgren had an especially difficult relationship with Stephen Clegg Rowan, his fleet captain and second in command until August 1864. At one point he suspected Rowan of involvement in a political plot to take over his post.[25] Dahlgren certainly had no shortage of troubles in his relationships with Fox and Welles.

Mission

Dahlgren carried out the first two parts of his overall mission—blockading the coast, defending the squadron and the base at Port Royal, capturing Charleston—successfully. He maintained a reasonably effective blockade, and the Confederates never really threatened Port Royal. The squadron lost five major vessels during his command. The *Housatonic* and *Patapsco* fell victim to torpedoes. The monitor *Weehawken* sank at her mooring because of her skipper's carelessness. A Confederate boat expedition surprised and captured the *Water Witch* while at anchor off Ossabaw Sound, Georgia. Confederate gunfire sank the *Dai Ching* while she was covering Sherman's crossing of the Savannah River. But because none of these losses hindered operations, Dahlgren may be said to have successfully defended his fleet.[26]

The principal reason for the Union's failure to capture Charleston was the lack of coordination within the high command. Welles and Fox's objective for the siege of Charleston—the fall of the symbolic cradle of the rebellion—cannot be faulted at the strategic level. Victory would have provided a tremendous boost to Northern morale and the political fortunes of the Lincoln administration whenever it might have occurred, and it would have deprived the Confederacy of a valuable port and dealt the Rebel cause a stunning psychological blow. In the absence of a unified command structure, the coordination of planning for such a large-scale campaign should have been handled jointly by the Navy and War Departments, but Welles and Fox never sat down with their counterparts in the War Department to do the necessary work. Again, Fox's rivalry with the army hindered interservice cooperation, as did Halleck's dislike of the very idea of joint operations and his desire to withdraw forces from the theater. Furthermore, Welles and Fox neither mustered sufficient forces nor appreciated the potential of Confederate underwater warfare to hinder offensive operations. After the war Admiral David D. Porter observed, "Naval success in an attack on Charleston was out of the question. The force supplied the naval commanders-in-chief was so small, and the obstructions, torpedoes and forts so numerous, that it would have been little less than a miracle for a hostile fleet to reach the city."[27] In sum, the Union's top leaders failed to reconcile political ends and military means at Charleston.

Evaluating Dahlgren's effort against Charleston is more difficult because Dahlgren did not always view the capture of the city as his primary mission. He regarded the support of army operations on Morris Island as his primary mission during the summer of 1863. He and Gillmore had an understanding that the ironclads would enter the harbor once Fort Sumter was rendered ineffective, but they defined *ineffective* differently. Gillmore claimed that the fort was ineffective as of 23 August 1863. Dahlgren believed that it remained effective as an infantry outpost until the bitter end. Between the fall of 1863 and the spring of 1864 Dahlgren assumed that he would receive more ironclads, and he intended to attack the city when they arrived. During his visit to Washington in the spring of 1864 he learned that he would not receive the ironclads as promised. From then until the following fall he regarded the blockade as his primary mission. From November 1864 until the end of the war he considered supporting Sherman to be his primary mission.

Dahlgren certainly deserved a share of the blame for the Union's frustration at Charleston. He did reasonably well in carrying out what he considered to be a changing mission, but he never perceived that the Navy Department had abandoned the idea of a naval attack by 1864, nor did he grasp the idea of using operations against Charleston to divert Confederate forces from Lee. Instead of devising operations in accord with this strategy, the glory-hungry admiral wished to avoid presiding over a stalemate and twice tried to resign when the situation did not suit his ambition to lead a glorious naval charge.

Control

War involves violent interaction between opposing forces, with each side endeavoring to exert its will over the other. A military commander seeks control of that interaction while denying such control to the enemy. To what extent did Dahlgren succeed in achieving control?

Underwater warfare afforded the Confederates a significant measure of control over Charleston harbor. After the city fell, Dahlgren made a study of the obstructions in the harbor. He believed that the Confederates had maintained piles, booms, chains, and rope obstructions at several different locations in the harbor throughout the siege. He also described torpedoes, torpedo boats, and the half-dozen Confederate ironclads in service or under construction during the siege. He concluded, "Quite sufficient it is certain to show that these several contrivances of obstructions and torpedoes would have been as troublesome as it was expected they would be in connection with the heavy batteries that lined the harbor and the rebel ironclads."[28]

But according to Roswell S. Ripley, the Confederate ordnance officer at Charleston, the obstructions in the main ship channel in Charleston harbor were not formidable, nor was the channel ever so obstructed as to prevent the passage of ships. Sam Jones, commander of the Confederate Department of South Carolina, Georgia, and Florida from April to October 1864, asserted that "in truth the obstructions were by no means so formidable as was supposed." By making Dahlgren think otherwise, the Confederates managed to deter an all-out naval attack on the city. They also controlled events by damaging the *New Ironsides* and sinking the *Housatonic* and *Patapsco* with torpedoes and submersibles.[29]

Dahlgren exerted the greatest measure of control over the enemy in joint operations. In the absence of a serious threat to his squadron outside Charleston harbor, he enjoyed nearly undisputed command of the sea. Confederate torpedo boats, submersibles, and ironclads could not prevent him from landing ground troops wherever he wanted. The fact that the land operations he supported often failed to achieve their objectives was not Dahlgren's fault. Until Sherman arrived, the Confederates managed to counter sea power by using interior lines, specifically railroad lines. But Dahlgren's fleet enabled the Union to retain the initiative.

In sum, Dahlgren was an admirable leader, but he was not perfect, and his performance as commander of the South Atlantic Blockading Squadron was good but flawed. His courage remained beyond question. He took care of his enlisted people but failed to inspire his officers. Although most commanders get along well with some officers and not so well with others, Dahlgren never managed to improve the low morale of his ironclad skippers, probably because the blows he had suffered—Gillmore's machinations, Henry Wise's betrayal, and, worst of all, Ully's death—had shattered his spirit, at least until Sherman arrived. Dahlgren excelled in joint operations but had difficulties with underwater warfare. He never took Charleston, but he attained the other objectives of his mission. In short, Dahlgren was no Farragut, but he was also no Du Pont.

FINAL DAYS IN COMMAND OF THE SOUTH ATLANTIC BLOCKADING SQUADRON

With Charleston in Union hands, there was little left for the South Atlantic Blockading Squadron to do. On 25 February a squadron of Dahlgren's vessels occupied the port of Georgetown, South Carolina, in order to establish a line of communication with Sherman's army as it advanced into North Carolina. Three days later Dahlgren reported to Welles that the only Confederate force remaining in South Carolina was a small troop of cavalry. He noted that bands of marauders were running rampant in the countryside. His own force patrolled as far up the rivers as possible to maintain order. "The State is completely on its back," he wrote.[30]

For the next few months Dahlgren's principal military tasks were clearing obstructions from Charleston harbor and disbanding his squadron. Tugs and boats swept the harbor for torpedoes. Dahlgren sent many of the larger vessels north or to distant stations. He discharged all of the private vessels under government charter as fast as their cargoes could be transferred or disposed of. He dismissed most of the workmen employed in the shops at Port Royal. By the end of the spring the South Atlantic Blockading Squadron had shrunk to a police force in both size and function.[31]

But Confederate defenses still packed a wallop. On the morning of 1 March the *Harvest Moon* steamed through Winyaw Bay near Georgetown, heading for Charleston. Dahlgren paced his cabin, awaiting breakfast and contemplating the lead-colored sky. Suddenly, at 7:45, he heard a loud crashing sound. The partition between the cabin and the wardroom shattered and fell in toward him. Things flew about. Hurried feet trampled on the deck. Someone began to scream. At first Dahlgren thought the boiler had burst. But then he smelled gunpowder and thought that the magazine had exploded. He donned a peacoat and cap and went outside. Frightened men struggled to lower the boats. The admiral squeezed past them, heading down the gangway to the upper deck ladder. Wood fragments cluttered the open spaces. The fleet captain, his white nightgown billowing behind, ran toward Dahlgren. They climbed the ladder to the upper deck to get a better view and saw a large hole in the deck between the main hatch and the wardroom bulkhead. Dahlgren rightly determined that the *Harvest Moon* had struck a torpedo and was sinking fast. A tug that had been following drew alongside the stricken steamer. Dahlgren and others stepped on board. The tug steamed for another ship, to which the admiral transferred his flag. The *Harvest Moon* sank in five minutes, but only one man died.[32]

As the operations of the South Atlantic Blockading Squadron wound down, Dahlgren's feud with Gillmore heated up. For a month they squabbled about an article published in the 22 February *New York Herald* by a correspondent attached to the general's headquarters. Dahlgren took offense at the article and accused Gillmore of condoning it. The general denied that it was provocative and accused Dahlgren of being overly sensitive to criticism. The admiral argued that Gillmore too might be sensitive to criticism if it originated from one of Dahlgren's ships and shaped public opinion "into a false estimate of your motives and actions." Gillmore claimed that he had never seen the article before it was published. Dahlgren argued that the general was nevertheless responsible for its "libels" because it had been written within the jurisdiction of his command.[33]

"Gillmore and the rest of the party have proved to be a lying skulking set of poor devils," Dahlgren noted in his diary. He ranted in a letter to Patty about Gillmore and the press. What particularly irked him was their claims that the obstructions in Charleston harbor had not really been formidable. After describing the torpedoes he had seen with his own eyes, he wrote:

And yet the papers say there is nothing here, not even obstructions, though one tug cut away [a] 100[-foot] section of Rope fixings between Sumter and Moultrie—

This is the work of that *ingenious Engineer* Gillmore who finding himself accountable for doing nothing unless some one else can shoulder the blame, gets the correspondents who are under his thumb to do the dirty work....

But that shall not save him—the truth will out—He is no General and was always beaten if not covered by the Navy[.] I doubt in fact if he has been under fire once—

So long as he was here the skunks were in activity[;] when he left, they disappeared[;] now he is back,—they show their dirty paws—one began the old tune the other day in the Herald,—so I wrote to Gillmore asking him to stop it—and I suppose the thunderer himself will be on my track: but I will make Gillmore answer for it—his machinery shall be exposed.[34]

Fox pointed the way for Dahlgren to achieve that end. The assistant secretary arrived in Charleston on 31 March for a visit. Dahlgren spoke with him the next evening, recounting the Gillmore business. Fox suggested that Dahlgren write a report on their joint operations and send it to Congress. The admiral vowed to do so as soon as he could.[35]

The symbolic end to Dahlgren's war came on Good Friday, 14 April 1865, the fourth anniversary of the surrender of Fort Sumter. President Lincoln had ordered a ceremony at Fort Sumter to commemorate the occasion. The surrender of Lee's army at Appomattox Court House on 9 April sweetened the celebration. At eight o'clock on the morning of the fourteenth, the vessels of the South Atlantic Blockading Squadron dressed ship and fired a twenty-one-gun salute. Fresh winds snapped the flags. Marines and soldiers lining the wharf and the walls of Fort Sumter presented arms to the beat of drums as Dahlgren stepped ashore. Generals and other luminaries, including William Lloyd Garrison, arrived shortly thereafter. Soon everyone sat down. There was a prayer, followed by a patriotic song. Then Major General Robert Anderson, who had surrendered the fort in 1861, ran up the Union flag, the same one he had hauled down four years earlier to the day. The crowd cheered. The fort, batteries ashore, and ships fired a one-hundred-gun salute. Sailors perched in the yards of each vessel in the harbor gave three cheers. The Reverend Henry Ward Beecher rose to address the assembly. One of the batteries delayed firing until he began. The reports were timed to punctuate the end of Beecher's sentences. Here is an extract from his speech:

Are we come to exult that Northern hands are stronger than Southern? No; but to rejoice that the hands of those who defend a just and beneficent government are mightier than the hands that assaulted it! Do we exult over fallen cities? We exult that a Nation has not fallen. We sorrow with the sorrowful. We sympathize with the desolate. We look upon this shattered fort, and yonder dilapidated city, with sad eyes. We exult, not for a passion gratified, but for a sentiment victorious; not for temper, but for conscience; not—as we devoutly believe—that *our* will is done, but that God's will hath been done.

The most famous photograph of Dahlgren. A Mathew B. Brady studio photographer captured this image on 21 April 1865. Dahlgren recorded the event in his diary:

Friday April 21' 1865

Fine day—cloud & shine—much wind from SW—
A day of photographs—Brady's man Mr. [—] called and asked to photo. me—had asked me in N.Y. two years ago, just as I was about to start for this,—but I declined—rather the first one I fancy who shunned such immortality—he had been so sorry—the Photo. had been so much asked for and would have sold so well—

So I went on board the Pawnee with all the Staff—and between big and little Photos—alone & with the Staff—there were a dozen or more Photos. taken—It used up the working part of a day.

This image portrays Dahlgren exactly as he wanted to be remembered: as a battle leader. He leans on a 50-pounder Dahlgren rifle on board the USS *Pawnee*.

Beecher's oration was "not too long," according to Dahlgren, "and moderate—seemingly acceptable." Another prayer ended the ceremonies. Afterward many people shook hands with Dahlgren. Several asked for his autograph. The ships fired another twenty-one-gun salute at sunset. The admiral ate dinner on board the *Iago,* then joined Fox for tea.[36]

Five days later an army transport flying its flag at half mast approached Dahlgren's flagship. The transport brought word that the president had been assassinated. On the evening of the flag-raising ceremony, Lincoln had gone to Ford's Theater to see *Our American Cousin,* an eccentric English comedy. During the third act John Wilkes Booth stepped into the box where the president was sitting, raised a derringer, and shot him in the back of the head. Lincoln died at 7:22 the next morning. Dahlgren ordered his vessels to fly their colors at half mast and to fire a gun every half hour from sunrise to sunset, and he directed his officers to wear black crepe on the left arm. He told Welles that the news of the assassination "produced a sensation of indignation and grief as universal as it was profound and sincere, far exceeding anything I have ever before witnessed." In his diary Dahlgren wrote, "I can say from an intimate acquaintance with the President that he was a man of rare sagacity—good genial temper and desirable firmness—that he possessed qualities of the highest order as a Ruler,—indeed we know of no man so well fitted to carry the country through her trial."[37]

Thus the Civil War ended for Dahlgren. He remained in the South two months longer, engaged primarily in disbanding the squadron. He faced with mixed emotions the prospect of returning home. His house on 4½ Street in Washington, he wrote in his diary, "has been a home to me & mine for 17 years—and brings to me now only the remembrance of sorrow—In that house my wife died—and dear Lizzie—and from it my beloved son went forth to his last battle—I never wish to look on it again, and yet at this time it is a most serious inconvenience—for I have not a spot where I can rest when I return and I have so much to do." Dahlgren was anxious to find

The ruins of Fort Sumter appear above his shoulder. The image is brimming with irony, however, for Dahlgren never took Charleston by storm, his heavy rifles were considered failures, and he had come to believe that rifled ordnance would never replace smoothbores. (Library of Congress; other photos taken that day are also preserved in the Library of Congress) a place where he could "get somewhere among my papers," as he put it to Patty, to write Ulric's memoir and to answer Gillmore's outrageous book.[38]

Dahlgren began making arrangements to leave the South in June. On the seventeenth, the day of his departure, he issued a farewell message to the squadron. "The Rebellion has been crushed," it began, "and the vast military and naval forces of the Union will now be made to conform to the peaceful condition of the country." He thanked everyone who had served under him. He reviewed the operations of the squadron during his command, hinting that Gillmore was responsible for the failure to capture Charleston. He told his men that the army could not have achieved what it had without their gallant efforts, and he congratulated them for maintaining an effective blockade. "In all these operations and in others which I cannot here enumerate," he concluded, "the personnel of this Squadron have manifested all that could be asked of the Navy, and if brilliant victory was not possible, the general results were not less useful, directly to the great end."[39]

Early that afternoon Dahlgren's officers came on board the flagship *Philadelphia* to shake hands and say good-bye. The admiral then boarded the *Pawnee,* which departed at four. The *Pawnee* steamed through the harbor, past Forts Sumter and Wagner, across the bar, and out into the open sea, heading north. As the ship ascended the Potomac, Dahlgren remarked on how splendid the river was. The *Pawnee* reached Washington late in the day on 21 June. The admiral spent the night on board, as he had sold the house on 4½ Street.[40]

At ten the next morning Dahlgren set out for the Navy Department. Welles gave him a warm welcome. The admiral visited the bureau chiefs, then had a brief but pleasant chat with President Andrew Johnson. Afterward he took a room on the corner opposite the Willard Hotel. He spent the next several days visiting government officials, naval officers, and old friends, and unpacking. On 12 July 1865 Rear Admiral John Adolphus Bernard Dahlgren hauled down his flag as commander of the South Atlantic Blockading Squadron for the last time.[41]

21

Washington and South America

July 1865–July 1868

Dahlgren had no specific assignment during his first days back in Washington in July 1865. It was his first time off duty in eighteen years. Rumor had it that he intended to return to the Bureau of Ordnance. "The Grand Admiral," wrote John D. Brandt, the bureau's chief clerk, "is cavorting about here, no one knows for what devilment—but of course with his eye open for the main chance[.] He is, however, looking quite well and seems to be in good spirits."[1] Richmond Aulick, assistant chief of the bureau, noted that he was "not sure whether [Dahlgren] means to turn us all out *now*, or wait for our natural demise, and come in then as *heir-at-law.*"[2]

But the father of naval ordnance spent little time around guns during the first three years after the Civil War. Instead he wrapped up business left over from the war and served on a series of ad hoc naval boards.

As ever, his greatest concern remained his reputation, which he set out to resurrect in a series of writing projects. The damage that Gillmore had done left him more sensitive than ever to the slightest insult. When David D. Porter received a promotion to vice admiral, Dahlgren protested loudly. Gideon Welles, who had grown tired of Dahlgren's complaints, shipped him off to the west coast of South America, where he served as a typical nineteenth-century naval diplomat.

321

WASHINGTON

But the first thing Dahlgren did after hauling down his flag as commander of the South Atlantic Blockading Squadron was to have a 15-inch shell mounted over the entrance to the Navy Department. Affixed to the shell were a bronze eagle with outspread wings and a plaque whose inscription said that the shell had been fired at Fort Moultrie by one of the monitors commanded by Rear Admiral John A. Dahlgren, Abraham Lincoln, president of the United States, and Gideon Welles, secretary of the navy—in that order.[3]

Madeleine

The second thing Dahlgren did was to marry Madeleine Vinton Goddard. Madeleine was born Sarah Madeleine Vinton on 13 July 1825 at Gallipolis, Ohio. Her mother died when she was six. Madeleine was educated at Monsieur Picot's boarding school in Philadelphia and the Convent of the Visitation in Georgetown, D.C. Her father, a wealthy congressman for whom Vinton County, Ohio, was named, made her his hostess in Washington as soon as she reached the proper age. In June 1846 she married Daniel C. Goddard, an Ohio lawyer and assistant secretary in the newly formed Interior Department. Daniel Goddard died five years later. Madeleine inherited a sizable estate when her father died in 1862. She and her two children remained in Washington.

An article published in 1886 in the *Chicago Tribune* described Madeleine as a "society star and novelist." She began writing in 1859 under the pen names Corinne and Cornelia. By the end of the Civil War she had published three books: *Identities* (1859), a translation of *Pius IX and France* (1861), and a translation of *An Essay on Catholicism, Authority, and Order* (1862). She moved in Washington's highest social circles and later wrote an article on social etiquette for debutantes. She was also well versed in "public affairs," as Dahlgren's friend William T. Sherman put it. For example, because she thought it unchristian for women to participate in politics, she wrote an article against women's suffrage for the Senate Committee on Privileges and Elections. Because "she was too modest to address the committee in person," as an article in *The Post* put it, she mailed her article to the senators.[4]

Dahlgren's papers reveal little about his courtship with Madeleine. She first appears in 1864 as "Mrs. Goddard," a friend of his sister Patty. Though John and Madeleine had both lived in Washington since before the Civil War and had moved in the same social circles, it is not known when they first met. His papers do indicate that he was contemplating marrying her as early

Madeleine Vinton Dahlgren, circa 1865 (Courtesy of Charles Peery)

as his first meeting with Sherman in December 1864. The papers contain no love poems for Madeleine. Dahlgren made a note of their marriage on 2 August 1865 in pencil in the margin of his diary. It is not that he loved her less than he had loved Mary; his relationship with Madeleine was different. Dahlgren was fifty-five when they married. He had seen much more of life than he had at twenty-nine when he wed Mary.[5]

Dahlgren's marriage elicited comment in naval circles. It was rumored that he had married Madeleine for her money. "You notice Dahlgren has committed hari kari in a rich widow," Fox wrote Farragut. Some of the comments were downright nasty. Richmond Aulick wrote Henry Wise:

[Their marriage] took us all by surprise—even busy Rumor had not heard a whisper of it before. Surely he had *"le besoin de la marier"* [the need to marry]. You may recollect the lady as one of the ugliest of her sex, though adorned with many golden charms! She has a very pretty daughter…and as the Admiral is also similarly provided, as well as with two sons, they will have a fine, well grown family ready made, to save them any future trouble that way![6]

Old Business

Dahlgren spent the rest of 1865 attending to business left over from the Civil War. Gillmore's attacks on his reputation concerned him most. The general's book *Engineer and Artillery Operations against the Defences of Charleston Harbor in 1863* charged that the navy could have taken Charleston at any time during the two weeks after 23 August, the day the general had declared Fort Sumter "ineffective," but that Dahlgren had failed to act. The admiral refuted this contention in yet another report to Congress, which he drafted during the summer and early fall of 1865 and sent to Welles on 16 October. The report did not put the matter to rest; Dahlgren would refight the siege of Charleston on paper over and over again for the rest of his life. These efforts resolved nothing and served no useful purpose. The massive amount of time he spent defending his reputation and honor would have been far better spent working on ordnance or studying the lessons of the Civil War. But in Dahlgren's mind, stains on one's reputation had to be rubbed out.[7]

With Gillmore answered for the time being, Dahlgren turned his attention to Ulric. Visions of his son, anger over the dishonor the Confederates had done him, and worries about the final disposition of his remains had haunted the admiral's thoughts ever since Ully's death. In July 1864 he wrote a long letter to the *Army and Navy Journal* declaring that the Confederates had forged the "orders" allegedly found on Ulric's body.[8] "My son, my son," he wrote on Thanksgiving Day, 1864, "how much better that I had passed away in your stead—The most loved & cherished of all things to me, in all life—gone,—and how sadly—It is the thanksgiving day of the Nation,—but what shall I be thankful for!—not for life surely nor for happiness."[9] On the first anniversary of Ulric's death he wrote, "This day one year since my dearly beloved Ully fell by the hands of assassins whose base work was fittingly concluded by the savage ferocity of the Rebel Gov. to his remains…. May God scourge them & send them to wander unpitied over the world."[10] Similar passages filled his diary and letters.

Dahlgren finally laid his son to rest, physically and mentally, in the autumn of 1865. Ulric's remains had been brought to Washington after the fall of Richmond. On 31 October a two-hour memorial service was held for Ulric at the First Presbyterian Church on 4¹/₂ Street. John and Madeleine Dahlgren, their children, President Johnson, nearly all of the cabinet members, and various army and navy officers attended. Henry Ward Beecher delivered a powerful sermon. "As long as our history lasts," said Beecher, "Dahlgren shall mean truth, honor, bravery, and heroic sacrifice." After the service, pallbearers placed the coffin on a hearse. A procession accompanied the hearse past silent crowds to the railroad depot, where the coffin was loaded onto a special car. At 4:30 P.M. the train set out for Philadelphia, arriving at midnight. A party of soldiers and army officers transferred the body to Independence Hall for the night. "Few dead are honored by resting there," the admiral noted in his diary. "The last who preceded was the body of…President Lincoln, Ully's friend." The next morning dawned clear and bright. General Meade, the mayor of Philadelphia, and numerous army and navy officers paid their respects. At eleven the preacher, Dr. Wilson, rose to speak. After a brief service, a procession accompanied the body to Laurel Hill Cemetery, a ride of two hours from Independence Hall. Dahlgren wrote of the ceremony:

> It was a striking spectacle, not easily forgotten—Among the evergreen & remaining leaves of other trees,—the many marble memorials crowding around,—were the long lines of troops—The gallant boy and Pall bearers preceded—then Dr. Wilson, Paul and myself—the officers followed[—]the notes of the dead march wailed plaintively—the rich banners of the Regiment drooped,—the troops presented Arms—nothing too much in honor for my gallant son—Silent around stood many spectators—We came to the grave—just by the side of his mother—on her other hand was poor Lizzie—and near by the two little boys—A mother & four children from my home group,—how sad!—
>
> How many memories weighed on my sad heart—they lowered the noble dead deep into his grave, and on his breast laid the cross of flowers sent by ladies—Every head was uncovered as the fine figure of the Clergyman appeared at the head of the grave…. A few words more closed his invocation—Then rang out the soldiers requiem in vollied peal.

The admiral continued to reflect upon Ulric from time to time, but the memory no longer tortured him as before.[11]

New Business

As 1865 drew to a close, Dahlgren began to look toward the future. The question of his next assignment arose in a meeting with Welles in December. The admiral asked for duty in Washington because he liked living there. He would not consider serving under Wise at the Bureau of Ordnance because, as he noted in his diary, "Wise was so much below me in rank." Welles offered to make Dahlgren chief of the bureau, but the admiral did not wish to displace his former friend.[12]

Instead of giving Dahlgren a long-term assignment such as command of a squadron, navy yard, or bureau, Welles placed him on three ad hoc boards. The first, which met in January 1866, was known as the Promotion Board. Besides Dahlgren, it included Farragut, Porter, and Rear Admiral Charles H. Davis. Its purpose was to examine the service records of the officers of the South Atlantic Blockading Squadron to determine which of them deserved promotion for outstanding service. Welles formed the board at Dahlgren's insistence because the admiral felt that some of his former subordinates had not received the recognition they deserved. Dahlgren proposed advancing every one of his officers who had been "near fire." The board approved twenty-three promotions.[13]

But mostly what the members of the Promotion Board did was gossip. Dahlgren was "sickened" by their "detestable" talk, remarking in his diary that the other admirals resembled "old women over their tea.... Farragut has no generosity—Porter gases tremendously—and Davis a cold calculating egotist.... These meetings on character are truly loathsome.... [The] most cruel and unfair reflections are common." Dahlgren noted only one specific item of gossip. It concerned Lieutenant William B. Cushing, whom the public regarded as a hero for having sunk the rebel ram *Albemarle* with a spar torpedo mounted on a small steam launch. Porter said that Cushing was to have brought several steam launches from New York for the attack on the *Albemarle* but had lost all but the one "owing to stupidity or drink." Porter intended to arrest Cushing but offered to suspend charges if he undertook the mission with the remaining launch. Cushing did so, succeeded, and became a hero.[14]

The second board on which Dahlgren served was a joint army-navy board on harbor defense. In February 1866 Gideon Welles wrote to War Secretary Stanton suggesting the organization of a board to study the implications of recent advances in ordnance, armored vessels, and underwater warfare for harbor defense. This study had the potential to yield abundant insights on joint warfare, technology, strategy, tactics, and doctrine. The board consisted of Rear Admiral Davis, Commodore James Alden, Brevet Major General J. G. Barnard, Brevet Brigadier Generals Z. B. Tower and B. S. Alexander, and Dahlgren. The army officers were engineers and the navy officers had commanded or served on ironclads. Gillmore was originally assigned to the board as well, but Dahlgren refused to serve with him, so Gillmore was detached.

The Harbor Defense Board met frequently between 1 March and 17 July 1866. Its members discussed ironclads, obstructions, and mines, but they reached no firm conclusions, citing a lack of data on ironclads and forts and a lack of money for experimentation. The board recommended placing one or more ironclads in each major harbor and experimenting with obstructions and torpedoes, but these recommendations were ignored because there were no funds to implement them. It was a less than halfhearted attempt to learn lessons from the Civil War.[15]

Finally, Dahlgren served as president of the Board of Visitors to the Naval Academy. The board met at Annapolis from 21 May to 9 June in order to review the discipline, management, and curriculum of the Naval Academy and to give examinations to midshipmen. In the board's report to the secretary of the navy, Dahlgren criticized the Academy for placing steam engineering above ordnance. "The ordnance of a ship-of-war alone gives it its distinctive character," he wrote in the board's report, "and its proper use gives victory." The report reflected views Dahlgren had held since before the Civil War.[16]

None of the boards on which Dahlgren served during the first half of 1866 made a significant contribution. Although each board provided an opportunity to study the implications of the Civil War for the future of naval warfare, Dahlgren—along with everyone else, it seems—remained too preoccupied with old business to pay much attention to the future. A golden opportunity was lost.

Since December 1865 Dahlgren had been working on his memoir of Ulric. He finished a draft—426 pages of manuscript—on 17 June 1866 and submitted it to Harpers for publication. To his surprise, Harpers turned it down. The editor said that it would not be "pecuniarily successful." Dahlgren submitted it to other publishers, but none accepted it. The reason was his style. He could write official reports clearly enough, but his style became turgid and ponderous in extended literary exercises. "So far as my experience of your pen goes," Henry Wise had once told him, "the first dash you make is always the best; and the more you reflect, revise, and correct, the less forcible the matter becomes." The publishers Ticknor and Fields—the same Ticknor who had so impressed Dahlgren during his visit on the eve of the *Cumberland* cruise more than twenty years before—told him that the manuscript was "full of inaccuracies both of composition and of fact" and needed to be "rewritten by some practiced writer." The *Memoir of Ulric Dahlgren* was published after the admiral's death, but only after Madeleine Dahlgren applied her skills as a novelist to revise and edit her husband's prose.[17]

The admiral had also begun writing his own memoirs. He intended not only to vindicate his reputation as commander of the South Atlantic Blockading Squadron but also to commemorate his contributions as an ordnance innovator. The "recognition he most ardently desired," Madeleine Dahlgren later noted, was "the recognition of posterity." He "always cared *much more* for posterity than for the present." This memoir was to be his legacy.[18]

The following excerpts are typical. On the coast survey, Dahlgren pursued his duties "with more zeal than care for himself" at the cost of his "uncommonly fine sight." He spent his first year of ordnance work "alone and unfriended." Nevertheless, he paid "earnest and patient attention to duty.... 1848—The organization that was to give form and substance to the Navy Ordnance was as yet but in dim outline;—the new comer felt that before him lay an ample field, unsown as yet by the seed that should yield results worth harvesting." On 21 February 1848 he submitted to Warrington the design of a boat gun: "Notwithstanding the increasing favorable disposition of the Commodore towards me, there were wiseacres about him who chilled propositions of this sort—men who had not the enterprise to undertake the matter, but were ever ready to criticize those who did." Dahlgren proudly noted that the boat guns never required a modification to their original design. He also boasted about the Ordnance Establishment, his heavy guns, his command of the Washington Navy Yard during the early months of the Civil War, and his command of the South Atlantic Blockading Squadron. He portrayed himself as a misunderstood martyr who was proven right time and again in battles against one wrongheaded opponent after another. As with the memoir of Ulric, Madeleine Dahlgren would have to rewrite Dahlgren's own memoir to make it publishable.[19]

In the second half of 1866 Dahlgren twice suffered what he considered professional affronts. The first occurred when he was not promoted to the newly established rank of vice admiral. David D. Porter, the naval hero of Vicksburg and Fort Fisher, attained this rank in July. When Dahlgren found out about Porter's promotion, he stormed into Welles's office, blustering that he should have been made vice admiral instead because of his seniority and "continued and faithful service." He also complained to several senators, including the chairman of the Naval Affairs Committee. He ranted about this "grievous wrong," this "outrage," in his diary. Not being promoted crushed Dahlgren, to whom recognition and rank meant everything.[20]

The second affront stemmed from the first. On 27 September, Dahlgren learned that Welles had slated him to command the South Pacific Squadron. This news came as an unexpected blow; Dahlgren was not ready to return to sea. The next day Welles ordered him to embark for Valparaiso, Chile, on the 1 December steamer. Dahlgren had no alternative but to go. Lincoln was dead, and there was no one above the secretary to whom he could appeal. Welles probably decided to ship Dahlgren off because of the fuss he had made over not being promoted. Whatever the reason, Dahlgren thought the order "unjust in its nature" and "rude in its manner." That "poor old imbecile" Welles, as he put it in his diary, had forgotten that Dahlgren had seen more duty at sea during the Civil War than any other rear admiral. He felt that someone with less time afloat should have been sent instead. A complication arose when Dahlgren asked Welles not to publish the order; Madeleine was ill and would be upset if she found out. But Welles insisted on publishing it because he kept receiving applications for the command. The news indeed upset Madeleine, who decided to accompany her husband.[21]

Welles then compounded the insult. On 15 September, Madeleine had given birth with great difficulty to twins, a boy and a girl whom the Dahlgrens named Eric and Ulrica, and she had not yet fully recovered. Dahlgren asked permission to give Madeleine and their babies passage in his flagship from Panama to Valparaiso, where they intended to establish residence. Welles denied the request. "How strange," Dahlgren noted in his diary. "I never asked the Gov. one cent for my guns with which the Navy is armed and am refused a passage for my wife!" The admiral decided to let the matter rest. Madeleine hounded Welles for a week, but to no avail. She resigned herself to remaining behind, at least temporarily.[22]

Before departing for South America, Dahlgren attended to personal matters, most of which, like his memoir, involved his image for posterity. Toward the end of October he commissioned a coat of arms, which included an anchor, a Dahlgren gun, an admiral's flag torn by a shot, and the motto

"Quorum pars fui." The anchor represented Dahlgren's life as a naval officer. The gun, of course, signified his ordnance work. The flag represented
the battle flag flown on the monitors in which he had led attacks on the forts
at Charleston in 1863. (He had sent that flag to his sister Patty in January
1864.) The motto was based on a line from Virgil's *Aeneid* in which Aeneas
recounts his role in the overthrow of Troy: "Quaeque ipse miserrima vidi, et
quorum pars magna fui" (Thrice piteous scenes which I myself beheld, And
was a mighty part of). The *Aeneid* is the national war poem of Rome. It
describes how the past has led to the present, celebrating a triumphant history culminating in the rule of Augustus. "Aeneas," writes historian Leo
Braudy, "is the hero as civic founder and pious citizen, who bows to the fates
that drive him onward to his destiny and who subordinates his own desires
to the commands of the gods." The parallels to his own role in history must
have struck Dahlgren as obvious. He no doubt remembered the quotation
from his prizewinning translation of Virgil as a boy. In an attempt at modesty he eliminated the word *magna,* so that the motto claimed only that he
had played "a part" in great events, not "a mighty part."[23]

At the end of October Dahlgren completed an autobiographical sketch
for Joel T. Headley's book *Farragut and Our Naval Commanders.* He was glad
to contribute to this work because, as Headley noted in the preface, "in
almost every case, the facts and personal details in the biographical sketches
have been furnished either by the commanders themselves, or their friends,
with their approval. Hence they can be relied on"—relied on, Headley might
have added, to tell the tale the commanders wanted told.[24]

Dahlgren's chapter was essentially a compression of the memoir he had
written earlier. Ordnance and Charleston were its salient themes. The following excerpt gives the flavor of the whole: "Dahlgren, by his inventive
genius in the construction of ordnance, and his bold and original plan of
arming vessels of war, has done more for the Navy of our country, than
probably any single man in it.... [Dahlgren's innovation marked] the most
important revolution in the arming of ships that ever occurred." The
account of the Charleston operations proceeded along similar lines. "The
Auto-Hagiography of John A. Dahlgren" would have been an appropriate
title. The chapters on the other officers were no less immodest.[25]

Two weeks before departing for South America, Dahlgren went down to
the Washington Navy Yard to secure his personal papers. He considered
them his most valuable possession. "No money can replace them," he wrote
his sister Patty. They were "the heir-loom for those who are to come."

Dahlgren spent several days sorting and arranging the papers and filled six wooden boxes with books, letters, notes, and memoranda. He purchased an iron safe for storing the most important.[26] Concern for personal papers was not unusual in Dahlgren's time. "In a social role constructed of such material as honor, fame and glory," notes historian Peter Karsten, "the guarding of sources that might aid one to reconstruct the past may have been deemed axiomatic."[27] Dahlgren, of course, went beyond most of his peers in such matters.

Dahlgren finished packing for his new assignment on 22 November. The next day he departed for New York, where he caught the mail steamer to South America on 1 December. His sister Patty and daughter Eva said goodbye the day before he left. His sons Charley and Paul saw their father off at the wharf.[28]

SOUTH AMERICA

Geographically, Dahlgren's new command was larger than the South Atlantic Blockading Squadron, but it was on a smaller scale in all other respects. The area of responsibility for the South Pacific Squadron stretched from Panama south to Cape Horn and across the Pacific to Malaysia, Indonesia, and Australia.

Under Dahlgren the South Pacific Squadron consisted of six Civil War–vintage sailing steamers. All but one patrolled along the west coast of South America, because it was the most troubled area of the command. Badly worn from their service in the war, the ships required almost constant attention to boilers, machinery, rotten spars, leaky hulls, and fouled bottoms. The supply of coal was so tight that upon issuing sailing orders, Dahlgren sometimes specified what sails to use, how much coal could be used, and what speed the vessel was to make.[29]

The mission of the South Pacific Squadron was to show the flag and protect American citizens and their interests in its area of responsibility. As commander of a squadron on a distant station, Dahlgren acted as a naval diplomat. American naval officers performed eight categories of diplomatic activities in the days of the wooden-ship navy: protection and enhancement of commerce; making war; peacetime aggression; treaty making or negotiating; nonbelligerent diplomacy; affiliation with American diplomats; humanitarianism; and expansion of American interests.

South America, from an 1867 map (Library of Congress)

The year 1866 marked the beginning of a period of political, economic, and social woes in South America. Civil and international violence erupted intermittently over the next fifteen years. Resident U.S. citizens who could not avoid the violence clamored for protection. U.S. naval officers stepped in where stability broke down, and their rescue missions often brought about confrontations with the governments concerned—Latin American, European, or both.[30]

Along the west coast of South America that year, Spain fought a war against Chile, Peru, Bolivia, and Ecuador. The conflict began when a big Spanish fleet appeared off Callao, Peru. The Spaniards demanded payment of a dubious claim and held the guano-rich Chincha Islands until the Peruvians paid the specified sum. Peru's President Juan Antonio Perez concluded a treaty with Spain, but its provisions angered his countrymen. When Chileans answered similar Spanish aggression by declaring war, Perez was driven out of office. His successor, Colonel Mariano Ignacio Prado, declared war on Spain in January 1866. Bolivia and Ecuador followed suit. Madrid's armada responded by assaulting first Chile, then Peru. On 31 March the Spanish squadron bombarded Valparaiso for three hours, inflicting an estimated $15 million in damage, then moved north against Callao. But when the Spanish moved in to shell the city, they found that the Peruvians had installed powerful, modern artillery there. Peruvian gunfire damaged all seven of the Spanish men-of-war, inflicting about two hundred casualties. Even though the Peruvians had lost many times that number, the Spanish departed for home, having accomplished nothing.[31]

The War of Salutes

Dahlgren arrived in these troubled waters eleven days after leaving New York and took command of the South Pacific Squadron on 12 December. The first episode in his new command could have come from the pages of a romantic novel.[32]

Dahlgren inherited a problem that had arisen on his predecessor's watch. John Randolph Tucker, a former U.S. naval officer and commander of the Confederate naval squadron at Charleston, had found postwar employment as admiral in chief of the Peruvian navy. The previous July, Captain Fabius Maximus Stanly, skipper of the USS *Tuscarora,* had made a courtesy call on Tucker. Although born in the South, Stanly had fought for the North in the Civil War. After the encounter he alleged to Rear Admiral George F. Pearson,

John Randolph Tucker, circa 1864 (Naval Historical Center)

Dahlgren's predecessor, that Tucker had given him a rude and insulting reception. Pearson viewed the incident as a violation of the "officer-like conduct" required between naval officers of friendly nations and reported it to Alvin P. Hovey, the U.S. minister in Lima. He threatened to suspend all courtesies to Peruvian naval officers unless Tucker made "an immediate and satisfactory apology." Hovey raised the matter with the Peruvian minister of foreign affairs, who in turn passed it on to Colonel Prado. Prado considered it a personal matter between Stanly and Tucker and hoped that Pearson would not suspend the traditional naval courtesies. Pearson did not see it that way, and he demanded redress. This was how things stood when Dahlgren took command.[33]

Washington sought to resolve the Tucker-Stanly affair with a minimum of controversy, but Dahlgren escalated the dispute into what historian David P. Werlich has called the "War of Salutes." As he noted in his diary, Dahlgren viewed Tucker as an unpardoned rebel "under parole & liable still to trial" for treason. Ulric's death and the failure at Charleston had bred in Dahlgren an intense hatred of the South, which he now focused on Tucker as a former opponent and symbol of the Confederacy.[34]

On 9 January 1867 Dahlgren ordered his captains to deny the usual courtesies to "all persons" still excluded from the presidential amnesty offered to Confederates after the Civil War. When the USS *Pensacola* entered the harbor of Valparaiso later that month, her skipper did not call on Tucker, whose flagship was in the harbor. Similarly, two U.S. vessels fired salutes to British and Chilean warships in the harbor, but not to the Peruvian flagship. Tucker thereupon suspended all courtesies to American warships. The Peruvian government regarded the incident as a slight to its flag and so informed Hovey.[35]

Hovey met with Dahlgren several times in January and February to discuss the war of salutes. Hovey argued that Tucker had not been tried or convicted of treason; as long as he remained a Peruvian admiral, he was entitled to traditional naval courtesies. Despite the minister's protests, Dahlgren refused to comply. The admiral believed that although Hovey had primary responsibility for representing the United States in Peru, naval officers were certainly not subordinate to him. Hovey argued that the State Department should decide the issue, and he sent a report to Seward. Dahlgren thought that the minister had "gone off half-cocked."[36]

The admiral heard from Washington in March. Welles privately regarded the Tucker affair as "a troublesome difficulty and not easy to dispose of, though not of great moment." The secretary ordered Dahlgren not to dispute the Peruvian position that the matter was a personal one between Stanly and Tucker. Besides, Stanly had been warned not to visit Tucker, and therefore he had no right to seek redress for grievances. Although Welles viewed Tucker as a "criminal fleeing from justice," the United States had no right to demand an apology from him.[37]

The State Department expressed a similar opinion. Although Seward praised Dahlgren's patriotic "sentiments" and regarded Tucker as "a fugitive, rebel, and traitor," he pointed out that Peru was a sovereign state and could employ in its fleet anyone it wished. He demanded that Dahlgren show proper respect for the flag of Peru, even though its agents might be "objectionable." Dahlgren viewed Seward's position as "a shameful & outrageous backdown."[38]

The affair ended late in March when Tucker resigned his commission in the Peruvian navy. It is unclear whether he did so because a campaign by a combined Peruvian-Chilean fleet that he was to mount against the Spaniards had been canceled, because of mounting domestic discontent facing Colonel Prado, or to prevent further deterioration of relations between Washington and Lima.[39]

In any case, the war of salutes had already disrupted U.S. diplomacy in Latin America. Seward wanted the United States to act as mediator in the war with Spain rather than Britain or France, thus enhancing the influence of Washington in Latin America while checking that of London and Paris. But early in March, Hugh J. Kilpatrick—the same Kilpatrick of the ill-fated Richmond raid, now the American minister at Valparaiso—wrote Dahlgren that the Chilean government perceived Dahlgren's refusal to salute Tucker as an affront to the flag of their ally and because of it had declined an American offer to mediate for peace with Spain. It took until 1871 for Seward and his successor to arrange an armistice between Spain, Peru, and Chile.[40]

Dahlgren and Prado

Apart from the Tucker affair, events proved that Dahlgren's personality suited his duties as commander of the South Pacific Squadron. His ease in moving among the rich and powerful helped him get along well with the American diplomats, European naval officers, and South American officials he encountered at every port of call. He frequently attended soirées and formal functions, where chats with foreign dignitaries yielded information he could use to detect diplomatic opportunities or threats to U.S. interests.

The best information came from local leaders. Dahlgren developed social and professional relationships with Latin American politicians, notably President Prado, as a matter of protocol. On 5 January 1867 he formally presented himself to Prado as the new commander of the South Pacific Squadron. The admiral wore a dress coat, epaulettes, cocked hat, and sword for the occasion, reflecting in his diary that it was the first time since New Year's Eve, 1861, that he had worn a full-dress uniform. The former occasion had been a reception for Abraham Lincoln. Hovey accompanied Dahlgren to the Peruvian president's palace—"a big name for a shabby building," as the admiral put it. They passed through the entrance into a large hall. Prado appeared several minutes later. He looked fit. He was forty years old, of medium height, and sported a black mustache and beard. He and Dahlgren shook hands and sat down. Dahlgren thought their conversation "brief & to the purpose." Half an hour later the admiral departed.[41]

Although Prado looked healthy to Dahlgren, his government seemed ill. In a report to Welles the admiral noted that political conditions in Peru remained unsettled. Prado's government, which had come to power in

January 1866 as the result of a revolution, had inaugurated "many salutary reforms," but its sudden and extensive actions had shocked established interests.[42]

While John Dahlgren had been establishing social contacts among the Peruvian elite, Madeleine Dahlgren had been clamoring to join her husband. The admiral wanted neither his wife nor their babies to come because they would have to cross Panama, where recently there had been an outbreak of yellow fever. Madeleine, however, would not be stopped. On 24 June 1867 she stepped on board his flagship, the *Powhatan,* with the twins.[43]

The Dahlgrens soon became active participants in Peruvian high society. Shortly after Madeleine's arrival the Dahlgrens attended a concert in Lima. President Prado and his wife sat in front of them. The two couples chatted during the breaks in the performance. Mrs. Prado and Madeleine hit it off immediately. The Prados began to invite the Dahlgrens to the opera and to state dinners and lunches at the presidential palace. Prado and Dahlgren became friends during that quiet summer of 1867.[44]

Revolution shattered the quiet in the fall. The revolt, led by Catholic priests and politicians, stemmed from religious objections to the newly pro-claimed constitution. It began with an uprising in the town of Arequipa. On 11 September government forces moved in, killing and wounding two hun-dred insurrectionists. Eleven days later the government troops murdered their officers and joined the insurrectionists. The leader of the revolution proclaimed the constitution of 1860 and formed his own government. His men dug in. On 12 October, Prado set out for Arequipa with some five thou-sand troops. Meanwhile, the revolution was spreading to other parts of the country.[45] Dahlgren moved his ships to the trouble spots in case the revo-lution threatened American lives or property, but no such threats emerged.[46]

Things did not go as well for Prado. On 27 December the colonel's troops assaulted Arequipa. The insurrectionists repulsed the attack. Prado's men fell back. A large proportion went over to the insurrectionists during the retreat. Prado withdrew and arrived in Lima on 5 January 1868. Desertion en route had whittled his army to nothing. He resigned two days later. "What a weak, wretched people," Dahlgren remarked of the Peruvians, "impatient of any government and Prado's was certainly the best they had."[47]

After stepping down, Prado went to the U.S. legation and asked for asy-lum. When a mob threatened to storm the legation, Prado slipped out and left Lima. On the night of 9 January the deposed president appeared in a boat alongside the USS *Nyack,* anchored in Callao harbor. Prado went on board and asked to be taken to Chile. Captain Garrett Pendergrast granted him asylum. The *Nyack* put to sea on the night of the eleventh and reached Valparaiso nine days later. Dahlgren, who had recently relocated there, soon learned of Prado's arrival. He went on board the *Nyack* to greet the former leader. Prado shook the admiral's hand, then hugged him "in the manner of his country," as Dahlgren put it. Prado, dressed in a plain black suit and straw hat, "showed entire firmness and unbroken spirit." The admiral offered his condolences. They stepped into the cabin, where Prado told him what had happened.[48]

Dahlgren deftly maneuvered around the legalities of providing Prado asylum on board a U.S. ship, which violated Peruvian law. On 9 February 1867 Dahlgren had issued an order, in response to a decree of Prado's government, forbidding his ships to grant asylum to Peruvian citizens. "It was little expected perhaps that the Head of that Government," he wrote in January 1868, "would be the first to ask for the protection of our Flag." But the leader of the revolution had unwittingly provided an out. Upon taking power he declared null all decrees, resolutions, and decisions that Prado's government had made. Dahlgren reasoned that this included the decree forbidding Peruvian citizens to take asylum on board foreign warships.[49]

The United States recognized the new government in February. By the end of the month, quiet had returned to Callao. Prado lived a few miles outside of Valparaiso, "seemingly taking no part whatever in passing events," as Dahlgren noted in a letter to Welles. No major repercussions resulted from Prado's escape on board the *Nyack*. No American citizens or property had been harmed during the revolution.[50]

Dahlgren's Personal Life

The revolt was the last significant event of Dahlgren's command of the South Pacific Squadron. The rest of his tour was uneventful, given over largely to the domestic life that he and his family were able to pursue. Until Madeleine arrived he lived on board the *Powhatan*. After her arrival the family lived in a hotel in Lima while they looked for a house. They did not intend to stay in Lima because of its cold, damp climate. Early in October 1867 the Dahlgrens moved to a big house on the side of a hill overlooking Valparaiso. The terrace in front provided a view of the snow-capped mountains as well as the sea. The rent was $200 per month, an enormous sum at that time and place. The Dahlgrens employed two nurses to help with the children. John and

Madeleine's third child, John Vinton Dahlgren, was born there on 22 April 1868.[51]

Dahlgren kept up with family affairs. He was especially close to his sister Patty, with whom he shared his feelings about everything. In October 1867 he learned that she had become engaged to Matthew M. Read, a judge from Philadelphia. The news pleased the admiral, who noted in his diary that it "releases her from a life of isolation to which she has been subjected and will give peace & contentment to the rest of her life." This prediction perhaps reflected Dahlgren's happiness in his own marriages.[52]

Charley and Paul, the only surviving sons from his marriage to Mary, had grown up. Charley, the elder, had studied ordnance and steam engineering at the West Point Foundry and had joined the navy's engineer corps on the eve of the Civil War. In 1861 he was transferred to the line and was serving on board the USS *San Jacinto* when that ship stopped the British vessel *Trent*. Thereafter he distinguished himself under Porter on the Mississippi, where he took part in the capture of New Orleans and, later, Vicksburg. Injuries sustained during the latter campaign required him to spend three months in a hospital. After recovering he served briefly under his father at Charleston, then went on to the North Atlantic Blockading Squadron and participated in the capture of Fort Fisher. After the war he had difficulties finding a job he liked, and he wrote about his "mishaps" to his father. The admiral offered him a job as secretary with the South Pacific Squadron, but Charley was determined to make his own way out west as an engineer.[53]

Paul too had joined the navy during the Civil War, but in 1864 he decided to transfer to the army and attend the Military Academy at West Point. The admiral disapproved of the change. Paul was made Adjutant of the Corps of Cadets upon passing into the fourth class in August 1867. It was the Military Academy's highest honor. The following October the admiral was distressed to learn that Paul had been accumulating demerits.[54]

An affair reminiscent of Shakespeare involving his daughter Eva distressed Dahlgren even more. In September 1867 the admiral learned that Eva was engaged to marry J. B. Rodman, the son of his archrival. Young Rodman was Paul's classmate at the Military Academy. The admiral objected to the engagement, explaining in a letter to young Rodman:

> It seems to me that both of you venture rather hastily upon so serious an undertaking, and it would be better to defer a conclusion for a year or so.
> But my chief objection is that Eva is not strong enough to endure the

privations and isolation of a frontier life and it is reasonable to suppose that you have much of this before you.

The rivalry with the elder Rodman was surely another reason. The young couple agreed to postpone their marriage at least until the admiral returned to the States.[55]

Back to Washington

Dahlgren's command of the South Pacific Squadron ended in the spring of 1868. On 28 May the Dahlgrens left their house in Valparaiso and began their journey homeward. They sailed to Panama, crossed the isthmus by train, then took a mail steamer to New York.[56]

Dahlgren contemplated his future as he headed home. He did not know for certain what his next assignment would be. Henry Wise had been ill and had resigned from the Bureau of Ordnance. In mid-June, newspapers reported that Dahlgren had been nominated as chief of the bureau. The news surprised him because of the latest difficulty with Welles. It was rumored that Dahlgren's enemies were trying to block his nomination. The admiral did not know who these people were or why they were doing this. On 9 July he read in the paper that the Senate had confirmed him as chief of ordnance. He decided to accept the post.[57]

Dahlgren arrived in New York City on 22 July 1868. Shortly after stepping ashore he notified the Navy Department of his return. Two days later he received official word that he was chief of ordnance and should begin duty at his earliest convenience.[58]

22

Dahlgren's Star Fades
July 1868–July 1870

Dahlgren's return to Washington from South America resembled his return from Charleston three years earlier in one crucial respect: he faced problems left over from the Civil War. This time, however, the problems concerned ordnance rather than his performance as commander of the South Atlantic Blockading Squadron. And, as before, he faced threats to his reputation. But this time the threats struck at its very core.

THE BUREAU OF ORDNANCE

Dahlgren arrived in Washington on 31 July 1868. The next day he reported to Welles, who greeted him warmly. The secretary handed Dahlgren his commission as chief of the Bureau of Ordnance. The admiral was not particularly excited about returning to his old berth. "The business of the Ordnance is contracted to nothing," he observed in his diary, "retrenchment being the order of the day."[1]

After the Civil War the United States Navy reverted to its antebellum size, technology, and strategic doctrine. Historians have described this as a decline or a retrogression and have characterized the period between the war and the

341

birth of the new steel navy in the 1880s as the "dark ages," the "doldrums," and the "days of our humiliation." In December 1864 the navy list included nearly seven hundred vessels. By the end of 1870 this force had shrunk to fewer than two hundred vessels, with only fifty-two in commission. The others, including the monitors, were laid up. Some historians point to the rejection of the steamer *Wampanoag,* the fastest ship of her day, as the quintessential example of the navy's postwar technological retrogression. Instead of furthering the development of steam power, the navy continued to rely upon obsolete but more economical wooden sailing steamers. The navy also returned to the strategic doctrine of coast defense and distant-station patrolling. As only the latter was practiced in peacetime, antiquated sailing steamers met the navy's operational needs. But the navy would remain technologically inferior to the major naval powers in most respects until World War I.[2]

Henry Wise had run the Bureau of Ordnance during Dahlgren's five-year absence, which began when Dahlgren had left Washington to take command of the South Atlantic Blockading Squadron. Wise had proven a competent administrator. "Everything in Captain Wise's bureau moved like clockwork," recalled Admiral David D. Porter, "and ships and squadrons lost no valuable time in waiting for guns and ammunition."[3] During the year ending on 1 November 1864, Wise oversaw the production of 1,522 naval cannon, a 26 percent increase in the navy's inventory. Commander William N. Jeffers, who was in charge of ordnance experiments at the Washington Navy Yard from the fall of 1863 until late 1865, complimented Wise on his efficiency: "The Ordnance while in your charge was always made to supply every requisition and the system and order [you] established saved hundreds of thousands of dollars."[4]

But Wise was no innovator. The pace and direction of development in the Bureau of Ordnance had always depended on the perceptions, energy, and motivation of the chief. Henry Wise lacked Dahlgren's inventive genius, political skill, and enthusiasm. Content with the performance of Dahlgren's guns during the Civil War, he perceived no need for innovation. In fact, Wise had backslid a little, manufacturing new 32-pounders and 8-inchers—the very calibers Dahlgren had sought to overthrow in the first place. Ironically, Wise had designed the new 32-pounders and 8-inchers with Dahlgren's soda-water-bottle shape. In reports to Gideon Welles, Wise advocated retaining the navy's current system of armament until the Europeans demonstrated conclusively that some other system was superior. For the time being, he was satisfied with the 15-inch gun and increased charges in the 11-incher as solutions to the armor question. He was also satisfied with cast iron as the material of choice for cannon. Although he occasionally stressed the necessity of resuming systematic experiments, he persuaded neither Welles nor Congress to provide the funds. As a result, American naval ordnance once again stagnated.[5]

Wise's complacency was not the only problem. The organization Dahlgren created bears as least some of the blame for the lack of innovation. Even without Dahlgren at the helm, the Bureau of Ordnance had sailed on the course he had set for it in the 1850s. The organization had been established not to innovate continuously, but to institute one particular innovation: the Dahlgren gun. Rather than innovate, the organization carried on with the existing program. Dahlgren had trained the "smart young fellers" to carry out his program, not to develop innovative programs of their own. They had merely observed and recorded; Dahlgren got the insights. And as with Dahlgren, although to a smaller degree, success in their careers depended on the success of the Dahlgren gun. In building a constituency from below for the gun, Dahlgren had created a group with a vested interest in the gun. To paraphrase historian Elting E. Morison, the "smart young fellers" had attached themselves to the products, not to the process, of change. Thus, in respect to the idea of continuous innovation, Dahlgren's ordnance organization, like early appearances of shells and steam engines, was to some degree a false start.[6]

DAHLGREN TAKES CHARGE

Dahlgren was horrified by what he found at the Bureau of Ordnance. Wise had encumbered the old berth with reams of administrative paperwork. "The quantity of this rubbish in appalling," Dahlgren ranted, "and threatens to engross all attention." The animosity between Dahlgren and Wise that had arisen after the latter's attempt to "Rodmanize" the former's inventions contributed to the gloomy atmosphere. Jeffers had been openly hostile to Dahlgren and had demoted the venerable John Holroyd, who had been Dahlgren's assistant in experiments since the late 1840s and had helped perfect the Dahlgren gun. "However," the admiral noted in his diary, "retribution at last brings me on the trail of these small fry."[7]

Dahlgren brought these matters to Welles's attention, but nothing came of it. For example, he asked for an assistant to help with the paperwork, arguing that without one he would not have time for "the real business of the Bureau—the great questions of the day." Welles turned the request down because of the navy's reduced budget.[8]

Dahlgren tried to resign when he learned why the Senate had delayed in approving him as bureau chief. His old friend Joseph Smith, now a rear admiral, told him that a group of private inventors had lobbied against him because they thought he would prevent adoption of their inventions. Insulted by the implication that he would be unscrupulous, Dahlgren asked Welles for command of the Washington Navy Yard when the berth became vacant. "I was indignant at such unworthy treatment," he wrote in his diary, "from the lies of a pack of plundering cormorants." The secretary refused to allow him to leave the Bureau of Ordnance.[9]

Dahlgren settled down to his unwanted job. He had to do much of the boring administrative work himself. He filled requisitions for ordnance, ammunition, handspikes, pistols, cutlass scabbards, and cutlass racks. He replaced worn-out parts and lost ordnance manuals. He reviewed the quarterly reports on the ordnance and ordnance stores of each ship in commission. He recommended changes when he felt that a particular vessel's armament was inadequate. He berated officers who he believed had not maintained their equipment properly. Despite his aversion to bureaucratic routine, he devised a printed form for ship captains to use in reporting the results of target practice.[10]

There was little else for him to do. The current appropriation provided inadequate funds for experimentation. Congress had begun to enforce a policy of strict economy to reduce the national debt. Welles had slashed his original budget proposal for the navy in fiscal 1869 from $47 million to $23 million. Congress gave him only $17 million. Consequently, Welles ordered his bureau chiefs to limit their estimates to the amount necessary to maintain only the authorized numbers of men and vessels already in service. Americans were focusing their attention on reconstruction and the West. Prewar naval expansion had given way to postwar reduction.[11]

In his section of the secretary's report for 1868, Dahlgren argued that it was a mistake not to fund ordnance experiments. He knew that Europeans were focusing their attention on the development of rifled ordnance, but he did not think that the United States should follow the European lead. "We cannot take the conclusions of foreign powers even if it were possible to know what they agree upon," argued Dahlgren, "but we must search for ourselves and be able, as well as others, to carry the experience of the practice ground into battle." Although peace now reigned, war in Europe was always a possibility. With war might come depredations to American commerce, resulting in a call to the navy. As had been the case in the War of 1812, the navy's strength would depend upon the qualitative superiority of individual ships. Experimentation, he concluded, was necessary to keep up the navy's strength.[12]

THE RIFLE QUESTION

It might seem "logical" or "natural" for Dahlgren to have pushed for the development of rifled ordnance, given its (in retrospect) obvious advantages over smoothbores and contemporary European efforts to develop them. The British had begun issuing Armstrong breechloading rifles to their fleet in 1861. By May 1862 every class of warship in the Royal Navy carried at least one Armstrong gun, from the 9-pounder used in launches to the 110-pounder carried in larger ships. The accuracy of the 32-pounder Armstrong at 3,000 yards was seven times better than that of a comparable muzzle-loader. Breech loading eliminated the possibility of double-charging the gun in battle as well as the possibility that burning fragments from the previous charge might ignite the next round. The Armstrong was the first modern breechloading rifle in regular service.[13]

Dahlgren, however, perceived no threat from the Armstrong gun, nor from any other piece of rifled ordnance. "The rifle has not entirely lost its interest," he wrote, "tho' with us it has so far abated as to leave much less pressure to improve than before—If rifle cannon had been safe—they might have ruled—but they have not."[14]

Dahlgren's disdain was not unfounded. Sir Alexander Milne, commander in chief of the British North American and West Indian Station from 1860 to 1864, was skeptical of the Armstrong gun from the beginning. Milne found that its breech was prone to explode during firing, and that its unreliable ventpiece, delicate ammunition, and low carriage made it difficult to operate. In a letter to the Admiralty written in December 1863, Milne declared the Armstrong gun "not suitable for naval service afloat." The Royal Navy returned to muzzleloaders as its main armament the next year. Not until 1880 was an improved breechloader introduced, finally ending the long reign of muzzleloaders.[15]

The Armstrong experience proved to be the rule rather than the exception during the 1860s. Historian Richard D. Glasow has pointed out that

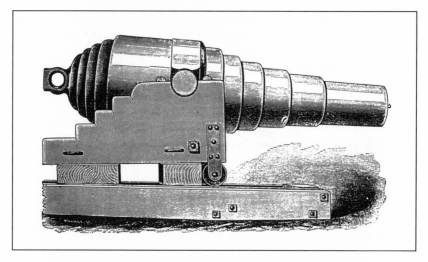

Six-hundred-pounder Armstrong muzzleloading rifle (From Holley, *Treatise on Ordnance and Armor*)

naval ordnance was in a state of flux during that decade. The future of rifled cannon seemed uncertain, and there were numerous competing systems. In 1865, for example, among the navies that had adopted the new built-up gun, there were three systems of rifling the barrel, at least four different combinations of the three principal gunmetals (cast iron, wrought iron, and steel), disagreements over the relative merits of breech loading and muzzle loading, and four approaches to the design and fabrication of the main tube and hoops. Steel remained unreliable. Neither Armstrong nor Krupp would develop a breechloading mechanism of adequate strength until the end of the decade. The reliable heavy all-steel breechloading rifled gun was still decades away.[16]

Although Dahlgren had been a proponent of rifled ordnance during the 1850s, he had begun to doubt its utility during the Civil War. In February 1864 Benjamin F. Wade, chairman of the Joint Committee on the Conduct of the War, which had launched an investigation of the "character and efficiency" of heavy ordnance both in the United States and abroad, asked him for information about rifled guns. "No heavy rifled cannon has been made," Dahlgren replied, "which meets the requirements for arming ships-of-war." "I always believed," he wrote Patty in August 1864, "that [rifles] would not supersede smooth bores,—and the proof comes in daily."[17]

The "proof" was the unreliability of rifled ordnance. By February 1862 at least six rifled cannon had burst in practice and in combat, killing several men.[18] Dahlgren rifles had proven so unreliable that production of them had ceased by early 1864.[19] During the attacks on Fort Fisher in the winter of 1864–65, so many 100-pounder Parrott rifles exploded in action that, according to Admiral David D. Porter, the commanders and men "lost confidence in them," and they were replaced with 11-inch Dahlgren guns.[20] On the other hand, not a single 9- or 11-inch gun ever burst prematurely in service.[21] Henry Wise said that "the advantages claimed for rifled cannon over smoothbores are in many respects visionary, and do not bear the test of actual combat."[22] Admiral Porter summed up the prevailing view in the United States Navy at the end of the Civil War: "Rifled cannon had not at that time made such an advance as to satisfy us that it would be the gun of the future."[23]

Dahlgren fully embraced this view. In December 1865 he argued his case in a paper entitled "Memorandum." The paper listed most of the rifles that had been introduced in the United States and in Europe, including breech- and muzzleloaders, banded and unbanded rifles, and steel, cast-iron, and wrought-iron rifles. Dahlgren argued that some of these "formidable rivals to my cannon" showed great promise, even of superseding the 9- and 11-inch guns. But despite the expenditure of millions, the breechloading Armstrong rifle was a failure. So many banded rifles exploded during the Civil War that the navy removed the heaviest of them from service. Wrought-iron guns fared so badly that they were abandoned altogether. "And so," he concluded,

> after long service in peace and War, the IX in and XI in Cannon that first saw light some fifteen years since, remain the dependence of our Naval power.
>
> Having seen a great deal of experimental practice, and witnessed as much protracted firing in action with the enemy as fell to the lot of most officers—I am satisfied that Naval smooth bore Ordnance will not be superseded by Rifles.[24]

Dahlgren often cited the battle between the famous Confederate commerce raider *Alabama* and the USS *Kearsarge* as evidence of the excellence of his smoothbores. The Union ship had sunk the Confederate raider after an hourlong gunnery duel on 19 June 1864. Dahlgren saw the battle as a duel between the *Kearsarge*'s two 11-inchers and the *Alabama*'s British-made 68-pounder and rifled 100-pounder. In the "Memorandum" he pointed out that British critics had jokingly referred to his guns as "soda-water bottles" and that the First Lord of the British Admiralty had poked fun at his theory of low velocity. The *Kearsarge*'s victory had proven, at least to Dahlgren, that his guns were no laughing matter.[25]

Dahlgren also cited the Union naval victories at New Orleans, Port Royal, Vicksburg, Mobile, and Fort Fisher as evidence of the excellence of his guns. "After the severe test of four years' War," he wrote in the "Memorandum," "the IX and XI in guns remain with unimpeached character and justly relied on by the whole navy, having carried the Flag of the union triumphantly through some of the hardest-fought battles that have occurred."[26] The last paragraph of Dahlgren's semi-autobiographical sketch in Joel Headley's *Farragut and Our Naval Commanders* noted, "Everything proceeding from Dahlgren's mind comes, like Minerva from the head of Jupiter, completely panoplied. Indeed, so perfect has every improvement he has made been, that he himself could hardly see where an alteration could be made."[27]

Naval officers, officials, and ordnance experts generally shared this view. The Dahlgren gun had become firmly embedded in the navy's culture. Gustavus Fox believed that the 9- and 11-inchers were the best shell guns in existence.[28] Captain James Alden, who commanded the USS *Brooklyn* at Mobile Bay and Fort Fisher, said that the 9-incher was "the best gun ever made.… The men stand around them and fight them with as much confidence as they drink their grog."[29] Alexander Lyman Holley, a steelmaker and ordnance expert, said that against nonarmored targets, Dahlgren's 9- and 11-inchers were "comparatively perfect."[30] Porter said that they were "the best of [their] kind in the world."[31] Writing in 1868, historian Charles B. Boynton predicted that "'built-up' guns of all kinds, will be abandoned…[and] the form of the Dahlgren cannon will in the main be adopted."[32] A letter from an anonymous naval officer to the editor of the *Army and Navy Journal* noted, "The present perfection of our naval artillery and its appurtenances, is, in large part, due to the skill and untiring industry of Rear-Admiral Dahlgren.… [He] devoted himself to the perfection of shells and shell-guns, with the result now universally acknowledged, of placing the American Navy ahead of the world in the perfection of this terrible arm."[33] Even George E. Belknap, the executive officer of the *New Ironsides* whom Dahlgren had suspected of insubordination, wrote in 1896, "In ordnance [Dahlgren] was unquestionably the ablest and most accomplished

USS *Kearsarge* versus CSS *Alabama*, 19 June 1864 (Beverley Robinson Collection, United States Naval Academy Museum)

officer of his time, whether in our service or in any other. To his genius and labors…the country was indebted for the best and most effective smoothbore guns the world had ever [seen]."[34]

Opinion on the 15-incher was divided. Some officers criticized its great weight, short range, and low rate of fire. Others thought that no enemy ironclad could withstand its power.[35] The jingoistic editor of the *Army and Navy Journal* proclaimed the 15-incher superior to "the service artillery of any other power."[36] The predominant view in the navy was that Dahlgren's guns were so good and rifles so bad that there was no immediate need for change.

In sum, Dahlgren did not pursue the development of rifled ordnance after the Civil War for many reasons. The wartime performance of his well-tested smoothbores had been excellent, while the performance of the infant rifles had been uneven. He believed that the Civil War had vindicated the strategic, tactical, and theoretical "principles" behind his smoothbores. Instead of studying actual wartime experience—blockading, underwater warfare, joint operations, naval assault on land fortifications, fleet operations, or the influence of sea power on war—he turned to the *Alabama-Kearsarge* duel, which was not representative of naval combat during the Civil War. In fact, single-ship duels had been rare. But the *Kearsarge*'s Dahlgren guns had done exactly what they were designed to do: defeat a wooden ship in single combat on the open sea. Most important of all,

Forward 11-inch Dahlgren pivot gun on USS *Kearsarge* (Library of Congress)

Dahlgren's reputation was inextricably intertwined with that of his smooth-bore guns. As Porter put it, "Having accomplished what he considered the grandest feat of gun-making in modern times, [Dahlgren] was contented to rest upon his laurels."[37]

With tremendous quantities of equipment remaining from the war, a Congress unwilling to spend money on experiments, the complacency born of victory, a return to the antebellum naval policy for which his guns had been designed, and the fact that his own identity and reputation were tied up in the highly successful 9- and 11-inchers, Dahlgren saw no need to develop rifled ordnance.

THE JOINT COMMITTEE ON ORDNANCE

But not everyone shared this view. In March 1867 a joint congressional com-mittee launched an investigation into the government's contracts with civil-ian arms inventors during the Civil War. Its aim was to discredit army and navy ordnance administrators and to compensate Horatio A. Ames and Norman Waird for alleged mistreatment by army and navy ordnance offi-cers during the war.[38]

Welles described the investigators as an "unprincipled set of scoundrels." In his diary Dahlgren called Waird a "charlatan" and Ames a "preposterous vaporing old bully of a Blacksmith." He suspected that Ames was one of the "plundering cormorants" who had attempted to block his return to the bureau.[39]

In 1862 the navy had contracted with Ames for six experimental wrought-iron rifles. Dahlgren put two to extreme proof. One endured 1,630 rounds. Dahlgren stopped firing the second after the 480th round, claiming that it had stretched out of shape. Proof of the remaining four was shelved when Dahlgren went to Charleston. The navy paid Ames for all six. In the fall of 1863 Lincoln contracted with Ames for fifteen more guns and ordered a board of army and navy ordnance officers to test one of them. The gun, a 7-inch rifle weighing about 19,000 pounds, endured seven hundred firings with heavy charges. Headed by none other than Quincy A. Gillmore, the board concluded that Ames's rifle was stronger and more reliable than any other gun of equal weight. Nevertheless, Ames received no compensation for the guns produced under the second contract. He sought redress by showing Gillmore's report to powerful friends in Congress. His friends got him a hearing before the Committee on the Conduct of the War. As a result of the hearing, Wise was ordered to test the untested guns produced under both contracts. Two burst in regular proof, one on the first round. Wise rejected them all, citing defective welds, cost, and the lack of uniformity in wrought iron. This closed the case as far as the navy was concerned, but the still uncompensated Ames alleged that some of the guns had been tested with excessive charges, and that others had been improperly rifled after he delivered them.[40]

Norman Waird had produced ten 50-pounder rifles for the navy in 1861. Three passed proof, two burst on the ninth round during proof, one failed the visual inspection, and the last four remained unproven. Waird was paid for only one. He later proposed to make 15-inch guns featuring external ribs intended to reduce both the strain of contraction while the gun cooled in the mold and the strain of expansion when the gun was fired. The navy ordered two of them in April 1863, with the understanding that if either proved satisfactory, twenty more would be ordered. The first failed the visual inspection. The second burst on the first proof fire. The navy decided not to order the twenty additional guns. Waird claimed that all of his guns had met the terms of their respective contracts. Like Ames, he claimed that his rifles had been tested with excessive charges.[41]

During 1867, 1868, and 1869 the joint committee on ordnance heard testimony from Ames, Waird, Gillmore, Thomas J. Rodman, various army and navy ordnance officers, and others connected with ordnance. The committee members' questions focused largely on the Ames guns. They asked whether the guns had been tested properly, how well they were made, and whether they were better than other kinds of rifles. Isaac French, a blacksmith who had worked for Ames for thirty years, said that the welds in the Ames guns were "perfect." Gillmore said that he could have done better at Charleston if his Parrott guns had been as good as the Ames gun. Waird fielded metallurgical questions. Ames simply stated his case. Rodman answered questions about his own work.[42]

Ames pursued his claim not only through the ordnance committee but also by writing letters to the secretary of the navy. In October 1868, after receiving a barrage of letters from the disgruntled inventor, Welles agreed to reopen the case if new facts came to light, or if the Bureau of Ordnance so recommended. Ames promptly informed Dahlgren of this. Unsure of Welles's intentions, Dahlgren inferred that the secretary wanted him to decide the issue. Keeping Ames's powerful friends in mind, the admiral took the safest course and recommended appointing a board of officers to investigate the matter. This decision enraged Welles, who had intended to keep the case closed. The secretary construed the admiral's decision as an attempt "to skulk from responsibility" and to damage Henry Wise's reputation, for Wise had rejected six of the Ames guns without inspecting them. Welles told Dahlgren that he should conduct the investigation himself. They bickered but resolved nothing.[43]

Dahlgren's relationship with Welles, which had never been smooth, finally disintegrated over the Ames case. "Admiral Dahlgren," wrote Welles in his diary, "is too timid and selfish for his position. He will not, if he can help it, give an opinion on any subject involving the slightest responsibility, for fear he shall in some way compromise himself, yet he is covetous of all honors." Welles later reflected that "Dahlgren was cold, and so calculatingly selfish that he feared to do anything lest he might injure his past reputation, which was on the 'gun line'—not in their use but the manufacture or make of them." For his part, Dahlgren compiled a list of what he considered to be Welles's blunders during the Civil War. He blamed the secretary for the loss of Norfolk, the delays in the construction of the monitors, the failure of the light-draft monitors, Du Pont's failure at Charleston, "tyrannical orders," and a host of other bad things. He probably intended to include the list in his own memoirs.[44]

Meanwhile, the joint committee on ordnance pressed on with its investigation. On 24 December 1868 Dahlgren received a letter from J. M. Howard, the chairman, asking questions about the armament of Union ironclads and ordnance testing methods, failures, and endurance. Dahlgren estimated that it would take six months to prepare a proper reply, but the committee had given him only one month. Welles urged him not to respond. Dahlgren nevertheless intended to do so, even though he rightly suspected that Ames and other disgruntled private inventors were behind the investigation, attempting to discredit him.[45]

He testified before the committee on 28 January 1869. He was asked to compare the endurance of his guns with Rodman's. "The history of the past," he said, "shows no endurance of other cannon equal to that of the 9 and 11-inch guns." He was asked about rifles. "I think the whole question of rifled guns is open," he said:

> Opinion has very much changed in our navy since the beginning of the war of the rebellion as regards the value of rifled guns. Then the demand was incessant. The idea seemed to be prevalent that smooth-bore cannon could not be pitted against rifle cannon under any circumstances. I think that sentiment is very much changed. My own experience, from repeated action, induces me to give preference to heavy smooth-bore guns. I always thought that they hurt our iron-clads more in battle than the rifles did, and I am inclined to believe that the same opinion prevails largely in the navy, independently of the distrust of the rifle guns which we now have.

He said that no reliable rifle had yet been invented in the United States, Britain, or France. He was also asked his opinion of the Ames gun. "It must be judged by its results," said Dahlgren; "they are before the committee."[46]

Dahlgren's written answers took "7 weeks incessant labor," as he noted in his diary, with "all the clerks in the Bureau assisting to collate from the record." Dahlgren reiterated the allegation that Rodman had plagiarized his design; said that he developed the 15-inch gun only because he had been ordered to; implied that Ingraham had prevented the development of rifled guns until after the Civil War began; stated that Parrott's rifles had been rushed into service without benefit of a comprehensive testing program because the demand for rifled ordnance during the war was so great; and repeated the position that no reliable rifle yet existed anywhere. He submitted the written reply on 11 February 1869.[47]

Four days later the committee issued its own report. It severely criticized both Dahlgren and Rodman. It quoted Dahlgren's section of the secretary of the navy's 1868 report to Congress:

Opinions differ quite as widely in regard to the preferable mode of developing ordnance power, whether it shall be by smooth or rifled bores, by loading at breech or muzzle, made from iron, cast or wrought, or from steel, solid or in connected parts. The relation of mass to velocity is also unsettled. In fact, the question involves the necessity of going back to fundamental principles, and starting thence by well-conducted experiments.

Dahlgren had been trying to justify funding for experiment, but the next paragraph of the committee's report said:

It therefore appears that, notwithstanding a series of elaborate experiments, extending over a long period of years, and the practical experience of our recent war, the ordnance officers of the government have not yet determined upon even the fundamental principles of their art, and possess no positive knowledge of the problem they have so long sought to solve. Mechanics is an exact science, and ignorance of that branch of it involved in the construction of guns would seem to show either want of knowledge of its principles, failure to understand their application, or superficiality of investigation, surprising in men whose minds have been from boyhood trained in the direction of a specialty.

The report cited two reasons why "the ordnance officers of the government find it necessary…to return to the rudiments of their art":

First, the ordnance officers, knowing their positions secure to them for life, have not felt the incentive to exertion and improvement which stimulates men not in government employ, and they have become attached to routine and to the traditions of their corps, jealous of innovation and new ideas, and slow to adopt improvements…. In the second place, these officers, educated to a specialty and proud of their positions, come to look upon themselves as possessing all the knowledge extant upon the subject of ordnance, and regard citizen inventors and mechanics who offer improvements in arms as ignorant and designing persons, and pretentious innovators, who have no claim to consideration. Instead of encouraging the inventive talent of the country, these officers seem to have constantly discouraged it.

The report made two other major criticisms:

> Another difficulty that has retarded progress in the science of ordnance has been the fact that prominent officers have been inventors of arms, and have possessed sufficient influence to secure the adoption and retention in service of their inventions, frequently without due regard to the question of real merit, and to the prejudice of other and better devices brought forward by citizens, or developed in other countries.… [Officers] in the two branches of the service have succeeded in securing the adoption of their own inventions, and the rivalry existing between them has prevented fair competitive trials of the various devices and systems advocated by each, neither being willing to admit the merit of the other's inventions, or to utilize the knowledge gained either by their successes or failures.[48]

In essence, the committee had charged Dahlgren with stifling innovation in ordnance.

Dahlgren got the gist. "Both my guns & Rodman's are condemned," he wrote in his diary. It was the ultimate indignity. The committee had questioned the very foundation of his reputation. It had leveled the same criticisms against him that he and the "smart young fellers" had leveled against Charles Morris. Dahlgren, who considered himself an innovator, was now being called an old fogy.[49]

Shattered, he drafted a letter of resignation from the Bureau of Ordnance. "I believe that the report of the Joint Committee on Ordnance has so far impaired my usefulness as Chf. of this Bureau," it began, "that it becomes my duty to withdraw from it and to sever my connection entirely with that branch of the public service." But Welles again refused to let him resign, perhaps out of spite.[50]

President Ulysses S. Grant's inauguration penetrated the gloom brought down by the committee's report. Grant would appoint a new secretary of the navy, who might let Dahlgren resign. "The Cabinet, the Cabinet," he noted in his diary, "how every one frets to get into that secret."[51]

Grant appointed Adolph E. Borie as the new secretary, but Vice Admiral David D. Porter became the real power in the navy. As Borie's "special assistant," Porter took control of the Navy Department at most visible levels, limited the power of bureaus to internal matters, and issued orders requiring full sailing power in all naval vessels.[52]

Dahlgren told Porter that he intended to resign because he was "tired of the eternal abuse, and disgusted at the report of the Committee." Porter dismissed the report and damned the committee. "We will whip them," he said. He thought Dahlgren was the best man for the ordnance job and did not want him to resign. Dahlgren told him that he wanted command of the Washington Navy Yard. For the next several months Dahlgren agitated to resign while Porter tried to persuade him not to. Porter finally gave in. On 10 August 1869 Dahlgren returned to the command of the Washington Navy Yard.[53]

Dahlgren spent the rest of his career engaged in the administrative routine of running the yard. He was through with ordnance forever. However, he still thought of ways to reform the navy. He made notes about improving the quality of enlisted men through better training, better pay, and better care for their families. These measures anticipated the creation of a professional enlisted service, still decades away. But thought did not spur Dahlgren to action this time. The joint committee had broken his spirit.[54]

DAHLGREN'S PERSONAL LIFE

What was to be Dahlgren's last birthday fell on 13 November 1869. "I complete Sixty years to-day," he noted in his diary. "Grateful to say, in good health and only the worse in point of time." His daughter Eva wrote him, "I can hardly realize that your birthday brings you to 60 years of age and thinking the matter over can only *hope* that I shall find the secret of keeping youth as you have." Eva thought her father looked young for an admiral.[55]

Dahlgren now had plenty of time for a personal life as well as the means to enjoy it. Madeleine had brought to their marriage a sizable estate, which Dahlgren administered. The Dahlgrens lived on the corner of Fourteenth and L Streets SE, in a house that had belonged to Madeleine's father. Since her return from South America, Madeleine had been overseeing extensive renovations, including the addition of a third floor. The house was finished at the end of September 1869.[56]

John and Madeleine attended dinners, soirées, and the like and hosted affairs of their own. They rubbed elbows with cabinet members, royalty, foreign dignitaries, naval and military officers, the president, senators, and congressmen. But socializing with the Washington elite had lost its appeal for the admiral. "The rush here is of the same kind," he wrote Patty, "every body inviting every body to dance, dine or be d—d—We touch it very lightly—accept a dinner or an 'evening' perhaps once a week—but I have declined most of the dinners."[57]

The largest event that the Dahlgrens hosted was the wedding of Romaine Goddard, Madeleine's daughter from her first marriage. The wedding took place on 16 March 1870 at the Dahlgrens' house. The guests included the president, the chief justice of the Supreme Court, the secretary of the navy, the secretary of war, the secretary of the interior, the British minister, the German minister, Sherman, Porter, Joseph Smith—some seventy people in all. After the short service, Grant stepped forward, awkwardly mumbling something about a kiss. "Romaine, kiss the president," Dahlgren said, and the awkward moment passed. A reception followed, with a magnificent spread set on the dining-room table. A marine band supplied the music. The affair lasted about three hours.[58]

Dahlgren delighted in his youngest son, John Vinton Dahlgren. "He is one of the finest babies I ever saw," he wrote Patty. Madeleine asked General Sherman and his wife Ellen to be the boy's godparents. The Shermans, friends of Madeleine since before her marriage to Dahlgren, accepted. "As the youngster grows up to the years of understanding," Sherman wrote the admiral, "you can impress upon his mind all sorts of terrible consequences from his dread Godfather if he dares to drink, gamble, or swear."[59]

Dahlgren and his sister Patty remained close, but he still referred to her husband Matthew as "Mr. Read." Dahlgren continued to share with her his feelings about work, family matters, and national events.

He worried about the rest of his family. "I dread to see a family letter," he wrote Patty; "they are all freighted with bad news." His brother Charles had turned up unexpectedly in John's study seven months after the war. Charles had left Philadelphia in 1830 and had gone to Natchez, Mississippi. He started out in banking but made his fortune as a cotton planter. When the Civil War broke out he raised and equipped the Third Mississippi Regiment. Jefferson Davis commissioned him a brigadier general. Charles served the Rebel cause at the battles of Vicksburg, Iuka, Corinth, Atlanta, and Chickamauga, and with Hood against Sherman. John had not seen his brother in nine years. Charles looked seedy. With only $10 to his name, he had come for a pardon under Lincoln's amnesty program. "So I have to get his pardon," John had noted in his diary, "rather hard after all I have done & suffered for four years in putting down the Rebellion."[60]

Charles was no better off in 1869. His children wore linsey and did not always have meat to eat. His twelve-year-old son could not read. The admiral frequently sent Charles money. John and Madeleine offered to take two of Charles's sons for two years "to school them at least in the ordinary elements of English education," as the admiral wrote his brother, but Charles's wife did not want to part with her sons. The admiral tried to get his brother a job, but Charles apparently never made the proper application. He continued to send money, and Patty's husband bought the mortgage on Charles's house to stave off a foreclosure. John did not like what had become of his brother.[61]

He was equally disappointed in his own older children. "I have lived long enough to see all my hopes in regard to my children fail utterly," he wrote Patty. "Charly has wasted ten years of life & is married without a cent.—Paul seems to see not beyond a mere soldier's life and Eva looks to her future in the barracks of some miserable fort in the Western wilds [in the event she married Rodman's son]—So that I have lived too long, truly.—For better things I had a right to hope."[62]

Charley had expressed an interest in mining coal on the estate of Madeleine's first husband near Athens, Ohio, but it did not work out. The admiral agreed to send $500 per year until Charley was "fairly afloat," as he put it. "Remember I am where I am," he wrote his son, "more by *steady hard work* than any thing else."[63]

Paul graduated twentieth in his class at the Military Academy. He would have been seventeenth but for demerits. "It is evident from the carelessness of his ways & habits," noted his father in his diary, "that ordinary exertion as a student would have [put him] a dozen numbers higher." Before going to South America the admiral had sent Paul $300, hoping he would resign from the army. But Paul stayed in and became an artillery instructor, a duty demanding only an hour a day. "The rest is idled away among the young ladies," observed his father. "Paul passed 20—rather below my expectations," he wrote Patty, "and I fear has no idea of being more than a mere soldier."[64]

The admiral prevented Paul from making what he considered a devastating social blunder. Here is his fatherly advice:

My dear Son

I have your note of the 4" and cannot say whether it astonished or pained me most.—Marry Mrs. Griffin!—why you might as well think of marry-

ing your grand mother—the woman is 6 or 8 years older than you are—
which alone would damn your prospects of happiness, if she had the
charms and virtues of an angel, which is very far from being the case.—
to be sure you hear her well spoken of "*every* where you go" which during
your acquaintance amounts to a circle of a mile in diameter with Roe's
Hotel as a centre;—which is more than I hear, except that she is thoroughly versed in the conventionalities of society.—What do you suppose
can be the opinion of every one whose opinion is worth having, in regard
to the conduct of a woman who after a nine months' widowhood, plunges
into a public affair with a young man just fledged from West Point! And,
yet upon this will o the wisp you think of building your future—My son,
you are beside yourself—Dismiss all idea of marrying until you can support a wife—and then let her be four to 8 years younger than yourself—
Believe me that even with these restrictions you will find abundance of
clever & worthy women from whom to choose the companion with
whom you shall share good or ill fortune through a long life. Mrs. Griffin
is very far from being that person, and I regret to think that even as far as
you have wandered [she] will often be to you a source of mortification.
This is the counsel of the friend that has never failed you.

Paul took the advice and did not marry Mrs. Griffin.[65]

Paul managed to please his father by finding employment with James B.
Eads, an engineer best known for his cantilevered steel bridge over the
Mississippi River at St. Louis, completed in 1874. "Since [Paul] has joined
Eads," the admiral wrote in his diary, "his whole tendency seems changed—
He works hard in his part of the Bridge enterprise and is in high favor with
Mr. Eads—His habits are changed wonderfully—dropping West Point
entirely, and looking with the hope of youth & the judgement of a man to
a future in civil life, which his trial so far fully approves."[66]

Dahlgren disapproved of Eva's intended marriage to Rodman's son. He
did not think Eva could stand the rigors of being the wife of a second lieutenant in the infantry. "I object because it would kill her," he wrote in his
diary, "to follow him to barrack, God knows where, and live as a soldier's
wife." "It is no doubt also sufficiently detrimental to my own views," he wrote
Patty, "because controversy cannot fail to arise between his father & myself
in regard to the gun question."[67]

Eva lived at her aunt Patty's house on Madison Avenue in New York and
spent most of her time in charity work. The admiral sent her $1,000 per year,

but she did not always live within her means. On Thursday, 28 April 1870, Madeleine walked down to the admiral's office with a telegram from Patty. Eva was gravely ill. The sickness had struck six days earlier, beginning with what the admiral described as "swelling in the Tonsils." Patty thought John should come at once. Dahlgren took the 12:45 train from Washington and arrived in New York at 10:00. His daughter was unconscious by the time he got there. "Dear Eva," he wrote in his dairy, "there she lay perfectly motionless, breathing hard—And so the sad spectacle continued until about 3. O. C Friday morning when a few sighs, no more, announced the departure of the innocent spirit."[68]

"Yesterday we laid my poor child in the cold ground near her beloved mother," he wrote Patty on 4 May:

> This morning I find that I do not recover from the shock, either in mind or body, as I have done before,—head & heart are both heavy—It has been a most sore affliction—and so unlooked for.... I cannot find words for my gratitude to Mr. Read in bestowing upon dear Eva unvarying fatherly kindness—He will understand however what I feel—For yourself I can measure the severity of the trial—and as a temporary alleviation from its instant sharpness, hope that you and Mr. Read will come down and pass some time with myself and Madeleine—The quiet of the place and the fresh greenness of the grass and shrubbery—will assist to divert the course of thought and to temper its sadness.[69]

Dahlgren consoled himself by spending time with his younger children. "The little fellows are very lively," he wrote Patty. "[John] grows more interesting every day—and picks up words amazingly—but quietly."[70]

He also consoled himself by writing yet another synopsis of the Charleston operations. The historian Lewis Hamersly had asked Dahlgren and other squadron commanders to write personal accounts of their experiences during the Civil War for a work tentatively entitled "Records of Living Officers." Dahlgren's account for Hamersly did not differ materially from his other accounts of the Charleston operations, but it was more openly critical of Gillmore. Dahlgren sent it off in mid-June.[71]

Dahlgren's greatest concern remained his reputation. Historian Charles B. Boynton wrote a favorable account of his operations at Charleston. "History will do me justice," Dahlgren noted in his diary, "and is doing me justice." Critics troubled him deeply. An author of a regimental history that made some negative statements about the navy at Charleston drew a sixty-five-page letter of rebuttal from the admiral. Growing tired of such statements, Dahlgren decided to set the record straight once and for all. After sending the manuscript off to Hamersly, he began to write his own book about Charleston. Command of the South Atlantic Blockading Squadron would be the last thing he would write about. He remained strangely silent about the congressional ordnance committee's devastating attack on the very core of his reputation, never putting pen to paper to answer its charges.[72]

In early July, John and Madeleine took the train to Pennsylvania to escape the Washington summer heat. After touring the Gettysburg battlefield they drove a carriage to the mountains west of town. The admiral was looking for a summer home. He wanted a cool, quiet place in the country where he could sit down to write his book. He found a house on the side of a mountain near Chambersburg and inquired about purchasing it. On the way back to the railroad station, a heavy rainstorm soaked the Dahlgrens to the skin. John caught a chill on the train back to Washington. His condition worsened over the next few days. Nevertheless, in a manner reminiscent of his mentor Ferdinand R. Hassler, he insisted upon working in his office at the yard. On 11 July he began having severe chest pain. He spent that evening in his study in his favorite chair. Perhaps realizing that the end was near, he said, "The officer should wear his uniform, as the judge his ermine, without a stain." He wanted no stain on his reputation to mar his image for posterity. The pain in his chest kept him awake for most of the night.[73]

On the morning of 12 July 1870 Dahlgren rose as usual at six. He had an egg, bread, and a glass of iced milk for breakfast. He told Madeleine that "the clear ring of the ice was refreshing." He then went to work in his office at the yard. At eight the pain in his chest suddenly worsened. Less than a half an hour later he died of heart failure.[74]

The funeral took place three days later. Flags at every navy yard and station and on board each U.S. naval vessel in commission flew at half mast. The officers on duty at the yard turned out early in dress-blue uniforms, epaulettes, swords, and caps. At 9:30 pallbearers moved the heavy casket with its silver-plated lid from Dahlgren's house to the hearse. Guns boomed as four gray horses pulled the hearse to the Presbyterian Church on 4½ Street. Numerous army and navy officers, including Sherman and Porter, rode in the funeral procession. At the church the Reverend Dr. Sunderland delivered a lengthy oration, filled with allusions to biblical figures and ancient

Romans. "[Dahlgren's] scientific experiments and practical inventions of ordnance," he said, "had made him a standard authority in that important branch of the national...defense." After the memorial service, a marine detachment escorted the casket to the railroad station. The 12:45 train carried Dahlgren's body to Philadelphia. He was buried at Laurel Hill Cemetery between the graves of his son Ulric and his first wife, Mary.[75]

Obituaries recounted the admiral's deeds, highlighting his ordnance career and command of the South Atlantic Blockading Squadron. The *Army and Navy Journal* gave him the most appropriate epitaph:

> With the exception of FARRAGUT and PORTER, no officer of our navy has enjoyed a wider reputation than DAHLGREN. For this he is indebted, less to his services at sea, than to those scientific studies which have associated his name both here and abroad with that improvement in ordnance which is one of the distinguishing features of modern advance in the art of war.... Our Navy has never had a more capable and accomplished ordnance officer than the departed Admiral.[76]

Conclusion

John Dahlgren's sister Patty remained happily married to "Mr. Read" until her death in 1904. John's brother Charles Gustavus Dahlgren eventually found employment in the insurance business. He died in 1888. Charles Bunker Dahlgren, John's son, became a successful engineer and wrote a book entitled *Historic Mines of Mexico,* which in its day was considered the standard work in the field. He also wrote *The Dahlgren Shell-Gun and Its Services during the Late Civil War,* a pamphlet that glorified and exaggerated the contribution of his father's guns to the war effort. During the Spanish-American War he served on board the USS *Resolute* and was present at the battle of Santiago harbor. Paul Dahlgren became the U.S. consul general to Italy and served in that capacity until his death in 1876. He never married.

John and Madeleine Dahlgren's children appeared frequently in the society column of the *New York Times.* In 1889 John Vinton Dahlgren, a distinguished lawyer, married Elizabeth Drexel of the wealthy banking Drexels of Philadelphia. Madeleine Dahlgren threw them a week-long "bridal reception" in the "Old English style" at her stately home atop South Mountain near Middletown, Maryland. A lengthy article in the *New York Times* listed the guests, including the great-grandson of the marquis de Lafayette and children of assorted diplomats, U.S. senators, and congressmen. The article also described Madeleine's furniture, including an "ancient mahogany table, once the property of Henry Clay." John Vinton Dahlgren died in 1899. One of the twins, Eric Bernard Dahlgren, married Elizabeth Drexel's sister Lucy in 1890. Although their wedding received relatively little attention in the *New York Times,* Eric's name frequently appeared in the paper later because of his exploits as a "millionaire yachtsman" and his nasty divorce in 1913. He died in 1922. Ulrica Dahlgren, the other twin, in 1891 married Josiah Pierce, Jr., a civil engineer and son of a U.S. diplomat in St. Petersburg.[1]

Madeleine Vinton Dahlgren did more to shape her husband's reputation for posterity than anyone else in the family except the admiral himself. Several years after his death she began working on the *Memoir of John A. Dahlgren, Rear-Admiral United States Navy.* Her motive was twofold. She wanted to vindicate her husband, whose reputation Gillmore and the congressional ordnance committee had tarnished. As she told Charles Cowley, who became a lawyer after serving on Dahlgren's staff at Charleston, "I was determined to…build the Admiral's monument as high as I could, for all Time."[2] She also wanted to finance her lifestyle as a Washington socialite. Soon after John's death she petitioned Congress for payment of royalties on his patented ordnance inventions. She spent seven years before Congress and two years in the courts battling for her claim. "*The least* sum for a just and proper compensation to our estate," she wrote Cowley, "would be $1,374,000." She was incensed about the final settlement: "an insolvent percentage of $65,000—and ten thousand…was at once required to meet the expenses of this prolonged suit!"[3] No doubt Madeleine hoped that the *Memoir* would support her arguments in Congress and in court. The book contains numerous extracts from Dahlgren's diary, which she edited to portray her husband in the best possible light. Most historians who have written about Dahlgren have relied largely on Madeleine's biased account. She died in 1898.[4]

As both Madeleine and John Dahlgren wished, the admiral's reputation long outlived him. The navy honored him by giving his name to three ships, a building at the Naval Academy, a building and a street at the Washington Navy Yard, and a naval weapons proving ground in Virginia. A bust of Dahlgren clad in a toga now stands in Dahlgren Hall at the Naval Academy.

John Adolphus Bernard Dahlgren was a forceful, uncompromising, hardworking, highly intelligent, and egotistical individual. He possessed enormous determination, persistence, and self-discipline. He had a well-developed sense of right and wrong, a healthy respect for wealth, a moderate sense of religion, a taste for martyrdom, and a reverence for knowledge. He considered himself a member of a superior race and social class. A shrewd and calculating climber, he actively sought recognition, promotion, social status, and military honor. He loved to bask in the limelight and to revel in his accomplishments, and he protested loudly when credit he thought belonged to him went to others.

Dahlgren always took offense at slights to his reputation, which remained of paramount importance to him. An individual with whom he had a disagreement usually became an object of scorn, if not an outright enemy. In Dahlgren's mind, Morris was an old fogy, Ingraham a well-meaning bumbler, Rodman a misguided plagiarist, Wise a traitor, Fox a meddlesome, insolent tyrant, Welles a vindictive, mean-spirited clod, and Gillmore, his ultimate adversary, a liar and a dirty scoundrel.

On the other hand, Dahlgren generally esteemed those who shared his point of view. Hassler was a father figure, Warrington an older officer with a young mind, Drayton a well-tried old companion, Lincoln a warm and respected superior, Sherman a crusty comrade in arms, and Foote, his best friend, a revered shipmate. To these people Dahlgren was a warm and devoted friend. At home he was a loving and romantic husband and a hard-to-please father deeply concerned about his children.

At work Dahlgren was a serious and sober officer. He considered enlisted men to be his social inferiors yet treated them kindly and looked after their needs. He was painfully meticulous, rigorous, careful, and thorough in carrying out his duty and was never afraid to take the initiative to right what he perceived as wrongs or to correct what he perceived as flaws. When faced with obstacles he chipped away at them patiently, often investing years to get what he wanted, all the while raging at what he believed was the stupidity of his opponents. Self-righteous about his own work, he distrusted that of others, especially when it impinged upon his own. In all that he did he honestly believed that he was acting in the navy's best interests.

Above all, he desired glory. The pace and direction of ordnance innovation in the United States Navy during the period 1848–69 depended more upon Dahlgren's quest for glory than upon any other single factor.

But Dahlgren did not set out to become an innovator. Born to potential high position in American society and frustrated when his father gave away the family's wealth, the ticket to that society, he turned toward a career in the United States Navy to redeem his social position. He wanted to command a ship, for during the age of sail, glory could be won only at sea, preferably in battle. Unfortunately, the limited opportunities in the antebellum navy prevented him from getting a command afloat.

Dahlgren sublimated his ambition in ordnance work. He came to believe that innovators were just as important to the navy as fighters and sought to win for his ordnance expertise the status accorded heroic feats of combat. He wanted high rank, honor, and the power to direct the development of ordnance.

During the late 1840s and 1850s he studied internal and external ballistics and metallurgy and invented a cannon that he manufactured and tested under the most comprehensive program of quality control the United States Navy had seen. Because its predecessors had been copies of European designs, the Dahlgren gun was the first truly American naval cannon, and it enjoyed a shining and well-deserved if short-lived reputation as the world's most powerful and reliable piece of naval ordnance. While perfecting his cannon he created the first organization in American naval history designed to improve a naval weapon by means of systematic research, development, and testing, and he contributed the idea of institutionalized innovation to the American naval tradition.

Dahlgren deserves the title "father of American naval ordnance" for these achievements. True, he borrowed existing ideas for the gun and the organization from the United States Army and from Europe. The army's Ordnance Department and European science may be called the grandfathers of American naval ordnance. However, Dahlgren reassembled army and European ideas into constructions that were new to the United States Navy and unique in American naval history.

In terms of continuous innovation, at least in the short term, however, the organization proved to be a false start. Ultimately, Dahlgren created the Ordnance Establishment not for ongoing research and development but to inaugurate a particular innovation. Dahlgren trained others not to develop programs of innovation but to carry out his own program. His goal was to institutionalize his gun, his ideas, and his own name. As a result, he curtailed what might have been his greatest contribution: an institution dedicated to continuous improvement of naval weapons by systematic research and development. But his goal was perfectly consistent with a naval culture in which individual deeds became institutional tradition.

Dahlgren's accomplishments demonstrated an individual's power and limits in effecting change in the nineteenth-century navy. He achieved what he did largely because of his talent as a bureaucratic entrepreneur. During midcentury, officers who had fought in the War of 1812 occupied the navy's highest berths. Dahlgren and officers of his generation called them "old fogies" because of their hidebound attitude toward technological innovation and administrative reform. Many of these elder officers fought Dahlgren's ideas. In order to overcome their resistance, he had to master the art of political salesmanship. The ambition, education, upbringing in the sailing navy, ordnance expertise, and political savvy that Dahlgren brought to the Bureau of Ordnance and Hydrography helped him construct a convincing sales pitch. Going over opponents' heads to higher authorities became a signature tactic. During the political and technical processes of development, he created constituencies for the gun from above and below. The constituency from above provided political support, helping overcome bureaucratic resistance. The constituency from below provided technical support, helped solve mechanical problems, and facilitated the fleet's acceptance of the gun. Dahlgren sold the buyers on the gun by linking it to their political interests, couching his proposals in terms of the national impulses of the day. He won over the workers by making the gun's success a criterion for success in their careers.

Because of his success, talent, dogged persistence, back-breaking work, masterful entrepreneurship, and extensive self-publicity, Dahlgren earned unparalleled renown as an internationally recognized scientific ordnance expert.

Despite this acclaim, however, the navy never fully empowered him to direct the development of ordnance as he saw fit. Dahlgren's own narrow vision was largely to blame. Despite his frustration with superiors, he turned down opportunities to become chief of ordnance after Morris's death and early in the Civil War. Dahlgren clung to the perception of the post as a strictly administrative berth; he never grasped its potential as a means for instituting change. As chief, he could have organized the bureau to minimize his role in administration and maximize the potential for R&D. If he had accepted the berth after Morris's death, for example, he could have initiated development of rifled ordnance in 1856. Unfortunately, both for himself and for the navy, he was unwilling to delegate administrative duties to a subordinate who might make a mistake for which the chief would be held responsible. Dahlgren's unwillingness to risk his reputation forced him to remain in a subordinate position within the bureau. That he continued to rankle under superiors who lacked ordnance expertise yet who refused to follow his advice was largely his own fault. As a result, he did not begin development of rifled ordnance until the eve of the Civil War. Fame without absolute power over R&D and without administrative responsibility seemed to him a dubious achievement.

Dahlgren's friendship with Abraham Lincoln promised to change this. The president supported Dahlgren's bid to reorganize the naval ordnance bureau exactly as he wanted it. But it was not to be. Dahlgren had no control over his superiors in the Navy Department. The duel between the *Monitor* and the *Virginia* indicated that his famous gun was inadequate against armored ships. Fox, a man devoid of ordnance expertise but empowered to make decisions, believed that the solution to the problem of armored warships lay in a much larger cannon than anything the navy had in its inventory: a 15-inch gun.

Fox's meddling was the last straw. Dahlgren strongly resisted the 15-incher, but the assistant secretary compelled him to develop it for the new monitors. Dahlgren realized that the navy would never accord him absolute power to determine the future shape of American naval ordnance, despite his unparalleled reputation. An old-fashioned successful combat record remained the one true path to glory and power; international acclaim as an ordnance expert was simply no substitute. Tradition dictated that naval glory be achieved on the quarterdeck of a fighting ship at sea, not at a bureau in Washington. Therefore, Dahlgren sought a fighting berth. At the moment his country needed him most for his expertise as an innovator, he forsook ordnance work to pursue his true ambition.

With the Lincoln's help he obtained command of the South Atlantic Blockading Squadron, potentially the most prestigious berth in the fleet. The squadron was slated to capture Charleston, the cradle of the rebellion. Success in this enterprise would give Dahlgren the kind of immortal fame he so desperately desired. He took command in June 1863.

On the whole, Dahlgren did reasonably well as commander of the South Atlantic Blockading Squadron. He failed to take Charleston, not only because he lacked support from the Navy and War Departments but also because he never found a way to cope with the harbor obstructions. But he maintained the blockade, defended his squadron to the satisfaction of his superiors, and excelled in joint operations.

Nevertheless, largely because of Quincy A. Gillmore, Dahlgren's reputation suffered a severe blow. The general, whose concern for reputation rivaled Dahlgren's, did not wish to be blamed for the failure to capture the city and secretly launched a campaign to make Dahlgren the scapegoat. When Dahlgren learned of this, Gillmore became a lifelong enemy.

Although the Civil War provided Dahlgren with a rich variety of experience, he made little effort to study and digest it, and certainly no real attempt to institutionalize its lessons. Personal needs came first. After the Civil War he focused the bulk of his attention on defending his reputation and had little inclination to do anything innovative. Gillmore's accusations made him more sensitive than ever to the slightest insult to his honor. When David D. Porter received a promotion to vice admiral instead of him, Dahlgren protested loudly. Welles, who had grown tired of his complaints, shipped him off to west coast of South America. Dahlgren did not wish to go, but with Lincoln dead he had no choice. In 1868 Welles summoned him back to Washington, where once again he took charge of the Bureau of Ordnance.

During Dahlgren's absence the bureau had continued on the course he had set for it in the 1850s. When the Civil War began, the bureau and the navy were wedded to Dahlgren's cast-iron muzzleloading smoothbore soda-water-bottle paradigm. During the war the exigencies of wartime production, the complacency of success, naval culture and tradition, and Dahlgren's personality precluded innovation. Production inhibited innovation because it absorbed most of the bureau's resources. The navy perceived no need for new weapons because the ordnance it already had met the demands of Civil War naval combat, and because rifles were relatively unreliable. The navy's cultural and traditional emphasis on sea service and combat inhibited innovation by precipitating the exodus of trained ordnance personnel to fighting berths. Dahlgren's desire for command of the South Atlantic Blockading Squadron resulted not only from an unquenchable thirst for glory and power but also from a tradition that to that time had failed to reward innovative talent adequately. Apart from driving him away from ordnance work to seek a fighting berth, Dahlgren's personality inhibited innovation in another important way. As bureau chief, his unwillingness to share either blame for others' failures or credit for his own successes prevented him from delegating authority, with the result that he spread himself too thin. Only urgent matters received his full attention. Because of production demands, because he did not perceive a need for new ordnance, and because he was bent on resurrecting the reputation of the 11-incher in the wake of the *Monitor-Virginia* duel, innovation in American naval ordnance did not occur during the Civil War.

Dahlgren returned to the bureau in 1868 with the intention of doing at least some experimental work, but he chose not to pursue the development of rifled ordnance. His guns had performed so well that the need for new weapons was not perceived until the late 1860s. By then the political climate had changed, with postwar retrenchment having overtaken wartime expansion. Although Dahlgren argued for experimentation during his second stint as ordnance chief, his postwar effort to innovate never matched the intensity of his prewar effort. By 1868, years of fighting his superiors and the Confederates had sapped the strength he needed to fight for change. More important, with his reputation as a naval commander at Charleston under siege, his reputation as an ordnance innovator was all he had left. The siege sapped his motivation to pursue change. Then came the ultimate blow. The congressional committee's charge that he had stifled innovation in ordnance during the war—in effect, the charge that he had become an old fogy—shattered the last vestige of his reputation. He resigned from the bureau and never worked with ordnance again. A year later he died a broken man.

At first, innovation in American naval ordnance stagnated in the wake of Dahlgren's death. Commodore Ludlow A. Case, Dahlgren's successor as chief of the Bureau of Ordnance, was uninterested in any but incremental improvements, despite mounting evidence of the obsolescence of American naval ordnance. Instead of stumping for a new development program, he persuaded Congress to provide money for ten 15-inch guns in fiscal 1871. A year later, Congress funded another ten 15-inchers. It was the last procurement of heavy smoothbores in American naval history. Nevertheless, Case's tenure marked the beginning of a rejuvenation of the naval ordnance R&D program. Although Case did not advocate major changes in naval armament, he established a new Naval Experimental Battery in Annapolis, Maryland, and he revived methods that Dahlgren had employed to educate specialists, sailors, and line officers, including the assignment of officers to foundries to learn about ordnance production and the use of a ship to train seamen in gunnery.[5]

Captain William N. Jeffers succeeded Case as chief of the Bureau of Ordnance in April 1873. Jeffers believed that Dahlgren smoothbores were no longer adequate armament against European men-of-war armed with rifled cannon. In each of his annual reports from 1874 on, he recommended rearmament of the navy with breechloading rifles. In 1875 he concluded that steel was the best metal for guns because it was lighter than cast or wrought iron and had better elasticity and hardness. He was, however, no Dahlgren when it came to selling a major rearmament program, and he failed to persuade Congress to provide the funds for new weapons. Without government backing, the American iron and steel industry would not risk capital in developing the manufacturing capability and technical expertise for making heavy steel guns. Legislators did not endorse a major program of naval rearmament until the following decade.

Jeffers, however, could claim significant achievements during his tenure as ordnance chief. He maintained and expanded Case's educational programs and forged partnerships between the navy and several small steel companies. Under Jeffers the Bureau of Ordnance converted a few 11-inch Dahlgren smoothbores into 8-inch rifles by drilling them out and inserting a steel sleeve; it developed the navy's first all-steel breechloading built-up rifle, a 6-incher produced in the late 1870s; and it laid the groundwork for subsequent production of modern steel ordnance. These efforts improved the firepower of the cannon, enabled the navy to acquire extensive expertise in modern guns, advanced the development of a domestic steel supply for heavy guns, and created a cadre of ordnance experts. Although Jeffers's achievements did not close the gap with Europe, they provided the foundation for the navy's rearmament program of the 1880s.[6]

Thus, Dahlgren's R&D organization outlived his gun. The Naval Gun Factory at the Washington Navy Yard and the Naval Experimental Battery in Annapolis stemmed from the organization Dahlgren created initially to test 32-pounders and, ultimately, to institute his gun. But it was the reputation of the gun that enabled the R&D organization to weather stagnation during the 1860s and retrenchment during the 1870s. Dahlgren had given American sailors something they had never had before: an unshakable faith in their guns, a faith justified by the existence of an organization founded on the idea that systematic research and development could produce safer and more powerful weapons. That idea was Dahlgren's most important contribution to the American naval tradition.

Tragically, Dahlgren's quest for glory prevented the navy from fully realizing the potential of this idea while he lived. His ambition produced spectacular success during the 1850s, but he proved unable to rise above it enough to see beyond his own initial achievement. His narrow vision stifled subsequent innovation, with unfortunate consequences for the fleet. Despite the efforts of his successors, the United States Navy lost its superiority in heavy ordnance to Europe during the 1870s and would not regain parity with the other major naval powers until the early 1890s.

*   *   *

In his memoirs Alfred Thayer Mahan describes an incident that happened while he was in command of a sailing steamer on the South Pacific Station in the mid-1880s. A French naval officer, making a courtesy call, paused upon leaving the ship to gaze wistfully at the Dahlgren smoothbores on her deck. They reminded him of his days as a midshipman, of his youth. He quoted a line from François Villon: "Où sont les neiges d'antan?" (Where are the snows of yesteryear?)[7]

Notes

ABBREVIATIONS

Annual Report. *Annual Report of the Secretary of the Navy.* Washington, D.C.: Government Printing Office, various years.

CWNC. U.S. Navy Department, Naval History Division. *Civil War Naval Chronology, 1861–1865.* Washington, D.C.: Government Printing Office, 1971.

DAB. Johnson, Allen, and Dumas Malone, eds. *Dictionary of American Biography.* 20 vols. New York: Charles Scribner's Sons, 1928–37.

DANFS. Mooney, James L., ed. *Dictionary of American Naval Fighting Ships.* 8 vols. Washington, D.C.: Government Printing Office, 1959–81.

DASHM. Rear Admiral John Adolphus Bernard Dahlgren Papers. American Swedish Historical Museum, Philadelphia, Pa.

DD. John A. Dahlgren Papers. Manuscripts Department, William R. Perkins Library, Duke University, Durham, N.C.

DFP. Dahlgren Family Papers. Julie Anne Young Johnson, Gaithersburg, Md. (private collection).

Diary. John A. Dahlgren Diaries, John A. Dahlgren Papers. George Arents Research Library at Syracuse University, Syracuse, N.Y.

DLC. John A. Dahlgren Papers. Manuscripts Division, Library of Congress, Washington, D.C.

DNHC. Rear Admiral John A. Dahlgren Papers, ZB File. Operational Archives, Naval Historical Center, Washington Navy Yard, Washington, D.C.

DNHFC. John Adolphus Bernard Dahlgren Papers, Naval Historical Foundation Collection. Manuscripts Division, Library of Congress, Washington, D.C.

DNL. Rear Admiral John A. Dahlgren, Letterbook of Correspondence between John A. Dahlgren and Henry A. Wise, 1855. Nimitz Library, United States Naval Academy, Annapolis, Md.

DNLC. John Adolphus Bernard Dahlgren Papers. Newberry Library, Chicago.

DNYPL. Rear Admiral John Adolphus Bernard Dahlgren Papers. Rare Books and Manuscripts Division, New York Public Library, New York.

DS. John A. Dahlgren Papers. George Arents Research Library at Syracuse University, Syracuse, N.Y.

DUSNAM. John Adolphus Bernard Dahlgren Papers. Manuscript Collections, Naval Academy Museum, United States Naval Academy, Annapolis, Md.

HSPA. Historical Society of Pennsylvania, Philadelphia.

MVDG. Madeleine Vinton Dahlgren Papers. Special Collections, Georgetown University Library, Washington, D.C.

NYHS. New-York Historical Society, New York.

ORA. *War of the Rebellion: A Compilation of the Official Records of the Union and Confederate Armies.* 128 vols. Washington, D.C.: Government Printing Office, 1880–1901. Cited as follows: series number, volume number, part number, page number.

ORN. U.S. Department of the Navy. *Official Records of the Union and Confederate Navies in the War of the Rebellion.* Edited by Richard Rush et al. 31 vols. and index. Washington, D.C.: Government Printing Office, 1894–1922. Cited as follows: series number, volume number, page number.

PDHSPA. Captain Percival Drayton Papers. Drayton Collection, Historical Society of Pennsylvania, Philadelphia.

RG45 NA. Naval Records Collection of the Office of Naval Records and Library, Record Group 45. National Archives, Washington, D.C.

RG74 NA. Records of the Bureau of Ordnance, Record Group 74. National Archives, Washington, D.C.

SFD. Du Pont, Samuel F. *Samuel Francis Du Pont: A Selection from His Civil War Letters.* Edited by John D. Hayes. 3 vols. Ithaca, N.Y.: Cornell University Press, 1969.

WNYHS. Henry Augustus Wise Papers. New-York Historical Society, New York.

PREFACE

1. Alden and Earle, *Makers of Naval Tradition;* Bradford, *Captains;* Macartney, *Mr. Lincoln's Admirals,* vi; McCollum, *Dahlgren,* 1–6; Peterson, *Admiral John A. Dahlgren.*

2. Madeleine Dahlgren, *Memoir;* Headley, *Farragut and Our Naval Commanders;* Schneller, "Intentional Omissions."

CHAPTER 1. THE QUEST BEGINS

1. Madeleine Dahlgren, *Memoir,* 4–7.

2. Ibid., 5–6; Scott, *Sweden,* 196–98, 316.

3. Madeleine Dahlgren, *Memoir,* 7.

4. Scott, *Sweden,* 287–93; Brown, *American Naval Heroes,* 485; Madeleine Dahlgren, *Memoir,* 7.

5. Madeleine Dahlgren, *Memoir,* 8–9; Diary, 3 August 1855 entry.

6. Madeleine Dahlgren, *Memoir,* 7–10; "List of Papers Delivered to B. Dahlgren," folder 7, box 11, General John Cadwalader Section, Cadwalader Collection, HSPA; petition for a bridge over the Susquehanna, 29 November 1810, folder 2, box 4b, "Petitions," Society Miscellaneous Collections, HSPA.

7. Madeleine Dahlgren, *Memoir,* 7–13; McIlwaine to Southard, 6 February 1823, box 1, DLC; [illegible] to Southard, 23 October 1824, box 1, DLC; Dahlgren to Cadwalader, 11 January 1815, Bernard Dahlgren folder, Thomas Cadwalader Section, Cadwalader Collection, HSPA.

8. "List of Papers Delivered to B. Dahlgren," folder 7, box 11, General John Cadwalader Section, Cadwalader Collection, HSPA; Dahlgren to Cadwalader, 11 January 1815, Bernhard Dahlgren folder, Thomas Cadwalader Section, Cadwalader Collection, HSPA; Pessen, *Jacksonian America,* 83–100; Madeleine Dahlgren, *Memoir,* 8–10, 17.

9. Charles G. Dahlgren, notes, DFP; Charles B. Dahlgren, "Genealogy," DFP; Madeleine Dahlgren, *Memoir,* 8–10; Martha M. Read, undated note, DFP; Diary, 9 November 1865 and 10 April 1869 entries; Dickson, *National Cyclopaedia of American Biography,* s.v. "de Rohan, William."

10. Madeleine Dahlgren, *Memoir,* 8–13, 415; Hindle, *Early American Science,* 173–77; Bartlett, *American Mind,* 20–22; Charles G. Dahlgren, notes, DFP; Diary, 8 June 1855 entry; B. H. Rand, note, 22 September 1824, box 1, DLC; school notebook, Memorabilia folder, box 2, DS; Colhoun to Southard, 25 December 1824, box 1, DLC; Joseph Roberts, Jr., note, 24 September 1824, box 1, DLC.

11. School notebook, Memorabilia folder, box 2, DS.

12. Madeleine Dahlgren, *Memoir,* 416; Diary, 3 August 1855 entry.

13. Pessen, *Jacksonian America,* 54–59; Larkin, *Reshaping,* 158; Dahlgren, journal/letter to Mary Dahlgren, 27 March 1845, DNHFC.

14. Brown, *American Naval Heroes,* 485; Charles B. Dahlgren, "Genealogy," DFP; Madeleine Dahlgren, *Memoir,* 9–10, 15–16; John Vaughan, "To Whom It May Concern," 31 December 1824, box 1, DLC.

15. Unlike other members of his family, Samuel F. Du Pont chose to capitalize the particle of his name. Merrill, *Du Pont,* 2.

16. Madeleine Dahlgren, *Memoir,* 9–10, 15–16; Victor du Pont to Bernhard Dahlgren, 7 June 1822, DFP; Charles G. Dahlgren, undated note, DFP.

17. Cooper, *The Pilot,* ed. House, xix–xxvii; Cooper, *The Pilot,* introd. Winterich, vi, viii; Axelrad, *History and Utopia,* vii; Philbrick, *Cooper,* 12, 44–82; Nelson, "Cooper's Maritime Nationalism," 129–30.

18. Philbrick, *Cooper,* vii, 1, 26–27; Larkin, *Reshaping,* 235; Guttridge and Smith, *Commodores,* ix–x.

19. McKee, *Gentlemanly and Honorable Profession,* 297.

20. Forgie, *Patricide,* 57–67; Bradford, *Command,* 77–79, 165, 178, 184–85, 214–16; Melville, *White Jacket,* 241; Philbrick, *Cooper,* vii, 1, 26–27.

21. Braudy, *Frenzy of Renown,* 10, 23–24, 30, 37–39, 366, 382, 595.

22. Madeleine Dahlgren to Cowley, 10 March 1890, DS.

23. Pessen, *Jacksonian America,* 91–92.

24. Bradford, *Command,* 251; Todorich, *Spirited Years,* 5; Valle, *Rocks and Shoals,* 13.
25. Madeleine Dahlgren, *Memoir,* 11–16; Willing to Southard, 23 February 1825, box 1, DLC; Pennsylvania General Assembly Members to Southard, 14 January 1825, box 1, DLC; Dahlgren to Southard, 13 February 1825, box 1, DLC.
26. Southard to Breck, 28 February 1825, box 1, DLC.
27. Bradford, *Captains,* 28; Certificate No. 28952 of District and Port of Philadelphia, 28 March 1825, box 1, DLC; Madeleine Dahlgren, *Memoir,* 18.
28. Madeleine Dahlgren, *Memoir,* 18; Dahlgren, "Thoughts on Cuba," 2 June 1825, box 1, DLC; Dahlgren, journal scraps, 16–18 June 1825, box 1, DLC.
29. Madeleine Dahlgren, *Memoir,* 16–20; Sutherland to Wurts, 29 December 1825, box 1, DLC.
30. Southard to Dahlgren, 1 February 1826, box 1, DLC.

Chapter 2. The Reefer, the Sailing Navy, and the Steam Navy

1. Keller, "Reflections on Politics and Generations," 123–25; Kriegel, "Generational Difference," 29.
2. McKee, *Gentlemanly and Honorable Profession,* 115, 167–70, 220.
3. Karsten, *Naval Aristocracy,* 385–95.
4. Southard to Dahlgren, 1 February 1826, box 1, DLC; Valle, *Rocks and Shoals,* 13–14, 90; Bradford, *Captains,* 27–28; Madeleine Dahlgren, *Memoir,* 21–22.
5. Morison, *Old Bruin,* 132; Huntington, *Soldier and the State,* 199; Bell, *Room to Swing a Cat,* 129–30.
6. Parker, *Recollections,* x; Guttridge and Smith, *Commodores,* 26–27; Bell, *Room to Swing a Cat,* 105–7.
7. Guttridge and Smith, *Commodores,* 26–27; Bell, *Room to Swing a Cat,* 105–7; Valle, *Rocks and Shoals,* 90.
8. Valle, *Rocks and Shoals,* 18, 90; Guttridge and Smith, *Commodores,* 75.
9. Schroeder, *Shaping a Maritime Empire,* 3, 17; Albion, *Makers of Naval Policy,* 5, 295; Weigley, *American Way of War,* 61.
10. Southard to Dahlgren, 12 April 1826, box 1, DLC; *DANFS,* 4:178–79.
11. Alden and Earle, *Makers of Naval Tradition,* 132; Madeleine Dahlgren, *Memoir,* 10; Dahlgren, "*Macedonian* Journal," box 32, DLC; Dahlgren, miscellaneous notes, 1855 folder, box 23, DLC.
12. Sands, *From Reefer to Rear Admiral,* 18–19; Bell, *Room to Swing a Cat,* 132–37.
13. Sands, *From Reefer to Rear Admiral,* 15–17; Harrod, *Manning the New Navy,* 155–56; Bell, *Room to Swing a Cat,* 207–8; Madeleine Dahlgren, *Memoir,* 24; Valle, *Rocks and Shoals,* 3.
14. Dahlgren, "*Macedonian* Journal," 13 October 1826 entry, box 32, DLC.
15. Ibid., 9 November 1826 entry; Madeleine Dahlgren, *Memoir,* 26–27.
16. Dahlgren, "*Macedonian* Journal," 31 May 1827 entry, box 32, DLC; Madeleine Dahlgren, *Memoir,* 31.
17. Dahlgren, "*Macedonian* Journal," 24 May and 3 June 1827 entries, box 32, DLC.
18. Ibid., 13–26 March and 26–28 May 1828 entries.

19. As a wooden ship aged, the bow and stern began to droop, and the keel began to curve upward. This was called hogging.

20. Dahlgren, "*Macedonian* Journal," 30 August–30 October 1828 entries, box 32, DLC; Dahlgren, journal/letter to Mary B. Dahlgren, 10 February 1845, DNHFC; Madeleine Dahlgren, *Memoir,* 39–43.

21. Southard to Dahlgren, 1 November and 1 December 1828, box 1, DLC; Madeleine Dahlgren, *Memoir,* 43, 124; Diary, *Ontario* cruise folder.

22. Branch to Dahlgren, 5 June 1829, DNYPL; Parker, *Recollections,* xi–xii; Bradford, *Captains,* 3; Albion, *Makers of Naval Policy,* 5; Madeleine Dahlgren, *Memoir,* 41–42.

23. Bradford, *Captains,* 143; *DANFS,* 5:160; Diary, *Ontario* cruise folder; Dahlgren, "Journal of a Cruise in the Mediterranean," DNYPL; Dahlgren, miscellaneous notes, 1855 folder, box 23, DLC.

24. Dahlgren, "Journal of a Cruise in the Mediterranean," DNYPL; Dahlgren, letter/journal to Mary B. Dahlgren, 31 October 1843, DNHFC.

25. Diary, *Ontario* cruise folder.

26. Dahlgren, "Journal of a Cruise in the Mediterranean," DNYPL; J. W. Plummer, note, 25 August 1831, box 1, DLC; Biddle to Dahlgren, 8 September 1831, DLC.

27. Dahlgren, notes, 14 September 1831, box 1, DLC; Dahlgren to Walker, 15 September 1831, box 1, DLC; Walker to Dahlgren, 15 September 1831, box 1, DLC; Parker to Dahlgren, 21 September 1831, box 1, DLC; Dahlgren, undated notes, 1831 file, box 1, DLC.

28. Bell, *Room to Swing a Cat,* 143–45; Duffy, *Military Experience in the Age of Reason,* 74–80; Janowitz, *Professional Soldier,* 215–25; Perret, *Country Made by War,* 191.

29. Bradford, *Captains,* 90–91; Morison, *Old Bruin,* 132–33; Todorich, *Spirited Years,* 8; Dahlgren, "Journal of a Cruise in the Mediterranean," DNYPL; Madeleine Dahlgren, *Memoir,* 65; Sands, *From Reefer to Rear Admiral,* 70–79.

30. Sands, *From Reefer to Rear Admiral,* 78–79.

31. Dahlgren, scrapbook titled "Ranges of Guns at Experimental Battery Washington and Other Miscellaneous Matter of South Atlantic Block. Squadron," box 32, DLC; Dahlgren, "Notebook 1843," box 32, DLC.

32. Bradford, *Captains,* 197; Callan to Dahlgren, 29 April 1832, box 1, DLC; Madeleine Dahlgren, *Memoir,* 65–66.

33. Miller, *Life of the Mind,* 136–44; Boyle to Dahlgren, 13 April 1833, box 1, DLC; Dahlgren, "Study Notes on Blackstone," 1832–33, box 20, DLC; Madeleine Dahlgren, *Memoir,* 66–67.

34. Dahlgren, Paul, and Lewis to Barron, 9 May 1833, box 1, DLC; Barron to Dahlgren, Paul, and Lewis, 14 May 1833, box 1, DLC; Karsten, *Naval Aristocracy,* 88.

35. Madeleine Dahlgren, *Memoir,* 67; Boyle to Dahlgren, 13 June 1833, box 1, DLC; Woodbury to Dahlgren, 10 February 1834, box 1, DLC; Hassler to Vaughan, 13 May 1834, box 1, DLC.

36. Madeleine Dahlgren, *Memoir,* 68–69; U.S. Congress, House, *Message from the President of the United States Transmitting the Rules and Regulations (Prepared by the Board of Revision) for the Government of the Navy of the United States,* H. Doc. 20, 23d Cong., 1st sess., 1833, 6, 10–11; *National Gazette* (Philadelphia), 11 and 25 February, 30 April 1834. Copies of the "Blue Jacket" articles may be found in the newspaper clippings folder in box 36, DLC.

37. Diary, 20 April 1834 entry; Madeleine Dahlgren, *Memoir,* 72.

38. Diary, 27 and 29 April 1834 entries.

39. McKee, *Gentlemanly and Honorable Profession*, 272, 286.

40. Bell, *Room to Swing a Cat*, 102–3; Duffy, *Military Experience in the Age of Reason*, 76; Karsten, *Naval Aristocracy*, 258; Langley, *Social Reform*, 22–23; Morison, *Old Bruin*, 135.

41. Langley, *Social Reform*, 24–25; Guttridge and Smith, *Commodores*, 300; Hagan, *In Peace and War*, 66; Valle, *Rocks and Shoals*, 24; Bradford, *Command*, 120.

42. Bartlett, *American Mind*, 42–43; Rogin, *Subversive Genealogy*, 71–73; for nationwide reform in this period, see Tyler, *Freedom's Ferment*.

43. Huntington, *Soldier and the State*, 217–20.

44. Mahan, *From Sail to Steam*, 11–12; Albion, *Makers of Naval Policy*, 70–71; Todorich, *Spirited Years*, 9–10; Morison, *Old Bruin*, 131; Valle, *Rocks and Shoals*, 26.

45. Albion, *Makers of Naval Policy*, 189, 194.

46. Ibid., 189–92; Baxter, *Introduction of the Ironclad Warship*, 46; Bradford, *Captains*, 7; Sprout and Sprout, *Rise of American Naval Power*, 111–15.

47. Dahlgren, trans., *Account of the Experiments Made in the French Navy for the Trial of Bomb Cannon*, 1–10.

48. Albion, *Makers of Naval Policy*, 193; Langley, *Social Reform*, 27–30; Coletta, *American Secretaries of the Navy*, 1:vii, 179–93.

49. Albion, *Makers of Naval Policy*, 193–94.

Chapter 3. The Young Officer

1. Daniels, *Nineteenth-Century American Science*, 26–30.

2. Bartlett, *American Mind*, 28; Cajori, *Hassler*, 15–95, 117–18, 236–40; Christman, *Naval Innovators*, 49–52; Daniels, *Nineteenth-Century American Science*, 26–30, 69; DuPree, *Science in the Federal Government*, 29–33, 51–56.

3. Cajori, *Hassler*, 178–87; Christman, *Naval Innovators*, 49–52; Bradford, *Captains*, 29.

4. Hassler to Vaughan, 13 May 1834, box 1, DLC; Dahlgren to Hassler, 15 May 1834, box 1, DLC.

5. Hassler to Vaughan, 13 May 1834, box 1, DLC; Diary, 15–18 May and 21 June 1834 entries.

6. Christman, *Naval Innovators*, 49–52; Dairy, 25 May 1834 entry; Sands, *From Reefer to Rear Admiral*, 88–91.

7. Bradford, *Captains*, 29; "Certificate of R. F. Hassler," 22 August 1838, box 1, DLC.

8. Hassler to Dahlgren, 6 April, 17 November, 10 and 19 December 1835, 13 December 1836, box 1, DLC.

9. Dahlgren to [Dickerson], 11 August 1835, box 1, DLC; Hassler to Dahlgren, 11 August 1835, box 1, DLC; Dickerson to Dahlgren, 16 September 1835, box 1, DLC; Dahlgren, draft of a letter to Dickerson, 17 September 1835, box 1, DLC.

10. Dickerson to Hassler, 25 March 1836, box 1, DLC; Dahlgren to Cuthbert, 18 April 1836, box 1, DLC; Dahlgren to Cist, 27 July 1865, DUSNAM.

11. Dickerson to Dahlgren, 23 September 1836, box 1, DLC; Dahlgren to Dickerson, 29 September and 13 October 1836, box 1, DLC; Dahlgren, letter/journal to Mary B. Dahlgren, 8 September 1845 entry, DNHFC.

12. DuPree, *Science in the Federal Government,* 53; "Extracts of Mr. Hassler's Letter to the President of the United States," 5 March 1837, box 1, DLC; Levi Woodbury, note, 18 March 1837, box 1, DLC; "Extracts of Mr. Woodbury's Letter to F. R. Hassler," 21 March 1837, box 1, DLC; Woodbury to Van Buren, 22 March 1837, box 20, DLC; Woodbury to Van Buren, 27 March 1837, box 1, DLC; "Extract of Letter from the Treasury Department to F. R. Hassler," 27 March 1837, box 1, DLC; "Extracts of Letter of Instructions to Captain Swift," 27 March 1837, box 1, DLC; Pickett to Dahlgren, 27 November 1837, box 1, DLC; Madeleine Dahlgren, *Memoir,* 73.

13. Headley, *Farragut and Our Naval Commanders,* 459; Hassler to Dahlgren, 2 August 1837, box 1, DLC; Ferguson to Butler, 4 November 1837, box 1, DLC.

14. Hassler to Dahlgren, 19 May, 3 June, and 2 August 1837, box 1, DLC; Dahlgren to Hassler, 10 September 1837, box 1, DLC; Hassler to Dahlgren, 27 September 1837, box 1, DLC; Woodbury to Hassler, 31 October 1837, box 1, DLC; Ferguson to Butler, 4 November 1837, box 1, DLC; Headley, *Farragut and Our Naval Commanders,* 459.

15. Woodbury to Cass, 7 November 1837, box 1, DLC; King to Rush, 22 November 1837, box 1, DLC; Hassler to Dahlgren, 19 May 1838, box 1, DLC; Dahlgren, extract of "Observations sur le danger et l'insuffisance des fortes épreuves…par le Colonel d'artillerie C. Frédérix," November 1836, box 20, DLC; Dahlgren, trans., *Bomb Cannon,* copy in box 37, DLC; Shaw to Dahlgren, 6 December 1838, box 1, DLC; [illegible] to Dahlgren, 15 December 1838, box 1, DLC; Headley, *Farragut and Our Naval Commanders,* 459.

16. Hassler to Dahlgren, 19 May 1838, box 1, DLC; Dickerson to Dahlgren, 16 June 1838, box 1, DLC; Dahlgren to Pickett, 18 June 1838, box 1, DLC; Hassler to Dahlgren, 20 June 1838, box 1, DLC; Ferguson to Van Buren, 12 August 1838, box 1, DLC; Ferguson to Dahlgren, 20 August 1838, box 1, DLC; "Certificate of R. F. Hassler," 22 August 1838, box 1, DLC; Dahlgren to Paulding, 31 August 1838, box 1, DLC.

17. Madeleine Dahlgren, *Memoir,* 78–79; Hassler to Dahlgren, 19 May 1838, box 1, DLC; Woodbury to Paulding, 18 July 1838, microcopy 517, roll 1, RG45 NA.

18. Thomas Harris, document, 14 October 1838, box 1, DLC; Madeleine Dahlgren, *Memoir,* 78; Dahlgren to Paulding, 30 January 1839, box 1, DLC; Paulding to Dahlgren, 6 February 1839, box 1, DLC; Dahlgren to Paulding, 11 February 1839, box 1, DLC.

19. [Illegible] to Dahlgren, 18 February 1839, box 1, DLC; Paulding to Dahlgren, 31 May 1839, box 1, DLC; Dahlgren, draft of a letter to Paulding, 4 June 1839, box 1, DLC.

20. Paulding to Dahlgren, 19 February and 27 May 1839, box 1, DLC; acting secretary of the navy to Dahlgren, 30 August 1839, box 1, DLC; Paulding to Dahlgren, 4 December 1839, 7 March, 8 June, 14 September, and 17 December 1840, box 1, DLC; acting secretary of the navy to Dahlgren, 23 March 1841, box 1, DLC; Badger to Dahlgren, 26 June 1841, box 1, DLC.

21. Title to lands in Bucks County, 1 January 1839, Judge John Cadwalader Papers, Cadwalader Collection, HSPA; Dahlgren, rough journal notes, 1848 folder, box 2, DLC; Hassler to Dahlgren, 7 February 1839, box 1, DLC; Diary, 28–29 December 1833 and 8 June 1855 entries; Dahlgren, journal/letter to Mary B. Dahlgren, 1 March 1844 entry, DNHFC; Dahlgren, undated valentine to Mary B. Bunker, DUSNAM; Dahlgren, *Memoir of Ulric Dahlgren,* 18–19; Diary, 26 September 1843–1 December 1844 entries, written by Mary B. Dahlgren; undated note by Patty Dahlgren, DFP.

22. Madeleine Dahlgren, *Memoir,* 78; Karsten, *Naval Aristocracy,* 124–28; Pessen, *Jacksonian America,* 93–94.

23. Diary, 6 January 1840–1 October 1842 and 8 June 1855 entries; Madeleine Dahlgren, *Memoir,* 80.

24. Madeleine Dahlgren, *Memoir,* 79–81; Upshur to Dahlgren, 3 May 1842, box 1, DLC; Diary, 25 March–17 May 1843 entries; Dahlgren to Henshaw, 29 August 1843, box 1, DLC.

25. Diary, 26 September 1843 entry; *DANFS,* 2:214–15; Dahlgren to Mary B. Dahlgren, 31 October 1843, DNHFC.

26. Morison, *Old Bruin,* 104; Dahlgren to Mary B. Dahlgren, 6 November 1843, DNHFC.

27. Madeleine Dahlgren, *Memoir,* 81; Dahlgren to Mary B. Dahlgren, 15 and 18 November 1843, DNHFC.

28. Bell, *Room to Swing a Cat,* 102; John A. Dahlgren, *Cumberland* notebook, 1844 folder, box 2, DS.

29. Madeleine Dahlgren, *Memoir,* 84–87, 97; Dahlgren to Mary B. Dahlgren, 29 September 1843, DNHFC; Dahlgren, letter/journal to Mary B. Dahlgren, 18 September 1844 entry, DNHFC; Alden and Earle, *Makers of Naval Tradition,* 133; Dahlgren, "Invention of Lock," 1847 folder, box 1, DLC.

30. Cajori, *Hassler,* 233–35; Dahlgren to Mary B. Dahlgren, 18 January 1844, DNHFC.

31. "Recollections of Admiral Dahlgren," *The State* (Boston), 28 November 1885, scrapbook, MVDG; Dahlgren, letter/journal to Mary B. Dahlgren, 29 November 1843 and 31 January 1844 entries, DNHFC; Madeleine Dahlgren, *Memoir,* 100–115.

32. Dahlgren, letter/journal to Mary B. Dahlgren, 1 April 1845 entry, DNHFC.

33. Bradford, *Captains,* 119–20; Langley, *Social Reform,* 61, 243.

34. Ibid.; Dahlgren, letter/journal to Mary B. Dahlgren, 18 December 1843 entry, DNHFC.

35. Langley, *Social Reform,* chaps. 6 and 9.

36. Bradford, *Captains,* 119–20; Langley, *Social Reform,* 243; Foote to Dahlgren, 26 November 1845, box 1, DLC; Dahlgren, letter/journal to Mary B. Dahlgren, 24 February, 18 May, 2 June, and 30 October 1844 entries, DNHFC.

37. Dahlgren, letter/journal to Mary B. Dahlgren, 14 April 1844 entry, DNHFC.

38. Valle, *Rocks and Shoals,* 16–18.

39. Dahlgren, letter/journal to Mary B. Dahlgren, 15 January 1845 entry, DNHFC.

40. Dahlgren to Mary B. Dahlgren, 26 December and 9 November 1843, DNHFC.

41. Dahlgren, letter/journal to Mary B. Dahlgren, 22 March 1845 entry, DNHFC.

42. Ibid., 4, 20, and 28 March 1844, 20 April 1845 entries.

43. Ibid., 23 May 1844 entry.

44. Ibid., 25 March and 10 October 1844, 5 August 1845 entries.

45. Ibid., 5 August 1845 entry.

46. Ibid., 22 February 1845.

47. Ibid., 22 September and 14 October 1845 entries.

48. Diary, 12 November 1845, 9 August 1846, and 8 June 1855 entries.

49. Madeleine Dahlgren, *Memoir,* 120–23; Smith to Dahlgren, 21 January 1846, box 1, DLC; Mason to Dahlgren, 6 January 1847, box 1, DLC.

CHAPTER 4. AMERICAN NAVAL ORDNANCE BEFORE 1850

1. Baxter, *Introduction of the Ironclad Warship*; Brodie, *Sea Power*.

2. Gardiner, *Steam, Steel, and Shellfire*, 8.

3. Ropp, *War in the Modern World*, 70–71.

4. Lavery, *Ship of the Line*, 122–54, quotation from 143.

5. Tucker, *Arming the Fleet*, 14–17, 89; Padfield, *Guns at Sea*, 13.

6. Garbett, *Naval Gunnery*, 14; Guilmartin, *Gunpowder and Galleys*, 38–39, 269; Hall, *Ballistics*, 54; Keegan, *Price of Admiralty*, 42–43, 90–95; Lambert, *Last Sailing Battlefleet*, 91–93; Padfield, *Guns at Sea*, 71–81; Robertson, *Evolution of Naval Armament*, 30–31; Ropp, *War in the Modern World*, 71–72.

7. Cowburn, *Warship in History*, 170.

8. Symonds, *Navalists and Antinavalists*, 1–12.

9. McCormick, "Dynamics of Doctrinal Change," 267–72.

10. Chapelle, *History of the American Sailing Navy*, 99–100.

11. Albion, *Makers of Naval Policy*, 181; Chapelle, *History of the American Sailing Navy*, 118–19; copy of a letter from Humphreys to Morris, 6 January 1793, from "Reminiscence of the Navy," 1826–47 folder, box 20, DLC; Symonds, *Navalists and Antinavalists*, chap. 2.

12. Boynton, *Navies*, 24; Chapelle, *History of the American Sailing Navy*, 316–18; Coles, *War of 1812*, chap. 3; MacBride, *Civil War Ironclads*, 2; Symonds, *Navalists and Antinavalists*, chap. 10; Valle, "Navy's Battle Doctrine," 172–78; Stanton's quotation comes from U.S. Congress, House, *Naval Service*, H. Rep. 35, 31st Cong., 2d sess., 1851, 1.

13. Lambert, *Last Sailing Battlefleet*, 11.

14. As for the other seven authorized liners, three were completed but saw service only as storeships, receiving ships, or training vessels, and four remained on the stocks until broken up or, in the case of the *New York*, burned at Norfolk in 1861 to prevent capture by the Confederates.

15. Laverly, *Ship of the Line*, 145–49; Sweetman, *American Naval History*, 28; U.S. Navy Department, *American Ships of the Line*.

16. Baxter, *Introduction of the Ironclad Warship*, 17; Comprato, *Age of Great Guns*, 66.

17. Baxter, *Introduction of the Ironclad Warship*, 18; Garbett, *Naval Gunnery*, 233–34; Comprato, *Age of Great Guns*, 66; Robertson, *Evolution of Naval Armament*, 162–67.

18. Browne, *Floating Bulwark*, 16–17, 132; Dahlgren, draft of a lecture delivered at the Naval School at Annapolis, 26 October 1847, box 1, DLC; Garbett, *Naval Gunnery*, 16–17; Robertson, *Evolution of Naval Armament*, 161–65; Tucker, *Arming the Fleet*, 111–12.

19. Baxter, *Introduction of the Ironclad Warship*, 25–26; Comprato, *Age of Great Guns*, 66; Robertson, *Evolution of Naval Armament*, 172.

20. Dahlgren, trans., *Bomb Cannon*, 11–92; Morison, *Men, Machines, and Modern Times*, chap. 2; Robertson, *Evolution of Naval Armament*, 166–71. *Bomb Cannon* is a compression and translation of Paixhans's works.

21. Ibid.

22. Robertson, *Evolution of Naval Armament,* 172–73; Tucker, *Arming the Fleet,* 177–78.

23. Garbett, *Naval Gunnery,* 17; Robertson, *Evolution of Naval Armament,* 164–76; Tucker, *Arming the Fleet,* 180–81.

24. Bolander, "Introduction," 110; Morison, *Old Bruin,* 207.

25. *Annual Report 1839,* 533; *Annual Report 1840,* 4; Bolander, "Introduction," 110–11; Morison, *Old Bruin,* 130; Tucker, *Arming the Fleet,* 146–48.

26. *Annual Report 1841,* 351–52, 371; Bolander, "Introduction," 110–11; Robertson, *Evolution of Naval Armament,* 178–79; Tucker, *Arming the Fleet,* 150–51, 186–90, 276–77.

27. Barber and Howe, *Historical Collections of the State of New York,* 449–50; Bathe, *Ship of Destiny,* 4, 12–13; Kennard, *Gunfounding and Gunfounders,* 32–33, 75, 145, 153; Temin, *Iron and Steel,* 90; Tucker, *Arming the Fleet,* 57–67, 274–81.

28. Jackson and De Beer, *Eighteenth-Century Gunfounding,* 16, 72–75; Kennard, *Gunfounding and Gunfounders,* 19–22; Simpson, *Treatise on Ordnance,* 38–75; Temin, *Iron and Steel,* 16–17, 58; Tucker, *Arming the Fleet,* 51–55.

29. Hall, *Ballistics,* 13; Kennard, *Gunfounding and Gunfounders,* 18–19; Sanders and Gould, *History Cast in Metal,* 365.

30. Hall, *Ballistics,* 9–11; McHugh, *Alexander Holley,* 81; Rosenberg, *Technology and American Economic Growth,* 77; Sanders and Gould, *History Cast in Metal,* 512–25.

31. Ferguson, *Engineering,* 121; Jackson and De Beer, *Eighteenth-Century Gunfounding,* 15–19; Pope, *Guns,* 117; Sanders, *History Cast in Metal,* 514–19; Vincenti, *What Engineers Know,* 200.

32. Gordon, *American Iron;* Sanders, *History Cast in Metal,* 390–91, 521–23.

33. Comprato, *Age of Great Guns,* 71; Ffoulkes, *Gun-Founders of England,* 98; Fisher, "Great Guns of the Navy," 284–85; Hall, *Ballistics,* 54–57, 164; Padfield, *Guns at Sea,* 102; Pope, *Guns,* 97–98.

34. Padfield, *Guns at Sea,* 102; Pope, *Guns,* 128; Robertson, *Evolution of Naval Armament,* 115–35.

35. Robertson, *Evolution of Naval Armament,* 84.

36. Lambert, *Last Sailing Battlefleet,* 101–2; Mauskopf, "Chief Support of War," 11.

37. Falk, "Soldier Technologist," 86–89, 139–45, 160–64, 228–29.

38. "Report of Experimental Firing at South Boston Point 1843," box 20, DLC; William Wade, "Fabrication, Inspection, and Extreme Proof of a 9-Pdr Trial Gun at the Tredegar Iron Works, Richmond, Virginia, February 1843," entry 159, RG74 NA.

39. Simpson, *Treatise on Ordnance,* 76–77; Lewis, "Ambiguous Columbiads," 118.

40. Falk, "Artillery for the Land Service," 97–110; Falk, "Soldier Technologist," 302–62.

41. *Annual Report 1842,* 552–54; U.S. Congress, House, *Naval Ordnance and Ordnance Stores,* H. Rep. 2, 27th Cong., 1st sess., 1841, 1–2.

42. Bradford, *Command,* 283–85; Hornsby, "Oregon and Peacemaker," 217; Miles, "*Princeton* Explosion," 2227–44; Pearson, "*Princeton* and the Peacemaker," 167–83.

43. A transverse breaking machine was used to determine the tensile strength of a bar of iron. The bar was screwed into the machine. A blade was placed on the bar. Weights were placed on top of the blade until it broke the bar. The tensile strength was calculated from the diameter of the bar and the weight required to break it.

44. *Reports of Experiments on Strength and Other Properties of Metals for Cannon,* 31–34, 338–46.

45. Coletta, *American Secretaries of the Navy,* 1:210; Hamersly, *Complete Army and Navy Register,* 4–5; Tucker, *Arming the Fleet,* 151; Crane to Bancroft, 17 March 1845, vol. 1, entry 1, RG74 NA; *Armament of Vessels of War,* 29 May 1845, box 37, DLC.

46. Tucker, *Arming the Fleet,* 101–20, 135, 145.

47. Coletta, *American Secretaries of the Navy,* 1:223.

48. *Armament of Vessels of War,* 29 May 1845, box 37, DLC; *Regulations for the Proof and Inspection of Cannon, Shot, and Shells, Adopted by a Board of Officers, Consisting of Commodore C. Morris, Commodore L. Warrington, Commodore W. M. Crane, Commodore A. S. Wadsworth, Commodore W. B. Shubrick, and Approved by the Secretary of the Navy, June 1845* (Washington, D.C.: J. and G. S. Gideon, 1848), copy in box 37, DLC.

49. Paullin, *History of Naval Administration,* 221; Tucker, *Arming the Fleet,* 68, 151–53, 190–96.

50. For examples of army/navy/gun-founder cooperation, see Harwood to Warrington, 16 September 1847, 1847–48–49 Official Correspondence file, box 1, DLC; Warrington to Mason, 12 May 1848, vol. 1, entry 1, RG74 NA; William Wade, "Report of Experiments Made to Ascertain the Durability of the New Model Heavy 8 and 10 Inch Howitzers, by Continuous Firing with Service Charges," 25 July 1844, in an untitled bound volume, 1848 folder, box 20, DLC.

51. Chauncey, Harwood, and Fairfax to Warrington, 13 November 1849, box 27, DLC.

CHAPTER 5. INVENTING THE DAHLGREN GUN

1. Bradford, *Captains,* 30; Karsten, *Naval Aristocracy,* 121–22; Todorich, *Spirited Years,* 8; Dahlgren to Mason, 20 January 1847, box 1, DLC; Appleton to Dahlgren, 21 January 1847, box 1, DLC; Dahlgren to [?], 7 February 1856 (1855 folder), box 2, DLC.

2. Madeleine Dahlgren, *Memoir,* 154; Smith to Dahlgren, 21 January 1846, box 1, DLC; Foote to Dahlgren, 17 June 1846, box 1, DLC; Diary, 28 August 1846 entry; Dahlgren, notebook titled "Memoranda 1847," box 36, DLC.

3. Peck, *Round-Shot to Rockets,* vii, 16–21, 72–75, 104; Spiller et al., *Dictionary of American Military Biography,* 1:231; Dahlgren to Mason, 10 February 1848, box 1, DLC; Navy Department Regulation, 26 November 1842, entry 41, RG45 NA; Christman, *Naval Innovators,* 103–8.

4. Bradford, *Command,* 83; Christman, *Naval Innovators,* 103–8; Guttridge and Smith, *Commodores,* 246–47, 253, 267; Hagan, *In Peace and War,* 70; Pratt, *Preble's Boys,* 276–95; Schroeder, *Shaping a Maritime Empire,* 16.

5. Winter, *First Golden Age of Rocketry,* 148–49; Dahlgren, notebook titled "Memoranda 1847," box 36, DLC.

6. Bruce, *Lincoln and the Tools of War,* 5; Christman, *Naval Innovators,* 103–8; Earle, "John Adolphus Dahlgren," 428; Falk, "Soldier Technologist," 302–62; Dahlgren, notebook titled "Memoranda 1847," box 36, DLC; Dahlgren, "Extract from the 'Nemesis in China' from Notes of Capt. Wm. H. Hall," 1847, box 1, DLC.

7. Dahlgren to Warrington, 13 February 1847, box 1, DLC; Foote to Dahlgren, 12 August 1847, box 1, DLC.

8. Christman, *Naval Innovators,* 103–8.

9. Dahlgren, notebook titled "Memoranda 1847," box 36, DLC; Dahlgren to Powell, [?] August 1847, box 1, DLC.

10. Warrington to Dahlgren, 27 July 1847, box 1, DLC; Dahlgren to Mason, 10 February 1848, box 1, DLC.

11. Dahlgren, document titled "General Laws of Mixtures," 1847, box 1, DLC; Dahlgren to Warrington, 1 October 1847, box 1, DLC; Dahlgren, draft of a letter, 26 November 1847, box 1, DLC; Dahlgren to Warrington, 8 December 1847 and [?] February 1848, box 1, DLC.

12. Alden and Earle, *Makers of Naval Tradition,* 134; Parker, *Recollections,* 130–31; Mason to Dahlgren, 12 October 1847, box 1, DLC; Upshur to Dahlgren, 19 October 1847, box 1, DLC; Dahlgren, draft of a lecture delivered at the Naval Academy, 26 October 1847, box 1, DLC; Foote to Dahlgren, 30 October 1847, box 1, DLC; Dahlgren to Lockwood, 11 February 1848, box 1, DLC.

13. Alden and Earle, *Makers of Naval Tradition,* 134; Hoppin, *Life of Andrew Hull Foote,* 64; Parker, *Recollections,* 130–31; Mason to Dahlgren, 12 October 1847, box 1, DLC; Upshur to Dahlgren, 19 October 1847, box 1, DLC; Dahlgren, draft of a lecture delivered at the Naval Academy, 26 October 1847, box 1, DLC; Foote to Dahlgren, 30 October 1847, box 1, DLC; Dahlgren to Lockwood, 11 February 1848, box 1, DLC.

14. *Armament of Vessels of War,* 29 May 1845, box 37, DLC; petition addressed to the secretary of the navy titled "To the Officers of the Navy," box 37, DLC; Dahlgren, "Report to Commodore L. Warrington Chief of Bureau of Ordnance and Hydrography on the Ranges of the 32 Pounder of 32 Cwt.," 1 November 1848, box 32, DLC. *Cwt.* is an abbreviation for *hundredweight,* a designation for a weight of 112 pounds. Thus, a 32-pounder of 32 cwt. was a gun weighing approximately 3,584 pounds (32 cwt. x 112 lbs./cwt.) that fired a 32-pound projectile. The six classes of 32-pounders were 27, 32, 42, 46, 51, and 57 cwt.

15. Dahlgren, untitled, undated bound notebook, 1848 folder, box 20, DLC; Dahlgren to Powell, 13 November 1847, box 1, DLC.

16. Dahlgren to Powell, 13 November 1847, box 1, DLC; Dahlgren to Warrington, 29 November 1847, box 1, DLC; Dahlgren, "Triangulation of the Anacostia to Determine Distances Required to Ascertain the Ranges of Navy Guns," 1848 folder, box 20, DLC.

17. Constant, *Origins of the Turbojet Revolution,* 20–26; Dahlgren, "Preliminary Practice to Ascertain the Practicability of Using the Plane Table in Determining Grazes of Shot in the Water," report in an untitled bound volume, 1848 folder, box 20, DLC.

18. Dahlgren, "Rough Notes of Practice at the Experimental Battery...Made on the Spot," 1848 folder, box 20, DLC; Dahlgren, "Preliminary Practice to Ascertain the Practicability of Using the Plane Table in Determining Grazes of Shot in the Water," report in an untitled bound volume, 1848 folder, box 20, DLC; Dahlgren, "Report to Commodore L. Warrington Chief of Bureau of Ordnance & Hydrography on the Ranges of the 32 Pounder of 32 Cwt.," 1 November 1848, box 32, DLC; Dahlgren, "Determination of the Ranges," 1 November 1848, box 32, DLC; Hunt to Dahlgren, [?] February 1848, box 1, DLC; Dahlgren to Powell, 13 April 1848, box 1, DLC; Dahlgren to Warrington, 18 April and 19 May 1848, box 1, DLC; Dahlgren, "Adjustment of Sights," 26 July 1848, box 20, DLC.

19. Diary, 8 October 1848 entry.

20. Dahlgren, draft of a report to Warrington, 1 November 1848, box 1, DLC; Dahlgren, "Report to Commodore L. Warrington Chief of Bureau of Ordnance & Hydrography on the Ranges of the 32 Pounder of 32 Cwt.," 1 November 1848, box 32, DLC.

21. Dahlgren, miscellaneous notes, 15 April 1848, box 20, DLC; Dahlgren to Warrington, 12 and 21 June 1848, 11 May 1849, box 1, DLC; Preston to Dahlgren, 21 June 1849, box 1, DLC; Dahlgren to Preston, 29 June 1849, box 1, DLC; Dahlgren to Warrington, 24 August and 2 October 1849, box 1, DLC; Fuller to Warrington, 29 March 1850, box 1, DLC.

22. Dahlgren, "Report to Commodore L. Warrington Chief of Bureau of Ordnance & Hydrog. on the Ranges of the 8 inch Shell Gun of 6000 lbs," box 21, DLC; Dahlgren to McCauley, 28 August 1848, box 1, DLC; Dahlgren to Warrington, 19 February 1849, box 1, DLC.

23. Tucker, *Arming the Fleet*, 200; unsigned and undated document titled "Boat Guns," 1847–48–49 Official Correspondence file, box 1, DLC; Dahlgren to Warrington, 30 September 1847, box 1, DLC.

24. Unsigned and undated document titled "Boat Guns," 1847–48–49 Official Correspondence file, box 1, DLC; Smith to Dahlgren, 23 April 1847, DS; Dahlgren, miscellaneous notes, 21 February and 12 October 1848, box 20, DLC; Fairfax, "Remarks upon the Report of Lt. J. A. Dahlgren Asst. Inspector of Ordnance—April 9th 1849—on the Subject of Boat Howitzers &c," box 21, DLC; Dahlgren, "Answers to Objections on Boat Howitzers," 21 May 1849, box 21, DLC; Dahlgren to McCauley, 4 June 1849, box 1, DLC; Dahlgren, "Rough Notes—Battery 32 Pdr of 57 Cwt—No. 361," 31 August 1849, box 21, DLC.

25. Dahlgren to Warrington, 30 September 1847, box 1, DLC; Dahlgren, miscellaneous notes, 21 September 1848, box 20, DLC; Dahlgren to Warrington, 22 September 1848 and 29 July 1850, box 2, DLC.

26. Dahlgren, "Trial of Boat Howitzer Carriage (No. 2)," 4 December 1848, box 1, DLC; Dahlgren, miscellaneous notes on boat guns, 1849 folder, box 21, DLC; Dahlgren, "Trial of Boat Howitzer No. 2," 6 January 1849, box 1, DLC; Dahlgren to Powell, 9 June 1849, box 1, DLC; Dahlgren to Warrington, 30 June 1849, box 1, DLC.

27. William Graham, "General Order," 17 December 1850, box 21, DLC.

28. Dahlgren, miscellaneous notes, January 1849 (1848 folder), box 20, DLC; Dahlgren, "Rough Notes—Battery 32 Pdr of 57 Cwt—No. 361," 31 August 1849, box 21, DLC; Dahlgren to Warrington, 15 October 1849, box 1, DLC.

29. Dahlgren to Warrington, 15 October 1849 (1859 folder), box 25, DLC; Diary, 12 November 1850 entry; Dahlgren, "Report to Bureau of Ordnance of Practice Made with the Experimental Nine-Inch Shell Gun 1850," 30 January 1851 (1850 folder), box 21, DLC; Dahlgren, "Reorganization of the U.S. Naval Ordnance (The Eleven Inch Shell-Gun) No. 2," 31 May 1853, box 22, DLC.

30. Dahlgren to Warrington, 15 October 1849 (1859 folder), box 25, DLC.

31. Ibid.

32. Dahlgren, "Rough Notes—Battery 32 Pdr of 57 Cwt—No. 361," 31 August 1849, box 21, DLC; Dahlgren to Warrington, 13 November 1849, box 1, DLC.

33. Dahlgren, "Rough Notes—Battery 32 Pdr of 57 Cwt—No. 361," 31 August 1849, box 21, DLC; Warrington to Dahlgren, 15 November 1849, box 1, DLC; Chauncey, Boutwell, and Fairfax to Warrington, 21 November 1849, box 1, DLC.

34. Dahlgren, "Specific Gravity Tensile & Transverse Strength of Metal from Iron & Bronze Guns," box 21, DLC; Harwood to Dahlgren, 5 December 1849, box 1, DLC; Dahlgren to Warrington, 26 February 1850, box 2, DLC.

35. Dahlgren, "Report on the Causes Which Produced the Bursting of a Long 32 Pounder Nov. 13 1849 during Practice at the Exper. Battery," 4 March 1850, box 2, DLC.

36. William Wade, "Reports of Experiments Made to Ascertain the Durability of the New Model Heavy 8 and 10 Inch Howitzers, by Continuous Firing with Service Charges," 25 July 1844, in an untitled bound volume, 1848 folder, box 20, DLC; William Wade, "Effects Produced by Different Charges of Powder, in 8 Inch and 10 Inch Columbiad Shells," 23 February 1849, box 1, DLC; Wade to Fairfax, 17 July 1849, box 1, DLC; Wade to Talcott, 19 June 1849 (1851 folder), box 21, DLC.

37. Dahlgren, undated document titled "Nine Inch Shell Guns Nos. 1 and 2," 1850 folder, box 21, DLC.

38. Dahlgren, *Shells and Shell Guns,* 14; Harwood to Dahlgren, 6 February 1850, box 2, DLC; Dahlgren, "Report to Bureau of Ordnance of Practice Made with the Experimental Nine-Inch Shell Gun 1850," 30 January 1851 (1850 folder), box 21, DLC; Dahlgren, "Notice of XI In Shell Gun No. 1," 1852, box 22, DLC; Dahlgren to Parrott, 30 May 1853, box 2, DLC.

39. Christman, *Naval Innovators,* 105, argues that Dahlgren drilled a gun barrel and inserted pressure gauges; Comprato, *Age of Great Guns,* 144, argues that Dahlgren drilled an 8-incher and inserted bullets.

40. Simpson, *Treatise on Ordnance,* 75–78.

41. Dahlgren to Thomas, 28 December 1859, box 4, DLC; Dahlgren, "Memorandum," 20 December 1865, box 6, DLC; Madeleine Dahlgren, *Memoir,* 251.

42. Cowley, *Leaves from a Lawyer's Life,* 208; Dahlgren, miscellaneous notes, 1852 folder, box 22, DLC.

43. Dahlgren, rough draft of a report and letter of resignation for the Bureau of Ordnance, 1869 folder, box 29, DLC.

44. Harwood to Dahlgren, 6 February 1850, box 2, DLC; Dahlgren, "Report to Bureau of Ordnance of Practice Made with the Experimental Nine-Inch Shell Gun 1850," 30 January 1851 (1850 folder), box 21, DLC; Dahlgren, "Notice of XI In Shell Gun No. 1," 1852, box 22, DLC; Dahlgren to Parrott, 30 May 1853, box 2, DLC.

45. Dahlgren, "Report to Bureau of Ordnance of Practice Made with the Experimental Nine-Inch Shell Gun 1850," 30 January 1851 (1850 folder), box 21, DLC; Dahlgren to Warrington, 19 March 1850, box 2, DLC; Dahlgren, "Notice of XI In Shell Gun No. 1," 1852, box 22, DLC.

46. See chaps. 9–10.

47. Boynton, *History of the Navy during the Rebellion,* 1:279, 286.

48. This discussion is informed by Daniels, *Nineteenth-Century American Science,* 26–30, 222–27; Ferguson, *Engineering,* 3–9, 70, 154–55; Gilfillan, *Sociology of Invention,* 6; Hughes, *Changing Attitudes toward American Technology,* 120–38; Hughes, "Development Phase of Technological Change," 432–36; Jewkes et al., *Sources of Invention,* 37–64, 169; Layton, "Mirror-Image Twins," 562–73; MacKenzie and Wajcman, *Social Shaping of Technology,* 9–10, 43–50; Merton, *Sociology of Science,* 346–51; Miller, *Life of the Mind,* 293–312; Morison, *Men, Machines, and Modern Times,* 9–12; Roland, "Secrecy, Technology, and War," 660.

49. Ferguson, *Engineering*, 13.
50. Ibid., 15.
51. Ibid., 22.

CHAPTER 6. EARLY DEVELOPMENT

1. Hughes, "Development Phase of Technological Change," 423–26.
2. MacKenzie, *Inventing Accuracy,* 28.
3. Dahlgren to Warrington, 15 October 1849 (1859 folder), box 25, DLC.
4. Albion, *Makers of Naval Policy,* 25, 178–79.
5. Ibid., 4, 29–32, 69–71, 169–71; Morison, *Admiral Sims,* 70–75.
6. Albion, *Makers of Naval Policy,* 30, 96–100, 114–25, 130–45, 153–55.
7. Ibid., 158–63.
8. Boynton, *Navies.*
9. Miller, *Life of the Mind,* 293–312; Hughes, *Changing Attitudes toward American Technology,* 120–38; Daniels, *Nineteenth-Century American Science,* 222–27; Layton, "Mirror-Image Twins," 562–73; Dairy, 8 October 1848 entry; Dahlgren, "Rough Notes—Battery 32 Pdr of 57 Cwt—No. 361," 31 August 1849, box 21, DLC.
10. Morison, *Old Bruin,* 255–56; Sprout and Sprout, *Rise of American Naval Power,* 127–28.
11. Sprout and Sprout, *Rise of American Naval Power,* 129–38.
12. Dahlgren, "Answers to Queries from Chairman of Naval Committee, U.S. Senate, in Relation to War Steamers," 19 March 1850 (1855 folder), box 23, DLC.
13. U.S. Congress, House, *Letter from the Secretary of War in Reference to Fortifications,* H. ExDoc. 5, 32d Cong., 1st sess., 1851, 200–218.
14. Madeleine Dahlgren, *Memoir,* 172.
15. Dahlgren, "Report to Bureau of Ordnance of Practice Made with the Experimental Nine-Inch Shell Gun 1850," 30 January 1851 (1850 folder), box 21, DLC.
16. Beach, *United States Navy,* 112; Dahlgren to Skinner, 31 July 1850, box 21, DLC; Dahlgren to Drayton, [August 1850], undated correspondence file, PDHSPA; Dahlgren to Smith, 17 August 1850, box 2, DLC; *Annual Report 1850,* 230–32.
17. Dahlgren to Warrington, 29 July 1850, box 2, DLC; Mordecai to his sister, 30 September 1850, series 2, container 3, Alfred Mordecai Papers, Library of Congress; Dahlgren to Warrington, 4 October 1850, box 2, DLC; *Annual Report 1850,* 209, 303.
18. Dahlgren to Brooks, [?] January 1851, box 21, DLC; Dahlgren to White, 11 January 1851, box 2, DLC; Dahlgren to Bayly, 13 January 1851, box 2, DLC; Dahlgren to Toombs, 14 January 1851, box 2, DLC.
19. Dahlgren, "Report to Bureau of Ordnance of Practice Made with the Experimental Nine-Inch Shell Gun 1850," 30 January 1851 (1850 folder), box 21, DLC.
20. Ibid.
21. *DAB,* s.v. "Stanton, Frederick P."; *Congressional Globe,* 31st Cong., 1st sess., 19 September 1850, 1864; Stanton, *Character of Modern Science,* 5–8, 20–21, 30–31; Dahlgren, "Reorganization of the U.S. Naval Ordnance, No. 1," 10 August 1852, box 22, DLC.
22. U.S. Congress, House, *Naval Service,* H. Rep. 35, 31st Cong., 2d sess., 1851;

Congressional Globe, 31st Cong., 2d sess., 28 February 1851, 754, and 1 March 1851, 761.

23. Sprout and Sprout, *Rise of American Naval Power,* 137–42; Tucker, *Arming the Fleet,* 205–6; *Congressional Globe,* 31st Cong., 2d sess., 1 March 1851, 761–62, and 3 March 1851, 836; Dahlgren to Dayton, 26 May 1851, DS.

24. Dahlgren, notes titled "Eleven-Inch Shell Gun for Frigate's Spar Deck," 20 January 1851, box 21, DLC; Dahlgren to Warrington, 19 March 1851, box 2, DLC; Dahlgren, notes clipped to a document dated 30 April 1851, box 21, DLC; Dahlgren, "Notice of XI In Shell Gun No. 1," 1852, box 22, DLC; Dahlgren, rough draft of a report and letter of resignation for the Bureau of Ordnance, 1869 folder, box 29, DLC.

25. Madeleine Dahlgren, *Memoir,* 153; *DAB,* s.v. "Alger, Cyrus"; Dahlgren, "Notice of XI In Shell Gun No. 1," 1852, box 22, DLC.

26. Dahlgren to Warrington, 14 April 1851, box 2, DLC; Warrington to Dahlgren, 15 April 1851, box 2, DLC; Dahlgren to Warrington, 17 June 1851, box 21, DLC; Dahlgren, "Notice of XI In Shell Gun No. 1," 1852, box 22, DLC.

27. *Annual Report 1851,* 9; Magruder to Warrington, 1 April 1851, box 2, DLC; Drayton to Dahlgren, 24 April 1851, box 2, DLC; Foote to Dahlgren, 19 July 1851, box 2, DLC; Dahlgren, "Notice of XI In Shell Gun No. 1," 1852, box 22, DLC.

28. Hamersly, *Complete Army and Navy Register,* 747; Dahlgren, "Sketch of Navy Boat Howitzers," 30 August 1866, box 28, DLC.

Chapter 7. Overcoming Entrenched Resistance

1. Bell, *Room to Swing a Cat,* 53; Bradford, *Command,* 88, 234, 257–59; Coletta, *American Secretaries of the Navy,* 1:207; Davenport, *Naval Officers,* 134–35; Guttridge and Smith, *Commodores,* 87–90, 197, 255, 301–2; McHenry, *Webster's American Military Biographies,* 290; Morris, "Autobiography of Commodore Charles Morris," 115–219; Von Doenhoff, *Versatile Guardian,* 165.

2. Ibid.

3. Dahlgren, letter/journal to Mary Dahlgren, 7 and 10 January 1844 entries, DNHFC; Dahlgren to Mary Dahlgren, 12 January 1844, DNHFC; Sands, *From Reefer to Rear Admiral,* 160.

4. Morris to Dahlgren, 20 January 1852, box 22, DLC; Morris to the secretary of the navy, 4 February 1852, box 22, DLC; Dahlgren to [?], 27 June 1855, box 2, DLC.

5. Morris to the secretary of the navy, 19 June 1852, 17 and 24 February 1853, vol. 1, entry 1, RG74 NA.

6. Dahlgren, "Reorganization of the U.S. Naval Ordnance, No. 1," 10 August 1852, box 22, DLC.

7. Morris to the secretary of the navy, 13 August 1852, box 22, DLC.

8. Stanton, "Speech of Hon. F. P. Stanton, of Tennessee, on Improvements in the Navy," 17 August 1852, box 2, DLC; *Congressional Globe,* 32d Cong., 1st sess., 17 August 1852, 2237–38; *Appendix to the Congressional Globe,* "Speech of Hon. F. P. Stanton, of Tennessee, on Improvements in the Navy," 32d Cong., 1st sess., 1049–53.

9. Coletta, *American Secretaries of the Navy,* 1:289; Madeleine Dahlgren, *Memoir,* 160–61; Dahlgren, undated document titled "Memorandum," 1865 folder, box 6, DLC.

10. Morris, "Autobiography of Commodore Charles Morris," 196–97; Farragut to Dahlgren, 4 November 1850 (1847 folder), box 1, DLC; Morris to the secretary of the navy, 29 April, 28 June, 19 August, and 3 September 1852, vol. 1, entry 1, RG74 NA; Farragut to Morris, 31 August 1853, 1852–53 letterbook, David G. Farragut Papers, Naval Historical Foundation Collection, Manuscripts Division, Library of Congress; *Annual Report 1852*, 446–47.

11. Smith to Dahlgren, 13 January 1852, box 2, DLC; Morris to Dahlgren, 24 January 1853, box 2, DLC; Kennedy to Dahlgren, 18 February 1853, box 2, DLC.

12. Dahlgren, *Naval Percussion Locks and Primers, Particularly Those of the United States,* copy in box 37, DLC.

13. Dahlgren, *System of Boat Armament in the U.S. Navy,* 1856 rev. ed.

14. Meehan to Dahlgren, 9 July 1853, box 2, DLC; Lee to Dahlgren, 15 July 1853, box 2, DLC.

15. Coletta, *American Secretaries of the Navy,* 1:289; Hagan, *This People's Navy,* 139–40; *Congressional Globe,* 25 February 1853, 32d Cong., 2d sess., 854–65.

16. Dahlgren to Morris, 8 March 1853, box 2, DLC; Morris to Dahlgren, 9 March 1853, box 2, DLC; Dahlgren, undated document titled "Nine Inch Shell Guns Nos 1 & 2," 1850 folder, box 21, DLC; Dahlgren to Morris, 3 May 1853, box 22, DLC.

17. *DAB,* s.v. "Parrott, Robert P."; Dahlgren, undated document titled "Nine Inch Shell Guns Nos 1 & 2," 1850 folder, box 21, DLC; Dahlgren to Parrott, 30 May and 14 June 1853, box 2, DLC.

18. Dahlgren, "Reorganization of the U.S. Naval Ordnance (The Eleven Inch Shell-Gun) No. 2," 31 May 1853, box 22, DLC.

19. Morris to the secretary of the navy, "Remarks upon Lieut. Dahlgren's Propositions for Substituting Heavier Guns for the Present Armaments of Our Ships of War," 30 May 1853, vol. 1, entry 1, RG74 NA.

20. Farragut to Morris, 9 August 1853, 1852–53 letterbook, David G. Farragut Papers, Naval Historical Foundation Collection, Manuscripts Division, Library of Congress; Dahlgren to Wade, 6 August 1855 (1854 folder), box 2, DLC; unprovenanced article pasted in a scrapbook and titled "It Saved the Union: The Dahlgren Shell Gun Explained and Eulogized," MVDG.

21. Morris, Smith, Haitt, Copeland, and Lenthall to Dobbin, 31 August 1853, vol. 1, entry 1, RG74 NA.

22. Sprout and Sprout, *Rise of American Naval Power,* 140–42.

23. Morris, Smith, Haitt, Copeland, and Lenthall to Dobbin, 31 August 1853, vol. 1, entry 1, RG74 NA.

24. Weigley, *American Way of War,* 64; *Annual Report 1853,* 302, 417–18.

Chapter 8. Arming the Fleet

1. Drayton to Dahlgren, 20 November 1853, box 2, DLC.

2. Dahlgren, "Reorganization of the U.S. Naval Ordnance No. 3: Comparative Accuracy at 1300 Yards, of Present and Proposed Cannon," 9 December 1853, box 22, DLC.

3. Lambert, *Battleships in Transition,* 122; Dahlgren, "Reorganization of the U.S. Naval Ordnance No. 3: Comparative Accuracy at 1300 Yards, of Present and Proposed Cannon," 9 December 1853, box 22, DLC.

4. Morris to Dobbin, 19 December 1853, vol. 1, entry 1, RG74 NA.

5. Dahlgren, "Reorganization of U.S. Naval Armament No. 4," 21 January 1854, box 22, DLC.

6. Morris to Dobbin, 30 January 1854, vol. 1, entry 1, RG74 NA.

7. Sprout and Sprout, *Rise of American Naval Power,* 142–44.

8. Diary, 12 May and 8 July 1854 entries.

9. Bathe, *Ship of Destiny,* 2; Chapelle, *History of the American Sailing Navy,* 354; *DAB,* s.v. "Lenthall, John"; Farr and Bostwick, *John Lenthall,* 7–8; Niven, *Gideon Welles,* 349–50.

10. Diary, 8 July 1854 entry.

11. Ibid., 11 July 1854 entry.

12. Dahlgren to Morris, 20 July 1854, vol. 15, entry 19, RG74 NA.

13. *DAB,* s.v. "Steers, George"; Morison, *Old Bruin,* 258.

14. Diary, 28 and 29 July 1854 entries.

15. Dahlgren, journal notes dated 31 July–18 September 1854, box 22, DLC; Diary, 5, 8, and 23 August 1854 entries; Dahlgren to Dobbin, 25 June 1855, box 2, DLC.

16. Dahlgren, journal notes dated 31 July–18 September 1854, box 22, DLC.

CHAPTER 9. THE CRISES OF 1855

1. Dahlgren to Wise, 17 August 1855 (1854 folder), box 2, DLC.

2. Dahlgren, notes dated 1846–52 (1852 folder), box 22, DLC; Wade to Fairfax, 17 July 1849, box 1, DLC; Wade to Harwood, 21 June 1851, box 2, DLC; Turner to Warrington, 20 October 1851, box 21, DLC.

3. Coulson, *Joseph Henry,* 247–49; Henry, *Scientific Writings,* 1:347–48.

4. Dahlgren, notes dated 1846–52 (1852 folder), box 22, DLC; Dahlgren to Warrington, 1 April 1851, box 2, DLC; Parrott to Dahlgren, 6 October 1853, box 2, DLC; Dahlgren to Alger, 18 October 1854, box 2, DLC; Dahlgren to Wade, 6 August 1855 (1854 folder), box 2, DLC; Dahlgren, "Endurance of Cannon: Unfinished Sketch Drawn up in 1855," box 23, DLC.

5. Gould, *Metalcasting Dictionary;* Schneller, "Development of Dahlgren's Heavy Cast-Iron Smoothbores," 48–75; Walton and Opar, *Iron Castings Handbook.*

6. Diary, 30 October and 1 November 1854 entries; Dahlgren, journal note dated 11 November 1854 (1851 folder), box 21, DLC; Dahlgren, undated document titled "Nine Inch Shell Guns Nos. 1 and 2," 1850 folder, box 21, DLC.

7. Madeleine Dahlgren, *Memoir,* 169; Morris to Dobbin, 13 November 1854, vol. 1, entry 1, RG74 NA; Diary, 28 November 1854 entry; "Rough Draft of Contract for Batteries of New Screw Frigates," 1854 folder, box 2, DLC; Morris to Knap and Wade, 28 November 1854, vol. 1, entry 4, RG74 NA; Morris to Parrott, 9 December 1854, vol. 1, entry 4, RG74 NA.

8. U.S. Navy Department, Bureau of Ordnance, *Instructions in Relation to the Preparation of Vessels of War for Battle,* 82–105; Chauncey, Harwood, and Fairfax to Warrington, 13 November 1849, box 21, DLC; contract of R. P. Parrott with the

Bureau of Ordnance and Hydrography, 20 December 1854, entry 162, RG74 NA; contract of Knap and Wade with the Bureau of Ordnance and Hydrography, 27 December 1854, entry 162, RG74 NA.

9. Morris to Dobbin, 25 May 1855, vol. 1, entry 1, RG74 NA.
10. Dahlgren, *Memoir of Ulric Dahlgren,* 28; Hagan, *This People's Navy,* 141; Langley, *Social Reform,* 34–35; Drayton to Dahlgren, 20 April 1855, DS; Wise to Dahlgren, 23 April 1855, DS; Morris to Dobbin, 25 May 1855, vol. 1, entry 1, RG74 NA; Drayton to Dahlgren, 28 June 1855, DS; Sinclair to Dahlgren, 23 January 1856, box 3, DLC.
11. Falk, "Soldier Technologist," 268–69.
12. Dahlgren, "Memorandum for Bureau," 27 January 1855, entry 201 #5, RG74 NA; Morris to Gregory, 13 February 1855, vol. 1, entry 4, RG74 NA; Wise to Dahlgren, 21 February 1855, DS.
13. Wise to Dahlgren, 21 February 1855, DS.
14. *DAB,* s.v. "Wise, Henry Augustus"; Wise to Dahlgren, 18 September 1855, DS.
15. Dahlgren to Wise, 5 March 1855 (1854 folder), box 2, DLC; Dahlgren to Wise, 5 March 1855, DNL.
16. Wise to Dahlgren, 17 March 1855, DS.
17. Dahlgren to Wise, 2 April 1855, DNL; Wise to Dahlgren, 4 April 1855, DS.
18. Dahlgren to Drayton, 21 March 1855, PDHSPA; Dahlgren to [?], 27 June 1855, box 2, DLC.
19. Dahlgren to Morris, 6 May 1855, entry 201 #5, RG74 NA; Dahlgren, draft of a report dated 22 May 1855, box 2, DLC.
20. Morris to Dobbin, 25 May 1855, vol. 1, entry 1, RG74 NA; Morris to Wise, 4 June 1855, vol. 1, entry 4, RG74 NA; Morris to Fairfax, 12 June 1855, vol. 1, entry 4, RG74 NA; Morris to Hitchcock, 12 June 1855, vol. 1, entry 4, RG74 NA; Morris to Renshaw, 20 June 1855, vol. 1, entry 4, RG74 NA.
21. Wise to Dahlgren, 16, 24, and 30 May, 29 August 1855, DS.
22. Hoppin, *Life of Andrew Hull Foote,* 76–78; Foote to Dahlgren, 25 October and 6 November 1849, box 1, DLC; and the following entries in the Diary: 17 and 27 September, 18–25 December 1847, 1 and 8 January, 19 March, 20 May 1848, 12 November 1850, undated entry made in summer 1853 in vol. 5, 25 December 1854, 8 June 1855.
23. Diary, 9 April and 6 June 1855 entries.
24. Ibid., 13, 16, 17, 21, 24, and 31 May 1855 entries.
25. Ibid., 6 June 1855 entry.
26. Dahlgren, *Memoir of Ulric Dahlgren,* 18; Diary, 7 June 1855 entry.
27. Diary, 8 June 1855 entry.
28. Drayton to Dahlgren, 23 March 1855, DS; Parrott to Dahlgren, 30 March 1855, DS.
29. Dahlgren to Drayton, 21 March 1855, PDHSPA; Dahlgren to Morris, 30 June 1855, box 2, DLC.
30. Wise to Dahlgren, 26 and 28 June 1855, DS.
31. Wade to Harwood, 23 June 1851, box 21, DLC; Dahlgren to Morris, 30 June 1855, box 2, DLC.
32. Morris to Dahlgren, 6 July 1855, box 2, DLC.

33. Drayton to Dahlgren, 9 August 1855, DS.

34. Dahlgren to Wise, 3 July 1855, DNL; Wise to Dahlgren, 5 July 1855, DS; Dahlgren to Morris, 9 July 1855, vol. 18, entry 19, RG74 NA; Dahlgren to Wise, 9 and 12 July 1855 (1854 folder), box 2, DLC.

35. Wade to Harwood, 23 June 1851, box 21, DLC; Morris to Alger, Parrott, Anderson, Knap, and Wade, 5 May 1855, vol. 1, entry 4, RG74 NA; Dahlgren to Wise, 19 July 1855, DNL; Dahlgren to Wade, 6 August 1855 (1854 folder), box 2, DLC; Dahlgren to Wise, 7 August 1855, DNL; Smith to Dahlgren, 25 September 1855, box 23, DLC.

36. Wade to Harwood, 23 June 1851, box 21, DLC; Dahlgren, "Notice of XI In Shell Gun No. 1," 1852, box 22, DLC; Dahlgren to Morris, 24 May 1854, box 22, DLC; Morris to Dahlgren, 27 June 1854, box 2, DLC; Dahlgren to Morris, 24 October 1854, box 2, DLC; Dahlgren to Hitchcock, 22 June 1855 (1854 folder), box 2, DLC; Dahlgren, "Memorandum for Bureau," 18 July 1855, box 23, DLC; Dahlgren to Wade, 6 August 1855 (1854 folder), box 2, DLC; Dahlgren to Wise, 7 August 1855 (1854 folder), box 2, DLC; Dahlgren to Morris, 9 August 1855, box 2, DLC; Diary, 16–18 and 24 October, 2 and 4 November 1854, 21 March, 12 and 18 July 1855 entries.

37. Morris to Alger, Parrott, Anderson, Knap, and Wade, 5 May 1855, vol. 1, entry 4, RG74 NA; Morris to Dornin, 12 July 1855, vol. 1, entry 4, RG74 NA; Dahlgren to Wise, 19 July 1855 (1854 folder), box 2, DLC; Dahlgren, journal note, 26 July 1855, box 2, DLC; Dahlgren, "Report to Bureau of Observations &c at the Tredegar Foundry," 30 July 1855, box 2, DLC.

38. Morris to Fairfax, 21 August 1855, vol. 1, entry 4, RG74 NA; Morris to Dahlgren, 19 September 1855, box 23, DLC; Wise to Dahlgren, 26 September 1855, DS.

39. Dahlgren, undated document titled "New Shell Guns Proved to Extreme," box 23, DLC; Diary, 29 August 1855 entry; Morris to Knap and Wade, 10 September 1855, vol. 1, entry 4, RG74 NA; Wise to Dahlgren, 18 and 26 September 1855, DS; Fairfax to Morris, 28 September 1855, box 2, DLC; Dornin to Morris, 20 December 1855, entry 43, RG74 NA; Ingraham to Dobbin, 2 May 1856, vol. 1, entry 1, RG74 NA.

40. Smith to Dahlgren, 25 September 1855, box 23, DLC; Missroon to Dahlgren, 18 October 1855, DS.

41. Fairfax to Morris, 4 October 1855, box 2, DLC; Wise to Dahlgren, 8 October 1855, DS.

42. Wise to Dahlgren, 26 September 1855, DS.

CHAPTER 10. DEVELOPMENT DURING PRODUCTION

1. Wade to Harwood, 21 June 1851, box 21, DLC; Wise to Dahlgren, 8 and 12 October 1855, DS; Dahlgren to Drayton, 24 October 1855, box 2, DLC.

2. Wade to Dahlgren, 28 July 1855, DS; Parrott to Morris, 27 September 1855, box 2, DLC; Parrott to Dahlgren, 4 October 1855, DS; Dahlgren to Parrott, 4 October 1855, box 2, DLC; Parrott to Dahlgren, 18 October 1855, DS.

3. Drayton to Dahlgren, 22 October 1855, DS.

4. Dahlgren to Drayton, 24 October 1855, box 2, DLC.

5. Dahlgren to Morris, 31 October 1855, box 2, DLC.

6. Dahlgren to Wise, 29 October 1855, DNL; Dahlgren to Morris, 31 October 1855, box 2, DLC.

7. Wade to Dahlgren, 6 June 1855, box 2, DLC; Knap and Wade to Renshaw, 12 July 1855, box 2, DLC; Parrott to Morris, 13 July 1855, box 2, DLC; Dahlgren to Morris, 17 July and 31 October 1855, box 2, DLC.

8. Dahlgren to Wise, 27 September 1855, DNL; Dahlgren to Parrott, 4 October 1855, box 2, DLC; Dahlgren to Wise, 10 October 1855, DNL; Dahlgren to Renshaw, 22 October 1855, box 2, DLC; Dahlgren to Missroon, 22 October 1855, box 2, DLC; Dahlgren to Morris, 31 October 1855, box 2, DLC.

9. Wade to Dahlgren, 6 June 1855, box 2, DLC; Knap and Wade to Renshaw, 12 July 1855, box 2, DLC; Parrott to Morris, 13 July 1855, box 2, DLC; Dahlgren to Morris, 17 July 1855, box 2, DLC; Dahlgren to Morris, 31 October 1855, box 2, DLC.

10. Morris to Dahlgren, 1 November 1855, box 23, DLC.

11. Morris to Dahlgren, 10 November 1855, box 23, DLC; Morris to Simpson, 12 November 1855, vol. 1, entry 4, RG74 NA; Dahlgren to Morris, 14 November 1855, box 23, DLC; Morris to Dahlgren, 14 November 1855, box 23, DLC; Morris to Missroon, 21 November 1855, vol. 1, entry 4, RG74 NA.

12. Parrott to Dahlgren, 9 November 1855, DS; Drayton to Dahlgren, 10 November 1855, DS; Drayton to Dahlgren, 13 November 1855, box 2, DLC; Parrott to Dahlgren, 15 November 1855, box 2, DLC.

13. Morris to Dahlgren, 22 November 1855, box 2, DLC.

14. Dahlgren to Drayton, 4 December 1855, PDHSPA.

15. Dahlgren to Morris, 24 November 1855, vol. 1, entry 4, RG74 NA.

16. Morris to Alger and Company, 27 November 1855, vol. 1, entry 4, RG74 NA; Morris to Parrott, 27 November 1855, vol. 1, entry 4, RG74 NA.

17. Alger to Morris, 7 and 24 December 1855, box 2, DLC; Dahlgren to Morris, 31 December 1855, box 2, DLC.

18. Dahlgren to Morris, 26 and 31 December 1855, box 2, DLC; Dahlgren to Morris, 3 January 1856 (August–December 1855 folder), box 2, DLC; Morris to Dahlgren, 5 January 1856, box 3, DLC; Alger to Morris, 12 January 1856, box 3, DLC; Dahlgren to Morris, 24 January 1856, box 3, DLC; Diary, 5, 8, and 16 January 1856 entries.

19. Bert Hall and Robert Gordon, conversation with author at the annual meeting of the Society for the History of Technology, Lowell, Mass., 9 October 1994.

20. Dahlgren, undated document titled "Nine Inch Shell Guns Nos. 1 and 2," 1850 folder, box 21, DLC; Diary, 7 January 1856 entry; *Brief Notice of the Late Commodore Charles Morris.*

21. Diary, 29 January 1856 entry; *Brief Notice of the Late Commodore Charles Morris.*

22. Wise to Dahlgren, 26 September 1855, DS; Dahlgren, journal notes, 29–30 January and 1 February 1856, box 23, DLC; Diary, 30 January and 1 February 1856 entries.

23. Dahlgren to [?], 7 February 1856 (1855 folder), box 2, DLC.

24. Dahlgren, undated document titled "Nine Inch Shell Guns Nos. 1 and 2," 1850 folder, box 21, DLC; Smith to Alger and Company, 25 January 1856, box 2, DLC; Dahlgren to Smith, 6 February 1856, box 3, DLC; Smith to Cyrus Alger and Company, Parrott, Knap and Wade, and Anderson, Delaney, and Company, 19 February 1856, vol. 1, entry 4, RG74 NA.

25. Tucker, *Arming the Fleet,* 43; Drayton to Dahlgren, 23 June 1850, box 2, DLC; Dahlgren to Drayton, 3 August 1850, PDHSPA.

26. Morris to Dobbin, 25 May 1855, vol. 1, entry 1, RG74 NA; Dahlgren, "Memorandum for Bureau," 25 January 1856, box 3, DLC; Smith to Dobbin, 26 January 1856, vol. 1, entry 1, RG74 NA; Diary, 8 February 1856 entry.

27. Dahlgren to Page, 18 September 1856, box 3, DLC.

28. Drayton to Dahlgren, 11 March 1855, box 1, DS.

29. *DAB,* s.v. "Jones, Catesby ap Roger" (the younger).

30. Bathe, *Ship of Destiny,* 7–8; Tucker, *Arming the Fleet,* 207; Dahlgren, undated document titled "Nine Inch Shell Guns Nos. 1 and 2," 1850 folder, box 21, DLC; Dahlgren, undated notes titled "Carriages," 1853 folder, box 22, DLC; Dahlgren to Paulding and Morris, 9 February 1854, box 22, DLC; Jones to Dahlgren, 15 March 1856, Jones Papers, Virginia Historical Society; Dahlgren to Smith, "Report on the Trial of the Merrimac's Battery at Sea," 24 March 1856, box 24, DLC; Jones to Dahlgren, 28 March 1856, Jones Papers, Virginia Historical Society.

31. Dahlgren to Dornin, 19 November 1855, box 2, DLC.

32. Dobbin to Dahlgren, 9 April 1856, box 3, DLC; Diary, 25 February–19 April 1856 entries.

33. Dahlgren to Dobbin, 25 April 1856, box 3, DLC; Dahlgren to Ingraham, 28 April 1856, entry 201 #5, RG74 NA.

34. *DAB,* s.v. "Ingraham, Duncan Nathaniel"; Dahlgren to Drayton, 12 March 1856, PDHSPA.

35. Dahlgren, "Proposed Conditions for Casting IX In Guns at Pittsburgh," 24 April 1856 (1848 folder), box 20, DLC; Hunt to Dahlgren, 10 May 1856, box 3, DLC; Diary, 21 July 1856 entry; Ingraham to Knap and Wade, 26 July 1856, vol. 1, entry 4, RG74 NA; Ingraham to Anderson, 28 July 1856, vol. 1, entry 4, RG74 NA; Ingraham to Archer, 28 July 1856, vol. 1, entry 4, RG74 NA; Austin to Dahlgren, 4 August and 27 September 1856, box 3, DLC; *Annual Report 1856,* 571; *Annual Report 1857,* 792.

36. Dahlgren to Sinclair, 26 January 1856, box 2, DLC.

Chapter 11. Dahlgren's Star Rising

1. Braudy, *Frenzy of Renown,* 3, 15, 584–87.

2. Foote to Dahlgren, 16 October 1855, box 1, DS.

3. Dahlgren to [?], 7 February 1856 (1855 folder), box 2, DLC.

4. Dahlgren, "Memorandum on Ordnance," 14 November 1856, box 23, DLC.

5. Dahlgren to Mallory, 12 January 1857, box 3, DLC.

6. Diary, 8 January 1857 entry.

7. Ibid., 8 May 1854 entry.

8. Quoted in Durkin, *Stephen R. Mallory,* 65.

9. *Annual Report 1856,* 410–13.

10. Foote to Dahlgren, 3 March 1855, DS.

11. Dahlgren to Jones, 15 August 1853, box 2, DLC; Foote to Dahlgren, 3 March 1855, DS; Dahlgren to Du Pont, 28 June 1855, W9-7400, Samuel Francis Du Pont

Collection of Winterthur Manuscripts, Eleutherian Mills Historical Library; Austin to Dahlgren, 20 December 1855, box 2, DLC; "(Extract), Trubner &c. Booksellers to Mr. Frank Taylor," 5 September 1856, box 3, DLC.

12. Bathe, *Ship of Destiny,* 7–8; Diary, 7 February 1856 entry; Jones to Dahlgren, 21 June, 2 August, and 29 November 1856, Jones Papers, Virginia Historical Society; document titled "Extract from British 'U. Service Journal,'" January 1857, box 24, DLC.

13. Wise to Dahlgren, 17 and 23 May 1855, DS; Dahlgren to Wise, 28 May 1855 (1854 folder), box 2, DLC; Wise to Dahlgren, 6 June 1855, DS.

14. Hoppin, *Life of Andrew Hull Foote,* 108.

15. "(Extract), Trubner &c. Booksellers to Mr. Frank Taylor," 5 September 1856, box 3, DLC.

16. Dahlgren, diary fragments dated 16 August 1856 and 9 March 1857, box 2, DS; Dobbin to Dahlgren, 18 August 1856, box 3, DLC; Dahlgren to Welsh, [?] March 1857, box 3, DLC; Hunt to Dahlgren, 30 March 1857, box 3, DLC; Dahlgren to King and Baird, 24 April 1857, box 3, DLC.

17. Dahlgren, *Shells and Shell Guns,* 11, 222, 275, 287.

18. Foote to Dahlgren, 8 December 1858, box 4, DLC.

19. Quoted in Alden and Earle, *Makers of Naval Tradition,* 138.

20. Dahlgren to Morris, 17 October 1855, box 2, DLC; Dobbin to [Dahlgren or Ingraham], 4 February 1856, box 3, DLC; Diary, 10 October 1856 entry; *Annual Report 1856,* 410–13; Walker to Dahlgren, 8 May 1857, box 3, DLC.

21. Toucey to Dahlgren, 22 June 1857, box 3, DLC; Dahlgren to Patty Dahlgren, 29 June 1857, DNLC. Incidentally, on board was Midshipman Alfred Thayer Mahan, taking his first naval cruise. Seager, *Alfred Thayer Mahan,* 12.

22. Alden and Earle, *Makers of Naval Tradition,* 139; Dahlgren, "Memoranda of Practice at Sea U.S. Ordnance Ship Plymouth," July–August 1857, box 24, DLC.

23. George Mifflin Dallas, note, 20 September 1857, George Mifflin Dallas Collection, HSPA; Hammond to Dallas, 22 September 1857, box 3, DLC; Stopford to Shubrick, 30 November 1857, box 3, DLC; Dahlgren, "Report on Cruise of Ordnance Ship Plymouth," 20 November 1857, box 24, DLC.

24. Dahlgren, "Report on Cruise of Ordnance Ship Plymouth," 20 November 1857, box 24, DLC.

25. *Annual Report 1857,* 579.

26. Mallory to Wise, 25 October 1857, box 3, DLC.

27. Missroon to Dahlgren, 19 January 1857, box 3, DLC; Dahlgren to Taylor, 12 December 1857, box 3, DLC; Dahlgren to Toucey, 24 March 1858, box 3, DLC; Diary, 3 May 1858 entry.

28. Diary, 13 April 1858 entry.

29. Sprout and Sprout, *Rise of American Naval Power,* 146–47; Coletta, *American Secretaries of the Navy,* 1:305; Toucey to Dahlgren, 28 May 1858, box 3, DLC.

30. Dahlgren to Patty Dahlgren, 3 June 1858, DNLC; Dahlgren to Foster, 23 June 1858, box 3, DLC; Dahlgren to Toucey, 24 June 1858, box 3, DLC; Dahlgren to McIntosh, 13 July 1858, box 4, DLC; Dahlgren to Patty Dahlgren, 15 July 1858, DNLC.

31. Cass to Toucey, 7 July 1858, box 4, DLC; McIntosh to Dahlgren, 22 July 1858, box 4, DLC; Dahlgren to Patty Dahlgren, 16 August 1858, DNLC; Dahlgren to Toucey, 29 September 1858, box 4, DLC.

32. Long, *Gold Braid,* 107–8.

33. Dahlgren to Toucey, 29 September 1858, box 4, DLC; Chase to Dahlgren, 1 October 1858, box 4, DLC.

34. Dahlgren to Toucey, 13 October 1858, box 4, DLC.

35. Dahlgren to Toucey, 17 October 1858, box 4, DLC; Chase to Dahlgren, 11 November 1858, box 4, DLC.

36. Chase to Dahlgren, 11 November 1858, box 4, DLC.

37. Dahlgren to Patty Dahlgren, 16 November 1858, DNLC; Toucey to Dahlgren, 8 December 1858, box 4, DLC.

38. "Casting Heavy Guns," *Scientific American* 14 (30 October 1858): 60.

39. Sprout and Sprout, *Rise of American Naval Power,* 146–47; "Record of Armament of Naval Vessels 1841–1903," vols. 1 and 2, entry 111, RG74 NA; Ingraham to Du Pont, [?] June 1858, W9-8955, and 8 July 1858, W9-8977, Samuel Francis Du Pont Collection of Winterthur Manuscripts, Eleutherian Mills Historical Library.

40. Diary, 4 April 1859 entry; Dahlgren to Duke Constantine, 5 December 1859, box 4, DLC.

41. Missroon to Dahlgren, 15 January 1857, box 3, DLC; Diary, 19 March 1859 entry.

42. Diary, 19 March 1859 entry; Dahlgren to Parrott, 13 February 1860, box 4, DLC.

43. Dahlgren to Toucey, 20 April 1859, box 4, DLC.

44. Dahlgren to the commissioner of patents, 16 March 1859, box 4, DLC.

45. Diary, 20 April 1859 entry; Dahlgren to Toucey, 20 April 1859, box 4, DLC.

46. Tucker, *Arming the Fleet,* 280–81; Wise to Dahlgren, 13 February 1864, box 6, DLC.

47. Farragut to Ingraham, 26 January and [?] November 1859, *Brooklyn* 1859–61 letter-book, David G. Farragut Papers, Naval Historical Foundation Collection, Manuscripts Division, Library of Congress; Dahlgren to Drayton, 20 October 1859, PDHSPA; Dahlgren to Ingraham, 2 November 1859, entry 201 #5, RG74 NA.

48. Dahlgren, document titled "Opinions Professional," 25 March 1859, box 4, DLC.

49. Samuel F. Du Pont, "Description of USS *Minnesota,*" 1859, W9-2084, Samuel Francis Du Pont Collection of Winterthur Manuscripts, Eleutherian Mills Historical Library.

50. *Annual Report 1858,* 6–7.

51. U.S. Congress, House, *Reports of the Board of Officers Ordered to Examine into the Condition of the Navy Yards,* H. ExDoc. 34, 36th Cong., 1st sess., 1859–60, 76.

52. Dahlgren, document titled "Opinions Professional," 25 March 1859, box 4, DLC.

53. Diary, 18 and 19 November 1859 entries.

54. Smith to Dahlgren, 29 February 1858, box 3, DLC.

55. Christman, *Naval Innovators,* 174.

Chapter 12. The Rifle Question

1. Skulski, *Battleship Yamato,* 17–19.

2. Bastable, "From Breechloaders to Monster Guns," 221, 244, quotation on 246.

3. Comprato, *Age of Great Guns,* 16–17.

4. Ibid., 17–18; Robertson, *Evolution of Naval Armament,* 199, 203.

5. Bastable, "From Breechloaders to Monster Guns," 218–20; Robertson, *Evolution of Naval Armament,* 203–9.

6. Prosser to Dahlgren, 18 March 1856, box 3, DLC; Dahlgren to Bormann, 26 April 1856, box 3, DLC; Bormann to Dahlgren, 20 September 1856, box 3, DLC.

7. Record of "council of works" meeting, 30 January 1855, box 23, DLC; Jones to Dahlgren, 8 September 1856, box 3, DLC; Dahlgren, notes clipped under the heading "New Ships & Armaments," 1857 folder, box 24, DLC; Diary, 24 September 1860 entry.

8. Dahlgren, document titled "Rifled Cannon of 16,000 Lbs," 1856, box 23, DLC; Dahlgren, "Preliminary IX In Rifled Shell Gun Adapted to the U.S. XI In Shell-Gun," 14 August 1856, box 23, DLC; Diary, 16 August 1856 and 24 September 1860 entries; Dahlgren to Maury, 27 January 1857, box 3, DLC; Dahlgren to Ingraham, 2 and 22 June 1857, entry 201 #5, RG74 NA; Dahlgren to Blakeley, 1 April 1858, box 3, DLC; Wise to Dahlgren, 20 July and 9 August 1858, box 4, DLC; Dahlgren to Drayton, 14 May 1859, PDHSPA; Jones to Dahlgren, 8 September 1865, box 3, DLC; various notes, box 25, DLC.

9. *DAB*, s.v. "Ingraham, Duncan Nathaniel."

10. Diary, 11 April 1856 entry.

11. Jones to Dahlgren, 30 August 1856, Jones Papers, Virginia Historical Society.

12. Diary, 24 September 1860 entry.

13. Hovgaard, *Modern History of Warships*, 387–88; Diary, 19 and 23 March, 4 April 1859, 24 September 1860 entries; Dahlgren, "Plan of Elongated Shell for Rifled Cannon," box 25, DLC; Toucey to Dahlgren, 26 March 1859, box 4, DLC.

14. Dairy, 26 September 1859 entry; Dahlgren to Thomas, 28 December 1859, box 4, DLC; Dahlgren to Ingraham, 11 January 1860, entry 201 #5, RG74 NA.

15. Ripley, *Artillery and Ammunition*, 104–5; "The New Guns for the Navy," *Scientific American* 6 (15 March 1862): 171.

16. Madeleine Dahlgren, *Memoir*, 226–27; Dahlgren to Buchanan, 27 August 1859, box 4, DLC; Dahlgren to Lynall Thomas, 28 December 1859, box 4, DLC; Dahlgren to Ingraham, 11 January 1860, entry 201 #5, RG74 NA; Dahlgren, miscellaneous notes on rifled cannon, Misc. John Dahlgren, Manuscript Collection, NYHS.

17. Bastable, "From Breechloaders to Monster Guns," 220–21.

18. Bradford, *Captains*, 148; Dahlgren to Du Pont, 23 August 1859, W9-9489, Samuel Francis Du Pont Collection of Winterthur Manuscripts, Eleutherian Mills Historical Library; Dahlgren to Drayton, 20 October 1859, PDHSPA.

19. Dahlgren to Drayton, 13 June 1860, PDHSPA.

20. Diary, 24 December 1859 entry.

21. Albion, *Makers of Naval Policy*, 39–40.

22. Madeleine Dahlgren, *Memoir*, 243–44.

23. Dahlgren to Porter, 20 June 1859, box 4, DLC; Dahlgren to Drayton, 20 October 1859, PDHSPA; Diary, 14 November 1859 entry; Dahlgren, miscellaneous notes on rifled cannon, Misc. John Dahlgren, Manuscript Collection, NYHS.

24. Dahlgren to Toucey, 15 December 1859 (1861 folder), box 26, DLC; Dahlgren to Toucey, 19 January 1860 (1861 folder), box 26, DLC; Diary, 3 May 1860 entry; Dahlgren to Welsh, 2 May 1860, box 4, DLC.

25. Dahlgren to Toombs, 18 February 1860, box 4, DLC; Dahlgren to Green, 27 March 1860, box 4, DLC; Dahlgren to Stanton, 30 March 1860, box 4, DLC; Dahlgren, "Statement Respectfully Submitted for the Information of the Committee," 31 March 1860, box 4, DLC; Dahlgren to Drayton, 13 June 1860, PDHSPA; Diary, 27 March and 2 July 1860 entries.

26. Dahlgren to Drayton, 9 October 1860, PDHSPA.

27. Dahlgren, "Practice with 50-Pdr & 15 Pdr Rifle Cannon," box 25, DLC; Dahlgren to Magruder, 12 December 1860, entry 201 #5, RG74 NA.

28. Diary, 14 September 1860 entry; Dahlgren to Smith, 14 September 1860, box 4, DLC.

29. Tucker, *Arming the Fleet,* 234–36; U.S. Congress, House, *Report of the Superintendent of Ordnance at the Washington Navy Yard on Rifled Cannon and the Armament of Ships of War,* H. ExDoc. 25, 36th Cong., 2d sess., 1860.

Chapter 13. Dahlgren and Lincoln

1. Lincoln quoted in Randall and Donald, *Civil War,* 117, 119.

2. Dahlgren to Drayton, 21 December 1859, PDHSPA.

3. Dahlgren to Foote, 23 January 1861, DNHC.

4. Bruce, *Lincoln and the Tools of War,* 10; Randall and Donald, *Civil War,* 133–89; Tindall, *America,* 608–23.

5. Dahlgren to Ulric Dahlgren, 26 November and 24 December 1860, box 19, DLC.

6. Diary, 1 January 1861 entry; Dahlgren to Paul, 9 January 1861, box 4, DLC; Dahlgren to Drayton, 18 January 1861, PDHSPA; Dahlgren to Badger, 14 March 1861, box 4, DLC.

7. Cooling, *Symbol,* 22–23; Buchanan to Dahlgren, 8 January 1861, box 4, DLC.

8. Dahlgren to Morse, 11 February 1861, box 4, DLC; Dahlgren to Grimes, 11 February 1861, box 4, DLC.

9. Dahlgren, "Card Re. the Suicide of Edward G. Tilton, Feb 8, 1861," DD; Diary, 11 February and 4 March 1861 entries.

10. Diary, 2 and 3 April 1861 entries.

11. West, *Gideon Welles,* 108–9; Cooling, *Symbol,* 30.

12. Cooling, *Symbol,* 30–38; Diary, 13 and 18 April 1861 entries.

13. Welles to Dahlgren, 22 April 1861, box 4, DLC; Diary, 3 May 1861 entry.

14. Dahlgren, *Memoir of Ulric Dahlgren,* 35.

15. Bruce, *Lincoln and the Tools of War,* 16–17; Cooling, *Symbol,* 30–38; Cooling, "Civil War Deterrent," 164–65; Welles to Dahlgren, 29 April 1861, box 4, DLC; Dahlgren, "Memoranda from Letters &c," 3 May 1861, box 26, DLC; Diary, 3 May 1861 entry; "A Graceful Tribute," *Army and Navy Journal* 7 (13 August 1870): 824.

16. Bruce, *Lincoln and the Tools of War,* 19; Cooling, "Civil War Deterrent," 173; Welles to Dahlgren, 29 April 1861, box 4, DLC; Eagle to Dahlgren, 29 May 1861, box 4, DLC; Dahlgren to Drayton, 3 June 1861, PDHSPA; Dahlgren, document, 21 June 1861, box 4, DLC; Ewbank to Dahlgren, 18 July 1861, box 4, DLC; Knap, Rudd, and Company to Dahlgren, 1 August 1861, box 4, DLC.

17. N. P. Willis, "Lookings-on at the War," *Home Journal,* 29 June 1861.

18. Dahlgren, "Memoranda from Letters &c," 28 April 1861, box 26, DLC.

19. Bruce, *Lincoln and the Tools of War,* 17–18; Diary, 9 May 1861 entry.

20. Diary, 12 and 18 May 1861 entries.

21. Cooling, *Symbol,* 45–50; Oates, *With Malice toward None,* 240–41; Diary, 23–24 May and 9 June 1861 entries.

22. Bruce, *Lincoln and the Tools of War,* 10–21; Coletta, *American Secretaries of the Navy,* 1:329; West, "Lincoln's Hand in Naval Matters," 178; Dahlgren, *Memoir of Ulric Dahlgren,* 32–33; Diary, 9 and 30 June, 14 July, 19 October, 26 November 1861 entries; Drayton to Hoyt, 12 October 1861, Percival Drayton Papers, Rare Books and Manuscripts Division, New York Public Library; "Rear-Admiral Dahlgren," *Army and Navy Journal* 7 (16 July 1870): 757. For other examples of Dahlgren's relationship with Lincoln, see Diary, 27–28 December 1861, 13 and 19 April, 10 July, 7 and 30 August 1862 entries; numerous other entries also illustrate the point.

23. Bruce, *Lincoln and the Tools of War,* 17; Diary, 2 August 1861 entry.

24. *SFD,* 1:118–19.

25. Bruce, *Lincoln and the Tools of War,* 16–21, 82; Welles to Dahlgren, 5 August 1861, box 4, DLC; Seward to Dahlgren, 5 August 1861, box 4, DLC; Diary, 5–6 August, 15, 19, and 30 November 1861 entries.

26. Dahlgren, *Memoir of Ulric Dahlgren,* 11–30; Dahlgren to [?], 13 September 1861, box 5, DLC; Diary, 12 September 1861 and 1–2 August 1862 entries.

27. Diary, 26 September 1861 entry.

28. Bruce, *Lincoln and the Tools of War,* 207; Lincoln to Hale, 28 January 1862, *Collected Works of Abraham Lincoln,* 5:112–13.

Chapter 14. *Monitor* versus *Virginia*

1. Brodie, *Sea Power,* 17. Although the proper spelling is *Merrimack,* the name often appears in the historical literature and source material without the *k.*

2. Albion, *Makers of Naval Policy,* 9; Paullin, *History of Naval Administration,* 250, 288; Sprout and Sprout, *Rise of American Naval Power,* 151–53.

3. Albion, *Makers of Naval Policy,* 38; *DAB,* s.v. "Welles, Gideon"; Niven, "Gideon Welles," 53–66; West, *Gideon Welles,* 11–12, 39, 63–64, 206.

4. *DAB,* s.v. "Fox, Gustavus Vasa"; Hayes, "Captain Fox," 64–71; Merrill, "Strategy Makers," 20–32; Niven, "Gideon Welles," 58–64; Coletta, *American Secretaries of the Navy,* 1:328.

5. Welles, *Diary,* 1:401.

6. Fox to Du Pont, 3 June 1862, *Confidential Correspondence of Gustavus Vasa Fox,* 1:126–28.

7. West, "Lincoln's Hand in Naval Matters," 176–81.

8. *CWNC,* I-5, I-11, I-12; Still, "Naval Sieve," 38–45.

9. Bathe, *Ship of Destiny,* 8; *CWNC,* xvi, I-9, I-10; Potter, *Sea Power,* 124.

10. Bathe, *Ship of Destiny,* 12–13; *CWNC,* I-13, I-15, I-17, I-19, II-23, II-26; Gardiner, *Steam, Steel, and Shellfire,* 65; McPherson, *Battle Cry of Freedom,* 373–74.

11. Albion, *Makers of Naval Policy,* 195–96; Dahlgren to Welles, 26 June 1861, box 4, DLC.

12. Baxter, *Introduction of the Ironclad Warship,* 245–47; Bennett, *Steam Navy,* 263–74; McPherson, *Battle Cry of Freedom,* 374.

13. "Reminiscences of the Late Captain Wise," *Army and Navy Journal* 6 (3 July 1869): 726; Dahlgren, untitled account of the battle of Hampton Roads, box 5, DLC; Diary, 8 March 1862 entry.

14. Quoted in Davis, *Duel between the First Ironclads,* 89.

15. *DANFS,* 6:533; Ketchum, *American Heritage Picture History of the Civil War,* 177; McPherson, *Battle Cry of Freedom,* 375–76.

16. Bathe, *Ship of Destiny,* 14; Baxter, *Introduction of the Ironclad Warship,* 287–93; quotations from Hoehling, *Thunder at Hampton Roads,* 100–119; Meissner, *Old Naval Days,* 244; Parker, *Recollections,* 279.

17. Diary, 9 March 1862 entry; Welles, *Diary,* 1:62–64.

18. Diary, 9 March 1862 entry; Welles, *Diary,* 1:66–67; Dahlgren to Lincoln, 9 March 1862, box 5, DLC; Dahlgren to McClellan, 9 March 1862, box 5, DLC.

19. Bathe, *Ship of Destiny,* 15–17; Baxter, *Introduction of the Ironclad Warship,* 293; Demaree, "*Merrimack,*" 68; Hoehling, *Thunder at Hampton Roads,* 158–63; Hovgaard, *Modern History of Warships,* 22; Ward, *Civil War,* 101; Stimers, "Aboard the *Monitor,*" 33–35; Diary, 9 March 1862 entry; Sanford to the telegraph operator at the Washington Navy Yard, 9 March 1862, box 5, DLC.

20. Welles to Dahlgren, 10 March 1862, box 5, DLC; Welles, *Diary,* 1:66–67; Diary, 10 March 1862 entry.

21. Parker, *Recollections,* 287–88.

22. Dahlgren, description of the battle of Hampton Roads, box 5, DLC.

23. Bathe, *Ship of Destiny,* 15–17; Baxter, *Introduction of the Ironclad Warship,* 285–95; Demaree, "*Merrimack,*" 68; Hovgaard, *Modern History of Warships,* 22; Robertson, *Evolution of Naval Armament,* 267; Stimers, "Aboard the *Monitor,*" 33–35.

CHAPTER 15. THE LAST STRAW

1. Canfield, *Civil War Naval Ordnance,* 8–10; Greene, "*Monitor* at Sea and in Battle," 1844–45; Hayes, "Captain Fox," 68; "Reminiscences of the Late Captain Wise," *Army and Navy Journal* 6 (3 July 1869): 726; Fox to Dahlgren, 11 March 1862, box 5, DLC; Fox to Harwood, 15 May 1862, roll 2, microcopy 480, entry 13, RG45 NA; Fox to Du Pont, 5 August 1862, *Confidential Correspondence of Gustavus Vasa Fox,* 1:144.

2. Church, *Life of John Ericsson,* 1:291; Foote, "DuPont Storms Charleston," 33; quotation from Hess, "Northern Response," 127–31.

3. *Passaic, Montauk, Catskill, Patapsco, Lehigh,* and *Sangamon.* Contracts for four other *Passaic*-class monitors (*Weehawken, Comanche, Nantucket,* and *Nahant*) were awarded to other builders.

4. Baxter, *Introduction of the Ironclad Warship,* 302–9; MacBride, *Civil War Ironclads,* 23–25.

5. The preponderance was the excess weight of the breech as the gun balanced on its trunnions. With the optimum preponderance, the breech was heavy enough to prevent bouncing when the gun was fired, but not so heavy as to make it hard for the crew to elevate the barrel. A difference of several inches in the placement of the trunnions, the pivot of balance, could mean a difference of hundreds of pounds of preponderance.

6. Fox to Ericsson, 18 March 1862, box 11, Ericsson Papers, American Swedish Historical Museum.

7. Welles to Harwood, 17 March 1862, no. 0368, roll 2, microcopy 480, entry 13, RG45 NA; Dahlgren to Harwood, 18 March 1862, vol. 14, entry 6, RG74 NA; Diary, 18

March 1862 entry; U.S. Congress, House, *Iron-Clad Ships, Ordnance, &c., &c.,* H. MisDoc. 82, 37th Cong., 2d sess., 1862.

8. Dahlgren to Harwood, 19 March 1862, box 5, DLC.

9. Holley, *Treatise on Ordnance and Armor,* 130–90; Hovgaard, *Modern History of Warships,* 393.

10. Dahlgren to Harwood, 19 March 1862, box 5, DLC.

11. *DAB,* s.v. "Rodman, Thomas J."; Dew, *Ironmaker to the Confederacy,* 44–49; Ripley, *Artillery and Ammunition,* 78–79. Rodman's ideas and methods are found in *Reports of Experiments on Strength and Other Properties of Metals for Cannon* and Rodman, *Reports of Experiments on Properties of Metals for Cannon, and Qualities of Cannon Powder.*

12. Turner to Warrington, 20 October 1851, box 21, DLC; Rodman, "Explanation of the Differences in the Endurance of the Experimental 8 and 10 In Guns, Cast and Proved at Pittsburgh Pa, in the Fall of 1851," 24 October 1851, box 21, DLC; Diary, 20 December 1856 entry; Holroyd to Dahlgren, 10 February 1863, box 5, DLC.

13. Dahlgren to Harwood, 19 March 1862, box 5, DLC.

14. Harwood to Dahlgren, 19 March 1862, vol. 14, entry 6, RG74 NA; Dahlgren to Harwood, 20 March 1862, vol. 14, entry 6, RG74 NA; Harwood to Knap, Rudd, and Company, 20 March 1862, vol. 14, entry 6, RG74 NA; Wise to Knap, 4 April 1862, vol. 15, entry 6, RG74 NA.

15. Diary, 26 July 1856 entry; Dahlgren to Davis, 26 July 1855, box 2, DLC; Dahlgren to Craig, [?] July 1855, box 2, DLC.

16. Dahlgren, "Report to Bureau of Ordnance on Thirty-one IX Inch Guns Cast at Algers Foundry 1857," 9 March 1858, box 24, DLC; Diary, 14 July 1859 entry.

17. Dahlgren, journal notes dated 9 November 1859 (1855 folder), box 23, DLC.

18. Dahlgren to Floyd, 13 October 1860, box 27, DLC.

19. Lewis, "Ambiguous Columbiads," 120; Rodman to Ripley, [?] September 1861, box 5, DLC.

20. Rodman to Ripley, [?] September 1861, box 5, DLC.

21. Dahlgren to Stanton, 31 March 1862 (1863 folder), box 27, DLC.

22. Dahlgren to Harwood, 4 April 1862, entry 201 #5, RG74 NA; Harwood to Knap and Rudd, 7 April 1862, vol. 2, entry 4, RG74 NA; Harwood to Knap, 8 April 1862, vol. 2, entry 4, RG74 NA; U.S. Congress, Senate, *Report to the Joint Committee on the Conduct of the War: Heavy Ordnance,* S. Rep. 121, 38th Cong., 2d sess., 1865, 128.

23. Dahlgren, "Memoranda, Connected with the Draft of XV^{in} Gun," 7 April 1862, box 27, DLC.

24. Dahlgren, "Ordnance Panic," 26 April 1862, box 27, DLC.

25. Diary, 28 March–6 May 1862 entries.

26. West, *Gideon Welles,* 216–17; Diary, 13–19 May 1862 entries.

27. Diary, 3 June 1866 entry.

28. Dahlgren to Hale, 24 March 1862, box 5, DLC.

29. Hale to Dahlgren, 29 May 1862, box 5, DLC; Dahlgren to Hale, 3 June 1862, box 5, DLC.

30. Reynolds, *Famous American Admirals,* v; West, *Gideon Welles,* 217–18; Dahlgren to Sedgwick, 26 February 1862, box 5, DLC.

31. Dahlgren to Kelley, 25 May 1862, box 5, DLC.

32. Dahlgren to Phelps, 3 June 1862, box 5, DLC.

33. Harwood to Dahlgren, 19 March 1862, vol. 14, entry 6, RG74 NA.

34. Quoted in *CWNC,* IV-95.
35. Janowitz, *Professional Soldier,* 21–36.
36. Karsten, *Naval Aristocracy,* 258; West, *Gideon Welles,* 217–18.
37. Diary, 25 May 1862 entry.
38. Lincoln to Stanton, 6 June 1862, *Collected Works of Abraham Lincoln,* 5:262.
39. Dahlgren, *Memoir of Ulric Dahlgren,* 63.
40. West, *Gideon Welles,* 189–91; *An Act to Reorganize the Navy Department of the United States, Statutes at Large,* vol. 12, chap. 134, 5 July 1862; Welles, *Diary,* 1:163–65; Diary, 5–23 July and 5 August 1862 entries; Dahlgren to Welles, 12 July 1862, box 5, DLC.
41. Albion, *Makers of Naval Policy,* 146–48; Reynolds, *Famous American Admirals,* v–vi; West, *Gideon Welles,* 189–91; *Annual Report 1862,* 39–41; Diary, 11–23 July 1862 entries; U.S. Congress, House, *Message from the President of the United States Recommending a Vote of Thanks by Congress to Naval Officers Named Therein,* H. ExDoc. 147, 37th Cong., 2d sess., 1862.
42. Albion, *Makers of Naval Policy,* 146–48; West, *Gideon Welles,* 190; Diary, 2 and 17 July 1862 entries.
43. Grimes to Du Pont, 1 July 1863, *SFD,* 3:191; Diary, 17 July 1862 entry.
44. Diary, 11–23 July and 5 August 1862 entries.

CHAPTER 16. THE BUREAU OF ORDNANCE

1. Diary, 6 February 1863 entry.
2. Fox to Harwood, 15 May 1862, roll 2, microcopy 480, entry 13, RG45 NA.
3. Harwood to Ericsson, 1 May 1862, vol. 17, entry 6, RG74 NA; Harwood to Welles, 13 May 1862, vol. 17, entry 6, RG74 NA; Harwood to Knap, Rudd, and Company, 16 May 1862, vol. 2, entry 4, RG74 NA; Harwood to Berrien, 21 May 1862, vol. 18, entry 6, RG74 NA.
4. Anderson, "Naval Strategy of the Civil War," 13; *CWNC,* I-27.
5. Burton, *Siege,* 99; Henig, "Admiral Samuel F. DuPont," 69; Luce, "Naval Administration, III," 817; Merrill, "Strategy Makers," 27–29; Reed, *Combined Operations,* 263–69; West, *Gideon Welles,* 218–20.
6. Berrien to Harwood, 14 June 1862, Fort Pitt vol. 3, entry 21, RG74 NA; Ericsson to Dahlgren, 20 August 1862, vol. 1, entry 51, RG74 NA; Dahlgren to Ericsson, 23 August 1862, vol. 22, entry 6, RG74 NA; Ericsson to Dahlgren, 29 August 1862, vol. 1, entry 51, RG74 NA; Dahlgren to Ericsson, 31 August 1862, vol. 22, entry 6, RG74 NA.
7. Knap to Dahlgren, 18 August 1862, vol. 1, entry 51, RG74 NA; Ripley to Dahlgren, 19 August 1862, box 5, DLC; Dahlgren to Knap, 20 August 1862, vol. 22, entry 6, RG74 NA; Dahlgren to Berrien, 2 September 1862, box 5, DLC; Berrien to Dahlgren, 13 September 1862, Fort Pitt vol. 4, entry 21, RG74 NA; Du Pont to Sophie Du Pont, 22 October 1862, *SFD,* 2:258; unsigned document titled "XV In Guns and XIII In Guns," 15 September 1868 (1863 folder), box 27, DLC.
8. Hinkley, Williams, and Company to Dahlgren, 23 August 1862, vol. 1, entry 51, RG74 NA; Sparrow to Dahlgren, 26 August 1862, vol. 1, entry 51, RG74 NA; Dahlgren to Matthews and Moore, 3 September 1862, vol. 22, entry 6, RG74 NA.

9. Harwood to Berrien, 25 June 1862, vol. 4, entry 4, RG74 NA; Dahlgren to Berrien, 30 August 1862, vol. 22, entry 6, RG74 NA; Diary, 5, 12, and 26 October 1862 entries; Wise to Dahlgren, 7 November 1862, Washington Navy Yard vol. 1, entry 3, RG74 NA.

10. Canfield, *Civil War Naval Ordnance*, 20.

11. West, *Gideon Welles*, 221.

12. Du Pont to Sophie Du Pont, 22 October 1862, *SFD*, 2:258.

13. Dahlgren to Welles, 22 November 1862, "Report to the Navy Department," box 27, DLC.

14. Canney, *Old Steam Navy, Volume Two: The Ironclads*, 78; West, *Gideon Welles*, 222; Ericsson to Harwood, 6 April 1862, vol. 1, entry 51, RG74 NA. The *Passaic* class was originally designed for either 11- or 13-inch guns; sources are unclear as to which.

15. West, *Gideon Welles*, 222; Diary, 3 November 1862 entry; Dahlgren to Ericsson, 4 November 1862, box 11, Ericsson Papers, American Swedish Historical Museum; Drayton to Dahlgren, 16 November 1862, box 5, DLC; Drayton to Hoyt, 16 November 1862, Drayton Papers, Rare Books and Manuscripts Division, New York Public Library; Drayton to Fox, 16 November 1862, *Confidential Correspondence of Gustavus Vasa Fox*, 2:439–41; Drayton to Dahlgren, 23 November 1862, box 5, DLC; Fox to Ericsson, 29 November 1862, box 11, Ericsson Papers, American Swedish Historical Museum.

16. Church, *Life of John Ericsson*, 2:136–37; Welles, *Diary*, 1:62; U.S. Congress, Senate, *Report to the Joint Committee on the Conduct of the War: Heavy Ordnance*, S. Rep. 121, 38th Cong., 2d sess., 1865, 128–29.

17. *Annual Report 1862*, 710; *Annual Report 1863*, 845.

18. Chandler, "Du Pont, Dahlgren, and the Civil War Nitre Shortage," 142–49; Dahlgren to Welles, 22 November 1862, "Report to the Navy Department," box 27, DLC.

19. Harwood to Dahlgren, 19 March 1862, vol. 14, entry 6, RG74 NA; Dahlgren to Harwood, 21 March 1862, entry 201 #5, RG74 NA; Dahlgren to Hale, 3 June 1862, box 5, DLC.

20. Chandler, "Du Pont, Dahlgren, and the Civil War Nitre Shortage"; *Annual Report 1862*, 710, 724; *Annual Report 1863*, 841–46.

21. Bruce, *Lincoln and the Tools of War*, 214–15.

22. Ibid., 89, 219.

23. Diary, 24 June 1862 entry.

24. *Annual Report 1862*, 711–20; Dahlgren, notes titled "Practice at Iron Plates May & June 1862," box 27, DLC; Mitchell to Dahlgren, 1 September 1862, box 5, DLC.

25. *Annual Report 1862*, 711–20; "Reports Concerning Target Practice on Iron Plates 1862–1864," entry 98, RG74 NA; Harwood to Knap, Rudd, and Company, 13 June 1862, vol. 19, entry 6, RG74 NA; Missroon to Wise, 29 October 1862, vol. 2, entry 51, RG74 NA; "Experiments with a New Gun," *Scientific American* 7 (29 November 1862): 342; Dahlgren to Knap, Rudd, and Company, 9 December 1862, Fort Pitt vol. 1, entry 4, RG74 NA.

26. [Illegible] to Harwood, 18 November 1861, vol. 33, entry 18, RG74 NA.

27. Thatcher to Harwood, 24 November 1861, vol. 33, entry 18, RG74 NA.

28. Tucker, *Arming the Fleet*, 235–36.

29. Ibid., 228–33; U.S. Congress, Senate, *Report to the Joint Committee on the Conduct of the War: Heavy Ordnance*, S. Rep. 121, 38th Cong., 2d sess., 1865, 2, 22, 34, 39.

30. *Annual Report 1862,* 711–21.

31. *Annual Report 1863,* 841.

32. Ammen to Dahlgren, 9 November 1862, box 5, DLC.

33. Missroon to Wise, 9 March 1864, WNYHS; Drayton to Wise, [?] September 1863, WNYHS; Sedgwick to Wise, 2 July 1863, WNYHS.

CHAPTER 17. DAHLGREN'S STAR ASCENDANT

1. Dahlgren, pamphlet titled "Extracts from Official Documents, 1853–1862" (1861 folder), box 27, DLC; Diary, 3 October 1862 entry.

2. Dahlgren to Lincoln, 1 October 1862, box 5, DLC.

3. Du Pont to Fox, 8 October 1862, *Confidential Correspondence of Gustavus Vasa Fox,* 1:160–61.

4. West, *Gideon Welles,* 220–21; Fox to Du Pont, 7 October 1862, *SFD,* 2:242; Welles to Dahlgren, 8 October 1862, box 5, DLC; Welles, *Diary,* 1:163–65.

5. Dahlgren to Wilmot and Cowan, [?] January 1863, box 5, DLC.

6. Quoted in "Rear-Admiral Dahlgren," *Army and Navy Journal* 7 (16 July 1870): 757.

7. Diary, 12, 17, and 25 February 1863 entries; Welles, *Diary,* 1:238–39; Lincoln to the Senate, 19 February 1863, *Collected Works of Abraham Lincoln,* 6:111–12; Dahlgren to Wilmot, 21 February 1863, box 5, DLC.

8. Diary, 27 and 28 February, 11 March 1863 entries.

9. Werlich, *Admiral of the Amazon,* 52; West, "Lincoln's Hand in Naval Matters," 178; Foote to Dahlgren, 13 July 1862, box 5, DLC; Rodgers to Du Pont, 18 July 1862, *SFD,* 2:164; Ammen to Dahlgren, 14 August 1862, DS; Knap to [illegible], 1 February 1863, WNYHS; Du Pont to Sophie Du Pont, 7 March 1863, *SFD,* 2:473; Farragut to Du Pont, 20 April 1863, *SFD,* 3:47–49; Welles, *Diary,* 1:239.

10. Bradford, *Captains,* 154; Burton, *Siege,* 132–36, 268–75; Jones, *Siege,* 198–99; Reed, *Combined Operations,* 289–91, 319; Still, *Iron Afloat,* 112. Fort Sumter stood approximately 1,760 yards from Fort Moultrie.

11. Still, *Iron Afloat,* 112–27, 219, 228.

12. Burton, *Siege,* 268; Melia, *Damn the Torpedoes,* 9–10; Perry, *Infernal Machines,* 49–62.

13. Reed, *Combined Operations,* 319.

14. Quoted in Wise, *Gate of Hell,* 28.

15. Bradford, *Captains,* 153–54; Burton, *Siege,* 135; Reed, *Combined Operations,* 263–69; West, *Gideon Welles,* 220.

16. Bradford, *Captains,* 154; Merrill, "Strategy Makers," 27–29; Reed, *Combined Operations,* 280.

17. Luce, "Naval Administration, III," 819.

18. Ely, "This Filthy Ironpot," 46–47; Still, "Common Sailor," 39; Drayton to Hoyt, 9 December 1862, and Drayton to Hamilton, 16 December 1862, Drayton Papers, Rare Books and Manuscripts Division, New York Public Library.

19. Du Pont to Sophie Du Pont, 11 February 1863, *SFD,* 2:430; Diary, 29 March 1863 entry; Ericsson to Fox, 10 April 1863, box 6, Ericsson Papers, American Swedish Historical Museum.

20. Bradford, *Captains,* 155–56; Foote, "DuPont Storms Charleston," 34; Henig, "Admiral Samuel F. DuPont," 71; Drayton to Hamilton, 11 February 1863, Drayton Papers, Rare Books and Manuscripts Division, New York Public Library; Du Pont to Fox, 7 March 1863, *Confidential Correspondence of Gustavus Vasa Fox,* 1:190–91.

21. Du Pont to Fox, 19 March 1863, *Confidential Correspondence of Gustavus Vasa Fox,* 1:190–91.

22. Reed, *Combined Operations,* 280–81; Diary, 29 March 1863 entry.

23. Bradford, *Captains,* 266; Hayes, "Fox versus DuPont," 11; Reed, *Combined Operations,* 271–87.

24. Hunter, *Year on a Monitor,* 49–59; Reed, *Combined Operations,* 292.

25. Reed, *Combined Operations,* 293–94; West, *Mr. Lincoln's Navy,* 233–37; Wise, *Gate of Hell,* 30.

26. Ammen to Du Pont, 14 April 1863, *Annual Report 1863,* 208–9; Drayton to Hamilton, 15 April 1863, Drayton Papers, Rare Books and Manuscripts Division, New York Public Library; Diary, 6 May 1863 entry.

27. Bradford, *Captains,* 156, 266–67; Du Pont to Sophie Du Pont, 8 April 1863, *SFD,* 3:3–4; Du Pont to McKean, ca. 29 April 1863, *SFD,* 3:66.

28. Welles, *Diary,* 1:273–77.

29. Ibid., 265.

30. Bradford, *Captains,* 156–57; Burton, *Siege,* 142–43; MacBride, *Civil War Ironclads,* 31–32; West, *Gideon Welles,* 232–39; West, *Mr. Lincoln's Navy,* 237–39.

31. Du Pont to Biddle, 4 May 1863, *SFD,* 3:87.

32. Welles, *Diary,* 1:311–12; Welles to Du Pont, 3 June 1863, reproduced in U.S. Congress, House, *Report of the Secretary of the Navy in Relation to Armored Vessels,* H. ExDoc. 69, 38th Cong., 1st sess., 1864, 112.

33. Du Pont to Dahlgren, 24 November 1861 and 19 February 1863, box 5, DLC; Diary, 21 April 1863 entry.

34. Bradford, *Captains,* 134; Welles, *Diary,* 1:312–16.

35. Diary, 28–29 May 1863 entries; Welles, *Diary,* 1:317–18.

36. Welles, *Diary,* 1:317–18.

37. Diary, 2 June 1863 entry.

38. Ibid., 3 and 4 June 1863 entries.

39. Bradford, *Captains,* 131–33; Diary, 19–20 June 1863 entries.

40. [Dahlgren] to Fox, 9 April 1863, box 5, DLC; Diary, 21–24 June 1863 entries; Welles, *Diary,* 1:337–38.

41. Welles, *Diary,* 1:341.

42. Albion, *Makers of Naval Policy,* 147–48; Grimes to Du Pont, 1 July 1863, *SFD,* 3:191.

43. Diary, 24–26 June 1863 entries; Dahlgren to Ulric Dahlgren, 22 June 1863, box 19, DLC; Dahlgren to [Wise], 27 June 1863, box 5, DLC.

44. Diary, 3 May 1858 and 27–30 June 1863 entries. Dahlgren's other daughter, Lizzie, had died in May 1858 of consumption at age seventeen.

45. Drayton to Wise, 25 October 1863, WNYHS.

46. Bradford, *Captains,* 267; Heitzmann, "Ironclad *Weehawken,*" 193–202; Welles, *Diary,* 1:342; U.S. Congress, Senate, *Report to the Joint Committee on the Conduct of the War: Heavy Ordnance,* S. Rep. 121, 38th Cong., 2d sess., 1865, 130–31; Dahlgren to Patty Dahlgren, 25 June 1863, DNLC; Dahlgren to Welles, 29 June 1863, box 8, DLC.

Chapter 18. Morris Island and Fort Sumter

1. "Distribution of the Vessels of the South Atlantic Blockading Squadron," 15 July 1863, box 5, DLC; Dahlgren to Welles, 28 January 1864, *ORN*, I:14:590–601; Dahlgren, General Order, 17 June 1865, box 28, DLC; Diary, 17 June 1865 entry.
2. Dahlgren to Welles, 1 August 1863, box 8, DLC.
3. Dahlgren, *Shells and Shell Guns*, 312–14, 387, 390, 405, 412; Dahlgren, "Attack on the Barrier Forts China by Captain Foote," 1856 folder, box 24, DLC.
4. Millett and Maslowski, *For the Common Defense*, 204; Randall and Donald, *Civil War*, 463–64; Reed, *Combined Operations*, 295–98.
5. *DAB*, s.v. "Gillmore, Quincy Adams"; Wise, *Gate of Hell*, 33.
6. Diary, 7–8 October 1863 entries.
7. Wise, *Gate of Hell*, 33–34.
8. Reed, *Combined Operations*, xix; Johnson and Buel, *Battles and Leaders*, 4:54–55; Gillmore, *Engineer and Artillery Operations*, 12–18; Gillmore to Cullum, 28 February 1864, *ORA*, I:28:1:5.
9. Diary, 6 July 1863 entry.
10. Welles to Du Pont, 6 June 1863, *ORN*, I:14:241; Du Pont to Welles, 11 April 1864, *ORN*, I:14:242; Welles to Dahlgren, 15 July 1863, *ORN*, I:14:343; Dahlgren to Welles, 16 October 1865, *ORN*, I:16:443.
11. Welles, *Diary*, 1:338.
12. McPherson, *Battle Cry of Freedom*, 406.
13. For examples of this confusion, see Dahlgren to Welles, 16 October 1865, *ORN*, I:16:442–44; Welles, *Diary*, 1:309, 313–14, 324, 330–31; Gillmore to Cullum, 28 February 1864, *ORA*, I:28:1:7.
14. Madeleine Dahlgren, *Memoir*, 392–93, 525–26; Diary, 4 and 5 July 1863 entries; Dahlgren to Welles, 6 July 1863, *ORN*, I:14:311; Dahlgren to Welles, 16 October 1865, *ORN*, I:16:442–43.
15. *CWNC*, III:112–13; Dahlgren, diary extract, 10 July 1863, *ORN*, I:14:325–26; Gillmore, *Engineer and Artillery Operations*, 26–31.
16. Burton, *Siege*, 158; Jones, *Siege*, 220; Wise, *Gate of Hell*, 78; Diary, 11 July 1863 entry; Gillmore, *Engineer and Artillery Operations*, 32; Dahlgren to Gillmore, 11 July 1863, *ORN*, I:14:319; Dahlgren to Welles, 12 July 1863, *ORN*, I:14:319–21; Welles, *Diary*, 1:380–81.
17. Burton, *Siege*, 161; Jones, *Siege*, 222–23; Wise, *Gate of Hell*, 80–81.
18. Burton, *Siege*, 162–71; Gillmore, *Engineer and Artillery Operations*, 34–42; Reed, *Combined Operations*, 307; Wise, *Gate of Hell*, 95–96; Diary, 18 July 1863 entry; Dahlgren to Welles, 19 July 1863, *ORN*, I:14:359–60.
19. Burton, *Siege*, 171–78.
20. Wise, *Gate of Hell*, 137–38.
21. Reed, *Combined Operations*, 308; Jones, *Siege*, 264.
22. Wise, *Gate of Hell*, 156–58.
23. For army-navy cooperation, see diary extracts, log extracts, and reports, 17–23 August 1863, *ORN*, I:14:472–509, and correspondence between Dahlgren and Gillmore, 19–21 August 1863, *ORA*, I:28:2:48–56; Dahlgren to Gillmore, 22 August 1863, *ORA*, I:28:2:54–55.

24. Gillmore to Dahlgren, 23 August 1863, *ORA*, I:28:2:56.

25. Dahlgren to Gillmore, 24 August 1863, *ORN*, I:14:506–7; "Extract from Diary of Rear-Admiral Dahlgren," 22–23 August 1863, *ORN*, I:14:507.

26. Gillmore to Dahlgren, 23 August 1863, *ORA*, I:28:2:56.

27. Gillmore, *Engineer and Artillery Operations*, 63–67, 324–25.

28. Reed, *Combined Operations*, 310–11; Wise, *Gate of Hell*, 150–51; Dahlgren to Welles, 28 January 1864, *ORN*, I:14:594–97.

29. Reed, *Combined Operations*, 310; Dahlgren to Welles, 28 January 1864, *ORN*, I:14:592–93.

30. Perry, *Infernal Machines*, 61–62, 168; Welles, *Diary*, 1:296; Ripley to Gillmore, 19 July and 16 August 1865, box 6, DLC; Dahlgren to Welles, 16 October 1865, *ORN*, I:16:430–34.

31. Dahlgren, "Order, No. 34," 26 August 1863, Orders to South Atlantic Blockading Squadron, HSPA; Diary, 26 August 1863 entry; Dahlgren to Gillmore, 27 August 1863, *ORN*, I:14:520.

32. Dahlgren to Gillmore, 29 August 1863, *ORN*, I:14:525; Dahlgren to Welles, 16 October 1865, *ORN*, I:16:430.

33. Reed, *Combined Operations*, 385.

34. "Extract from Diary of Rear-Admiral Dahlgren," 1 September 1863, *ORN*, I:14:566; Dahlgren to Welles, 2 September 1863, *ORN*, I:14:531–33.

35. Reed, *Combined Operations*, 309–10; Wise, *Gate of Hell*, 189; Dahlgren to Gillmore, 3 September 1863, *ORN*, I:14:534; Gillmore to Dahlgren, 3 September 1863, *ORN*, I:14:534–35.

36. Burton, *Siege*, 178–80; Jones, *Siege*, 268–73; Johnson and Buel, *Battles and Leaders*, 63–64.

37. Gillmore to Dahlgren, 7 September 1863, 5:10 A.M., *ORA*, I:28:2:86.

38. Diary, 7 September 1863 entry.

39. Burton, *Siege*, 194–97; Reed, *Combined Operations*, 312–14; various communications between Dahlgren and Gillmore, 8 September 1863, *ORN*, I:14:608–10; Diary, 8 September 1863 entry.

40. Belknap, "Reminiscent of the Siege of Charleston," 189; Reed, *Combined Operations*, 312–13; Wise, *Gate of Hell*, 97, 205–9.

41. Burton, *Siege*, 195–97; Dahlgren to Welles, 11 September 1863, *ORN*, I:14:610–11; Gillmore to Cullum, 28 February 1864, *ORN*, I:14:636.

42. Diary, 8–9 September 1863 entries; Dahlgren to Welles, 11 September 1863, *ORN*, I:14:610–11; Welles, *Diary*, 1:434–35; Du Pont to Davis, 18 September 1863, *SFD*, 3:239; Dahlgren to Fox, 24 September 1863, *ORN*, I:14:671–72.

43. Diary, 12, 15, 26, and 28 August, 2 and 19 September 1863 entries.

44. Wise to Dahlgren, 4 September 1863, box 6, DLC; Dahlgren to Wise, 22 September 1863, WNYHS; Dahlgren to Ulric Dahlgren, 30 September 1863, box 19, DLC.

45. Diary, 27 September 1863 entry.

46. *CWNC*, III-143–44; Roland, *Underwater Warfare*, 162–63.

47. Perry, *Infernal Machines*, 85; Diary, 5–6 October 1863 entries.

48. Diary, 6 October 1863 entry; Dahlgren to Welles, 7 October 1863, *ORN*, I:15:10–11; Dahlgren to Fox, 7 October 1863, box 6, DLC.

49. Dahlgren to Welles, 29 September 1863, *ORN*, I:14:680–81; Dahlgren to Welles, 18 October 1863, *ORN*, I:15:52–53.

50. Welles to Dahlgren, 9 October 1863, *ORN,* I:15:26–27.

51. "Gen. Gillmore and Admiral Dahlgren," *Army and Navy Journal* 1 (31 October 1863); Welles, *Diary,* 1:434–35; Du Pont to Davis, 18 September 1863 and 3 March 1864, *SFD,* 3:239, 316.

52. Dahlgren to Ulric Dahlgren, 22 September 1863, box 19, DLC.

53. Dahlgren to Welles, 2 September 1863, *ORN,* I:14:531–33; Johnson and Buel, *Battles and Leaders,* 4:67.

54. Quoted in Wise, *Gate of Hell,* 189.

55. Gillmore to Dahlgren, 27 September 1863, *ORN,* I:14:675; Dahlgren to Gillmore, 29 September 1863, *ORN,* I:14:683.

56. Jones, *Siege,* 290–91; Gillmore to Dahlgren, 17 October 1863, *ORN,* I:15:49–50; Dahlgren to Welles, 17 October 1863, box 6, DLC; Dahlgren to Gillmore, 18 October 1863, *ORN,* I:15:56–57; Diary, 22 October 1863 entry; unsigned document, 22 October 1863, box 6, DLC.

57. Welles to Dahlgren, 2 November 1863, *ORN,* I:15:96–97; Diary, 8 November 1863 entry.

58. Diary, 11 and 13 November 1863 entries; Dahlgren to Welles, 15 November 1863, *ORN,* I:15:114–15.

59. Du Pont to Grimes, 11 September 1863, *SFD,* 3:235–36; Dahlgren to Wise, 18 October 1863, WNYHS.

60. Diary, 11 and 19 October 1863 entries; Dahlgren to Ulric Dahlgren, 19 October 1863, box 19, DLC; Dahlgren to Welles, 20 October 1863, *ORN,* I:15:63.

61. Welles, *Diary,* 1:474–75.

62. Dahlgren to Welles, 29 December 1863, *ORN,* I:15:212–13.

63. Belknap, "Reminiscent of the Siege of Charleston," 205.

64. Lincoln to Stanton, 21 December 1863, *Collected Works of Abraham Lincoln,* 7:84; Wise to Dahlgren, 23 December 1863, DS.

65. Wilson, *Ironclads in Action,* 1:100–101; Luce, "Naval Administration, III," 818.

66. Wise to Dahlgren, 1 September 1863, box 6, DLC; Wise to Dahlgren, 10 September and 6 October 1863, WNYHS.

67. Welles, *Diary,* 1:440, 520.

68. Wise to Dahlgren, 23 December 1863, DS.

69. Dahlgren to [?], 13 January [1864], box 3, War 1861–65, NYHS.

70. Diary, 31 December 1863 entry.

Chapter 19. Stalemate

1. Braudy, *Frenzy of Renown,* 28.

2. Welles to Dahlgren, 11 January 1864, *ORN,* I:15:236–37; Dahlgren, journal note, 16 January [1864], box 27, DLC; Diary, 16 January 1864 entry.

3. Diary, 16 January 1864 entry.

4. Dahlgren to Wise, 29 November 1863, WNYHS.

5. Reed, *Combined Operations,* 314–16; Diary, 4 and 29 March, 18–24 April 1864 entries.

6. Luce, "Naval Administration, III," 816.

7. Perry, *Infernal Machines*, 86; Werlich, *Admiral of the Amazon*, 57.

8. Diary, 7 January 1864 entry; Order of Rear-Admiral Dahlgren, 7 January 1864, *ORN*, I:15:226–27; Dahlgren to Welles, 13 January 1864, *ORN*, I:15:238–39.

9. Werlich, *Admiral of the Amazon*, 59; Higginson to Dahlgren, 18 February 1864, *ORN*, I:15:328; Dahlgren to Welles, 19 February 1864, *ORN*, I:15:329–30; Diary, 19 February 1864 entry.

10. Dahlgren to Welles, 19 February 1864, *ORN*, I:15:329–30.

11. Diary, 20 February 1864 entry; Dahlgren to Ulric Dahlgren, 20 February 1864, DNLC.

12. Werlich, *Admiral of the Amazon*, 59; Dahlgren to Welles, 19 February 1864, *ORN*, I:15:329–30.

13. Perry, *Infernal Machines*, 168; Dahlgren, "Order No. 45," 7 September 1863, Orders to South Atlantic Blockading Squadron, HSPA; Dahlgren to Fox, 24 September 1863, *ORN*, I:14:671–72; Dahlgren to Welles, 21 December 1863, *ORN*, I:15:185; Johnson to Dahlgren, 1 February 1864, box 6, DLC; Dahlgren to Welles, 18 February 1864, box 6, DLC; Dahlgren to Dichman, 21 May 1864, *ORN*, I:15:437; Dahlgren to Welles, 19 October 1864, *ORN*, I:16:19–25; Diary, 15 December 1864 entry; Dahlgren to Welles, 16 January and 1 June 1865, *ORN*, I:16:171–75, 380–89. The *Patapsco* incident occurred on 15 January 1865.

14. Diary, 21 February 1864 entry.

15. Dahlgren to Welles, 18 February 1864, box 6, DLC; Dahlgren to Ulric Dahlgren, 20 February 1864, DNLC.

16. Welles to Dahlgren, 15 February 1864, Cabinet Members' Letters, Louis A. Warren Lincoln Library and Museum; Diary, 23 and 27 February 1864 entries.

17. Diary, 2 March 1864 entry.

18. Ibid., 3–4 March 1864 entries.

19. Ibid., 5 March 1864 entry; Dahlgren, "Memorandum," [?] March 1864, box 27, DLC.

20. Welles, *Diary*, 1:520.

21. Dahlgren, document titled "Memorandum," [?] March 1864, box 27, DLC; Diary, 29 March 1864 entry.

22. Diary, 8 March 1864 entry.

23. Jones, *Eight Hours before Richmond*, 31–33; Wilson and Fiske, *Appleton's Cyclopaedia of American Biography*, s.v. "Dahlgren, Ulric"; Dahlgren, *Memoir of Ulric Dahlgren*, 11–47, 68, 179; Macartney, *Mr. Lincoln's Admirals*, 164; Diary, 29 May, 28 September 1862, 20 and 22 July, 7 August 1863 entries; Lincoln to Stanton, 6 June 1862, *Collected Works of Abraham Lincoln*, 5:262; Dahlgren to Ulric Dahlgren, 15 and 23 June 1863, box 19, DLC; Wise to Dahlgren, 16 July 1863, box 5, DLC; Dahlgren to Ulric Dahlgren, 20 July 1863, box 19, DLC; Dahlgren to Wise, 29 July 1863, WNYHS; Dahlgren to Ulric Dahlgren, 19 August 1863, box 19, DLC.

24. Dahlgren to Ulric Dahlgren, 20 July 1863, box 19, DLC; Dahlgren to Wise, 29 July 1863, WNYHS.

25. Dahlgren, *Memoir of Ulric Dahlgren*, 175, 255; Jones, *Eight Hours before Richmond*, 32. For Ulric Dahlgren's relationship with Lincoln, see, for example, Diary, 3 September 1862 entry.

26. Dahlgren to Ulric Dahlgren, 19 August 1863, box 19, DLC.

27. Dahlgren, journal note about the first time he saw Ulric after the amputation, box 19, DLC.

28. Diary, 13 November 1863 entry; Ulric Dahlgren, notes dated 25 November 1863, box 19, DLC.

29. Ulric Dahlgren to Wise, 13 December 1863, WNYHS.

30. Jones, *Eight Hours before Richmond*, vii–viii, 91; Thomas, "Kilpatrick-Dahlgren Raid," 4–5.

31. Quoted in Macartney, *Mr. Lincoln's Admirals*, 165.

32. Welles, *Diary*, 1:538.

33. Diary, 8 March 1864 entry.

34. Dahlgren, *Memoir of Ulric Dahlgren*, 227; Jones, *Eight Hours before Richmond*, 99–126; Diary, 9–10 March 1864 entries.

35. Jones, *Eight Hours before Richmond*, 123–39; Diary, 9, 10, and 16 March 1864 entries.

36. Diary, 15–16 July 1864 entries; Dahlgren to Patty Dahlgren, 6 May 1867, DNLC.

37. Dahlgren to Patty Dahlgren, 3 June 1858 and 10 March 1864, DNLC; Diary, 3 May 1858 and 9–15 March 1864 entries.

38. Diary, 17–24 March 1864 entries; unprovenanced article titled "A Boy Hero" in Charles B. Dahlgren scrapbook, DFP; Sullivan, "Sacrificial Limb."

39. Diary, 25 March 1864 entry.

40. Sedgwick to Wise, 2 July 1863 and 30 July [1863], WNYHS; Townsend to Wise, 15 September 1863, WNYHS; Missroon to Wise, 9 March 1864, WNYHS; Diary, 29 March 1864 entry; Watkinson to Wise, 25 April 1864, WNYHS.

41. Welles, *Diary*, 2:7.

42. Diary, 5–17 April 1864 entries.

43. Welles, *Diary*, 2:7; Diary, 18 April 1864 entry.

44. Diary, 29 March and 18–24 April 1864 entries; Welles to Stanton, 21 April 1864, *ORN*, I:15:408–9; Welles to Dahlgren, 23 April 1864, *ORN*, I:15:412.

45. Jones, *Eight Hours before Richmond*, 141; Diary, 26 April 1864 and 5 May 1869 entries.

46. Diary, 28 April–2 May 1864 entries.

47. Ibid., 3–4 May 1864 entries.

48. Ibid., 14 and 28 January 1864 entries; Welles, *Diary*, 1:547.

49. Belknap, "Reminiscent of the Siege of Charleston," 196–97; Diary, 6, 8–10, and 17 May 1864 entries.

50. Dahlgren, "Memoranda for Consideration," 9 May 1864, box 27, DLC; Dahlgren to Welles, 14 May 1864, *ORN*, I:15:430–32.

51. Luce, "Naval Administration, III," 819.

52. Diary, 10–12 May 1864 entries; Dahlgren to Welles, 14 May 1864, *ORN*, I:15:430–32.

53. Diary, 21 and 25 August 1863, 2 and 21 February 1864 entries.

54. Dahlgren to Welles, 14 May 1864, *ORN*, I:15:430–32; Diary, 17 May 1864 entry.

55. Wise, *Lifeline of the Confederacy*, 121–24, 251–59; Wise, *Gate of Hell*, 214.

56. Dahlgren, order of 21 June 1864, Orders to South Atlantic Blockading Squadron, HSPA; Dahlgren to Welles, 4 August 1863, box 8, DLC; for examples of ship-movement letters, see May–July 1863 folders in box 5, DLC.

57. Diary, 24 October 1863, 12 and 17 August 1864 entries; Dahlgren to Patty Dahlgren, 4 June and 11 October 1864, DNLC.

58. Joshua D. Warren, "Journal of Joshua D. Warren," 7–8 July 1864 and June 1870 entries, box 8, Civil War ZO files, Operational Archives, Naval Historical Center.

59. Diary, 30 July 1863 entry; Dahlgren to Welles, 4 August 1863, box 8, DLC; Dahlgren

to Welles, 22 September 1863, *ORN,* I:14:658–59; Dahlgren to Welles, 21 June 1865, *ORN,* I:16:348–49. Alfred Thayer Mahan served as Dahlgren's ordnance officer from October 1864 to May 1865. See Seager, *Alfred Thayer Mahan,* 40–41.

60. Kuly to Dahlgren, 10 July 1863, box 5, DLC; Dahlgren, order of 24 October 1863, *ORN,* I:15:70; Diary, 10 and 21 December 1863, 31 May 1864 entries; Rowan to Welles, 1 July 1864, Stephen Clegg Rowan Papers, Naval Historical Foundation Collection, Manuscripts Division, Library of Congress; Dahlgren, order of 24 August 1864, Orders to South Atlantic Blockading Squadron, HSPA; Dahlgren to Welles, 24 August 1864, *ORN,* I:15:644–45.

61. Diary, 30 July 1863 entry; Dahlgren to the crews of the monitors, 16 August 1863, *ORN,* I:14:444; Dahlgren, order of 18 August 1863, Orders to South Atlantic Blockading Squadron, HSPA; Dahlgren to Dorrance, 22 September 1863, box 8, DLC; Dahlgren to Welles, 17 November 1863, *ORN,* I:15:117–20; Dahlgren, announcement to the fleet, 17 May 1864, box 6, DLC; Dahlgren, orders of 15 and 17 August 1864, Orders to South Atlantic Blockading Squadron, HSPA.

62. Dahlgren to Bridge, 30 July 1863, box 8, DLC; Dahlgren to Welles, 9 August 1863, *ORN,* I:14:431–32; Dahlgren, orders of 11 August 1863, 23 and 28 June, 14 July 1864, Orders to South Atlantic Blockading Squadron, HSPA.

63. Ely, "This Filthy Ironpot," 46–47; Still, "Common Sailor," 39.

64. Still, "Common Sailor," 37; Wise, *Gate of Hell,* 151; Dahlgren to Clymer, 17 July 1863, box 8, DLC; Dahlgren to Bradford, 17 July 1863, box 8, DLC; Dahlgren to Welles, 20 July 1863, *ORN,* I:14:376; Diary, 13 August 1863 entry.

65. Receipt for Dahlgren from Thomas R. Patton, box 27, DLC; Dahlgren to Patty Dahlgren, 11 July 1864, DNLC; Diary, 9 October and 23 November 1864 entries.

66. Albion, *Makers of Naval Policy,* 104–7; Reid, "Historians and the Joint Committee," 319; Williams, "Navy and the Committee," 1751–55.

67. Albion, *Makers of Naval Policy,* 198; Bradford, *Captains,* 157; Coletta, *American Secretaries of the Navy,* 1:341–43; Henig, "Admiral Samuel F. DuPont," 72–73.

68. Bradford, *Captains,* 157; Coletta, *American Secretaries of the Navy,* 1:341–43.

69. Welles to Dahlgren, 12 January 1864, Cabinet Members' Letters, Louis A. Warren Lincoln Library and Museum.

70. Diary, 21 January 1864 entry; Dahlgren to Welles, 28 January 1864, *ORN,* I:14:590–601; Dahlgren to [?], 28 May 1864, Ferdinand J. Dreer Autograph Collection, HSPA.

71. Dahlgren to Welles, 28 January 1864, *ORN,* I:14:590–601.

72. Coletta, *American Secretaries of the Navy,* 1:341–42; U.S. Congress, House, *Report of the Secretary of the Navy in Relation to Armored Vessels,* H. ExDoc. 69, 38th Cong., 1st sess., 1864.

73. Williams, "Navy and the Committee," 1752; Dahlgren to [?], 28 May 1864, Ferdinand J. Dreer Autograph Collection, HSPA.

74. Dahlgren to [?], 28 May 1864, Ferdinand J. Dreer Autograph Collection, HSPA.

75. Dahlgren to Wade, 20 June 1864, box 27, DLC; U.S. Congress, Senate, *Operations against Charleston,* S. Rep. 142, 38th Cong., 2d sess., 1864.

76. Welles to Dahlgren, 15 July 1864, Cabinet Members' Letters, Louis A. Warren Lincoln Library and Museum; Diary, 22 July 1864 entry.

77. Welles, *Diary,* 1:62 and 2:128–29, 147.

78. Potter, *Sea Power,* 150.

79. Ibid.; Welles to Dahlgren, 9 September 1864, box 6, DLC; Diary, 21 October 1864 entry.

80. Dahlgren to Wise, [?] September 1864, WNYHS; Dahlgren to Welles, 10 November 1864, *ORN,* I:16:49–50.

81. Diary, 16 November 1864 entry; Dahlgren to Welles, 20 November 1864, box 27, DLC. After the war Dahlgren learned that all of the 9-, 10-, and 11-inch Dahlgren guns in service had been cast solid. Only the 15-inchers, a few experimental 16,000-pound 10-inchers, and an experimental 12,000-pound 9-incher had been cast by Rodman's method. The latter two types were designed for use against ironclads but never saw service. See Diary, 27 March 1865 entry; Aulick to Dahlgren, 17 July 1865, box 6, DLC.

82. Diary, 24 May 1864 entry.

Chapter 20. The Fall of Charleston and the End of the War

1. Welles to Dahlgren, 22 November 1864, *ORN,* I:16:57; Dahlgren, general order, 22 November 1864, *ORN,* I:16:58–59.

2. Diary, 25 November 1864 entry.

3. Diary, 12–15 December 1864 entries; Dahlgren to Welles, 12 December 1864, *ORN,* I:16:127–28; Dahlgren to Lincoln, 12 December 1864, *ORN,* I:16:127.

4. Sherman, *Memoirs,* 1:225, 2:203.

5. Diary, 12–15 December 1864 entries.

6. Davis, *Sherman's March,* 106; Diary, 14–15 December 1864 entries.

7. Davis, *Sherman's March,* 102–19; Dahlgren to Fillebrown, 13 December 1864, *ORN,* I:16:129–30; Dahlgren to Scott, 13 December 1864, *ORN,* I:16:130; Dahlgren to Welles, 23 December 1864, *ORN,* I:16:140–42.

8. Sherman, *Memoirs,* 2:231.

9. Ibid., 1:225.

10. Luce, "Naval Administration, III," 820.

11. Burton, *Siege,* 313; Davis, *Sherman's March,* 139; Diary, 2–15 January 1865 entries; Dahlgren to Welles, 4 January 1865, *ORN,* I:16:156–58; Dahlgren, general instructions, 15 January 1865, *ORN,* I:16:169; Sherman to [Dahlgren], undated, 1865 folder, box 6, DLC.

12. Diary, 15 January 1865 entry.

13. *CWNC,* V-18, V-27; Dahlgren to Welles, 22 January 1865, *ORN,* I:16:185; Diary, 18–24 January 1865 entries.

14. Diary, 6 February 1865 entry.

15. Gillmore, *Engineer and Artillery Operations.*

16. Quoted in Madeleine Dahlgren, *Memoir,* 516–17.

17. Diary, 7 February 1865 entry; Dahlgren to Welles, 7 February 1865, DS; Dahlgren to Patty Dahlgren, 7 February 1865, DNLC.

18. Diary, 11 February 1865 entry.

19. Burton, *Siege,* 314–17; *CWNC,* IV-14, 62–63, 138, 142, 150 and V-6, 11, 37, 39–40; Diary, 1–11 July 1864 entries.

20. Diary, 11–15 February 1865 entries; Dahlgren to Welles, 14 February 1865, *ORN,* I:16:243–44.

21. "Monthly Record of Current Events," *Harper's New Monthly Magazine* 30 (April 1865): 668; Burton, *Siege,* 317–20.

22. Diary, 17–18 February 1865 entries; Dahlgren to Welles, 18 February 1865, *ORN,* I:16:250; Dahlgren to Patty Dahlgren, 18 February 1865, DNLC.

23. Horsfield, *Art of Leadership,* 160–70; Linderman, *Embattled Courage,* 7–22.

24. Badger to Dahlgren, 12 April 1865, box 6, DLC; Schimmelfennig to Dahlgren, 10 April 1865, Schoff Civil War Collection, Manuscripts Department, William L. Clements Library, University of Michigan; Diary, 20 April 1865 entry; Cowley to Madeleine Dahlgren, 2 August 1870, box 7, DLC; Joshua D. Warren, "Journal of Joshua D. Warren," 11 September 1864 entry, box 8, Civil War ZO files, Operational Archives, Naval Historical Center.

25. Diary, 15 January 1865 entry.

26. *CWNC,* V-31; Sweetman, *American Naval History,* 81–82, 85.

27. Porter, *Naval History of the Civil War,* 769.

28. Dahlgren to Welles, 1 June 1865, *ORN,* I:16:380–89; Dahlgren to Faxon, 24 August 1865, DUSNAM.

29. Jones, *Siege,* 289; Gillmore to Ripley, 17 July 1865, box 6, DLC; Ripley to Gillmore, 19 July 1865, box 6, DLC; Gillmore to Ripley, 15 August 1865, box 6, DLC; Ripley to Gillmore, 16 August 1865, box 6, DLC.

30. Dahlgren to Welles, 25 and 28 February 1865, *ORN,* I:16:272, 273–75, 301–2.

31. Dahlgren to Welles, 8 and 12 March 1865, *ORN,* I:16:288, 291; Diary, 17 March 1865 entry; Dahlgren to Welles, 21 March and 10 April 1865, *ORN,* I:16:296–97, 311; Gray to Dahlgren, 15 May 1865, box 6, DLC; Dahlgren to Welles, 21 June 1865, box 6, DLC.

32. Diary, 1 March 1865 entry; Dahlgren to Welles, 1 March 1865, *ORN,* I:16:282–83; abstract log of the USS *Harvest Moon,* 1 March 1865, *ORN,* I:16:283–84.

33. Dahlgren to Gillmore, 27 February 1865, box 6, DLC; Gillmore to Dahlgren, 1 March 1865, box 6, DLC; Dahlgren to Gillmore, 11 March 1865, box 6, DLC; Gillmore to Dahlgren, 19 March 1865, box 6, DLC; Dahlgren to Gillmore, 27 March 1865, box 6, DLC.

34. Diary, 8 June 1865 entry; Dahlgren to Patty Dahlgren, 12 March 1865, DNLC.

35. Diary, 31 March, 1 and 25 April 1865 entries; Dahlgren to Patty Dahlgren, 30 April 1865, DNLC.

36. Cowley, *Leaves from a Lawyer's Life,* 182–85; Stanton, General Order No. 50, 27 March 1865, *ORN,* I:16:314–15; Welles to Dahlgren, 28 March 1865, *ORN,* I:16:314; Dahlgren, General Order, 5 April 1865, *ORN,* I:16:315–16; Dahlgren, General Orders, 10 and 13 April 1865, box 37, DLC; Diary, 14 April 1865 entry.

37. Oates, *With Malice toward None,* 426–34; Diary, 19 April 1865 entry; Dahlgren, General Orders, 19 and 21 April 1865, box 37, DLC; Dahlgren to Welles, 22 April 1865, *ORN,* I:16:319.

38. Diary, 10 May and 6 June 1865 entries; Dahlgren to Patty Dahlgren, 24 and 25 May 1865, DNLC; Fox to Dahlgren, 31 May 1865, *ORN,* I:16:340.

39. Diary, 14–16 June 1865 entries; Dahlgren, General Order, 17 June 1865, box 28, DLC.
40. Diary, 17 and 21 June 1865 entries.
41. Ibid., 22 June–12 July 1865 entries.

CHAPTER 21. WASHINGTON AND SOUTH AMERICA

1. Brandt to Wise, 16 July 1865, WNYHS.
2. Aulick to Wise, 17 July 1865, WNYHS.
3. Dahlgren to Cist, 27 July 1865, DUSNAM.
4. *DAB,* s.v. "Dahlgren, Madeleine Vinton"; Sherman to Madeleine Dahlgren, 5 September 1875, box 7, DLC; "The Voice of the Voiceless: Mrs. Dahlgren's Argument against Woman Suffrage," *The Post,* 7 March 1878, scrapbook, MVDG; "Mrs. Dahlgren's New Novel," *Chicago Tribune,* 8 September 1886, scrapbook, MVDG; "How to Behave in Society: Mrs. Admiral Dahlgren Gives Advice to Debutantes," *New York World,* 18 November 1888, scrapbook, MVDG; *New York Times,* 17 October 1914, 8.
5. Madeleine Dahlgren to Patty Dahlgren, 10 July 1864, DNHFC; Diary, 15 November 1864 and 24 June 1865 entries; Smith to Dahlgren, 1 December 1864, box 6, DLC; Sherman to Dahlgren, 9 August 1865, box 6, DLC.
6. Aulick to Wise, 8 August 1865, WNYHS; Fox to Farragut, 28 September 1865, WNYHS.
7. Gillmore, *Engineer and Artillery Operations,* 63–66; Dahlgren to Welles, 16 October 1865, *ORN,* I:16:429–55.
8. John A. Dahlgren, "Vindication of Colonel Ulric Dahlgren," *Army and Navy Journal* 1 (13 August 1864): 836–38.
9. Diary, 24 November 1864 entry.
10. Ibid., 2 March 1865 entry.
11. Beecher quoted in Dahlgren, *Memoir of Ulric Dahlgren,* 283; Welles to Dahlgren, 12 April 1865, box 6, DLC; Dahlgren to Patty Dahlgren, 18 April 1865, DNLC; Diary, 27 October–1 November 1865 entries; undated scrap from *City News,* box 35, DLC. The "little boys" were John, their fourth child, who had died in infancy, and Lawrence, their seventh child, who also died at an early age.
12. Diary, 14 December 1865 entry.
13. Ibid., 14 December 1865 and 23 January 1866 entries.
14. Ibid., 23–27 January 1866 entries.
15. Welles to Dahlgren, 15 February 1866, box 6, DLC; Diary, 20 and 26 February, 15 and 27 March 1866 entries; *Annual Report 1866,* 29–30.
16. Welles to Dahlgren, 11 May 1866, box 6, DLC; Dahlgren to Welles, 1 June 1866, box 6, DLC; Diary, 3 June 1866 entry; U.S. Congress, Senate, *Report of the Board of Visitors to the United States Naval Academy for the Year 1866,* S. ExDoc. 53, 39th Cong., 1st sess., 1865–66.
17. Wise to Dahlgren, 11 February 1864, box 6, DLC; Diary, 17 June and 5 November 1866 entries; Dahlgren to Ticknor and Fields, 11 August and 1 September 1868, box 7, DLC; Dahlgren, *Memoir of Ulric Dahlgren.*

18. Schneller, "Intentional Omissions," 6; Cowley to Madeleine Dahlgren, 2 August 1870, box 7, DLC; Madeleine Dahlgren to Cowley, 19 April 1880 and 10 March 1890, DS.

19. Dahlgren, undated manuscript titled "Memoir," 1866 folder, box 28, DLC; Dahlgren, "Sketch of Navy Boat Howitzers," 30 August 1866, box 28, DLC.

20. Diary, 24–31 July 1866 entries.

21. Ibid., 27 September–9 October 1866 entries; Welles to Dahlgren, 28 September 1866, box 6, DLC.

22. Dahlgren to Welles, 29 October 1866, box 6, DLC; Diary, 30 October, 4 and 8 November 1866, 14 September 1867 entries.

23. Braudy, *Frenzy of Renown*, 122–23; Virgil, *Aeneid*, book 2, line 5; Dahlgren to Patty Dahlgren, 14 January 1864, DNLC; Cluss to Dahlgren, 26 October 1866, box 6, DLC; Diary, 31 October 1866 entry.

24. Headley, *Farragut and Our Naval Commanders*, ix; Diary, 29 October 1866 entry.

25. Headley, *Farragut and Our Naval Commanders*, 456–95.

26. Dahlgren to Patty Dahlgren, 20 July 1864, DNLC; Diary, 12–14 November 1866 entries.

27. Karsten, *Naval Aristocracy*, 76.

28. Diary, 15–23 November and 1 December 1866 entries.

29. Letterbook 2, box 17, DLC; Dahlgren to Welles, 1 and 8 April 1867, DNYPL; *Annual Report 1866*, 20; *Annual Report 1867*, 13; *Annual Report 1868*, xvi.

30. Long, *Gold Braid*, 341, 413–16.

31. Dupuy and Dupuy, *Encyclopedia of Military History*, 912; Long, *Gold Braid*, 356–58.

32. Dahlgren to Welles, 12 December 1866, box 17, DLC.

33. Werlich, *Admiral of the Amazon*, 115–21; Diary, 22 November 1866 entry; "Memoir.— Captain Stanly & Mr. Tucker," 16 October–10 December 1866, box 28, DLC.

34. Werlich, *Admiral of the Amazon*, 115–25; Dahlgren to Welles, 12 October 1866, box 17, DLC; Diary, 13 January 1867 entry.

35. Werlich, *Admiral of the Amazon*, 115–25; Diary, 9 January 1867 entry; "Admiral Dahlgren and the Peruvian Admiral," *Army and Navy Journal* 4 (22 June 1867): 698.

36. Werlich, *Admiral of the Amazon*, 123–28; Diary, 2, 8, and 13 January, 6 and 11 February 1867 entries.

37. Welles, *Diary*, 3:37; Welles to Dahlgren, 18 March 1867, DNYPL.

38. Seward to Hovey, 18 March 1867, DNYPL; Welles to Dahlgren, 25 March 1867, DNYPL; Diary, 20 April 1867 entry.

39. Werlich, *Admiral of the Amazon*, 129–33; Diary, 27 March 1867 entry; Dahlgren to Welles, 22 April 1867, DNYPL.

40. Long, *Gold Braid*, 356–58; Werlich, *Admiral of the Amazon*, 122; Dahlgren to Kilpatrick, 5 March 1867, DNYPL; Dahlgren to Welles, 26 April 1867, DNYPL.

41. Diary, 5 January 1867 entry.

42. Dahlgren to Welles, 1 February 1867, box 17, DLC.

43. Madeleine Dahlgren, *Memoir*, 622; Welles, *Diary*, 3:92–93; Diary, 14 March, 6 May, 16–24 June, 20 July, and 14 September 1867 entries.

44. Diary, 31 July–2 August 1867 entries.

45. Diary, 6 October, 28 October–13 November 1867 entries; Dahlgren to Welles, 30 January 1868, box 17, DLC.

46. Madeleine Dahlgren, *Memoir,* 633–34; Dahlgren to Spicer, 22 January 1868, box 17, DLC.

47. Diary, 18–20 January 1868 entries; Dahlgren to Welles, 30 January 1868, box 17, DLC.

48. Diary, 20–22 January 1868 entries; Dahlgren to Brasher, 22 January 1868, box 17, DLC.

49. Dahlgren to Welles, 30 January 1868, box 17, DLC.

50. Dahlgren to Brasher, 25 February 1868, box 17, DLC; Dahlgren to Welles, 1 March 1868, box 17, DLC.

51. Madeleine Dahlgren, *Memoir,* 637; Diary, 29 March, 4 April, 24 June, 20 July, 10 and 24 August, 21 September, 9 October 1867, 28 May 1868 entries.

52. Diary, 30 June 1861 and 21 October 1867 entries.

53. Dickson, *National Cyclopaedia of American Biography,* and Johnson, *Twentieth Century Biographical Dictionary of Notable Americans,* s.v. "Dahlgren, Charles Bunker"; Dahlgren to Patty Dahlgren, 30 July 1864 and 6 May 1867, DNLC.

54. Dahlgren to Patty Dahlgren, 6 July and 11 September 1864, DNLC; Diary, 9 August and 21 October 1867 entries.

55. Diary, 8 September 1867 entry; Dahlgren to J. B. Rodman, 1 December 1867, box 6, DLC.

56. Madeleine Dahlgren, *Memoir,* 637–39; Diary, 28 May, 14 June, and 6 July 1868 entries.

57. "Obituary: Captain Henry A. Wise," *Army and Navy Journal* 6 (1 May 1869): 581; Diary, 30 April, 17 June, 2, 5, 9, and 10 July 1868 entries; Dahlgren to Patty Dahlgren, 18 August 1868, box 7, DLC.

58. Diary, 22–24 July 1868 entries.

CHAPTER 22. DAHLGREN'S STAR FADES

1. Diary, 31 July–1 August 1868 entries.

2. Buhl, "Mariners and Machines," 704–26; Harrod, "New Technology in the Old Navy," 5; Morison, *Men, Machines, and Modern Times,* 116–19; Sandler, "Navy in Decay," 138–40; Sprout and Sprout, *Rise of American Naval Power,* 165–75.

3. Porter, *Naval History of the Civil War,* 364.

4. *Annual Report 1863,* 843; "Naval Ordnance," *Army and Navy Journal* 2 (17 December 1864): 260; Jeffers to Wise, 25 August 1866, WNYHS.

5. Glasow, "Prelude," 17–18, 34–39, 50; "Naval Ordnance," *Army and Navy Journal* 2 (17 December 1864): 260; *Annual Report 1866,* 149.

6. Morison, *Men, Machines, and Modern Times,* 43.

7. Still, *Ironclad Captains,* 45–46; Diary, 3–6 August and 23 September 1868 entries.

8. Diary, 28 August 1868 entry.

9. Madeleine Dahlgren, *Memoir,* 640; Diary, 12 September 1868 entry.

10. Dahlgren to Davis, 1 September 1868, entry 2, RG74 NA; Dahlgren to Hoff, 5 September 1868, entry 2, RG74 NA; Dahlgren to Turner, 8 September 1868, entry 2, RG74 NA; Dahlgren to Haggerty, 11 September 1868, entry 2, RG74 NA; Dahlgren to Davis, 22 September 1868, entry 2, RG74 NA; Dahlgren to Davis, 12 November 1868, entry 2, RG74 NA; Dahlgren to Craven, 12 November 1868, entry 2, RG74 NA;

Dahlgren to Turner, 24 November 1868, entry 2, RG74 NA; Dahlgren to Pennock, 2 December 1868, entry 2, RG74 NA; Dahlgren to Wildes, 24 December 1868, entry 2, RG74 NA.

11. Glasow, "Prelude," 39–41.

12. *Annual Report 1868,* 71–73; Dahlgren, notes titled "Report for 1868," box 29, DLC.

13. Courtemanche, *No Need of Glory,* 161–62.

14. Dahlgren, notes titled "Report for 1868," box 29, DLC.

15. Courtemanche, *No Need of Glory,* 165–66.

16. Glasow, "Prelude," 18, 51–56.

17. U.S. Congress, Senate, *Report to the Joint Committee on the Conduct of the War: Heavy Ordnance,* S. Rep. 121, 38th Cong., 2d sess., 1865, 112–27; Wade to Dahlgren, 3 February 1864, box 6, DLC; Welles to Dahlgren, 5 February 1864, box 6, DLC; Dahlgren to Patty Dahlgren, 17 August 1864, DNLC.

18. Dahlgren to Fox, 14 February 1862, *Confidential Correspondence of Gustavus Vasa Fox,* 1:423–24.

19. Tucker, *Arming the Fleet,* 236.

20. Porter, *Naval History of the Civil War,* 726.

21. U.S. Congress, Senate, *Report of the Joint Committee on Ordnance on Experiments on Heavy Ordnance,* S. Rep. 266, 40th Cong., 3d sess., 1869, 159.

22. Ibid., 158.

23. Porter, *Naval History of the Civil War,* 361.

24. Dahlgren, "Memorandum," 20 December 1865, box 6, DLC.

25. Diary, 11 July 1864 entry; Dahlgren, "Memorandum," 20 December 1865, box 6, DLC.

26. Dahlgren, "Memorandum," 20 December 1865, box 6, DLC.

27. Headley, *Farragut and Our Naval Commanders,* 495.

28. U.S. Congress, Senate, *Report to the Joint Committee on the Conduct of the War: Heavy Ordnance,* S. Rep. 121, 38th Cong., 2d sess., 1865, 170.

29. Ibid., 172.

30. Holley, *Treatise on Ordnance and Armor,* 133.

31. Porter, *Naval History of the Civil War,* 361.

32. Boynton, *History of the Navy during the Rebellion,* 2:480–81.

33. "Naval Ordnance," letter to the editor, *Army and Navy Journal* 2 (21 January 1865): 342.

34. Belknap, "Reminiscent of the Siege of Charleston," 205.

35. U.S. Congress, Senate, *Report to the Joint Committee on the Conduct of the War: Heavy Ordnance,* S. Rep. 121, 38th Cong., 2d sess., 1865, 13, 24, 90–92.

36. "American Ordnance," *Army and Navy Journal* 4 (1 December 1866): 237.

37. Porter, *Naval History of the Civil War,* 361.

38. Glasow, "Prelude," 43–44; U.S. Congress, Senate, *Report of the Joint Committee on Ordnance on Experiments on Heavy Ordnance,* S. Rep. 266, 40th Cong., 3d sess., 1869, 1.

39. Welles, *Diary,* 3:122; Diary, 1 April 1863, 10 June 1865, 31 August 1868, and 15 February 1869 entries.

40. Tucker, *Arming the Fleet,* 236; Welles, *Diary,* 3:447–48; U.S. Congress, Senate, *Report to the Joint Committee on the Conduct of the War: Heavy Ordnance,* S. Rep. 121, 38th Cong., 2d sess., 1865, 1–6, 29, 132–38, 147–52; U.S. Congress, Senate, *Report of the*

Joint Committee on Ordnance on Experiments on Heavy Ordnance, S. Rep. 266, 40th Cong., 3d sess., 1869, 9–11.

41. U.S. Congress, Senate, *Communication of Norman Waird to the Joint Committee on the Conduct of the War upon the Subject of Great Guns,* S. MisDoc. 47, 38th Cong., 2d sess., 1865, 25–29; Dahlgren, notes titled "Waird's XV In Guns, Smooth-Bore," 1868 folder, box 29, DLC; U.S. Congress, House, *Norman Waird,* H. Rep. 6, 40th Cong., 3d sess., 1869, 1–18.

42. See various testimonies in U.S. Congress, Senate, *Report of the Joint Committee on Ordnance on Experiments on Heavy Ordnance,* S. Rep. 266, 40th Cong., 3d sess., 1869: French quotation, 61; Gillmore quotations, 42–44; Rodman testimony, 63–89; Waird testimony, 37–39 and 102–17; Ames testimony, 9–11.

43. Welles, *Diary,* 3:447–49, 451; Diary, 2–16 October 1868 entries.

44. Welles, *Diary,* 3:484–85, 562; Dahlgren, notes titled "Naval Administration" [1869], "Writings—Misc. Fragments" folder, box 2, DS.

45. Diary, 22 December 1868 entry; Howard to Dahlgren, 24 December 1868 and Dahlgren to Howard, 11 February 1869, in U.S. Congress, Senate, *Report of the Joint Committee on Ordnance on Experiments on Heavy Ordnance,* S. Rep. 266, 40th Cong., 3d sess., 1869, 122–23.

46. Testimony of Rear-Admiral Dahlgren, 28 January 1869, U.S. Congress, Senate, *Report of the Joint Committee on Ordnance on Experiments on Heavy Ordnance,* S. Rep. 266, 40th Cong., 3d sess., 1869, 89–97.

47. Diary, 11 February 1869 entry. Dahlgren's written reply is in U.S. Congress, Senate, *Report of the Joint Committee on Ordnance on Experiments on Heavy Ordnance,* S. Rep. 266, 40th Cong., 3d sess., 1869, 123–48.

48. U.S. Congress, Senate, *Report of the Joint Committee on Ordnance on Experiments on Heavy Ordnance,* S. Rep. 266, 40th Cong., 3d sess., 1869, 1–7.

49. Diary, 15 February 1869 entry.

50. Dahlgren, undated letter, 1869 folder, box 29, DLC.

51. Diary, 4 March 1869 entry.

52. Bradford, *Captains,* 230–45; Borie to Dahlgren, 12 March 1869, entry 16, RG74 NA.

53. Diary, 10 and 30 March, 12 July, 10 August 1869 entries; Robeson to Dahlgren, 23 July 1869, entry 16, RG74 NA.

54. Dahlgren, undated notes, 1868 folder, box 29, DLC. For the creation of the professional enlisted service, see Harrod, *Manning the New Navy.*

55. Diary, 13 November 1869 entry; Eva Dahlgren to Dahlgren, 21 November 1869, DD.

56. Dahlgren to Patty Dahlgren, 18 August 1868, box 7, DLC; Diary, 24 May, 8 June, and 20 September 1869 entries; Dahlgren to Cox, 30 September 1869, Society Collection, John A. Dahlgren folder, HSPA.

57. Diary, 15 and 21 October 1868, 16–23 January, 5 May 1869, 29 January 1870 entries; Dahlgren to Eva Dahlgren, 28 January 1870, DFP; Dahlgren to Read, 5 and 20 February 1870, DNLC.

58. Diary, 16 March 1870 entry.

59. Sherman to Dahlgren, 4 August 1868, box 7, DLC; Dahlgren to Read, 18 and 25 August 1868, box 7, DLC.

60. Diary, 9 November 1865 entry; Dahlgren to Read, 11 June 1869, DNLC; obituary of Charles G. Dahlgren, *New York Times,* 19 December 1888, 2.

61. Diary, 1 January, 26 March, and 18 May 1869 entries; Dahlgren to Read, 1 February 1869, box 7, DLC; John Dahlgren to Charles Dahlgren, 3 March, 4 May, and 1 June 1869, box 7, DLC.

62. Dahlgren to Read, 25 August 1868, box 7, DLC.

63. Diary, 24 July 1868 entry; John Dahlgren to Charles Dahlgren, 4 September and 12 November 1868, box 7, DLC.

64. Diary, 24 July 1868; Dahlgren to Read, 18 August 1868, box 7, DLC.

65. Dahlgren to Paul Dahlgren, 8 September 1868, box 7, DLC.

66. Diary, 7 April 1870 entry; "Death of Paul Dahlgren," *New York Times,* 28 March 1876, 5.

67. Dahlgren to Read, 18 and 25 August 1868, box 7, DLC; Diary, 1 January 1869 entry.

68. Dahlgren to Read, 1 December 1868, box 7, DLC; Diary, 28 April 1870 entry. This is the last entry in Dahlgren's diary.

69. Dahlgren to Read, 4 May 1870, DNLC.

70. Dahlgren to Read, 17 June 1870, DNLC.

71. Hamersly to Dahlgren, 2 June 1870, DS; Dahlgren to Hamersly, 14 June 1870, letterbook dated 15 December 1858, box 18, DLC; Dahlgren to Read, 17 June 1870, DNLC; Dahlgren, manuscript titled "Minutes for Hamersly's 'Records of Living Officers,'" 14 June 1870, letterbook dated 15 December 1868, box 18, DLC.

72. Dahlgren to Davis, 28 October 1869, letterbook dated 15 December 1868, box 18, DLC; Diary, 22 December 1868 and March 1870 entries; Dahlgren, manuscript bound in letterbook dated 15 December 1868, box 18, DLC; Dahlgren to Draper, 10 May 1869, bound in letterbook dated 15 December 1868, box 18, DLC; Dahlgren, manuscript dated 21 June 1870 (1866 folder), box 28, DLC.

73. Macartney, *Mr. Lincoln's Admirals,* 171; Dahlgren to Read, 26 June 1870, DNLC; undated document titled "Forum," DASHM; Madeleine Dahlgren, *Memoir,* 646–49.

74. Madeleine Dahlgren, *Memoir,* 648; Johnson to Patterson, 12 July 1870, entry 201 #5, RG74 NA; "Sudden Death of Admiral Dahlgren," *New York Herald,* 13 July 1870, 3; "Death of Admiral Dahlgren," *Philadelphia Inquirer,* 13 July 1870, 1.

75. "The Late Admiral Dahlgren," *Philadelphia Inquirer,* 14 July 1870, 1; "Burial of Rear Admiral Dahlgren," *Philadelphia Inquirer,* 16 July 1870, 2; "The Late Admiral Dahlgren: The Funeral Discourse," unprovenanced article in the Charles B. Dahlgren Scrapbook, DFP.

76. "Obituary: Rear Admiral John A. Dahlgren," *New York Tribune,* 13 July 1870, 2; "Rear-Admiral Dahlgren," *Army and Navy Journal* 7 (16 July 1870): 757.

Conclusion

1. Charles B. Dahlgren, *Dahlgren Shell-Gun;* Dickson, *National Cyclopaedia of American Biography,* s.v. "Dahlgren, Charles Bunker," "Dahlgren, John Vinton," and "Pierce, Josiah, Jr."; Charles B. Dahlgren, "Genealogy," DFP; Davenport, *Naval Officers,* 134–35; *New York Times,* 28 March 1876, 5; 19 December 1888, 2; 7 July 1889, 5; 12 December 1890, 8; 17 October 1914, 8; 22 November 1922, 21; and 1 January 1944, 13.

2. Madeleine Dahlgren to Cowley, 17 December 1882, DS.

3. Madeleine Dahlgren to Cowley, 10 March 1890, DS; Madeleine V. Dahlgren, *The Petition of Madeleine Vinton Dahlgren, Widow of the Late Rear-Admiral Dahlgren, Asking Compensation for Property Taken and Used by the United States, with Proof of the Facts Set Forth in the Petition* (Lancaster, Pa.: Inquirer Printing and Publishing Company, 1874), copy in box 37, DLC; Madeleine Dahlgren to Cowley, 21 and 22 November 1877, 19 April 1880, DS.

4. *DAB,* s.v. "Dahlgren, Madeleine Vinton"; Schneller, "Intentional Omissions."

5. Glasow, "Prelude," 58–64, 100, 116–17, 297.

6. Ibid., 50, 99, 119–24, 158–59, 225, 239–45, 298–99; Still, *Ironclad Captains,* 47–48.

7. Cited in Knorr, *Historical Dimensions,* 274.

Bibliography

PRIMARY SOURCES

Manuscripts

Cabinet Members' Letters. Louis A. Warren Lincoln Library and Museum, Fort Wayne, Ind.

Cadwalader Collection. Historical Society of Pennsylvania, Philadelphia.

Dahlgren, John A. Letterbook of Correspondence between John A. Dahlgren and Henry A. Wise, 1855. Nimitz Library, United States Naval Academy, Annapolis, Md.

———. Orders to the South Atlantic Blockading Squadron, 1863–65. Historical Society of Pennsylvania, Philadelphia.

———. Papers. American Swedish Historical Museum, Philadelphia, Pa.

———. Papers. George Arents Research Library at Syracuse University, Syracuse, N.Y.

———. Papers. Manuscript Collections, Naval Academy Museum, United States Naval Academy, Annapolis, Md.

———. Papers. Manuscripts Department, South Caroliniana Library, University of South Carolina, Columbia.

———. Papers. Manuscripts Department, William R. Perkins Library, Duke University, Durham, N.C.

———. Papers. Manuscripts Division, Library of Congress, Washington, D.C.

———. Papers. Naval Historical Foundation Collection, Manuscripts Division, Library of Congress, Washington, D.C.

———. Papers. Newberry Library, Chicago.

———. Papers. New-York Historical Society, New York.

———. Papers. Rare Books and Manuscripts Division, New York Public Library, New York.

———. Papers. ZB File, Operational Archives, Naval Historical Center, Washington Navy Yard, Washington, D.C.

Dahlgren, Madeleine Vinton. Papers. Special Collections, Georgetown University Library, Washington, D.C.

Dahlgren Family Papers. Julie Anne Young Johnson, Gaithersburg, Md. (private collection).

Drayton, Percival. Papers. Drayton Collection, Historical Society of Pennsylvania, Philadelphia.

———. Papers. Rare Books and Manuscripts Division, New York Public Library, New York.

Dreer, Ferdinand J. Autograph Collection. Historical Society of Pennsylvania, Philadelphia.

Du Pont, Samuel Francis. Samuel Francis Du Pont Collection of Winterthur Manuscripts. Eleutherian Mills Historical Library, Greenville, Del.

Ericsson, John. Papers. American Swedish Historical Museum, Philadelphia, Pa.

Farragut, David Glasgow. Papers. Naval Historical Foundation Collection, Manuscripts Division, Library of Congress, Washington, D.C.

Gratz Collection. Historical Society of Pennsylvania, Philadelphia.

Jones, Catesby ap Roger. Papers. Virginia Historical Society, Richmond.

Mordecai, Alfred. Papers. Manuscripts Division, Library of Congress, Washington, D.C.

Naval Records Collection of the Office of Naval Records and Library, Record Group 45. National Archives, Washington, D.C.

> Entry 13. Microfilm Copy 480. "Letters Sent by the Secretary of the Navy to the Chiefs of Naval Bureaus, 1842–1886."
>
> Entry 41. "Directives."
>
> Microfilm Copy M517. "Letters Received by the Secretary of the Navy from the President and Executive Agencies, 1837–1886."

Records of the Bureau of Ordnance, Record Group 74. National Archives, Washington, D.C.

> Entry 1. "Letters Sent to the Secretary of the Navy and the Chiefs of Naval Bureaus."
>
> Entry 2. "Letters and Telegrams Sent to Naval Officers, 1842–1882."
>
> Entry 3. "Letters Sent to Navy Yards and Stations, 1842–1884."
>
> Entry 4. "Letters and Telegrams Sent to Inspectors, 1852–1883."
>
> Entry 6. "Letters and Telegrams Sent, 1861–1911."
>
> Entry 16. "Letters Received from the Secretary of the Navy and Navy Department Bureaus, 1842–1885."
>
> Entry 18. "Letters Received from Naval Officers, 1842–1884."
>
> Entry 19. "Letters Received from Navy Yards and Stations."
>
> Entry 21. "Letters Received from Inspectors of Ordnance, 1861–1884."
>
> Entry 36. "Reports of Experiments with 32-Pounder Guns, 1846."
>
> Entry 43. "Report of Extreme Proof of IX-Inch Gun, Tredegar Foundry, Richmond, Virginia, 1855."
>
> Entry 51. "Letters Relating to 15-Inch Guns, 1862–1866."
>
> Entry 98. "Reports Concerning Target Practice on Iron Plates, 1862–1864."

Entry 111. "Record of Armament of Naval Vessels, 1841–1903."

Entry 159. "Memoranda of Naval Appropriation Acts, 1844–1847."

Entry 162. "Ordnance Contracts, 1845–1876."

Entry 201 #5. "Reports and Letters on Ordnance Subjects by John Dahlgren, 1855–1870."

Rowan, Stephen Clegg. Papers. Naval Historical Foundation Collection, Manuscripts Division, Library of Congress, Washington, D.C.

Schoff Civil War Collection. Manuscripts Department, William L. Clements Library, University of Michigan, Ann Arbor.

Society Miscellaneous Collections. Historical Society of Pennsylvania, Philadelphia.

Warren, Joshua D. "Journal of Joshua D. Warren." Box 8, Civil War ZO Files, Operational Archives, Naval Historical Center, Washington, D.C.

Wise, Henry Augustus. Papers. New-York Historical Society, New York.

Printed Manuscripts

Du Pont, Samuel F. *Samuel Francis Du Pont: A Selection from His Civil War Letters.* Edited by John D. Hayes. 3 vols. Ithaca, N.Y.: Cornell University Press, 1969.

Fox, Gustavus V. *Confidential Correspondence of Gustavus Vasa Fox: Assistant Secretary of the Navy, 1861–1865.* Edited by Robert Mears Thompson and Richard Wainwright. 2 vols. New York: Naval History Society, 1919.

Henry, Joseph. *Scientific Writings of Joseph Henry.* Washington, D.C.: Smithsonian Institution, 1886.

Lincoln, Abraham. *The Collected Works of Abraham Lincoln.* Edited by Roy P. Basler. 8 vols. New Brunswick, N.J.: Rutgers University Press, 1953.

Stanton, Frederick Perry. *The Character of Modern Science; or, The Mission of the Educated Man. An Address Delivered before the Alumni Association of Columbian College, July 21, 1852.* Washington, D.C.: R. A. Waters, 1852.

———. *A Lecture Delivered by the Hon. F. P. Stanton, on the Navy of the United States, before the Mercantile Library Association, February 3, 1854.* New York: S. T. Callahan, 1854.

Welles, Gideon. *The Diary of Gideon Welles.* Edited by Howard K. Beale. 3 vols. New York: W. W. Norton, 1960.

Printed Government Documents

An Act to Reorganize the Navy Department of the United States. Statutes at Large. Vol. 12 (1859–63).

Brief Notice of the Late Commodore Charles Morris. Washington, D.C., 1856. (Pamphlet taken from the *Providence (Rhode Island) Journal* of 29 January 1856.)

Congressional Globe. 46 vols. Washington, D.C., 1834–73.

Reports of Experiments on Strength and Other Properties of Metals for Cannon, with Description of Machines for Testing Metals and of Classification of Cannon in Service. Philadelphia: H. C. Baird, 1856.

U.S. Congress. House. *Iron-Clad Ships, Ordnance, &c., &c.* H. MisDoc. 82, 37th Cong., 2d sess., 1862.

———. *Letter from the Secretary of War in Reference to Fortifications.* H. ExDoc. 5, 32d Cong., 1st sess., 1851.

———. *Message from the President of the United States Recommending a Vote of Thanks by Congress to Naval Officers Named Therein.* H. ExDoc. 147, 37th Cong., 2d sess., 1862.

———. *Message from the President of the United States Transmitting the Rules and Regulations (Prepared by the Board of Revision) for the Government of the Navy of the United States.* H. Doc. 20, 23d Cong., 1st sess., 1833.

———. *Naval Ordnance and Ordnance Stores.* H. Rep. 2, 27th Cong., 1st sess., 1841.

———. *Naval Service.* H. Rep. 35, 31st Cong., 2d sess., 1851.

———. *Norman Waird.* H. Rep. 6, 40th Cong., 3d sess., 1869.

———. *Report of the Secretary of the Navy in Relation to Armored Vessels.* H. ExDoc. 69, 38th Cong., 1st sess., 1864.

———. *Report of the Superintendent of Ordnance at the Washington Navy Yard on Rifled Cannon and the Armament of Ships of War.* H. ExDoc. 25, 36th Cong., 2d sess., 1860.

———. *Reports of the Board of Officers Ordered to Examine into the Condition of the Navy Yards.* H. ExDoc. 34, 36th Cong., 1st sess., 1859–60.

U.S. Congress. Senate. *Communication of Norman Waird to the Joint Committee on the Conduct of the War, upon the Subject of Great Guns.* S. MisDoc. 47, 38th Cong., 2d sess., 1865.

———. *Operations against Charleston.* S. Rep. 142, 38th Cong., 2d sess., 1864.

———. *Report of the Board of Visitors to the United States Naval Academy for the Year 1866.* S. ExDoc. 53, 39th Cong., 1st sess., 1865–66.

———. *Report of the Joint Committee on Ordnance on Experiments on Heavy Ordnance.* S. Rep. 266, 40th Cong., 3d sess., 1869.

———. *Report to the Joint Committee on the Conduct of the War: Heavy Ordnance.* S. Rep. 121, 38th Cong., 2d sess., 1865.

U.S. Department of the Navy. *Annual Reports of the Secretary of the Navy.* Washington, D.C.: Government Printing Office, 1839–69.

———. *Official Records of the Union and Confederate Navies in the War of the Rebellion.* Edited by Richard Rush et al. 31 vols. and index. Washington, D.C.: Government Printing Office, 1894–1922.

———. *Regulations for the Proof and Inspection of Cannon, Shot, and Shells, Adopted by a Board of Officers, Consisting of Commodore C. Morris, Commodore L. Warrington, Commodore W. M. Crane, Commodore A. B. Wadsworth, Commodore W. B. Shubrick, and Approved by the Secretary of the Navy, June 1845.* Washington, D.C.: C. Alexander, 1845.

———. Bureau of Ordnance. *Instructions in Relation to the Preparation of Vessels of War for Battle: To the Officers and Others When at Quarters: And to Ordnance and to Ordnance Stores.* Washington, D.C.: C. Alexander, 1852.

———. *Ordnance Instructions for the United States Navy.* Washington, D.C.: Government Printing Office, 1866.

War of the Rebellion: A Compilation of the Official Records of the Union and Confederate Armies. 128 vols. Washington, D.C.: Government Printing Office, 1880–1901.

Contemporary Books

Barber, John W., and Henry Howe. *Historical Collections of the State of New York.* Port Washington, N.Y.: Kennikat, 1841.

Belknap, George E. "Reminiscent of the Siege of Charleston." In *Naval Actions and History, 1798–1898.* Vol. 12 of *Papers of the Military Historical Society of Massachusetts.* Boston: Griffith-Stillings, 1902.

Benton, James G. *Course of Instruction in Ordnance and Gunnery.* 3d ed. New York: D. Van Nostrand, 1867.

Boynton, Charles Brandon. *The History of the Navy during the Rebellion.* 2 vols. New York: D. Appleton, 1870.

———. *The Navies of England, France, America, and Russia, Being an Extract from a Work on English and French Neutrality, and the Anglo-French Alliance.* New York: J. F. Trow, 1865.

Cooper, James Fenimore. *The Pilot.* With an introduction by John T. Winterich. New York: Heritage, 1968.

———. *The Pilot: A Tale of the Sea.* Edited and with a historical introduction and explanatory notes by Kay Seymour House. Albany: State University of New York Press, 1986.

Cowley, Charles. *Leaves from a Lawyer's Life, Afloat and Ashore.* Lowell, Mass.: Penhallow, 1879.

Dahlgren, Charles Bunker. *The Dahlgren Shell-Gun and Its Services during the Late Civil War.* Trenton, N.J.: [private printing], 1887.

Dahlgren, John A. *A Few Hints to Captains of the New IX. Inch Shell Guns.* Boston: Ticknor and Fields, 1856.

———. *Maritime International Law.* Boston: B. B. Russell, 1877.

———. *Memoir of Ulric Dahlgren, by His Father, Rear Admiral Dahlgren.* Edited by Madeleine Vinton Dahlgren. Philadelphia: J. B. Lippincott, 1872.

———. *Naval Percussion Locks and Primers, Particularly Those of the United States.* Philadelphia: A. Hart, 1853.

———. *Report on the Thirty-two Pounder of Thirty-two cwt. to Commodore Warrington, Chief of the Bureau of Ordnance and Hydrography, by Lieut. Jno. A. Dahlgren.* Washington, D.C.: C. Alexander, 1850.

———. *Shells and Shell Guns.* Philadelphia: King and Baird, 1856.

———. *The System of Boat Armament in the United States Navy.* Philadelphia: A. Hart, 1852. Rev. ed. 1856.

———, trans. *An Account of the Experiments Made in the French Navy for the Trial of Bomb Cannon, etc. By H. J. Paixhans, Lieut. Colonel of Artillery.* Philadelphia: E. G. Dorsey, 1838.

Dahlgren, Madeleine Vinton. *Memoir of John A. Dahlgren, Rear-Admiral United States Navy.* Boston: James R. Osgood, 1882.

Gillmore, Quincy Adams. *Engineer and Artillery Operations against the Defences of Charleston Harbor in 1863; Comprising the Descent upon Morris Island, the Demolition of Fort Sumter, the Reduction of Forts Wagner and Gregg. With Observations on Heavy Ordnance, Fortifications, Etc.* New York: D. Van Nostrand, 1865.

Hamersly, Thomas Holdup Stevens. *Complete Army and Navy Register of the United States of America, from 1776 to 1887.* New York: Hamersly, 1888.

Headley, Joel T. *Farragut and Our Naval Commanders.* New York: E. B. Treat, 1867.

Holley, Alexander Lyman. *A Treatise on Ordnance and Armor.* New York: D. Van Nostrand, 1865.

Hoppin, James Mason. *The Life of Andrew Hull Foote, Rear-Admiral United States Navy.* New York: Harper and Brothers, 1874.

Hunter, Alvah Folsom. *A Year on a Monitor and the Destruction of Fort Sumter.* Edited and with an introduction by Craig L. Symonds. Columbia: University of South Carolina Press, 1987.

Johnson, Robert Underwood, and Clarence Clough Buel, eds. *Battles and Leaders of the Civil War: Being for the Most Part Contributions by Union and Confederate Officers.* 4 vols. New York: Century, 1887.

Melville, Herman. *White Jacket; or, The World in a Man-of War.* With an introduction by Stanton Garner. Annapolis: Naval Institute Press, 1988.

Morris, Charles. "The Autobiography of Commodore Charles Morris, U.S.N." United States Naval Institute *Proceedings* 6 (1880): 111–219.

Paixhans, Henri Joseph. *An Account of the Experiments Made in the French Navy for the Trial of the Bomb Cannon.* Translated by John A. Dahlgren. Philadelphia: Dorsey, 1838.

Parker, William Harwar. *Recollections of a Naval Officer, 1841–1865.* With an introduction and notes by Craig L. Symonds. Annapolis: Naval Institute Press, 1985.

Porter, David Dixon. *The Naval History of the Civil War.* 1886. Rpt. Secaucus, N.J.: Castle, 1984.

Rodman, Thomas J. *Reports of Experiments on Properties of Metals for Cannon, and Qualities of Cannon Powder, with Account of Fabrication and Trial of 15-Inch Gun.* Boston: Charles H. Crosby, 1861.

Sands, Benjamin F. *From Reefer to Rear Admiral.* New York: Frederick A. Stokes, 1899.

Sherman, William T. *Memoirs of General William T. Sherman.* 2 vols. New York: D. Appleton, 1875.

Simpson, Edward. *A Treatise on Ordnance and Naval Gunnery, Compiled and Arranged as a Text-book for the U.S. Naval Academy.* 2d ed. New York: D. Van Nostrand, 1862.

Articles by Contemporaries

Ely, Robert B. "This Filthy Ironpot: Ironclads in the Battle of Mobile Bay." *American Heritage* 19 (February 1968): 46–51, 108–11.

Greene, Dana S. "The *Monitor* at Sea and in Battle." United States Naval Institute *Proceedings* 49 (November 1923): 1839–47.

Luce, Stephen B. "Naval Administration, III." U.S. Naval Institute *Proceedings* 29 (December 1903).

Stimers, Alban C. "Aboard the *Monitor.*" Edited by John D. Milligan. *Civil War Times Illustrated* 9 (April 1970): 28–35.

Periodicals

Army and Navy Journal: Gazette of the Regular and Volunteer Forces.
Home Journal.
New York Herald.
New York Tribune.
The Philadelphia Inquirer.
Scientific American.

SECONDARY SOURCES

Books

Albion, Robert Greenhalgh. *Makers of Naval Policy, 1798–1947.* Edited by Rowena Reed. Annapolis: Naval Institute Press, 1980.

Alden, Carroll S., and Ralph Earle. *Makers of Naval Tradition.* Rev. ed. Boston: Ginn, 1943.

Anderson, Bern. *By Sea and by River: The Naval History of the Civil War.* New York: Knopf, 1962.

Axelrad, Allan M. *History and Utopia: A Study of the World View of James Fenimore Cooper.* Norwood, Pa.: Norwood, 1978.

Bartlett, Irving H. *The American Mind in the Mid-Nineteenth Century.* 2d ed. Arlington Heights, Ill.: Harlan Davidson, 1982.

Barzun, Jacques. *Clio and the Doctors: Psycho-History, Quanto-History, and History.* Chicago: University of Chicago Press, 1974.

Bathe, Greville. *Ship of Destiny: A Record of the U.S. Steam Frigate "Merrimac," 1855–62. With an Appendix on the Development of U.S. Naval Cannon from 1812–1865.* Philadelphia: Allen, Lane, and Scott, 1951.

Baxter, James Phinney, III. *The Introduction of the Ironclad Warship.* Cambridge: Harvard University Press, 1933.

Beach, Edward L. *The United States Navy: 200 Years.* New York: Henry Holt, 1986.

Bell, Frederick J. *Room to Swing a Cat: Being Some Tales of the Old Navy.* New York: Longman, 1938.

Bennett, Frank M. *The Steam Navy of the United States.* Pittsburgh: Warren, 1896.

Biographical Directory of the United States Congress, 1774–1989. Washington, D.C.: Government Printing Office, 1989.

Bradford, James C., ed. *Captains of the Old Steam Navy: Makers of the Naval Tradition, 1840–1880.* Annapolis: Naval Institute Press, 1986.

———. *Command under Sail: Makers of the American Naval Tradition, 1775–1850.* Annapolis: Naval Institute Press, 1985.

Braudy, Leo. *The Frenzy of Renown: Fame and Its History.* New York: Oxford University Press, 1986.

Brodie, Bernard. *Sea Power in the Machine Age.* Princeton: Princeton University Press, 1941.

Brown, John Howard. *American Naval Heroes, 1775–1812–1861–1898.* Boston: Brown, 1899.

Browne, Douglas G. *The Floating Bulwark.* New York: St. Martin's, 1963.

Bruce, Robert V. *Lincoln and the Tools of War.* Indianapolis: Bobbs-Merrill, 1956.

Burton, E. Milby. *The Siege of Charleston, 1861–1865.* Columbia: University of South Carolina Press, 1970.

Cajori, Florian. *The Chequered Career of Ferdinand Rudolph Hassler, First Superintendent of the United States Coast Survey: A Chapter in the History of Science in America.* Rpt. New York: Arno, 1980.

Canfield, Eugene B. *Civil War Naval Ordnance.* Washington, D.C.: Government Printing Office, 1969.

Canney, Donald L. *The Old Steam Navy, Volume Two: The Ironclads, 1842–1885.* Annapolis: Naval Institute Press, 1993.

Chapelle, Howard I. *The History of the American Sailing Navy: The Ships and Their Development.* New York: W. W. Norton, 1949.

Church, William Conant. *The Life of John Ericsson.* 2 vols. New York: Charles Scribner's Sons, 1890.

Coles, Harry L. *The War of 1812.* Chicago: University of Chicago Press, 1965.

Coletta, Paolo Enrico, ed. *American Secretaries of the Navy.* 2 vols. Annapolis: Naval Institute Press, 1980.

Comprato, F. C. *Age of Great Guns: Cannon Kings and Cannoners Who Forged the Firepower of Artillery.* Harrisburg: Stackpole, 1965.

Constant, Edward W. *The Origins of the Turbojet Revolution.* Baltimore: Johns Hopkins University Press, 1980.

Cooling, Benjamin Franklin. *Gray Steel and Blue Water Navy: The Formative Years of America's Military-Industrial Complex, 1881–1917.* Hamden, Conn.: Archon, 1979.

———. *Symbol, Sword, and Shield: Defending Washington during the Civil War.* Hamden, Conn.: Archon, 1975.

Coulson, Thomas. *Joseph Henry: His Life and Work.* Princeton: Princeton University Press, 1950.

Courtemanche, Regis A. *No Need of Glory: The British Navy in American Waters, 1860–1864.* Annapolis: Naval Institute Press, 1977.

Cowburn, Philip. *The Warship in History.* New York: Macmillan, 1965.

Christman, Albert B. *Naval Innovators, 1776–1900.* Dahlgren, Va., and Silver Spring, Md.: Naval Surface Warfare Center, 1989.

Daniels, George H., ed. *Nineteenth-Century American Science: A Reappraisal.* Evanston, Ill.: Northwestern University Press, 1972.

Davenport, Charles Benedict. *Naval Officers: Their Heredity and Development.* Washington, D.C.: Carnegie Institute of Washington, 1919.

Davis, Allen F., and Harold D. Woodman, eds. *Conflict and Consensus in Early American History.* 7th ed. Lexington, Mass.: D. C. Heath, 1988.

Davis, Burke. *Sherman's March.* New York: Vintage, 1988.

Davis, William C. *Duel between the First Ironclads.* Garden City, N.Y.: Doubleday, 1975.

Dew, Charles B. *Ironmaker to the Confederacy.* New Haven: Yale University Press, 1966.

Dickson, John, ed. *National Cyclopaedia of American Biography.* 47 vols. New York: J. T. White, 1892–.

Duffy, Christopher. *The Military Experience in the Age of Reason*. New York: Atheneum, 1988.

DuPree, Hunter. *Science in the Federal Government: A History of Policies and Activities to 1940*. Cambridge, Mass.: Belknap Press, 1957.

Dupuy, R. Ernest, and Trevor N. Dupuy. *The Encyclopedia of Military History from 3500 B.C. to the Present*. 2d rev. ed. New York: Harper and Row, 1986.

Durkin, Joseph T. *Stephen R. Mallory: Confederate Navy Chief*. Chapel Hill: University of North Carolina Press, 1954.

Farr, Gail E., and Brett F. Bostwick. *John Lenthall, Naval Architect: A Guide to Plans and Drawings of American Naval and Merchant Vessels, 1790–1874*. Philadelphia: Philadelphia Maritime Museum, 1991.

Ferguson, Eugene S. *Engineering and the Mind's Eye*. Cambridge: MIT Press, 1992.

Ffoulkes, Charles John. *The Gun-Founders of England*. Cambridge: Cambridge University Press, 1937.

Forgie, George B. *Patricide in the House Divided: A Psychological Interpretation of Lincoln and His Age*. New York: W. W. Norton, 1979.

Garbett, Herbert. *Naval Gunnery*. London: G. Bell, 1897. Rpt. with a new preface by Geoffrey Bennett. Wakefield: S. R. Publishers, 1971.

Gardiner, Robert, ed. *Steam, Steel, and Shellfire*. London: Conway Maritime Press, 1992.

Gilfillan, S. Colum. *The Sociology of Invention*. Cambridge: MIT Press, 1970.

Gordon, Robert. *American Iron*. Baltimore: Johns Hopkins University Press, forthcoming.

Gould, Dudley C., ed. *Metalcasting Dictionary*. Des Plaines, Ill.: American Foundrymen's Society, 1968.

Grob, Gerald N., and George Athan Billias. *Interpretations of American History: Patterns and Perspectives*. 5th ed. 2 vols. New York: Free Press, 1987.

Guilmartin, John. *Gunpowder and Galleys: Changing Technology and Mediterranean Warfare at Sea in the Sixteenth Century*. New York: Cambridge University Press, 1974.

Guttridge, Leonard F., and Jay D. Smith. *The Commodores*. With an introduction by James C. Bradford. Annapolis: Naval Institute Press, 1986.

Hagan, Kenneth J. *This People's Navy: The Making of American Sea Power*. New York: Free Press, 1991.

———, ed. *In Peace and War: Interpretations of American Naval History, 1775–1978*. Westport, Conn.: Greenwood, 1978.

Hall, Alfred Rupert. *Ballistics in the Seventeenth Century: A Study of the Relations of Science and War with Reference Principally to England*. Cambridge: Cambridge University Press, 1952.

Harrod, Frederick S. *Manning the New Navy: The Development of a Modern Naval Enlisted Force, 1899–1940*. Westport, Conn.: Greenwood, 1978.

Hindle, Brooke, ed. *Early American Science*. New York: Science History Publications, 1976.

Hoehling, Adolph A. *Thunder at Hampton Roads*. Englewood Cliffs, N.J.: Prentice-Hall, 1976.

Hook, Sidney. *The Hero in History: A Study in Limitation and Possibility*. New York: John Day, 1943.

Horsfield, John. *The Art of Leadership in War: The Royal Navy from the Age of Nelson to the End of World War II*. Westport, Conn.: Greenwood, 1980.

Hovgaard, William. *Modern History of Warships, Comprising a Discussion of Present Standpoint and Recent War Experiences.* London: E. and F. Spon, 1920.

Hughes, Thomas Parke, ed. *Changing Attitudes toward American Technology.* New York: Harper and Row, 1975.

Huntington, Samuel P. *The Soldier and the State: The Theory and Politics of Civil Military Relations.* Cambridge, Mass.: Belknap Press, 1957.

Jackson, Melvin H., and Carel De Beer. *Eighteenth-Century Gunfounding: The Verbruggens at the Royal Brass Foundry—A Chapter in the History of Technology.* Washington, D.C.: Smithsonian Institution Press, 1974.

Janowitz, Morris. *The Professional Soldier: A Social and Political Portrait.* Glencoe, Ill.: Free Press, 1960.

Jewkes, John, et al. *The Sources of Invention.* 2d ed. London: Macmillan, 1969.

Johnson, Allen, and Dumas Malone, eds. *Dictionary of American Biography.* 20 vols. New York: Charles Scribner's Sons, 1928–37.

Johnson, Rossiter, ed. *The Twentieth Century Biographical Dictionary of Notable Americans.* 1904. Rpt. Detroit: Gale Research, 1968.

Jones, Samuel. *The Siege of Charleston.* New York: Neale, 1911.

Jones, Virgil Carrington. *Eight Hours before Richmond.* New York: Holt, 1957.

Karsten, Peter. *The Naval Aristocracy: The Golden Age of Annapolis and the Emergence of Modern American Navalism.* New York: Free Press, 1972.

Keegan, John. *The Price of Admiralty: The Evolution of Naval Warfare.* New York: Viking, 1989.

Kennard, Arthur Norris. *Gunfounding and Gunfounders: A Directory of Cannon Founders from Earliest Times to 1850.* London and New York: Arms and Armour, 1986.

Ketchum, Richard M., ed. *The American Heritage Picture History of the Civil War.* New York: American Heritage, 1960.

Knorr, Klaus, ed. *Historical Dimensions of National Security Problems.* Lawrence: University of Kansas Press, 1976.

Knox, Dudley W. *A History of the United States Navy.* New York: Van Rees, 1936.

Kuhn, Thomas S. *The Structure of Scientific Revolutions.* 2d ed. Chicago: University of Chicago Press, 1970.

Lambert, Andrew. *Battleships in Transition: The Creation of the Steam Battlefleet, 1815–1860.* Annapolis: Naval Institute Press, 1984.

———. *The Last Sailing Battlefleet: Maintaining Naval Mastery, 1815–1850.* London: Conway Maritime Press, 1991.

Langley, Harold P. *Social Reform in the United States Navy, 1798–1862.* Urbana: University of Illinois Press, 1967.

Larkin, Jack. *The Reshaping of Everyday Life, 1790–1840.* New York: Harper and Row, 1988.

Lavery, Brian. *The Ship of the Line, Volume 1: The Development of the Battlefleet, 1650–1850.* Annapolis: Naval Institute Press, 1983.

Linderman, Gerald F. *Embattled Courage: The Experience of Combat in the American Civil War.* New York: Free Press, 1987.

Long, David F. *Gold Braid and Foreign Relations: Diplomatic Activities of U.S. Naval Officers, 1798–1883.* Annapolis: Naval Institute Press, 1988.

Macartney, Clarence Edward Noble. *Mr. Lincoln's Admirals.* New York: Funk and Wagnalls, 1956.

MacBride, Robert. *Civil War Ironclads: The Dawn of Naval Armor.* Philadelphia: Chilton, 1962.

McCollum, Kenneth G., ed. *Dahlgren.* Dahlgren, Va.: Naval Surface Weapons Center, 1977.

McHenry, Robert, ed. *Webster's American Military Biographies.* Springfield, Mass.: G. and C. Merriam, 1978.

McHugh, Jeanne. *Alexander Holley and the Makers of Steel.* Baltimore: Johns Hopkins University Press, 1980.

McKee, Christopher. *A Gentlemanly and Honorable Profession: The Creation of the U.S. Naval Officer Corps, 1794–1815.* Annapolis: Naval Institute Press, 1991.

MacKenzie, Donald. *Inventing Accuracy: A Historical Sociology of Nuclear Missile Guidance.* Cambridge: MIT Press, 1991.

MacKenzie, Donald, and Judy Wajcman. *The Social Shaping of Technology: How the Refrigerator Got Its Hum.* Philadelphia: Open University Press, 1985.

McPherson, James M. *Battle Cry of Freedom: The Civil War Era.* New York: Oxford University Press, 1988.

Mahan, Alfred Thayer. *From Sail to Steam: Recollections of a Naval Life.* New York: Harper and Brothers, 1907. Rpt. New York: DeCapo, 1968.

———. *The Influence of Seapower upon History.* With an introduction by Louis M. Hacker. New York: Hill and Wang, 1957.

Meissner, Sophie Radford de. *Old Naval Days: Sketches from the Life of Rear Admiral William Radford, U.S.N.* New York: Henry Holt, 1920.

Melia, Tamara Moser. *Damn the Torpedoes: A Short History of U.S. Naval Mine Countermeasures, 1777–1991.* Washington, D.C.: Naval Historical Center, 1991.

Merrill, James M. *Du Pont: The Making of an Admiral.* New York: Dodd, Mead, 1986.

Merton, Robert K. *The Sociology of Science: Theoretical and Empirical Investigations.* Edited and with an introduction by Norman W. Storer. Chicago: University of Chicago Press, 1973.

Miller, Perry. *The Life of the Mind in America from the Revolution to the Civil War.* London: Victor Gollancz, 1965.

Millett, Allan R., and Peter Maslowski. *For the Common Defense: A Military History of the United States of America.* New York: Free Press, 1984.

Mooney, James L., ed. *Dictionary of American Naval Fighting Ships.* 8 vols. Washington, D.C.: Government Printing Office, 1959–81.

Morison, Elting E. *Admiral Sims and the Modern American Navy.* Boston: Houghton Mifflin, 1942.

———. *Men, Machines, and Modern Times.* Cambridge: MIT Press, 1966.

Morison, Samuel Eliot. *"Old Bruin": Commodore Matthew C. Perry.* Boston: Little, Brown, 1967.

Niven, John. *Gideon Welles: Lincoln's Secretary of the Navy.* New York: Oxford University Press, 1973.

Oates, Stephen B. *With Malice toward None: The Life of Abraham Lincoln.* New York: Harper and Row, 1977.

O'Connell, Robert L. *Sacred Vessels: The Cult of the Battleship and the Rise of the U.S. Navy.* Boulder, Colo.: Westview Press, 1991.

Padfield, Peter. *Guns at Sea.* New York: St. Martin's, 1974.

Paullin, Charles Oscar. *Paullin's History of Naval Administration, 1775–1911.* Annapolis: Naval Institute Press, 1968.

Peck, Taylor. *Round-Shot to Rockets: A History of the Washington Navy Yard and U.S. Naval Gun Factory.* Annapolis: U.S. Naval Institute, 1949.

Perret, Geoffrey. *A Country Made by War, from the Revolution to Vietnam: The Story of America's Rise to Power.* New York: Random House, 1989.

Perry, Milton F. *Infernal Machines: The Story of Confederate Submarine and Mine Warfare.* Baton Rouge: Louisiana State University Press, 1965.

Pessen, Edward. *Jacksonian America: Society, Personality, and Politics.* Rev. ed. Homewood, Ill.: Dorsey, 1978.

Peterson, C. Stewart. *Admiral John A. Dahlgren, Father of U.S. Naval Ordnance.* Cynthiana, Ky.: Hobson, 1945.

Peterson, Harold Leslie. *Round Shot and Rammers.* Harrisburg: Stackpole, 1969.

Philbrick, Thomas. *James Fenimore Cooper and the Development of American Sea Fiction.* Cambridge: Harvard University Press, 1961.

Pope, Dudley. *Guns: From the Invention of Gunpowder to the Twentieth Century.* New York: Delacorte, 1965.

Potter, E. B., ed. *Sea Power: A Naval History.* 2d ed. Annapolis: Naval Institute Press, 1981.

Pratt, Fletcher. *Preble's Boys: Commodore Preble and the Birth of American Sea Power.* New York: Sloane, 1950.

Randall, J. G., and David Herbert Donald. *The Civil War and Reconstruction.* Lexington, Mass.: D. C. Heath, 1969.

Reed, Rowena. *Combined Operations in the Civil War.* Annapolis: Naval Institute Press, 1978.

Reynolds, Clark G. *Famous American Admirals.* New York: Van Nostrand Reinhold, 1978.

Ripley, Warren. *Artillery and Ammunition of the Civil War.* New York: Van Nostrand Reinhold, 1970.

Robertson, Frederick Leslie. *The Evolution of Naval Armament.* London: Harold Storey and Sons, 1968.

Rogin, Michael P. *Subversive Genealogy: The Politics and Art of Herman Melville.* New York: Knopf, 1983.

Roland, Alex. *Underwater Warfare in the Age of Sail.* Bloomington: Indiana University Press, 1977.

Ropp, Theodore. *War in the Modern World.* Rev. ed. New York: Collier, 1962.

Rosenberg, Nathan. *Technology and American Economic Growth.* Armonck, N.Y.: M. E. Sharpe, 1972.

Sanders, Clyde A., and Dudley C. Gould. *History Cast in Metal: The Founders of North America.* Des Plaines, Ill.: Cast Metals Institute, American Foundrymen's Society, 1976.

Saum, Lewis O. *The Popular Mood of Pre–Civil War America.* Westport, Conn.: Greenwood, 1980.

Schroeder, John. *Shaping a Maritime Empire: The Commercial and Diplomatic Role of the American Navy, 1829–1861.* Westport, Conn.: Greenwood, 1985.

Scott, Franklin D. *Sweden: The Nation's History.* Minneapolis: University of Minnesota Press, 1977.

Seager, Robert, II. *Alfred Thayer Mahan: The Man and His Letters.* Annapolis: Naval Institute Press, 1977.

Skulski, Janusz. *The Battleship Yamato.* London: Conway Maritime Press, 1988.

Spiller, Roger, et al., eds. *Dictionary of American Military Biography.* 3 vols. Westport, Conn.: Greenwood, 1984.

Sprout, Harold, and Margaret Sprout. *The Rise of American Naval Power, 1776–1918.* Princeton: Princeton University Press, 1939.

Still, William N., Jr. *Iron Afloat: The Story of the Confederate Armorclads.* Nashville: Vanderbilt University Press, 1971.

———. *Ironclad Captains: The Commanding Officers of the USS "Monitor."* Washington, D.C.: Government Printing Office, 1988.

Sweetman, Jack. *American Naval History: An Illustrated Chronology of the U.S. Navy and Marine Corps, 1775–Present.* Annapolis: Naval Institute Press, 1984.

Symonds, Craig L. *Navalists and Antinavalists: The Naval Policy Debate in the United States, 1785–1827.* Newark: University of Delaware Press, 1980.

Temin, Peter. *Iron and Steel in Nineteenth Century America: An Economic Inquiry.* Cambridge: MIT Press, 1964.

Tindall, George Brown. *America: A Narrative History.* 2 vols. New York: W. W. Norton, 1984.

Todorich, Charles M. *The Spirited Years: A History of the Antebellum Naval Academy.* Annapolis: Naval Institute Press, 1984.

Tucker, Spencer. *Arming the Fleet: U.S. Navy Ordnance in the Muzzle-Loading Era.* Annapolis: Naval Institute Press, 1989.

Tyler, Alice Felt. *Freedom's Ferment: Phases of American Social History from the Colonial Period to the Outbreak of the Civil War.* Rpt. New York: Harper and Row, 1962.

U.S. Navy Department. *American Ships of the Line.* Washington, D.C.: Government Printing Office, 1969.

U.S. Navy Department, Bureau of Naval Personnel. *Principles of Naval Ordnance and Gunnery.* Washington, D.C.: Government Printing Office, 1971.

U.S. Navy Department, Naval History Division. *Civil War Naval Chronology, 1861–1865.* Washington, D.C.: Government Printing Office, 1971.

Valle, James E. *Rocks and Shoals: Order and Discipline in the Old Navy, 1800–1861.* Annapolis: Naval Institute Press, 1980.

Van Creveld, Martin. *Command in War.* Cambridge: Harvard University Press, 1985.

Vincenti, Walter G. *What Engineers Know and How They Know It: Analytical Studies from Aeronautical History.* Baltimore: Johns Hopkins University Press, 1990.

Von Doenhoff, Richard A., ed. *Versatile Guardian: Research in Naval History.* Washington, D.C.: Howard University Press, 1979.

Walton, Charles F., and Timothy J. Opar, eds. *Iron Castings Handbook.* Rocky River, Ohio: Iron Castings Society, 1981.

Ward, Geoffrey C. *The Civil War: An Illustrated History.* New York: Alfred A. Knopf, 1990.

Warner, Ezra J. *Generals in Blue: Lives of the Union Commanders.* Baton Rouge: Louisiana State University Press, 1964.

———. *Generals in Gray: Lives of the Confederate Commanders.* Baton Rouge: Louisiana State University Press, 1959.

Weigley, Russell F. *The American Way of War: A History of United States Military Strategy and Policy.* Bloomington: Indiana University Press, 1977.

Werlich, David P. *Admiral of the Amazon: John Randolph Tucker, His Confederate Colleagues, and Peru.* Charlottesville: University Press of Virginia, 1990.

West, Richard S., Jr. *Gideon Welles, Lincoln's Navy Department.* Indianapolis: Bobbs-Merrill, 1943.

————. *Mr. Lincoln's Navy.* New York: Longman's Green, 1957.

Wilson, Herbert W. *Ironclads in Action: A Sketch of Naval Warfare from 1855 to 1898, with Some Account of the Development of the Battleships in England.* 2 vols. Boston: Little, Brown, 1896.

Wilson, J. G., and John Fiske, eds. *Appleton's Cyclopaedia of American Biography.* 7 vols. New York: D. Appleton, 1888–1900.

Winter, Frank H. *The First Golden Age of Rocketry: Congreve and Hale Rockets in the Nineteenth Century.* Washington, D.C.: Smithsonian Institution Press, 1991.

Wise, Stephen R. *Gate of Hell: Campaign for Charleston Harbor, 1863.* Columbia: University of South Carolina Press, 1994.

————. *Lifeline of the Confederacy: Blockade Running during the Civil War.* Columbia: University of South Carolina Press, 1988.

Articles

Anderson, Bern. "The Naval Strategy of the Civil War." *Military Affairs* 26 (Spring 1962): 11–21.

Bastable, Marshall J. "From Breechloaders to Monster Guns: Sir William Armstrong and the Invention of Modern Artillery, 1854–1880." *Technology and Culture* 33 (April 1992): 213–47.

Bolander, Louis H. "The Introduction of Shells and Shell Guns in the United States Navy." *Mariner's Mirror* 17 (April 1931): 105–12.

Bracken, Paul. "Defense Organization and Management." *Orbis* 27 (Summer 1983): 253–66.

Buhl, Lance C. "Mariners and Machines: Resistance to Technological Change in the American Navy, 1865–1869." *Journal of American History* 59 (December 1974): 703–27.

Chandler, Alfred D., Jr. "DuPont, Dahlgren, and the Civil War Nitre Shortage." *Military Affairs* 13 (Fall 1949): 142–49.

Conti, Gerald. "Motivation." *Civil War Times Illustrated* 23 (April 1984): 18–23.

Cooling, B. Franklin, III. "Civil War Deterrent: Defenses of Washington." *Military Affairs* 29 (Winter 1965–66): 164–78.

Demaree, Albert L. "The *Merrimack*—Our Navy's Worst Headache." United States Naval Institute *Proceedings* 88 (March 1962): 66–84.

Earle, Ralph. "John Adolphus Dahlgren." United States Naval Institute *Proceedings* 51 (1925): 424–36.

Falk, Stanley L. "Artillery for the Land Service: The Development of a System." *Military Affairs* 28 (Fall 1964): 97–110

Fisher, Charles R. "The Great Guns of the Navy, 1797–1843." *American Neptune* 36 (1976): 276–95.

Foote, Shelby. "DuPont Storms Charleston." *American Heritage* 14 (June 1963): 28–34, 89–92.

Foster, G. A. "Woman Who Saved the Union Navy: M. Louvestre's Drawings of Warship *Merrimac.*" *Ebony* 33 (December 1977): 131–32.

Harrod, Frederick S. "New Technology in the Old Navy: The United States Navy during the 1870s." *American Neptune* 53 (Winter 1993): 5–19.

Hayes, John D. "Captain Fox—*He* Is the Navy Department." United States Naval Institute *Proceedings* 91 (September 1965): 64–71.

———. "Fox versus DuPont: The Crisis in Civil-Military Relations, 7 April 1863." *Shipmate* 26 (April 1963): 10–11.

Heitzmann, William Ray. "The Ironclad *Weehawken* in the Civil War." *American Neptune* 42 (1982): 193–202.

Henig, Gerald S. "Admiral Samuel F. DuPont, the Navy Department, and the Attack on Charleston, April 1863." *Naval War College Review* 31 (February 1979): 68–77.

Hess, Earl J. "Northern Response to the Ironclad: A Prospect for the Study of Military Technology." *Civil War History* 31 (June 1985): 126–43.

Hornsby, Thomas. "Oregon and Peacemaker: 12-Inch Wrought-Iron Guns." *American Neptune* 6 (July 1946): 212–22.

Hughes, Thomas Parke. "The Development Phase of Technological Change." *Technology and Culture* 17 (July 1976): 423–31.

Keller, Morton. "Reflections on Politics and Generations in America." *Daedalus* 107 (Fall 1978): 123–35.

Kriegel, Annie. "Generational Difference: The History of an Idea." *Daedalus* 107 (Fall 1978): 23–38.

Layton, Edwin. "Mirror-Image Twins: The Communities of Science and Technology in 19th-Century America." *Technology and Culture* 12 (October 1971): 562–80.

Lewis, Emanuel R. "The Ambiguous Columbiads." *Military Affairs* 28 (Fall 1964): 111–22.

Lewis, Kevin N. "On the Appropriate Use of Technology." *Orbis* 27 (Summer 1983): 274–85.

Lockhart, Paul D. "The Confederate Naval Squadron at Charleston and the Failure of Naval Harbor Defense." *American Neptune* 44 (Fall 1984): 257–75.

McCormick, Gordon H. "The Dynamics of Doctrinal Change." *Orbis* 27 (Summer 1983): 266–74.

Merrill, James M. "Strategy Makers in the Union Navy Department, 1861–1865." *Mid America* 44 (January 1962): 19–32.

Miles, Alfred H. "The *Princeton* Explosion." United States Naval Institute *Proceedings* 52 (1926): 2225–45.

Nelson, Paul David. "James Fenimore Cooper's Maritime Nationalism, 1820–1850." *Military Affairs* 41 (October 1977): 129–32.

Niven, John. "Gideon Welles and Naval Administration during the Civil War." *American Neptune* 35 (January 1975): 53–66.

Paret, Peter. "Nationalism and the Sense of Military Obligation." *Military Affairs* 34 (February 1970): 2–6.

Pearson, Lee M. "The *Princeton* and the Peacemaker: A Study of 19th Century Naval Research and Development Procedures." *Technology and Culture* 7 (Spring 1966): 163–83.

Roland, Alex. "Secrecy, Technology, and War: Greek Fire and the Defense of Byzantium, 678–1204." *Technology and Culture* 33 (October 1992): 655–79.

Reid, Brian Holden. "Historians and the Joint Committee on the Conduct of the War, 1861–1865." *Civil War History* 38 (December 1992): 319–41.

Sandler, Stanley. "A Navy in Decay: Some Strategic Technological Results of Disarmament, 1865–69, in the U.S. Navy." *Military Affairs* 35 (December 1971): 138–42.

Schneller, Robert J., Jr. "Intentional Omissions from the Published Civil War Diaries of Admiral John A. Dahlgren." *Syracuse University Library Associates Courier,* Spring 1990.

Still, William N., Jr. "The Common Sailor, Part I: Yankee Blue Jackets." *Civil War Times Illustrated* 23 (February 1985): 25–39.

———. "A Naval Sieve: The Union Blockade in the Civil War." *U.S. Naval War College Review* 36 (May–June 1983): 38–45.

Sullivan, Dwight. "Sacrificial Limb." *Washington Post Magazine,* 27 January 1991.

Thomas, Emory M. "The Kilpatrick-Dahlgren Raid." *Civil War Times Illustrated* 16 (February 1978): 4–9, 46–48; 17 (April 1978): 26–33.

Valle, James E. "The Navy's Battle Doctrine in the War of 1812." *American Neptune* 44 (Summer 1984): 171–78.

West, Richard S., Jr. "Lincoln's Hand in Naval Matters." *Civil War History* 4 (June 1958): 175–83.

Williams, T. Harry. "The Navy and the Committee on the Conduct of the War." United States Naval Institute *Proceedings* 65 (December 1939): 1751–55.

Unpublished Manuscripts

Falk, Stanley L. "Soldier Technologist: Major Alfred Mordecai and the Beginnings of Science in the United States Army." Ph.D. diss., Georgetown University, 1959.

Glasow, Richard Dwight. "Prelude to a Naval Renaissance: Ordnance Innovation in the United States Navy during the 1870s." Ph.D. diss., University of Delaware, 1978.

Klingler, Marion H. "A Failure to Learn: The Union Navy and Bombarding Shore Fortifications in the Civil War." Student paper, NW 518, American Military University, Fall 1994.

Mauskopf, Seymour H. "The Chief Support of War Must, after Money, Be Now Sought in Chemistry." Paper presented at the Johns Hopkins Colloquium in the History of Science, 13 March 1991.

Schneller, Robert J., Jr. "The Contentious Innovator: A Biography of Rear Admiral John A. Dahlgren, U.S.N. (1809–1870): Generational Conflict, Ordnance Technology, and Command Afloat in the Nineteenth-Century Navy." Ph.D. diss., Duke University, 1991.

———. "The Development of Dahlgren's Heavy Cast-Iron Smoothbores and Their Adoption by the Navy." M.A. thesis, East Carolina University, 1986.

Thiesen, William H. "A Fond Farewell to 'Practical Shipbuilding': The Introduction of Iron Ship Construction to Great Britain and the United States." Paper presented at the annual meeting of the Society for the History of Technology, Lowell, Mass., 9 October 1994.

Index

About the Author

Robert J. Schneller, Jr., has been a historian in the Contemporary History Branch of the Naval Historical Center since 1991. He holds a Ph.D. in military history from Duke University and an M.A. in history from the Maritime History and Underwater Research Program at East Carolina University.

The **Naval Institute Press** is the book-publishing arm of the U.S. Naval Institute, a private, nonprofit society for sea service professionals and others who share an interest in naval and maritime affairs. Established in 1873 at the U.S. Naval Academy in Annapolis, Maryland, where its offices remain, today the Naval Institute has more than 100,000 members worldwide.

Members of the Naval Institute receive the influential monthly magazine *Proceedings* and discounts on fine nautical prints and on ship and aircraft photos. They also have access to the transcripts of the Institute's Oral History Program and get discounted admission to any of the Institute-sponsored seminars offered around the country.

The Naval Institute also publishes *Naval History* magazine. This colorful bimonthly is filled with entertaining and thought-provoking articles, first-person reminiscences, and dramatic art and photography. Members receive a discount on *Naval History* subscriptions.

The Naval Institute's book-publishing program, begun in 1898 with basic guides to naval practices, has broadened its scope in recent years to include books of more general interest. Now the Naval Institute Press publishes more than seventy titles each year, ranging from how-to books on boating and navigation to battle histories, biographies, ship and aircraft guides, and novels. Institute members receive discounts on the Press's nearly 400 books in print.

For a free catalog describing Naval Institute Press books currently available, and for further information about subscribing to *Naval History* magazine or about joining the U.S. Naval Institute, please write to:

Membership & Communications Department
U.S. Naval Institute
118 Maryland Avenue
Annapolis, Maryland 21402-5035

Or call, toll-free, (800) 233-USNI.

THE NAVAL INSTITUTE PRESS
A QUEST FOR GLORY
A Biography of Rear Admiral John A. Dahlgren
Designed by Karen L. White
Set in Minion with Fournier Ornaments
on a Macintosh Quadra
Printed on 60-lb. Booktext natural
and bound in Kingston Natural with Rainbow cotton
by BookCrafters
Fredericksburg, Virginia